Financial Markets and Institutions

Written for undergraduate and graduate students of finance, economics and business, the third edition of *Financial Markets and Institutions* provides a fresh analysis of the European financial system. Combining theory, data and policy, this successful textbook examines and explains financial markets, financial infrastructures, financial institutions and the challenges of financial supervision and competition policy. The third edition features greater discussion of the financial and euro crises, including extensive analysis of their causes and impact, as well as their remedies. New material covers unconventional monetary policies, the Banking Union, the Basel 3 capital adequacy framework for banking supervision, macroprudential policies and state aid control applied to banks. The new edition also features wider international coverage, with greater emphasis on comparisons with countries outside the European Union.

Visit the companion website at www.cambridge.org/de_Haan3e for exercises and solutions for each chapter, and copies of the figures and tables used in the book.

Jakob de Haan is Head of Research of De Nederlandsche Bank and Professor of Political Economy at the University of Groningen.

Sander Oosterloo is Deputy Head of the Financial Stability Department at the Netherlands Ministry of Finance.

Dirk Schoenmaker is Dean of the Duisenberg School of Finance, Amsterdam, and Professor of Finance, Banking, and Insurance at the VU University Amsterdam.

Financial Markets and Institutions

A European Perspective

Third Edition

Jakob de Haan

Sander Oosterloo

Dirk Schoenmaker

CAMBRIDGE
UNIVERSITY PRESS

CAMBRIDGE
UNIVERSITY PRESS

University Printing House, Cambridge CB2 8BS, United Kingdom

Cambridge University Press is part of the University of Cambridge.

It furthers the University's mission by disseminating knowledge in the pursuit of education, learning and research at the highest international levels of excellence.

www.cambridge.org
Information on this title: www.cambridge.org/9781107539365

First edition 2009
Second edition 2012
Third edition 2015

Printing in the United Kingdom by TJ International Ltd. Padstow Cornwall

A catalogue record for this publication is available from the British Library

Library of Congress Cataloguing in Publication data
Haan, Jakob de.
[European financial markets and institutions]
Financial markets and institutions : a European perspective / Jakob de Haan, Sander Oosterloo, Dirk Schoenmaker. – Third Edition.
pages cm
Includes index.
ISBN 978-1-107-11999-4
1. Financial institutions – Europe. 2. Europe – Economic policy.
3. Europe – Economic integration. I. Oosterloo, Sander. II. Schoenmaker, Dirk. III. Title.
HG186.A2H33 2015
332′.0415094–dc23

2015006130

ISBN 978-1-107-11999-4 Hardback
ISBN 978-1-107-53936-5 Paperback

Additional resources for this publication at www.cambridge.org/de_Haan3e

Contents

Boxes

Figures

Tables

Countries

Member States of the European Union

	Country	Official abbreviation	Year of accession
1	Austria	AT	1995
2	Belgium	BE	1951
3	Bulgaria	BG	2007
4	Croatia	HR	2013
5	Cyprus	CY	2004
6	Czech Republic	CZ	2004
7	Denmark	DK	1973
8	Estonia	EE	2004
9	Finland	FI	1995
10	France	FR	1951
11	Germany	DE	1951
11	Greece	EL	1981
13	Hungary	HU	2004
14	Ireland	IE	1973
15	Italy	IT	1951
16	Latvia	LV	2004
17	Lithuania	LT	2004
18	Luxembourg	LU	1951
19	Malta	MT	2004
20	Netherlands	NL	1951
21	Poland	PL	2004
22	Portugal	PT	1986
23	Romania	RO	2007
24	Slovakia	SK	2004
25	Slovenia	SI	2004
26	Spain	ES	1986
27	Sweden	SE	1995
28	United Kingdom	UK	1973

The European Union (EU) consists of 28 Member States as of 2015 (EU 28). Before the accession of the New Member States in 2004, 2007 and 2013, the EU consisted of 15 Member States, which are usually indicated by EU-15. The 10 New Member States in 2004 are indicated by NMS-10 and the total of 12 New Member States in 2004 and 2007 are indicated by NMS-12. EU-25 refers to the EU-15 and NMS-10. EU-27 refers to the EU-15 and NMS-12.

There are 19 countries in the euro area.

Countries in the euro area

	Country	Year of accession
1	Austria	1999
2	Belgium	1999
3	Cyprus	2008
4	Estonia	2011
5	Finland	1999
6	France	1999
7	Germany	1999
8	Greece	2001
9	Ireland	1999
10	Italy	1999
11	Latvia	2014
12	Lithuania	2015
13	Luxembourg	1999
14	Malta	2008
15	Netherlands	1999
16	Portugal	1999
17	Slovakia	2009
18	Slovenia	2007
19	Spain	1999

Abbreviations

ABP	Algemeen Burgerlijk Pensioenfonds
ABS	Asset-Backed Securities
ACP	Asset-backed Commercial Paper
ACP	Autorité de Contrôle Prudentiel
AIG	American International Group
ALM	Asset and Liability Management
AMF	Autorité des Marchés Financiers
ASC	Advisory Scientific Committee
ATM	Automated Teller Machine
BaFin	Bundesanstalt für Finanzdienstleistungsaufsicht
BCBS	Basel Committee on Banking Supervision
BHB	Bond Home Bias
BIS	Bank for International Settlements
BME	Bolsas y Mercados Españoles
BoE	Bank of England
BoJ	Bank of Japan
BRRD	Bank Recovery and Resolution Directive
BU	Banking Union
CalPERS	California Public Employees Retirement Scheme
CAPM	Capital Asset Pricing Model
CB	Central Bank
CBPP	Covered Bond Purchase Programme
CCP	Central Counterparty
CD	Certificate of Deposit
CDC	Collective Defined Contribution
CDO	Collateralised Debt Obligation
CDS	Credit Default Swap
CEA	Comité Européen des Assurances
CEO	Chief Executive Officer
CESR	Committee of European Securities Regulators

CET1	Common Equity Tier 1
CFO	Chief Financial Officer
CLS	Continuous Linked Settlement
CMBS	Commercial Mortgage-Backed Securities
CRA	Credit Rating Agency
CRAAC	CRA Assessment Centre
CRD	Capital Requirements Directive
CRO	Chief Risk Officer
CRR	Capital Requirements Regulation
CSD	Central Securities Depository
DB	Defined Benefit
DC	Defined Contribution
DG	Directorate General
DGS	Deposit Guarantee Scheme
DNB	De Nederlandsche Bank (Dutch Central Bank)
DTB	Deutsche Terminbörse
EBA	European Banking Authority
EBRD	European Bank for Reconstruction and Development
EC	European Commission
ECB	European Central Bank
ECFI	European Court of First Instance
ECJ	European Court of Justice
ECN	European Competition Network
Ecofin	Council of Economic and Finance Ministers
ECSC	European Coal and Steel Community
ECU	European Currency Unit
EDP	Excessive Deficit Procedure
EEA	European Economic Area
EEC	European Economic Community
EFAMA	European Fund and Asset Management Association
EFSF	European Financial Stability Facility
EFSM	European Financial Stabilisation Mechanism
EHB	Equity Home Bias
EIOPA	European Insurance and Occupational Pensions Authority
EMI	European Monetary Institute
EMIR	European Market Infrastructure Regulation
EMS	European Monetary System
EMU	Economic and Monetary Union
EOE	European Options Exchange

EONIA	Euro Overnight Index Average
EP	European Parliament
EPC	European Payments Council
ERM	Exchange Rate Mechanism
ESA	European Supervisory Authority
ESCB	European System of Central Banks
ESFS	European System of Financial Supervisors
ESM	European Stability Mechanism
ESMA	European Securities and Markets Authority
ESRB	European Systemic Risk Board
ETF	Exchange Traded Funds
EU	European Union
Euratom	European Atomic Energy Community
EUREPO	Repo Market Reference Rate for the Euro
EURIBOR	Euro Interbank Offered Rate
FCA	Financial Conduct Authority
FDI	Foreign Direct Investment
Fed	Federal Reserve
FESE	Federation of European Securities Exchanges
FOMC	Federal Open Market Committee
FPC	Financial Policy Committee
FRA	Forward Rate Agreement
FSA	Financial Services Authority
FSAP	Financial Services Action Plan
FSB	Financial Stability Board
FSF	Financial Stability Forum
FSOC	Financial Stability Oversight Council
FSR	Financial Stability Review
FTO	Fine Tune Operation
FX	Foreign Exchange
GDP	Gross Domestic Product
GIIPS	Greece, Ireland, Italy, Portugal, Spain
GLAC	Gone-concern loss-absorbing capacity
GMI	Governance Metrics International
GVA	Gross Value Added
HI	Herfindahl Index
IAIS	International Association of Insurance Supervisors
IAS	International Accounting Standards
IASB	International Accounting Standards Board

ICI	Investment Company Institute
ICMA	International Capital Market Association
ICSD	International Central Securities Depository
IFRS	International Financial Reporting Standards
IMF	International Monetary Fund
IOSCO	International Organisation of Securities Commissions
IPO	Initial Public Offering
IRS	Interest Rate Swap
ISD	Investment Services Directive
ISDA	International Swaps and Derivatives Association
IT	Information Technology
LCR	Liquidity Coverage Ratio
LI	Lerner Index
LIBOR	London Interbank Offered Rate
LIFFE	London International Financial Futures and Options Exchange
LoLR	Lender of Last Resort
LSE	London Stock Exchange
LTCM	Long-Term Capital Management
LTRO	Longer-Term Refinancing Operation
LVPS	Large-Value Payment System
M&As	Mergers and Acquisitions
MBS	Mortgage-Backed Securities
MFI	Monetary Financial Institution
MIF	Multilateral Interchange Fee
MiFID	Markets in Financial Instruments Directive
MiFIR	Markets in Financial Instruments Regulation
MMF	Money Market Fund
MoU	Memorandum of Understanding
MPC	Monetary Policy Committee
MREL	Minimum requirements for own funds and eligible requirements
MRO	Main Refinancing Operation
MSCI	Morgan Stanley Capital International
MTF	Multilateral Trading Facility
MTO	Medium-Term Objective
NAV	Net Asset Value
NCA	National Competition Authority
NCB	National Central Bank

NFC	Non-financial corporations
NMS	New Member States
NSA	National Supervisory Authority
NSFR	Net Stable Funding Ratio
NYSE	New York Stock Exchange
OECD	Organisation for Economic Co-operation and Development
OFT	Office of Fair Trading
OIS	Overnight Interest Rate Swap
OMTs	Outright Monetary Transactions
OMX	Options Maklarna Exchange
OTC	Over-the-Counter
PAYG	Pay-As-You-Go
P&C	Property and Casualty
PCA	Prompt Corrective Action
PSD	Payment Services Directive
PvP	Payment versus Payment
QE	Quantitative Easing
RAROC	Risk Adjusted Return On Capital
RBB	Regional Bond Bias
REB	Regional Equity Bias
RMBS	Residential Mortgage-Backed Securities
ROE	Return On Equity
RQMV	Reverse qualified majority voting
RTGS	Real-Time Gross Settlement
SBA	Stand-by Arrangement
SCP	Structure-Conduct-Performance
SEA	Single European Act
SEC	Securities and Exchange Commission
SEPA	Single Euro Payments Area
SETS	London Stock Exchange's premier Electronic Trading System
SFTs	Securities Financing Transactions
SGP	Stability and Growth Pact
SIB	Systemically Important Bank
SIFI	Systemically Important Financial Institution
SIV	Structured Investment Vehicle
SMEs	Small and Medium Enterprises
SMP	Securities Markets Programme

SOFFEX	Swiss Options and Financial Futures Exchange
SPO	Secondary Public Offering
SPV	Special Purpose Vehicle
SRI	Socially responsible investing
SRB	Single Resolution Board
SRO	Self Regulatory Organisation
SRM	Single Resolution Mechanism
SSM	Single Supervisory Mechanism
SSNIP	Small, but Significant Non-transitory Increase in Prices
SSP	Single Shared Platform
STP	Straight-Through Processing
TARGET	Trans-European Automated Real-Time Gross Settlement Express Transfer System
TBTF	Too-big-to-fail
TEU	Treaty on European Union
TFEU	Treaty on the Functioning of the EU
TLAC	Total loss-absorbing capacity
TLTROs	Targeted Longer-Term Refinancing Operations
TSCG	Treaty on Stability, Coordination and Governance in the Economic and Monetary Union
T2S	TARGET2-Securities
UCITS	Undertakings for Collective Investments in Transferable Securities
UK	United Kingdom
US	United States
VaR	Value-at-Risk
ZLB	Zero Lower Bound

Preface

As a team of authors we have followed the building of the European financial system from different angles. We have contributed to the academic literature on this topic. Moreover, one of us has been teaching a course on European Financial Integration, from which this book has emerged. On the policy side, the authors have been directly involved in the work of national administrations (i.e. the Ministry of Finance, the Ministry of Economic Affairs in the Netherlands, and the Dutch central bank) as well as the European institutions (i.e. the Council, the European Commission, and the European Central Bank). As part of our job, two of us have participated in many meetings in Brussels discussing the future of European financial markets and institutions, and negotiating new European financial services directives.

The authors would like to thank Wilco Bolt, Jean Frijns, Ronald Heijmans, Iman van Lelyveld, Albert Menkveld, Almoro Rubin de Cervin, Martijn Schrijvers, Casper de Vries and Peter Wierts for their advice on specific chapters. We thank Martin Admiraal, René Bierdrager and Henk van Kerkhoff for their statistical support.

What is new in the third edition?

Since the first edition of this book, the world's financial system has been through its greatest crisis for a century. What made this crisis unique is that severe financial problems emerged simultaneously in many different countries, and its economic impact was felt throughout the world as a result of the increased interconnectedness of the global economy. Financial innovation also played an important part in the financial crisis. Two chapters deal with (1) financial crises, including an overview of the causes and consequences of the 2007–2009 financial crisis as well as the more recent euro crisis, and (2) financial innovation, including the role of securitisation and the shadow banking system.

In the third edition, the chapters on financial markets and institutions have been updated with new data through 2014 whenever possible. These extensive updates illustrate the impact of the financial crisis and the euro crisis on the process of European financial integration: a breakdown of integration, followed by a partial reversal. On the policy side, the third edition features an extensive analysis of the euro crisis, unconventional monetary policies, the Banking Union, the Basel 3 capital adequacy framework for banking supervision, macroprudential policies and state aid control applied to banks. Compared to the previous editions, more emphasis is put on the comparison with countries outside the European Union.

How does this textbook compare with other books?

Different from other textbooks, *Financial Markets and Institutions: A European Perspective* has a wide coverage dealing with the various elements of the European financial system supported by recent data and examples. This wide coverage implies that we treat not only the functioning of financial markets where trading takes place but also the working of supporting infrastructures (clearing and settlement) where trades are executed. Turning to financial institutions, we cover the full range of financial intermediaries, from institutional investors to banks and insurance companies. Based on new data, we document the gradual shift of financial intermediation from banks towards institutional investors, such as pension funds, mutual funds, and hedge funds. In this process of re-intermediation, the assets of institutional investors have tripled over the last two decades. As to policy making, we cover the full range of monetary policy, financial regulation and supervision, financial stability, and competition. We deal with the challenges of European financial integration for monetary, financial supervision and financial stability policies. Competition is a new topic for a finance textbook.

The existing textbooks in the field of financial markets and institutions generally describe the relevant theories and subsequently relate these theories to the general characteristics of financial markets. An excellent example of a more in-depth textbook is *The Economics of Financial Markets* by Roy E. Bailey. The broad coverage of our book is comparable to the widely used textbook *Financial Markets and Institutions* by Frederic S. Mishkin and Stanley G. Eakins. Whereas our book focuses on the EU, Mishkin and Eakins analyse the US financial system. The early European textbooks (e.g. *The Economics of Money, Banking and Finance – A European Text*, by Peter

Howells and Keith Bain) typically contain chapters on the UK, French, and German banking systems, but do not provide an overview of European banking. More advanced textbooks that do discuss the specifics of the European financial system mostly do this in the context of monetary policy making.

Finally, the excellent *Handbook of European Financial Markets and Institutions*, edited by Xavier Freixas, Philipp Hartmann, and Colin Mayer, has a broad coverage of the European financial system, but deals with topics on a stand-alone basis in separate chapters and is not constructed as an integrated textbook. Nevertheless, this handbook contains very useful material for further study of particular aspects of the European financial system.

How to use this book

Financial Markets and Institutions: A European Perspective is an accessible textbook for both undergraduate and graduate students of Finance, Economics, and Business Administration. Each chapter first gives an overview and identifies learning objectives. Throughout the book we use boxes in which certain issues are explained in more detail, by referring to theory or practical examples. Furthermore, we make abundant use of graphs and tables to give students a comprehensive overview of the European financial system. At the end of each chapter we provide suggestions for further reading. Cambridge University Press provides a supporting website for this book. This website contains exercises (and their solutions) for each chapter. The website also provides regular updates of figures and tables used in the book, and identifies new policy issues.

A basic understanding of finance is needed to use this textbook, as we assume that students are familiar with the basic finance models, such as the standard Capital Asset Pricing Model (CAPM). The book can be used for third-year undergraduate courses as well as for graduate courses. More advanced material for graduate students is contained in special boxes marked by a star (*). Undergraduate students can skip these technical boxes.

Jakob de Haan
Sander Oosterloo
Dirk Schoenmaker

Part I

Setting the Stage

CHAPTER

1

Functions of the Financial System

OVERVIEW

Having a well-functioning financial system in place that directs funds to their most productive uses is a crucial prerequisite for economic development. The financial system consists of all financial intermediaries and financial markets, and their relations with respect to the flow of funds to and from households, governments, business firms, and foreigners, as well as the financial infrastructure.

The main task of the financial system is to channel funds from sectors that have a surplus to sectors that have a shortage of funds. In doing so, the financial sector performs two main functions: (1) reducing information and transaction costs, and (2) facilitating the trading, diversification, and management of risk. These functions are discussed at length in this chapter.

The importance of financial markets and financial intermediaries differs across Member States of the European Union (EU). An important question is how differences in financial systems affect macroeconomic outcomes. Atomistic markets face a free-rider problem: when an investor acquires information about an investment project and behaves accordingly, he reveals this information to all investors, thereby dissuading other investors from devoting resources towards acquiring information. Financial intermediaries may be better able to deal with this problem than financial markets.

This chapter discusses these and other pros and cons of bank-based and market-based systems. A specific element in this debate is the role of corporate governance, i.e. the set of mechanisms arranging the relationship between stakeholders of a firm, notably holders of equity, and the management of the firm. Investors (the outsiders) cannot perfectly monitor managers acting on their behalf since managers (the insiders) have superior information about the performance of the company. So there is a need for certain mechanisms that prevent the insiders of a company using the profits of the firm for their own benefit rather than returning the money to the outside investors. This chapter outlines the various mechanisms in place.

While there is considerable evidence that financial development up to some point is good for economic growth, there is no clear evidence that one type of financial system is better for growth than another. However, various recent studies suggest that differences in financial systems may influence the type of activity in which a country specialises. The reason is that different forms of economic activity may be more easily provided by one financial system than another.

In the years before the financial crisis, the banking system in industrial countries saw two major changes. First, the traditional banking model, in which the issuing banks hold loans until they are repaid, was increasingly replaced by the 'originate and distribute' banking model. In this model, banks pool loans (like mortgages) and then tranch and sell them via securitisation. Second, this securitisation led to a non-regulated shadow banking system. The shadow banking system refers to institutions that support bank-style maturity transformation – funding of long-term assets (primarily highly rated tranches of asset-backed securities) with short-term debt – outside banks and without access to a central bank liquidity backstop.

Finally, the chapter discusses the 'law and finance' view according to which legal system differences are key in explaining international differences in financial structure. According to this approach, distinguishing countries by the efficiency of national legal systems in supporting financial transactions is more useful than distinguishing countries by whether they have bank-based or market-based financial systems.

LEARNING OBJECTIVES

After you have studied this chapter, you should be able to:

- explain the main functions of a financial system
- differentiate between the roles of financial markets and financial intermediaries
- explain why financial development may stimulate economic growth and why this relationship may become negative
- explain why government regulation and supervision of the financial system is needed
- describe the advantages and disadvantages of bank-based and market-based financial systems
- explain the various corporate governance mechanisms
- describe recent changes in the banking system of several industrial countries
- explain the 'law and finance' view.

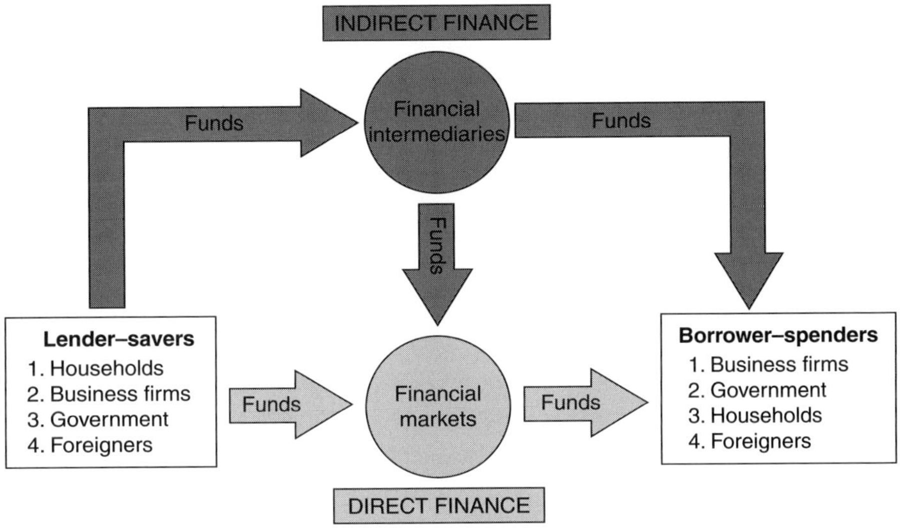

Figure 1.1 Working of the financial system
Source: Mishkin (2006)

1.1 Functions of a financial system

The financial system

This section explains why financial development matters for economic welfare. To understand the importance of financial development, the essentials of a country's *financial system* will first be outlined. The financial system encompasses all financial intermediaries and financial markets, and their relations with respect to the flow of funds to and from households, governments, business firms, and foreigners, as well as the financial infrastructure. *Financial infrastructure* is the set of institutions that enables effective operation of financial intermediaries and financial markets, including such elements as payment systems, credit information bureaus, and collateral registries.

The main task of the financial system is to channel funds from sectors that have a surplus to sectors that have a shortage of funds. Figure 1.1 offers a schematic diagram explaining the working of the financial system.

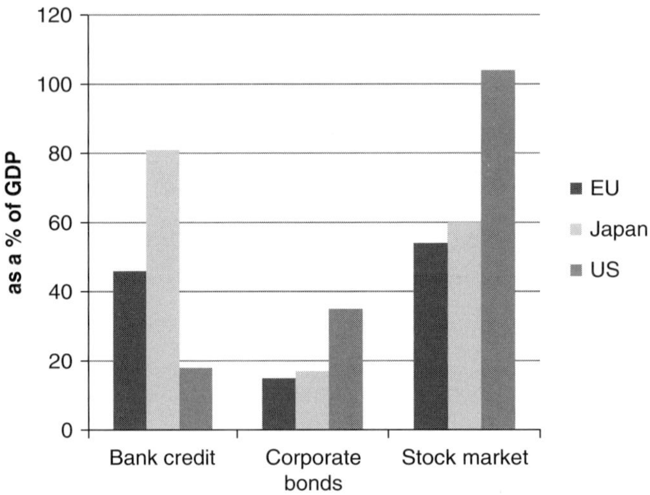

Figure 1.2 Bank credit, corporate bonds and stock market capitalisation in the EU, US and Japan, 2011 (% of GDP)
Source: Authors' calculations based on Bijlsma and Zwart (2013)

Sectors that have saved and are lending funds are on the left, and those that must borrow to finance their spending are on the right. *Direct finance* occurs if a sector in need of funds borrows from another sector via a financial market. A *financial market* is a market where participants issue and trade securities. This direct finance route is shown at the bottom of Figure 1.1. With *indirect finance*, a financial intermediary obtains funds from savers and uses these savings to make loans to a sector in need of finance. *Financial intermediaries* are coalitions of agents that combine to provide financial services, such as banks, insurance companies, finance companies, mutual funds, pension funds, etc. (Levine, 1997). This indirect finance route is shown at the top of Figure 1.1. In most countries, indirect finance is the main route for moving funds from lenders to borrowers. These countries have a *bank-based system*, while countries that rely more on financial markets have a *market-based system*.

Figure 1.2 shows the importance of bank credit, bond, and equity finance in the EU, Japan, and the United States in 2011 as a share of GDP. Clearly, in the EU banks are more important as a source of finance for non-financial corporations than in the US, but in Japan bank credit to non-financial firms is higher than in the EU. Stock market capitalisation and corporate bonds as a share of GDP are highest in the US.

The financial system transforms household savings into funds available for investment by firms. However, the importance of financial markets and financial intermediaries differs across Member States of the EU, as will be explained in some detail in this chapter. Also, the types of assets held by households differ among the various European countries. Despite all these differences, there is one feature that is common to all the financial systems in these countries and that is the importance of *internal finance*. Most investments by firms in industrial countries are financed through retained earnings, regardless of the relative importance of financial markets and intermediaries (Allen and Gale, 2000).

The past 30 years have seen revolutionary changes in the structure of the world's financial markets and institutions. Some financial markets have become obsolete, while new ones have emerged. Similarly, some financial institutions have gone bankrupt, while new entrants have emerged. However, the functions of the financial system have been more stable than the markets and institutions used to accomplish these functions (Merton, 1995). This first chapter of the book discusses at length the functions of the financial system. The later chapters discuss the changes in the financial markets and financial institutions in Europe.

At times, major disruptions occur in the financial system which are characterised by sharp declines in asset prices and the failure of financial intermediaries. Such financial crises have been a feature of capitalist economies for hundreds of years. Often they are followed by severe economic downturns. Chapter 2 will discuss financial crises, zooming in on the most recent banking and debt crises which have hit the euro area since 2008.

Having a well-functioning financial system in place that directs funds to their most productive uses is a crucial prerequisite for economic development. If sectors with surplus funds cannot channel their money to sectors with good investment opportunities, many productive investments will never take place. Indeed, cross-country, case-study, industry- and firm-level analyses suggest that the functioning of financial systems is vitally linked to economic growth. Specifically, countries with larger banks and more active stock markets grow faster over subsequent decades, even after controlling for many other factors underlying economic growth (Levine, 2005). Box 1.1 discusses some studies coming to this conclusion, as well as some recent studies showing that above some threshold financial development no longer has a positive impact on growth.

Box 1.1 Financial development and economic growth

King and Levine (1993a, 1993b) were among the first to argue that financial development is related to economic development. King and Levine (1993b) suggest that current financial depth can predict economic growth over the subsequent 10–30 years and conclude that 'better financial systems stimulate faster productivity growth and growth in per capita output by funnelling society's resources to promising productivity-enhancing endeavours' (King and Levine, 1993b, p. 540).

However, Papaioannou (2008) points out that evidence based on cross-country cross-sectional regressions faces various problems in establishing causality. First, it is almost impossible to account for all possible factors that may foster growth. Second, the effect of financial development may be heterogeneous across countries. Third, there can be reverse causation: financial development can be both the cause and the consequence of economic growth. Finally, the indicators of financial development as generally used in these studies (such as private domestic credit to GDP and market capitalisation as a share of GDP) lack a sound theoretical basis.

Rajan and Zingales (1998) argue that financial development should be most relevant to industries that depend on external finance and that these industries should grow fastest in countries with well-developed financial systems. They therefore focus on 36 individual industries in 41 countries and analyse the influence of the interaction between the external financial dependence of those industries and the financial development of the countries on the growth rates of those industries in the different countries over the period 1980 to 1990. Using various measures of financial development of a country (the ratio of market capitalisation to GDP, domestic credit to the private sector over GDP, and accounting standards), they report a strong relation between economic growth in different industries and countries and the interaction of financial development of countries and the financial dependence of industries. Rajan and Zingales (1998, p. 584) conclude that their results 'suggest that financial development has a substantial supportive influence on the rate of economic growth and this works, at least partly, by reducing the cost of external finance to financially dependent firms'.

Other important studies include Levine *et al.* (2000), who address the endogeneity problems inherent in finance and growth regressions, and the papers in Demirgüç-Kunt and Levine (2001) that use a number of different econometric techniques on datasets ranging from micro-level firm data to international comparative studies. All these studies, and many others, report evidence that financial development stimulates economic growth (Levine, 2005; Papaioannou, 2008).

However, some recent studies come to different conclusions. For instance, Arcand *et al.* (2012) report that at intermediate levels of financial depth, there is a positive relationship between the size of the financial system and economic growth, but at high levels of

Box 1.1 (cont.)

financial depth, more finance is associated with less growth. In fact, the marginal effect of financial depth on output growth becomes negative when credit to the private sector reaches 80–100 per cent of GDP. Likewise, Cecchetti and Kharroubi (2012) report that financial development has a non-linear impact on aggregate productivity growth. Based on a sample of developed and emerging economies, they show that the level of financial development is good only up to a point, after which it becomes a drag on growth.

There are several possible reasons why large financial systems may have a negative effect on economic growth. First, countries with a large financial sector are more prone to severe financial crises which are followed by financial recession or even depression (see Chapter 2). Second, a large financial sector may lead to misallocation of resources as the financial sector may 'steal' talents from the productive sectors of the economy and therefore be inefficient from society's point of view.

Main functions

Let us focus on the two main *functions of the financial system*, i.e. (1) reducing information and transaction costs, and (2) facilitating the trading, diversification, and management of risk, to explain why the financial sector may stimulate capital formation and/or technological innovation, two of the driving forces of economic growth.

Reducing information asymmetry and transaction costs

The financial system helps overcome an information asymmetry between borrowers and lenders. An information asymmetry can occur ex ante and ex post, i.e. before and after a financial contract has been agreed upon. The ex-ante information asymmetry arises because borrowers generally know more about their investment projects than lenders. Borrowers most eager to engage in a transaction are the most likely ones to produce an undesirable outcome for the lender (*adverse selection*). It is difficult and costly to evaluate potential borrowers. Individual savers may not have the time, capacity, or means to collect and process information on a wide array of potential borrowers. So high information costs may keep funds from flowing to their highest productive use. Financial intermediaries may reduce the costs of acquiring and processing information and thereby improve resource allocation (see Chapters 9, 10, and 11). Without intermediaries, each investor would face the large fixed cost associated with evaluating investment projects. Also, financial markets may reduce information costs (see Chapter 5). Economising on information-acquisition costs facilitates the gathering of information about investment opportunities and thereby improves resource allocation. Besides identifying the best investments, financial intermediaries may boost the rate of technological innovation by identifying those entrepreneurs with the best chances of successfully initiating new goods and production processes (Levine, 2005).

The information asymmetry problem occurs ex post when borrowers, but not investors, can observe actual behaviour. Once a loan has been granted, there is a risk that the borrower will engage in activities that are undesirable from the perspective of the lender (*moral hazard*). Financial markets and intermediaries also mitigate the information acquisition and enforcement costs of monitoring borrowers. For example, equity holders and banks will create financial arrangements that compel managers to manage the firm in their best interest (see section 1.2 for more details).

Furthermore, the financial system reduces the time and money spent in carrying out financial transactions (*transaction costs*). Financial intermediaries can reduce transaction costs as they have developed expertise and can take advantage of economies of scale and scope. A good example of how the financial system reduces transaction costs is *pooling*, i.e. the (costly) process of agglomerating capital from disparate savers for investment. By pooling the funds of various small savers, large investment projects can be financed. Without pooling, savers would have to buy and sell entire firms (Levine, 1997). Mobilising savings involves (1) overcoming the transaction costs associated with collecting savings from different individuals, and (2) overcoming the informational asymmetries associated with making savers feel comfortable in relinquishing control of their savings (Levine, 2005).

By reducing information and transaction costs, financial systems lower the cost of channelling funds between borrowers and lenders, which frees up resources for other uses, such as investment and innovation. In addition, financial intermediation affects capital accumulation by allocating funds to their most productive uses. However, higher returns on investment ambiguously affect saving rates, as the income and substitution effects work in opposite directions. A higher return makes saving more attractive (substitution effect), but fewer savings are needed to receive the same returns (income effect). Similarly, lower risk – to which we will turn below – also ambiguously affects savings rates. Thus, the improved resource allocation and lower risk brought about by the financial system may lower saving rates (Levine, 2005).

Trading, diversification, and management of risk

The second main service the financial sector provides is facilitating the trading, diversification, and management of risk. Financial systems may mitigate the risks associated with individual investment projects by providing opportunities for trading and diversifying risk which – in the end – may affect long-run economic growth. In general, high-return projects tend to be riskier than low-return projects. Thus, financial systems that make it easier for people to diversify risk by offering a broad range of high-risk (like equity) and low-risk (like government bonds) investment opportunities tend to induce a portfolio shift towards projects with higher expected returns. Likewise, the ability to hold a diversified portfolio of innovative projects reduces risk and promotes investment in growth-enhancing innovative activities (Levine, 2005).

One particular way in which financial intermediaries and markets reduce risk is by providing *liquidity*, i.e. the ease and speed with which agents can convert assets into purchasing power at agreed prices (Levine, 1997). Savers are generally unwilling to delegate control over their savings to investors for long periods, so less investment is likely to occur in high-return projects that require a long-term commitment of capital. However, the financial system creates the possibility for savers to hold liquid assets – like equity, bonds, or demand deposits – that they can sell quickly and easily if they seek access to their savings, simultaneously transforming these liquid financial instruments into long-term capital investments. Without a financial system, all investors would be locked into illiquid long-term investments that yield high payoffs only to those who consume at the end of the investment. Liquidity is created by financial intermediaries as well as financial markets. For instance, a bank transforms short-term liquid deposits into long-term illiquid loans, therefore making it possible for households to withdraw deposits without interrupting industrial production. Similarly, stock markets reduce liquidity risks by allowing stock holders to trade their shares, while firms still have access to long-term capital.

Risk measurement and management is a key function of financial intermediaries. The traditional role of banks in monitoring the credit risk of borrowers has evolved towards the use of advanced models by all types of financial intermediaries to measure and manage financial risks. Progress in information technology has facilitated the development of advanced risk-management models, which rely on statistical methods to process financial data (see Chapters 10 and 11 for more details).

Securitisation is an important means for the financial system to perform the function of trading, diversification, and management of risk. *Securitisation* is the packaging of particular assets and the redistribution of these packages by selling securities, backed by these assets, to investors (see also section 1.3). For instance, an intermediary may create a pool of mortgage loans (bundling) and then issue bonds backed by those mortgage loans (unbundling). Securitisation thereby converts illiquid assets into liquid assets. While residential mortgages were the first financial assets to be securitised, many other types of financial assets have undergone the same process. A recent example is so-called catastrophe bonds (also known as cat bonds). If insurers have built up a portfolio of risks by insuring properties in a region that may be hit by a catastrophe, they could create a special-purpose entity that would issue the cat bond (see Chapter 11 for more details). Investors who buy the bond make a healthy return on their investment, unless a catastrophe, like a hurricane or an earthquake, hits the region, because then the principal initially paid by the investors is forgiven and is used by the sponsors to pay their claims to policy holders.

While the focus of finance is traditionally on fostering economic growth, more recently there is also attention for social and environmental factors. Under the heading of finance and sustainability, a new field stresses the role of finance in accelerating the transition towards a sustainable economy (see Box 1.2).

Box 1.2 Finance and sustainability

The allocation role of finance plays an important role in the transition towards a sustainable economy. The Brundtland Commission defines sustainable development as development that meets the needs of the present generation without compromising the ability of future generations to meet their own needs. Resource scarcity and climate change are reaching planetary boundaries and may reduce consumption of future generations. Population growth is speeding up this process. In addition to economic and financial factors, sustainable finance also looks at social and environmental factors (see Figure 1.3). Social factors encompass inequality and (child) labour conditions, while environmental factors include the intensity of resource use, pollution, and ecosystem decline. The impact of economic activities on the environment is typically felt in the long term. By contrast, conventional finance is mostly focused on the short term, which is reinforced by quarterly reporting of financial results (though life insurance companies and pension funds tend to have a long-term focus; see Chapter 9).

Box 1.2 (cont.)

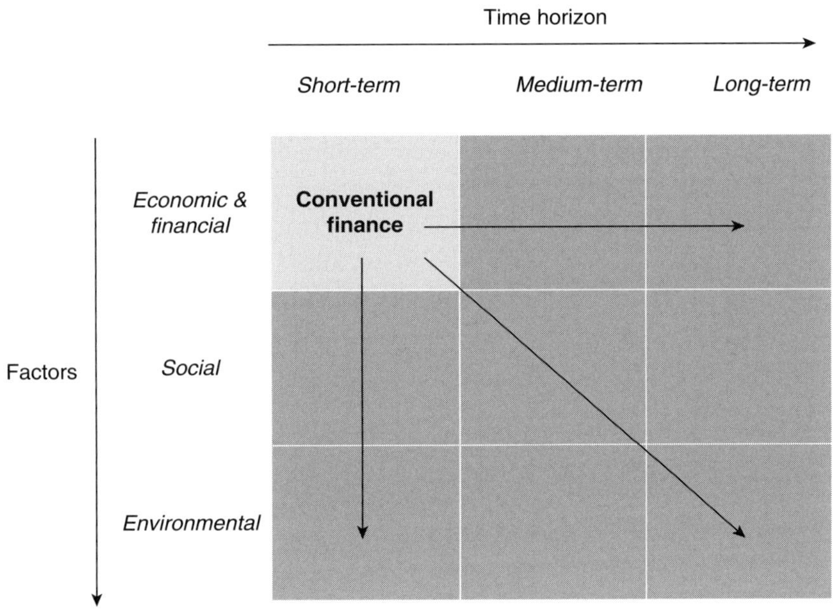

Figure 1.3 Time horizon and factors in sustainable finance
Source: Sikken (2014)

The challenge is to integrate social and environmental factors in decision-making. Some institutional investors have adopted socially responsible investing (SRI), which incorporates environmental, social, and governance information into investment decisions. Companies are integrating sustainability principles into business strategies by adopting integrated governance and integrated reporting. While environmental and social reports used to be stand-alone reports (and were therefore not much read), the newly emerging integrated reports show how a company's strategy, governance, performance, and prospects, in the context of its external environment, lead to the creation of value in the short, medium, and long term.

In a meta-study on the performance of SRI funds, Renneboog *et al.* (2008) report that existing studies hint but do not univocally demonstrate that SRI investment funds perform worse than conventional funds. Bauer *et al.* (2005) find little evidence that the average performance of SRI funds in the US and UK is different from that of conventional funds. But restricting the investment universe to SRI can limit the diversification possibilities and negatively influence the risk-return trade-off (Geczy *et al.*, 2006).

Role of government

A well-functioning financial system requires particular government actions. First, government regulation is needed to protect *property rights* and to *enforce* contracts. Property rights refer to control of the use of the property, the right to any benefit from the property, the right to transfer or sell the property, and the right to exclude others from the property. Absence of secure property rights and enforcement of contracts severely restrict financial transactions and investment, thereby hampering financial development. If it is not clear who is entitled to perform a transaction, exchange will be unlikely. As the financial system allocates capital across time and space, contracts are needed to connect providers and users of funds. If one of the parties does not adhere to the content of a contract, an independent enforcement agency (for instance, a court) is needed; otherwise contracts would be useless.

Second, government regulation is needed to encourage proper information provision (*transparency*) so that providers of funds can take better decisions on how to allocate their money. Government regulation can reduce adverse selection and moral hazard problems in financial systems and enhance their efficiency by increasing the amount of information available to investors, for instance by setting and enforcing accounting standards. Although government regulation to increase transparency is crucial to reducing adverse selection and moral hazard problems, borrowers have strong incentives to cheat, so government regulation may not always be sufficient, as various corporate scandals, such as WorldCom, Parmalat, and Ahold, illustrate.

Third, in view of the importance of financial intermediaries, government should arrange for regulation and supervision of financial institutions in order to ensure their *soundness*. Savers are often unable to properly evaluate the financial soundness of a financial intermediary as that requires extensive effort and technical knowledge. Financial intermediaries have an incentive to take too many risks. This is because high-risk investments generally bring in more revenues that accrue to the intermediary, while if the intermediary fails a substantial part of the costs will be borne by the depositors. Government regulation may prevent financial intermediaries from taking too much risk. Depositors may also be protected by introducing some deposit-guarantee system, but this may provide the intermediary with an even stronger incentive for risky behaviour. Finally, there is a risk that a sound financial intermediary may fail when another intermediary goes bankrupt due to taking too much risk (*contagion*). Since the public cannot distinguish between sound and unsound financial institutions, they may withdraw their money once a financial intermediary fails, thereby perhaps destroying a sound institution. Chapter 12 discusses *financial supervision* in the EU, while Chapter 13 deals with *financial stability* in the EU. The latter can be defined as a situation in which the financial system is capable of withstanding shocks and the unravelling of financial imbalances, thereby mitigating the likelihood of disruptions in the financial-intermediation process, which are severe enough to significantly impair the allocation of savings to profitable investment opportunities (ECB, 2006). An important prerequisite for financial stability is a well-functioning financial infrastructure, which is discussed in Chapter 7.

New regulatory and supervisory policies are increasingly designed at the global level. The Basel Committee on Banking Supervision (BCBS), the International Association of Insurance Supervisors (IAIS), and the International Organisation of Securities Commissions (IOSCO) are traditionally setting the international standards. While these committees are more technical, the Financial Stability Board (FSB), which comprises ministers of finance, central banks, and supervisors of the Group of Twenty countries, has set the international financial reform agenda after the financial crisis. The FSB is more political and aims to tackle thorny issues such as too-big-to-fail (TBTF). To that end, the FSB has produced a list of global systemically important financial institutions that have to follow stricter regulations (see Chapters 12 and 13).

Finally, governments are responsible for *competition policy* to ensure competition. There are many ways that competition may be hampered. For instance, competitors may agree to sell the same product or service at the same price (*price fixing*), leading to profits for all the sellers. Another example is that banks may receive support from the government (*state aid*), leading to an unfair advantage over their competitors. In the EU, competition policy is based on the Treaty on the Functioning of the European Union, particularly Articles 101 (Restrictive practices), 102 (Abuse of dominant market power), and 107 (State aid control). The Treaty states: 'The following shall be prohibited . . . : (a) directly or indirectly fix purchase or selling prices . . . (b) limit or control production . . . (c) share markets or sources of supply . . ..' Chapter 14 provides further details on EU competition policy for the financial sector.

Foreign participants

Figure 1.1 assumes that foreigners also participate in the financial system and that domestic sectors can borrow from or lend to foreigners. What are the benefits if it becomes possible to lend or borrow in foreign financial markets and to do business with foreign financial intermediaries? Following Mishkin (2006), we may differentiate between the direct and indirect effects of (international) *financial liberalisation*, i.e. the opening up of domestic financial markets to foreign capital and foreign financial intermediaries.

Allowing foreign capital to freely enter domestic markets increases the availability of funds, stimulating investment and economic growth. Furthermore, competition in the financial system may be enhanced when foreign financial intermediaries enter a country, stimulating domestic financial intermediaries to become more efficient.[1] Finally, opening up to foreign capital and foreign financial institutions may lead to a constitution for institutional reforms that stimulate financial development (see also Box 1.3). For instance, when domestic financial intermediaries lose customers to foreign intermediaries, they may support institutional reforms, such as improved transparency regulation, helping them to compete better (Mishkin, 2006).

As will be explained in some detail in Chapter 3, the EU has gone beyond financial liberalisation and has taken various steps to promote the creation of a single market for financial services. Chapter 6 will analyse *financial market integration* in the EU. According to Baele *et al.* (2008), a market for a given set of financial instruments or services is fully integrated when all potential market participants in such a market (1) are subject to a single set of rules when they decide to deal with those financial instruments or services, (2) have equal access to this set of financial instruments or services, and (3) are treated equally when they operate in the market.

1.2 Bank-based versus market-based financial systems

There are important differences among the financial systems of the Member States of the EU. For instance, the size of financial markets and the importance of bank and non-bank financial intermediaries (such as mutual funds, private pension funds, and insurance companies) differ substantially across countries. Bijlsma and Zwart (2013) have applied principal component analysis on 23 indicators related to the structure of individual countries' financial systems, such as household deposits, bank credit to non-financial

Box 1.3 The political economy of financial reform

Reform of the financial system may foster financial development, which, in turn, may stimulate economic growth. For instance, Bekeart *et al.* (2005) study countries that liberalised their equity markets in the period 1980–1997. They report that these policies resulted in an overall increase of the annual per-capita GDP growth of approximately 1 per cent. This finding is robust to controlling for other reforms, such as capital-account liberalisation.

Some countries have reformed earlier and also more extensively than others. What explains these policy differences? A small but highly relevant line of research has examined the forces driving financial reform. The basis of the analysis is that there are winners and losers in financial reform. The status quo will persist as long as the benefits of no reform outweigh the costs of no reform for those who determine the timing and pace of policies. Fernandez and Rodrik (1991) explain the tendency to retain the status quo on the basis of uncertainty faced by individuals with respect to the benefits of the reform. If it is not known ex ante who will benefit from reform, a majority may oppose the policy change even if they will benefit ex post from reform. So even if some of the existing financial institutions may prosper after the reform, uncertainty regarding the identities of the winners and losers may cause the sector as a whole to oppose the reform. Learning, made possible by the accumulation of new information, is particularly relevant in this context (Abiad and Mody, 2005). If the reform takes place in various stages, then early reform may help agents assess whether they will benefit or lose so that they may change their views. Consequently, some agents who initially opposed reforms may become advocates for further reforms.

Abiad and Mody (2005) use a newly constructed financial-reform index, covering 35 countries over the period 1973–1996, to examine the driving forces of financial reform. The index captures six dimensions of financial liberalisation, including the degree of controls on international financial transactions. On each dimension, a country is classified as being fully repressed, partially repressed, largely liberalised, or fully liberalised. When they relate their index to various explanatory variables, Abiad and Mody (2005) find that countries with highly repressed financial sectors tend to stay that way, but once reforms are initiated, the likelihood of additional reforms increases. This suggests that learning plays an important role. Also, the occurrence of crises plays a role. While balance-of-payments crises tend to increase the likelihood of financial reforms, banking crises tend to increase the likelihood of reversals of reform. According to Abiad and Mody (2005), left-wing and right-wing governments are seen to operate similarly in similar situations, and openness to trade does not, on average, increase the pace of reform.

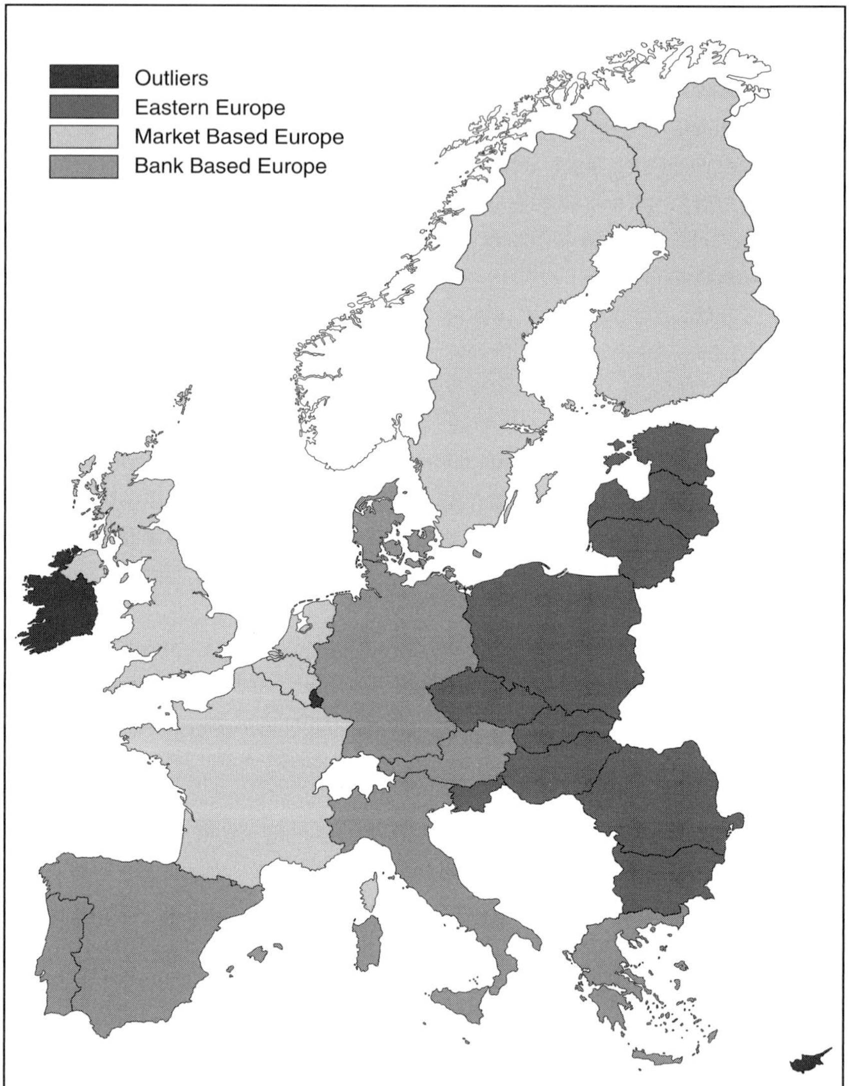

Figure 1.4 Classification of EU Member States
Source: Bijlsma and Zwart (2013)

firms, market capitalisation of listed firms, the size of the banking sector, the volume of initial public offerings, venture capital investment activity, the size of foreign banking assets, bank concentration levels, and bank profitability, to classify countries as more bank-based or more market-based. As Figure 1.4 shows, they distinguish four groups of countries:

1. The Netherlands, United Kingdom, Belgium, France, Finland, and Sweden (market-based countries);
2. Austria, Denmark, Germany, Greece, Italy, Portugal, and Spain (bank-based countries);
3. Bulgaria, Czech Republic, Estonia, Hungary, Latvia, Lithuania, Poland, Romania, Slovakia, and Slovenia (Eastern Europe);
4. Ireland, Malta, Cyprus, and Luxembourg (outliers).

Countries in the first group are closer to the US than other EU Member States. The second group consists of EU countries that resemble Japan more closely. The third group includes the Eastern European countries that accessed the EU more recently. These countries generally have smaller financial systems than those in the old Member States. Still, also in these countries firms rely more on financing by banks than on market finance. Finally, Ireland, Cyprus, Malta, and Luxembourg are classified as outliers. These countries have banking sectors that are both very large and extend a large amount of credit compared to their national economies. Arguably, these countries can also be classified as bank-based, in view of the size of their banking sector.

However, even within each group there are sometimes important differences. For instance, among bank-based countries the importance of bank credit for financing non-financial firms differs substantially as shown by Figure 1.5. For instance, in Spain bank credit to non-financial firms was much higher than in Italy over the 2007–2011 period.

A key question is how these differences in financial systems affect macroeconomic outcomes. For instance, do bank-based financial systems (like that of Germany) lead to higher rates of economic growth than market-based systems (like that of the UK)? The post-war high growth rates of Germany and Japan – where banks are dominant in the financial system – were often considered as 'evidence' that bank-based systems outperform market-based systems. However, more detailed empirical work, using micro-level data, has frequently failed to identify the superiority of bank-based systems. Also, the much better growth performance of Anglo-American countries during the 1990s raised scepticism about the acclaimed advantages of bank-based systems (Carlin and Mayer, 2000).

Providing financial functions

What are the theoretical reasons explaining differences in the growth performance of countries with bank-based or market-based systems? As Levine (2005) pointed out, the case for a bank-based system refers to the

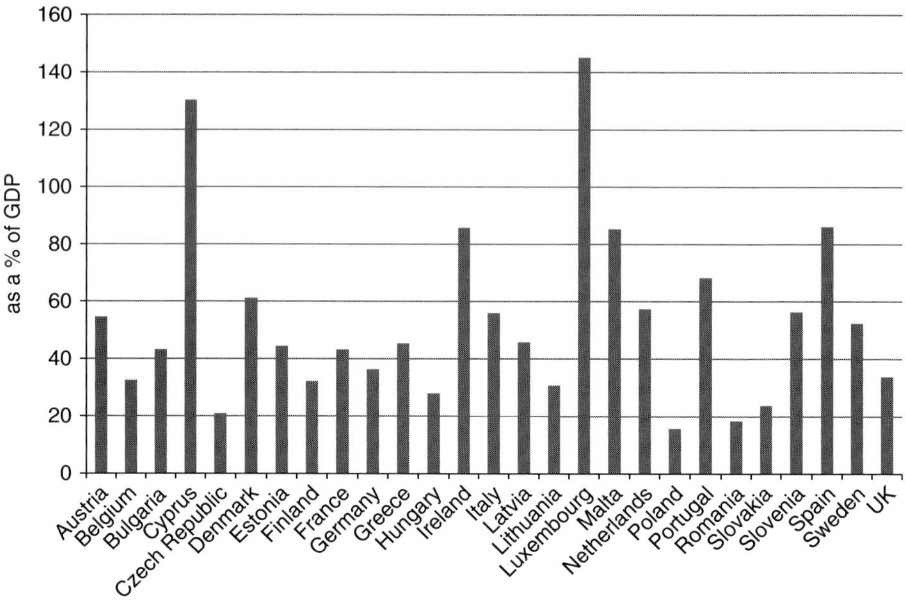

Figure 1.5 Bank credit to non-financial firms (average 2007–2011) as percentage of GDP
Source: Authors' calculation using data provided by Bijlsma and Zwart (2013)

role of markets in providing financial functions. Atomistic markets face a *free-rider problem*: when an investor acquires information about an investment project and behaves accordingly, he reveals this information to all investors, thereby dissuading other investors from devoting resources towards acquiring information. So investors do not have strong incentives to properly acquire information, as they cannot keep the benefits of this information. Consequently, innovative projects that foster growth may not be identified. Banks, however, may keep the information they acquire, often by having long-run relationships with firms, and use it in a profitable way. Since banks can make investments without revealing their decisions immediately in public markets, they have the right incentives to do research on investment projects. Furthermore, banks with close ties to firms may be more effective than atomistic markets at exerting pressure on firms to repay their loans. Often, firms obtain a variety of financial services from their bank and also maintain checking accounts with it, thereby increasing the bank's information about the borrower. For example, the bank can learn about the firm's sales by monitoring the cash flowing through its checking account or by factoring the firm's accounts receivables. Firms may profit from these long-term relationships in the form of access to credit at lower prices.[2]

The problem of free riding that occurs due to diffuse shareholders may be less in the case of large, concentrated ownership. However, concentrated owners may maximise the private benefits of control at the expense of minority shareholders. Furthermore, large equity owners may stimulate the firm to undertake higher-risk activities since shareholders benefit on the upside, while debt holders share the costs of failure. Finally, concentrated control of corporate assets produces market power that may distort public policies (Levine, 2005). Empirical evidence does not suggest that international differences in concentrated ownership are associated with disciplining firms' management (Carlin and Mayer, 2000).

Corporate governance

A second element in the debate on the pros and cons of bank-based vs. market-based systems refers to *corporate governance*, i.e. the set of mechanisms arranging the relationship between stakeholders of a firm, notably holders of equity, and the management of the firm. Principal-agent theory predicts that the managers, the agents, may not always act in the best interest of the owners, the principal (Jensen and Meckling, 1976). Investors (the outsiders) cannot perfectly monitor managers acting on their behalf since managers (the insiders) have superior information about the performance of the company. So there is a need for certain mechanisms that prevent the insiders of a company using the profits of the firm for their own benefit rather than returning the money to the outside investors. Corporate governance systems differ across the EU Member States (see Box 1.4).

Investors can use several tools to ensure that the management of a firm acts in their interest. The most important of these are the appointment of the board of directors, executive compensation, the market for corporate control, concentrated holdings, and monitoring by financial intermediaries (Allen and Gale, 2000).

By appointing the board of directors,[3] shareholders have an instrument to control managers and ensure that the firm is run in their interest. The way that boards are chosen differs across countries. In many countries, the management of the firm effectively determines who is nominated for the board, so that an incestuous relationship may blossom between boards of directors and management (Jensen, 1993). Boards may, for instance, approve various protection mechanisms that reduce the attractiveness of

Box 1.4 Corporate governance in EU Member States

Governance Metrics International (GMI) publishes ratings of the corporate governance of firms on a scale of 1.0 (lowest) to 10.0 (highest). Each GMI rating report includes a summary of the company's overall governance profile and commentary on each of the six research categories employed by GMI: board accountability, financial disclosure and internal controls, shareholder rights, executive compensation, market for control and ownership base, and corporate-behaviour and corporate-social-responsibility issues. All company ratings are calculated relative to the 3,400+ companies rated by GMI worldwide ('global rating'). A GMI rating of 9.0 or higher is considered to be well above average. A rating of 7.5–8.5 is considered to be above average, 6.0–7.0 is considered average, 3.5–5.5 is considered to be below average, and 3.0 or less is considered well below average.

The number of firms with a GMI rating differs across countries – ranging from 14 for Poland to 394 for the UK. Figure 1.6 shows the average GMI score for various EU Member States. The figure shows that the corporate governance regimes differ substantially. While the average score for Spain (14 firms) is only 3.97, in the UK it amounts to 7.60.

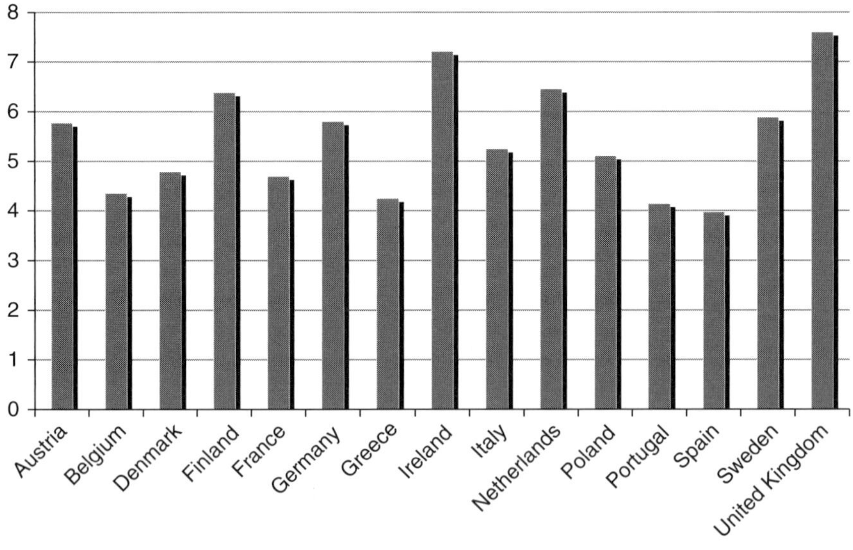

Figure 1.6 Corporate governance rating in EU Member States (averages), 2010
Source: GMI

a takeover, one of the mechanisms in the market for corporate control (see below).

A second method of ensuring that managers pursue the interests of shareholders is to structure executive compensation appropriately. By making managers' compensation depend on the firm's performance, shareholders can provide incentives for the management of the firm. Examples include direct ownership of shares, stock options, and bonuses dependent on the share price. However, contingent compensation may also have a less desirable effect. If the managers' compensation is sensitive to the performance of the firm, they will have an incentive to take excessive risks as they benefit greatly from good performance, while the penalties for poor performance are limited (Allen and Gale, 2000).

Probably the most important mechanism to control firm management is the market for corporate control that can operate in three ways: proxy contests, friendly mergers and takeovers, and hostile takeovers. In *proxy contests*, a shareholder tries to persuade other shareholders to act in concert with him and force the management of the firm to change course or even to unseat the board of directors. Whether proxy contests work depends, among other things, on the dispersion of shareholding. *Friendly mergers and takeovers* occur when the management of both firms agree that combining the firms would create additional value. The transaction can occur in various ways, such as an exchange of stock or a tender offer by one firm for the other firm's stock (Allen and Gale, 2000).

The potentially most important device in the market for corporate control forcing managers to behave in accordance with the interests of stock holders is a hostile takeover. A *takeover bid* is an attempt by a potential acquirer to obtain a controlling block of shares in a target firm, and thereby gain control of the board and, through it, the firm's management. If a firm does not exploit all of its growth potential, some outsiders may consider the firm an attractive takeover target. After a takeover, they will try to improve the performance of the firm by replacing the current management. This threat gives managers the right incentives to behave in the interest of current stock holders. However, a takeover threat may not be effective for various reasons. First, a takeover threat may not work well due to the information asymmetry between insiders and outsiders: ill-informed outsiders will outbid relatively well-informed insiders for control of firms only when they pay too much. Second, there may again be a free-rider problem. If an outsider spends resources obtaining information, other market participants will observe the results of this research when the outsider bids for shares of the firm. Third, firms often take various actions that deter takeovers and thereby weaken the market as a disciplining device. For instance, a firm may issue rights to existing shareholders to acquire a large number of new securities.

Since the market for corporate control may not always ensure that managers behave in accordance with the interest of shareholders, proponents of a bank-based system argue that monitoring by financial institutions may be more effective in this regard. The agency problem is solved by financial institutions acting as the outside monitor for firms (Allen and Gale, 2000). The main characteristics of this system are a long-term relationship between banks – but potentially also other financial intermediaries like institutional investors (see Chapter 9) – and firms, the holding of both equity and debt by the financial intermediary, and the active intervention by the financial intermediary should the firm become financially distressed.

The case for a market-based system focuses on the problems created by powerful banks. While firms with close ties to a 'main bank' have greater access to capital and are less cash constrained than firms without such a bank, the dependence on an influential bank may have various negative effects. Bankers act in their own best interests, not necessarily in the best interests of all stakeholders. For instance, banks with power can extract part of the expected future profits from potentially profitable investments, which may reduce the firm's effort to undertake innovative investments. Influential banks may also prevent outsiders from removing inefficient managers if these managers are particularly generous to the bankers. Bank managers may also be more reluctant to bankrupt firms with which they have had long-term ties (Levine, 2005).

Furthermore, there may be difficulties in governing banks themselves. The information asymmetries between bank insiders and outsiders may be larger than with non-financial corporations. Therefore, banks are even more likely than non-financial firms to have a large, controlling owner.

Finally, proponents of market-based financial systems claim that markets provide a richer set of instruments to manage risks. While bank-based systems may provide inexpensive, basic risk-management services for standardised situations, market-based systems provide greater flexibility to tailor make products.

Types of activity

While there is considerable evidence that financial development is good for economic growth, there is no clear evidence that one kind of financial system is better for growth than another. For instance, Levine (2002) finds that the quality of the financial services produced by the entire financial system (intermediaries and markets) matters for economic growth. However, various recent studies suggest that differences in financial systems may influence the type of activity in which a country specialises. The reason is that different forms of economic activity may be more easily provided by one financial system than the other. Box 1.5 summarises a study providing support for this view.

Economies of scale in monitoring make banks more efficient monitors than individual market participants. However, securities markets have the advantage of aggregating diverse views of a large number of market participants and are therefore more likely to support activities where there is a high degree of uncertainty in production, while banks are more likely to support

Box 1.5 Does the financial system matter after all?

To pursue the hypothesis that different financial systems might favour industries with different kinds of characteristics, Carlin and Mayer (2003) examine the interrelation between types of systems, the nature of different industries, and the levels of activity in those industries in different countries. They evaluate whether there is a relationship between the growth rates of industries in different countries and the interaction between country structures (e.g. the degree of market and bank orientation of their financial systems) and industry characteristics (the dependence of industries on external equity or bank-debt sources of finance and inputs of skilled labour). The sample comprises 14 OECD countries and 27 industries over the period from 1970 to 1995. The financial structure of different countries is measured by the size of their stock markets, accounting standards, the ratio of bank credit to GDP, and the degree of bank ownership of corporate equity. The structure of corporate systems is captured by the degree of concentration of ownership and by the extent of pyramid ownership. The characteristics of legal systems are measured by indicators of legal protection of investors or creditors and by the common- or civil-law origin of the legal system as indicated by its source in English, German, Scandinavian, or French law (see below). Carlin and Mayer report strong evidence of a relation between industry growth rates in different countries and the interaction of country financial structures with industry characteristics. Market-oriented financial systems are associated with high growth of external equity-financed and skill-intensive industries. The effect comes through investment in R&D rather than fixed capital expenditures.

activities in which uncertainty is low but gestation periods are long (Carlin and Mayer, 2000). Banks may be effective at eliminating duplication of information gathering and processing, but may not be effective gatherers and processors of information in new, uncertain situations involving innovative products and processes, in which case securities markets work better. Similarly, Dewatripont and Maskin (1995) argue that banks will find it difficult to credibly commit not to renegotiate contracts in the case of long-run contacts with firms. The credible imposition of tight budget constraints may be necessary for the funding of newer, higher-risk firms.

Complements

Some authors argue that financial markets and financial intermediaries may provide complementary growth-enhancing financial services to the economy. Intermediaries may be necessary for the successful functioning of markets. A historical perspective shows that financial markets did not develop spontaneously. The earliest financial transactions involving loans were handled by financial intermediaries. It was not until the Amsterdam Bourse was founded at the start of the seventeenth century that anything like a formal financial market existed (Allen and Gale, 2000). Stock markets may complement banks by spurring competition for corporate control and by offering alternative means of financing investment, thereby reducing the potentially harmful effects of excessive bank power. Indeed, banks have increasingly moved away from their traditional deposit-taking and lending role into fee-generating activities, such as the securitisation of loans and the sale of risk-management products (see section 1.3). Financial markets, of course, also compete with banks. Consumers can invest directly in securities (government and private bonds, and stocks) rather than leaving their money in savings accounts, while borrowers can go to the capital markets rather than to banks. This is often called *dis-intermediation.*

Allen and Santomero (1997) forcefully argue that financial intermediaries reduce what they call *participation costs*, i.e. the costs of learning about effectively using financial markets as well as participating in them on a day-to-day basis. As financial markets have become increasingly complex over time, financial intermediaries offer various services to the uninformed investors, such as providing information, investing on their behalf, or offering a fixed-income claim against the intermediary's balance sheet. Investors get access to financial markets through the intermediary's services, which add value to the transaction by reducing the (perceived) participation costs of uninformed investors. Allen and Santomero argue that the increase in the breadth and depth of financial markets has been the result of greater use of these instruments by financial intermediaries and firms. The increased size of financial markets has coincided with a dramatic shift away from direct participation by individuals in financial markets towards participation through various kinds of intermediaries. The importance of different types of intermediary has also undergone a significant change. While the share of assets held by banks has fallen, that of institutional investors has dramatically increased in size (see Chapter 9 for a further analysis). Also, in countries with a bank-dominated financial system, like France and Italy, the role of institutional investors has increased. As a consequence, institutional investors have also become more dominant in corporate governance issues.

Legal systems

Finally, some recent research suggests that legal system differences are key in explaining international differences in financial structure. In this approach, the financial system is a set of contracts that is defined and made more or less effective by legal rights and enforcement mechanisms. A well-functioning legal system facilitates the operation of both financial markets and intermediaries. According to this literature, distinguishing countries by the efficiency of national legal systems in supporting financial transactions is more useful than distinguishing countries by whether they have bank-based or market-based financial systems. La Porta *et al.* (1997) argue that financial systems offer different levels of creditor and shareholder protection depending on the origin of the legal rules in place, i.e. English, French, German, or Scandinavian origin. Common-law countries of the English tradition protect both shareholders and creditors the most, French civil-law countries the least, and German and Scandinavian civil-law countries somewhere in the middle. La Porta *et al.* (1997, p. 1149) find that 'civil law, and particularly French civil law, countries, have both the weakest investor protections and the least developed capital markets, especially as compared to common law countries'.

Table 1.1 summarises some of the measures as developed by La Porta *et al.* (1997) and extended and updated by Djankov *et al.* (2007; 2008) for the EU Member States. Column (2) shows the legal family to which the country belongs. The rationale of the other measures is as follows. Those who control a firm, whether they are managers, controlling shareholders, or both, can use their power to deliver firm wealth to themselves, without sharing it with the

Table 1.1 Indicators of investor and creditor protection, 2003

(1)	(2)	(3)	(4)	(5)
Country	Law family	Creditor rights	Shareholder rights	Anti-self dealing index
Austria	German	3	2.5	0.21
Belgium	French	2	3	0.54
Bulgaria	German	n.a.	3	0.65
Czech Republic	German	3	4	0.33
Denmark	Scandinavian	3	4	0.46
Finland	Scandinavian	1	3.5	0.46
France	French	0	3.5	0.38
Germany	German	3	3.5	0.28
Greece	French	1	2	0.22
Hungary	German	1	2	0.18
Ireland	English	1	5	0.79
Italy	French	2	2	0.42
Latvia	German	3	4	0.32
Lithuania	French	2	4	0.36
Luxembourg	French	n.a.	2	0.28
Netherlands	French	3	2.5	0.20
Portugal	French	1	2.5	0.44
Slovakia	German	2	3	0.29
Slovenia	German	3	n.a.	n.a.
Spain	French	2	5	0.37
Sweden	Scandinavian	1	3.5	0.33
United Kingdom	English	4	5	0.95

Note: n.a. means not available
Source: Djankov *et al.* (2007, 2008)

other investors. The measures quantify the extent to which various investors are protected. Column (3) presents a creditor rights index that measures powers of secured lenders in bankruptcy (Djankov *et al.*, 2007). The creditor rights index varies between 0 (poor creditor rights) and 4 (strong creditor rights). For their full sample, Djankov *et al.* report that the index of creditor rights for 2003 is lowest in French legal-origin countries and highest in German legal-origin ones.

Column (4) shows an index reflecting shareholder rights. The original index, reported in La Porta *et al.* (1997), has been criticised by a number of scholars for its ad hoc nature, for mistakes in its coding, and for conceptual ambiguity in the definitions of some of its components. Therefore, Djankov *et al.* (2008) came up with a revised and extended index that is shown in column (4) of Table 1.1. This index is available for 72 countries and is based on laws and regulations applicable to publicly traded firms in May 2003. The index summarises the protection of minority shareholders in the corporate decision-making process, including the right to vote. This index varies between 0 (poor shareholder rights) and 6 (strong shareholder rights). For their full sample, Djankov *et al.* (2008) report that the index of shareholder rights is lowest in French legal-origin countries and highest in English legal-origin ones.

A recent alternative measure of shareholder protection quantifies their rights against expropriation by corporate insiders through self-dealing (see Djankov *et al.*, 2008). Various forms of such self-dealing include executive perquisites to excessive compensation, transfer pricing, self-serving financial transactions such as directed equity issuance or personal loans to insiders, and outright theft of corporate assets. This index ranges between 0 (poor protection) and 1 (high protection) and is shown in column (5) of Table 1.1. For their full sample, Djankov *et al.* report that the index is lowest in French legal-origin countries and highest in English legal-origin ones.

Various conclusions can be drawn from Table 1.1. First, the EU Member States clearly have different legal traditions. So, if the finance and law view is correct (see Box 1.6 for some discussion), financial differences in the EU are likely to remain in place, despite attempts to create one single financial market (see Chapter 3 for further details on the various policy initiatives to create such a single market). Second, the various indicators vary widely across EU Member States, suggesting that the degree that investors are protected differs substantially across these countries. For instance, the creditor rights index ranges between 0 (France) and 4 (the UK), while the shareholder index ranges between 1 (Luxembourg) and 5 (Spain and the UK).

1.3 Recent changes

In the years before the financial crisis (which will be discussed in Chapter 2), the banking system in industrial countries saw two major changes. First, the traditional banking model, in which the issuing banks hold loans until they are repaid, was increasingly replaced by the '*originate and distribute*' banking model. As will be explained in more detail below, in this model banks pool loans (like mortgages) and then tranch and sell them via securitisation. Starting

Box 1.6 Legal origin or political institutions?

According to the law and finance literature, the financial development of countries can be traced back to their legal origins (La Porta *et al.*, 1997). There is some evidence in support of this view. Beck *et al.* (2001) investigate the relative effects of political arrangements, legal origin, and different historical factors on financial development. They conclude that legal origin offers a substantially stronger explanation of financial development than political conditions. However, Keefer (2007) challenges this conclusion. He uses total credit extended to the private sector by banks and other financial institutions as a measure of financial-sector development. This is the preferred way of Beck *et al.* (2001) to measure financial development. Keefer reports that various political variables, including his measure of political checks and balances (i.e. how many political actors can block proposed legislation, therefore tracking whether formal institutions exist that potentially impose constraints on arbitrary behaviour by the executive branch) and newspaper circulation (a proxy for the extent of voter information), have a significant influence on financial-sector development. More importantly, these variables remain significant determinants of financial-sector development, even controlling for legal origin. In fact, the legal-origin variables often become insignificant once political variables are included in the regression model.

with mortgages, securitisation gradually grew to encompass trade receivables, credit card receivables, lease payments, and even future royalty payments.

Second, this securitisation led to a non-regulated *shadow banking system.* The shadow banking system refers to institutions that support bank-style maturity transformation – funding of long-term assets (primarily highly rated tranches of asset-backed securities) with short-term debt – outside banks and without access to a central bank liquidity backstop. It includes hedge funds, investment banks, and other non-depository financial firms. To facilitate securitisation, banks set up off-balance sheet vehicles, like conduits and *special purpose vehicles* (SPVs). These are shell companies holding financial assets such as securitised mortgages. They generally have no employees or headquarters. Their management is outsourced to an administrator, typically a commercial bank that sets up the conduit in the first place. The administrator manages the asset portfolio according to pre-specified investment guidelines and issues asset-backed commercial paper to finance the conduit's assets. Banks often provided liquidity enhancement and credit enhancement to these off-balance sheet vehicles. So if the quality of their assets deteriorated, the investors in these off-balance sheet vehicles often had recourse to banks. The economic rationale for setting up these vehicles was to reduce capital requirements imposed by bank regulation. Banks were not required to hold up equity capital for these vehicles' assets but instead needed to hold equity against liquidity and credit enhancement provided to them. And these requirements were lower (Acharya and Schnabl, 2009).

Under the 'originate and distribute' model, banks pool and repackage loans and then pass them on to other financial investors (including conduits created for this purpose). Banks create 'structured' products often referred to as *collateralised debt obligations* (CDOs). The first step is to form diversified portfolios of mortgages and other types of loans. The next step is to slice these portfolios into different tranches. These tranches are then sold to investors. The safest tranche – known as the 'super senior tranche' – offers investors a (relatively) low interest rate, but it is the first to be paid out of the cash flows of the portfolio. In contrast, the most junior tranche – referred to as the 'equity tranche', 'toxic waste', or 'stub' – will be paid only after all other tranches have been paid. The mezzanine tranches are between these extremes. In terms of loss absorption, the most junior security, or stub, absorbs the first loss; once this class of security is wiped out, the mezzanine securities bear loss; then the senior securities, and then finally the super-senior securities.

The exact cutoffs between the tranches are typically chosen to ensure a specific rating for each tranche. These ratings are provided by credit rating agencies (see Chapter 8 for further details). For example, the top tranches are constructed to receive the highest rating. The more senior tranches are then sold to various investors, while the issuing bank usually (but not always) holds the toxic waste (see Figure 1.7).

The increasing complexity of securitised credit required that credit rating techniques were applied to new varieties of structured security, where no historic record existed. These ratings proved highly imperfect predictors of risk and were subject to rapid rating downgrades once the crisis broke (see Chapter 2).

Buyers of securitised instruments can protect themselves by purchasing *credit default swaps* (CDSs), which are contracts insuring default. The buyer of these contracts pays a periodic fixed fee in exchange for a contingent payment in the event of credit default. Anyone who purchased a tranche of a collateralised debt obligation with the highest rating combined with a credit default swap had reason to believe that the investment had low risk because

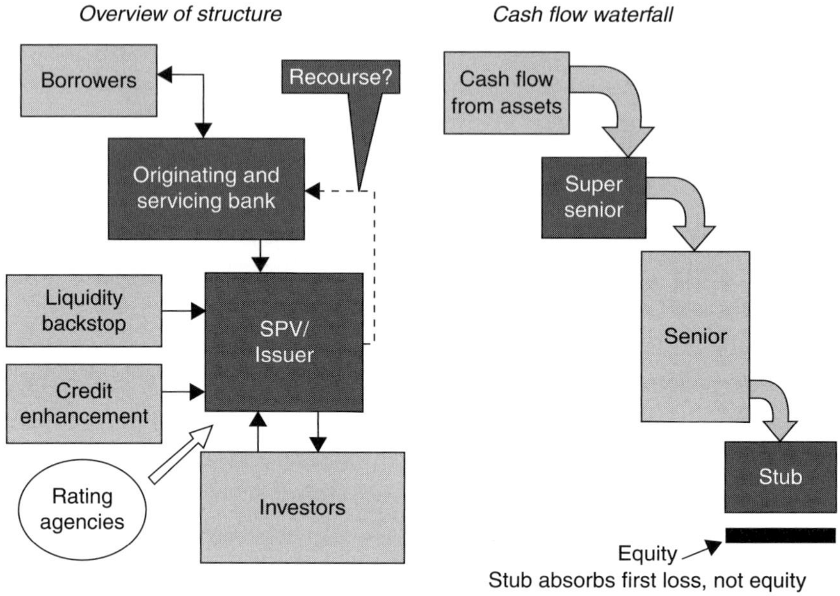

Figure 1.7 Securitisation
Source: Huertas (2010)

the probability of the CDS counterparty defaulting was considered to be small (Brunnermeier, 2009). However, the financial crisis showed them to be wrong (see Chapter 2).

It was not only via SPVs and conduits that a growing proportion of aggregate maturity transformation has been occurring outside regulated banks with central bank access. Investment banks increasingly funded holdings of long-term to maturity assets with much shorter-term liabilities. In addition, particularly in the US, mutual funds increasingly performed a bank-like form of maturity transformation. They have held long-term credit assets against liabilities to investors which promise immediate redemption (Turner, 2009).

As pointed out by Adrian and Shin (2010), these changes in the financial system of some countries, notably the US, have changed the mode of financial intermediation as well. A characteristic feature of financial intermediation that operates through the capital market is the long chain of financial intermediaries involved in channelling funds from the ultimate creditors to the ultimate borrowers. Figure 1.8, taken from Adrian and Shin (2010), illustrates this by showing one possible chain of lending relationships in a market-based financial system.

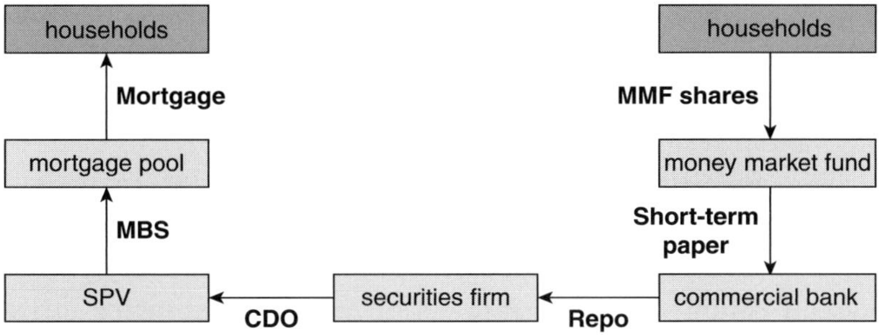

Figure 1.8 Long intermediation chain
Source: Adrian and Shin (2010)

In this illustration, banks issue mortgages that are then pooled. These pooled mortgages are then packaged to form mortgage-backed securities (MBS), which are liabilities issued against the mortgage assets. The MBS might then be owned by an SPV which pools and tranches them into another layer of claims, such as collateralised debt obligations. A securities firm (e.g. an investment bank) might hold collateralised debt obligations on its own books for their yield but will finance such assets by collateralised borrowing through repurchase agreements (i.e. repos) with a larger commercial bank. (In a repo, the borrower sells a security today for below the current market price on the understanding that it will buy it back in the future at a pre-agreed price. The difference between the current market price of the security and the price at which it is sold is called the haircut in the repo.) In turn, the commercial bank would fund its lending to the securities firm by issuing short-term liabilities. Money market mutual funds would be natural buyers of such short-term paper, and, ultimately, the money market fund would complete the circle, as household savers would own shares of these funds.

1.4 Conclusions

The financial system encompasses all financial intermediaries and financial markets, and their relations with respect to the flow of funds to and from households, governments, business firms, and foreigners (including the financial infrastructure). The main task of the financial system is to channel funds from sectors that have a surplus to sectors that have a shortage of funds. The importance of financial markets and financial intermediaries differs across Member States of the European Union. However, most investments by firms in the EU are financed through retained earnings, regardless of the relative importance of financial markets and intermediaries.

The financial system helps overcome an information asymmetry between borrowers and lenders. An information asymmetry can occur ex ante and ex post, i.e. before and after a financial contract has been agreed upon. The ex-ante information asymmetry arises because borrowers generally know more about their investment projects than lenders. The ex-post information asymmetry arises because borrowers, but not investors, can observe actual behaviour. Furthermore, the financial system reduces the time and money spent in carrying out financial transactions.

A well-functioning financial system requires particular government actions. First, government regulation is needed to protect property rights and to enforce contracts. Second, government regulation is needed to encourage proper information provision so that providers of funds can take better decisions on how to allocate their money. Third, government should arrange for regulation and supervision of financial institutions in order to ensure their soundness. Finally, governments are responsible for competition policy to ensure competition.

An important question is how differences in financial systems affect macroeconomic outcomes. Atomistic markets face a free-rider problem: when an investor acquires information about an investment project and behaves accordingly, he reveals this information to all investors, thereby dissuading other investors from devoting resources towards acquiring information. Financial intermediaries may be better able to deal with this problem than financial markets.

Another element in the debate on the pros and cons of bank-based vs. market-based systems refers to corporate governance, i.e. the set of mechanisms arranging the relationship between stakeholders of a firm, notably holders of equity, and the management of the firm. Investors (the outsiders) cannot perfectly monitor managers acting on their behalf since managers (the insiders) have superior information about the performance of the company. So there is a need for certain mechanisms that prevent the insiders of a company using the profits of the firm for their own benefit rather than returning the money to the outside investors.

While there is considerable evidence that financial development – up to some point – is good for economic growth, there is no clear evidence that one

Table 1.2 Bank-based vs. market-based financial systems

	Bank-based	Market-based
Economic growth	++	++
High-uncertainty investment	– –	++
Low-uncertainty investment	++	– –

kind of financial system is better for growth than another. However, various recent studies suggest that differences in financial systems may influence the type of activity in which a country specialises. The reason is that different forms of economic activity may be more easily provided by one financial system than the other. Table 1.2 summarises these issues.

Some authors argue that financial markets and financial intermediaries provide complementary growth-enhancing financial services to the economy. Intermediaries are necessary for the successful functioning of markets. Due to several recent changes, market-based financial intermediaries have become very important in some countries, notably the US, making the chain of intermediation much longer.

Finally, according to the 'law and finance' view, legal system differences are key in explaining international differences in financial structure. Therefore, distinguishing countries by the efficiency of national legal systems in supporting financial transactions is more useful than distinguishing countries by whether they have bank-based or market-based financial systems.

Notes

1. Whether competition increases depends on the entry strategy of foreign intermediaries. For instance, if a foreign intermediary acquires various domestic intermediaries and merges them, competition may decrease.
2. Various studies examine this issue. A good example is Petersen and Rajan (1994) who, on the basis of a large-scale sample of US firms with less than 500 employees, found evidence that relationships increase the availability and reduce the price of credit to firms. The empirical results suggest that the availability of finance increases as the firm spends more time in a relationship, as it increases ties to a lender by expanding the number of financial services it buys from it, and as it concentrates its borrowing with the lender.
3. There are two main types of board of directors. The UK and the US have a so-called one-tier board, which consists of a mix of outside (non-executive) directors and inside (executive) directors, who are the top executives of the firm. The role of management is to implement

the business policies that the board has determined. Continental European countries apply the two-tier board system with a supervisory board and a management board. The supervisory board is the controlling body and elected by the shareholders (and sometimes also by the employees). The management board is appointed by the supervisory board.

Suggested Reading

Allen, F. and D. Gale (2000), *Comparing Financial Systems*, MIT Press, Cambridge (MA).

Carlin, W. and C. P. Mayer (2003), Finance, Investment and Growth, *Journal of Financial Economics*, **69**(1), 191–226.

Papaioannou, E. (2008), Finance and Growth. A Macroeconomic Assessment of the Evidence from a European Angle, in: X. Freixas, P. Hartmann, and C. Mayer (eds.), *Handbook of European Financial Markets and Institutions*, Oxford University Press, 68–98.

References

Abiad, A. and A. Mody (2005), Financial Reform: What Shakes It? What Shapes It?, *American Economic Review*, **95**(1), 66–88.

Acharya, V. V. and P. Schnabl (2009), How Banks Played the Leverage Game, in: V. V. Acharya and M. Richardson, *Restoring Financial Stability*, Wiley, Hoboken (NJ), 83–100.

Adrian, T. and H. S. Shin (2010), The Changing Nature of Financial Intermediation and the Financial Crisis of 2007–09, Federal Reserve Bank of New York Staff Reports 439.

Allen, F. and D. Gale (2000), *Comparing Financial Systems*, MIT Press, Cambridge (MA).

Allen, F. and A. M. Santomero (1997), The Theory of Financial Intermediation, *Journal of Banking and Finance*, **21**, 1461–1485.

Arcand, J.-L., E. Berkes, and U. Panizza (2012), Too Much Finance? IMF Working Paper 12/161.

Baele, L., A. Ferrando, P. Hördahl, E. Krylova, and C. Monnet (2008), Measuring European Financial Integration, in: X. Freixas, P. Hartmann, and C. Mayer (eds.), *Handbook of European Financial Markets and Institutions*, Oxford University Press, 165–194.

Bauer, R., K. Koedijk, and R. Otten (2005), International Evidence on Ethical Mutual Fund Performance and Investment Style, *Journal of Banking and Finance*, **29**, 1751–1767.

Beck, T., A. Demirgüç-Kunt, and R. Levine (2001), Law, Politics and Finance, World Bank, Policy Research Working Paper 2585.

Bekeart, G., C. R. Harvey, and C. Lundblad (2005), Does Financial Liberalization Spur Growth? *Journal of Financial Economics*, **77**, 3–55.

Bijlsma, M. J. and T. J. Zwart (2013), The Changing Landscape of Financial Markets in Europe, the United States and Japan, CPB Discussion Paper 238.

Brunnermeier, M. K. (2009), Deciphering the Liquidity and Credit Crunch 2007–2008, *Journal of Economic Perspectives*, **23**(1), 77–100.

Carlin, W. and C. P. Mayer (2000), How Do Financial Systems Affect Economic Performance?, in: X. Vives (ed.), *Corporate Governance: Theoretical and Empirical Perspectives*, Cambridge University Press, 137–168.

(2003), Finance, Investment and Growth, *Journal of Financial Economics*, **69**(1), 191–226.

Cecchetti, S. and E. Kharroubi (2012), Reassessing the Impact of Finance on Growth, BIS Working Paper 381.

Demirgüç-Kunt, A. and Levine, R. (eds.) (2001), Financial Structure and Economic Growth: A Cross-Country Comparison of Banks, *Markets and Development*, MIT Press, Cambridge (MA).

Dewatripont, M. and E. Maskin (1995), Credit Efficiency in Centralized and Decentralized Economies, *Review of Economic Studies*, **62**, 541–555.

Djankov, S., C. McLiesh, and A. Shleifer (2007), Private Credit in 129 Countries, *Journal of Financial Economics*, **84**, 299–329.

Djankov, S., R. La Porta, F. Lopez-de Silanes, and A. Shleifer (2008), The Law and Economics of Self-dealing, *Journal of Financial Economics*, **88**(3), 430–465.

European Central Bank (2006), *Financial Stability Review* (December), ECB, Frankfurt am Main.

(2011), *Financial Integration in Europe* (May), ECB, Frankfurt am Main.

Fernandez, R. and D. Rodrik (1991), Resistance to Reform: Status Quo Bias in the Presence of Individual-specific Uncertainty, *American Economic Review*, **81**, 1146–1155.

Geczy, C., R. Stambaugh, and D. Levin (2006), Investing in Socially Responsible Mutual Funds, Working Paper, Wharton School.

Governance Metrics International (2006), *Ratings on 3800 Global Companies*, GMI, New York.

Huertas, T. F. (2010), *Crisis: Cause, Containment and Cure*, Palgrave MacMillan, Houndsmills.

International Monetary Fund (2006), *World Economic Outlook*, Chapter 4, IMF, Washington DC.

Jensen, M. (1993), The Modern Industrial Revolution, Exit, and the Failure of Internal Control Systems, *Journal of Finance*, **48**, 831–880.

Jensen, M. and W. Meckling (1976), Theory of the Firm: Managerial Behavior, Agency Costs, and Capital Structure, *Journal of Financial Economics*, **3**, 287–322.

Keefer, P. (2007), Beyond Legal Origin and Checks and Balances: Political Credibility, Citizen Information and Financial Sector Development, World Bank Policy Research Working Paper 4154.

King, R. G. and R. Levine (1993a), Finance and Growth: Schumpeter Might Be Right, *Quarterly Journal of Economics*, **108**, 717–737.

(1993b), Finance, Entrepreneurship, and Growth: Theory and Evidence, *Journal of Monetary Economics*, **32**, 513–542.

La Porta, R., F. Lopez-de-Silanes, A. Shleifer, and R. Vishny (1997), Legal Determinants of External Finance, *Journal of Finance*, **52**, 1131–1150.

Levine, R. (1997), Financial Development and Economic Growth: Views and Agenda, *Journal of Economic Literature*, **35**, 688–726.

(2002), Bank-Based or Market-Based Financial Systems: Which is Better?, *Journal of Financial Intermediation*, **11**, 398–428.

(2005), Finance and Growth: Theory, Mechanisms and Evidence, in: P. Aghion and S. N. Durlauf (eds.), *Handbook of Economic Growth*, Elsevier, Amsterdam, 865–923.

Levine, R., N. Loayza, and T. Beck (2000), Financial Intermediation and Growth: Causality and Causes, *Journal of Monetary Economics*, **46**, 31–77.

Merton, R. C. (1995), Financial Innovation and the Management and Regulation of Financial Institutions, *Journal of Banking and Finance*, **19**, 461–481.

Mishkin, F. S. (2006), *The Next Great Globalization*, Princeton University Press.

Papaioannou, E. (2008), Finance and Growth. A Macroeconomic Assessment of the Evidence from a European Angle, in: X. Freixas, P. Hartmann, and C. Mayer (eds.), *Handbook of European Financial Markets and Institutions*, Oxford University Press, 68–98.

Petersen, M. A. and R. G. Rajan (1994), The Benefits of Lending Relationships: Evidence from Small Business Data, *The Journal of Finance*, **49**(1), 3–37.

Rajan, R. and L. Zingales (1998), Financial Dependence and Growth, *American Economic Review*, **88**, 559–586.

Renneboog, L., J. ter Horst, and C. Zhang (2008), Socially Responsible Investments: Institutional Aspects, Performance, and Investor Behavior, *Journal of Banking and Finance*, **32**, 1723–1742.

Sikken, B. J. (2014), Lecture Series Finance & Sustainability, Duisenberg School of Finance, Amsterdam.

Turner, A. (2009), *The Turner Review: A Regulatory Response to the Global Banking Crisis*, Financial Services Authority, London.

CHAPTER

2

Financial Crises

OVERVIEW

Financial crises have been pervasive phenomena throughout history. This chapter starts by exploring the different types of crises: banking crises, sovereign debt crises, and currency crises. In a banking crisis a significant part of a country's banking sector has become insolvent after heavy investment losses, banking panics, or both. A sovereign default occurs when a government fails to meet interest or principal payments on its debt obligations. Finally, in a currency crisis the value of a country's currency falls precipitously.

This chapter first provides facts and figures about financial crises, after which some theoretical models are discussed. A first set of models is related to the liability side of banks. As banks finance long-term loans with short-term deposits, they are vulnerable to massive withdrawals cumulating in a banking run. A second set of models looks at the asset side of banks. Banking problems arise from deteriorating asset quality. This decline in assets is closely related to the business cycle, resulting from shocks to fundamentals.

In 2007–2009, the world's financial system went through its greatest crisis for at least a century. What made this crisis unique was that severe financial problems emerged simultaneously in many different countries, and its economic impact was felt throughout the world as a result of the increased interconnectedness of the global economy. The second part of this chapter offers an overview of the causes and consequences of this crisis. This crisis was followed by a sovereign and banking crisis in Europe, to which we will refer as the euro crisis, which is discussed in the final part of this chapter.

LEARNING OBJECTIVES

After you have studied this chapter, you should be able to:

- explain the characteristics of different types of financial crises
- understand the link between sovereign and banking crises
- explain the main theoretical models of banking crises
- understand the pro-cyclicality of the financial system
- explain the main drivers and contagion mechanisms of the 2007–2009 financial crisis
- explain the euro crisis.

2.1 Introduction

Financial crises have been around since the development of money and financial markets. They come in different forms: banking crises, sovereign debt crises, and currency crises.

In a *banking crisis* a significant part of a country's banking sector has become insolvent after heavy investment losses, banking panics, or both. Often a distinction is made between systemic and non-systemic banking crises. Following Laeven and Valencia (2013), we may define a *systemic banking crisis* as follows: In a systemic banking crisis, a country's corporate and financial sectors experience a large number of defaults and financial firms face great difficulties repaying contracts on time. As a result, non-performing loans increase sharply and all or most of the aggregate banking system capital is exhausted.

A *sovereign debt crisis* involves outright default on payment of debt obligations, i.e. repudiation or the restructuring of debt into terms less favourable to the lender than in the original. A sovereign default occurs when a government fails to meet interest or principal payments on its debt obligations. A distinction can be made here between external and domestic debt obligations. External debt consists of loans issued under another country's jurisdiction and is often denominated in a foreign currency and held by foreign creditors. Domestic debt is issued under a country's own jurisdiction and is typically denominated in the local currency and held by domestic creditors. In a default sometimes countries repudiate their debt, but it is more common that a government restructures debt on terms less favourable to the lender than those in the original contract (like a longer maturity and a lower interest rate). Although debt crises are often believed to occur mainly in emerging countries, only a few industrial countries (like Denmark and the US) have managed to avoid default on their government debt (Reinhart and Rogoff, 2009).

Finally, in a *currency crisis* the value of a country's currency falls precipitously. Countries maintaining an (almost) fixed exchange rate regime are vulnerable to sudden crises of confidence, leading to speculative attacks that can blow up seemingly stable regimes overnight. Although currency crises are often believed to be a phenomenon of emerging countries, they also occurred in the European Union (EU). Before the start of the Economic and Monetary Union (EMU) in 1999 (see Chapter 4), several European countries tried to stabilise their exchange rates through the so-called Exchange Rate Mechanism (ERM). However, the track record of this system is mixed at best; in 1992–1993 several participating currencies plummeted vis-à-vis the German mark, the anchor of the system (see Box 2.1).

The remainder of this section will focus on debt and banking crises. Figure 2.1 plots the incidence of government external debt defaults and banking crises according to the data of Reinhart and Rogoff (2010). These data are for a large sample of countries, accounting for about 90 per cent of world income. The graphs show the percentage of all independent countries that experienced a crisis in any given year from 1800 through 2008–2009.

The first graph identifies five episodes with many external debt defaults. The first is during the Napoleonic War, while the second runs from the 1820s through the late 1840s, when nearly half the countries in the world were in default. The third episode begins in the early 1870s and lasts for two decades, while the fourth episode begins in the Great Depression of the 1930s and extends through the 1950s, when almost 50 per cent of all countries stood in default. The most recent default episode encompasses the emerging market debt crises of the 1980s and 1990s. The median duration of default spells after the Second World War is three years (Reinhart and Rogoff, 2010).

The second graph shows that the highest incidence of banking crises occurred during the Great Depression of the 1930s. The share of countries with banking difficulties began to expand in the 1970s, while in the early 1980s there were severe banking crises in emerging economies, notably in Latin America. During the early 1990s, the Nordic countries as well as Japan experienced some of the worst banking crises. In the second half of the 1990s, crises in Mexico and Argentina (in 1994–1995) were followed by the Asian crisis of 1997–1998. A brief tranquil period came to an abrupt halt in the summer of 2007 when the subprime crisis in the United States began (see section 2.3 for further details). Although the frequency of banking crises

Box 2.1 The EMS crisis

The European Monetary System (EMS) started in March 1979. The cornerstone of the EMS was the *Exchange Rate Mechanism* (ERM). Within the ERM each currency was kept within a band defined by a grid of central rates for the various pairs of currencies. For most countries, this band was defined as plus and minus 2.25 per cent of the central parity. These parities could be changed by mutual consent. Whenever an exchange rate reached the edge of the band, the central banks of both countries concerned were supposed to intervene on the foreign exchange market. The ERM went through a number of phases that can be clearly distinguished:

- a turbulent start, 1979–1983
- a calmer intermediate phase, 1983–1987
- no realignments, 1987–1992
- crises, 1992–1993
- tranquillity restored, 1993–1998.

Initially, there were frequent and substantial realignments. For instance, already in September 1979 a number of currencies were devaluated vis-à-vis the German mark. This was a pattern to be repeated many times. Although some devaluations occurred in the second phase, both their frequency and magnitude were substantially lower than in the previous phase. In the period 1987–1992 the sequence of devaluations came to a halt. The parities and the bands of the ERM were considered to be very credible. This third phase of the ERM was also marked by new entries: the Spanish peseta in June 1989, the British pound in October 1990, and the Portuguese escudo in April 1992. During this period it looked as if exchange rates were almost fixed. However, this turned out to be illusionary. The fourth phase of the ERM was very turbulent. There was a severe currency crisis. In August 1992 the British pound fell close to the ERM floor and the Italian lira even fell below it. Eventually, the two currencies left the system. Except for the Dutch guilder, all currencies came under attack between September 1992 and August 1993. Only after the fluctuation margins were increased to 15 per cent did the foreign exchange markets become more tranquil. During the fifth phase, ERM membership broadened again as participation in the exchange rate system was one of the convergence criteria for participation in the EMU (see Chapter 3).

Source: Eijffinger and de Haan (2000)

drops off markedly in the advanced economies, all except Portugal experienced at least one post-War crisis prior to the current episode.

Reinhart and Rogoff (2009) report that systemic banking crises are typically preceded by *credit booms* (growth of credit above the trend of GDP growth) and *asset price bubbles* (a rise of asset prices above their fundamental

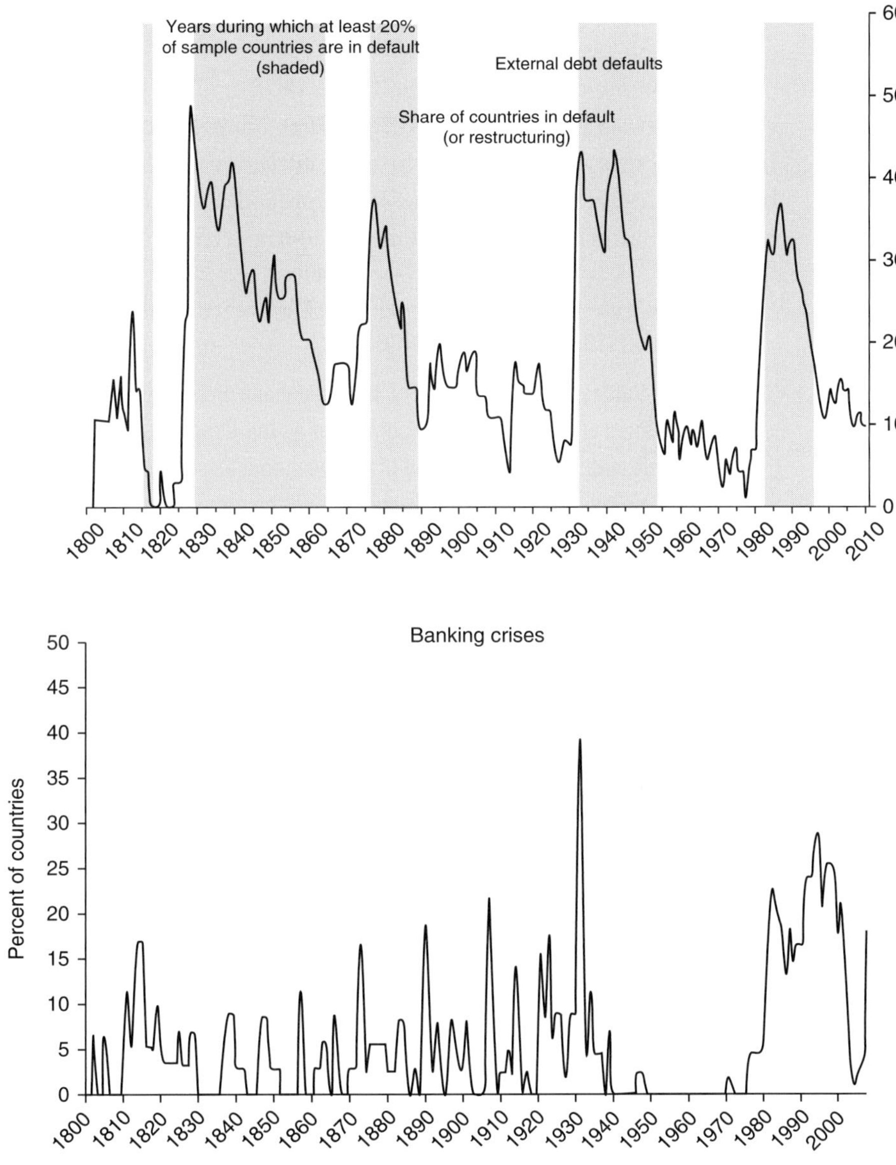

Figure 2.1 Incidence of financial crises, 1800–2009
Source: Reinhart and Rogoff (2010) and Qian *et al.* (2010)

economic value). As will be explained in section 2.3, the crisis that started in 2007–2008 is no exception. In addition, they find that crises result, on average, in a 35 per cent real drop in housing prices spread over a period of six years, while equity prices decline by 55 per cent over three-and-a-half years. The costs of banking crises in terms of output lost and the fiscal costs are very high (see Box 2.2).

Many financial crises, especially those in countries with fixed exchange rates, are so-called *twin crises* with currency depreciation exacerbating banking sector problems through foreign currency exposures of borrowers or banks themselves. Banking crises often precede or accompany sovereign debt crises. The aftermath of a systemic banking crisis often involves protracted

Box 2.2 Costs of banking crises

Laeven and Valencia (2013) have compiled a database on banking crises which they use to estimate the fiscal costs of a crisis (computed as the direct fiscal outlays due to financial sector rescue packages in per cent of GDP), the output losses (computed as the cumulative loss in income relative to a pre-crisis trend), and the increase in public debt (measured in per cent of GDP over [T–1, T+3], where T is the starting year of the crisis). Table 2.1 is reproduced from their study.

The median output loss for emerging and advanced economies is very similar and both are statistically significantly larger than that in developing countries. As pointed out by Laeven and Valencia, output losses in advanced and emerging economies are larger because a banking crisis is more disruptive in countries with deeper financial systems. The fiscal costs of banking crises are larger in developing and emerging economies than in advanced countries. Increases in public debt tend to be larger in advanced economies than in emerging and developing economies. While increases in public debt during banking crises in emerging and developing economies are mostly due to fiscal outlays associated with financial sector intervention policies, in advanced economies such fiscal outlays constitute only a relatively small fraction of the overall increase in public debt. In these countries discretionary fiscal policy and the impact of reduced economic growth due to the crisis on government revenues and outlays play a much more important role.

Table 2.1 Costs of banking crises (medians)

	Output loss (% trend income)	Fiscal costs (% of GDP)	Increase in public debt (% of GDP)
All countries	23.2	6.8	12.1
Advanced	32.4	4.2	23.6
Emerging	33.6	8.3	9.1
Developing	0.7	10.0	10.9

Source: Laeven and Valencia (2013)

and pronounced contraction in economic activity and puts important strains on the government's financial position. The government often has to bail out financial institutions in a crisis. However, the most important driver of the worsening fiscal position after a systemic banking crisis is the economic downturn following the crisis. The data provided by Reinhart and Rogoff (2009) suggest that after a banking crisis output falls by 9 per cent over two years, while unemployment rises 7 per cent over a period of four years. The indirect fiscal consequences of a banking crisis are thus much larger than the costs of bank bailouts. Government debt, on average, increases by 86 per cent in the three years following a systemic banking crisis. The experience of Finland and Sweden stand out in this regard. Both countries experienced a systemic banking crisis at the beginning of the 1990s (see Box 2.3). In Sweden the government's budget balance increased from a surplus of 3.8 per cent of GDP before the crisis to a deficit of 11.6 per cent at the peak of the crisis, i.e. a deterioration of 15.4 per cent. Likewise, in Finland the fiscal position worsened by almost 12 per cent (Reinhart and Rogoff, 2009).

Now let's zoom in on crises in Europe. Drawing on the seminal work by Reinhart and Rogoff (2009), Table 2.2 presents four crisis indicators for European countries: the share of years a country was in default since 1800 or the year in which it became independent, the share of years with a banking crisis, and the number of banking crises since 1800 and 1945. Four conclusions can be drawn from this table. First, the share of years in default varies considerably among European countries. Second, whereas several countries have been able to avoid a debt crisis, all countries have spent some time in a banking crisis since 1800. Third, the average length of time a country spends in a state of average default exceeds the average amount of time spent in banking crisis. Finally, the number of banking crises has dropped off markedly after the Second World War. Nevertheless, except for Portugal, all countries included in Table 2.1 experienced at least one banking crisis since 1945.[1] One such crisis is described in more detail in Box 2.3.

2.2 Theory

Broadly speaking, theoretical models either focus on the asset or the liability side of the bank balance sheet to explain banking crises. We first describe how problems at the liability side may cause a banking crisis, after which we discuss some theories focusing on the asset side.

Box 2.3 The banking crisis in Sweden

The financial system in Sweden was liberalised in the 1980s. At the time, the financial system was dominated by a few, large commercial banks offering wide-ranging financial services leading to predominance of debt financing of the non-financial sector. The financial deregulation and liberalisation of capital flows led to a credit-financed surge in investment. The credit surge also contributed to a jump in asset prices, especially real-estate prices. Before the liberalisation, banks relied almost exclusively on deposits for funding but, in the course of time, they relied increasingly on (more expensive) money market and foreign funding. As monetary policy was not able to stem the credit boom due to its focus on maintaining the stability of the exchange rate, losses from defaulted bank loans began to mount rapidly in the early 1990s after asset prices collapsed and a severe recession set in. While losses on real estate loans represented a significant part of the problem, other sectors also experienced financial distress when economic growth slowed down. The major Swedish banks were hit by massive credit losses totalling around 7 per cent of GDP in 1992. These losses threatened to quickly put all but one of the seven major Swedish banks, controlling most of the Swedish market, below the capital requirement of 8 per cent. Consequently, the government had to intervene heavily to preserve financial stability. Initially, the crisis was dealt with in an ad hoc manner but in September 1992 the conservative Swedish government decided to guarantee the debt of the banks. The guarantee did not cover equity capital; in case of financial support by the government, owners generally lost their equity stakes. The guarantee was formulated in an explicit and transparent way and received wide support in the parliament; also the social-democratic opposition supported the measures. A new agency under the finance ministry, the Bank Support Authority, was created in 1993 to implement the programme.

The banking crisis in Sweden started with the largest savings bank, Första Sparbanken. The Swedish government provided a lending guarantee to the bank but this was later converted into a loan. Eventually, the bank was merged into the Savings Bank of Sweden together with several other savings banks. The second problem bank was Nordbanken, the third largest commercial bank at the time, which was largely owned by the government. The government guaranteed a new share issue and the bank was restructured. An asset management company, Securum, took over the bad assets, while Nordbanken received in return a capital injection of 1 per cent of GDP. Also Gota Bank, the fourth largest commercial bank, got into difficulties. The government decided to meet all the commitments of Gota Bank but not those of the parent company, which was declared bankrupt. Again, as part of restructuring, non-performing assets, largely in the form of commercial real estate, were put in a separate asset management company (Retriva, which merged with Securum in December 1995). In 1993, Gota Bank was merged with Nordbanken, retaining the name Nordbanken.

Nordbanken became part of the pan-Nordic bank, Nordea.

Source: De Haan *et al.* (2009)

Table 2.2 Debt and banking crises in European countries

Country	Share of years in default since independence or 1800 (in %)	Share of years in banking crisis since independence or 1800 (in %)	Number of banking crises since independence or 1800	Number of banking crises since independence or 1945
Austria	17.4	1.9	3	1
Belgium	0	7.3	10	1
Denmark	0	7.2	10	1
Finland	0	8.7	5	1
France	0	11.5	15	1
Germany	13.0	6.2	8	2
Greece	50.6	4.4	2	1
Hungary	37.1	6.6	2	2
Italy	3.4	8.7	11	1
Netherlands	6.3	1.9	4	1
Norway	0	15.7	6	1
Poland	32.6	5.6	1	1
Portugal	10.6	2.4	5	0
Romania	23.3	7.8	1	1
Spain	23.7	8.1	8	2
Sweden	0	4.8	5	1
United Kingdom	0	9.2	12	4

Source: Reinhart and Rogoff (2009)

As explained in Chapter 1, banks transform short-term deposit funding into long-term loans. They borrow in the form of short-term savings and demand deposits which can be withdrawn at short notice. At the same time, they lend at longer maturities in the form of loans to firms and households. This makes them vulnerable. In normal times, banks hold more than sufficient reserves to handle withdrawals of deposits. However, during a run, depositors lose confidence in the bank and withdraw their deposits en masse. As withdrawals increase, the bank is forced to liquidate assets, typically against 'fire sale' prices, especially if the assets are illiquid. As banks often hold broadly similar portfolios of assets the market can dry up completely if all banks try to sell at once. This typically happens during a systemic banking crisis. Assets that are liquid during normal times can suddenly become highly illiquid at the time that banks need them most. So even a bank that would be solvent in the absence of a bank run may see its balance sheet destroyed, so that the bank run becomes self-fulfilling.

If everyone expects a problem and acts as if one is about to occur, then the run becomes a self-fulfilling prophecy. Conversely, if no one expects a bank to be in crisis, this expectation is also self-fulfilling and no run occurs (Reinhart and Rogoff, 2009).

As has been explained in Chapter 1, modern banking systems have increased in complexity over the last two decades. Despite running off-balance sheet vehicles or using various financial instruments to transfer credit risk, banks remained sensitive to panics and runs. In the summer of 2007 holders of short-term liabilities refused to fund US banks, expecting losses on subprime and subprime-related securities. So there were runs on banks. The difference is that modern runs typically involve the drying up of liquidity in the short-term markets (a wholesale run) instead of retail depositor withdrawals (Allen *et al.*, 2009). Still, also in modern times classical bank runs may occur, as the example of Northern Rock as described in Box 2.4 illustrates.

From a theoretical perspective, events as described above imply that there are *multiple equilibria.* A confidence shock can cause a jump from the good equilibrium to the bad equilibrium. According to the Diamond and Dybvig (1983) model, bank runs are self-fulfilling prophecies. In this model, agents have uncertain needs for consumption in an environment in which long-term investments are costly to liquidate. If depositors believe that other depositors will withdraw then they all find it rational to redeem their claims and a panic occurs. Another equilibrium exists where everybody believes no panic will occur and depositors withdraw funds according to their consumption needs. In this case, their demand can be met without costly liquidation of assets (Allen *et al.*, 2009). While this model explains how panics may occur, it does not explain which of the two equilibria will be selected. Depositors' beliefs are self-fulfilling and are coordinated by so-called 'sunspots'.

In the second line of argument, banking problems do not arise from the liability side, but from a protracted deterioration in asset quality due to poor fundamentals arising from the business cycle, like a collapse in real estate prices or increased bankruptcies in the non-financial sector. Some authors consider crises as an intrinsic part of the business cycle, resulting from shocks to economic fundamentals. When the economy goes into a recession, borrowers will have difficulty repaying loans. So, an economic downturn will reduce the value of bank assets, raising the possibility that banks are unable to meet their commitments. If depositors anticipate financial difficulties in the banking sector they will try to withdraw their bank deposits. The result is the same as in the panic story, but the cause is different. According to this interpretation, crises are not random events but a response of depositors to the arrival of some negative news on economic circumstances (Allen *et al.*,

Box 2.4 The run on the Rock

Northern Rock was formerly a building society in the UK, but it demutualised on 1 October 1997. At the end of 1997, Northern Rock had assets on a consolidated basis of £15.8 billion, but by 2006 its consolidated balance sheet had grown to £101.0 billion. It comprised mainly secured lending on residential properties. Wholesale markets became an important source of funding, making up some 25 per cent of total funding, of which half had a duration of less than one year. Northern Rock had not foreseen all its funding markets closing simultaneously, as happened after 9 August 2007. It also had insufficient insurance and standby facilities to cover this risk. It soon became evident that Northern Rock would face severe problems if the markets stayed frozen for long. Initially, the Bank of England refused to provide support to financial institutions, including Northern Rock. In a letter of 12 September 2007, the Governor of the Bank of England (BoE) pointed to the risk of 'moral hazard': should the central bank provide extra liquidity against weaker collateral, markets would take it as a signal that the central bank would always rescue them. And such a signal would lead to ever more risk taking by banks.

On the evening of Thursday 13 September 2007, the BBC leaked that Northern Rock had asked for and received emergency financial support from the Bank of England. The next day, long queues began to form outside some of Northern Rock's branches; later, its website collapsed and its phone lines were reported to be jammed. The first bank run in the United Kingdom since Victorian times was underway. The momentum of the run on Northern Rock deposits once it had begun was caused by two factors. First, depositors were becoming aware that, were the run to continue, Northern Rock would eventually cease to be a going concern. Second, public awareness increased that deposits above £2,000 were not guaranteed in full. Only after four days did the BoE announce that it would guarantee all the existing deposits in Northern Rock. On 9 October, the BoE announced that 'additional facilities' would be available to Northern Rock and, on 18 December, the government granted a further extension of the earlier guarantee arrangements. Eventually, on 22 February 2008 Northern Rock was taken into state ownership as a result of two unsuccessful private sector bids to take over the bank.

Source: Treasury Committee (2008)

2009). Allen and Gale (1998) develop a model in which they assume that depositors can observe a leading economic indicator that provides public information about future bank asset returns. If returns are high, depositors will want to keep their funds in the bank. However, if returns are low, depositors will withdraw their money in anticipation of low returns and there is a crisis. Box 2.5 presents the Allen–Gale model.

Box 2.5 Bank runs and the business cycle*

Allen and Gale (1998) developed a model to show how cyclical fluctuations in asset values can produce bank runs. Time is divided in three periods: t = 0, 1, 2. There are early consumers c_1 at date 1 and late consumers c_2 at date 2, each with probability half. The consumer's utility function is as follows:

$$U(c_1, c_2) = \begin{cases} u(c_1) \text{ with probability } 1/2 \\ u(c_2) \text{ with probability } 1/2 \end{cases} \tag{2.1}$$

where c_t denotes consumption at date t = 1, 2. Consumers want to maximise consumption. Their objective function is given by:

$$\max \quad E\left[u\left(c_1(R)\right) + u\left(c_2(R)\right)\right] \tag{2.2}$$

where c_1 (R) and c_2 (R) give the consumption of the early and late consumers conditional on the return to the risky asset R (see below). Let E denote the consumer's total endowment of the consumption good at date 0. The role of banks is to make investments on behalf of consumers. Banks have two assets: a safe asset L and a risky asset X. The total amount invested must be less or equal to the amount deposited:

$$L + X \leq E \tag{2.3}$$

The return r on the safe asset is zero and that is why r = 1. The return R on the risky asset X is stochastic, where R is a non-negative random variable. The risky asset is more productive than the safe asset L but cannot be liquidated at date 1. The expected return is thus larger than zero: $E[R]>1$. At date 1, depositors receive a signal about R, which can be thought of as a leading economic indicator representing the state of the business cycle. The signal is realised at date 2. The holding of the safe asset must be sufficient to provide for consumption of the early consumers:

$$c_1(R) \leq L \tag{2.4}$$

The consumption of the late consumers cannot exceed the total value of the risky asset plus the amount of the safe asset left over after the early consumers are paid off. Together with the previous constraint in equation 2.4, this condition gives:

$$c_1(R) + c_2(R) \leq L + RX \tag{2.5}$$

The deposit contract needs to be incentive compatible. For each value of R, the late consumers must be at least as well off as the early consumers. Since late consumers are paid off at date 2, an early consumer cannot imitate a late consumer. But a late consumer can imitate an early consumer, obtain c_1 (R) at date 1, and consume that at date 2. It will be optimal to do so unless:

Box 2.5 (cont.)

$$c_1(R) \leq c_2(R) \tag{2.6}$$

Until now, the deposit contract is assumed to be contingent on the return on the risky asset R. But a standard deposit contract is non-contingent. Allen and Gale (1998) take a standard deposit contract that promises a fixed amount at each date. In the event that the bank does not have enough liquid assets to make the promised payment, the bank pays out all available liquid assets, divided equally among those withdrawing. Let $\bar{c}$ denote the fixed payment promised to the early consumers. The amount promised to the late consumers can be ignored, since they are always paid what is available at the last date.

Next, the equilibrium conditions of the standard contract and the possibility of bank runs are analysed. Let c_{21} and c_{22} denote the equilibrium consumption of late consumers who withdraw from the bank at dates 1 and 2. Let $\alpha(R)$ denote the fraction of late consumers who decide to withdraw early, conditional on the risky return R. So, a bank run is dependent on the signal about R and thus related to the business cycle.

If a run does not occur, the feasibility conditions in equations 2.4 and 2.5 still apply as before. If there is a run, then the early consumers and the early-withdrawing late consumers share the liquid assets available at date 1:

$$c_1(R) + a(R)c_{21}(R) = L \tag{2.7}$$

And the late-withdrawing late consumers get the returns to the risky asset at date 2:

$$\Big(1 - a(R)\Big)c_{22}(R) = RX \tag{2.8}$$

Since early consumers and early-withdrawing late consumers are treated the same in a run and all late consumers must have the same utility in equilibrium:

$$c_1(R) = c_{21}(R) = c_{22}(R) \tag{2.9}$$

The final condition comes from the standard deposit contract, which promises the early consumers $c_1(R) = \bar{c}$ or, if that is infeasible, an equal share of the liquid assets L, where it has to be borne in mind that some of the late consumers may want to withdraw early as well. In the latter case $c_1(R) < \bar{c}$, the early withdrawers (including the early-withdrawing late consumers) exhaust the liquid assets of the bank:

$$\begin{cases} & c_1(R) = \bar{c} \quad \textit{no bank run} \\ c_1(R) < \bar{c} \Rightarrow & c_1(R) + a(R) \cdot c_{21}(R) = L \quad \textit{bank run} \end{cases} \tag{2.10}$$

Box 2.5 (cont.)

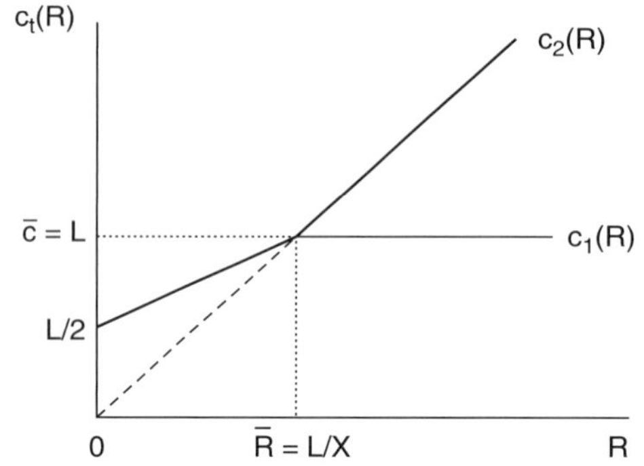

Figure 2.2 The standard deposit contract with bank runs
Source: Allen and Gale (1998)

The optimal deposit contract is solved for $\bar{c} = L$. In that case, the bank holds exactly sufficient liquid assets to pay the early consumers. The remainder is invested in risky assets with a positive expected return. Figure 2.2 illustrates the optimal deposit contract. The figure plots consumption $c_1(R)$ *and* $c_2(R)$ against the return on the risky asset R. Remember that R can be observed at date 1 but not at date 0. When $R = 0$ the only consumption available is from the safe asset. To maximise expected utility at t=0, this safe asset is split equally between the two groups so $c_1(0)=c_2(0)=L/2$. As R increases both groups can consume more. At $\bar{R} = L/X$, L is consumed by the early consumers and $\bar{R}X$ is consumed by the late consumers. Note that at $\bar{R} = L/X$, the consumption of the early and late consumers is still equal. As R increases above $\bar{R}$, it is not possible for the early consumers to have more than L since this is the only consumption available at date 1. At date 2, the late consumers are able to consume $RX > L$.

One particular theory linking the business cycle to financial crises is Minsky's 'financial-instability' hypothesis (see Minsky, 1986). While his views were initially often regarded as radical, if not crackpot, the credit crisis of 2007–2009 (see section 2.3) has revived interest in his theory. In the Minsky model the events leading up to the crisis start with a 'displacement' – some exogenous, outside shock to the macroeconomic system – an invention or an abrupt change of economic policy about which investors get excited. Subsequently there are five stages to the boom and eventual bust:

1. credit expansion, characterised by rising assets prices;
2. euphoria, characterised by overtrading;
3. distress, characterised by unexpected failures;

4. discredit, characterised by liquidation; and
5. panic, characterised by the desire for cash.

The displacement sets in a boom fuelled by credit. As a boom leads to euphoria, banks extend credit to ever more dubious borrowers, often creating new financial instruments to do the job. Then, at the top of the market, some smart traders start to cash in their profits. The onset of panic is usually heralded by a dramatic event, such as a bank not being able to meet its obligations. Losses on loans begin to mount, and the drop in the value of the loans falls relative to liabilities, driving down the capital of financial institutions. With less capital, financial institutions cut back on their lending (*deleveraging*).

Minsky's financial-instability hypothesis highlights the *pro-cyclicality* of the financial system. Several factors contribute to this pro-cyclicality. First, the role of risk assessment is important. While risk tends to be underestimated in good times (euphoria with 'low risk'), it is overestimated in bad times (distress with 'high risk'). Moreover, risk can be endogenous. For example, when financial institutions sell a particular asset to reduce risk, the price of that asset may fall further. Second, the amount of debt (leverage) is a key factor explaining the depth of the financial crisis. The more debt is built up in the upswing, the more severe is the deleveraging in the downswing. Third, Gorton and Ordonez (2014) stress the pro-cyclical role of collateral. Investors are willing to lend short term (e.g. via repos) against collateral without collecting costly information about the collateral backing the debt. When the economy relies on such informationally insensitive debt, firms with low quality collateral can borrow, generating a credit boom. Financial fragility builds up over time as information about counterparties decays. A crisis occurs when a (possibly small) shock causes investors to suddenly have incentives to collect information. Fourth and last, capital requirements play a role. Banks have to keep minimum capital against new loans (see Chapter 12). In good times, retained earnings boost capital, which enables banks to increase lending. In bad times, capital shrinks through losses, which may hamper the granting of new credit.

Figure 2.3 illustrates how the financial cycle (measured by credit and house prices) and the business cycle (measured by GDP) diverge. The amplitude of the financial cycle over the 1970–2011 period is five times that of the business cycle in the US. Moreover, the duration of the financial cycle tends to be longer than that of business cycle. While Figure 2.3 represents the US cycle, similar patterns can be found across Europe. Financial cycles may not move synchronously across countries. As will be explained in section 2.5, one of the

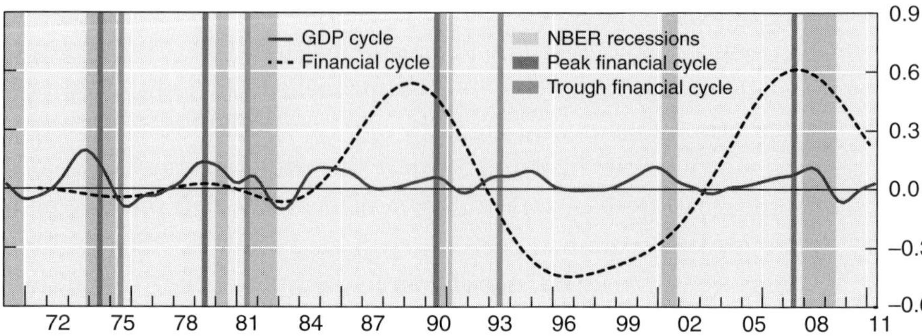

Figure 2.3 Business cycle (GDP) versus financial cycle in the US, 1970–2011
Source: Borio (2014)

factors that played a role in the euro crisis was that financial cycles in euro-area Member States were not in sync.

Finally, some recent theories on financial instability focus on information problems. For example, Mishkin (1992) argues that a financial crisis is a disruption to financial markets in which adverse selection and moral hazard problems become much worse, so that financial markets are unable to efficiently channel funds to those who have the most productive investment opportunities. Uncertainty about the future (e.g. business prospects of firms) increases in a financial crisis, which widens the information asymmetry between contracting parties (e.g. information on the repayment capacity of a counterparty or information on the behaviour of a counterparty) and worsens the incentives of parties. *Adverse selection* occurs when investments that are most likely to produce an undesirable outcome are the most likely to be selected. *Moral hazard* arises when a borrower has the incentive to invest in high-risk projects, in which the borrower does well if the project succeeds but the lender bears a substantial loss if the project fails.

2.3 The financial crisis of 2007–2009

The crisis of 2007–2009 started with the bursting of the housing market bubble in the US forcing banks to write down several hundred billion dollars in bad loans caused by mortgage delinquencies, especially in the subprime part of the market. *Subprime mortgages* are housing loans to high-risk borrowers with a weak or a bad credit history who do not qualify for a conventional mortgage. Although these loans are relatively risky, subprime mortgages represented about 20 per cent of all newly issued mortgages in the US in 2005–2006. The mortgages were initially sold at bargain rates, but would be reset after some time (i.e. these contracts had a low or zero starting interest rate, which would rise significantly after a year or two). Due to the housing boom in the US – which began around 2001 – these mortgages could be refinanced before the interest rates were reset at market rates (thereby averting the high interest costs). However, when housing prices started to fall in 2006, many subprime owners could not refinance their mortgage and a significant number of them were unable to continue payments. This resulted in many defaults among subprime borrowers.

Why did financial institutions provide these mortgages? In the years before the crisis, interest rates in the US were very low. Low interest rates were caused by both large capital inflows from abroad, especially from Asian countries, and the policies of the Federal Reserve, the central bank of the US. Several Asian countries, including Japan and China, accumulated large current account surpluses prior to the crisis. As China and several other surplus countries were committed to (more or less) fixed exchange rates, the rising claims on other countries due to their current account surpluses took the form of central bank reserves. These are typically invested not in a wide array of equity, property, or fixed income assets, but almost exclusively in risk-free government securities (Turner, 2009). The loose policies by the Federal Reserve were caused by fears of deflation after the bursting of the Internet bubble. Between October 2007, when the stock market reached an all-time high, and October 2008 $8 trillion of US stock-market wealth was lost (Brunnermeier, 2009). As inflation was also low, real interest rates in the US were at a historically low level. Low interest rates in turn led to a rapid growth of credit extension, particularly for residential mortgages, which fuelled the property price boom. For banks (and other providers), subprime loans were interesting as a relatively high interest rate could be charged while (at that time) the default rate was very low because of the housing boom.

As of 2004, the Federal Reserve began to raise interest rates gradually from 1 per cent to 5.25 per cent in order to cool down the economy and keep inflation under control. As a result, it became more expensive to buy a house as mortgage rates increased substantially. This led to a slowdown in the housing market and eventually a housing-price crash. As the subprime mortgages were sold under the (false) assumption that housing prices would continue to increase, many subprime mortgage holders defaulted as they were unable to refinance their loans. This created a domino effect, as a result of which problems spread through the financial system. Summing up, the US banking crisis followed Minsky's model, starting with cheap credit ('low risk') and rising house prices, euphoria with overextension, distress with defaults, forced liquidations and fire sales, and finally panic with a freezing of short-term funding markets ('high risk').

But how did problems in the US housing market lead to a global financial crisis? Even though banks initially faced serious losses, they were small compared to the wealth losses of the dotcom bubble which did not lead to a serious recession. There is one particular aspect of the subprime crisis that makes this crisis different from previous financial crises (Brunnermeier, 2009). As discussed in Chapter 1, banks traditionally finance their mortgage loans through the deposits received from depositors and keep the mortgage loans (as well as the associated risks) on their balance sheet. In return, banks receive an upfront fee as well as interest income. However, in this case the providers of subprime loans bundled the mortgage loans and sold them to investors via collateralised debt obligations (CDOs). As mortgage providers were merely interested in receiving the upfront fee, they tried to sell as many mortgages as possible and there was no incentive to perform a proper credit check as the risks were transferred to third parties. The process of pooling, packaging, and reselling the loans as securities is referred to as *securitisation*.[2] The securitised instruments were in high demand by investors searching for as much as possible spread above the risk-free rate, to offset at least partially the declining risk-free rate (Turner, 2009).

Before the securitised instruments were sold, they were rated by credit rating agencies (CRAs). The agencies reviewed the proposed transactions prior to their coming to market, and placed their seal of approval on the deals in the form of a rating on the various tranches (see Chapter 8 for a discussion of CRAs). The most critical rating was the one for the senior tranche, which was almost invariably AAA, i.e. the highest possible rating. Indeed, deals were constructed so as to be sure that the senior tranches would get this rating. Although the ratings for securitisation issues were not directly comparable with ratings on sovereign or corporate bonds, the use of the same rating scale for securitisation issues as for sovereign and corporate bonds created exactly the opposite impression. Consequently, AAA-rated securitisation issues would pass the same investment and regulatory screens as AAA-rated corporate bonds, thereby opening the door to selling securitisation issues to investors (Huertas, 2010). However, during the crisis it became clear that the CRAs had not adequately assessed the risks related to the subprime mortgages. Moreover, there was poor investor due diligence as investors relied excessively on credit ratings. The poor credit assessment by CRAs

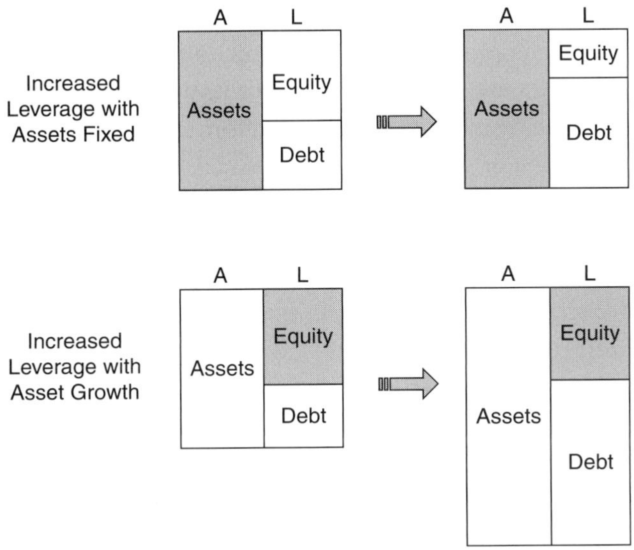

Figure 2.4 Two modes of levering up
Source: Hahm *et al.* (2011)

and over-reliance on credit ratings by investors clearly contributed to the build-up of the crisis.

As pointed out by Turner (2009), securitisation led to a remarkable growth in the relative size of wholesale financial services within the overall economy, with activities internal to the banking system growing far more rapidly than end services to the real economy. This growth of the relative size of the financial sector, and in particular of securitised credit activities, increased the potential impact of financial system instability on the real economy. This growing size of the financial sector was accompanied by an increase in total system *leverage*, which played an important role in driving the boom and in creating vulnerabilities that have arguably increased the severity of the crisis (see Figure 2.4). Moreover, there was a maturity transformation, as the SPVs and conduits through which the securities were distributed (see Chapter 1) were often funded with (short-term) asset-backed commercial paper. By contrast, the dotcom bubble was predominantly financed by equity.

Not only the volume of securitised instruments increased; also the volume of credit derivatives grew extremely fast. During the 1990s and the first years of the twenty-first century they increased to over $45 trillion in notional value by mid-2007. Credit derivatives (like Credit Default Swaps, see

Chapter 1) allow an investor to take a position with respect to the possibility that the so-called reference entity will default. The investor can either buy protection, in which case he or she will receive a payment if the reference entity defaults, or the investor can sell protection, in which case he or she will make a payment if the reference entity defaults. In return for providing this protection, the seller of protection receives a premium from the buyer of protection (Huertas, 2010).

Financial guarantee insurance performed a similar function to credit derivatives. In exchange for a premium, financial guarantee insurance companies (generally they only wrote this type of insurance and they were therefore known as *monolines*) provided protection against the possibility that an issuer would not be able to make timely payments of interest and/or principal on its securities.

When the crisis broke, it became apparent that diversification of risk holding that securitisation was supposed to deliver had not been achieved. Instead in the books of end investors intending to hold the assets to maturity, many instruments were on the books of banks and bank-like institutions. Instruments were not simply sold through to an end investor, but bought by the propriety trading desk of another bank, or sold by the first bank but with part of the risk retained via the use of credit derivatives, or 'resecuritised' into increasingly complex and opaque instruments (Turner, 2009). According to Acharya and Schnabl (2009), in the US about 30 per cent of all AAA asset-backed securities remained within the banking system, and if conduits (see Box 2.6) are included as part of the banking system, then this fraction rises to 50 per cent. Consequently, most of the risk was still somewhere on the balance sheets of banks (be it directly or indirectly via guarantees or insurances) but not in a transparent fashion.

The uncertainty as to who was exposed to these risks disturbed the functioning of many financial markets, including the interbank money market. Problems started to occur in the money market due to the damage done to two hedge funds affiliated with the US investment bank, Bear Stearns. Increasingly, banks started to be reluctant to lend to each other (which resulted in a liquidity crisis). Apart from this so-called *funding liquidity*, also *market liquidity* became a problem. A wide range of institutions – both banks and near banks – developed an increasing reliance on 'liquidity through marketability', believing that it would be safe to hold long-term assets funded by short-term liabilities as these assets could be sold rapidly in liquid markets if needed. This assumption was valid at the level of firms individually in non-crisis conditions, but became rapidly invalid in

Box 2.6 Off-balance sheet vehicles

As explained in Chapter 1, banks used off-balance sheet vehicles like conduits in the securitisation process. These conduits were funded with some equity and the rest in roll-over finance in the form of asset-backed commercial paper (ACP). They had recourse to bank balance sheets. Recourse is the institutional arrangement through which risks of the conduit get transferred back to the commercial bank setting up the conduit. This recourse could consist of liquidity enhancement and credit enhancement. Liquidity enhancement provides a backup credit line or commitment to repurchase non-defaulted assets in case a conduit cannot roll over maturing commercial paper. Credit enhancement covers credit losses on a conduit's assets.

Acharya and Schnabl (2009) distinguish three types of off-balance sheet vehicles:

Fully supported conduits, which have liquidity enhancement that covers the entire amount of commercial paper outstanding and credit enhancement that covers all assets in the conduit.

Partially supported conduits, which have liquidity enhancement and partial credit enhancement.

Structured investment vehicles (SIVs), which have only partial liquidity and credit enhancement. The extent of liquidity and credit enhancement varies depending on the underlying assets.

Table 2.3 shows the ten largest conduit administrators in 2007.

mid-2007, as many firms attempted simultaneously to liquidate their positions. So often they had to sell assets at fire sale prices. In 2007 several hundred non-bank mortgage lenders collapsed, while others were merged into larger banking institutions.

Increased *risk aversion* and *deleveraging* amplified the initial shock. Central banks were forced to inject liquidity into the financial system to ensure that banks were not exposed to long periods of tight liquidity. Banks reported substantial losses as they had invested directly in structured securities or had contracts requiring them to support conduits. Many firms were, however, unable to rapidly assess their exposures as their assets had become illiquid (since the underlying market had imploded). This resulted in a loss spiral for the financial system, as illustrated in Figure 2.5. When banks mark their balance sheet to market, changes in prices lead to losses for all banks holding these assets. Losses worsen funding liquidity for many banks forcing

Table 2.3 Ten largest conduit administrators by size (January 2007)

	Conduits		Administrator			
	Number	CP (in $ bn)	Assets	Equity	CP/Asset	CP/Equity
Citibank	23	93	1,884	120	4.9%	77.5%
ABN AMRO	9	69	1,300	34	5.3%	202.9%
Bank of America	12	46	1,464	136	3.1%	33.8%
HBOS	2	44	1,160	42	3.8%	104.8%
JPMorgan Chase	9	42	1,352	116	3.1%	36.2%
HSBC	6	39	1,861	123	2.1%	31.7%
Société Générale	7	39	1,260	44	3.1%	88.6%
Deutsche Bank	14	38	1,483	44	2.6%	86.4%
Barclays	3	33	1,957	54	1.7%	61.1%
WestLB	8	30	376	9	8.0%	333.3%

Source: Acharya and Schnabl (2009)

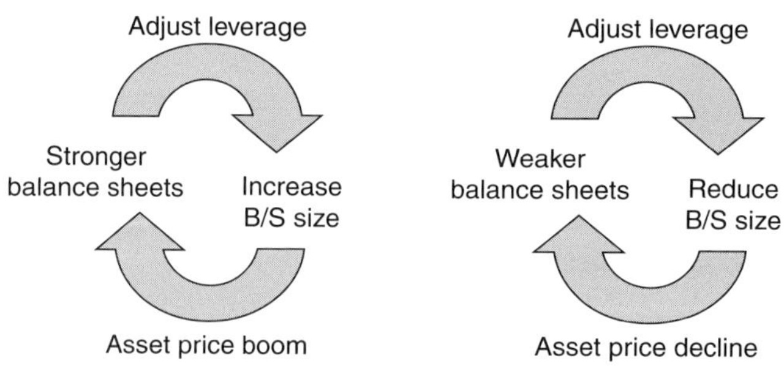

Figure 2.5 Loss spiral through the balance sheet
Source: Brunnermeier *et al.* (2009)

them to shed even more assets which further depresses prices and increases losses. The loss spiral can thus lead to sharp asset price movements (Brunnermeier *et al.*, 2009).

In 2008, problems worsened and the US authorities were forced to bail out Bear Stearns, the fifth largest investment bank in the US. It was highly leveraged and exposed significantly to the subprime mortgage market. The US government helped engineer JPMorgan Chase's purchase of the bank by guaranteeing $29 billion of subprime-backed securities. Later, the mortgage agencies Fannie Mae and Freddie Mac, accounting for nearly half of the outstanding mortgages in the US, were nationalised. When problems occurred at the fourth largest investment bank, Lehman Brothers, the authorities tried persuading rival institutions to take over the troubled firm. In the absence of a buyer, the government felt that an example had to be set to combat 'moral hazard', and decided to allow Lehman Brothers to fail in September 2008. The subsequent fears over counterparty risk turned into panic (if Lehman Brothers was not too big to fail, other investment banks might fail as well). In addition, several institutions had an exposure on Lehman that became virtually worthless. For instance, the Reserve Primary Fund, one of the largest money market funds, owned $700 million of Lehman Brothers' short-term paper and came into serious financial difficulties due to Lehman's collapse. This, in turn, led to uncertainty about all money market funds. As money market funds are the primary source for funding repos and commercial paper in the US, money markets came close to a breakdown (Richardson, 2009). Central banks in the US and elsewhere had to step in and eventually became vital suppliers in the money market.

Both in the EU and the US, authorities were eventually forced to rescue financial institutions to prevent a systemic meltdown. The world's largest insurance company, American International Group (AIG), received an emergency loan in return for an 80 per cent public stake in the firm. The landscape of American finance was changed radically. The investment bank Merrill Lynch was bought by Bank of America. Two investment banks, Goldman Sachs and Morgan Stanley, converted themselves into commercial banks. In a rescue deal backed by US authorities, Washington Mutual and Wachovia were sold to JPMorgan Chase and Citigroup respectively.

Moving to Europe, Box 2.7 highlights the concerted crisis management of the governments. Benelux authorities had to bail out Fortis. Eventually the Dutch activities of Fortis were nationalised by the Dutch government, while the other activities were sold to the French banking group, BNP Paribas. The French, Belgian, and Luxembourg authorities also had to recapitalise the financial conglomerate, Dexia. In the UK, the authorities were forced to take over the mortgages and loans of Bradford & Bingley, while its savings operations and branches were sold to the Spanish banking group, Santander. The UK authorities also took a major equity stake in two large banks: RBS and Lloyds-HBOS. Germany's Hypo Real Estate, a large commercial property lender, received a €50 billion secured-credit facility by a consortium of German banks and the government. The Icelandic authorities had to nationalise their entire banking system, leading to a near bankruptcy of the country itself.

Box 2.7 Financial crisis management in Europe

In a historical summit of the euro-area leaders in October 2008, Sarkozy (then president of the EU) presented an impressive concerted European action plan of the euro-area countries to face the challenges of the financial crisis. The declaration of this euro-area summit introduced an action plan with three main measures:

1. Ensuring appropriate liquidity conditions for banks. The ECB provides ample liquidity to banks against adequate collateral.
2. Facilitating the funding of banks. National governments provide a guarantee for medium-term funding of banks. These government guarantees cover medium-term bank debt issuance with a maturity ranging from three months up to three to five years.
3. Recapitalising banks. Governments provide capital injections to restore Tier 1 capital (see Chapter 12) at an appropriate level. Furthermore, governments may allow for an efficient recapitalisation of distressed banks, including nationalisation as an ultimate remedy.

Between end-September and end-October 2008, several EU countries announced bank rescue schemes which complemented the exceptional liquidity support provided by the ECB (see Chapter 4 on the liquidity support). In order to ensure respect of the EU state aid rules, the European Commission provided guidance on how to design these measures (see also Chapter 14). In particular, the measures under (2) and (3) should avoid any discrimination against financial institutions based in other Member States and should ensure that beneficiary banks do not unfairly attract new additional business solely as a result of the government support. Although individual governments provided the funding guarantees under (2), the ECB managed to broker a common fee across the EU. The market for bank funding is integrated and a common fee ensures a level playing field. For maturities up to one year, there was a flat fee of 50 basis points. The fee for maturities from one year up to three to five years was based on the credit default swap spread of the involved bank plus 50 basis points.

Initially, public support targeted the liabilities side of banks' balance sheets. In early 2009, public support to the banking sector began to target the assets side of banks' balance sheets, with the aim of providing relief for impaired bank assets. This support complemented existing measures and was mainly motivated by the persisting uncertainty regarding asset valuations and the risk that new asset write-downs could impair banks' balance sheets, thus undermining confidence in the banking sector. Asset relief schemes include: (1) asset removal schemes, which aim at removing impaired assets from a bank's balance sheet either via direct government purchases or by transferring them to independent asset management companies (which are sometimes referred to as 'bad banks'); and (2) asset insurance schemes, which keep the assets on the banks' balance sheets but insure them against tail risk.

Source: Van Riet (2010)

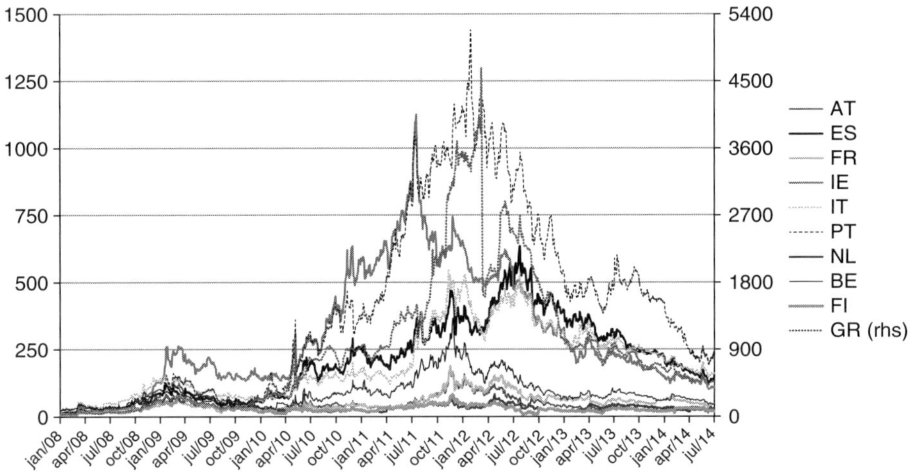

Figure 2.6 10-year government bond spreads against German bunds, 2008–2014
Source: Datastream

2.4 The euro crisis

The crisis unfolded

In 2009 the euro had its tenth anniversary. Yet, amidst the celebrations in 2009, in Greece a shock was unfolding that, by the end of the year, would materialise into a full-blown financial crisis. After several revisions of previously announced deficit figures (even going back to the time of admission of Greece in the euro area) had been published it became clear that public finances in Greece were unsustainable. On 10 May 2010, the 10-year yield spread between Greek and German government bonds reached about 1,000 basis points. Similar concerns arose in Ireland, Portugal, and, later, Spain and Italy (see Figure 2.6).

On 2 May 2010, the euro countries agreed to provide bilateral loans for a total amount of €80 billion to be disbursed over the period May 2010 through June 2013, with the International Monetary Fund (IMF) financing additional €30 billion under a stand-by arrangement (SBA). The European Commission was entrusted with the coordination and administration of the pooled bilateral loans, including their disbursement to Greece. The loans are subject to strict conditions aimed at consolidating Greek public finances and restoring competitiveness.

Why was Greece rescued? Several economists argued that Greece and other countries facing insolvency should default as quickly as possible, to allow for a substantial debt restructuring (haircut) aimed at restoring sustainable debt levels and stabilising financial markets. Delaying such a decision – according to this logic – would make things even worse. European policy makers did not follow this advice, as they were worried that a Greek default would have serious consequences. First, a Greek default was considered to easily spread to other countries (contagion). A worsening of the Greek crisis could further aggravate the situation in Portugal and Ireland – two other countries facing severe financial problems at the time – also pushing them into default and the crisis might spread even to Spain or Italy, pushing them to ask for a rescue. This would over-burden the abilities and willingness of the other EU countries to come to the rescue. A major default would also activate CDSs, with unforeseeable consequences not only for European but also for global financial markets.

Second, many banks and other financial institutions had a large exposure on Greece. It was feared that a sovereign default would lead to another banking crisis as many banks were just recovering from the 2007–2009 crisis and would not be able to absorb the substantial losses that a Greek default would imply. More generally, financial institutions had extensive exposures to European governments (see Table 2.4) and to each other. In turn, owing to their efforts to contain the banking crisis, governments hold considerable participations in banks or stand guarantee for large amounts. The governments' involvement is essential to preserve market confidence in vulnerable institutions. At the same time, this involvement could give rise to doubt about the sustainability of fiscal policy, especially if there are other factors that knock public finances off course, like poor economic growth rates. If this happens, risk premiums rise and downgrades occur, jeopardising the (re)financing of debt (DNB, 2011).

But the support to Greece proved insufficient to stabilise the markets and prevent contagion between countries. Tensions in financial markets continued to mount; the euro tumbled to a 14-month low against the US dollar. In view of these mounting instabilities, in May 2011 the euro-area countries agreed to establish two facilities to provide financial support to EU countries experiencing severe economic or financial disturbances. First, the European Financial Stabilisation Mechanism (EFSM) was set up, which allows the European Commission to raise up to €60 billion on behalf of the EU for providing financial assistance to EU Member States experiencing serious financial difficulties. Second, the euro countries established the European Financial Stability

Table 2.4 Exposure of euro-area banks on euro-area countries ($ million), March 2011

	Greece	Ireland	Italy	Portugal	Spain
Austria	104	3,193	105,097	187	5,288
Belgium	240	4,689	4,173	465	4,441
Cyprus	11,351	–	1,729	82	92
Estonia	3	–	399	–	12
Finland	2	–	1,271	59	3,014
France	1,675	15,955	41,153	7,411	28,790
Germany	5,246	62,664	266,138	3,910	58,840
Greece	–	773	4,694	10,158	1,265
Ireland	544	–	14,324	22,250	11,052
Italy	537	13,182	–	2,998	35,190
Luxembourg	7,687	3,088	28,598	2,613	8,325
Malta	382	–	890	848	166
Netherlands	4,502	5,986	25,908	13,111	19,892
Portugal	92	2,475	4,331	–	89,932
Slovakia	–	–	19,711	86	167
Slovenia	2	–	8,778	43	110
Spain	361	13,737	31,764	25,616	–

Source: BIS

Facility (EFSF). The EFSF was set up as a limited liability company authorised to issue debt securities, guaranteed up to a total of €440 billion by euro-area countries on a pro rata basis, for lending to euro-area countries.[3] The IMF committed itself to adding half of the funding provided by Europe. Moreover, the IMF is closely involved in designing adjustment programmes for a country that seeks recourse to the safety net (*conditionality*).

Also, the ECB announced far-reaching measures. On 10 May 2010, it announced the launch of the Securities Markets Programme (SMP). Under the SMP, the ECB makes purchases in secondary public and private bond markets in order to enhance depth and liquidity in dysfunctional markets. This improves the monetary transmission in the euro area. In line with the provisions of the Treaty on the Functioning of the European Union, ECB purchases of government bonds are strictly limited to secondary markets. To ensure that liquidity conditions will not be affected, all purchases are fully sterilised by conducting liquidity-absorbing operations (see Chapter 4). In May and June 2010, ECB interventions amounted to €64.5 billion. At end-2010, purchases under the SMP ran up to a total of €73.5 billion (DNB, 2011).

Following the statements by euro-area governments and by the ECB, tensions in financial markets abated for a short period of time. Market sentiment improved in the summer. New debt issues by European governments were successful. This revival was short-lived, however. The country risk premiums in notably Greece, Ireland, and Portugal expanded substantially relative to countries with a stronger economic recovery and healthier financial positions, such as Germany and the Netherlands.

On 21 November 2010, Ireland requested EU financial assistance. The problems in Ireland are completely different, although no less serious than those in Greece. For many years, Ireland had high growth rates, climbing up among the top ten richest countries in the world. However, the tide began to turn in 2007. Up until that year, there were sharp rises in the prices of real estate, which in turn resulted in substantial investments in the construction sector. As abundant credit was available to accommodate this process, a bubble arose, which began to deflate when the subprime crisis broke out. Since then, house prices have fallen by close on 40 per cent and the prices of commercial real estate by even more than 50 per cent. This caused an exceptionally deep recession during which unemployment doubled. The Irish banking sector had to absorb unprecedented losses on mortgage lending and was confronted with extensive withdrawals from the international liabilities, so that state support was unavoidable. Serious concerns arose about the sustainability of Irish public finances in particular when the extent of the Irish government's support to the banking sector became clear, forcing Ireland to ask for European support. The EU, the EFSF, the IMF, and some non-euro-area EU countries (UK, Denmark, and Sweden) promised Ireland financial support amounting to €67.5 billion. In return for aid, Ireland had to commit itself to an ambitious programme aiming to restructure the financial sector and restoring public finances (DNB, 2011).

In 2011 the problems continued. First, Portugal had to seek international financial assistance in April. Portugal had not performed well since its accession to EMU: it had sluggish growth, pronounced credit expansion, seriously eroding competitiveness, and excessive government and current account deficits. Following the Portuguese request, the terms and conditions of the financial assistance package were agreed upon by the EU's Council of Economics and Finance Ministers on 17 May 2011. The financial package covered Portugal's financing needs of up to €78 billion. The EFSM and the EFSF each provided up to €26 billion to be disbursed over three years. Further support was made available through the IMF for up to €26 billion, as approved by the IMF Executive Board on 20 May.

In the course of 2011 it also became obvious that Greece would require a second major rescue package because it would not be able to return to financial markets in 2012 when the first assistance package ran out. At their summit in July 2011, the Heads of State or Government of the euro-area countries announced several measures to alleviate the Greek debt crisis and ensure the financial stability of the euro area as a whole. The support was conditional not only on the implementation of another austerity package (combined with the continued demands for privatisation and structural reforms outlined in the first programme), but it also demanded that all private creditors holding Greek government bonds should sign a deal accepting lower interest rates and a 53.5 per cent face-value loss. The most contentious part of the deal was the involvement of the private sector. Germany, strongly supported by the Netherlands and Finland, insisted that private investors should be involved in any new package. It was only in February 2012 that the deal was ratified. In mid-May 2012, the crisis and impossibility of forming a new coalition government after elections led to strong speculation that Greece would leave the eurozone (*Grexit*). A second election in mid-June ended with the formation of a new government supporting a continued adherence to the main principles outlined by the signed bailout plan.

Again, the agreement did not have a lasting effect on financial market volatility. This time, interest rates on Italian and Spanish government bonds started to rise, without a clear change in the underlying fundamentals. In response, in August 2011 a majority of the Governing Council of the ECB decided to purchase government bonds again under the Securities Market Programme after the Spanish and Italian governments had agreed to additional fiscal consolidation measures. In the week thereafter, the ECB purchased €22 billion of government bonds.

The Belgian-French Dexia bank was the first large bank which had to be rescued in this phase of the crisis due to its heavy exposure on sovereign debt. In October 2011, a bailout was arranged in which the Belgian government assumed control of 100 per cent of the company's Belgian operations. Some units of the bank were put up for sale, while the remaining troubled assets would remain in a 'bad bank' that received funding guarantees of up to €90 billion provided by the governments of Belgium (60.5 per cent), France (36.5 per cent), and Luxembourg (3 per cent).

In July 2012, a programme was agreed upon with Spain for a period of 18 months, providing external financing of up to €100 billion to support Spanish banks. The newly established European Stability Mechanism

(ESM, see below) disbursed a total of €41.3 billion to the Spanish government for the recapitalisation of the country's banking sector. This was the first financial assistance programme carried out by the ESM. It also was the first time that the instrument of recapitalising banks through loans granted to a government was used. There were no contributions from other lenders.

The Cypriot Government requested a bailout on 25 June 2012, citing difficulties in supporting its banking sector to deal with the exposure to the Greek debt. It was only in May 2013 that the final deal under which Cyprus would receive €10 billion, making it the fifth country – after Greece, Ireland, Portugal, and Spain – to receive money from the EU-IMF, was formally agreed. Measures were put in place to prevent withdrawal or transfer of moneys representing the prescribed levy. This was necessary, as equity, bond, and deposit holders of the two largest banks in Cyprus (the Bank of Cyprus (BoC) and the Cyprus Popular Bank (Laiki)) also had to contribute to the restructuring of these banks (bail-in). The BoC was capitalised through the full contribution of the shareholders and bondholders of the bank and through the conversion of 47.5 per cent of uninsured deposits (over €100,000) into equity. The resolution of Laiki minimised the use of taxpayers' money with a full bail-in of equity shareholders and bondholders, and a partial bail-in of uninsured depositors. A *bail-in* means that a financial institution is recapitalised by writing down or converting (or both) its unsecured debt, while maintaining the institution's legal entity (Enoch *et al.*, 2014). All deposits under €100,000 were fully protected. Laiki was split in two units. While all uninsured deposits were kept in a legacy unit (Legacy Laiki), the insured deposits were transferred together with certain assets and liabilities to the BoC.

It was only after ECB President Draghi told an investment conference in London in July 2012: 'Within our mandate, the ECB is ready to do whatever it takes to preserve the euro. And believe me, it will be enough' that bond spreads of *GIIPS countries* (Greece, Ireland, Italy, Portugal, and Spain) started to decline substantially.[4] To live up to those words, the ECB introduced the Outright Monetary Transactions (OMTs) programme in September 2012 (see Chapter 4). With this instrument, the ECB made clear that scenarios involving the collapse of the monetary union are out of the question. After European political leaders finally showed their commitment as well by agreeing on further support for Greece, financial markets calmed down. Interest rate spreads between the core countries and the periphery, which had to that point reflected increased risk of a euro break-up, narrowed sharply in the second half of 2012 (see Figure 2.6).

Meanwhile, Ireland, Portugal, and Spain have successfully exited their support programmes (limited to the financial sector in the case of the latter). Greece returned to the capital markets in April 2014, when it successfully issued 5-year bonds.

Causes[5]

Lack of fiscal discipline

Several important fault lines that had existed under the surface since the launch of the euro, notably weak public finances and persistent imbalances in some countries, unexpectedly became clearly visible during the euro crisis. Especially during its first stages, the sovereign debt crisis in the eurozone was often primarily attributed to a lack of budgetary discipline. This might in part be due to the fact that the initial phase of the crisis was dominated by Greece, whose budgetary troubles could indeed be clearly attributed to a lack of budgetary discipline (and even deliberate statistical misreporting). Spain and Ireland, however, had stellar fiscal records when the crisis erupted before they too ran into budgetary problems. So a lack of budgetary discipline was not the only issue at play. Diverging financial cycles played a major role. In multiple Member States, macroeconomic and financial imbalances that had built up in the years prior to the crisis were a major factor behind the deterioration of public finances. We will discuss these issues in turn, starting with lack of budgetary discipline.

The Stability and Growth Pact (SGP) as discussed in Chapter 3 aims to ensure budget discipline. Its major shortcoming has been weak enforcement. As a result, the SGP was a dire failure. Financial markets also did not discipline governments, as they hardy differentiated between sovereign bonds treating them all as (almost) risk-free. General risk aversion was very low before the crisis and financial markets apparently did not consider the no bailout clause as stipulated in the Maastricht Treaty (see Chapter 3) as credible, expecting that the Union would renege on this clause, if needed, to avert a financial crisis. When market discipline eventually came by the end of the decade, it took the form of a 'sudden stop' (Buti and Carnot, 2012).

Diverging financial cycles

Although the euro crisis is a sovereign debt crisis, it was not only caused by unsustainable fiscal policies. In fact, fiscal policies in countries like Ireland and Spain looked relatively healthy when the financial crisis started. So why then did the economic downturn following the financial crisis cause such a large swing in

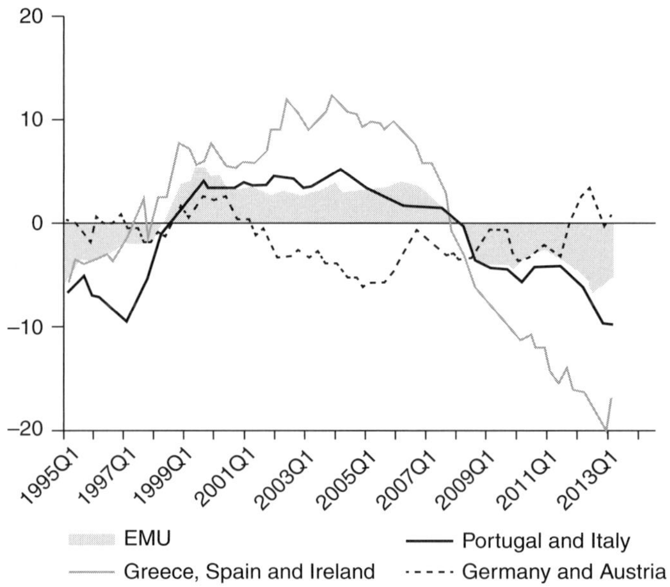

Figure 2.7 Diverging financial cycles in the euro area
Note: Financial cycle is calculated as the first principal component of the output gap, real credit growth and real house price growth.
Source: De Haan *et al.* (2014)

the budgetary position of Member States? De Haan *et al.* (2014) argue that this reflects differences in the financial cycle across Member States. Characteristics of the financial cycle are that (1) it is driven by growth in credit and house prices, (2) it has a much longer duration than business cycles: 16–20 years instead of up to 8 years, and (3) it has a wider amplitude while the correction of the financial cycle is often accompanied by a financial crisis (Drehmann *et al.*, 2012).

In the euro area, the financial cycle was asymmetric (see Figure 2.7). It was strongest in a number of countries in the periphery, notably in Ireland, Spain, and to a lesser extent Greece. In the run-up to the financial crisis multiple countries had experienced strong credit booms, in part because joining the eurozone meant that their banks could raise funds from international sources in their own currency. Also, these countries were – at least initially – experiencing a process of real convergence, while lower interest rates related to EMU-membership fuelled consumption-related and property-related borrowing (Obstfeld, 2013). By contrast, the financial cycle was much more contained in Germany and Austria, where interest rates had already been low before EMU-membership.

When cross-border financial flows dried up, countries with the greatest reliance on external funding were disproportionately affected. This applies especially to Ireland and Spain, where the resulting decline in construction was a major shock to domestic economic activity, while abandoned projects and falling property prices indicated large prospective losses for banks that had made too many property-backed loans (Lane, 2012). Recent research shows that a turn of the financial cycle has a much larger negative impact on public finances than a turn of the normal business cycle (Bénétrix and Lane, 2013). This is mostly due to its effect on government revenues. Rising asset prices increase revenues in capital gains and transaction taxes. In addition, high wage growth increases income tax revenue, especially when the system is progressive. Finally, wealth effects stimulate domestic demand and thereby the revenues from indirect taxes. All these factors reverse when the financial cycle turns, resulting in a large budgetary deterioration.

Diverging competitiveness

The credit boom fuelled by capital inflows in much of Southern Europe and Ireland facilitated another development that would come back to haunt EMU: diverging competitiveness positions. In the run-up to the crisis, several countries saw their competitiveness deteriorate. Between 2001 and 2011 per unit labour costs rose by 33 per cent in Greece, 31 per cent in Italy, 27 per cent in Spain, and 20 per cent in Ireland. By contrast, they grew by only 0.9 per cent in Germany, partly because the country needed to restore its price competitiveness after reunification. Although the large current-account deficits of some countries signalled a competitiveness problem, the deficits were relatively easy to finance as financial integration increased the availability of foreign funding (Obstfeld, 2013). In fact, capital inflows continued pushing up money and credit growth, which, in turn, increased inflation and had further negative effect on competitiveness. Growing current account deficits in the periphery were accompanied by increasing surpluses in core countries like Germany and the Netherlands.

As countries in the euro area no longer have the possibility to devalue their currency or to use national monetary policy, external imbalances can only be restored by improving competitiveness. However, relative price adjustments without a change in the nominal exchange rate will be difficult when average euro-area inflation is low; it will be a rather slow and painful route to rebalancing (Shambaugh, 2012). The conventional wisdom before the crisis was that balance-of-payments of individual euro-area countries would become as irrelevant as among regions within a country. Yet the euro crisis has challenged the wisdom of this view (Merler and Pisani-Ferry, 2012). Still, it took a while before this was realised. In fact, the financing of external positions in a monetary union could be interpreted as proof of successful integration of capital markets and of real convergence within a monetary union. However, if capital inflows fuel investments that have little effect on future productivity growth (such as real estate) and delay adjustment to structural shocks, they pose risks (Giavazzi and Spaventa, 2011).

Doom loop

The funding problems of sovereigns were reinforced by a negative feedback loop with the banking sector. The banking system in the euro area is large (see Chapter 1). The largest banks in the euro area are large in proportion to their home economies. Furthermore, most banks heavily invested in government bonds, with a home bias which is particularly strong for banks of troubled sovereigns (Greece, Ireland, Italy, Portugal, and Spain). In Spain, Portugal, and Italy domestic banks owned around 25 per cent of the outstanding stock of government debt. This is the basis for what came to be known as the 'doom loop' (or 'diabolic loop'). The essence of the problem is as follows. During the financial crisis, governments in several euro-area countries engaged in large-scale, sometimes blanket, financial sector bailouts. Such bailouts require immediate issuance of additional debt by the sovereign causing an increase in the sovereign's credit risk. This has two possible consequences. First, the government runs the risk that this debt-overhang will affect the private sector. Households and corporations may anticipate that the high level of government debt will require higher taxes in the future, thereby diluting long-run returns on real-sector and human-capital investments. The resulting under-investment in the economy can cause economic growth to slow down, thereby further increasing the sovereign's credit risk. Second, the deterioration in the sovereign's creditworthiness may feed back adversely onto its financial sector through four channels. In the first place, the market value of the government debt on the balance sheet of the financial institutions reduces, causing the financial sector's creditworthiness to decline. In the second place, higher sovereign risk reduces the value of collateral that financial institutions can use for funding purposes. In the third place, if sovereigns are downgraded by credit rating agencies this normally translates into lower ratings for banks located in the downgraded country. Finally, as the sovereign's creditworthiness declines, the value of the explicit and implicit government guarantees to the financial sector also declines, and this adversely impacts the financial sector's credit quality (Acharya *et al.*, 2012; 2014; Obstfeld, 2013). One of the goals of the

Banking Union is to break the links between sovereigns and banks. Now that the Single Supervisory Mechanism (SSM; see Chapter 12) is fully operational, the European Stability Mechanism (ESM; see below) will be able to directly capitalise problematic banks without impacting national debt and reducing the likelihood of a similar phenomenon in the future.

During the course of the euro crisis the exposure of foreign banks on sovereign debt of the GIIPS reduced, whereas the exposure of domestic banks increased. Whereas, for instance, in December 2010 67 per cent of Greek sovereign debt was held by domestic banks, in June 2013 this percentage had risen to 99 (de Haan *et al.*, 2014). This made the problem of the doom loop even more pressing. Due to the doom loop, funding problems on sovereign bond markets in the periphery went hand in hand with funding problems for banks in these countries. As a result, many countries in the periphery at some point experienced an outflow of capital which constituted a sudden stop in external financing (Merler and Pisani-Ferry, 2012). Most of the capital fled to so-called core countries that were considered a safe haven. It made banks in vulnerable countries very dependent on ECB funding, which was also reflected in growing imbalances in the Target2 settlement system (see Chapter 7). Target2 liabilities (and assets) reached around €1,000 billion in the summer of 2012.

According to the European Commission (2014), throughout the period 2008–2012, public capital injections in EU banks amounted to €413.2 billion. Banks from the UK, Germany, Ireland, and Spain received the largest injections with €60 billion or more each. In relative terms, total injections represent 3.2 per cent of the EU GDP in 2012, but they represent more than 10 per cent of the country's GDP in Ireland, Greece, and Cyprus. Problems in the banking systems eroded public finance in those countries and ultimately led governments to ask for support for their partners. Public capital injections were also significant (over 4 per cent of GDP) in Belgium, Luxembourg, Spain, Denmark, the UK, and Portugal.

Some of the banks which received support in the early stages of the crisis have started to pay back the capital injected (notably in the Netherlands, Denmark, Germany, and Italy); however, in other Member States (Spain, Greece, Portugal, Belgium, and France, among others), new injections were needed still in 2012 or 2013 (European Commission, 2014).

Policy reactions

The reaction of European leaders to the crisis was twofold. Initially, several ad hoc support programmes were initiated to support the countries that faced financial difficulties. Also more structural measures were taken, including reform of the Stability and Growth Pact, the creation of a permanent fund to support countries facing financial difficulties, and the creation of a Banking Union. Fear that the sovereign debt crisis would spread further, thereby undermining the stability of the euro area and perhaps even the sustainability of the currency union, created the political willingness to take these steps.

In view of the compelling need for a reform of the fiscal policy governance framework, European policy makers have taken several steps, including the introduction of the 'Six-Pack', 'Two-Pack', and the Treaty on Stability, Coordination, and Governance in the Economic and Monetary Union (TSCG) as discussed in Chapter 3.

In October 2010 European politicians decided to create a permanent crisis mechanism, the European Stability Mechanism (ESM) as of 2013. The ESM replaces both the European Financial Stability Facility (EFSF) and the European Financial Stabilisation Mechanism (EFSM). The ESM is a permanent last-resort rescue mechanism set up among euro-area countries and able to issue triple-A bonds to provide assistance to euro countries in difficulty, on the basis of strict conditionality. The ESM has an effective lending capacity of €500 billion and seeks to supplement its lending capacity through the participation of the IMF and non-euro EU countries. The ESM will only provide financial assistance if this is deemed indispensable to safeguard the stability of the euro as a whole. The decision to activate the ESM and the terms under which assistance will be made available will be taken unanimously by its Board of Governors, which is made up of the finance ministers of the euro-area countries. Unanimous means that abstentions do not prevent the decision from being adopted. ESM assistance will predominantly take the form of loans that will be conditional on agreement to and compliance with a strict macroeconomic adjustment programme. The interest rate on the loans will be the sum of the funding cost to the ESM and a charge of 200 basis points.

The crisis has made clear that national supervision in a monetary union is not a viable arrangement, notably in an environment with a large banking sector and high interconnectedness among national banking systems as well as between banking systems and sovereigns (Obstfeld, 2013). Furthermore, a banking union with a common safety net can break the doom loop between national governments and banks. Under a common safety net, government support to banks will no longer be provided through national budgets, so that problems in the banking sector will not immediately affect the governments' fiscal positions. The European Council therefore decided in June 2012 to establish a European Banking Union. Chapter 12 discusses this in more detail.

2.5 Conclusions

Crises are a permanent feature of the financial system. While a good functioning financial system can contribute to economic growth as discussed in Chapter 1, crises may temporarily hamper economic growth.

In a systemic banking crisis, a significant part of a country's banking system becomes insolvent after heavy investment losses and/or banking panics. Theory suggests that such banking crises are often rooted in the business cycle. In the upswing credit is expanded, while credit is reduced in the downswing ('credit crunch'). The financial system can thus amplify the business cycle. Banking crises can have a large impact on the economy. While problem banks may need to be refinanced by the government, the real cost of a banking crisis is the loss of economic growth.

The financial crisis of 2007–2009 was a banking crisis, which started with the bursting of the housing market bubble in the US. A particular feature of the crisis was the role of securitised credit. In the process of securitisation, subprime mortgages (i.e. housing loans to high risk borrowers) were repackaged by originating banks and sold to other financial institutions across the world. In that way, the crisis spread very fast and also became very deep.

In a sovereign crisis, governments default on their debt obligations. While countries sometimes repudiate their debt in a default, it is more common that a government restructures debt on less favourable terms to the lender. Debt crises are a common feature of emerging countries, but can also happen in industrial countries. The euro crisis was not only caused by unsustainable fiscal policies, but also by diverging financial cycles and competitiveness.

Notes

1. Only Austria, Belgium, the Netherlands, and Portugal managed to escape banking crises from 1945 to 2007. Except for Portugal, even these countries had massive bailouts in 2008.
2. As Turner (2009, p. 14) points out, securitised credit has existed for almost as long as modern banking. But from the mid-1990s the scale of securitisation increased rapidly. In

addition, there was 'an explosion in the complexity of the securities sold, with the growth of the alphabet soup of structured credit products'. See also Chapter 8.
3. In practice, however, the capacity of the EFSF is only around half of the €440 billion announced, primarily because only a limited part of the governments' guarantees may actually be used to raise funding.
4. See https://www.ecb.europa.eu/press/key/date/2012/html/sp120726.en.html.
5. This part heavily draws on de Haan *et al.* (2014).

Suggested Reading

Allen, F. and D. Gale (1998), Optimal Financial Crises, *Journal of Finance*, **53**, 1245–1284.

Brunnermeier, M. K. (2009), Deciphering the Liquidity and Credit Crunch 2007–2008, *Journal of Economic Perspectives*, **23**(1), 77–100.

Reinhart, C. M. and K. S. Rogoff (2009), *This Time Is Different: Eight Centuries of Financial Folly*, Princeton University Press.

References

Acharya, V. V. and P. Schnabl (2009), How Banks Played the Leverage Game, in: V. V. Acharya and M. Richardson, *Restoring Financial Stability*, Wiley, Hoboken (NJ).

Acharya, V. V., I. Drechsler, and P. Schnabl (2012), A Tale of Two Overhangs: The Nexus of Financial Sector and Sovereign Credit risks, *Banque de France Financial Stability Review*, 16, April 2012.

Acharya, V. V., I. Drechsler, and P. Schnabl (2014), A Pyrrhic Victory? Bank Bailouts and Sovereign Credit Risk, *Journal of Finance*, **69**(6), 2689–2739.

Allen, F. and D. Gale (1998), Optimal Financial Crises, *Journal of Finance*, **53**, 1245–1284.

Allen, F., A. Babus, and E. Carletti (2009), Financial Crises: Theory and Evidence, *Annual Review of Financial Economics*, **1**, 97–116.

Bénétrix, A. and P. Lane (2013), Financial Cycles and Fiscal Cycles, *Journal of International Money and Finance*, **34**, 164–176.

Borio, C. (2014), The Financial Cycle and Macroeconomics: What Have We Learnt?, *Journal of Banking and Finance*, **45**, 182–198.

Brunnermeier, M. K. (2009), Deciphering the Liquidity and Credit Crunch 2007–2008, *Journal of Economic Perspectives*, **23**(1), 77–100.

Brunnermeier, M., A. Crockett, C. Goodhart, A. Persaud, and H. Shin (2009), *The Fundamental Principles of Financial Regulation*, Geneva Report on the World Economy 11, ICBM, Geneva, and CEPR, London.

Buti, M. and N. Carnot (2012), The EMU Debt Crisis: Early Lessons and Reforms, *Journal of Common Market Studies*, **50**(6), 899–911.

de Haan, J., J.-E. Sturm, and E. Zandberg (2009), The Impact of Financial and Economic Crises on Economic Freedom, in: *Economic Freedom of the World Report 2009*, Fraser Institute, Vancouver.

de Haan, J., J. Hessel, and N. Gilbert (2014), Reforming the Architecture of EMU: Ensuring Stability in Europe, DNB Working Paper 446.

De Nederlandsche Bank (2011), *Annual Report 2010*, DNB, Amsterdam.

Drehmann, M., C. Borio, and K. Tsatsaronis (2012), Characterizing the Financial Cycle: Don't Lose Sight of the Medium Term!, BIS Working Paper 380.

Diamond, D. and P. H. Dybvig (1983), Bank Runs, Deposit Insurance, and Liquidity, *Journal of Political Economy*, **91**(3), 401–419.

Eijffinger, S. C. W. and J. de Haan (2000), *European Monetary and Fiscal Policy*, Oxford University Press.

Enoch, C., L. Everaert, T. Tressel, and J. Zhou (eds.) (2014), *From Fragmentation to Financial Integration in Europe*, IMF, Washington.

European Central Bank (2011), *Monthly Bulletin*, July 2011, ECB, Frankfurt.

European Commission (2014), *European Financial Stability and Integration Report* 2013, EC, Brussels.

Giavazzi, F. and L. Spaventa (2011), Why the Current Account Matters in a Monetary Union, in: Beblavy, M., D. Cobham, and L. Odor (eds.), *The Euro Area and The Financial Crisis*, Cambridge University Press.

Gorton, G. and G. Ordoñez (2014), Collateral Crises, *American Economic Review*, **104**(2), 343–378.

Hahm, J., H. S. Shin, and K. Shin (2011), Non-Core Bank Liabilities and Financial Vulnerability, paper presented at Federal Reserve Board conference, Regulation of Systemic Risk, Washington, 15–16 September, 2011.

Huertas, T. F. (2010), *Crisis: Cause, Containment and Cure*, Palgrave MacMillan, Houndsmills.

Laeven, L. and F. Valencia (2013), Systemic Banking Crises Database, *IMF Economic Review*, **61**, 225–270.

Lane, P. R. (2012), The European Sovereign Debt Crisis, *Journal of Economic Perspectives*, **26**(3), 49–68.

Merler, S. and J. Pisani-Ferry (2012), Sudden Stops in the Euro Area, Bruegel Policy Contribution 2012/6, March 2012.

Minsky, H. P. (1986), *Stabilizing An Unstable Economy*, Yale University Press.

Mishkin, F. S. (1992), Anatomy of a Financial Crisis, *Journal of Evolutionary Economics*, **2**(2), 115–130.

Obstfeld, M. (2013), Finance at Center Stage: Some Lessons of the Euro Crisis, European Economy – Economic Papers 493.

Qian, R., C. M. Reinhart, and K. S. Rogoff (2010), On Graduation from Default, Inflation and Banking Crisis: Elusive or Illusion? NBER Working Paper 16168.

Reinhart, C. M. and K. S. Rogoff (2009), *This Time Is Different: Eight Centuries of Financial Folly*, Princeton University Press.

(2010), From Financial Crash to Debt Crisis, NBER Working Paper 15795.

Richardson, M. (2009), Causes of the Financial Crisis, in: V. V. Acharya and M. Richardson, *Restoring Financial Stability*, Wiley, Hoboken (NJ).

Shambaugh, J. (2012), The Euro's Three Crises, *Brookings Papers on Economic Activity*, **44**(1), 157–231.

Treasury Committee of the House of Commons (2008), The Run on the Rock, Fifth Report of Session 2007–08, Volume I.

Turner, A. (2009), *The Turner Review: A Regulatory Response to the Global Banking Crisis*, Financial Services Authority, London.

Van Riet, A. (2010), Euro Area Fiscal Policies and the Crisis, ECB Occasional Paper 109.

CHAPTER

3

European Financial Integration: Origins and History

OVERVIEW

The European Union (EU) consists of 28 Member States at the time of writing and has supranational and intergovernmental forms of cooperation. The EU has its origins in the European Coal and Steel Community (ECSC) formed by six European countries in 1951. Since then, it has grown in size through the accession of new Member States, while it has also increased its powers by the addition of new policy areas to its remit.

This chapter describes the major steps towards monetary and financial integration in the European Union. In addition, it explains the most important EU institutions (European Commission, Council of the EU, European Council, the European Parliament, and the European Court of Justice) and legal instruments (like directives and regulations).

A major step in the history of European integration was the publication of the report of the Committee for the Study of Economic and Monetary Union in 1989. In this so-called Delors Report, named after the chairman of this committee, a three-phase transition towards monetary unification was proposed. The main conclusions of the Delors Committee were incorporated in the 1992 Treaty on European Union and finally led to the introduction of the single currency (the euro) as well as the European Central Bank (ECB). To protect monetary policy, the Stability and Growth Pact restricts fiscal policy of the Member States in the currency union.

An important milestone for financial integration was the launch of the Financial Services Action Plan (FSAP) by the European Commission in May 1999. The purpose of the FSAP was to remove regulatory and market barriers that limit the cross-border provision of financial services and the free flow of capital within the EU, and to create a level playing field among market participants. During the euro crisis, it was decided to create a Banking Union, which started in 2014. The ECB is now also responsible for banking supervision.

LEARNING OBJECTIVES

After you have studied this chapter, you should be able to:

- outline the various steps in the process of European monetary and financial integration
- explain the Stability and Growth Pact
- describe the fundamental principles underlying the financial integration process
- explain the functioning of the most important EU institutions and their responsibilities
- describe the various EU legal instruments
- explain the main elements of the Banking Union.

3.1 European integration: introduction

Although the idea of economic integration of European countries was proposed earlier, it was put into practice only after the Second World War. The major impetus was the Schuman plan of May 1950 that foresaw the establishment of the so-called European Coal and Steel Community (ECSC). It was very much inspired by political considerations as the ECSC was seen as the basis for Franco–German reconciliation. To ensure that reconstruction in the western part of Germany would not endanger peace, the ECSC intended to integrate the coal and steel sectors, which were at the time considered to be of central importance for the defence industry. The main objective of the ECSC was the elimination of barriers and the encouragement of competition in these sectors.

The ECSC that started in 1951 was in many ways characteristic for the European integration process of the years to come. First, its membership was limited. Only Belgium, Germany, France, Italy, Luxembourg, and the Netherlands were members. The United Kingdom and various other European countries remained outside the organisation. It was only in 1973 that Denmark, Ireland, and the UK joined what was then called the European Communities, to be followed by Greece (1981) and Spain and Portugal (1986). Austria, Finland, and Sweden became members in 1995. After the collapse of communism at the end of the 1980s, various Eastern- and Central-European countries became candidate members of what was by then called the European Union. In 2004, Cyprus, the Czech Republic, Estonia, Hungary, Latvia, Lithuania, Malta, Poland, Slovakia, and Slovenia acceded to the EU, followed in 2007 by Bulgaria and Romania. Croatia joined the EU on 1 July 2013. At the time of writing, the EU is negotiating EU membership with several other countries in the Balkans and Turkey.

Second, much of the organisational structure of the EU as we know it today (see section 3.2) is very similar to that of the ECSC. For instance, the High Authority, the ECSC's supranational executive organ, was the predecessor of the European Commission. The first president of this High Authority was Jean Monnet. Other institutions of the ECSC were the Council of Ministers (representing member governments), the Assembly (composed of 68 delegates from the national parliaments, later transformed into the European Parliament), and the European Court of Justice.

With the entering into force of the Treaty of Rome in 1958 (see Box 3.1), the European Economic Community (EEC) and the European Atomic

Box 3.1 The role of treaties

Treaties form the basis of the European integration process. The basic treaty is the *Treaty of Rome* (1957) establishing the European Economic Community. The Treaty of Rome contains the legal basis for most decisions taken by the institutions of the European Union (see section 3.2) and is still the main source of communitary legislation. The original Treaty of Rome has been amended by subsequent treaties.

A first major amendment is the *Single European Act* (1986) completing the internal market. The chief objective of the Single European Act was to add new momentum to the process of European integration. An important innovation was that it moved away from the principle of unanimity for the harmonisation of legislation. Another major treaty is the *Maastricht Treaty on European Union (TEU)* (1992) launching Economic and Monetary Union. The Maastricht Treaty also created the European Union.

Next, the *Treaty of Amsterdam* (1997) puts a greater emphasis on security and justice matters and contains the beginning of a common foreign and security policy. A further amendment is the *Treaty of Nice* (2001). This Treaty deals with reforming the institutions so that the EU could continue to function effectively after its enlargement to 25 Member States in 2004 and subsequently to 27 Member States in 2007.

The final change is the *Treaty of Lisbon* (2007), which entered into force on 1 December 2009. This Treaty further streamlines the institutions of the EU and upgrades the powers of the European Parliament (see Box 3.2). The Treaty of Lisbon amends the EU's two core treaties: the Treaty on European Union (TEU) and the Treaty establishing the European Community (also known as the Maastricht Treaty and the Treaty of Rome, respectively). The latter is renamed the Treaty on the Functioning of the European Union (TFEU). The Treaty of Lisbon was drafted as a replacement for the Constitutional Treaty which was rejected by French and Dutch voters in 2005.

Energy Community (Euratom) came into being. Of the three communities (i.e. the ECSC, the EEC, and Euratom), the EEC was by far the most important in terms of scope and instruments.[1] The Treaty paved the way for the creation of a common market where goods, services, labour, and capital could move freely. It directed Europe towards a single financial market, but it was not until the 1980s that major steps were taken in this direction.

In 1985, the European Commission published a White Paper on the Completion of the Internal Market, which provided for the free circulation of persons, goods, services, and capital in the European Union. Economies of scale and scope would result from decreased border controls, unified technical standards, reduced distribution and marketing costs, and standardised rules and regulations in the manufacturing and services sectors. To provide an economic underpinning of the Internal Market Project, the Cecchini Report (1988) calculated the costs of nationally fragmented markets, i.e. the costs of 'non-Europe', and estimated the benefits of the internal market at approximately 4–7 per cent of GDP. The White Paper led to the adoption of the so-called Single European Act (SEA) in 1986 that aimed at completing the internal market by 1992.

Another major step in the history of European integration was the publication of the report of the Committee for the Study of Economic and Monetary Union in 1989. In the *Delors Report* – named after the chairman of this committee and then-president of the European Commission, Jacques Delors – a three-phase transition towards monetary unification was proposed. The main conclusions of the Delors Committee were incorporated in the 1992 Treaty on European Union, better known as the Maastricht Treaty, named after the Dutch city where the final negotiations took place. As a consequence, the Economic and Monetary Union (EMU) started on 1 January 1999 with the irrevocable fixing of the exchange rates of the then 11 participating countries and the start of the common monetary policy by the ECB. Euro notes and coins were introduced in January 2002.

In May 1999, the European Commission launched the Financial Services Action Plan (FSAP). The purpose of the FSAP was to remove regulatory and market barriers that limit the cross-border provision of financial services and the free flow of capital within the EU, and to create a level playing field among market participants.

This chapter outlines the most important steps taken towards European financial integration. The next section goes on to explain the most important European institutions and the legal instruments used to shape integration. As full financial integration requires monetary integration, section 3.3 describes first how monetary integration has evolved. Section 3.4 discusses coordination of fiscal and economic policies. Section 3.5 sets out the major steps towards financial integration and discusses the Banking Union.

3.2 European institutions and instruments

There are two basic approaches towards integration. In the *supranational approach*, an international institution that is independent from national governments is responsible for policy making, while in the *intergovernmental approach* an international institution basically fulfils a secretariat role for the governments and has no real power. The key difference in the two approaches is the transfer of sovereignty from the Member States to that institution. Whereas in the intergovernmental approach no sovereignty is transferred, in the supranational approach Member States lose their power to enact legislation. Interestingly, in the EU both types of integration exist (Craig and De Burca, 2007).

Institutions

The *European Commission* is the EU institution that is most independent from the Member States. Its most important task is to initiate legislation. Only the Commission can come up with formal proposals for legislation (the so-called right of initiative). The Council and Parliament, to be explained below, are only able to request legislation. The formal legislative process starts with the presentation of a proposal by the European Commission to the European Parliament and the European Council, after which the process of negotiation between the latter parties starts. Currently, the Commission consists of 28 Commissioners, one from each Member State, who are appointed for a five-year term. Commissioners are expected to detach themselves from national interests. The President of the Commission and the other Commissioners are first nominated by the European Council and are officially approved by the European Parliament. The Commission has its own staff, sometimes referred to as 'the Brussels bureaucracy'. Although this name suggests otherwise, the size of the Commission staff is relatively small – the Commission employs about 33,000 officials. Each Commissioner is responsible for a particular policy area, and politically responsible for a Directorate General (DG).[2] The most important departments for financial services are DG Financial Stability, Financial Services and Capital Markets Union, DG Internal Market, DG Economic and Financial Affairs, and DG Competition.

The *Council* of the European Union consists of representatives of each Member State at the ministerial level. When the Council meetings comprise ministers of economics and finance, it is known as *Ecofin*. Decision-making in the Council is on the basis of unanimity, simple majority, or qualified majority. Decisions on financial services policy are mainly taken by qualified majority. Under the voting scheme of the Nice Treaty the number of votes of the Member States reflected their size and ranged between 29 (for Germany, France, Italy, and the UK) and 3 (for Malta). The new voting rules of the Treaty of Lisbon (see Box 3.2) are based on population size. Figure 3.1 shows the difference between the percentage of votes held by each Member State

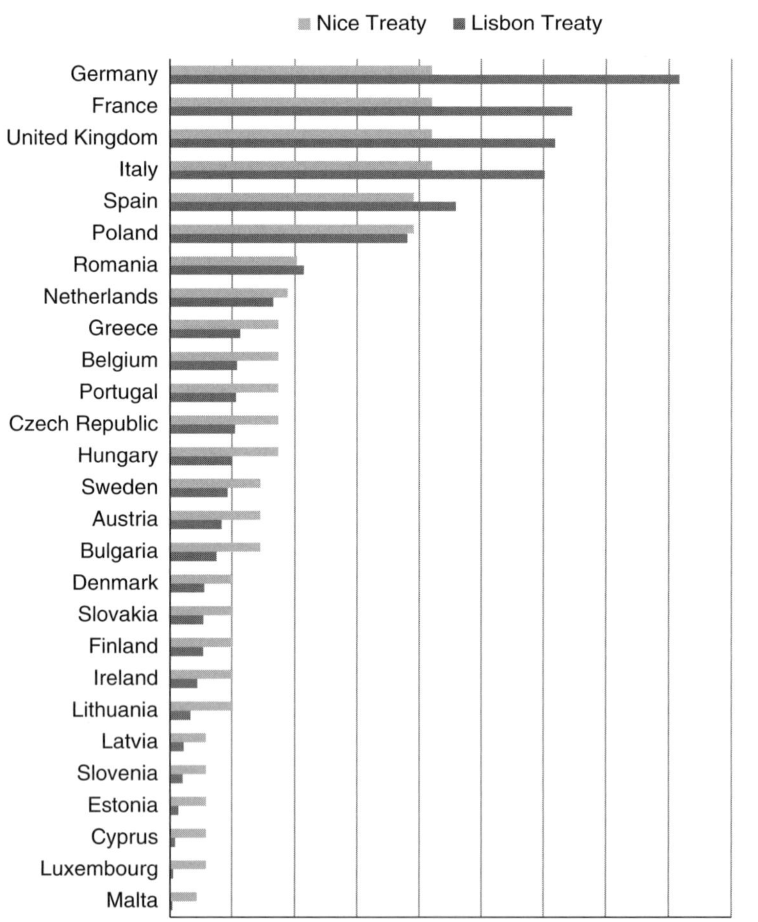

Figure 3.1 The changes in vote weights for the 28 EU countries under qualified majority voting
Source: Häge (2014)

under the old system, and the percentage of the total EU population in each state. The figure shows that larger and smaller Member States are better able to shape the outcome of negotiations than they were under the Nice Treaty (large Member States have a larger vote and small Member States are needed to form a majority of 55 per cent of Member States), while medium-sized Member States have less influence. However, it is important to realise that, on average, only about 20 per cent of legislative acts are adopted against the expressed dissatisfaction, in form of an abstention or a negative vote, of a minority of Member States (Häge, 2014).

The *European Council* has become a very powerful body. Comprised of the heads of government or state, and the President of the European Commission, it 'shall provide the Union with the necessary impetus for its development' (Article 15 TEU). Essentially, it defines the Union's policy agenda. Major policy initiatives, such as the Internal Market Programme, the Maastricht Treaty, and the Banking Union, were adopted by the European Council. The European Council also comes into play when the ministers are caught in stalemate. When the Council cannot reach a decision, the issue concerned is typically transferred to the European Council.

The role of the *European Parliament* (EP), which since 1979 is elected by the people of the EU Member States in direct elections every five years (coinciding with the term of the Commissioners of the European Commission), is more limited than that of national parliaments. Still, over time, the influence of the EP has increased. Currently, it has 751 members. The EP has veto power over the appointment of the Commission. It can also dismiss the Commission. The EP also has the right to reject the EU Budget. It plays an important role in legislation, which may go through different procedures. Under the *consultation procedure*, the EP only gives its opinion. Under the *cooperation procedure* it has the right to amend or even reject legislation, but these decisions may be overruled by the Council. Under the *co-decision procedure*, acceptance by the EP is necessary. The Commission presents a proposal to Parliament and the Council, then the EP sends amendments to the Council, which can either adopt the text with those amendments or send back a 'common position'. That proposal may be approved or further amendments may be tabled by the EP. If the Council does not approve those, a 'Conciliation Committee' is formed that seeks agreement. Finally, under the *assent procedure* the Council is required to obtain the European Parliament's assent before certain important decisions are taken. The assent principle is based on a single reading. The EP may accept or reject a proposal but cannot

Box 3.2 The Lisbon Treaty

After the French and Dutch electorate had rejected a proposal for a 'European Constitution' in Spring 2005, it took until October 2007 before the Heads of State and Government agreed in the Portuguese capital on the text of the Lisbon Treaty that amends the existing Treaties. The Treaty of Lisbon amends the EU's two core treaties, the Treaty on European Union (TEU) and the Treaty establishing the European Community. The latter is renamed the Treaty on the Functioning of the European Union (TFEU) and implies the following changes with respect to the institutions of the EU as outlined above.

The Lisbon Treaty originally intended to reduce the size of the European Commission to 18 Commissioners. However, negotiations following Ireland's rejection of the Treaty in 2008 led to an agreement that all Member States will keep their Commissioner unless national governments decide otherwise unanimously.

Like the European Parliament and the Commission, the European Council has become an EU institution with its own full-time president who will not be able to assume a national mandate. The president is elected by qualified majority by the European Council for two and a half years; this term can be renewed once. The president of the European Council represents the EU in the international arena and chairs and coordinates the European Council's work. The Lisbon Treaty also provides for a so-called 'High Representative of the Union for Foreign Affairs and Security Policy' who is responsible in the Council for the EU's common foreign and defence policies.

There are new decision-making rules within the Council. A decision is adopted within the Council if it wins the approval of 55 per cent of the EU Member States representing at least 65 per cent of the EU's population. Furthermore, a blocking minority has to include at least 4 Member States. The new double-majority voting rule that emerged with the Lisbon Treaty has come into force in November 2014 with a transitional period until March 2017. During this period it is possible for the Members of the Council to ask that decisions that need to be adopted by qualified majority as stipulated in the Treaty of Nice. It is also possible to suspend decisions using the so-called 'Ioannina mechanism', a mechanism which was included during negotiations in order to win over Poland. If Member States that are against a text are significant in number but still insufficient to block the decision (one-third of the Member States or 25 per cent of the population), all of the Member States commit to seeking a solution to rally opponents while reserving the option to vote at any time. The efficiency of the decision-making process is also enhanced by the extension of the qualified majority vote to new areas. The qualified majority replaces unanimity in several areas, such as the adoption of measures relating to external border control, asylum, and immigration.

Box 3.2 (cont.)

Finally, the powers of the European Parliament have been extended. In the legislative domain, the co-decision procedure is applied in nearly 50 new areas, including the internal market. As to the budget, the European Parliament has been given the same right to decision as the Council, notably with regard to the adoption of the entire annual budget.

amend it. If the EP does not give its assent, the act in question cannot be adopted. The assent procedure applies mainly to the accession of new Member States, association agreements, and other fundamental agreements with third countries. It is, among others, also required with regard to the specific tasks of the ECB and amendments to the Statutes of the European System of Central Banks (ESCB) and the ECB. Parliament's assent is given by a majority of votes cast, but a majority of Members is also required in case of the accession of a new Member State and the electoral procedure.

The *European Court of Justice* (ECJ) consists of 28 judges (one judge per Member State) and 9 advocates-general. Judgments of the ECJ on matters relating to the interpretation and application of European law have been of great importance for the development of the EU. As the supreme court of the EU, the ECJ gives a coherent and uniform interpretation of Community law and ensures compliance by the Member States. The ECJ has rejected protectionism in many judgments and thus contributed significantly to the realisation of the internal market.

Legal instruments

Legislative measures in the EU are proposed by the European Commission and – in the case of nearly all the measures under the Financial Services Action Plan (see section 3.5) – are adopted by co-decision under which the Council and the European Parliament consider, amend, and agree on the final content of each legislative measure. These measures are published in the *Official Journal of the European Union* and can take the form of:

- *regulations* – a regulation is binding in its entirety and directly applicable in all Member States, and does not require transposition into the respective national laws (although there may be changes required in Member States' laws to achieve the full effect of the regulation);
- *directives* – a directive is binding upon each Member State to which it is addressed, but gives national authorities the choice of form and methods.

In other words, directives must be incorporated in the national law of each Member State, generally by introducing or amending national laws, within a deadline of usually 18 or 24 months after publication.

In addition to regulations and directives, the Commission or the Council can take *decisions* which are binding upon those to whom they are addressed. The Commission and the Council can also formulate *recommendations* or deliver *opinions*. These are not legally binding, although politically they can be important. The Treaty of Lisbon has created *delegated acts* under which the legislator delegates the power to the European Commission to adopt acts amending non-essential or technical elements of a legislative act. The Treaty of Lisbon also strengthens the implementing powers of the Commission, by authorising the Commission to adopt *implementing acts*. Such acts are aimed at ensuring uniform implementation of specific measures across the EU.

The various instruments have a different impact on integration (see also Box 3.3). A regulation fosters full integration, because of its direct application. Basically, the rules are uniform and overrule national legislation, to the

Box 3.3 Dynamics of integration

The combination of the choice of the decision-making procedure (supranational or intergovernmental) and the choice of legal instrument (regulation or directive) determines to a large extent the degree of integration. In the area of competition policy and monetary policy, the EU has chosen for regulations to ensure uniformity across the EU. A good example is the Regulation on the Introduction of the Euro (EC/974/98), according to which the national currencies participating in the euro could only be converted into the euro in a uniform way. If the euro denomination of the German D-Mark, for example, were calculated differently across countries, there would be scope for arbitrage. A supranational institution (the European Central Bank) is responsible for policy making.

In the area of financial services policy, in the past the EU often opted for directives. These directives are mostly implemented in a different way by each Member State. An example is the definition of 'capital' under the Banking Directive (2006/48/EC), which has been replaced by a new legislative package known as CCR/CRD IV, which applies from 1 January 2014 (see Chapter 12). This directive determined how much capital banks must maintain in view of the risks that a bank faces. All Member States used their own definition of capital. Moreover, banking supervision was executed by national supervisory authorities. Since the start of the Banking Union in November 2014, the European Central Bank has become responsible for banking supervision as will be discussed in more detail in section 3.5.

extent that the latter is not consistent with the regulation. By contrast, a directive needs to be implemented by the Member States, leaving scope for minor or major differences. The rules are then harmonised and are generally not uniform.

The adoption or implementation of legal instruments is only the first element of the legislative framework. The second element is the putting in place of the relevant administrative arrangements to ensure that the new rules are observed. The third element, sometimes referred to as enforcement, is ensuring that the new rules work effectively and are complied with across the EU.

3.3 Monetary integration

During the initial phase of European integration, the emphasis was on integration of goods markets. As far as monetary issues were concerned, the Rome Treaty described exchange rate policies as a matter of 'common concern', but did not offer substantive contents as to its meaning. It was only at the summit in 1969 in The Hague that the European governments agreed on monetary union. Pierre Werner, prime minister of Luxembourg at the time, was appointed to chair a committee that was to draw up a plan. The Werner Report was completed in 1970. It called for the completion of a monetary union by 1980. The Werner Committee proposed a three-stage approach towards monetary union, leading eventually to fixed exchange rates and a common monetary policy.

Although the Council adopted the plan, the turmoil in the currency markets at the time made it falter. The mid-1970s can be characterised as a low point in European monetary integration. However, at the end of the 1970s the then French president, Valéry Giscard d'Estaing, and German chancellor, Helmut Schmidt, took the initiative for the European Monetary System (EMS). The aim of the EMS was to create a 'zone of monetary stability' in Europe. The core was the so-called *Exchange Rate Mechanism* (ERM). Currencies participating in the ERM were supposed to fluctuate vis-à-vis one another within a band of plus and minus 2.25 per cent around agreed-upon central rates. These central rates could be adjusted. Although this system brought some stability for the participating currencies, there were, at times, frequent adjustments of the central rates. Within the system, the German D-Mark functioned as the anchor. Countries that pegged their currency to the German one had little room for manoeuvre in monetary policy making. If the German monetary authorities decided to change their interest rates, the other countries had to follow if they wanted to maintain their peg. Various countries, notably France, felt that the German-dominated ERM did not always serve their interests as the German monetary authorities, in deciding on interest rates, took into account only the economic situation in Germany. A monetary union was considered the proper answer to this problem.

During the 1980s, the discussion therefore focused again on monetary integration. There is no doubt that the signing of the Single European Act (SEA) in 1986 and the commitment to complete the internal market by 1992 were important in furthering monetary union. Initially regarded as rather modest in nature, the SEA succeeded in developing renewed momentum for European integration, not least by establishing a clear deadline for completion of the internal market. It was argued that in order to reap the full gains from the internal market, exchange-rate risks and transaction costs were to be banished by introducing a common currency. This view is apparent from the title of an important study by the European Commission: 'One Market, One Money' (Emerson *et al.*, 1992). Although many economists do not subscribe to the view that fixed exchange rates are needed to fully capture the gains from the Single Market, the argument gained popularity under policy makers.

At the Hannover summit in June 1988, the European Council decided to establish a committee that should propose concrete stages leading to Economic and Monetary Union (EMU). The committee was chaired by Jacques Delors. A year later the committee presented its report. Although it did not offer a specified timetable, the committee proposed a gradual process towards EMU, eventually leading to monetary union, but stressed that the timing of each stage required a political decision. In the final stage, there would be a single currency under a new central bank's authority. Although not strictly necessary for the creation of monetary union, the Delors Committee argued in favour of a single currency, as this would demonstrate the irreversibility of the union. The countries participating were not only supposed to have a common currency but would also coordinate their economic policies, notably fiscal policy (see section 3.4). That is why the system is called Economic and Monetary Union.[3]

Subsequent negotiations eventually led to the adoption of the 1992 Treaty on European Union, signed in Maastricht, where the leaders of the EU countries met to take a decision on EMU. The negotiations were difficult, as the United Kingdom had strong reservations about moving towards an EU-wide currency union. The compromise that was reached was to give the

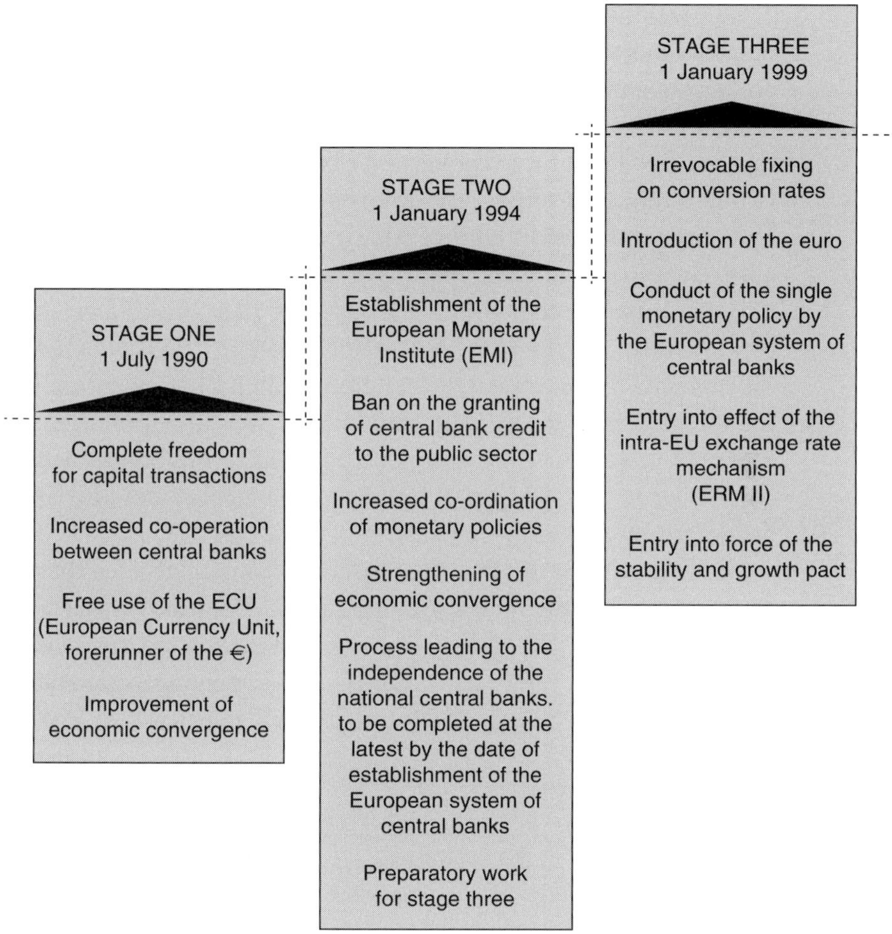

Figure 3.2 The three stages leading to EMU
Source: ECB

UK a so-called 'opt-out clause', i.e. even if the UK meets the convergence criteria for entering the euro area as stipulated in the Maastricht Treaty, it is up to the UK government to decide about entry.

Many of the suggestions of the Delors Committee found their way into the Treaty, including a three-stage approach (see Figure 3.2). As suggested in the Delors Report, the first stage of EMU started on 1 July 1990 with the liberalisation of capital controls (see section 3.5 for further details).

However, ratification of the Treaty turned out to be difficult. Denmark rejected the Maastricht Treaty in a referendum in June 1992.[4] The rejection, with a slight majority, came as a huge shock. In France, where the Maastricht

Treaty was put to a referendum after the Danes initially had said no, the majority in favour was a wafer-thin 51 per cent. Ratification was tortuous and contentious in some other countries too.

Perspectives for EMU became dim when serious currency crises occurred in 1992–1993 that forced governments to broaden the ERM fluctuation band to plus and minus 15 per cent. Many sceptics asked what hope there could be for a monetary union among countries unable to keep national currencies aligned. Sometimes EMU was perceived as an ambitious project that would never fly, just like the emu, the large Australian bird. For instance, the then prime minister of the UK, John Major, wrote in *The Economist* that continuing 'to recite the mantra of full economic and monetary union . . . will have all the quaintness of a rain dance and about the same potency'. Although the currency crises for some time led to lingering doubts, with the start of the second stage of EMU on 1 January 1994 it became clear that EMU was becoming more and more likely.

At the beginning of 1998, the European Council decided that 11 of the then 15 EU Member States could join the currency union. This decision was based on the so-called convergence criteria as outlined in the Maastricht Treaty that refer to inflation, long-term interest rates, exchange rate stability, and the public deficit and debt-to-GDP ratios (see Table 3.1).

Table 3.1 Convergence criteria

Inflation	Member State has a price performance that is sustainable and an average rate of inflation, observed over a period of one year before the examination, that does not exceed by more than 1½ percentage points that of, at most, the three best-performing Member States in terms of price stability.
Interest rate	Member State has had an average nominal long-term interest rate that does not exceed by more than 2 percentage points that of, at most, the three best-performing Member States in terms of price stability.
Exchange rate	Member State has observed the normal fluctuation margins provided for by the ERM for at least two years, without devaluing against the currency of any other Member State on its own initiative.
Budget deficit	Member State's planned or actual government deficit to GDP ratio must not exceed 3 per cent unless: – either the ratio has declined substantially and continuously and reached a level that comes close to the reference value; or, alternatively, – the excess over the reference value is only exceptional and temporary and the ratio remains close to the reference value.
Debt	Member State's government debt to GDP ratio must not exceed 60 per cent, unless the ratio is sufficiently diminishing and approaching the reference value at a satisfactory pace.

Box 3.4 Lithuania introduces the euro

On 23 July 2014 the Council of the European Union adopted a decision allowing Lithuania to adopt the euro as its currency on 1 January 2015. As will be explained in more detail in section 3.5, euro-area countries participate automatically in the Single Supervisory Mechanism (SSM), and Lithuania therefore also joined the SSM on the same date that it adopted the euro. Lithuania was the first country to join both the euro area and the SSM in this way.

Both the ECB and the European Commission published their respective Convergence Reports on 4 June 2014, in line with the requirement laid down in Article 140 of the Treaty on the Functioning of the European Union to report to the EU Council at least once every two years, or at the request of an EU Member State with a derogation 'on the progress made by the Member States with a derogation in fulfilling their obligations regarding the achievement of economic and monetary union'. (A Member State with a derogation is an EU Member State outside the euro area.) Based on the findings of the Convergence Reports, the Commission concluded that Lithuania fulfilled all of the necessary conditions for adopting the euro.

At the same time, the EU Council also adopted a regulation on the conversion rate to the euro for Lithuania. The irrevocable conversion rate is set at 3.45280 Lithuanian litas to one euro, which corresponds to the central rate of the litas in the Exchange Rate Mechanism II. (ERM II is the successor of the ERM after the introduction of the euro, which aims to stabilise exchange rates of participating countries vis-à-vis the euro.) This rate is unchanged from that agreed at the time the litas entered ERM II in 2004. Over the reference period the litas continued to be stable and did not exhibit any deviation from its central rate within ERM II.

Source: ECB Monthly Bulletin August 2014

On 1 January 1999 Europe entered a new era with the adoption of a single currency – the euro – by 11 Member States of the EU. It was the first time that countries of anything like this number, size, or global economic weight had gathered together on a voluntary basis to share a currency and to pool their monetary sovereignty. Greece joined the euro area in 2001 and Slovenia in 2007, while Cyprus and Malta introduced the euro in 2008 and Slovakia in 2009. Estonia joined the euro area in 2011, Latvia in 2014, and Lithuania in 2015 (see Box 3.4). 19 out of the 28 EU Member States have thus adopted the euro at the time of writing.

With the start of EMU, participating countries no longer had their own monetary sovereignty. As of 1 January 1999, monetary policy in the euro area was delegated to the European Central Bank (ECB). The *Governing Council of the ECB* is responsible for taking monetary policy decisions. This Council consists of the Executive Board of the ECB – made up of the president, the vice-president, and four other members – and the Central Bank governors from the countries in the euro area. Together with National Central Banks (NCBs), the ECB is part of the European System of Central Banks (ESCB). While the ECB is responsible for policy decisions, NCBs play a role in implementing monetary policy. The central banks of the EU Member States that do not participate in the euro area are members of the ESCB but they do not take part in the decision-making on the single monetary policy for the euro area and the implementation of such decisions.

The ECB's primary objective as laid down in the Treaty on the Functioning of the EU (TFEU), is price stability. The ECB has announced its interpretation of price stability (maintaining inflation in the euro area below but close to 2 per cent in the medium term) and has developed a monetary policy strategy to accomplish this objective (see Chapter 4 for further details).

3.4 Coordination of fiscal and economic policies

Stability and Growth Pact

Whereas monetary policy in EMU is conducted at the supranational level, fiscal policy has remained largely the competence of national governments. According to ECB (2011), a well-functioning monetary union requires the maintenance of fiscal discipline among its member countries. High deficits can give rise to demand and inflationary pressures that may force the ECB to keep short-term interest rates at a higher level than would otherwise be necessary. Furthermore, fiscal policies may undermine confidence in the ECB's monetary policy if markets come to expect that excessive government borrowing will ultimately be financed through money creation, and thus adjust their inflation expectations accordingly.

Therefore, the Maastricht Treaty contains provisions for the monitoring and coordination of EU Member States' fiscal policies which were further specified in the Stability and Growth Pact (SGP) that was adopted in 1997. It contains a preventive and a corrective arm. The preventive arm prescribes the path for sound fiscal policies, while the corrective arm is intended to prevent 'gross policy errors' by deterring excessive deficits and requiring their prompt correction should they occur.

Under the preventive arm of the SGP, Member States submit stability or convergence programmes in which they detail their medium-term budgetary plans. Under the original SGP, Member States were required to pursue the medium-term objective of budgetary positions that were 'close to balance or in surplus'.

The corrective arm of the SGP specifies the Excessive Deficit Procedure (EDP). When the Ecofin decides that an excessive deficit exists in a Member State, the procedure provides for a sequence of steps to be taken that should intensify the pressure on the Member State concerned to take effective action to correct its excessive deficit. For each step, the Ecofin has to take decisions on the basis of recommendations by the Commission. If a Member State does not take (sufficient) action to redress an excessive deficit, sanctions may be imposed. Sanctions include the requirement for the Member State concerned to make a non-interest-bearing deposit, which, if non-compliance persists, is eventually turned into a fine.

Critics of the SGP pointed to a major weakness of the rules in place: the Ecofin will not automatically impose sanctions, as each step requires a discretionary decision by the Council, thus following an intergovernmental approach. And the same ministers who are responsible for drafting national budgets also have to decide whether one of their colleagues breaches the rules. There are no strong incentives for Member States to prevent other Member States from deviating from the objective to strive for a balanced budget in the medium term. Furthermore, the Member States have no other means than peer pressure in the multilateral surveillance part of the SGP. No wonder, therefore, that various Member States did not adhere to this medium-term objective. Large countries, in particular, did not bring down their deficit sufficiently. As a consequence, they exceeded the 3 per cent deficit threshold once the economic downturn set in during 2000–2001. It then became clear that the enforcement mechanism in the excessive deficit procedure is also weak. Its major shortcoming is the lack of an impartial enforcement mechanism, as the Ecofin is responsible for enforcing the rules.

In 2005 the SGP was amended and this introduced more discretion and flexibility into the surveillance procedures, but made the corrective arm slightly more stringent. Each Member State will present its own country-specific medium-term objective (MTO) in its stability programme. These country-specific MTOs will be differentiated and may diverge from the close to balance or in surplus requirement depending on the current debt ratio and potential growth. The adjustment effort should be greater in good times and could be more limited in bad times. As a benchmark, the Member States should pursue an annual adjustment in cyclically adjusted terms, net of one-off and temporary measures, of 0.5 per cent of GDP. Under the amended SGP more emphasis is also put on the government debt ratio. This was important, as in implementing the SGP until then the Ecofin had only focused on the government budget deficit. However, the reform has not introduced any fundamental institutional changes.

Recent changes to the Stability and Growth Pact

In view of the compelling need for a reform of the fiscal policy governance framework, European policy makers have taken several steps, including the introduction of the Six-Pack, Two-Pack, and the Treaty on Stability, Coordination, and Governance in the Economic and Monetary Union (TSCG).

The *Six-Pack*, consisting of five Regulations and one Directive, hence its name, entered into force on 13 December 2011. It does not only cover fiscal policy surveillance, but also macroeconomic surveillance under the new Macroeconomic Imbalance Procedure (see below). In the fiscal field, the Six-Pack reinforces both the preventive and the corrective arm of the SGP. For instance, it defines quantitatively what a 'significant deviation' from the medium term objective (MTO) or the adjustment path towards it means. Moreover, it enables an EDP to be launched if a country does not meet the rule for the government debt ratio (i.e. the ratio is above 60 per cent of GDP and does not diminish towards the Treaty reference value at a satisfactory pace). Financial sanctions are imposed in a gradual way, from the preventive arm to the latest stages of the EDP, and may eventually reach 0.5 per cent of GDP. Most importantly, the Six-Pack introduces *reverse qualified majority voting* (RQMV) for decisions on most sanctions. RQMV implies that a recommendation or a proposal of the Commission is considered adopted by the Council unless a qualified majority of Member States votes against it, thereby bringing some automaticity in the procedure.

The *Two-Pack* added two more Regulations, entering into force on 30 May 2013. Its main contribution lies in the preventive arm of the SGP: it obliges governments to submit their (draft) budgetary plan for the coming year to the European Commission. It allows the European Commission to check beforehand whether the budgetary plan is in line with its recommendations. If the Commission detects serious shortcomings, it can require a revision of the budget.

On 1 January 2013, the Treaty on Stability, Coordination, and Governance in the Economic and Monetary Union (TSCG) entered into force. The articles in Title III of the Treaty referring to fiscal policy are referred to as *Fiscal Compact*. The two most important elements are a balanced budget rule, including an automatic correction mechanism, and a strengthening of the excessive deficit procedure. The contracting parties commit to implementing in their national legislation a fiscal rule, which requires the general government structural budget balance to be in line with the country-specific MTO with a lower limit of a deficit of 0.5 per cent of GDP. (This limit is 1 per cent if the government debt-to-GDP ratio is significantly below 60 per cent and risks to long-term fiscal sustainability are low.) The balanced budget rule must include a correction mechanism, which is automatically triggered in the event of significant deviations from the MTO or the adjustment path towards it. More importantly, the balanced budget rule must be introduced in the national law of the countries concerned. This must be done in a binding and permanent way, preferably at the constitutional level.

The Fiscal Compact also further strengthens the EDP of the SGP, in particular by increasing its automaticity if a euro-area Member State is in breach of the deficit criterion. Most importantly, at each stage of the EDP euro-area Member States will support the Commission's proposals or recommendations in the Council if a euro-area Member State is in breach of the deficit criterion, unless a qualified majority of them is against it. However, reverse qualified majority voting will not be applied following a breach of the debt criterion by a euro-area Member State.

Macroeconomic Imbalance Procedure

European policy makers have also enhanced the possibilities to monitor and prevent large macroeconomic and financial imbalances within the euro area. Particularly important is the introduction of the *Macroeconomic Imbalance Procedure* (MIP). The MIP is based on a continuous monitoring of a 'scoreboard', consisting of a set of 11 indicators covering the major sources of macroeconomic imbalances. These include the current account balance, price competitiveness as measured by the change in the real effective exchange rate, as well as the growth of credit and house prices. For each indicator, thresholds have been defined to identify potential imbalances. According to the European Commission, the scoreboard and the thresholds are not applied mechanically, as the scoreboard is complemented by an economic interpretation. The aim of the scoreboard is to identify countries that warrant in-depth analysis in order to determine whether the potential imbalances identified in the early-warning system are benign or problematic. By analogy with the SGP, the MIP has a preventive arm and a corrective arm. Under the preventive arm policy recommendations can be issued by the Council to tackle imbalances early on. Under the corrective arm an Excessive Imbalance Procedure (EIP) may be opened for a Member State if it is deemed to experience excessive imbalances. In that case, the Member State concerned will have to submit a corrective action plan with a clear roadmap consisting of concrete policy measures and deadlines for implementing corrective action. Non-compliance with the Council recommendations may lead to financial sanctions that could eventually reach 0.2 per cent of GDP. All decisions on sanctions are made in the Council via Reversed Qualified Majority Voting (RQMV) in order to increase automaticity. The MIP has some overlap with the emerging macroprudential policy framework of the ECB and the national central banks (see Chapter 13), as both are *inter alia* examining financial variables such as capital flows, credit growth, and house prices. This calls for close cooperation between the Commission and the ECB.

3.5 Financial integration

The Treaty of Rome of 1957 identified the 'creation of a unified economic area with a common market' as a task of the Community. As for the creation of a single market for financial services, policy primarily focused on the banking system in the first decades. The first step towards harmonisation of prudential standards for supervision of banks was set with the First Banking Directive (77/780/EEC). This directive required full harmonisation of relevant banking standards, such as solvency, liquidity, and internal controls. But the national approaches to basic prudential standards, including capital requirements, continued to diverge. Major subsequent steps were taken under the Internal Market Programme and the Financial Services Action Plan. Finally, a major step towards financial integration was made with the start of the Banking Union on 4 November 2014.

The Internal Market Programme

As pointed out in section 3.1, in the second half of the 1980s completion of the internal market was high on the agenda of European policy makers. In the context of banking, the European Commission called for a single banking licence and home-country control. Accordingly, the Second Banking Directive (89/646/EEC) determines that a credit institution that is authorised in any EU Member State is allowed to establish branches or supply cross-border financial services in the other EU Member States. Such a *single banking licence* is necessary and sufficient for cross-border provision of banking services and the establishment of branches in other Member States. The single banking licence has therefore significantly contributed to stimulating cross-border banking in Europe. However, the main limitation of the Second Banking Directive is that the single licence does not extend to subsidiaries in host Member States. This is unfortunate, as the process of cross-border European banking more often takes place via subsidiaries, especially when the cross-border operations involve major banking operations (see Chapter 10).

Importantly, the Second Banking Directive also introduced the principle of *home-country control* in supervision of branches with some exceptions, notably the supervision of branch liquidity. The authorities in the home country were responsible for supervision on solvency that extends to the bank itself, its foreign and national subsidiaries, which have to be consolidated for supervisory purposes, and its foreign branches. The authorities in the host state retained the right to regulate a foreign bank's activities in that state only to the extent that such regulation is necessary for the protection of 'public interest'.

The European legal framework incorporates the international banking standards of the Basel Committee on Banking Supervision (see Box 3.5). An important element in banking supervision is the so-called *capital adequacy requirements*, i.e. regulations on the minimum amount of capital that banks have to provide for. The Solvency and Own Funds Directives (89/647/EEC and 89/299/EEC) that laid down the solvency rules for banks were based on the 1988 Basel Capital Accord. Likewise, Basel III forms the basis for new EU regulation (see Chapter 12).

An important principle underlying European financial integration is *minimum harmonisation*. Instead of fully harmonising rules, a common minimum is defined that Member States have to implement. However, they are free to move beyond this minimum. A good example of this approach is the Directive on Deposit Guarantee Schemes (94/19/EEC) that was accepted by the Council in 1994. This directive provides for mandatory coverage per depositor with a minimum of €20,000. The directive does not deal with funding, so that the financing has to be arranged at the national level (e.g. ex-ante or ex-post funding). Deposits of a branch are covered by the deposit-

Box 3.5 Basel Committee on Banking Supervision

The Basel Committee on Banking Supervision (BCBS) provides a forum for regular cooperation on banking supervisory matters. Its objective is to enhance understanding of key supervisory issues and improve the quality of banking supervision worldwide. It seeks to do so by exchanging information on national supervisory issues, approaches, and techniques, with a view to promoting common understanding. At times, the Committee develops guidelines and supervisory standards in areas where they are considered desirable. Examples include Standards on Capital Adequacy (Basel I, Basel II, and Basel III; see below), the Core Principles for Effective Banking Supervision, and the Concordat on cross-border banking supervision.

The Committee's members come from Argentina, Australia, Belgium, Brazil, Canada, China, France, Germany, Hong Kong SAR, India, Indonesia, Italy, Japan, Korea, Luxembourg, Mexico, the Netherlands, Russia, Saudi Arabia, Singapore, South Africa, Spain, Sweden, Switzerland, Turkey, the United Kingdom, and the United States. Countries are represented by their central bank and also by the authority with formal responsibility for the prudential supervision of banking business where this is not the central bank. The Committee's Secretariat is located at the Bank for International Settlements in Basel, Switzerland.

One of the issues that the Committee frequently discusses is minimum capital requirements for banks. In 2004, an agreement was reached, generally referred to as the *Basel II Accord*. It uses a three-pillars concept: (1) minimum capital requirements, (2) supervisory review, and (3) market discipline. Its predecessor, the *Basel I Accord* of 1988, dealt with only parts of each of these pillars. Basel II aimed to improve on these existing rules by aligning regulatory capital requirements more closely to the underlying risks that banks face. In response to the financial crisis, the Committee proposed several changes in 2010, generally referred to as *Basel III* (see Chapter 12 for further details).

insurance system of the home country. All EU countries adopted an explicit deposit-insurance scheme with compulsory participation. Practical arrangements with respect to coverage limits, funding, and co-insurance differed substantially across EU Member States. During the crisis, the EU rules were changed. Directive 2009/14/EC of 11 March 2009 determines that Member States are required to increase the coverage level to eventually €100,000. According to the European Commission, the new level would cover an estimated 90 per cent of deposits.

So far, this section has discussed banking integration under the Internal Market Programme. Similar developments have taken place in the fields of insurance and securities. The Third Insurance Directives (92/49/EEC and 92/96/EEC) and the Investment Services Directive (93/22/EEC) also adopted the principles of a single licence, home-country control, and minimum harmonisation of standards.

Another important milestone for European financial integration was the Directive on Liberalisation of Capital Flows (88/361/EEC). Starting from 1 July 1990 – i.e. the start of the first phase of EMU – capital controls were, as a rule, no longer allowed. Only in the case of large, speculative movements could the European Commission authorise capital controls.

The Financial Services Action Plan

The European Council of Cardiff in 1998 underlined the importance of financial market integration as a political priority. In reaction, the European Commission published a Communication entitled 'Financial Services: Building a Framework for Action' which set out a series of measures to strengthen integration. This resulted in May 1999 in the launch of the *Financial Services Action Plan (FSAP)* by the European Commission. The purpose of the FSAP, endorsed by the European Council in March 2000, is to remove regulatory and market barriers that limit the cross-border provision of financial services and the free flow of capital within the EU, and to create a level playing field among market participants. It consists of a set of 42 measures to fill gaps and remove remaining barriers to provide a legal and regulatory environment that supports the integration of financial markets across the EU.

The FSAP has four objectives. The first objective is a single EU wholesale market. The Markets in Financial Instruments Directive (MiFID, 2004/39/EC) is, to a large extent, the cornerstone of the FSAP. This directive provides securities firms with an updated EU passport, allowing them to offer a range of financial services across Member States on a 'home-country control' basis (Haas, 2005). Under the passport principle, a firm licensed to provide financial services in its home country has the right to provide these same services throughout the EU, without the need for an additional licence. MiFID applies the passport to a broader range of financial instruments and significantly extends the list of financial services that can be 'passported' across European countries.

The second objective of the FSAP is open and secure retail markets. The Commission acknowledged that certain barriers prevented consumers and suppliers from reaping the single-market benefits of increased choice and competitive terms.

Examples of FSAP directives in the domain of retail financial services include the Distance Selling Directive and the Insurance Mediation Directive. The Distance Marketing Directive (2002/65/EC) aims to protect retail customers who deal with a financial services firm or acquire a financial product through the exclusive use of distance means such as telephone, Internet, fax, or post. It ensures that retail customers are given minimum specified information about financial services or products before contracting and have the right to cancel some types of contracts after entering into them. The Insurance Mediation Directive (2002/92/EC) aims to improve choice and reinforce protection for customers while helping insurance intermediaries (like insurance brokers and banks) to market their services cross-border in the EU. The directive sets common minimum standards across the EU for the regulation of the sale and administration of insurance. It provides rights for an insurance intermediary established in one Member State to operate in another Member State.

The third objective of the FSAP is state-of-the-art prudential rules and supervision. The Capital Requirements Directive (CRD) lays down these new capital adequacy rules for banks and is based on the 2004 Basel II Capital Accord. Capital requirement rules stipulate the minimum amounts of own financial resources that credit institutions and investment firms must have in order to cover the risks to which they are exposed. The aim is to ensure the financial soundness of these institutions – in particular to ensure that they can weather difficult periods, thereby protecting depositors and clients, and fostering the stability of the financial system. The CRD introduces capital requirements to ensure that institutions are resilient to several risks. Similarly, the Solvency II Directive (2009/138/EC) introduces risk-based capital requirements for insurance companies (see Chapter 12).

The final objective of the FSAP is related to wider conditions for an optimal single financial market, e.g. addressing disparities in tax treatment and creating an efficient and transparent legal system for corporate governance. An example is the Savings Directive (2003/48/EC) that aims to enable interest on savings received in one Member State, by individuals who are resident for tax purposes in another Member State, to be made subject to effective taxation in accordance with the laws of the latter Member State. It establishes automatic exchange of information as the way of combating cross-border tax evasion on savings income.

In 2004, the European Commission concluded that the Financial Services Action Plan was delivered on time, with 40 out of 42 measures being adopted before the 2005 deadline.

The Banking Union

Before the crisis, national authorities in the Member States were responsible for supervising the banking system and ensuring its stability. The crisis has made clear that this is not a viable arrangement. A decentralised system of bank supervision and resolution is inadequate in an environment with a large banking sector and high interconnectedness among national banking systems as well as between banking systems and sovereigns (Obstfeld, 2013). Experience of the near-failure of cross-border banks in Europe suggests that in times of crisis national authorities focus on preserving the national parts, while the integrated value of a bank is neglected (Gros and Schoenmaker, 2014).

The European Council therefore decided in June 2012 for a European Banking Union, which involves four elements. First, a Single Rulebook, consisting of a set of harmonised legislative texts that all financial institutions in the EU must comply with. These legislative texts range from capital requirements to rules for the recovery and resolution of banks.

Second, under the so-called *Single Supervisory Mechanism* (SSM) micro-prudential supervision of banks has moved from national supervisors to the ECB since November 2014. The single supervisor applies a single approach to supervision by harmonising practices and methodologies, which increases comparability across borders and reduces compliance costs for banks. Under the SSM, every bank is supervised according to a single supervisory model and use of the same data-reporting template. This ensures a harmonised and consistent implementation of prudential regulation. Single supervision under the aegis of the ECB also credibly addresses long-standing home-host coordination problems. Finally, owing to the supranational structure of decision-making, the predominance of 'national bias' should be diminished (ECB, 2014). Chapter 12 offers a more extensive discussion of the SSM.

Third, a *Single Resolution Mechanism* (SRM) has been introduced to deal with bank resolution, i.e. the orderly restructuring and/or liquidation of ailing financial institutions. A situation in which only supervision is delegated to the European level, but in which the resolution mechanism remains national, could give rise to conflicts of interest. For example, supervisory decisions to withdraw the licence of a bank would be taken at a central level whereas the bill of such decisions would have to be footed at a national level. This would put tremendous pressure on the European supervisor not to pull the trigger but instead to exercise forbearance. The political agreement concluded in March 2014 about a SRM was therefore a major step. The SRM Regulation will be applicable from 2016, together with the bail-in provisions under the Bank Recovery and Resolution Directive (BRRD). Under this mechanism, losses are initially borne by shareholders and creditors. If necessary, a new Single Resolution Board (SRB) can make temporary financing available from the newly established Resolution Fund. Chapter 13 offers a more extensive discussion of the SRM.

Fourth, a European deposit guarantee scheme has been introduced. A first step in this direction was the agreement on the Deposit Guarantee Scheme Directive (DGSD). The DGSD will ensure that deposits in all Member States will continue to be guaranteed up to €100,000 per depositor and bank. The DGSD will also ensure faster pay-outs with specific repayment deadlines, which would be gradually reduced from 20 to 7 working days. It will also ensure strengthened financing of national DGSs, notably by requiring a significant level of ex ante funding (0.8 per cent of covered deposits) to be met in 10 years.

Finally, the European Stability Mechanism (ESM) created as a permanent last-resort rescue mechanism among euro-area countries (see Chapter 2) can, under very strict conditions, recapitalise banks in the Banking Union.

Figure 3.3 illustrates the new governance framework for financial supervision and stability in the Banking Union. The bottom line shows the agency for each function. The first two stages are preventive with the European Commission (EC) responsible for legislation and the ECB for supervision. The latter three stages form the crisis management arrangements. The ECB is

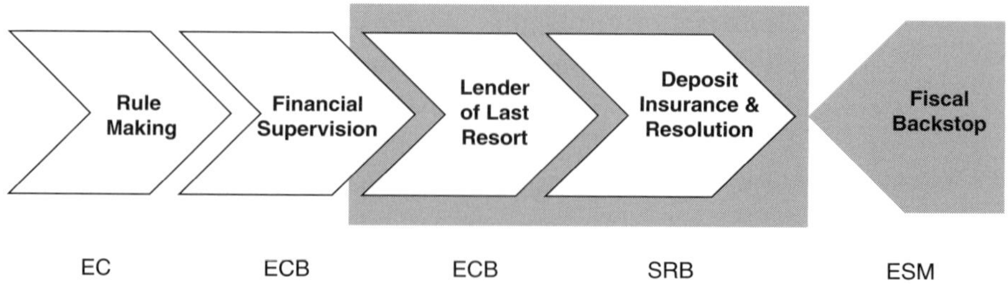

Figure 3.3 European bodies in the Banking Union
Source: Schoenmaker (2013)

the lender of last resort, just as the national central banks used to be the lender of last resort under the national regime. This lender of last resort role is typically not written down in legislation to reduce moral hazard. Finally, the SRB is responsible for resolution and the ESM is the fiscal backstop to the banking system in the Banking Union.

3.6 Conclusions

The EU has its origins in the European Coal and Steel Community, formed by six European countries in 1951. Since then, the EU has grown in size through the accession of new Member States, while it has also increased its powers by the addition of new policy areas to its remit. At the time of writing, the European Union consists of 28 Member States and has supranational and intergovernmental forms of cooperation.

Legislation has been the main mechanism for fostering economic integration. Treaties are the milestones in the integration process. An example is the Maastricht Treaty establishing the European Central Bank (ECB). Within the broader framework of these treaties, legislative measures are proposed by the European Commission and adopted by the Council and the European Parliament. These legislative measures include regulations, which apply directly in each Member State, and directives, which need to be incorporated in the national law of each Member State. While regulations ensure a uniform regulatory framework throughout the EU, the implementation of directives by Member States leaves scope for differences.

Monetary integration is characterised by two major steps. In 1979, the European Monetary System (EMS) was introduced. A key element of the EMS was the Exchange Rate Mechanism, within which the currencies of participating countries were supposed to fluctuate within a band of plus and minus 2.25 per cent. In the early 1990s, the EMS was strained by the differing economic policies and conditions of its members and the band of fluctuation was subsequently widened to plus and minus 15 per cent. In 1999, the European Central Bank took over responsibility for monetary policy making, and a common currency, the euro, was introduced in 11 EU Member States. Currently, 19 Member States are part of the euro area.

Whereas monetary policy has been delegated to the supranational ECB, fiscal policy has remained largely the competence of national governments. In order to protect monetary policy, the Stability and Growth Pact has introduced restrictions on national fiscal policy of the countries in the monetary union.

While monetary integration in Europe took place with some major steps, financial integration is a more gradual process. In 1992, the EU created an internal market by a system of laws which apply in all Member States, guaranteeing the freedom of movement of people, goods, services, and capital. In the area of financial services, the internal market introduced a single licence and home-country control for financial institutions. With a licence from the home country, financial institutions can expand throughout the EU. To strengthen financial integration further, the Commission launched the Financial Services Action Plan (FSAP) in 1999 with the purpose of removing any remaining barriers that limit the cross-border provision of financial services. A major step is the creation of the Banking Union. Under the so-called Single Supervisory Mechanism (SSM) microprudential supervision of banks has moved from national supervisors to the ECB since November 2014. The other pillars of the Banking Union are a Single Resolution Mechanism (SRM), a European deposit guarantee scheme, and the European Stability Mechanism (ESM). A deposit guarantee system has received a low priority as national schemes had been harmonised in the early stages of the financial crisis.

Notes

1. The three communities were merged in 1967. Since then, one often referred to the European Communities, later to be changed to European Community. Since the Maastricht Treaty one generally refers to the European Union.
2. Sometimes a Commissioner is responsible for more than one DG.
3. So EMU does not mean European Monetary Union. Unfortunately, this is how the abbreviation is often explained, sometimes in academic publications.
4. After Denmark attained a similar position to the UK, the Danes voted again about the Treaty in a second referendum in 1993, in which 57 per cent of the voters favoured ratification.

Suggested Reading

Decressin, J., H. Faruqee, and W. Fonteyne (eds.) (2007), *Integrating Europe's Financial Markets*, IMF, Washington DC.

Dermine, J. (2006), European Banking Integration: Don't Put the Cart before the Horse, *Financial Markets, Institutions & Instruments*, **15**(2), 57–106.

Drudi, F., A. Durré, and F. P. Mongelli (2012), The Interplay of Economic Reforms and Monetary Policy: The Case of the Eurozone, *Journal of Common Market Studies*, **50**(6), 881–898.

References

Cecchini, P. (1988), *The European Challenge, 1992: The Benefits of a Single Market*, Gower, Aldershot.

Craig, P. and G. de Burca (2007), *EU Law: Text, Cases, and Materials*, 4th edition, Oxford University Press.

Dermine, J. (2006), European Banking Integration: Don't Put the Cart before the Horse, *Financial Markets, Institutions & Instruments*, **15**(2), 57–106.

Emerson, M., D. Gros, A. Italianer, J. Pisani-Ferry, and H. Reichenbach (1992), *One Market, One Money: An Evaluation of the Potential Benefits and Costs of Forming an Economic and Monetary Union*, Oxford University Press.

European Central Bank (2011), The Reform of Economic Governance in the Euro Area – Essential Elements, *ECB Monthly Bulletin*, March 2011, 99–119.

European Central Bank (2014), *Financial Integration in Europe*, ECB, Frankfurt.

European Commission (2011), *Regulating Financial Services for Sustainable Growth. A Progress Report*, February 2011, EC, Brussels.

Gros, D. and D. Schoenmaker (2014), European Deposit Insurance and Resolution in the Banking Union, *Journal of Common Market Studies*, **52**(3), 529–546.

Haas, F. (2005), The Integration of European Financial Markets, in: *Euro Area Policies: Selected Issues*, IMF Country Report 05/266, IMF, Washington DC.

(2007), Current State of Play, in: J. Decressin, H. Faruqee, and W. Fonteyne (eds.), *Integrating Europe's Financial Markets*, IMF, Washington DC.

Häge, F. (2014), The Lisbon Treaty's Change to Council Voting Rules Will Have Important Implications for the Democratic Legitimacy of the EU, available at: http://blogs.lse.ac.uk/europpblog/2014/02/03/the-lisbon-treatys-change-to-council-voting-rules-will-have-important-implications-for-the-democratic-legitimacy-of-the-eu/.

Obstfeld, M. (2013), Finance at Center Stage: Some Lessons of the Euro Crisis, European Economy – Economic Papers 493.

Schoenmaker, D. (2013), *Governance of International Banking: The Financial Trilemma*, Cambridge University Press, New York.

CHAPTER

4

Monetary Policy of the European Central Bank

OVERVIEW

This chapter describes the monetary policy of the European Central Bank (ECB). Since the start of the monetary union in 1999, the ECB has been responsible for monetary policy making in the euro area. The ECB and the National Central Banks (NCBs) of the EU Member States whose currency is the euro make up the Eurosystem. Under the Maastricht Treaty, the primary objective of the ECB is 'price stability'. The ECB specifies this objective as inflation 'below but close to' 2 per cent in the euro area in the medium term. The ECB has an array of instruments available of which interest rate decisions generally attract most attention. Policy decisions are the outcome of the monetary policy strategy. The ECB has a 'two-pillar' strategy that explicitly pairs the discussion of monetary factors ('monetary analysis') with a broad-based non-monetary analysis of the risks to price stability in the short to medium run ('economic analysis').

During the financial crisis the ECB adopted several non-standard (or unconventional) policy measures. Next, the chapter discusses the ECB's communication policy. Nowadays, central bank communication is widely believed to enhance the effectiveness of monetary policy. The ECB has always regarded its communication policies as an integral part of its monetary policy. Finally, forward guidance by central banks is discussed. Forward guidance means that a central bank communicates about its future policy rate.

LEARNING OBJECTIVES

After you have studied this chapter, you should be able to:

- explain the functioning of the ECB
- describe the monetary policy strategy of the ECB
- explain the monetary policy instruments of the ECB

- describe the unconventional policy measures of the ECB
- describe the ECB's communication policies
- explain forward guidance policies.

4.1 The European Central Bank

On 1 January 1999 a new currency – the euro – was created and the European Central Bank (ECB) became responsible for monetary policy in the euro area – the second largest economic area in the world after the United States. At the time of writing, the euro is the official currency of 19 EU Member States with more than 330 million citizens. It is also used in five small European countries outside the EU.

The ECB and the National Central Banks (NCBs) of the EU Member States whose currency is the euro make up the Eurosystem. While the ECB is responsible for monetary policy decisions, the NCBs of the countries in the euro area play a role in implementing monetary policy through open market operations (see section 4.3 for further details). In addition to the definition and implementation of the monetary policy of the euro area, the Eurosystem is responsible for:

- the conduct of foreign exchange operations;
- the holding and management of the official foreign reserves of the EU Member States;
- the promotion of the smooth operation of payment systems.

Structure

The three decision-making bodies of the ECB are the Governing Council, the Executive Board, and the General Council (see Figure 4.1).

The *Governing Council* of the ECB is the most important decision-making body of the ECB. It consists of the six members of the Executive Board and the governors of the euro-area NCBs (19 governors in 2015), who have been appointed by their respective governments. However, when taking monetary policy decisions, the members of the Governing Council of the ECB should not act as national representatives, but in a fully independent personal capacity. In other words, when taking policy decisions they are supposed to focus on the euro area as a whole and not on their own country. The Governing Council is responsible for formulating monetary policy, including decisions about interest rates. Since 2015, the Governing Council decides about monetary policy every

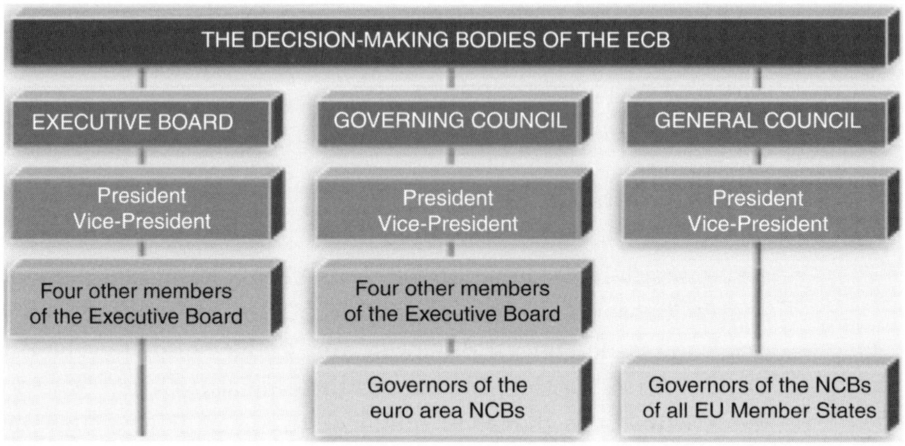

Figure 4.1 Structure of the ECB
Source: ECB (2011)

six weeks (instead of every four weeks). After the entry of Lithuania in 2015 a rotation system has been introduced for decision-making within the Governing Council (see Box 4.1). Compared to other central banks, the ECB's Governing Council's size and the proportion of outsiders appear rather large (see Table 4.1), especially if one takes into account that 7 out of the 12 Federal Reserve Presidents do not vote as a result of the rotation system in place at the Federal Open Market Committee (FOMC).

The *Executive Board* of the ECB consists of the President, the Vice-President, and up to four other members. Its members are appointed by the European Council, acting by a qualified majority, on a recommendation from the Council of the European Union. Their term in office is eight years and is not renewable. The Executive Board prepares the meetings of the Governing Council and implements monetary policy decisions taken by the Governing Council. In doing so, it may give instructions to National Central Banks. Both the Governing Council and the Executive Board are chaired by the President of the ECB or, in his or her absence, by the Vice-President (ECB, 2011).

As long as not all EU Member States use the euro as their currency, the *General Council* will also play a role. It consists of the President and Vice-President of the ECB and the governors of the National Central Banks of all EU member countries. As the central banks of the EU countries that have not (yet) adopted the euro continue to pursue national monetary policies, they do not participate in decisions related to the single monetary policy for the euro area. In the General Council, however, they have the opportunity to discuss monetary policy issues and their exchange rate relations with the euro.

Box 4.1 Decision making within the ECB Governing Council

Under the Maastricht Treaty, the ECB Governing Council takes monetary policy decisions by a simple majority of the votes cast by the members who are present in person. In practice, monetary policy decisions have generally been supported by a 'consensus' among members of the Governing Council (ECB, 2011). Each member of the Governing Council has one vote. The principle of 'one member, one vote' reflects that all the members, including the governors of the NCBs, are appointed in their personal capacity and not as representatives of their Member States. At some point in time, the new EU Member States will join the euro area. Furthermore, three 'old' EU Member States that are currently not members of the euro area – the United Kingdom, Sweden, and Denmark – could decide to adopt the euro.[1] So membership in the Eurosystem might increase to 28. The size of the ECB Governing Council could therefore increase to 34, making it by far the largest monetary policy-making institution among OECD countries. Due to this increase in membership, discussion and voting procedures would likely become more time-consuming and complicated.

Back in 2002, new voting rules were therefore agreed upon. Since the entry of Lithuania as 19th member of the euro area in 2015, these rules are in place.

There are two groups with rotating voting rights. Governors will rotate in and out of voting rights every month. The first group consists of the 5 governors of the largest Member States. They will share four voting rights. Currently, the countries in this group are Germany, France, Italy, Spain, and the Netherlands. The second group consists of all other governors, who share 11 voting rights.

Once there are 22 euro-area members, there will be 3 groups with rotation. The first group with 4 votes consists of the 'big 5'. The second group, with 8 voting rights, will consist of half of all National Central Bank governors selected from the subsequent positions in a ranking primarily determined by size of the economy. The third group will be composed of the remaining governors. They will share 3 voting rights.

The new decision-making rules have met considerable criticism from academic observers. Apart from critique on the size of the Governing Council, Gros (2003) argues that the new rules give up the principle of equality of Member States, thus potentially undermining the idea that all members of the Governing Council should forget the particular interests of their home country and act only in the interest of the entire euro area.

Objectives

The Maastricht Treaty made price stability the ECB's primary objective, but left it to the ECB to give a precise meaning to this objective. Moreover, and 'without prejudice to the objective of price stability', the ECB shall

Table 4.1 Main characteristics of selected Monetary Policy Committees

Country	MPC size	Number of outsiders	De jure decision rule	Non-voting MPC members
Euro area	25	19	Simple majority	4
United States	19	12	Simple majority	7
Japan	9	6	Simple majority	0
United Kingdom	9	4	Simple majority	0

Note: Data as of January 2015. 'Outsider' means committee member without full-time managerial position within the central bank.

'support the general economic policies in the Community with a view to contributing to the achievement of the objectives of the Community', which include a 'high level of employment', and 'sustainable and non-inflationary growth'. The primary objective, first specified by the ECB as inflation less than 2 per cent in the euro area, was made more precise in 2003 following an internal evaluation of the ECB's monetary policy strategy. Today, the ECB aims for maintaining inflation below but close to 2 per cent in the euro area in the medium term. The ECB has developed a monetary-policy strategy to accomplish this objective (see section 4.2 for further details).

Inflation is measured by the Harmonised Index of Consumer Prices (HICP) for the euro area. The HICP is a comprehensive measure for prices of consumption goods. The aim of an inflation rate 'below but close to' 2 per cent clearly delineates the maximum rate of inflation deemed to be consistent with price stability. Price decreases – deflation – are also not consistent with price stability. Price stability is to be maintained over the medium term. This implies that price levels may be temporarily distorted by short-term factors. Euro-area-wide developments, instead of specific national or regional factors, are the only determinants of decisions regarding the single monetary policy. A year-on-year increase of the HICP for the euro area as a whole below 2 per cent represents price stability, even if increases in national price indices are above 2 per cent per year. Box 4.2 discusses why price stability is deemed so important.

With the start of the Banking Union in 2014, the ECB has become responsible for supervision of banks (see Chapter 12). The ECB also plays an important role in the European Systemic Risk Board (ESRB), an independent EU body, responsible for the macroprudential oversight of the financial system within the EU. The responsibilities of the ESRB will be discussed in detail in Chapter 13.

Box 4.2 Price stability

Not all central banks have price stability as their primary objective. For instance, the Federal Reserve's mandate is 'to promote effectively the goals of maximum employment, stable prices, and moderate long-term interest rates'. Because long-term interest rates can remain low only in a stable macroeconomic environment, these goals are often referred to as the *dual mandate*; that is, the Federal Reserve seeks to promote maximum employment and price stability. Why is price stability the primary objective of the ECB's policies? The ECB (2011) provides several reasons.

First, price stability makes it easier for people to disentangle changes in relative prices (i.e. movements in prices of any individual good or service) from changes in the general price level. This allows markets to allocate resources efficiently. Second, with price stability creditors can be sure that prices will remain stable in the future and they will therefore not demand an inflation risk premium to compensate them for the risks associated with holding nominal assets over the longer term. Third, price stability makes it less likely that individuals and firms will divert resources from productive uses in order to hedge against inflation. For example, high inflation provides an incentive to stockpile real goods since they retain their value better in such circumstances than money or certain financial assets. Fourth, as tax and welfare systems are not fully indexed, inflation (or deflation) exacerbates the perverse incentives of these systems which distort economic behaviour. For instance, a nominal increase of income to compensate for inflation may cause someone to move to a higher marginal tax rate which, in turn, may affect this person's labour supply. Fifth, inflation acts as a tax on holdings of cash because households have an incentive not to use cash as often in order to reduce transaction costs. These so-called shoe-leather costs arise because individuals have to visit the bank (or cash machine) more frequently to withdraw banknotes.

Sixth, unexpected inflation causes considerable and arbitrary redistribution of wealth and income (e.g. redistribution effects from creditors to debtors). Typically, the weakest groups of society often suffer the most from inflation, as they have only limited possibilities for hedging against it. Finally, inflation leads to sudden revaluations of financial assets which may undermine the soundness of the banking sector's balance sheets and decrease households' and firms' wealth, leading to financial instability.

According to the ECB (2011), the previous discussion suggests that a central bank that maintains price stability makes a substantial contribution to the achievement of broader economic goals, such as high levels of economic activity and better employment prospects. Indeed, several empirical studies suggest the existence of a negative relationship between inflation and economic growth. However, this relationship is less clear at low rates of inflation. One may therefore wonder why the ECB has defined price stability as inflation below but close to 2 per cent. Several arguments have been put forward in support of the

Box 4.2 (cont.)

view that a maximum inflation rate of 2 per cent (even if it refers to the medium term) may be too low (de Haan *et al.*, 2005).

In the first place, there may be an upward measurement bias in inflation. It has long been recognised that due to *measurement bias*, measured inflation may overstate actual inflation. There are several reasons for this. For instance, improvements in the quality of goods may cause price changes to be overestimated. The quality of goods typically increases over time, and this, for example, makes computers bought at two different points in time not directly comparable. Ignoring this quality change will induce a measurement error in the price index. Likewise, prices of new goods often fall rapidly in the first years after their introduction. It may be several years before goods are included in the basket of goods used to calculate the price index, and thus the fall in their prices may be missed. According to the Governing Council of the ECB, the quality of the HICP makes it possible to set a precise definition of price stability in the euro area (Issing, 2001).

In the second place, even if an inflation objective of 'below but close to 2 per cent' seems high enough to forego deflation in the euro area as a whole, it is possible that deflation occurs in an individual country, depending on how large inflation differentials are in the monetary union. Deflation shares many of the costs of inflation. However, Sibert (2003) argues that the redistribution due to unexpected deflation may be more costly than the redistribution resulting from unanticipated inflation. Defaults may occur and the resulting bankruptcies and restructurings destroy real wealth. The deterioration in debtors' balance sheets brought about by unexpected deflation may thus lower both consumption and investment demand. Persistent deflation may turn into a deflationary spiral of falling prices, output, profits, and employment. Aggregate demand-induced deflation can reduce employment when nominal wages are rigid downwards. With sticky wages, price declines cause real wages to rise, profit margins to fall, and employment to be cut back. This may set off a deflationary cycle. So how large are inflation differentials in the euro area? Before the start of EMU, the inflation dispersion in the founding countries of EMU decreased over time, especially during the second half of the 1990s. The non-weighted standard deviation declined from around 4 percentage points at the beginning of the 1990s to about 1 percentage point at the start of the monetary union. Since then the standard deviation initially declined, but more recently inflation dispersion slightly increased.

In the third place, it has been argued that since nominal interest rates cannot fall (far) below zero, *monetary policy faces a trade-off between a very low level of inflation and stabilising the economy.* If the economy is faced with a recession when inflation is zero, the monetary authority is constrained in its ability to engineer a negative short-term real interest rate to counter the output loss. This constraint reflects the fact that the nominal short-term interest

Box 4.2 (cont.)

rate cannot be lowered (much) below zero, the so-called zero interest rate bound. Japan is often mentioned as an example of a country where this problem has occurred. However, even if the zero bound is hit, this may not imply that monetary policy is impotent as there may be other mechanisms through which monetary policy may influence the real economy. As will be discussed in more detail in sections 4.4 and 4.5, central banks have other instruments at their disposal when short-term interest rates are close to zero.

Finally, Akerlof *et al.* (2000) argue that *a moderate level of inflation provides 'grease' to the price and wage setting process.* The economic adjustment of relative prices to shocks can become sluggish in the presence of downward nominal rigidities in wages and prices. For instance, with a zero inflation rate, individual firms facing an adverse firm-specific shock will not be able to secure real wage reductions in the presence of downward nominal wage rigidity and will, instead, lay off workers. Likewise, at low levels of inflation, a significant part of the price and wage setters probably ignore or underweight anticipated inflation in setting future prices. A moderate level of inflation provides for some real wage flexibility, which reduces the natural, or long run, rate of unemployment. According to the ECB (2003), however, the empirical evidence on the importance of downward nominal rigidities for the euro area is not conclusive. Evidence based on the distribution of changes in the euro-area price indices indicates that nominal price cuts are not as uncommon as often believed. According to micro-based studies a substantial proportion of wage earners have experienced wage cuts. However, even if downward nominal rigidities were pervasive, one may wonder whether 'accommodating' them with a higher inflation rate makes this undesirable structural feature of some economies not even more 'entrenched' (ECB, 2003).

4.2 Monetary policy strategy

The ECB's monetary policy is based on a 'two-pillar' strategy that explicitly pairs the discussion of monetary factors ('monetary analysis') with a broad-based non-monetary analysis of the risks to price stability in the short to medium run ('economic analysis'). Figure 4.2 provides a schematic overview. According to the ECB (2011, p. 69), 'the two-pillar approach is designed to ensure that no relevant information is lost in the assessment of the risks to price stability and that appropriate attention is paid to different perspectives and the cross-checking of information in order to reach an overall judgement on the risks to price stability'. The two-pillar approach provides a cross-check of the indications that stem from the shorter-term economic analysis with

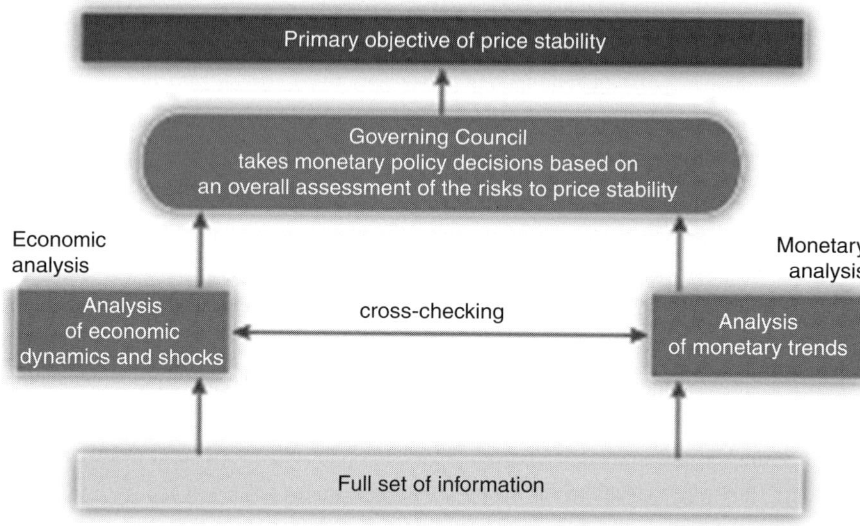

Figure 4.2 The monetary policy strategy of the ECB
Source: ECB (2011)

those from the longer-term-oriented monetary analysis, which, according to the ECB, ensures that monetary policy does not overlook important information relevant for assessing future inflation trends. By taking policy decisions and evaluating their consequences not only on the basis of the short-term indications stemming from the analysis of economic and financial conditions but also on the basis of money and liquidity considerations, the ECB arguably will not be tempted to take an overly activist course in determining the monetary policy stance (ECB, 2011).

The 'economic analysis' focuses on the assessment of current economic and financial developments and the implied short- to medium-term risks to price stability. The economic and financial variables that are the subject of this analysis include, for example: developments in overall output; aggregate demand and its components; fiscal policy; capital and labour market conditions; a broad range of price and cost indicators; developments in the exchange rate, the global economy, and the balance of payments; financial markets and the balance sheet positions of euro-area sectors (ECB, 2011). Moreover, macroeconomic staff projections play an important role in the economic analysis, although their role is different from that of inflation forecasts in an inflation-targeting strategy (see Box 4.3). The ECB publishes these projections for the euro area four times a year in its *Monthly Bulletin*. (At the beginning of 2015, the Monthly Bulletin was replaced by the

Box 4.3 Inflation targeting

Inflation targeting has become a very popular monetary policy strategy. Central banks in among others Australia, Canada, New Zealand, Norway, Sweden, and the UK have adopted this strategy. Also central banks in several emerging and developing countries (such as Brazil, Indonesia, and South Africa) use an inflation targeting strategy. According to Mishkin and Savastano (2001), *inflation targeting* involves the public announcement of numerical targets for inflation, a strong commitment of the central bank to price stability as a final monetary policy objective, and a high degree of transparency and accountability. The distinctive feature of this strategy is a forward-looking decision-making process known as 'inflation-forecast targeting'. It means that the central bank sets its policy instruments in such a way that its inflation forecast (after some time) equals the inflation target. Although in practice, different forms of inflation targeting exist, they all have in common a published numerical inflation target and a predefined policy horizon. Central banks using this approach communicate monetary policy decisions in terms of a reaction to deviations in a forecast for a particular measure of inflation from the inflation target at a particular horizon. The central bank's forecast for inflation is therefore centrepiece both when it comes to decision making and in communicating to the public.

The ECB (2011) provides several arguments against using this approach. First, focusing entirely on a forecast inflation figure does not provide a comprehensive and reliable framework for identifying the nature of threats to price stability. Second, various aspects of the textbook inflation targeting approach – such as the fixed horizon of the forecast from which monetary policy decisions feed back – are somewhat arbitrary and in many circumstances do not appear to be optimal. Third, it is difficult to integrate the information contained in monetary aggregates into inflation forecasts that are based on conventional macroeconomic models. Finally, the ECB takes the view that relying on a single forecast would not be appropriate, given the considerable uncertainty relating to the structure of the euro-area economy. It is considered preferable to adopt a diversified approach to the analysis of economic data based on a variety of analytical methodologies.

Economic Bulletin, to mirror the six-week cycle for the Governing Council's monetary policy meetings.) The Governing Council uses them with many other pieces of information to assess the risks to price stability, but it neither assumes responsibility for the projections nor does it use the staff projections as its only tool for organising and communicating its assessment as done under inflation targeting.

In the economic analysis, due attention is paid to the need to identify the nature of shocks hitting the economy, their effects on cost and pricing behaviour, and the short- to medium-term prospects for their propagation in the economy. For example, the appropriate monetary policy response to a temporary rise in the international price of oil might be different from the appropriate response to wage increases that are not in line with productivity growth. The former results in a transient and short-lived increase in inflation which quickly reverses, whereas the latter entails the risk of a self-sustaining spiral of higher costs, higher prices, and higher wage demands. The ECB also carries out several surveys that provide further input into the economic analysis. Also, asset prices and financial yields are analysed to derive information about the expectations of financial markets, including expected future price developments. Likewise, developments in the exchange rate are closely assessed for their implications for price stability as exchange rate movements have a direct effect on price developments through their impact on import prices (ECB, 2011).

The so-called 'monetary analysis' focuses on a medium- to long-term horizon. When the ECB's monetary policy strategy was introduced in 1998, the ECB Governing Council announced a quantitative 'reference value' for the annual growth rate of a broad monetary aggregate (M3). This focus on money growth was motivated by the view that inflation in the long run is considered to be a mostly monetary phenomenon. The choice for M3 growth was justified by its perceived favourable empirical properties, especially a relatively stable money demand relationship. Furthermore, M3 growth was shown to exhibit leading indicator properties for future inflation. However, the ECB has always stressed that monetary policy does not react mechanically to deviations of M3 growth from the reference value. Such deviations, however, trigger increased efforts to identify and assess the underlying driving forces. Nowadays, the monetary analysis entails a comprehensive analysis of the liquidity situation, going well beyond M3 growth. For instance, the composition of M3 growth (i.e. the components and sectoral contributions) is extensively analysed.

In December 2002 the ECB Governing Council decided to evaluate this strategy in the light of the experience, taking into account the public debate and the outcomes of research undertaken by ECB and NCB staff. The results of this evaluation were published in May 2003. Although many observers had expected that the ECB would abandon the monetary pillar, the Governing Council made it clear that the ECB would continue to include monetary analysis in its policy strategy, although it needed some 'clarification'. As the Governing Council explained, the monetary analysis was to mainly serve as a means of 'cross-checking', from a medium- to long-term perspective, the short- to medium-term indications from the economic analysis. To underscore the longer-term nature of the reference value for monetary growth, the Governing Council decided to discontinue the practice of an annual review of the reference value for M3 growth.

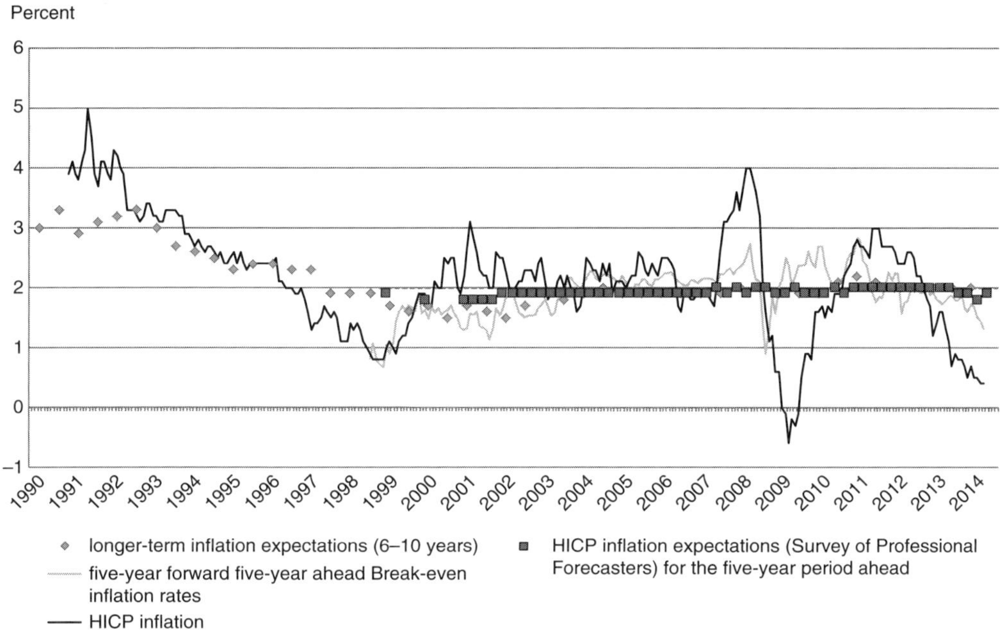

Figure 4.3 Long-term inflation expectations and actual inflation in the euro area, 1990–2014
Source: ECB

According to the ECB (2011), its policies have contributed to keeping longer-term inflation expectations in the euro area firmly anchored at levels consistent with the ECB's definition of price stability (see Figure 4.3).

4.3 Monetary policy instruments

The ECB has several instruments at its disposal. By using these instruments, the ECB is able to affect inflation and output (see Box 4.4 for a further discussion of how monetary policy affects the economy). This section discusses the ECB's policy instruments, starting with a description of the ECB policy rates which signal the ECB's monetary policy stance. Then we turn to open market operations and minimum reserve requirements.

Policy rates

To understand ECB interest rate decisions, it is important that we first explain the so-called standing facilities, i.e. the marginal lending facility and the deposit facility. Banks can use these facilities if they need liquidity

Box 4.4 Monetary policy transmission

Monetary policy decisions affect the real economy and inflation through various channels. Changes in money market rates due to ECB policy measures in turn affect other short-term interest rates (*interest channel*). For example, changes in money market rates have an impact on the interest rates set by banks on short-term loans and deposits.

Furthermore, changes in central bank interest rates may also affect the supply of credit (*credit channel*). The credit channel has three mechanisms: the bank lending channel, the balance sheet channel, and the risk-taking channel.

Following an increase in interest rates, the risk that some borrowers cannot safely pay back their loans may increase to a level such that the bank will not grant a loan to these borrowers (the *bank lending channel*). As a consequence, such borrowers are forced to postpone their consumption or investment plans.

Interest rate changes also affect firms' balance sheets. An increase in interest rates leads to a lower net worth of assets which means a lower collateral value and thus a reduced ability to borrow (the *balance sheet channel*).

Whereas the bank-lending channel focuses on the quantity of loans supplied, the *risk-taking channel* zooms in on banks' incentive to bear risk related to the provision of loans. The risk-taking channel is thought to operate mainly via two mechanisms. First, low interest rates boost asset and collateral values. This, in conjunction with the belief that the increase in asset values is sustainable, leads both borrowers and banks to accept higher risks. Second, low interest rates make riskier assets more attractive, as agents search for higher yields. In the case of banks, these two effects usually translate into a softening of credit standards, which can lead to an excessive increase in loan supply.

Interest rate changes may also affect the exchange rate which, in turn, will normally affect inflation in three ways (*exchange rate channel*). First, exchange rate movements may directly affect the domestic price of imported goods. If the exchange rate appreciates, the price of imported goods tends to fall, thus helping to reduce inflation directly, insofar as these products are directly used in consumption. Second, if these imports are used as inputs into the production process, lower prices for inputs might, over time, feed through into lower prices for final goods. Third, an appreciation in the exchange rate may make domestically produced goods less competitive in terms of their price on world markets; this tends to constrain external demand and thus reduce overall demand pressure in the economy. All other things being equal, an appreciation of the exchange rate would thus tend to reduce inflationary pressures, and vice versa. The strength of exchange rate effects depends on how open the economy is to international trade. Exchange rate effects are in general less important for large economies than for small open economies. Furthermore, financial asset prices like the exchange rate depend on many other factors in addition to monetary policy.

Box 4.4 (cont.)

The *expectations channel* mainly works by influencing the private sector's longer-term expectations. It has gained particular relevance for the conduct of monetary policy over past decades. Its effectiveness crucially depends on the credibility of central bank communication (see section 4.5). For instance, if a central bank enjoys a high degree of credibility in pursuing its objective, monetary policy can exert a powerful direct influence on price developments by guiding economic agents' expectations of future inflation and thereby influencing their wage- and price-setting behaviour. The credibility of a central bank to maintain price stability in a lasting manner is crucial in this respect. If economic agents believe in the central bank's ability and commitment to maintain price stability, inflation expectations will remain firmly anchored to price stability. This, in turn, will influence wage-and price-setting, as wage- and price-setters will not have to adjust their prices upwards for fear of higher inflation in the future.

According to the ECB (2011), monetary policy transmission in the euro area has several characteristics. First, long and uncertain lags exist in the transmission of monetary impulses to the domestic price level. Second, in normal times, monetary policy works mainly through the interest rate channel: a tightening of monetary policy leads to a transitory decrease in output, which is estimated to reach its maximum between one and two years after the interest rate increase. Prices tend to decline more gradually, and respond more sluggishly, to the tightening of monetary policy than output. Third, interest rate changes also affect economic activity via their impact on firms' cash flows and the supply of bank loans, hence confirming the relevance of the credit channel of monetary policy.

Source: ECB (2011)

or if they want to stall liquidity. Both facilities have an overnight maturity and are available to banks on their own initiative. The deposit facility is used for mopping up liquidity from the banks at rates which normally are substantially below market rates. The marginal lending facility provides liquidity to the banks at rates that are usually substantially above market rates.

As the interest rates on the standing facilities are normally substantially higher (for borrowing) or lower (for depositing) than the corresponding money market rate, banks normally only use the standing facilities in the absence of other alternatives. As there are no limits on access to these facilities (except for the collateral requirements of the marginal lending facility), the rate on the marginal lending facility and the rate on the deposit facility normally provide a ceiling and a floor, respectively, for the overnight

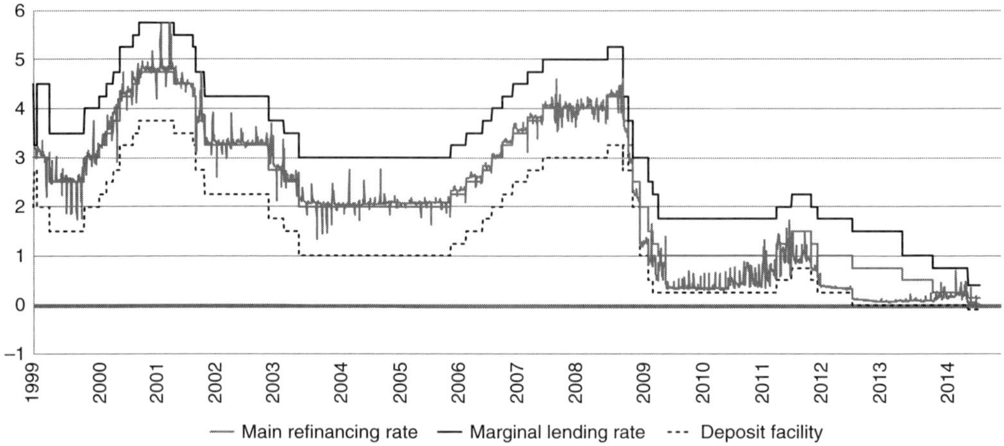

Figure 4.4 ECB policy rates and EONIA, 1999–2014 (percentage per annum; daily data)
Source: ECB

rate in the interbank money market. The standing facilities thus constitute a corridor for the interbank money market rate. By setting the rates on the standing facilities, the ECB effectively determines the corridor within which the overnight money market rate can fluctuate.

Figure 4.4 shows the development of key ECB interest rates since January 1999 and illustrates how the interest rates on the standing facilities have provided a ceiling and a floor for the overnight interbank market interest rate, measured by EONIA (euro overnight index average). EONIA represents the average rate on unsecured overnight euro lending transactions in the interbank market. It is the (weighted) average rate on transactions reported to the ECB on that day by a representative panel of banks, known as the EONIA Panel.

Figure 4.4 shows that in the past EONIA generally remained close to the rate on the main refinancing operations, one of the ECB's open market operations explained below. This changed in October 2008, when the ECB adopted non-standard measures to counter the negative effects of the financial crisis (see section 4.4).

The ECB also changed policy rates at the time when unconventional monetary policies as discussed in the next section were in place. For instance, on 5 July 2012 the Governing Council decided to decrease the interest rate on the main refinancing operations by 25 basis points to 0.75 per cent. In addition, it decided to cut the interest rates on both the marginal lending facility and the deposit facility by 25 basis points, to 1.50 per cent and 0.00 per cent, respectively. Likewise, in May 2013 the

Governing Council decreased the interest rate on the marginal lending facility by 50 basis points to 1.00 per cent and cut the rate on the main refinancing operations to 50 basis points, narrowing the spread to the rate on the deposit facility to 50 basis points. In November 2013, the Governing Council narrowed the policy corridor further by cutting the MRO rate by 25 basis points and leaving the deposit facility at 0 per cent. In addition, it decided to decrease the interest rate on the marginal lending facility by 25 basis points to 0.75 per cent.

In June 2014 the Governing Council decided:

- to decrease the interest rate on the main refinancing operations by 10 basis points to 0.15 per cent;
- to cut the interest rate on the marginal lending facility by 35 basis points to 0.40 per cent;
- to decrease the interest rate on the deposit facility by 10 basis points to –0.10 per cent.

In September 2014 it was decided to decrease all interest rates by another 10 basis points. On that occasion, ECB President Draghi said that 'now we are at the lower bound, where technical adjustments are not going to be possible any longer'.

Open market operations

The Eurosystem affects money market interest rates by providing more (or less) liquidity to banks if it wants to decrease (increase) interest rates. It allocates an amount of liquidity that allows banks to fulfil their liquidity needs at a price that is in line with the ECB policy intentions. To manage liquidity in the money market and steer short-term interest rates, it uses *open market operations*, i.e. it buys (or sells) financial assets. If assets are bought from (sold to) a bank, the reserves of that bank at the central bank increase (decrease).

The Eurosystem's open market operations can be divided into the following four categories (ECB, 2011): main refinancing operations (MROs), longer-term refinancing operations (LTROs), fine tune operations (FTOs), and structural operations (see Table 4.2). Lending through open market operations normally takes place in the form of reverse transactions. In these reverse transactions, the central bank buys assets from a bank under a repurchase agreement (i.e. the bank buys the asset back) or grants a loan against assets pledged as collateral. Reverse transactions are therefore temporary open market operations which provide funds for a limited, pre-specified period only.

Table 4.2 Monetary policy instruments

Monetary policy operations	Liquidity provision	Liquidity absorption	Maturity	Frequency
Open market operations				
Main refinancing operations	Reverse transactions	–	One week	Weekly
Longer-term refinancing operations	Reverse transactions	–	Three months	Monthly
Fine tune operations	Reverse transactions	Reverse transactions	Non-standardised	Non-regular
		Several fixed-term deposits		
	Foreign exchange swaps	Foreign exchange swaps		
Structural operations	Reverse transactions	Issuance of ECB debt certificates	Standardised/ Non-standardised	Regular and non-regular
	Outright purchases	Outright sales	–	Non-regular
Standing facilities				
Marginal lending facility	Reverse transactions	–	Overnight	Access at discretion of counterparties
Deposit facility	–	Deposits	Overnight	Access at discretion of counterparties

Source: ECB (2011)

The Eurosystem accepts instruments issued by both private and public debtors as collateral.

In addition to the weekly MROs, the Eurosystem also executes regular monthly LTROs with various maturities (e.g. 6 months or 12 months). These operations are aimed at providing longer-term liquidity to the banking system. After October 2008, when the ECB took several measures to combat the financial crisis (see section 4.4), the weight of the refinancing operations shifted towards LTROs (see Figure 4.5).

The Eurosystem may also carry out open market operations on an ad hoc basis, the so-called fine tune operations (FTOs). The frequency and maturity of such operations are not standardised. FTOs are aimed at managing the liquidity situation in the money market and steering interest rates, in particular in order to smooth the effects on interest rates of unexpected liquidity

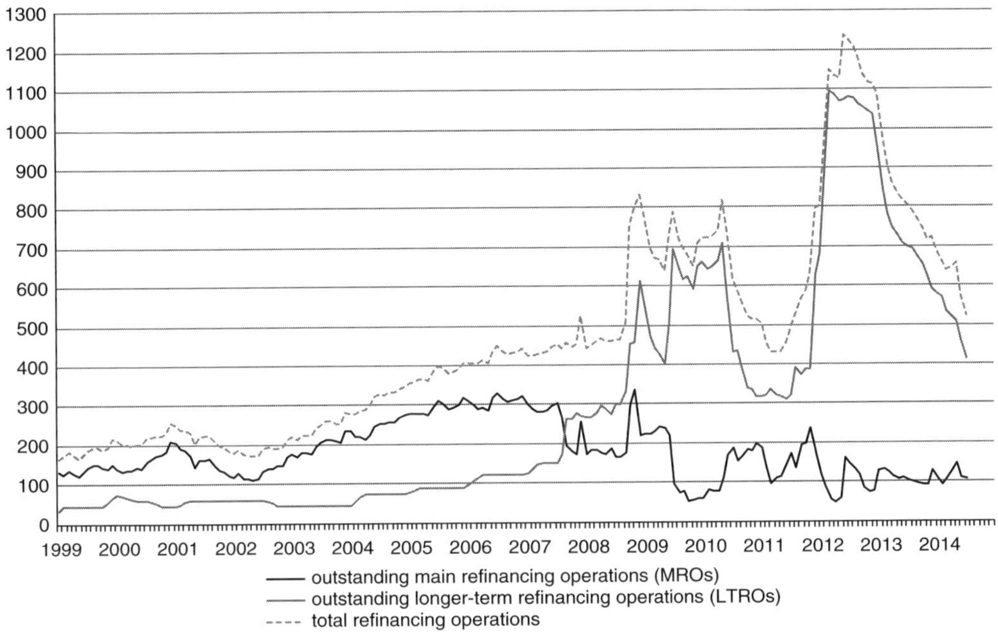

Figure 4.5 Refinancing operations, 1999–2014 (EUR billions, averages of daily positions over maintenance period)
Source: ECB

fluctuations in the market. Finally, the Eurosystem may issue debt certificates and carry out reverse or outright transactions whenever it wishes to adjust the structural position of the Eurosystem vis-à-vis the financial sector (ECB, 2011).

While monetary policy decisions are centralised and taken by the ECB's Governing Council, their implementation is more decentralised. The 19 national central banks of the euro-area countries play an important role in implementing refinancing operations. This reflects the largely bank-based structure of the euro-area economy. The involvement of NCBs aims to ensure that the single monetary policy reaches the banking system in all the euro-area countries. There are about 6,300 credit institutions established in the euro area, of which around 2,200 fulfil the operational criteria for participation in open market operations. Approximately 200–400 institutions usually participate. This differs from the US set-up, where the Federal Reserve Bank of New York implements monetary policy on behalf of the entire Federal Reserve System and the operations consist mainly of outright purchases and sales of assets in the open market, in line with the essentially market-based structure of the economy (Cour-Thiman and Winkler, 2014).

Minimum reserve requirements

The final instrument that we discuss is the *minimum reserve requirements* imposed on banks. Under the minimum reserve system banks are required to hold compulsory deposits with NCBs. The amount of the required reserves is determined by the size and composition of the liabilities on the balance sheet of the bank concerned. For most liabilities included in the reserve base the reserve ratio used to be 2 per cent. The minimum reserve system serves two main purposes: (1) to create sufficient structural demand for central bank credit, and (2) to contribute to the stabilisation of money market interest rates.

The minimum reserve system enlarges the structural liquidity shortage of the banking system. The need for banks to hold reserves with the NCBs contributes to increasing the demand for central bank credit which, in turn, makes it easier for the ECB to steer money market rates through regular liquidity-providing operations.

Interest rates are stabilised by allowing banks to use averaging provisions, i.e. to comply with reserve requirements on the basis of average daily reserve holdings over the maintenance period. This allows banks to smooth out daily liquidity fluctuations, since transitory reserve imbalances can be offset by opposite reserve imbalances generated within the same maintenance period. The averaging provision implies that banks can profit from lending in the market and run a reserve deficit whenever the money market rates are above those expected to prevail for the remainder of the maintenance period. In the opposite scenario, they can borrow in the market and run a reserve surplus. Since March 2004, the timing of the reserve maintenance period has been such that it will always start on the settlement day of the main refinancing operation following the Governing Council meeting at which a monetary decision is taken. Furthermore, as a rule, the implementation of changes to the standing facility rates will be aligned with the start of the new reserve maintenance period. The averaging provision works very smoothly during the maintenance period. However, at the end of the period, the reserve requirement becomes binding and banks can no longer transfer a liquidity surplus or deficit into the future. This explains the spikes in the EONIA towards the end of each maintenance period, which can be seen in Figure 4.4. It also explains why the use of the standing facilities is most extensive towards the end of the maintenance period.

4.4 Unconventional monetary policy

ECB's unconventional monetary policies

In describing the ECB's unconventional monetary policies it is useful to distinguish between four phases:

- the start of the global financial crisis in September 2008 (Lehman collapse);
- the start of the euro crisis in May 2010 (Greek crisis);
- the reintensification of the euro crisis, coupled with increased banking sector strain from mid-2011 on;
- declining inflation and sluggish economic recovery after 2013.

At the beginning of the financial crisis, the ECB, like other major central banks, reduced its key interest rates to historically low levels. The main refinancing rate was cut by a total of 325 basis points to 1 per cent between October 2008 and May 2009. In addition, the Governing Council adopted a number of temporary non-standard measures, subsequently referred to as Enhanced Credit Support. These measures focus primarily on banks, reflecting the financial structure of the euro area (see Chapter 1). Due to uncertainty about the creditworthiness of other banks, the interbank market did not function properly. After the failure of Lehman Brothers in September 2008 the interbank market effectively shut down. Amid significantly impaired markets and elevated counter-party credit concerns, demand for liquidity rose sharply while interbank lending declined rapidly. The start and intensification of the euro crisis forced the ECB to intervene also in sovereign debt markets. In the latter phase, worries about deflation became important.

Enhanced Credit Support

There are five main building blocks of the Enhanced Credit Support:

(1) unlimited provision of liquidity through 'fixed rate tenders with full allotment';
(2) extension of the (already long) list of collateral assets, so that the share of private sector assets increased to 56 per cent of the nominal value of securities on the list;
(3) extension of the maturity of long-term refinancing operations, initially to 6 months, and then, in late June 2009, to 12 months, aiming to decrease uncertainty in commercial banks' liquidity planning;

(4) liquidity provision in foreign currencies, particularly US dollars, through swap lines with the Federal Reserve; and
(5) outright purchases of covered bonds in order to revive that market, which is important for banks' funding.

Fixed rate full allotment

A fixed rate full allotment tender procedure was adopted for all refinancing operations during the financial crisis. Thus, contrary to normal practice, banks had unlimited access to central bank liquidity at the main refinancing rate, subject to adequate collateral. In November 2013 the Governing Council decided to prolong the framework of fixed rate full allotment for all operations as long as it was needed, and at least until 7 July 2015.

Collateral requirements

The list of eligible collateral accepted in Eurosystem refinancing operations was extended, allowing banks to use a larger range and proportion of their assets to obtain central bank liquidity. The ability to refinance illiquid assets through the central bank provides an effective remedy to liquidity shortages caused by a sudden halt in interbank lending. This includes, for instance, asset-backed securities, which became illiquid when the market collapsed after the default of Lehman Brothers.

Extension of the maturity of liquidity provision

The Eurosystem had already increased the amount of liquidity provided in longer-term refinancing operations (LTROs) after the ECB's decision to introduce supplementary refinancing operations with maturities of 3 and 6 months during the period of financial turmoil. After the collapse of Lehman Brothers, the maximum maturity of the LTROs was temporarily extended to 12 months. This increased the Eurosystem's intermediation role aimed at easing refinancing concerns of the euro-area banking system. Reduced uncertainty and a longer liquidity planning horizon were expected to encourage banks to continue providing credit to the economy. Moreover, the measures were expected to contribute to keeping money market interest rates at low levels.

Currency swap agreements

The Eurosystem also temporarily provided liquidity in foreign currencies during the financial crisis, most notably in US dollars, at various maturities. It used reciprocal currency arrangements with the Federal Reserve System to provide funding in US dollars against Eurosystem eligible collateral at various maturities at fixed interest rates with full allotment. This measure supported banks which otherwise faced a massive shortfall in US dollar funding during the period of financial crisis.

Covered bond purchase programme

The Eurosystem purchased euro-denominated covered bonds issued in the euro area at a value of €60 billion over the period between May 2009 and June 2010. The covered bonds market (see Chapter 5) had virtually dried up in terms of liquidity, issuance, and spreads. The aim of the programme was to revive the covered bond market, which is a very important financial market in Europe and a primary source of financing for banks.

In October 2011, the ECB announced a new covered bond purchase programme (CBPP2). Purchases of about €16 billion have been conducted in the primary and secondary markets between November 2011 and October 2012. In September 2014 another covered bond purchase programme was announced (CBPP3).

As a result of the non-standard measures taken during the financial crisis, the relationship between the main refinancing rate and money market rates changed. Whereas in normal circumstances the EONIA rate closely follows movements in the main refinancing rate, the high demand from banks for central bank liquidity in refinancing operations with full allotment has resulted in the deposit rate playing a greater role in steering the EONIA rate, as can be seen in Figure 4.4.

Securities Markets Programme

In addition to the Enhanced Credit Support, the ECB introduced the *Securities Markets Programme* in response to tensions in the euro-area sovereign bond markets in May 2010 (see Chapter 2). The spreads between the yields on ten-year bonds of some euro area governments (notably Greece, Ireland, and Portugal) and the German Bund yield increased sharply. Interest rates reached levels that would have quickly become unsustainable for any sovereign. Given the crucial role of government bonds as benchmarks for private-sector lending rates and their importance for bank balance sheets and liquidity operations, this development was considered to impair the transmission of policy interest rate decisions to the real economy (Cour-Thiman and Winkler, 2014).

Under the programme, Eurosystem interventions were carried out in the euro-area public and private debt securities markets to ensure depth and liquidity in dysfunctional market segments and to restore the proper functioning of the monetary policy transmission mechanism. Purchases of government bonds were strictly limited to secondary markets. To ensure that liquidity conditions are not affected, all purchases were fully neutralised through liquidity-absorbing operations.

When the sovereign debt crisis struck Italy and Spain in the summer of 2011 and their government bond markets risked becoming dysfunctional, the ECB reactivated its Securities Markets Programme that had been dormant for several months. Significant and sustained interventions at varying intensity temporarily eased the situation in government bond markets.

Even though the SMP was used for monetary policy purposes, it also provided time for governments to find a durable solution to the crisis and restore the sustainability of public finances. According to Cour-Thiman and Winkler (2014), governments did not use the time effectively. For instance, in the Greek programme, significant implementation shortfalls emerged and the fundamental issues of substantially improving tax collection and strengthening competitiveness were not addressed sufficiently. Cour-Thiman and Winkler (2014) argue that these developments illustrated the limits of central bank actions on government bond markets without explicit conditionality on adjustment efforts for the benefiting sovereigns.

The SMP was terminated after the introduction of Outright Monetary Transactions (see below).

Further unconventional measures: LTROs, OMTs, and TLTROs

LTROs

In November and December 2011, the ECB Governing Council reduced interest rates by 25 basis points. The refinancing interest rate came down from 1.50 to 1.00 per cent. These rate cuts were deemed necessary in view of the worsened economic forecasts which indicated increased recession risk. The ECB in addition introduced liquidity-enhancing measures in order to strengthen the liquidity position of European banks. The interest rate cuts were expected by the market, but the liquidity-enhancing measures were not. The ECB introduced two longer-term refinancing operations (LTROs) with a maturity of 36 months and the option of early repayment after one year. In December 2011, the ECB lent almost €490 billion to banks. In February 2012, the ECB lent almost €530 billion. Whereas the number of banks participating in the first LTRO was 523, in the second LTRO 800 banks asked for and received three-years loans. Banks considered three-years central bank funding at favourable rates as a very attractive way of funding current and new business. In addition to introducing these LTROs, the Governing Council in its December 2011 meeting decided to extend the list of eligible collateral and to temporary reduce the reserve ratio from 2 to 1 per cent.

OMTs

Despite these liquidity arrangements for banks, in the summer of 2012 there were signs that the ability of banks to provide credit was seriously hampered with consequences for the real economy. Bank funding costs were pushed up by continued tensions in sovereign debt markets. Some government bond yields started to incorporate the risk that the country concerned might abandon the euro area. In other words, markets had doubts about the sustainability of EMU.

Against this background, the ECB announced on 2 August 2012 its intention to perform *Outright Monetary Transactions* (OMTs) in secondary sovereign bond markets.[2] A necessary condition for OMTs is strict and effective conditionality attached to an appropriate European Financial Stability Facility/European Stability Mechanism (EFSF/ESM) programme or a precautionary programme (Enhanced Conditions Credit Line). This means that the ECB would wait for the euro-area governments collectively to be ready to put their money first before deciding whether central bank money would be used in the sovereign bond markets, if this is warranted from a monetary policy perspective (Cour-Thiman and Winkler, 2014). Transactions are focused on the shorter end of the yield curve, and in particular on sovereign bonds with a maturity of between one and three years. Importantly, no ex ante quantitative limits are set on the size of OMTs. OMTs will be fully sterilised.

The measure enables the ECB to address severe distortions in government bond markets, which originate from, in particular, unfounded fears on the part of investors of the reversibility of the euro. By signalling its readiness to intervene in government bond markets, the ECB could help, in particular, to reduce the likelihood of adverse self-fulfilling equilibria.

The ECB has always emphasised that OMTs are aimed at ensuring the proper transmission of the ECB's interest rates to the euro-area economy and the singleness of its monetary policy (Cour-Thiman and Winkler,

2014). The reason is that the Maastricht Treaty's prohibition of monetary financing prevents the ECB from purchasing government bonds in the primary market. Moreover, secondary market intervention cannot be used to circumvent the prohibition of primary market intervention. According to the ECB, OMTs are consistent with the ECB's mandate as the Governing Council acts in full independence, which guarantees that the purpose in OMTs is one of monetary policy. OMTs are limited to transactions in secondary markets for sovereign bonds: the money goes to investors, not to the sovereign issuer. Finally, and most importantly, OMTs require explicit conditionality to ensure that governments make the necessary efforts to restore the sustainability of public finances. The ECB has explicitly committed itself to suspending the OMTs if the government concerned fails to comply with conditionality, or if the OMT objectives are achieved (Cour-Thiman and Winkler, 2014).

Besides strict conditionality and explicit reference to an exit, there are three other modalities that make OMTs different from the SMP: focus on the short-term maturities in government bond markets, explicit acceptance of *pari passu* status (equal claims on rights), and transparency with regard to the disclosure of transactions for the countries concerned. With those differences, the ECB aimed at addressing a number of concerns relating to the SMP, which was terminated at the same time as the OMT was announced (Cour-Thiman and Winkler, 2014). OMTs have not been activated.

TLTROs

In view of the outlook for inflation, on 5 June 2014 the ECB announced a further reduction in policy rates. The outlook for inflation had been downwardly adjusted in the previous months, increasing fears for deflation (see Box 4.5). As part of a package of measures (see below), the ECB therefore lowered all of its policy rates. This means that the deposit rate turned negative (–0.1 per cent), as it already stood at zero. A negative deposit interest rate means that the ECB will charge banks to park their surplus liquidity with it.

The ECB also announced new measures to enhance the functioning of the monetary policy transmission mechanism by supporting lending to the real economy. In particular, the ECB decided to conduct a series of *Targeted Longer-Term Refinancing Operations* (TLTROs). The package in particular aims at improving bank lending to the euro-area non-financial private sector and at stimulating economic growth and inflation. At the

Box 4.5 Deflation in the euro area?

Overall annual HICP inflation in the euro area has declined significantly in recent years. This has triggered discussions about the extent to which there is a risk of deflation in the euro area. According to the ECB, deflation should not be defined as a negative inflation rate during a short period. A period of negative annual inflation does not in itself imply deflation, in a meaningful economic sense, unless the price declines become generalised and entrenched in inflation expectations. In assessing the risk of deflation, it is crucial to identify the nature and persistence of the determining factors and, in particular, to assess the degree to which inflation developments can be attributed to supply-side or demand-side forces. The overall price index may turn negative for a short period on the back of transitory supply-side shocks, such as commodity price movements. This occurred in the euro area and in other countries, for example, in 2009. But if longer-term inflation expectations remain stable, the ebbs and flows in commodity prices are bound to exert only transitory effects on inflation. Likewise, structural reforms may initially lead to downward pressures on inflation rates, reflecting also supply-side improvements in the economy, but inflation can be expected to pick up over time as aggregate demand gradually recovers. Negative inflation rates in individual countries may, on occasion, be consistent with the normal functioning of a monetary union, as they help to restore competitiveness, i.e. they may be symptomatic of supply-side induced relative price adjustments.

According to the ECB, the low inflation rates in the euro area are the result of a confluence of both supply and demand-side factors. Global supply-side factors, including a deceleration in energy and food prices, have played the most important role. The appreciation in the euro effective exchange rate has also contributed to the decline in inflation, amplifying the effect of commodity prices. Local factors, such as the impact of structural reforms in labour and product markets, have contributed to weakening price pressures as well. At the same time, demand-side factors have weighed on inflation, particularly in those countries where pre-crisis excesses are still unwinding.

However, according to the ECB, the situation in the summer of 2014 does not suggest that an outright deflationary episode is imminent for the following reasons:

- the share of items with negative annual growth rates is not exceptionally high compared with earlier episodes of disinflation;
- there is no evidence of an unanchoring of medium to long-term inflation expectations (see Figure 4.3);
- the latest Eurosystem staff macroeconomic projections for the euro area suggest that, although price pressures will remain subdued for a prolonged period, HICP inflation is projected to increase gradually;

Box 4.5 (cont.)

- in addition, economic growth is projected to gradually pick up, while unemployment is falling slowly from high levels.

But after the summer of 2014 the situation worsened and also long-term inflation expectations started edging down. This motivated the decisions on quantitative easing taken in the second half of 2014 (see below).

Source: ECB Monthly Bulletin June 2014

time, the ECB expected inflation to remain below target for quite some time. Banks were entitled to an initial TLTRO borrowing allowance equal to 7 per cent of the total amount of their loans to the euro-area non-financial private sector, excluding loans to households for house purchase, outstanding on 30 April 2014. If banks have borrowed under the TLTROs and their net lending to the euro-area non-financial private sector, excluding loans to households for house purchase, in the period from 1 May 2014 to 30 April 2016 is below the benchmark, they have to pay back borrowings in September 2016.

The initial operations were conducted on 18 September and 11 December 2014, with additional operations scheduled for March, June, September, and December 2015 and March and June 2016. Banks can borrow additional amounts in these TLTROs up to a limit which is determined by taking into account the bank's net lending to the euro-area non-financial private sector, excluding loans to households for house purchase, provided between 30 April 2014 and the respective allotment reference date in excess of a specified benchmark. For most banks, the benchmark is determined by taking into account each counterparty's net lending to the euro-area non-financial private sector, excluding loans to households for house purchase, recorded in the 12-month period up to 30 April 2014. Banks that have borrowed under the TLTROs, while their net lending to the euro-area non-financial private sector, excluding loans to households for house purchase, in the period from 1 May 2014 to 30 April 2016 is below the benchmark, have to pay back borrowings in September 2016.

All TLTROs will mature in September 2018. The interest rate on the TLTROs will be fixed over the life of each operation at the rate on the Eurosystem's main refinancing operations (MROs) prevailing at the time of take-up, plus a fixed spread of 10 basis points.

Why did the ECB introduce new monetary policy measures? Despite better financial conditions since the summer of 2012, bank lending in the euro area was still weak. This is attributable to both weaker credit demand due to households and companies trying to reduce their debt levels, and tighter bank lending conditions. As pointed out by DNB (2014), banks are strict in their assessment of new loan applications, given the risks they observe in the financing of companies and the necessity to maintain sufficient capital buffers. In addition, banks in the euro area are being faced with losses and bad loans resulting from the crisis, which limits room on the balance sheet to extend new loans. Targeted central bank funding may help prevent limited availability of bank loans from slowing down economic recovery. This especially holds true for the euro area, where businesses largely depend on bank loans for their external financing (see Chapter 1). TLTROs offer banks temporary access to cheap and longer-term central bank funding. This is expected to contribute to a further decrease of the financing costs of banks and may lead to lower interest rates on loans in the euro area. Contrary to earlier liquidity measures taken by the ECB, these measures incentivise banks more strongly to extend their loans to the real economy, as the size of the funding depends on outstanding and new bank loans to companies and consumers. Loans to households for house purchase are excluded from this measure in order to avoid financial imbalances on the housing market. Banks may increase lending but can also use the funding for purchases of other assets, such as corporate bonds, commercial paper, and government paper, which will help bring down rates across the board. However, this can only be done to a limited extent, as banks are obliged to repay the loans obtained if they do not keep lending to companies and households in line with the benchmark determined by the ECB.

As the accommodative monetary policy may have unwanted side effects, the new liquidity support to banks is temporary and targeted to address bottlenecks in lending. De Nederlandsche Bank (2014) points to the following risks. First, the prolonged low interest rate and the sizeable non-standard liquidity support necessary to kick-start the economy and inflation may unintentionally reduce the incentive for governments and private institutions to make structural adjustments and reforms. The low interest rates dampen the debt burden on the budget, which may trigger governments to postpone measures to restore sound public finances. Second, accommodative monetary policy could induce excessive risk-seeking behaviour with investors in their search for better returns. This may give rise to undesirable build-up of bubbles in some market segments.

Box 4.6 A comparison of unconventional monetary policies

As a consequence of unconventional policy measures, central bank balance sheets have expanded substantially. In advanced economies, central bank assets now exceed 20 per cent of GDP (see Figure 4.6). Still, the unconventional measures differed. After the collapse of Lehman Brothers, the balance sheets of the Fed and the Bank of England initially developed very similarly to that of the Eurosystem. Both central banks offered loans at longer maturities and with a broader spectrum of collateral. For this purpose, the Fed introduced its Term Auction Facility, thereby deviating from its usual way of providing liquidity through outright purchases of government securities. As the crisis progressed, the Fed increasingly provided liquidity through outright purchases of securities. Although this is the Fed's traditional form of liquidity provision, the purchases of federal agency securities and mortgage-backed securities changed its composition and its volume increased, especially from November 2010 onwards.

The Federal Reserve began to purchase assets with long maturities to lower long-term interest rates. There were several rounds of what came to be known as *quantitative easing* (QE1, QE2, and QE3). Quantitative easing entails an expansion of the central bank balance sheet, while it does not alter the composition of the asset side of the balance sheet. So the portfolio of assets held by the central bank is not changed: the share of each asset category in total holdings does not alter substantially and no new asset classes are added to the portfolio. In September 2011, the Federal Reserve decided to conduct a maturity extension programme, i.e. it sold shorter-term Treasury securities and used the proceeds to buy longer-term Treasury securities. This is an example of qualitative easing. Under *qualitative easing*, the overall size of the central bank balance sheet is left untouched, but the composition of asset holdings is changed. Market participants often refer to this programme as 'Operation Twist'. This operation was intended to put downward pressure on longer-term interest rates and contribute to a broad easing in financial market conditions. In 2013, then Fed-chairman Ben Bernanke announced that the Federal Reserve would lower the amount of assets purchased by the Fed each month if economic conditions, such as inflation and unemployment, were favourable. This came to be known as *tapering.*

The Bank of England set up the Asset Purchase Facility Fund to help achieve monetary policy objectives. Losses incurred by the fund are offset by the state and its accounts are not consolidated with those of the Bank of England, but the Bank finances this fund with loans that appear on its own balance sheet. The Bank mainly purchased British government bonds – known as gilts – under the Asset Purchase Facility.

Thus, compared with the Federal Reserve and the Bank of England, the Eurosystem until recently had only a very limited monetary policy portfolio resulting from outright purchases. This reflects that most of the ECB's non-standard policies were aimed at providing liquidity support to banks.

Box 4.6 (cont.)

The ECB's non-standard policies differ also in another dimension from those of other major central banks. The US Federal Reserve and the Bank of England consider unconventional monetary policy, centred on outright asset purchases, a substitute for interest rate decisions and therefore a way to provide extra stimulus to the economy and mitigate deflationary pressures once policy rates have reached a lower bound. By contrast, the ECB has always considered these non-standard policies a complement to standard monetary policies. This is also reflected in the timing of these policies. Already early in the crisis the ECB introduced non-standard measures, whereas the US Federal Reserve and the Bank of England started focusing on non-standard measures since the spring of 2009, once policy interest rates had reached a lower bound (Cour-Thiman and Winkler, 2014).

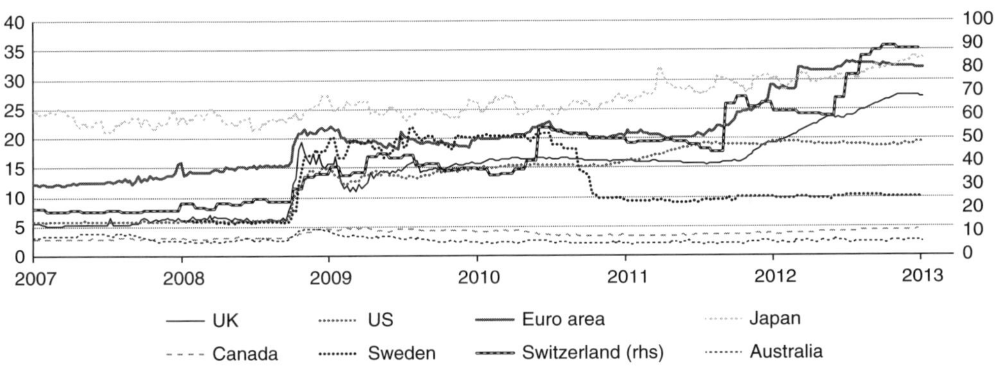

Figure 4.6 Central bank assets as percentage of GDP
Source: Pattipeilohy *et al.* (2013)

Quantitative easing

Outright purchases of ABS

The ECB also decided in June 2014 to intensify preparatory work related to outright purchases in the ABS market to enhance the functioning of the monetary policy transmission mechanism, given the role of this market in facilitating new credit flows to the economy. Under this initiative, the Eurosystem will purchase simple and transparent ABS with underlying assets consisting of claims against the euro-area non-financial private sector.

Quantitative Easing

In January 2015, the ECB decided to launch an expanded asset purchase programme, encompassing its existing purchase programmes for asset-backed securities and covered bonds.[3] The ECB followed other central banks (such as the Federal Reserve, the Bank of England and the Bank of Japan), which have used outright purchases as part of their monetary policy already for several years. This policy is often referred to as quantitative easing, or QE.

The ECB's Governing Council took this decision in order to address the risks of a prolonged period of too low inflation. At the time, most indicators of actual and expected inflation in the euro area had drifted towards fresh lows. And this situation required a forceful monetary policy response. According to the ECB, "the interest rate instrument alone has not been sufficient to steer inflation closer to 2 per cent. If the ECB still had room to cut interest rates, it would have done so already. Given that this option was no longer possible, the asset purchase programme was the only appropriate tool to enable the ECB to achieve a similar result. To fulfil its mandate, the ECB needs to make use of all instruments at its disposal."

From March 2015 onwards, each month up to €60 billion of public and private sector securities will be purchased until end-September 2016 under this expanded programme. The ECB announced that the purchases "will in any case be conducted until we see a sustained adjustment in the path of inflation which is consistent with our aim of achieving inflation rates below, but close to, 2 per cent over the medium term". The securities, euro-denominated investment-grade securities issued by euro area governments and agencies and European institutions, will be bought in the secondary market. The amount of government bonds bought will be based on the Eurosystem NCBs' shares in the ECB's capital key. Importantly, there will be two limits. First, there is an issuer limit of 33 per cent. This means that the Eurosystem will not buy more than one third of each issuer's debt. Second, there is an issue limit, which is 25 per cent. This limit implies that the Eurosystem will not buy more than 25 per cent of each issue of a particular security. The maturities of the securities to be purchased will range between 2 and 30 years. NCBs will play a key role in implementing the programme, while the ECB will coordinate the purchases.

Risk sharing under QE

To explain risk sharing under QE, we first have to explain capital keys. The ECB has its own capital, subscribed by the NCBs in the participating Member States of the European Union (EU). Each NCB accounts for a fixed percentage of this total capital and this percentage is called the capital key. The key is calculated according to the relative size of a Member States' population and gross domestic product. So the ECB is owned by the participating NCBs in the EU. When a country joins the EU, its central bank automatically becomes a member of the European System of Central Banks (ESCB). That means it is immediately factored into the calculation of the capital key. This last happened in July 2013, when Croatia became the 28th Member State of the EU. NCBs in the euro area have to pay up the full amount of capital. When the ECB makes gains or losses in a given year, these are passed on to the NCBs in line with their capital key, after deduction of an accumulated safety buffer. However, the gains and losses arising from the Eurosystem's (the ECB and the NCBs of the countries in the euro area) monetary policy operations are distributed only to those central banks, which have paid up their subscribed capital in full – i.e. the NCBs of the countries in the euro area. It is important to realise, however, that apart from this rule, the ECB's Governing Council, in accordance with the Statute of the ESCB, decides the way in which and the extent to which losses incurred by NCBs are shared within the Eurosystem. Although the "default mode is a full risk-sharing mode", as pointed out by Draghi in his January 2015 press conference, there is no automatic loss-sharing rule.

Indeed, risk sharing under QE will be different than under other monetary policy operations. The Governing Council decided that purchases of securities of European institutions (which will be 12 per cent of the additional asset purchases, and which will be purchased by NCBs) will be subject to loss sharing. The rest of the NCBs' additional asset purchases will not be subject to loss sharing. The ECB will hold 8 per cent of the additional asset purchases. This implies that 20 per cent of the additional asset purchases will be subject to a regime of risk sharing. The remaining 80 per cent is for the account and risk of the NCBs.

Effects and risks

The effectiveness of QE on aggregate demand in the euro area is uncertain. First, banks, households and firms are still deleveraging, which makes them reluctant to issue or take new credit or to spend. Second, QE1 of the Fed was particularly effective because of the adverse market conditions in 2008–09. At the time the ECB introduced QE, the euro area faced a strong risk-on environment and interest rates and credit spreads are already extremely low. This means that the market conditions at the start of QE in the euro area are very different from those in the US. This makes the potential effects of QE in the euro area likely smaller. Finally, the economy of the euro area structurally differs from the US economy. The latter is a market-based economy, while the euro area can be characterised as a bank-based economy. Since QE mainly works through financial market channels, its effects in the euro area will likely be smaller than in the US.

QE implies several risks. By encouraging risk-taking by market participants, QE can create financial imbalances that are out of line with economic fundamentals. For instance, in the UK and US, stock prices rose strongly after announcements of new QE programs. In the euro area, risk-taking in financial markets and in the economy seem out of sync: the confidence of financial investors is much higher than that of manufacturers. Another risk of QE is that by prolonging very loose monetary conditions, it may lead to a misallocation of resources by, for instance, discouraging write-downs of loans that would not be profitable in normal market conditions. And last but not least, the large-scale central bank interventions on financial market reduce market discipline and take away incentives for governments and private entities to conduct fundamental adjustments. Since investors seem to price in an improvement of economic fundamentals, this constellation raises the risk of a sharp reversal in financial market prices.

4.5 ECB communication policies

Theory

Since its inception, the ECB has regarded communication as an integral part of its monetary policy. It has communicated frequently to the public on various issues, such as its objective, its policy decisions, and the economic outlook. In doing so, the ECB has used various communication channels. For instance, the ECB extensively uses press conferences to inform the public on its decisions almost on a real-time basis. In addition, the ECB employs other communication channels, like the *Economic Bulletin*, its website, as well as speeches by and interviews with ECB policy makers.

This emphasis on communication is not unique to the ECB. Over the past two decades, a true revolution in thinking and practice has occurred with respect to central bank openness. For a number of reasons – including the greater independence from the political process and the related increased need for accountability – central banks have shed their previous shrouds of mystery. Most importantly, communication has become important because it has the potential to affect private sector expectations. As such, it offers central banks an additional instrument to achieve their monetary policy objectives. By now, communication has developed into a key instrument in the toolbox of many central bankers (Blinder *et al.*, 2008).

Central bank communication has two main objectives. First, it contributes to the accountability of the central bank and, second, it helps the central bank in managing expectations. Here we leave the first objective aside and focus upon the second objective of central bank communication (see de Haan *et al.*, 2005 for a further discussion on the accountability of the ECB).

Why are expectations relevant? Nowadays, it is widely accepted that the central bank's ability to affect the economy critically depends upon the degree to which it can influence market expectations regarding the *future path* of overnight interest rates. The reason is simple: few, if any, economic decisions hinge on the overnight bank rate, which is the only market interest rate that is effectively controlled by the central bank. Long-term interest rates, reflecting expected future short-term interest rates, affect saving and investment decisions by households and firms. Therefore, the public's perception of future policy rates is critical for the effectiveness of monetary policy.

Still, from a theoretical point of view, it is not obvious that communication may help the central bank to realise its ultimate objective(s), like price stability and stable economic growth. For instance, communication has little value added if the central bank credibly commits to a policy rule. Assuming that the public has rational expectations, any systematic pattern in the way that policy is conducted should be correctly inferred from the central bank's observed behaviour (Woodford, 2005). Thus, when it comes to predicting future interest rates, the public merely has to interpret (forecasts of) economic data in view of the central bank's policy rule; there is no role for central bank communication. A central bank can be fully transparent without any communication.

This reasoning is highly stylised. Still, it points out three conditions under which central bank communication may matter: non-rational expectations, absence of commitment to unchanging policy rules, and asymmetric information.

First, the assumption that the public will understand monetary policy perfectly regardless of the efforts that are made to explain it may be unrealistic. As a correct understanding of the central bank's policy commitments does not occur automatically, it is clearly desirable for the central bank to explain the rule that it follows (Woodford, 2005). By communicating to the public, the central bank may help anchor inflation expectations.

Second, it is unlikely that the central bank would stick to an unchanged policy rule for long. Former ECB President Trichet has repeatedly emphasised that the ECB takes its decisions one step at a time, rather than following a rule.

Third, financial market participants generally do not have as much information as monetary policy makers on a number of key inputs to policy making, including the weights policy makers assign to possible objectives, or their assessment of the economic situation. If there is *asymmetric information*, so that the public and the central bank dispose of different information, it may be perfectly rational for the public to adjust their expectations if the central bank provides new information. Here it is important that we distinguish between the types of information on which asymmetries may exist.

In the first place, the central bank may provide *information about its reaction function*. This should lead, *ceteris paribus*, to an increase in the private sector's ability to forecast the central bank's policy decisions. One possibility is that the central bank provides information about its long-run inflation target. Likewise, central banks could also provide information on the relative weights that the central bank places on its objectives if it has more than one objective.

By publicly announcing its monetary policy strategy and communicating its regular assessment of economic developments, the central bank provides guidance to the markets so that expectations can be formed more efficiently and accurately. This helps markets to understand the systematic response pattern of monetary policy to economic developments and shocks and thus to anticipate the broad direction of monetary policy over the medium term.

Furthermore, the central bank may have better information on the economic outlook. Several studies find that financial markets not only react to macroeconomic news, but also to *information on the economic outlook* provided by the central bank. Apparently investors update their own views in response to the information conveyed by the central bank. Private agents may lend special credence to the economic pronouncements of the central bank, particularly if the central bank has established credibility as an effective forecaster of the economy.

Even though there are good reasons why communication may be beneficial, it is by no means clear what constitutes an optimal communication strategy. The literature on central bank transparency has shown that full disclosure of all available information is often not optimal. Unfortunately, the theoretical literature has not come up with clear-cut conclusions regarding the optimal level of transparency.

ECB communications policy

Most central banks nowadays inform the public about their monetary policy decisions on the day they are taken. Many central banks do so by releasing short press statements. The ECB has been rather unique in detailing the motives behind a particular policy decision at elaborate press conferences after policy meetings. Since 2015 the ECB also publishes minutes of the policy meeting. Press conferences may provide less detail than minutes, but they are timelier and more flexible, especially if the media are allowed to ask questions.

Following a Governing Council meeting, the ECB announces the monetary policy decisions at 13:45 CET. Some 45 minutes later, the ECB President and Vice-President hold a press conference that comprises two elements: a prepared introductory statement containing the background considerations for the monetary policy decision, and a Questions & Answers (Q&A) part during which the President and the Vice-President are available to answer questions by the attending journalists. The introductory statement is understood to reflect the position and views of the Council, agreed upon on a word-by-word basis by its members. While providing background information on the rationale for its decision, the ECB press conference is generally less detailed than the minutes of the Bank of England or the Federal Reserve (Blinder *et al.*, 2008). In particular, it does not provide information on voting. However, the press conference avoids the substantial time delay of the minutes. The minutes (or 'accounts' as the ECB calls them) of the Governing Council meeting are published four weeks after the meeting. Furthermore, the Q&A session allows the press to ask follow-up questions and thus can help clarify open issues.

A second important communication device for the ECB is its *Economic Bulletin*, which is usually published two weeks after the meeting of the Governing Council and contains the information that the Governing Council possessed when it took its policy decisions. The *Economic Bulletin* provides the general public and the financial markets with a detailed and comprehensive analysis of the economic environment. It also contains articles which provide insights into long-term developments, general topics, or into the analytical tools used by the Eurosystem within the framework of the monetary policy strategy.

The testimonies of the ECB President to the European Parliament (EP) offer a third opportunity to communicate. Four times a year, the President appears before the EP's Committee on Economic and Monetary Affairs and explains the ECB's policy decisions and its economic outlook. Subsequently, he answers questions posed by Committee members. These testimonies are open to the public and the transcripts of the presentations are published on the websites of both the EP and the ECB.

Finally, ECB officials often give speeches or interviews on monetary policy. Communications by individual central bankers offer greater flexibility in timing than pre-scheduled events. Speeches and interviews by individual committee members between meetings offer a way to communicate changes in views rapidly, if so desired (Blinder *et al.*, 2008).

One perceived benefit of central bank transparency is that it will contribute to predictability of monetary policy. Such predictability is important for the conduct of monetary policy: while central banks only directly control very short-term interest rates, the expected path of these rates over longer horizons and the premia for uncertainty are significant for the transmission of monetary policy to the economy. If agents can broadly anticipate policy responses, this allows a rapid incorporation of any (expected) changes in monetary policy into financial variables. This in turn can shorten the process by which monetary policy is transmitted into investment and consumption decisions and accelerate any necessary economic adjustments, thus potentially enhancing the effectiveness of monetary policy (ECB, 2011). Indeed, empirical evidence points out that ECB monetary policy generally has been quite predictable. Also, predictability of ECB policy decisions has increased over time (see Blattner *et al.* 2008 for an overview).

An important line of research focuses on the impact of central bank communications on financial markets. The basic idea is that if communications steer expectations, asset prices should react. There is a broad consensus that ECB communication affects financial markets. There is substantive evidence that various forms of ECB communication affect volatility, which implies that expectations changed. This holds true for short-term interest rates, the bond market, the stock market, and the swap markets. The strongest effects are generally found for the President's introductory statements at the ECB press conference following the Governing Council's meeting. There is also substantive evidence that financial markets also moved in the intended direction (Blinder *et al.*, 2008).

4.6 Forward guidance

In recent years central banks frequently reduced the policy interest rate to such a low level that it could not be reduced any further. This is called the *zero-lower bound* (ZLB). Several economists have argued that by offering what is called 'forward guidance' monetary policy may be effective even under the ZLB. *Forward guidance* means that a central bank communicates about its future policy rate. If a central bank can commit to future values of the policy rate, it can work around the ZLB constraint by promising monetary accommodation in the future once the ZLB ceases to bind (Eggertsson and Woodford, 2003). We can explain this using Figure 4.7, which is taken from Den Haan (2013). The solid line in the figure shows what would happen with the policy rate under the central bank's normal strategy, that is, the strategy without forward guidance. T_0 is the current period. The central bank would prefer a negative policy rate in view of the economic situation, but cannot reduce its rate further. In period T, the economy has recovered to the extent that the bank's reaction function no longer calls for a negative policy

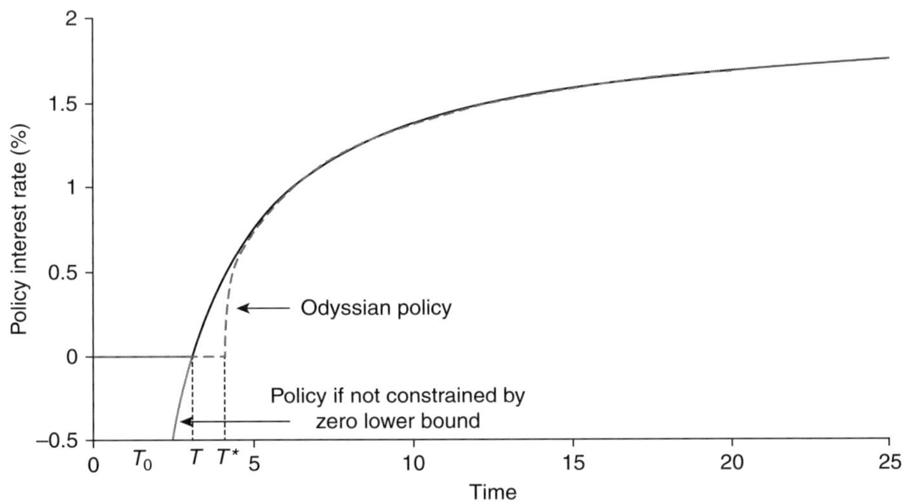

Figure 4.7 Odyssean forward guidance
Source: Den Haan (2013)

interest rate. Now suppose that the central bank could lower the expected values of future (strictly positive) interest rates. The long-term interest rate reflects expected future short-term rates. So reducing expected future policy rates would reduce the long-term interest rate in the current period. This in turn would stimulate consumption and investment. The central bank can accomplish lower long-term interest rates by promising to keep the policy interest rate 'lower for longer', i.e. keep the future policy rates below levels consistent with its reaction function. The corresponding time path is the dashed line in Figure 4.7. The policy interest rate remains at zero until T^* and then catches up to the level which is in line with the bank's standard reaction function. However, there is a time-inconsistency problem. That is because between T and T^*, the central bank's normal reaction function calls for a positive interest rate, whereas the bank had promised to keep the interest rate at zero during this period. So the central bank has an incentive to break its promise. And if markets believe that the central bank will break its promise, they will not adjust their expectations of future policy rates downward so that long-term rates will not come down. In other words, this forward guidance policy can only be effective if the central bank can convince markets that – like Odysseus who tied him self to the mast to withstand the song of the Sirens – it commits to this policy and will not change course.

Despite its popularity in academic writings, this concept of '*Odyssean forward guidance*' is not put in practice by central banks. Instead, central banks use what Campbell *et al.* (2012) call *Delphic forward guidance.*[4] Under this policy, central banks publish their forecasts of macroeconomic developments and their likely monetary policy actions without any commitment. However, this type of forward guidance also may affect private-sector expectations. As long-term rates are more relevant for economic decisions than the current level of the overnight rate, any action by the central bank that influences interest rate expectations could be a potential tool for monetary policy, even if current short-term rates cannot be reduced any further (Blinder *et al.*, 2008). As pointed out in Section 4.5, there are several reasons why markets may respond to central bank communication. For instance, the central bank may be perceived to have superior forecasting ability or better knowledge about its own monetary policy intentions.

In practice, central banks apply three broad forms of Delphic forward guidance (Filardo and Hoffman, 2014): (1) *qualitative* (or open-ended) *forward guidance*, where the central bank does not provide detailed quantitative information about the envisaged time frame for their policy intentions; (2) *calendar-based* (or time contingent) *forward guidance*, where the central bank refers to a clearly specified time horizon for its policies; and (3) *threshold-based* (state contingent) *forward guidance*, where the central bank links future rates to specific quantitative economic thresholds.

Table 4.3 summarises forward guidance by some major central banks. The Bank of Japan (BoJ) was a pioneer in using (open-ended) forward guidance. In 1999, the BoJ announced that interest rates would stay at zero until deflationary concerns were dispelled. When it faced deflationary pressure in 2013, the BoJ again relied on forward guidance, stating that it has a time period, namely two years, for achieving the objective of the 2 per cent inflation rate (Den Haan, 2013).

When the Monetary Policy Committee (MPC) of the Bank of England (BoE) announced its forward guidance based on a threshold for unemployment, it announced that the guidance would cease to hold if some 'knockouts' were breached. However, instead of any of these 'knockouts', the unexpectedly strong decline in unemployment to even below the threshold forced the BoE already in May 2014 to change its forward guidance. Despite the increased levels of economic activity, the MPC was still worried about the slack in the economy. According to the minutes of the MPC 'all members agreed that, in the absence of other inflationary pressures, it would be necessary to see more evidence of slack reducing before an increase in Bank Rate would be warranted'.

In December 2008, the Federal Open Market Committee (FOMC) of the Federal Reserve announced that '[t]he Committee anticipates that weak economic conditions are likely to warrant exceptionally low levels of the federal funds rate for some time'. In March 2009, 'for some time' was replaced by 'for an extended period'. In August 2011, the Fed switched from open-ended to time contingent forward guidance, while in December 2012 it turned to state contingent forward guidance (see Table 4.3 for details).

The forward guidance by the ECB is open-ended. While after previous Governing Council meetings it was stated that monetary policy would be accommodative 'for as long as necessary', in July 2013 the ECB announced that interest rates would remain at present or lower levels 'for an extended period of time'. Likewise, in June 2014 the ECB stated that 'key ECB interest rates will remain at present levels for an extended period of time in view of the current outlook for inflation'.

Table 4.3 Forward guidance by some central banks

Central bank	Type of guidance	Date	Statement
Bank of England	State contingent (with threshold)	August 2013	MPC 'agreed its intention not to raise Bank Rate from its current level of 0.5% at least until . . . the unemployment rate has fallen to a "threshold" of 7 per cent . . .'
	State contingent (without threshold)	May 2014	'all members agreed that, in the absence of other inflationary pressures, it would be necessary to see more evidence of slack reducing before an increase in Bank Rate would be warranted'.
Bank of Japan	Open-ended	April 1999	Having lowered the policy rate to 0.15 per cent in February 1999, the BOJ indicated in April 1999 that it would maintain it at that rate until 'deflationary concerns' were 'dispelled'.
	Time contingent	April 2013	BOJ states that it would continue with its programme of 'qualitative and quantitative easing, aiming to achieve the price stability target of 2 per cent, as long as it is necessary for maintaining that target in a stable manner'.
ECB	Open-ended	July 2013	'Governing Council expects the key ECB interest rates to remain at present or lower levels for an extended period of time.'
Federal Reserve	Open-ended	August 2003	FOMC stated that it believed that 'policy accommodation' could 'be maintained for a considerable period'.
		December 2008	'[t]he Committee anticipates that weak economic conditions are likely to warrant exceptionally low levels of the federal funds rate for some time'.
		March 2009	'for some time' was replaced by 'for an extended period'.
	Time contingent	August 2011	Exceptionally low rates expected to last 'at least through mid-2013'.
		January 2012	'at least through late 2014'.
		September 2012	'at least through mid-2015'.
	State contingent	December 2012	Exceptionally low level of the federal funds rate would 'be appropriate at least as long as the unemployment rate remains above $6\frac{1}{2}$ per cent, inflation between one and two years ahead is projected to be no more than a half percentage point above the Committee's 2 per cent longer-run goal, and longer-term inflation expectations continue to be well anchored'.

Source: Den Haan (2013); (update of) Bank of England (2013)

4.7 Conclusions

Since 1999, the ECB has been responsible for monetary policy making in the euro area. The Governing Council takes monetary policy decisions. The Governing Council consists of the six members of the ECB's Executive Board and the governors of the central banks of the EU Member States in the euro area. Under the Maastricht Treaty, the primary objective of the ECB is 'price stability', which the ECB specifies as inflation 'below but close to' 2 per cent in the euro area in the medium term. The ECB has been quite successful in keeping inflation and inflation expectation in the euro area in line with this target. The ECB's monetary policy is based on a 'two-pillar' strategy that explicitly pairs the discussion of monetary factors ('monetary analysis') with a broad-based non-monetary analysis of the risks to price stability in the short to medium run ('economic analysis'). The ECB's policy instruments are (1) policy rates which signal the ECB's monetary policy stance; (2) open market operations to steer liquidity and thereby money market rates; and (3) minimum reserve requirements. In the beginning of the financial crisis, the ECB reduced its policy interest rates to historically low levels. In addition, the ECB introduced several temporary non-standard measures, subsequently referred to as Enhanced Credit Support, as the interbank money market does not function properly in times of financial distress. Later on, several other non-standard measures were introduced, such as Outright Monetary Transactions and Targeted Longer-Term Refinancing Operations. The ECB recently also introduced quantitative easing. Another instrument of modern central banking is central bank communication. The ECB has a very active communication strategy. The most important communication instrument is the press conference following the policy meeting of the ECB's Governing Council. Since July 2013 the ECB also communicates about its future policy rates (forward guidance).

Notes

1. As explained in Chapter 3, Denmark and the UK may decide to remain outside the euro area even if they meet the convergence criteria. Sweden does not meet all the convergence criteria, notably the exchange rate criterion.
2. See http://www.ecb.int/press/pr/date/2012/html/pr120906_1.en.html.

3. The programme will encompass the asset-backed securities purchase programme (ABSPP) and the covered bond purchase programme (CBPP3), which were both launched in 2014. Under these programmes assets were bought at a rate of around €10 billion a month. So the decision implies that the Eurosystem will buy an additional €50 billion-a-month of bonds of national governments and European institutions.
4. Named after Delphi, where, according to ancient Greek mythology, the oracle Pythia predicted the future.

Suggested Reading

de Haan, J. and H. Berger (eds.) (2010), *The European Central Bank at Ten*, Heidelberg, Springer.

Den Haan, W. (ed.) (2013), *Forward Guidance. Perspectives from Central Bankers, Scholars and Market Participants*, CEPR, London.

European Central Bank (2011), *The Monetary Policy of the ECB*, ECB, Frankfurt.

References

Akerlof, G. A., W. T. Dickens, and G. L. Perry (2000), Near-rational Wage and Price Setting and the Long-Run Phillips Curve, *Brookings Papers on Economic Activity*, 2000–1, 1–44.

Bank of England (2013), *Monetary Policy Trade-offs and Forward Guidance*, Bank of England, London.

Blattner, T., M. Catenaro, M. Ehrmann, R. Strauch, and J. Turunen (2008), The Predictability of Monetary Policy, European Central Bank Occasional Paper No. 83.

Blinder, A. S., M. Ehrmann, M. Fratzscher, J. de Haan, and D. Jansen (2008), Central Bank Communication and Monetary Policy: A Survey of Theory and Evidence, *Journal of Economic Literature*, **46**(4), 910–945.

Campbell, J., C. Evans, J. Fisher, and A. Justiniano (2012), Macroeconomic Effects of FOMC Forward Guidance, *Brookings Papers on Economic Activity*, Spring, 1–54.

Cour-Thiman, P. and B. Winkler (2014), The ECB's Non-Standard Monetary Policy Measures. The Role of Institutional Factors and Financial Structure, European Central Bank Working Paper 1528.

de Haan, J. and H. Berger (eds.) (2010), *The European Central Bank at Ten*, Heidelberg, Springer.

de Haan, J., S. C. W. Eijffinger, and S. Waller (2005), *The European Central Bank Credibility, Transparency, and Centralization*, MIT Press, Cambridge (MA).

De Nederlandsche Bank (2014), Targeted Central Bank Funding to Support Bank Lending, available at: http://www.dnb.nl/en/news/news-and-archive/dnbulletin-2014/dnb308896.jsp.

Den Haan, W. (ed.) (2013), *Forward Guidance. Perspectives from Central Bankers, Scholars and Market Participants*, CEPR, London.

Eggertsson, G. and M. Woodford (2003), The Zero Bound on Interest Rates and Optimal Monetary Policy, *Brookings Papers on Economic Activity*, **1**, 193–233.

European Central Bank (2003), *Background Studies for the ECB's Evaluation of its Monetary Policy Strategy*, ECB, Frankfurt.

(2011), *The Monetary Policy of the ECB*, ECB, Frankfurt.

Filardo, A. and B. Hoffman (2014), Forward Guidance at the Zero Lower Bound, *BIS Quarterly Review*, March 2014, 37–53.

Gros, D. (2003), Reforming the Composition of the ECB Governing Council in View of Enlargement: How Not to Do It!, Briefing paper for the Monetary Committee of the European Parliament, February.

Issing, O. (2001), Why Price Stability?, in: A. Garcia Herrero, V. Gaspar, L. H. Hoogduin, J. Morgan, and B. Winkler (eds.), *Why Price Stability?*, ECB, Frankfurt.

Mishkin, F. S. and M. Savastano (2001), Monetary Policy Strategies for Latin America, *Journal of Development Economics*, **66**, 415–444.

Pattipeilohy, C., J. W. van den End, M. Tabbae, J. Frost, and J. de Haan (2013), Unconventional Monetary Policy of the ECB during the Financial Crisis: An Assessment and New Evidence, in: M. Balling and E. Gnan (eds.), *50 Years of Money and Finance: Lessons and Challenges*, SUERF 50th Anniversary Volume, SUERF, Vienna, 117–155.

Sibert, A. (2003), The New Monetary Policy Strategy of the ECB, Briefing paper for the Committee on Economic and Monetary Affairs of the European Parliament, May 2003.

Woodford, M. (2005), Central-bank Communication and Policy Effectiveness, in: *The Greenspan Era: Lessons for the Future*, Federal Reserve Bank of Kansas City, 399–474.

Part II

Financial Markets

CHAPTER

5

European Financial Markets

OVERVIEW

This chapter starts off by reviewing the functions that financial markets perform. First, financial markets release information to aid the price discovery process. Second, markets provide a platform to trade. The main trading mechanisms, i.e. quote-driven and order-driven markets, are discussed. Finally, markets provide an infrastructure to settle trades. The remainder of the chapter describes the main financial markets in the EU (the money, bond, equity, derivatives, and foreign exchange markets).

The euro money market is the market for euro-denominated short-term funds and related derivative instruments. It consists of various segments, including unsecured deposit contracts with various maturities, ranging from overnight to one year, and repurchase agreements (so-called repos, i.e. reverse transactions secured by securities) also ranging from overnight to one year. Banks account for the largest share of the euro money market. The ECB has a major influence on the money market via its use of various monetary policy instruments (reserve requirements, standing facilities, and open market operations). There are three main market interest rates for the money market: EONIA (euro overnight index average), EURIBOR (euro interbank offered rate), and EUREPO (the repo market reference rate for the euro).

The bulk of euro-denominated bonds (i.e. debt securities with a maturity of more than one year) is issued by euro-area issuers. Although the share of private-sector securities (corporate bonds) in all euro-denominated debt securities outstanding has risen, securities issued by public authorities (government bonds) still form the most important market segment. The introduction of the euro in 1999 created a pan-European capital market, making government-debt managers small to medium-sized players in a larger European market, instead of being the dominant player in the national market. Before the financial crisis, long-term interest rates were very similar in the euro area. Especially after the crisis differentials vis-à-vis the German yield vary considerably across countries, while for each country the yield differential varies considerably over time.

The importance of equity finance in the EU is growing, although there are large differences across exchanges. The market capitalisations of Euronext and the London Stock Exchange (LSE) are much higher than those of other exchanges in the EU. Despite the increase in equity finance, public equity markets play a limited role as a source of new funds as firms generally raise external financing via bank loans and, to a lesser extent, debt securities.

Next, the chapter discusses derivatives, i.e. financial instruments whose value is derived from the value of the underlying financial instruments. They can be based on different types of assets (such as equities or commodities), prices (such as interest rates or exchange rates), or indexes (such as a stock market index). They are traded on organised exchanges or over-the-counter (OTC). Derivatives can provide a source of income but are also important risk-management tools. The most important derivatives are futures, forwards, options, and swaps.

Finally, the foreign exchange market is discussed.

LEARNING OBJECTIVES

After you have studied this chapter, you should be able to:

- explain the purpose and structure of financial markets
- describe the essentials of the euro money market, including its functions and main interest rates
- explain how the monetary policy of the ECB affects the money market
- discuss the most important developments in the money market since the start of the monetary union
- discuss the most important developments in the bond markets since the start of the monetary union
- discuss the most important developments in the equity markets since the start of the monetary union
- describe the essentials of the derivatives market
- describe the foreign exchange market.

5.1 Financial markets: functions and structure

Functions

A *financial market* is a market where individuals issue and trade securities and derivatives. *Securities* are fungible, negotiable instruments representing financial value, and are broadly categorised in debt securities and equity securities. In financial markets, funds are channelled from those with a surplus, who buy securities, to those with a shortage, who issue new securities or sell existing securities (see Chapter 1). A financial market can be seen as a set of arrangements that allows trading among its participants. The following functions are performed by a financial market depending on the phase of trading (Bailey, 2005):

- Price discovery: the market facilitates the dissemination of information. This enables participants who want to buy or sell to find out the prices at which trades can be agreed upon (pre-trading phase).
- Trading mechanism: the market provides a mechanism to facilitate the making of agreements. There must be a means by which those who want to sell can communicate with those who want to buy (trading phase).
- Clearing and settlement arrangements: the agreements are executed. The market must ensure that the terms of each agreement are honoured (post-trading phase).

Price discovery involves the incorporation of new information into asset prices (O'Hara, 2003). Securities represent a promise of future payments. The value of a security depends on expectations of the size and the risk of these future payments. New information can affect these expectations. In an efficient market, prices reflect all (publicly) available information.[1] Although insiders of a company may have more information than outsiders, regulation typically forbids insider trading (see Chapter 12). Markets also provide liquidity. Market liquidity refers to the matching of buyers and sellers (O'Hara, 2003). Liquidity is inter-temporal in nature as buyers and sellers may enter the market at different points in time. The trading mechanism is the means of matching those buyers to sellers. Below we discuss the main trading mechanisms in more detail. Finally, clearing and settlement arrangements include: (1) confirmation of the terms of the transactions; (2) clearing of the trades to establish the obligations of buyers and sellers; (3) settlement of the accounts to finalise the delivery of securities against payment of money. These post-trading arrangements are discussed in Chapter 7.

The participants in financial markets can be classified into various groups, according to their motive for trading:

1. *Public investors*, who ultimately own the securities and who are motivated by the returns from holding the securities. Public investors include private individuals and institutional investors, such as pension funds and mutual funds.
2. *Brokers,* who act as agents for public investors and who are motivated by the remuneration received (typically in the form of commission fees) for

the services they provide. Brokers thus trade for others and not on their own account.

3. *Dealers*, who do trade on their own account but whose primary motive is to profit from trading rather than from holding securities. Typically, dealers obtain their return from the differences between the prices at which they buy and sell the security over short intervals of time.

In practice the three groups are not mutually exclusive. Some public investors may occasionally act on behalf of others; brokers may act as dealers and hold securities on their own, while dealers often hold securities in excess of the inventories needed to facilitate their trading activities. The role of these three groups differs according to the trading mechanism adopted by a financial market.

Another important group of firms are the credit rating agencies (CRAs) that assess the credit risk of borrowers (see Chapter 8).

Trading mechanisms

Financial markets use a trading mechanism for matching buyers to sellers. As the trading mechanism is a defining characteristic, financial markets are often classified by their trading mechanism (Harris, 2003). The two main types are quote-driven markets and order-driven markets, while hybrid markets use some combination of the two.

Quote-driven markets

In *quote-driven markets* (also known as dealer markets), dealers quote bid and ask prices at which they are prepared to buy or sell, respectively, specified amounts of the security (Bailey, 2005). Quote-driven markets require little formal organisation, but need mechanisms for publishing the dealers' price quotations and for regulating the conduct of dealers. Stock exchanges normally grant dealers (or market makers) privileged access to certain administrative procedures or market information. In return for these privileges, dealers have particular obligations, most importantly to quote 'firm' bid and ask prices at which they guarantee to make trades of up to specified volumes. Anyone who wants to trade in a quote-driven market must trade with a dealer. Either the investors negotiate with the dealers themselves or their brokers negotiate with the dealers.

When a security is traded, the buyer pays the ask price, p_a, and the seller receives the bid price, p_b. The difference is the *bid-ask spread*: $s = p_a - p_b$ received by the dealer. The dealer typically holds an inventory of securities during the day to be able to sell (and buy) immediately. From his return (i.e. the bid-ask spread), the dealer has to cover the costs of holding his inventory (e.g. interest costs of financing the securities inventory) and the risks (e.g. prices may move while the securities are in the inventory). While bid and ask prices are published, dealers may negotiate special prices for large transactions. The spread could be broader for particularly large transactions (i.e. block trades) to cover the price risk of such block trades before the dealer can sell on (or buy) the bought (sold) securities to (from) other dealers in the market.

Order-driven markets

In *order-driven markets* (also known as auction markets), participants issue orders to buy or sell at stated prices, which can be modelled as 'double auctions'. Participants issue instructions that specific actions should be taken in response to the arrival of publicly verifiable price observations. The price is then adjusted by an 'auctioneer' until the total orders to buy equal the total orders to sell (Bailey, 2005). There are different forms of order-driven markets. In call markets, the price is determined at a limited number of specified times. In that way, orders can be collected and the auction takes place at the specified time. This type of auction is widely used for new issues of government debt (see section 5.3) and initial public offerings of equity (see section 5.4). The call-market mechanism has disappeared in secondary markets for bonds and equity and has been replaced by continuous trading systems.

In continuous auction markets, public investors send their instructions ('orders') to buy or sell to brokers. There are different sorts of order. The most well-known are the *limit order*, which specifies purchase or sale at maximum buying prices or minimum selling prices, respectively, and the *market order*, which specifies purchase or sale at the best available price. The outstanding limit orders are generally listed in a limit order book. The existence of a limit order book implies automatic trade matching, though in practice some element of discretion remains (e.g. in setting the priority of orders). Order-driven markets are highly formalised as the auction rules for matching trades have to be specified in great detail to ensure an orderly and fair trading process.

Hybrid markets

Trading mechanisms are often compared with respect to transparency and liquidity (Bailey, 2005). In terms of fundamental principles, quote-driven markets and order-driven markets should result in the same market prices if all trades are made public. But in practice quote-driven markets tend to be more fragmented. Dealers quote different bid and ask prices, and deals that have been executed are not necessarily public information or may be published with some delay (to allow dealers some time to off-load large trades in the market). Thus, order-driven markets tend to be more transparent than quote-driven markets.

Liquidity does not depend only on the trading mechanism. In a call market, investors must wait until the next price fixing takes place. By contrast, they can trade immediately in continuous order-driven markets. The price, however, depends on the availability of sufficient orders on the other side of the market. Investors may therefore sometimes prefer the opportunity to negotiate individual agreements with dealers in quote-driven markets. Also, quote-driven markets may allow a delay of publication so that deals can be kept secret, if only for a limited time.

In practice, we observe *hybrid markets*, which combine characteristics of quote-driven and order-driven markets. Advances in IT have spurred the development of order-driven markets, in particular for equity trading. The combination of smart trading rules (software) with fast computers (hardware) allows an almost instantaneous matching of orders. Euronext, for example, applies an order-driven trading mechanism with a centralised electronic order book. Nevertheless, Euronext also enables small and medium sized listed companies to hire a designated market maker to act as 'liquidity provider' in their stock. Similarly, the London Stock Exchange's premier electronic trading system (SETS) combines electronic order-driven trading with liquidity provision by market makers. While stock exchanges are becoming more order-driven, bond markets tend to be more quote-driven (making use of dealers). Sections 5.3 and 5.4 discuss the main bond markets and stock exchanges in more detail.

Overview of financial markets

Generally, a distinction can be made between primary and secondary markets. At a *primary market* new issues of a security are sold to investors. At a *secondary market* securities that have been previously issued are traded. Secondary markets can be organised in exchanges, where buyers and sellers meet in one central location to conduct trade, or *over-the-counter (OTC) markets* in which dealers at different locations stand ready to sell and buy securities 'over-the-counter'.

The principal financial markets that we discuss in the remainder of the chapter are:

- The money market – this is the market for short-term funds up to one year. In particular, banks use the money market for the management of their short-term liquidity positions.
- The bond markets – these are the most important segment of the market for debt securities with a maturity of more than one year. Governments and firms issue bonds to raise medium- and long-term debt against a fixed or flexible interest rate.
- The equity markets – firms may raise funds by issuing equity that grants the investor a residual claim on the company's income.
- The derivatives market – derivatives are financial instruments whose value is derived from the value of the underlying financial instruments. Derivatives are important risk-management tools.
- The foreign exchange market, where the relative values of currencies are determined.

Figures 5.1 and 5.2 compare the size of the main funding markets, the equity and bond markets, in the EU and the US. These figures demonstrate the fundamental difference between the financial systems of the EU and the US (see also Chapter 1). The US financial system is primarily market-based. Nevertheless, the importance of equity finance is growing in the EU though less than in the US. The equity market capitalisation was €10 trillion in 2013. The large fluctuations in market capitalisation reflect the dotcom bubble in 2000–2001 and the 2007–2009 financial crisis.

At the time of the introduction of the euro, the EU bond market amounted to €9 trillion compared with €15 trillion in the US (see Figure 5.2). The EU bond market has experienced spectacular growth since then so that the EU and US bond markets have become similar in size, with the outstanding value of bonds equal to around €25 trillion in 2013.

5.2 Money market

In a broad sense, the *money market* consists of the market for short-term funds, usually with maturity up to one year. The '*euro money market*' is the market for euro-denominated short-term funds and related derivative instruments (i.e. contracts, such as options and futures, whose value is derived from the value of the underlying instrument). Credit institutions (i.e. banks) account for the largest share of the euro money market. As will be

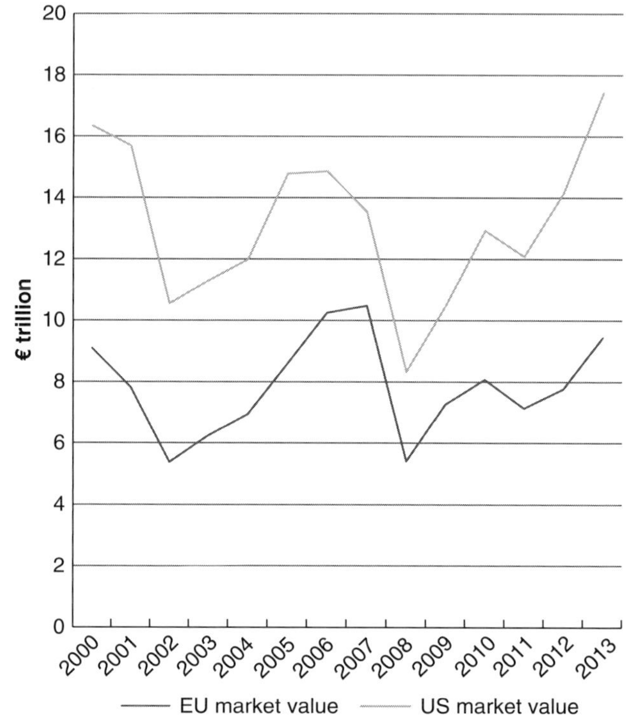

Figure 5.1 Size of the equity markets, year-end market value (€ trillion), 2000–2013
Source: World Federation of Exchanges

explained below, these institutions rely on the euro money market for the management of their short-term liquidity positions and for the fulfilment of their minimum reserve requirements. Other important market participants are money market funds, other financial intermediaries (such as investment funds other than money market funds), insurance companies and pension funds, as well as large non-financial corporations.

The most important money-market segments are the unsecured deposit markets (with various maturities, ranging from overnight to one year) and the secured repo markets (often called repos) with maturities also ranging from overnight to one year.[2] A *repurchase agreement* is an arrangement whereby an asset is sold while the seller simultaneously obtains the right and obligation to repurchase it at a specific price on a future date or on demand (ECB, 2008b). The most important difference between the secured and the unsecured segments is the amount of risk involved. When providing unsecured interbank deposits, a bank transfers funds to another bank for a specified period of time during which it assumes full counterparty credit risk.

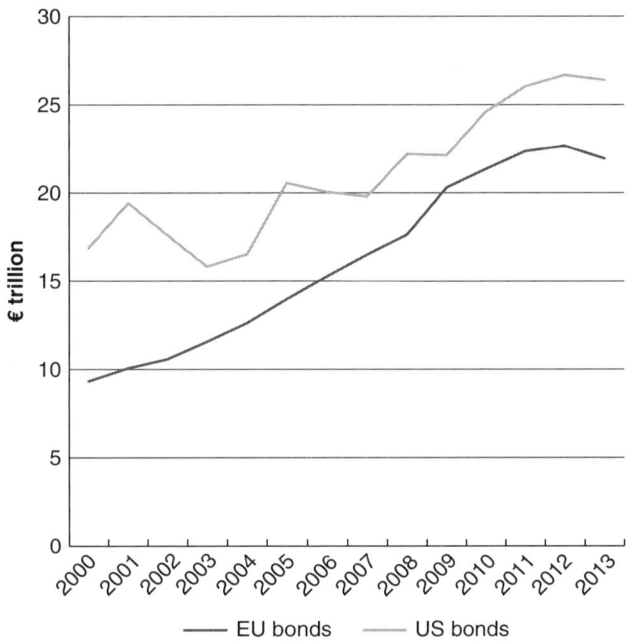

Figure 5.2 Bond markets, amounts outstanding year-end (€ trillion), 2000–2013
Source: Bank for International Settlements, Quarterly Reviews

In the secured repo markets, this counterparty credit risk is mitigated as the bank that provides liquidity receives collateral (e.g. bonds) in return. In the event of a credit default, the liquidity-providing bank can utilise the collateral received to satisfy its claim against the defaulting bank. Because of this lower credit risk, secured repo rates are usually somewhat lower than unsecured deposit rates (ECB, 2008a).

Apart from transactions with the central bank, money market participants trade with each other to take positions in relation to their short-term interest rate expectations, to finance their securities trading portfolios (bonds, shares, etc.), to hedge their more long-term positions with more short-term contracts, and to square individual liquidity imbalances (Hartmann *et al.*, 2001).

As explained in Chapter 4, the euro money market is strongly influenced by the monetary policy of the ECB. In addition to decisions concerning interest rates, the ECB influences the euro money market through three monetary policy instruments:

- reserve requirements
- open market operations
- standing facilities.

The ECB requires banks to hold *required reserves*. Currently, banks established in the euro area have to keep 1 per cent of the total amount of overnight deposits, other deposits with maturity below two years, debt securities with maturity below two years, and money market paper (excluding interbank liabilities) at reserve accounts with their National Central Banks. Reserve requirements have to be fulfilled on average over a one-month maintenance period (averaging).

The minimum reserve system helps to stabilise money market interest rates by the *averaging provision*, i.e. banks' compliance with reserve requirements is judged on the basis of the average of the daily balances on their reserve accounts over a reserve maintenance period. As a consequence, banks can smooth out daily liquidity fluctuations since transitory reserve imbalances can be offset by opposite reserve imbalances within the same maintenance period. The averaging provision also implies that if institutions believe that money market rates are currently higher than in the remainder of the maintenance period, they can profit from lending in the market and run a reserve deficit. If they believe that money market rates will go up, they can borrow in the market and run a reserve surplus. This mechanism stabilises the overnight interest rate during the maintenance period.

Open market operations are the general instruments used to manage the liquidity situation and to steer interest rates. The *main refinancing operations* (MROs) are the most important instrument. During the crisis, notably LTROs have become very important (see Chapter 4 for further details).

The *standing facilities* provide or absorb liquidity with an overnight maturity when unforeseen liquidity shocks occur. Therefore they provide a type of insurance mechanism for banks, but at penalty interest rates. The initiative in these transactions is on the side of the credit institution.

Apart from the ECB interest rates on the standing facilities and the MROs, there are three main market interest rates for the money market:

- EONIA (euro overnight index average). The *EONIA* is the effective overnight reference rate for the euro. It is computed daily as a volume-weighted average of unsecured euro overnight lending transactions in the interbank market, as reported by a representative panel of large banks.[3]
- EURIBOR (euro interbank offered rate). The *EURIBOR* is the benchmark rate of the large unsecured euro money market for maturities longer than overnight (one week to one year) that has emerged since 1999. It is based on information provided by the same panel of banks.
- EUREPO (the repo market reference rate for the euro) for different maturities. The *EUREPO* is the benchmark rate of the euro repo market

and has been released since March 2002. It is the rate at which one prime bank offers funds in euros to another prime bank when the funds are secured by a repo transaction using general collateral.

Developments in money-market segments

Figure 5.3 shows the development of turnover (turnover in 2003 is 100). The figure shows turnover at unsecured and secured segments. After 5 years of continuous growth, total activity in the unsecured market began to shrink in 2008. In 2013 average turnover figures for unsecured cash lending and borrowing reached their lowest level since 2003. According to the ECB (2012), this was caused by two factors. First, the euro crisis and its spillover to the banking sector increased risk aversion, making credit quality of borrowing banks a primary source of concern for lenders: investors do not seem to have lent to borrowers below a certain credit quality regardless of the price. Second, the substantial liquidity injected through the three-year

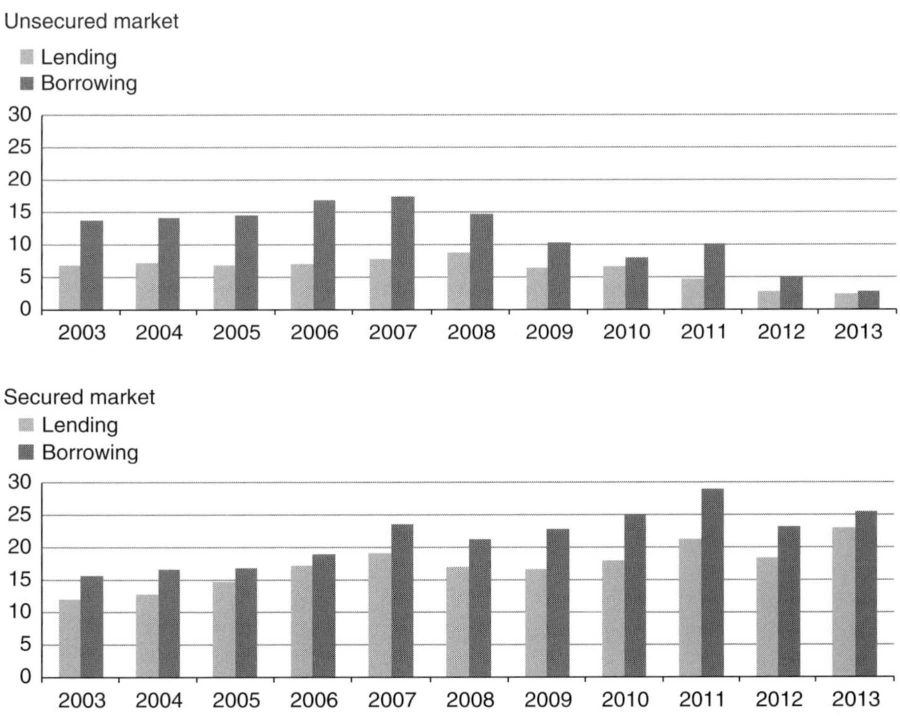

Figure 5.3 Turnover in money market segments (2003 = 100), 2003–2013
Source: ECB (2013)

LTROs (see Chapter 4) covered funding needs in the banking system on the one hand, and on the other drove money market rates to historically low levels. As a consequence of very low market rates relative to the deposit facility and amid concerns over the credit quality of counterparties, a clear preference emerged for using the central bank's deposit facility or banks' current accounts at the central bank (ECB, 2012).

Declining unsecured volumes were in 2012 not balanced with an increase in secured turnover, which decreased for the first time since 2008. However, the decline in secured volumes was less pronounced than in the unsecured segment. This decline in the secured market can be attributed mainly to continued banks' balance sheet adjustments and elevated risk aversion (ECB, 2012). In 2013, turnover in the secured segment recovered.

A breakdown by maturity shows that turnover is concentrated in short maturities. Most of the turnover in the unsecured market is concentrated in the overnight (O/N) maturity segment, both in lending and borrowing as O/N is the maturity which banks typically use to adjust their day-to-day cash imbalances. The overnight tenure accounted for roughly 83 per cent of total lending in 2012 and 66 per cent per cent of total borrowing (ECB, 2012).

The average maturity of secured transactions is comparatively longer than that for unsecured transactions. A breakdown by maturity in the unsecured market shows that turnover is concentrated in the bucket 'tomorrow/next to one month'. In 2012 this maturity bucket accounted for roughly 83 per cent of total lending and 66 per cent per cent of total borrowing. In the secured market, transactions in the maturity bucket 'tomorrow/next up to one month' increased to a share of 79 per cent in 2012 (ECB, 2012).

5.3 Bond markets

A *bond* is a debt security that promises that payments will be made periodically for a specified time. The re-denomination of debt from former national currencies into euros at the beginning of the monetary union paved the way for a European debt securities market. The increased role of the euro as an international investment currency has made the market in euro-denominated issues attractive for both investors and issuers. The bulk of euro-denominated debt securities is issued by euro-area issuers. However, for issuers outside the euro area it has also become attractive to borrow in euros.

As Table 5.1 shows, debt securities issued by public authorities still form the most important market segment, closely followed by bank bonds

Table 5.1 Bonds by issuer, September 2013 (€ trillion)

	Government	Financials	Corporates	Total
Euro area	6.9	7.9	1.0	15.8
EU	9.3	11.0	1.6	21.9
US	10.6	10.6	5.0	26.2
Japan	7.0	1.9	0.6	9.5
Total	33.8	31.5	8.2	73.5

Source: Bank for International Settlements

(financials). In Europe, bank bonds have overtaken government bonds in size. Corporate bonds have become important in the US, but (yet) form a small market segment in Europe and Japan.

Bonds are the main instrument of governments (mainly central governments, but also regional and local government authorities, and social securities funds) within the euro area to finance their budget deficits. Furthermore, government bonds often serve as a benchmark for pricing other assets and they are also frequently used as collateral in various financial transactions.

The non-government bond market is dominated by bank debt securities. This segment encompasses numerous different types of bonds, including unsecured bank debt securities and covered bonds. *Covered bonds* are claims of the bond holders against the issuing bank that are secured by a pool of cover assets on the bank's balance sheet, such as mortgage loans or loans to the public sector.

Government bonds

Issuance

The introduction of the euro in 1999 had a major impact on the operations of government-debt managers as the disappearance of exchange-rate risks within the euro area created the conditions for a pan-European capital market. As a result, debt managers have become small to medium-sized players in a larger European market, instead of being the dominant player in the national market. Investors now focus more on credit risk and liquidity, while bond portfolios have become increasingly internationally diversified, especially in the smaller euro-area countries. Consequently, competition among debt managers has increased, stimulating a more efficient primary market and a deeper, more liquid secondary market. Governments have put great effort into making their outstanding debt and new issues more attractive to international bond investors. To this end, they have adopted a number of supply-side innovations (see Box 5.1 for further details). These innovations were enabled by the rapid expansion of electronic trading systems. In

Box 5.1 Government-debt management

The primary objective of debt-management agencies in the euro area is to ensure financing of the government's annual borrowing at the lowest possible (medium-term) cost with acceptable risks, although precise wordings and emphasis differ from country to country. The operational targets or guidelines for debt-management units differ more substantially. Often, these are based on asset-liability studies or cost-at-risk models, weighing interest costs against budgetary risks. Targets can take the form of a target (range) for the average maturity or the (modified) duration,[4] subject to certain restrictions such as quantitative limits on the use of interest rate swaps.

Debt-management units were generally given more independence in the 1990s. A stronger focus on 'narrow' debt-management goals allowed for delegation to separate units. In addition, higher product complexity and competition among debt managers require a higher degree of operational independence and professionalism, which is easier to accomplish in a non-government unit. Cost considerations sometimes also played a role in the decision to delegate tasks to more independent units (Wolswijk and de Haan, 2005).

The increased competition has led to increasing liquidity of government securities and larger volumes of outstanding issues. While issues of around €2 billion were standard in smaller countries before the start of EMU, the minimum is now €5 billion, with large countries in the euro area having bond issuances of over €20 billion.[5] Governments sometimes focus on 'niches' targeting particular investor needs. For instance, Spain and France have introduced constant-maturity bonds, while France (followed by Greece and Italy) has taken the lead in the issuance of index-linked bonds (Baele *et al.*, 2004). The return of an index-linked bond is depending on the development of a price index. In 2006, Germany issued an index-linked bond. Outside the euro area, the UK and the US are major issuers of index-linked bonds. In the segment of long-term debt securities, securities with a maturity of ten years or more play the major role. The 3-, 5-, and 30-year segments also remained attractive, with about half of the debt managers issuing at least one security in those segments. More recently, debt managers have selected a somewhat wider spectrum of maturities, including some reversion to issuing short-term securities (Wolswijk and de Haan, 2005). At the end of March 2014, securities with a residual maturity of up to one year accounted for 21 per cent of total outstanding debt securities in the euro area, or 15.4 per cent of GDP. Around one third of outstanding debt securities will mature within two years,

Box 5.1 (cont.)

and some 60 per cent within five years. The average residual maturity of outstanding euro-area government securities was 6.4 years, ranging from 3.1 years in Cyprus to 12.3 years in Ireland (ECB, 2014).

Debt managers have also made issuance activity more regular and predictable by introducing pre-announced auction calendars, which has improved market transparency. Increased competition in the primary and secondary government bond markets has also led to changes in distribution channels. Primary dealers and bank syndicates are now popular means to reach more non-domestic investors. Primary dealers mediate between the debt agency and buyers in both the primary and secondary markets. All euro-area countries (except Germany) now use primary dealers to distribute government bonds. Tasks for primary dealers usually include the obligation to bid at auctions or to buy a certain amount of newly issued bonds, promotion of government debt, and market making. In all countries concerned, many foreign financial institutions are included as primary dealers, reflecting the wish to spread ownership of government securities widely. Bank syndicates have also become increasingly popular as a way to distribute new government debt, particularly when approaching new market segments. Syndicate participants may select specific investors to whom the government security to be issued may be especially interesting. For smaller countries, a particular advantage is that a significant amount can be placed at once, thus immediately creating liquidity.

addition to local systems, the European electronic platform for government securities, EuroMTS, was introduced in 1999, enabling quotation and trading of some European benchmark bonds (see Chapter 7 for further details).

Figure 5.4, showing the indebtedness of euro-area countries, illustrates that despite progress with fiscal consolidation, fiscal policies of only a few Member States meet the targets of the Stability and Growth Pact (see Chapter 3).

Government bond yields

Figure 5.5 shows the euro-area yield curve for AAA-rated government bonds with different remaining maturities at 8 August 2014. Yields of government bonds are influenced by expected short-term interest rates and the term premium. Risk-averse investors demand a risk premium (*term premium*) for investments in long-term bonds to compensate them for the risk of losses due to (unexpected) interest rate hikes; those losses increase with bond

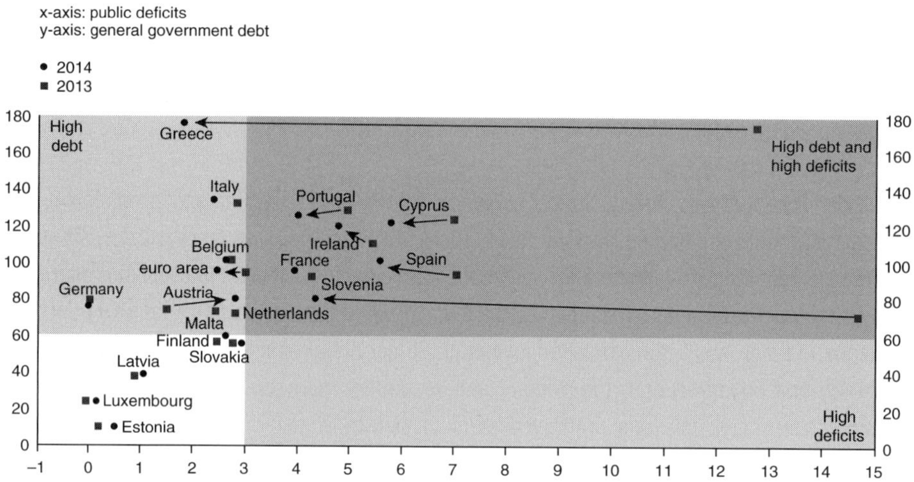

Figure 5.4 Government debt and deficits in the euro area, 2013/14 (% GDP)
Source: ECB (2014)

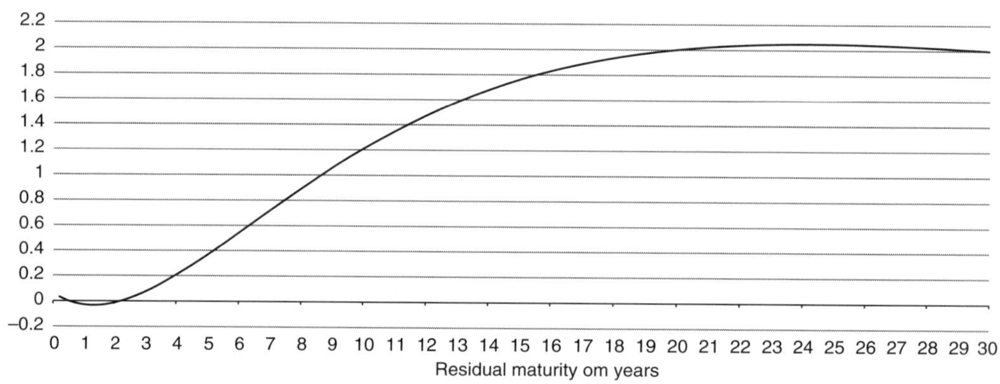

Figure 5.5 Yield curve at 8 August 2014 (%)
Source: ECB

duration. The *term premium* leads to a positive *term spread*, i.e. the spread of yields for bonds with longer maturity over yields for bonds with shorter maturity, even when markets expect increasing and decreasing interest rates to be equally likely. The term spread in the euro area has been mostly positive since 1999, reflecting what is often called a 'normal' yield curve (ECB, 2007). However, the term spread has been changing over time.

Apart from interest rate expectations and the term premium, credit risk and liquidity also influence government bond yields. *Credit risk* is the risk of loss because of the failure of a counterparty to perform according to a contractual arrangement, for instance due to a default by a borrower. The spread between the yield of a particular bond and the yield of a bond with similar characteristics but without credit risk is the credit risk premium. Rating agencies – like Moody's, Standard & Poor's (S&P), and Fitch – indicate issuers' credit risk by assigning them a rating (see Chapter 8 for further details).

Liquidity is the ease with which an investor can sell or buy a bond immediately at a price close to the mid-quote (i.e. the average of the bid-ask spread, as defined in section 5.1). The spread between the yield of a bond with liquidity and a similar bond with less liquidity is referred to as the liquidity premium.

Figure 2.6 in Chapter 2 shows that yield differentials vis-à-vis German government bond yields vary considerably across countries, while for each country the yield differential varies considerably over time. Pagano and Von Thadden (2008) discuss studies that try to explain these yield differentials,

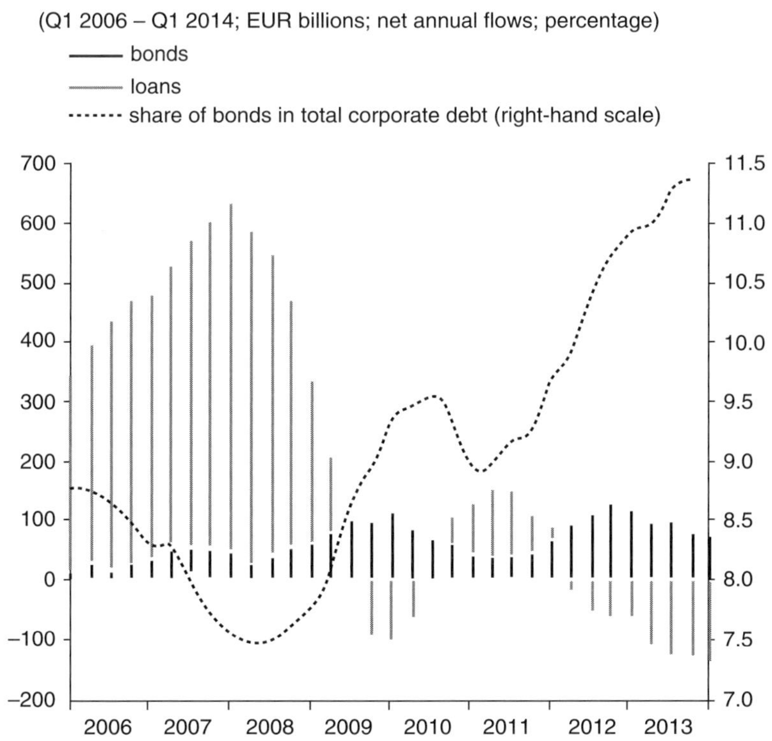

Figure 5.6 External financing of euro-area non-financial corporations, 2006–2013
Source: ECB (2014)

arguing that they may arise from (1) intrinsic differences in country-specific default risk or different sensitivities of bonds' future payoffs to common shocks, or (2) market frictions, like trading costs, clearing and settlement fees, and taxes. As Pagano and Von Thadden (2008) point out, these factors may also interact. For instance, if an asset on which a transaction tax has to be paid becomes riskier, the effect on the price will be smaller the larger the tax, since the initial after-tax price is correspondingly lower. Pagano and Von Thadden (2008) conclude that credit risk explains a considerable portion of cross-country yield differences but explains very little of their variation over time.

As Figure 2.6 shows, since 2012 yield spreads of euro-area government bonds vis-à-vis German government bonds have come down. According to the ECB (2014), two main factors have underpinned this recent decline in yield spreads. First, continued progress towards weakening the links between sovereigns by building a Banking Union (see Chapter 3) has contributed to the improved sentiment towards euro-area sovereigns. Second, euro-area countries have made significant adjustment towards more sustainable fiscal positions. Public deficits are expected to fall to 2.5 per cent of GDP in the euro area as a whole in 2014, with notable improvements compared with 2013 expected in several countries (see also Figure 5.4). Still, euro-area public debt-to-GDP ratio is expected to peak in 2014 at 96 per cent of GDP.

Corporate bonds

In recent years the European corporate bond market has grown rapidly and the market's structure has undergone some important changes. Before 1998, the market was dominated by debt issued by highly rated financial corporations, whereas since that date industrial corporations have increasingly found their way to the corporate bond market (Baele *et al.*, 2004). Nevertheless, financials are still more important than non-financial firms, being the second largest group of issuers of debt securities in the euro-area economy after governments. Notably when bank credit is constrained, issuance of bonds may be an alternative for (large) firms to finance investment. However, as Figure 5.6 shows, after the start of the financial crises gross issuance of long-term securities other than shares by non-financial firms also declined in the euro area. Still, as loans to non-financial firms dropped substantially, the share of bonds in total corporate debt increased (right-hand side scale in Figure 5.6). Banks in the euro area have reduced their holdings of non-financial corporate debt (from 40 per cent of the outstanding stock of these

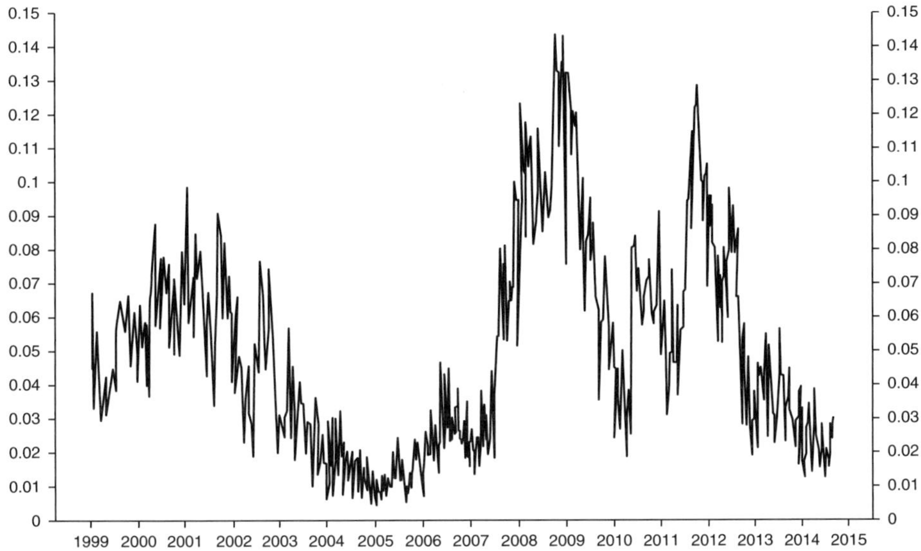

Figure 5.7 Spreads of AAA-rated corporate bonds over AAA-rated government bonds (percentage points), 1999–2014
Source: ECB

bonds in September 2007 to 13 per cent by February 2014). The share of open-ended euro-area investment funds has risen to 21 per cent in February 2014 (ECB, 2014). Open-ended investment funds are investment funds, the units or shares of which are, at the request of the holders, repurchased or redeemed directly or indirectly out of the undertaking's assets.

Yields of AAA-rated corporate bonds are generally higher than AAA-rated government bond yields as shown in Figure 5.7. This mainly reflects the perceived credit risk that results from an investment in corporate bonds. When the corporate outlook deteriorates, these spreads increase. For example, spreads were high during the years 2001 and 2002 when economic growth was low, but decreased significantly in 2003. After the start of the financial crisis and during the euro crisis spreads increased. Corporate bond spreads are higher for bonds of lower-rated issuers than for bonds of higher-rated issuers. The ECB (2007) identifies two possible explanations for this. First, the default probabilities of lower-rated corporate issuers may be more closely linked to the business cycle than the default probabilities of higher-rated corporations. Second, bond spreads widen when bonds become less liquid. During recessions, lower-rated corporate bonds may suffer and might be traded less actively, thus reducing their liquidity, leading to higher liquidity premia. More generally, there is a trade-off between liquidity and transparency in bond markets, which are quote-driven. Dealers quote prices at which they are prepared to trade bonds. To protect dealers with large positions, deals may be published with some delay. Box 5.2 discusses the optimal amount of trade transparency in bond markets.

Box 5.2 How much transparency is optimal?

Transparency refers to the absence or elimination of information asymmetries. In a fully transparent market, all relevant market information is common knowledge for all participants. The debate on bond market transparency is a difficult one. According to Dunne *et al.* (2006), the very existence of most financial markets depends on striking a balance between transparency, thought to promote competition, fairness, investor protection, and opacity, in the interest of encouraging ongoing participation of both end-customers and liquidity providers. If market participants do not obtain adequate fairness, protection, and incentives, they will not participate in sufficient numbers and the market will not function properly.

This can be illustrated by the so-called Winner's Curse, according to which the highest bidder has probably bid too much. If the highest bidder wants to resell the product immediately after the auction, the best price he will obtain is the underbidder's price. Because of incomplete information or subjective factors, bidders will form a range of estimates of the item's 'intrinsic value'. As a result, the largest overestimation of an item's value ends up winning the auction. With perfect information and fully rational participants skilled in valuation, no overpayments should occur. A number of dealers submit quotes and the highest-bidding dealer secures the bonds. Typically, the successful dealer enters the inter-dealer market to hedge his risk. The underbidders are aware of this and can benefit by taking up contrarian positions in the market, thereby making it difficult for the successful bidder to square his position. The more transparent the inter-dealer market, the more difficult it is for the successful bidder to hedge his risk. Consequently, an increase in market transparency makes dealers more cautious about participating.

Yet there are powerful arguments in favour of enhancing transparency. Transparency can facilitate 'best execution', i.e. it allows investors to verify whether dealers and others indeed execute orders at the best price available. Goldstein *et al.* (2007) observe a decrease in transaction costs which is consistent with investors' ability to negotiate better terms of trade with dealers once investors have access to broader bond-pricing data. Costs may also be lower for bonds with transparent prices (see Edwards *et al.*, 2007). Greater price transparency can enhance investor protection as price movements signal default probabilities. Strengthening overall transparency may also create a level playing field between

Box 5.2 (cont.)

large institutional and smaller investors. Large institutional investors may already be able to obtain all relevant information, while smaller investors are not able to exert the same pressure on dealers.

Finally, transparency may improve liquidity. As for municipal bond trades, Harris and Piwowar (2006) argue that ongoing regulatory initiatives to increase transparency in the municipal bond market will lead to liquidity improvements. These improvements should have the greatest impact on retail investors. Next to this, Goldstein *et al.* (2007) find that adding transparency to corporate bond markets has either a neutral or a positive effect on liquidity. These findings seem contradictory to what has been argued by Dunne *et al.* (2006). However, Casey (2006) stresses that pre- and post-trade transparency may equally enhance or harm market liquidity and efficiency, depending on how they are applied, by whom, for what instruments, in which markets, and at which latency.

Bond yields of sovereigns and bond yields of firms are related. However, according to the ECB (2014), the link between the bond yields of sovereigns and financial and non-financial corporations is varying over time. Experience since the inception of EMU suggests that they tend to co-move strongly during market tensions and recovery periods. Notably in crisis periods when yields on sovereign bonds rose, correlations between sovereign and corporate bonds increased.

An important type of debt securities are covered bonds, i.e. debt securities backed by cash flows from mortgages or public sector loans. Covered bonds provide investors with two layers of protection: recourse first to the underlying assets (mainly composed of good quality instruments) and second to the other unsecured assets of the issuing bank. By issuing covered bonds, banks retain the assets on their balance sheet or provide guarantees on dedicated structures to which the assets are transferred (ECB, 2011c). Covered bonds also form an important part of collateral used for Eurosystem operations. Germany is by far the most important euro-area country for covered bonds (so-called *Pfandbriefe*), followed by Spain and France. Maturities of covered bonds typically range from 2–10 years. The majority of covered bonds are rated AAA. In 2012 and 2013 issuance activity for covered bank bonds was very low (see Figure 5.8).

Another type of bonds that has recently become more popular is *contingent convertible bonds* (CoCos). CoCos are hybrid capital securities that

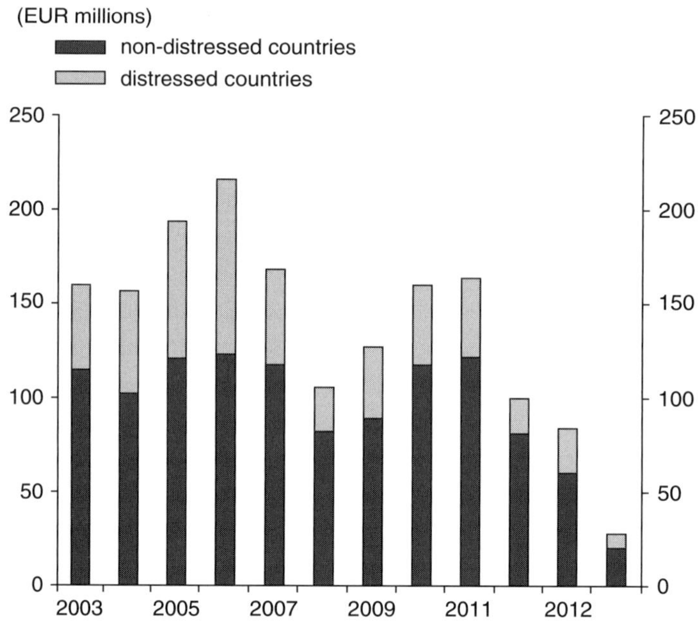

Figure 5.8 Covered bond issues, 2003–2013
Source: ECB (2014)

absorb losses in accordance with their contractual terms when the capital of the issuing bank falls below a certain level. CoCos are attractive for banks because of their potential to satisfy regulatory capital requirements. The CoCo market in Europe is relatively recent but not entirely new. EU banks have issued since 2009 a variety of contingent capital instruments in the amount of approximately €45 billion, of which €26 billion were issued by banks in the euro area (ECB, 2014). CoCo issuance activity by banks picked up strongly in 2013 and 2014, due to banks' efforts to issue CRR/CRD IV-compliant instruments (see Chapter 12 for further details).

Securitised instruments

Despite similarities, covered bonds are different to securitised products. The key difference between covered bonds and securitisation is that covered bonds do not involve credit risk transfer. The credit risk stays with the originator, which has to hold capital (against the risk of losses) but typically obtains cheaper funding through the covered bond issuance (ECB, 2007).

According to the ECB (2007), there are two objectives for the issuance of asset-backed securities, i.e. fund raising and credit risk transfer. Both objectives can be achieved through a 'true sale' securitisation or through a funded synthetic securitisation. In a *'true sale' securitisation*, the originator (typically a bank) transfers the ownership of a pool of assets to a special purpose vehicle (SPV), which issues securities backed by the pool of assets and transfers the funds raised through selling these securities to the originator. In a *funded synthetic securitisation* process, the ownership of the asset pool is not transferred to the SPV but remains on the balance sheet of the originator.

Securitisation markets grew dramatically in the run up to the crisis, with amounts outstanding peaking at €2 trillion in Europe and US$11 trillion in the United States. They have since contracted sharply (see Figure 5.9); especially in Europe aggregate issuance has been notably lower since the crisis, with only €174 billion issued in 2013 (including retained issuance), equivalent to roughly 40 per cent of the pre-crisis annual rate (BoE/ECB, 2014). In particular, new issuance of residential mortgage-backed securities in Europe has fallen markedly. *Mortgage-backed securities* (MBSs) are backed by mortgages loans, be it residential (RMBS) or commercial (CMBS). But issuance of Asset Backed Securities backed by auto loans and consumer loans, for example, has held up reasonably well.

The outstanding amount of securitisations in the EU at the end of 2013 was about €1.4 trillion (Figure 5.10), or around one fifth of the size of the US

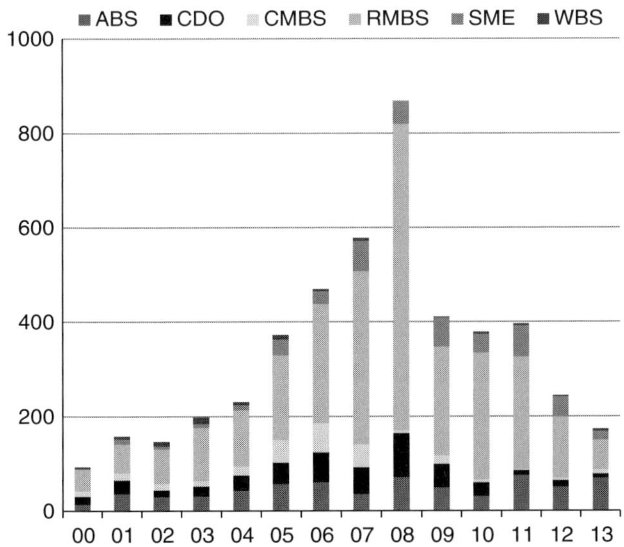

Figure 5.9 Securitisation (new issues) in Europe, 2000–2013 (€ billion)
Source: SIFMA and own calculations

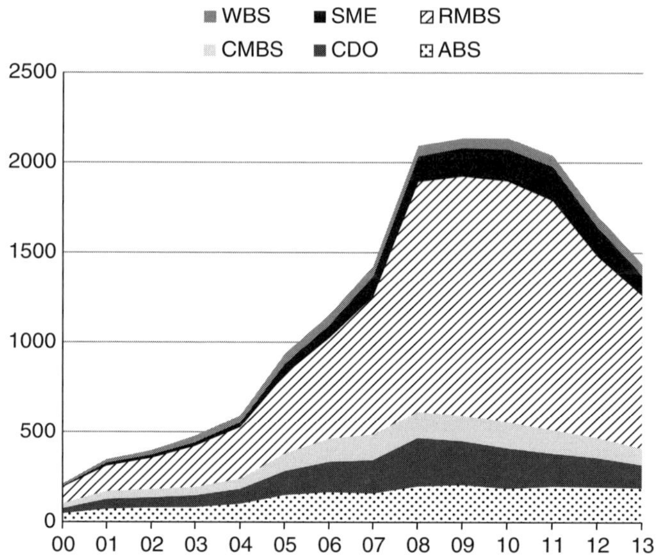

Figure 5.10 Securitisation (amounts outstanding) in Europe, 2000–2013 (€ billion)
Source: SIFMA and own calculations

securitisation market. RMBS formed by far the largest segment, accounting for 59 per cent (BoE/ECB, 2014).

5.4 Equity markets

Equities grant the investor a residual right to receive income from the company's earnings. Equity can be issued either privately (unquoted shares) or publicly via shares that are listed on a stock exchange (quoted shares). The importance of equity finance in the EU is lower than in the US, as reflected by the size of European equity markets as shown in Table 5.2 (see also Figure 5.1). Also within Europe, there are large differences. As Table 5.2 shows, the market capitalisations of Euronext and the LSE are much higher than those of other exchanges in the EU.

Consolidation

The EU stock market is highly concentrated. This high level of concentration may be explained by the fact that financial exchanges exhibit network externalities, as higher participation of traders on both sides of the market positively affects market liquidity and increases traders' utility.

Table 5.2 The world's largest equity exchanges, 2013

Exchange	Market capitalisation ($ billion)	Traded firms (number)	Turnover ($ billion)
NYSE	17,950	2,371	15,309
NASDAQ OMX (US)	6,085	2,637	26,644
Japan Exchange Group – Tokyo	4,543	3,419	6,496
London SE Group	4,429	2,736	3,732
Euronext	3,584	1,062	3,123
Hong Kong Exchanges	3,101	1,643	1,447
Shanghai SE	2,497	953	3,800
Toronto Stock Exchange	2,114	3,886	1,333
Deutsche Börse	1,936	720	1,500
SIX Swiss Exchange	1,541	272	794
Shenzhen SE	1,452	1,536	3,939
Australian SE	1,366	2,055	976
NASDAQ OMX (Europe)	1,269	755	738
Korea Exchange	1,235	1,813	1,361
Bombay Stock Exchange India	1,139	5,294	82
BME Spanish Exchanges	1,117	3,245	1,202

Source: World Federation of Exchanges

There has been an intensive regional cross-border consolidation. First, Euronext resulted from a merger of the Paris, Amsterdam, Brussels, and Lisbon stock exchanges during 2000–2002. Next, the stock exchanges of Copenhagen, Stockholm, Helsinki, Tallin, Riga, Vilnius, and Iceland merged between 2004 and 2006, creating the OMX Nordic Exchange. In 2006, the first trans-Atlantic stock exchange merger took place between Euronext and the New York Stock Exchange (NYSE), strengthening its position as the largest securities trading venue in the world. This merger was subsequently unravelled in 2014. Euronext is now the largest stock exchange in the eurozone. In 2008, a merger between Nasdaq and OMX was completed, while Italy's stock-exchange operator Borsa Italiana accepted a takeover from the LSE. In 2011, BATS Global Markets acquired Chi-X Europe. Chi-X Europe is a London-based, order-driven pan-European equity exchange. BATS (Better Alternative Trading System) is operator of the third largest stock exchange in the US.

There is an advantage in consolidation. Bigger exchanges enjoy economies of scale that reduce trading costs, which in turn attracts more traders and listed companies (Wharton, 2006). The market capitalisation of Euronext

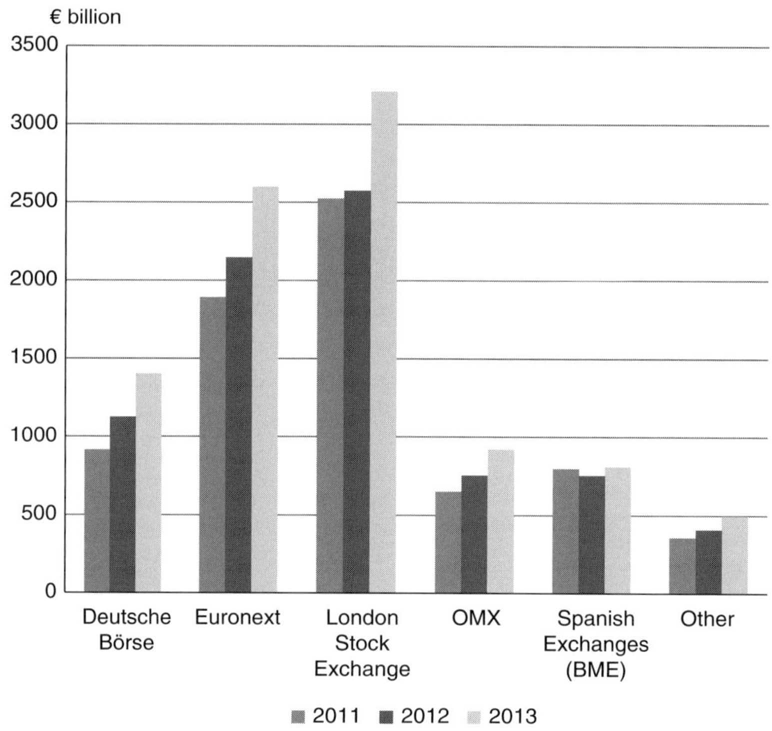

Figure 5.11 Market capitalisation of some exchanges in the EU, 2011–2013 (€ billion)
Source: World Federation of Exchanges

and the LSE has grown faster than that of its smaller competitors (see Figure 5.11). While consolidation allows an exchange to exploit economies of scale, it may also reduce competition and thus lower an exchange's incentive for financial innovation (in the form of developing new, cheaper, trading mechanisms). The impact of competition is interesting in equity trading. Competition may reduce trading fees, but fragmentation of the order flow between exchanges may reduce the liquidity of equity trading. Examining the competition between Euronext and the LSE in the Dutch equity market, Foucault and Menkveld (2008) find evidence of reduced fees and improved liquidity. Liquidity is improved as some brokers automate the routing decision between the two exchanges to obtain the best execution price. In that way, the order flow at the two exchanges is indirectly combined.

There are still some challenges. First, the clearing and settlement infrastructure in Europe has remained fragmented so far. As documented in Chapter 7, post-trading costs per transaction in the EU are substantially higher than in the US. Next, cross-border exchanges like Euronext and

Table 5.3 Liabilities of non-financial firms in the euro area, 2009–2013 (€ billion)

	2009	2010	2011	2012	2013
Debt	9,460	9,709	9,864	9,991	9,899
– of which bank loans	4,684	4,659	4,698	4,474	4,289
– of which debt securities	814	882	876	1,035	1,085
Equity	12,588	13,149	12,459	13,378	15,018
– quoted shares	3,509	3,805	3,287	3,748	4,515
– other equity	9,080	9,344	9,172	9,630	10,503

Source: ECB *Monthly Bulletin* July 2014

OMX force national financial supervisors to cooperate. This challenge is discussed further in Chapter 12.

Initial public offerings

In Europe, public equity markets play a limited role as a source of new funds for listed corporations. Table 5.3 shows the liabilities side of the aggregated balance sheet of non-financial corporations in the euro area for 2009–2013. The table shows that debt financing via bank loans or bonds is more important than financing via quoted shares. This pattern is in line with the pecking-order theory (Myers and Majluf, 1984), which suggests that companies adopt a hierarchy of financial preferences. Due to asymmetric information, companies prefer internal financing (i.e. retained earnings) to external financing. If external financing is needed, companies first seek debt funding. Equity is issued only as a last resort.

When issuing public equity, a firm may obtain a listing on a stock exchange for the first time, the *initial public offering* (IPO). If a firm is already listed and issues additional shares, this is called *seasoned equity offering* (SEO) or *secondary public offering* (SPO). A firm issuing equity at a stock exchange may decide to substitute existing unquoted shares for quoted ones, or issue newly created shares. In the latter case, the funds raised accrue to the firm, while in the first case the proceeds are directed to the initial investors.

There are various motives for IPOs. One of the main reasons, of course, is to obtain funds to finance investment. Moreover, the listing of a firm's shares on a stock exchange also increases its financial autonomy, as the firm becomes less dependent on a single financial provider (like a bank). Further, by issuing equity the firm's owners can diversify their investment risk by selling stakes in the company in a liquid market. Another advantage of public issuance is increased recognition of the company name. In addition, from the time of the IPO investors receive better information due to improved transparency and the disclosure requirements that are part of the listing conditions. At the same time, the price of a company's stock acts as a measure of the company's value and as a disciplining mechanism for managers.

However, there are a number of disadvantages for a company inherent in listing its shares on a stock exchange. To start with, equity issuance is an expensive procedure, incurring costs such as underwriters' commission, legal fees, and other charges resulting primarily from the need to satisfy the additional disclosure requirements. From the perspective of investors, going public implies that the ownership of the company is likely to be shared more widely, resulting in a larger gap between external investors and managers. This separation of ownership and control could cause 'agency problems', where company insiders hold more accurate information on the prospects of the firm than external equity investors, resulting in a divergence of managers' and outside investors' interests. Lastly, by going public, a company exposes itself to scrutiny by shareholders, who may be excessively focused on short-term results.

While it is difficult to disentangle the different factors motivating a company's decision to issue public equity, the economic cycle is likely to play a significant role. This is mainly because equity is often used to finance capital formation, which fluctuates over the business cycle. Furthermore, significant increases in stock-market prices generally preceded increases in equity issuance. In the literature on behavioural finance (Shiller, 2003), a related factor explaining the timing of equity issuance is the effect of investor sentiment. Developments in investor optimism over time may have an impact on the cost of equity, thereby influencing the amount of equity issued. For example, excessive increases in risk aversion resulting in falling stock-market prices could raise the cost of equity, thereby dissuading companies from issuing equity. Although investor sentiment will inevitably change over time, it is difficult to measure risk aversion empirically, and/or investors' willingness to invest in the stock market. Companies also issue equity in order to finance the acquisition of other companies, either by using the cash proceeds of public offerings or by issuing shares, which are subsequently exchanged for the shares of a target company. Consequently, merger and acquisition (M&A) cycles can also be expected to correlate with equity issuance activity.

Figure 5.12 shows that the IPO market contracted in 2008 and 2009 (in line with the economic downturn after the start of the financial crisis) and again

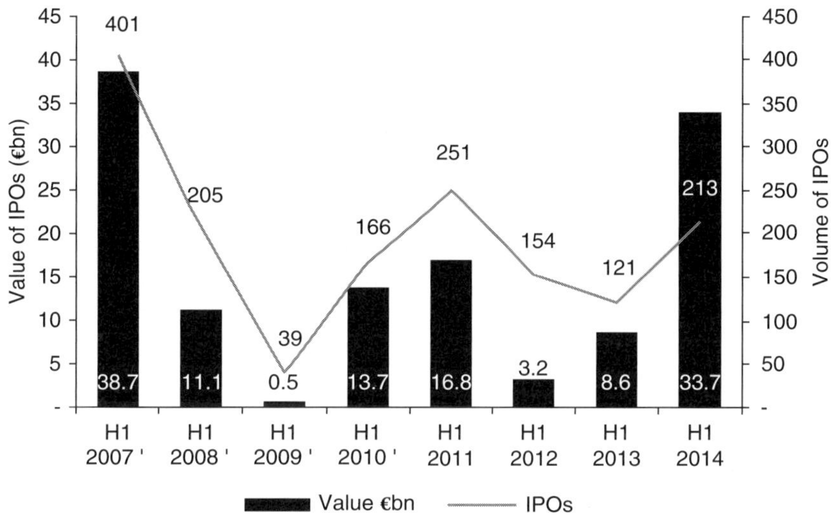

Figure 5.12 IPOs in Europe: value (left) and number (right), 2007–2014 (up to Q2)
Source: PwC

in 2012 and 2013 (after the euro crisis). The IPO market only started to recover in 2014.

5.5 Derivatives

Derivatives are financial instruments whose value is derived from the value of the underlying financial instruments. They can be based on different types of assets (such as equities or commodities), prices (such as interest rates or exchange rates), or indexes (such as a stock market index). Derivatives can be used as a source of revenue but are also important risk-management tools (see Batten *et al.*, 2004). As for the latter, the BIS (1994) stresses that derivatives allow parties to identify, isolate, and manage the market risk in financial instruments and commodities, i.e. changes in market prices of financial instruments and changes in interest and exchange rates. When used properly, derivatives can reduce risks through hedging. This is done by transferring the cost of bearing the risk from one party to the other; the former wants to reduce the exposure to risk, whereas the latter is willing to assume that exposure in the expectation of making a profit (Reilly, 2005). Financial innovation and increased market demand led to a rapid growth of derivatives trading until 2007 (see Figure 5.13). After the onset of the

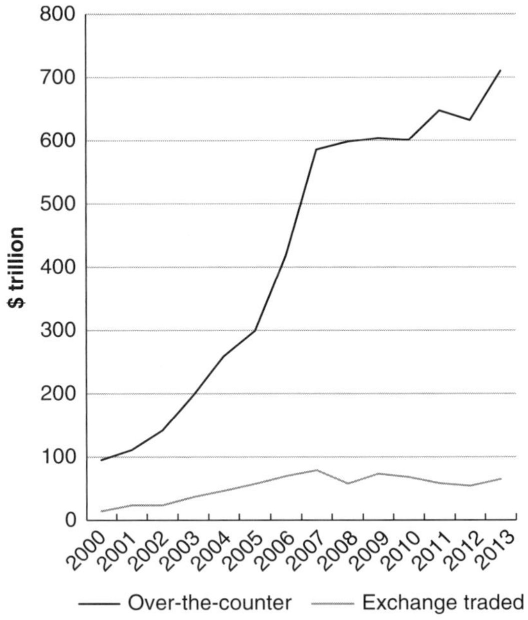

Figure 5.13 Global derivatives markets ($ trillion), notional amounts, 2000–2013
Source: Bank for International Settlements

financial crisis, the global derivatives markets stabilised albeit at a very high level. The notional amount of OTC trading was around $700 trillion, while exchange traded derivatives amounted to $65 trillion in 2013.

The use of derivatives has a major impact on asset management and risk management. A portfolio manager can, for example, change its risk profile through derivative transactions at a very low cost. Without derivatives, the portfolio manager would have to conduct transactions in the underlying cash markets (i.e. money, bond, or equity markets) at a higher cost, including the costly transfer of securities. Derivatives are thus a low-cost tool for risk management. Moreover, derivatives can be tailor-made in the over-the-counter market (see below). The spectacular growth of hedge funds can also be explained by the rise of low-cost derivatives markets. Hedge funds typically exploit small price differences of similar financial products, as explained in Chapter 9. Only when the transaction cost is smaller than the price differential will hedge funds take a position.

There are two broad types of derivatives: forwards and options. A *forward contract* gives the holder the obligation to buy or sell a certain underlying instrument (like a bond) at a certain date in the future (i.e. the delivery or final settlement date), at a specified price (i.e. the settlement price). Two examples are futures and swaps. *Futures contracts* are forward contracts traded on organised exchanges. *Swaps* are forward contracts in which counterparties agree to exchange streams of cash flows according to predetermined rules. For example, an *interest rate swap* is a derivative in which one party exchanges a stream of interest payments for another party's stream of cash flows. The most important difference with options is that *options* give the holder the right (but not the obligation) to buy or sell a certain underlying instrument at a certain date in the future at a specified price.

Derivatives are traded on *organised exchanges* or *over-the-counter*. The oldest official derivatives market in Europe is the European Options Exchange (EOE) in Amsterdam, which started to trade options on stocks in 1978. EOE became part of the Amsterdam Exchanges and subsequently of Euronext. Next, the London International Financial Futures and Options Exchange (LIFFE) began its operations in 1982. LIFFE used a system of open-outcry floor trading. Later on, derivatives exchanges were opened in continental Europe. While some of these also adopted open-outcry floor trading, others (like the DTB, i.e. Deutsche Terminbörse) introduced electronic trading. DTB was founded in 1991. It introduced trading of futures on the Bund, i.e. German government bonds, in direct competition with a contract already trading at LIFFE. By 1998, the DTB had competed the Bund contract away from LIFFE (Anderson and McKay, 2008). Also, LIFFE moved to electronic trading.

EUREX is a serious competitor to LIFFE in the area of bond and short-term interest rate futures and options trading in Europe. This German–Swiss joint venture came about through the merger of the DTB and SOFFEX, the Swiss Options and Financial Futures Exchange, in 1998. Today, it trades a wide range of bond and money market derivative products. Access to the market is available in a number of major cities, including Chicago, New York, London, and Tokyo (Batten *et al.*, 2004).

OTC contracts are traded (and privately negotiated) directly between two parties. All contract terms, such as delivery quality, quantity, location, date, and price, are negotiable (Anderson and McKay, 2008). As Figure 5.13 shows, trade in OTC derivatives dwarfs trade in derivatives via exchanges. The United Kingdom is the leading OTC derivative market in the world. Derivatives such as swaps and forward rate agreements are generally traded on OTC markets. Derivative contracts (such as futures contracts and options) that are transacted on an organised futures exchange are standardised. However, Anderson and McKay (2008) point out that the traditional distinction between exchange-based and OTC derivatives has become less

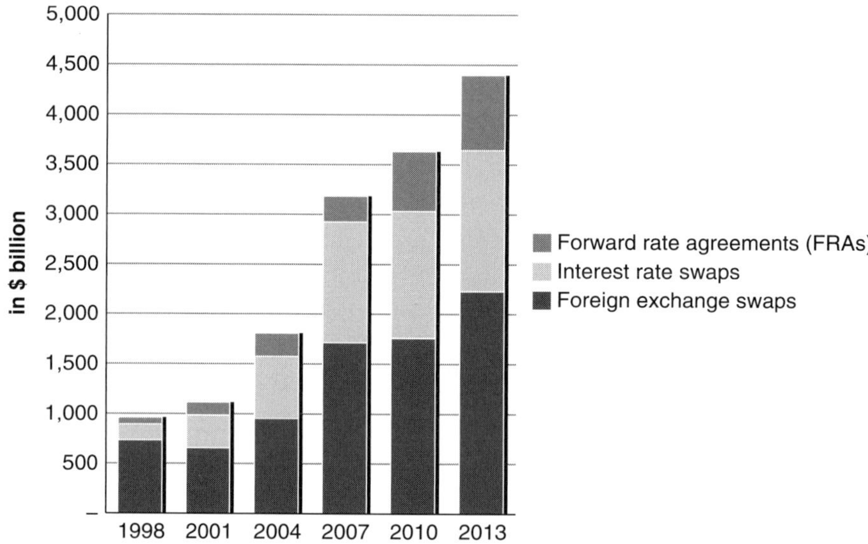

Figure 5.14 Average daily turnover in various OTC derivatives markets ($ billion), 1998–2013
Source: BIS Triennial Central Bank Survey

clear. For instance, the International Swaps and Derivatives Association (ISDA) has provided a contract with standard pre-conditions. This standardisation has made it easier for more participants to access the OTC markets. Furthermore, OTC trades are increasingly being cleared through clearing-houses in much the same way as exchange-based contracts.

Table 5.4 shows the outstanding amounts of the different types of OTC derivatives. Interest rate derivatives dominate the market, followed by foreign exchange derivatives. Financial institutions, corporates, and government agencies use these derivatives to manage their interest rate and foreign exchange risks. Credit default swaps are a more recent phenomenon and will be discussed below.

Figure 5.14 shows that the average daily turnover in the various OTC derivatives markets increased rapidly at the beginning of the 2000s. In addition to the forward rate agreement (FRA) market and interest rate swap (IRS) market – comprising overnight interest rate swaps (OISs, also referred to as EONIA swaps) and other IRSs – the figure shows the share of OTC derivatives linked to the foreign exchange market, comprising FX swaps and cross-currency swaps (Xccy swaps). The figure shows that measured by volume, the foreign exchange swaps are by far the most important OTC derivatives market segments, followed by other IRSs.

Table 5.4 Amounts of outstanding OTC derivatives ($ trillion), 2003–2013

	2003	2005	2007	2009	2011	2013
Interest rate derivatives	142	212	393	450	504	584
Foreign exchange derivatives	24	31	56	49	63	71
Credit default swaps	–	14	58	33	29	21
Equity-linked derivatives	4	6	8	6	6	7
Commodity derivatives	1	5	8	3	3	2
Other OTC derivatives	26	31	61	63	43	26
Total contracts	197	299	586	604	648	710

Source: Bank for International Settlements

Credit derivatives

As can be seen in Table 5.4, an important development in the OTC derivatives markets has been the emergence of credit derivatives. The essence of a *credit derivative* is a contract in which a credit-protection seller promises a payment to a credit-protection buyer contingent upon the occurrence of a credit event (Anderson and McKay, 2008). The various types of contracts differ according to the terms and conditions that govern the promised payment, such as the definition of the 'credit event'. Various definitions are used, including formal bankruptcy and default. Increasingly diverse and complex products have appeared, but the most popular type of credit derivatives is the single-name *credit default swap* (CDS). Under this contract, the protection seller promises to buy at par from the protection buyer a specified bond (Anderson and McKay, 2008). A CDS requires fixed and regular premium payments from the protection buyer to the protection seller until a credit event occurs or the CDS matures. The premium is calculated as a percentage (called *credit spread*) of the nominal value of the reference obligation (the *notional amount*). Apart from single-name CDSs, the multi-name contract may refer to more reference entities (i.e. the underlying names on which credit risk is exchanged). A CDS resembles an insurance contract, in that it protects the 'protection buyer' against predefined credit events, in particular the risk of default in return for a periodic fee paid to the protection seller. Following a credit event, contracts settle either physically (i.e. through the delivery to the protection buyer of defaulting bonds and/ or loans for an amount equivalent to the notional value of the swap) or in cash, with the net amount owed by the protection seller determined after the credit event. CDSs are an attractive instrument for risk management. Protection

Table 5.5 Notional amounts of CDSs outstanding ($ trillion), 2003–2013

	June 2003	June 2005	June 2007	June 2009	June 2011	June 2013
Credit default swaps (BIS data)	–	10.2	42.6	36.1	32.4	24.3
– Single-name instruments	–	7.3	24.2	24.2	18.1	13.1
– Multi-name instruments	–	2.9	18.3	11.9	14.3	11.2
– of which index products	–	–	–	–	12.5	10.2
Credit default swaps (ISDA data)	2.7	12.4	45.5	31.2	29.1	24.3

Source: BIS, ISDA

buyers can transfer credit risks without transferring credit claims or debt securities, while protection sellers can assume credit risks without granting credit or buying debt securities. So, both sides can optimise credit risk portfolios relatively efficiently (ECB, 2007).

Data on notional amounts of CDSs on euro-denominated reference obligations are not available. Table 5.5 describes the development in notional CDS amounts outstanding worldwide from two different sources, i.e. the ISDA and the BIS. The data from the two sources differ substantially. Nevertheless, they all indicate average annual growth rates in the CDS markets of 100 per cent or more. However, after 2008, the market shrank very quickly.

The most common maturities of CDSs are three, five, seven, and ten years, with the five-year maturity serving as a benchmark. The most active market participants in CDS markets, both as protection buyers and sellers, have been banks, hedge funds, and insurance companies. The majority of reference obligations are bonds or loans that are rated A or better (ECB, 2007).

5.6 Foreign exchange market

Funds transferred from one country to another have to be converted if the countries do not share the same currency. This takes place at the foreign exchange market which is an over-the-counter market, where most trading is done by banks. If countries have a floating exchange rate regime, transactions at the foreign exchange market determine the rate at which currencies are exchanged. These transactions consist of the buying and selling of different currencies. There are two types of transactions: *spot* and *forward transactions.* Spot transactions involve the immediate exchange of currency, while forward transactions involve the exchange of currency at some specified future date.

Box 5.3 The role of the euro-dollar exchange rate in the ECB's policies

The euro-dollar exchange rate is one of the indicators of future inflationary developments in the monetary policy strategy of the ECB. The ECB has at various occasions made it clear that it closely monitors the euro-dollar exchange rate. Several studies have examined the so-called *exchange rate pass-through* (ERPT), i.e. the degree to which exchange rate changes are passed through in (domestic) prices. ERPT is defined as the percentage change of import prices (in local currency) resulting from a one per cent change in the exchange rate between the exporting and importing countries. Firms may choose to pass exchange rate alterations fully into their selling prices (*complete* ERPT). At the other extreme, firms may decide to absorb the shock by reducing their profit margins, so the selling prices will be unchanged (*no* ERPT). The relationship between exchange rates and prices is given by the following equation:

$$P_t = a + \delta X + \gamma E_t + \psi Z_t + \varepsilon_t \tag{5.1}$$

In equation (5.1), P is the local currency import price; X is a measure of the export costs. Z may include import demand-shifting factors, such as competing prices or income, and E is the exchange rate (importer's currency per unit of exporter currency). Taking the logarithm of both sides yields the elasticity of ERPT with which γ is referred to as the *pass-through coefficient*. Campa and Goldberg (2005) report that in the long run ERPT is higher than in the short run, but for all European countries in their sample the ERPT is less than one both in the short and long run. They also find huge differences across the countries of the euro area.

When a country's currency appreciates, i.e. rises in value vis-à-vis other currencies, the country's goods become more expensive in other countries, while foreign goods become cheaper. Likewise, a depreciation makes foreign goods more expensive. In other words, the exchange rate affects the rate of inflation. That is why central banks keep a close eye on the exchange rate. Box 5.3 discusses the role of the euro-dollar exchange rate in the monetary policy of the ECB.

Figure 5.15 shows the euro exchange rate vis-à-vis the US dollar, the British pound and the Japanese yen between 1999 and 2014. Since 1999, the euro initially depreciated against the dollar, but since 2002 it appreciated. However, during the recent financial crises the euro strongly fluctuated, reflecting changing market perceptions of the financial problems in the US and the euro area. In the beginning of 2015, the euro strongly depreciated against the dollar, reflecting the ECB's quantitative easing policies (see Chapter 4).

Not all countries have a floating exchange rate regime. Until 1971 most countries pegged their currency against the dollar. Also, after the demise of

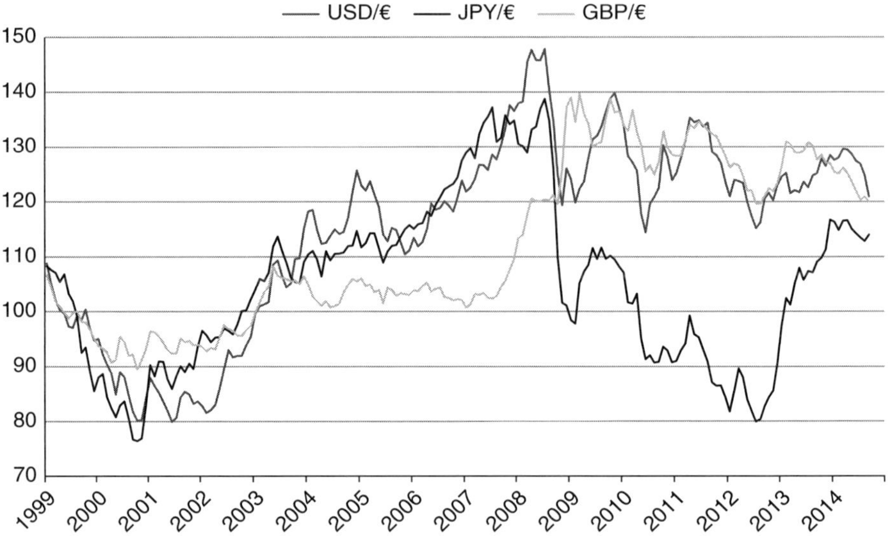

Figure 5.15 The euro exchange rate, 1999–2014
Source: ECB

the Bretton Woods system several countries decided to peg their currency to another currency, like the euro. Other countries have a 'floating' or 'crawling' peg whereby they adjust the value of the peg periodically.

The *real exchange rate* is the rate at which domestic goods can be exchanged for foreign goods, i.e. the price of domestic goods relative to the price of foreign goods denominated in the domestic currency. So, the real exchange rate (r) can be defined as the nominal exchange rate (e) that is adjusted by the ratio of the foreign price level (P_f) to the domestic price level (P):

$$r = e * P_f / P \qquad (5.2)$$

5.7 Conclusions

Financial markets release information to aid the price discovery process, they provide a platform to trade, and they provide an infrastructure to settle trades. The main trading mechanisms are quote-driven and order-driven markets.

The euro money market is the market for euro-denominated short-term funds and related derivative instruments. It consists of various segments, including unsecured deposit contracts with various maturities, ranging from overnight to one year, and repurchase agreements (repos, i.e. reverse transactions secured by securities) also ranging from overnight to one year. Credit institutions account for the largest share of the euro money market. The ECB has a major influence on the money market via its use of various monetary policy instruments (reserve requirements, standing facilities, and open market operations). There are three main market interest rates for the money market: EONIA (euro overnight index average), EURIBOR (euro interbank offered rate), and EUREPO (the repo market reference rate for the euro).

The EU bond market has experienced spectacular growth since the introduction of the euro and is now matching the US bond market in size. The bulk of euro-denominated bonds (i.e. debt securities with a maturity of more than one year) is issued by euro-area issuers. Although the share of corporate bonds in all euro-denominated bonds outstanding has risen, government bonds still form the most important market segment. Also, since the introduction of the euro, yield differentials vary considerably across countries, while for each country the yield differential varies considerably over time. The issuance of asset-backed securities has increased rapidly during the last decade.

The importance of equity finance in the EU is growing, although there are large differences across exchanges. The market capitalisation of Euronext and the London Stock Exchange, which are the biggest exchanges in terms of turnover, are much higher than those of other exchanges in the EU. Despite the increase in equity finance, public equity markets play a limited role as a source of new funds for corporations that raise external financing generally via bank loans or debt securities.

Derivatives are financial instruments whose value is derived from the value of underlying financial instruments. They are traded on organised exchanges or over-the-counter. Derivatives can provide for a source of income but are also important risk-management tools. The most important derivatives are futures, forwards, options, and swaps. During recent years credit derivatives have become important. These are contracts in which a credit-protection seller promises a payment to a credit-protection buyer contingent upon the occurrence of a credit event.

If countries have a floating exchange rate regime, transactions at the foreign exchange market determine the rate at which currencies are exchanged. As changes in the exchange rate affect the rate of inflation, central banks keep a close eye on the exchange rate.

Notes

1. Insiders of a company may have more information than outsiders. Regulation typically forbids insider trading (see Chapter 12).
2. In addition, the derivatives market has become increasingly important over recent years. The derivative money-market segments can be grouped into exchange-traded instruments, such as short-term interest rate futures and options, and instruments that are typically traded over-the-counter. This section will focus on the unsecured deposit markets and the secured repo markets.
3. See www.euribor-ebf.eu/euriborg-org/panelbanks.html for an overview of the banks in the panel.
4. The modified duration measures the change in the current value of the debt portfolio when the yield of the portfolio changes by 1 basis point.
5. The lower limit for government securities to be eligible for trading on EuroMTS is €5 billion.

Suggested Reading

Harris, L. E. (2003), *Trading and Exchanges: Market Microstructure for Practitioners, An Introductory Textbook to the Economics of Market Microstructure*, Oxford University Press.

Hull, J. C. (2005), *Options, Futures, and Other Derivatives*, 6th edition, Prentice Hall, Upper Saddle River (NJ).

Pagano, M. and E. Von Thadden (2008), The European Bond Markets under EMU, in: X. Freixas, P. Hartmann, and C. Mayer (eds.), *Handbook of European Financial Markets and Institutions*, Oxford University Press, 488–518.

References

Anderson, R. W. and K. McKay (2008), Derivatives Markets, in: X. Freixas, P. Hartmann, and C. Mayer (eds.), *Handbook of European Financial Markets and Institutions*, Oxford University Press, 568–596.

Baele, L., A. Ferrando, P. Hördahl, E. Krylova, and C. Monnet (2004), Measuring Financial Integration in the Euro Area, ECB Occasional Paper 14.

Bailey, R. E. (2005), *The Economics of Financial Markets*, Cambridge University Press.

Bank for International Settlements (1994), Risk Management Guidelines for Derivatives, BIS, Basel.

Bank of England/European Central Bank (2014), The Case for a Better Functioning Securitisation Market in the European Union, A Discussion Paper, Bank of England/ECB, London/Frankfurt am Main.

Batten, J., T. Fetherson, and P. G. Szilagi (2004), *European Fixed Income Markets: Money, Bonds, and Interest Rate Derivatives*, John Wiley & Sons Ltd, Chichester.

Bearing Point (2007), The Electronic Bond Market – New Perspectives for Electronic Fixed Income Trading, May.

Campa, J. M. and L. S. Goldberg (2005), Exchange Rate Pass-Through into Import Prices, *The Review of Economics and Statistics*, **87** (4), 679–690.

Casey, J. P. (2006), Bond Market Transparency: To Regulate or not to Regulate . . ., ECMI Policy Brief, Brussels.

Committee of European Securities Regulators (2008), The Role of Credit-Rating Agencies in Structured Finance, CESR, Paris.

Dunne, P., M. Moore, and R. Portes (2006), *European Government Bond Markets: Transparency, Liquidity, Efficiency*, CEPR, London.

Edwards, A. K., L. E. Harris, and M. S. Piwowar (2007), Corporate Bond Market Transaction Costs and Transparency, *Journal of Finance*, **62** (3), 1421–1454.

European Central Bank (2007), *The Euro Bonds and Derivatives Markets*, ECB, Frankfurt am Main.

(2008a), The Analysis of the Euro Money Market from a Monetary Policy Perspective, *ECB Monthly Bulletin*, February.

(2008b), *Bond Markets and Long-term Interest Rates in Non-euro Area Member States of the European Union – Statistical Tables*, ECB, Frankfurt am Main.

(2010), *Euro Money Market Study December 2010*, ECB, Frankfurt am Main.

(2011a), *Financial Stability Review June 2010*, ECB, Frankfurt am Main.

(2011b), *Euro Money Market Study September 2011*, ECB, Frankfurt am Main.

(2011c), *Recent Developments in Securitisation*, ECB, Frankfurt am Main.

(2012), *Euro Money Market Study December 2012*, ECB, Frankfurt am Main.

(2013), *Euro Money Market Survey November 2013*, ECB, Frankfurt am Main.

(2014), *Financial Stability Review May 2014*, ECB, Frankfurt am Main.

Financial Stability Forum (2008), *Report on Enhancing Market and Institutional Resilience*, FSF, Basel.

Foucault, T. and A. J. Menkveld (2008), Competition for Order Flow and Smart Order Routing Systems, *Journal of Finance*, **63**, 119–158.

Goldstein, M. A., E. Hotchkiss, and E. Sirri (2007), Transparency and Liquidity: A Controlled Experiment on Corporate Bonds, *Review of Financial Studies*, **20** (2), 235–273.

Harris, L. E. (2003), *Trading and Exchanges: Market Microstructure for Practitioners*, Oxford University Press.

Harris L. E. and M. S. Piwowar (2006), Secondary Trading Costs in the Municipal Bond Market, *Journal of Finance*, **61** (3), 1361–1397.

Hartmann, P., M. Manna, and A. Manzanares (2001), The Microstructure of the Euro Money Market, ECB Working Paper 80.

Kyle, A. S. (1985), Continuous Auctions and Insider Trading, *Econometrica*, **53**, 1315–1336.

Myers, S. and N. Majluf (1984), Corporate Financing and Investment Decisions when Firms Have Information that Investors Do Not Have, *Journal of Financial Economics*, **13**, 187–221.

O'Hara, M. (2003), Presidential Address: Liquidity and Price Discovery, *Journal of Finance*, **58**, 1335–1353.

Pagano, M. and E. Von Thadden (2008), The European Bond Markets under EMU, in: X. Freixas, P. Hartmann, and C. Mayer (eds.), *Handbook of European Financial Markets and Institutions*, Oxford University Press, 488–518.

Reilly, A. (2005), Over-the-Counter Derivatives Markets in Ireland – An Overview, *CBFSAI Quarterly Bulletin*, Dublin, July.

Shiller, R. J. (2003), From Efficient Markets to Behavioral Finance, *Journal of Economic Perspectives*, **17**, 83–104.

Wharton (2006), LSE, NYSE, OMX, Nasdaq, Euronext ... Why Stock Exchanges Are Scrambling to Consolidate, Knowledge@Wharton, Wharton School, University of Pennsylvania.

Wolswijk, G. and J. de Haan (2005), Government Debt Management in the Euro Area: Recent Theoretical Developments and Changes in Practices, ECB Occasional Paper 25.

CHAPTER

6

The Economics of Financial Integration

OVERVIEW

This chapter begins by defining financial integration and identifying its drivers. Financial integration may be defined as a situation without frictions that discriminate between economic agents in their access to – and their investment of – capital, particularly on the basis of their location. Not only market forces but also collective action and public action are shown to be driving financial integration.

The second part of the chapter deals with measuring financial integration. Three categories of measures have been used for this purpose. The first category consists of price-based indicators that measure discrepancies in prices or returns on assets caused by the geographic origin of the assets. The second category consists of news-based measures. The underlying idea is that in a financially integrated area, portfolios should be well diversified so that news (i.e. arrival of new economic information) of a regional character has little impact on prices, whereas common or global news is relatively more important. The third category of measures are quantity-based indicators that measure the effects of frictions faced by the demand for and supply of investment opportunities, like cross-border activities or listings, and statistics on the cross-border holdings of investors.

The third part of the chapter gives an overview of the extent to which various financial markets in the EU are integrated. The financial crisis and the euro crisis were a serious setback for European financial integration. An important reason why the European Union put the creation of a single financial market high on the policy agenda is that it widely believed that financial integration may stimulate economic growth. This growth effect and other consequences of financial integration are discussed at the end of the chapter.

LEARNING OBJECTIVES

After you have studied this chapter, you should be able to:

- define financial integration
- explain what drives financial integration
- describe the various ways of measuring financial integration, their shortcomings, and the reasoning underlying these various approaches
- assess the extent to which various financial markets in the EU are integrated
- discuss the consequences of financial integration.

6.1 Financial integration: definition and drivers

Definition of financial integration

While legal restrictions on international capital flows were already abolished in the late 1980s (see Chapter 3), financial market segmentation due to exchange-rate risk persisted until the start of the monetary union in 1999. The introduction of the euro was a powerful catalyst for the creation of integrated financial markets by removing one of the most important obstacles to the cross-border provision of financial services. At the same time, it became clear that there are other impediments to truly integrated financial markets, such as different regulations and institutions across the Member States of the EU.

Following Baele *et al.* (2008), the following definition of an *integrated financial market* is adopted: the market for a given set of financial instruments and/or services is fully integrated if all potential market participants with the same relevant characteristics:

(1) face a single set of rules when they decide to deal with those financial instruments and/or services;
(2) have equal access to the above-mentioned set of financial instruments and/or services; and
(3) are treated equally when they are active in the market.

Full integration requires the same access to banks or trading, clearing, and settlement platforms for both borrowers and lenders, regardless of their country of origin. In addition, full integration requires that there is no discrimination among comparable market participants based solely on their location of origin (Baele *et al.*, 2004).

This definition of financial integration is closely linked to the law of one price. According to the law of one price, assets with identical risks should be priced identically regardless of where they are transacted. As Baele *et al.* (2004) point out, the law of one price is very attractive since it allows for quantitative measures of financial integration, but it only can be tested for markets for instruments that are listed or quoted. Hence, the analysis based on the law of one price cannot serve as a basis for measuring integration of markets for unlisted instruments.

Drivers of financial integration

What drives financial integration? Following the ECB (2003), a differentiation can be made between (1) market forces, (2) collective action, and (3) public action.

Market forces

The first driver of financial integration is market forces. Firms benefit from the lower cost of capital that enhanced competition brings about, allowing a better allocation of capital. More productive investment opportunities will become available, and a reallocation of funds to the most productive investment opportunities will take place. Investors also benefit from access to a broader range of financial instruments and more opportunities to diversify their portfolios. The complete elimination of barriers to trading, clearing, and settlement platforms will allow firms to choose the most efficient trading, clearing, and/or settlement platforms. Also, financial intermediaries may profit by exploiting the potential economies of scale and scope that a larger market offers. But financial intermediaries may also face pressure on their profit margins.

Figure 6.1 illustrates the impact of enhanced competition with an example. The starting position is a market rate of 4 per cent. In a segmented market with low competition, a bank lends to firms at 6 per cent and offers depositors a return of 2 per cent. The bank earns a margin of 4 per cent. As markets integrate, increased competition forces the bank to reduce its lending rate to 5 per cent and to increase its deposit rate to 3 per cent. The lending firms experience a lower cost of capital, while depositors receive a higher return. The margin for the bank is reduced to 2 per cent. The bank can (partly) offset the reduction of its profit margin by increasing its business in an integrated market.

Since investors and financial intermediaries may benefit from financial integration, market forces could lead to the elimination of market segmentation. For

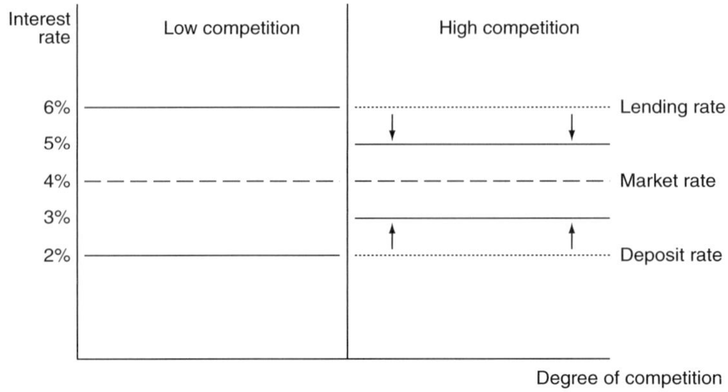

Figure 6.1 Impact of enhanced competition

instance, issuance practices of government bond issuers converged towards what was perceived as 'best' practice because they had to compete to attract investors (Wolswijk and de Haan, 2005). Likewise, mergers of stock exchanges, clearinghouses, and securities settlement systems are often motivated by efforts to exploit the economies of scale and scope potentially available within a broader market. Of course, market forces can foster integration only if there are no legislative or regulatory obstacles standing in the way.

Collective action

Sometimes market forces alone are not sufficient to remove obstacles to integration. This may happen, for instance, due to network externalities in the financial system. The more participants use a particular market, the more benefits it generally brings to its users. These benefits include greater depth and liquidity, reduced transaction costs, as well as easier and more effective opportunities for risk management (ECB, 2003). Individual market participants will not take these externalities into account. Through collective action, market participants can, for instance, agree on standard technical features of financial instruments, the definition of common practices and conventions, or the establishment of reference indices. However, the existence of powerful network externalities may also hamper integration as strong network effects are often associated with high switching costs, i.e. the cost of switching from one set of organisation, practices, conventions, rules, and infrastructure to another. A switch to a pan-European market entails costs – at least in the short term – for participants in national markets (ECB, 2003).

In 1998 a series of market conventions sponsored by several market organisations stimulated financial integration. A good example is the rules applicable to the basic market interest reference rate, the EURIBOR (the rate at which euro interbank term deposits are offered by one prime bank to another at 11 am CET). A similar initiative permitted the establishment of the other basic interest reference rate for overnight unsecured interbank deposits, the EONIA. In 2002, another market convention added a new reference index, the EUREPO, i.e. the rate at which one prime bank offers funds in euros to another prime bank if in exchange the former receives eligible assets as collateral from the latter (see Chapter 5 for further details).

Another good example of collective action is the creation of the Single Euro Payments Area (SEPA) that allows customers to make non-cash euro payments to any beneficiary located anywhere in the euro area using a single bank account and a single set of payment instruments. In other words, there will no longer be any differentiation between national and cross-border retail payments within the euro area. This is a major step towards integration. Despite the introduction of the euro in 1999 and the development of TARGET (the EU-wide large-value payment system operated by the ESCB; see Chapter 7), retail payments continued to be processed differently throughout the euro area. However, in 2002, the banking industry took the initiative to create the European Payments Council (EPC), which defined the new rules and procedures for euro payments. The goal of SEPA is an integrated, competitive, and innovative retail payments market for all non-cash euro payments.

Public action

While financial integration benefits first and foremost the market community, its effects are much more widespread (see section 6.4). The pervasive effects of financial integration on the whole economy justify the involvement of public authorities to support its development towards an optimal outcome, e.g. in situations where a public good cannot be supplied privately or where a market or coordination failure occurs (ECB, 2003). In both cases, neither market forces alone nor collective action within the private sector is sufficient to deliver the desirable level of integration. In this context, action by public authorities may come in many forms. It can be a catalyst or facilitator of collective action to help overcome coordination problems. It can also extend to direct intervention, as in the case of the development of TARGET. An essential responsibility of public action is the establishment of an appropriate legislative and regulatory framework. The European Commission's FSAP, described in Chapter 3, aimed to create a single wholesale market and an open and secure retail market.

A good example of 'FSAP in action' is the regulation on cross-border euro payments (No. 2560/2001, later replaced by regulation No 924/2009) that gives EU consumers a guarantee that when they make a payment in euros to an account in another EU Member State, it will cost the same as it would to make a payment within their own Member State. As of 1 January 2006, the regulation applies to payments of up to €50,000. According to the European Commission (2006), prior to this regulation charges for cross-border euro payments were often excessive, with a €100 transfer costing the consumer on average €24. According to the Commission, charges for cross-border euro payments have reduced significantly since the introduction of the regulation, with a €100 transfer now costing on average less than €2.50.

6.2 Measuring financial integration

Following Baele *et al.* (2004, 2008), integration of financial markets can be assessed using three categories of measures. The first broad category consists of *price-based indicators*, which measure discrepancies in prices or returns on assets caused by the geographic origin of the assets. Most empirical research on financial market integration in Europe compares rates of return on assets. To properly test for integration, assets should have identical cash flows and risk characteristics but be traded in different countries. The risk of an asset's return is composed of a systematic part and an idiosyncratic part; the latter can be diversified away, the former cannot. While this type of risk may be considered negligible in some cases, for example in the money market before the crisis, it is crucial to control for it in the corporate bond and equity markets (Baele *et al.*, 2004).

The second category of measures consists of *news-based indicators*. The underlying idea is that in a financially integrated area, portfolios should be well diversified so that news (i.e. arrival of new economic information) of a regional character has little impact on prices, whereas common or global news is relatively more important. This presumes that the degree of systematic risk is identical across assets in different countries.

The third category consists of *quantity-based indicators*, which quantify the effects of frictions faced by the demand for and supply of investment opportunities. Examples are statistics giving information on the ease of market access, such as cross-border activities or listings, and cross-border holdings of securities. However, cross-border activity is an imperfect measure of integration. Increased cross-border traffic typically indicates an increase in integration. But there is no need for cross-border activity in a fully integrated market, as prices are the same everywhere.

The remainder of this section will provide further details on some measures of financial integration.

Price-based measures

The construction of price-based integration measures for the money and government bond markets is facilitated by the fact that relatively homogeneous assets are available across countries. A widely used measure in research on integration of government bond markets is the *difference between local yields and some benchmark*, which is often the German yield. In the market for ten-year government bonds, for instance, market participants consider German bonds to be the reference bond. Consequently, it seems reasonable to measure integration in this segment of the bond market by calculating the spread between the yield on a local asset and the German benchmark asset. In perfectly integrated markets the spread should be equal to zero. The time variation in the size of the spread serves as a good indicator of how integration is proceeding in a particular country and market.[1] However, under stressed market conditions price-based measures may be problematic, because they may not adequately control for underlying risk characteristics, and therefore do not clearly distinguish effects stemming from changes in the credit standing of the issuers from the effects of financial integration (ECB, 2011).

A second price-based indicator of financial integration refers to the *dispersion of prices.* It can be calculated at each point in time by taking the standard deviation of yields across countries. If the cross-sectional standard deviation $sd(i)_t$ is zero, the law of one price applies fully. The degree of financial integration increases when the cross-sectional standard deviation has a downward trend (moves towards zero).

$$sd\,(i)_t = \sqrt[2]{\frac{(R_{i,t} - \overline{R}_t)^2}{n}} \tag{6.1}$$

where $R_{i,t}$ is the yield in country i at time t and $\bar{R}_t$ is the average yield across countries at time t.

A third measure has been proposed by Pukthuanthong and Roll (2009) and used by the ECB in its most recent report on financial integration (ECB, 2014). This indicator measures integration via the explanatory power of common factor portfolios. For each calendar year, these portfolios are formed on the basis of a principal component analysis and used in a simple regression framework to explain market returns for each country. The measure for integration is then computed as an average (or median) R-square across countries. In general, a higher measure indicates a more integrated market, where 1 implies perfect integration and 0 entails no integration (ECB, 2014). The following regression is estimated for each country *i*:

$$R_{i,t,\pi} = a_{i,t} + \sum_{k=1}^{K} \beta_{i,t}^{k} \theta_{i,t}^{k} + \varepsilon_{i,t,\pi} \tag{6.2}$$

where $R_{i,t,\pi}$ is the market return in country i on trading day π within year t, and $\theta_{i,t}^{k}$ is the return on the k-th common factor portfolio on the same day. The K common factor portfolios are obtained via principal component analysis.

News-based measures

To make news-based measures operational, one needs to provide a proxy for common news. Baele *et al.* (2004) argue that yield changes in the benchmark asset could be used to proxy all relevant common news. They suggest running the following regression:

$$\Delta R_{i,t} = \alpha_{i,t} + \beta_{i,t} \Delta R_{b,t} + \varepsilon_{i,t} \tag{6.3}$$

where $\Delta R_{i,t}$ is the change in the yield on an asset in country i at time t, $\Delta R_{b,t}$ is the yield change on a comparable asset in the benchmark country b, $\alpha_{i,t}$ is a time-varying intercept, $\beta_{i,t}$ is the time-dependent beta with respect to the benchmark asset, and $\varepsilon_{i,t}$ denotes a country-specific shock. When integration increases, the proportion of the variance in $\Delta R_{i,t}$ explained by the common factor $\Delta R_{b,t}$ will increase towards one, so that *the proportion of local variance explained by the common factor* can be used as another measure of integration.

For the purpose of examining integration in euro-area equity markets, Baele *et al.* (2004) distinguish between global and euro-area-wide effects on equity returns in the euro area. To this end, Baele *et al.* use the return on US stock markets as a proxy for world news, while the return on a euro-area-wide stock market index, corrected for US news, is used as the euro factor.

Quantity-based measures

Baele *et al.* (2004) classify these measures into two groups. The first group includes measures dealing with cross-border activities in a specific market, and the second group refers to measures for the home bias.

One way to assess the progress made towards integration is to consider whether the existing barriers to entry imposed on foreign economic agents willing to invest in a specific region have been reduced over time. If so, cross-border ownership of securities should increase over time. In Chapters 10 and 11, the cross-border activity of banks and insurers is discussed.

Baele *et al.* (2004) regard the extent of the *home bias*, i.e. the degree to which agents invest in domestic assets even though risk is shared more effectively if foreign assets are held, as a sign that financial integration is still not complete. In Chapter 9, the home bias of the portfolios of institutional investors are discussed.

6.3 Integration of European financial markets

This section summarises the main findings of empirical research on European financial integration. The available evidence suggests that the degree of integration varies depending on the market segment and is correlated with the degree of integration of the underlying financial infrastructure (see Chapter 7 for further details). The financial crisis and the euro crisis affected various financial markets to different degrees, resulting in a temporary retrenchment of market activity within domestic borders (ECB, 2011). Despite substantial recent improvements, in most market segments a relatively high degree of fragmentation still remains at the time of writing. In many market segments, financial integration has not yet returned to pre-crisis levels (ECB, 2014).

Money market

To assess the extent to which the various segments of the money market rate are integrated, Figure 6.2 shows the price-based indicator explained in Equation 6.1, namely the (unweighted) standard deviation of the average daily interest rates prevailing in each euro-area country.

As Figure 6.2 shows, the unsecured money market reached a stage of 'near-perfect' integration almost immediately after the introduction of the euro. The cross-sectional standard deviation of the EONIA lending rates and the 1-month and 12-month EURIBOR rates across euro-area countries fell sharply to close to zero following the introduction of the euro, and remained stable until the financial crisis.

Although the euro-area money market was the financial market which achieved the fastest and most complete integration after the introduction of

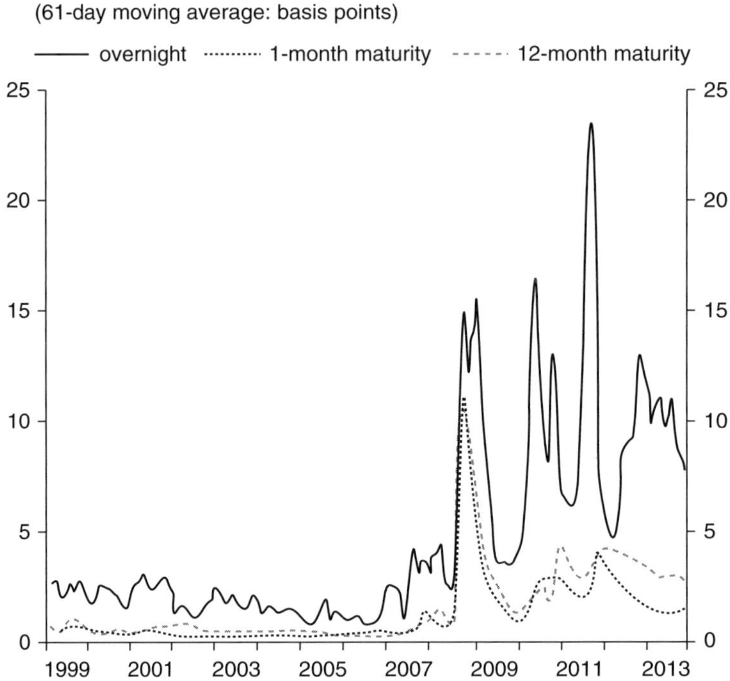

Figure 6.2 Integration of the money market: cross-country standard deviation of interest rates (average of unsecured interbank lending rates; in basis points; 61-day moving average), 1999–2013
Source: ECB (2014)

the euro, it was also the hardest hit during the financial crisis and the euro crisis (ECB, 2011). The collapse of the subprime mortgage market in the United States in the summer of 2007 led to rising yields on a variety of money market instruments. The deepening of the crisis due to the bankruptcy of Lehman Brothers in September 2008 had a sharp negative impact on the measured integration of the euro-area money market. During 2009, the money market gradually reverted to more stable conditions. However, the euro crisis led again to rising tensions in the money market, as reflected in increases in the cross-country standard deviation of the EONIA.

More recently, standard deviations have come down. Particularly after ECB President Draghi's speech in July 2012 in London and the announcement of the outright monetary transactions (OMTs) in September 2012 (see Chapter 4), market conditions in the unsecured money market have improved noticeably.

Also in the secured euro money market, dispersion of EUREPO has come down (not shown). Notably, for both short- and long-term maturities, dispersion in rates decreased. At the end of 2013, they even reached levels not seen since the start of the financial crisis. Thus, the secured market is leading the unsecured market in terms of market integration, which is in line with the structural shift between these markets since the financial crises.

In 2013, intra euro-area transactions accounted for almost 60 per cent of all lending. This reflects a renewed increase in banks' willingness to engage in cross-border lending, and thus a reintegration of intra-euro-area money markets. Despite this progress, at the time of writing, fragmentation of money markets in the euro area is still quite evident (ECB, 2014).

Government bond market

After the introduction of the euro, differences in government bond yields among euro-area countries were never more than 50 basis points until the financial crisis. After August 2007, some sovereign bond markets benefited from a 'flight to safety', while other euro-area sovereign bond spreads rose sharply relative to the German benchmark (see Figure 2.6). The increase in yield spreads therefore does not necessarily reflect a decline in bond market integration, as it is likely to incorporate a reassessment and repricing of risk for the respective sovereign issuers.

Figure 6.3 shows the results of the integration measure based on Equation 6.2. Until the crisis, the indicator was close to one but after the crisis the indicator declined sharply. More recently, it increased, but less so for the GIIPS countries than for the other countries in the euro area. Still, integration of the government bond market is not back to pre-crisis levels.

Corporate bond market

In analysing corporate bond market integration, yield differentials relative to a benchmark cannot be used, as corporate bonds are generally not sufficiently homogeneous to allow for easy comparison. The yield on a corporate bond typically depends on a number of factors, such as the bond's credit rating, time-to-maturity, liquidity, and cash-flow structure. The ECB (2014) assesses progress in integration in the corporate bond market using the dispersion (see Equation 6.1) of CDS premia in the euro area for two groups of firms producing relatively homogeneous products, i.e. the leading communications firms and the largest commercial banks in each country. The higher the dispersion is at industry level for the euro area, the lower the integration is for the financing of these entities (banks and telecoms) at the euro-area level. As

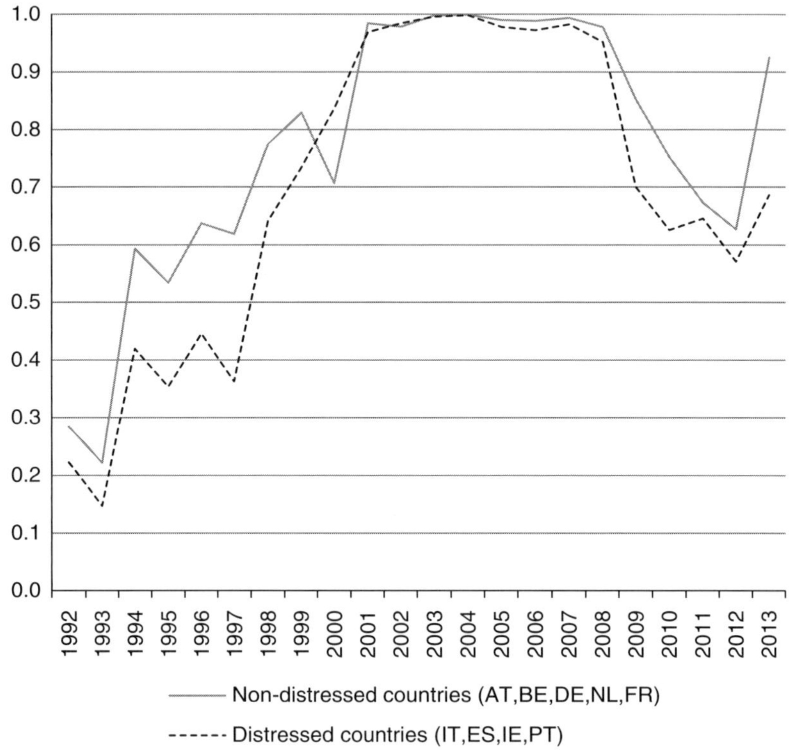

Figure 6.3 Government bond market integration based on common factor portfolios, 1992–2013
Source: ECB (2014)

Figure 6.4 shows, the dispersion of CDS spreads in the euro area for both commercial banks and telecommunications firms was close to zero before the financial crisis. But then it rose sharply. However, since 2012 the indicator has declined sharply, although it is not back to pre-crisis levels.

Equity market

If the equity markets in the euro area were integrated, prices should be mainly driven by common euro-area factors rather than country-specific ones. Assuming that equity returns in euro-area countries react to both a local and a global factor – proxied respectively by shocks in aggregate euro-area and US equity markets – it is possible to measure the proportion of the total domestic equity volatility that can be explained by local and global factors, respectively (see Equation 6.3). *Ceteris paribus*, a higher variance ratio associated with euro-area-wide changes is an indication of a more integrated euro-area equity market, signalling that national stock-market returns are increasingly driven

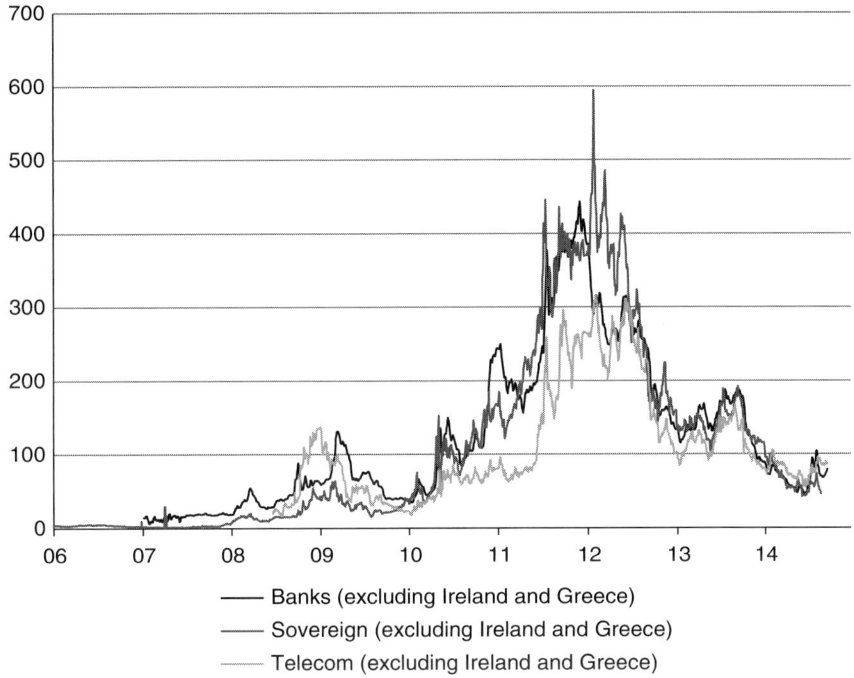

Figure 6.4 Dispersion in five-year CDS premia across the euro area, 2006–2014 (daily data; basis points)
Source: ECB (2014)

by common news. Figure 6.5 shows that between 2004 and 2012 only 17 per cent of euro-area local equity market volatility could be attributed to US volatility, while this reached 25 per cent in the period from 2012 to 2014 after the euro crisis.

Also quantity-based measures of euro-area equity market integration indicate a rising degree of integration in the equity markets (see Figure 6.6). By 2012 more than 40 per cent of the equity holdings of euro-area residents were issued in other euro-area countries (as a share of their total holdings of shares), whereas the share of euro-area equity assets held outside the euro area remained at a much lower level and increased only slightly.

6.4 The consequences of financial integration

According to Baele *et al.* (2004), financial integration has three benefits: more opportunities for risk sharing and diversification, better allocation of capital,

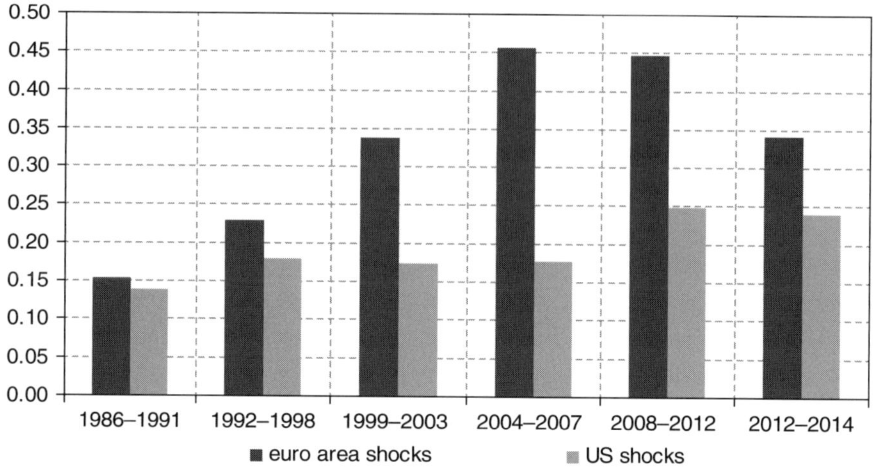

Figure 6.5 Proportion of variance in local equity returns explained by euro-area and US shocks, 1986–2013
Source: ECB (2014)

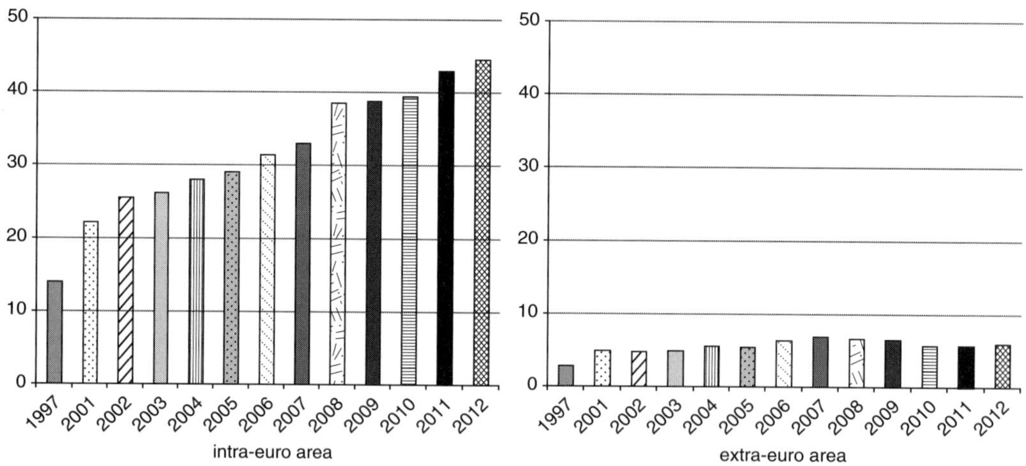

Figure 6.6 Cross-border holdings of equity issued by euro-area residents (share), 1997–2012
Source: ECB

and the potential for higher growth. Financial integration may also have implications for financial stability and the structure of the EU financial system. These consequences of financial integration will be discussed in turn.

Financial integration will provide additional possibilities to diversify portfolios and share idiosyncratic risk across regions. When agents in an area fully share risk, the consumption of agents in one region co-moves with that of agents located in other regions of that area, while consumption does not co-move with region-specific shocks. There is some evidence suggesting that in the euro area consumption in the various countries is still affected by country-specific shocks. For instance, Adjaouté and Danthine (2003) find that consumption growth rates in the euro area are less correlated than are GDP growth rates, suggesting that risk-sharing opportunities are far from fully exploited. Likewise, Adam *et al.* (2002) reject the hypothesis that consumption growth rates are unaffected by idiosyncratic changes in GDP growth rates.

Greater financial integration may also allow a better allocation of capital. Due to the elimination of barriers to trading, clearing, and settlement platforms, firms will be able to choose the most efficient trading, clearing, and/or settlement platforms. In addition, investors can invest their funds wherever they believe these funds will be allocated to the most productive uses (Baele *et al.*, 2004).

Financial integration may also affect economic growth, due to improved capital allocation and its contribution to financial development. As discussed in Chapter 1, recent studies show that financial development is associated with higher economic growth. Why would integration spur financial development?

Integration will stimulate local financial markets and foster internal competition, as well as open these markets to competitive pressure from foreign intermediaries. Guiso *et al.* (2004) argue that financial integration should increase the supply of funds in the less financially developed countries of the integrating area. This may occur for two reasons. First, integration facilitates the entry of more efficient intermediaries to firms in backward areas. Second, integration enables these firms to access more distant financial markets. In both cases, firms in less financially developed countries will face easier and cheaper access to external finance and this should spur capital accumulation and economic growth. Another reason why financial integration may affect financial development runs via improved regulation (Guiso *et al.*, 2004). A 'level playing field' in regulation is an essential prerequisite for an integrated market, and this convergence in regulatory standards is likely to result in an improvement in the regulatory standards of less developed financial markets. All of this will contribute to further financial development, which in turn may affect economic growth. Therefore, financial integration can have a 'growth dividend' in Europe (see also Box 6.1).

Guiso *et al.* (2004) provide an estimate of this growth dividend, based on the empirical relationship between financial market development and growth in the manufacturing industry. These authors examine a scenario where EU countries raise their regulatory standards to the highest current EU standard.

Box 6.1 Financial integration and economic growth[2]

Theoretically, the economic growth effects of international financial integration are ambiguous. On the one hand, integration facilitates risk sharing and thereby enhances production specialisation, capital allocation, and economic growth. It also eases the flow of capital to capital-scarce countries with positive output effects. Finally, financial integration may enhance the functioning of domestic financial systems, through the intensification of competition and the importation of financial services, with positive growth effects. On the other hand, in the presence of pre-existing distortions, integration can actually retard growth. For instance, in countries with weak institutions – like weak financial and legal systems – integration may induce capital outflows from capital-scarce countries to capital-abundant countries with better institutions. This line of reasoning suggests that financial integration will promote growth only in countries with sound institutions.

Empirical research on the impact of integration on growth is complicated by the difficulty in measuring integration across a wide array of countries that may impose a complex array of price and quantity controls on a broad assortment of financial transactions. Researchers have used (1) proxies for government restrictions on capital flows, (2) measures of actual international capital flows, or (3) the accumulated stock of foreign assets and/or liabilities.

The IMF's restriction measure is the most commonly used proxy of government restrictions on international financial transactions. It classifies countries on an annual basis by the presence or absence of restrictions, i.e. it is a dummy variable. The advantage of this variable is that it proxies directly for government impediments. Its disadvantage stems from the difficulty in accurately gauging the magnitude and effectiveness of government restrictions (Edison *et al.*, 2002).

Measures of actual international capital flows are also employed to proxy for international financial openness. These measures are based on the assumption that more capital flows indicate more integration. The advantage of these measures is that they are widely available and they are not subjective measures of capital restrictions, but a disadvantage is that many factors influence capital flows, including economic growth (Edison *et al.*, 2002).

Lane and Milesi-Ferretti (2001) have computed the accumulated stock of foreign assets and liabilities for an extensive sample of countries. These stock measures are less sensitive to short-run fluctuations in capital flows associated with factors that are unrelated to integration.

Empirical evidence yields conflicting conclusions about the growth effects of financial integration. While, for instance, Quinn (1997) finds that his measure of capital account openness is positively linked with growth, others report that this relationship is not robust (see Edison *et al.*, 2002 for a more detailed review). Edison *et al.* (2002) examine the growth impact of international financial integration, which they define as

Box 6.1 (cont.)

the degree to which an economy does not restrict cross-border transactions, using new data and new econometric techniques. The authors want not only to investigate the impact of international financial integration on economic growth but also to assess whether this relationship depends on the level of economic development, financial development, legal system development, government corruption, and macroeconomic policies. They use a wide array of measures of international financial integration for 57 countries, including (variants of) the IMF-restriction measure, various measures of capital flows (FDI, portfolio, and total capital flows), and the accumulated stock of liabilities (as a share of GDP) and the accumulated stock of liabilities and assets (as a share of GDP). Interestingly, the authors find that international financial integration does not accelerate economic growth even when controlling for particular economic, financial, institutional, and policy characteristics. However, Abiad *et al.* (2007) present research on the impact of financial integration in the NMS that comes to more optimistic conclusions. The authors find that financial integration raises growth in the new EU Member States and thus contributes to speeding up the convergence process.

They estimate that the effect of achieving full financial integration on the growth of European manufacturing industry is around 0.7 percentage points per year. As EU manufacturing accounts for about one-fourth of EU total value added, this estimate translates into 0.2 percentage points of GDP growth. This overall growth effect results from markedly different country and sector effects, reflecting the heterogeneity of the EU in terms of sector composition and level of financial development. Especially smaller businesses are the main beneficiaries of integration as they get access to a larger and more developed financial market than that within their national borders. There is also some evidence that financial integration has benefited the new EU Member States.

Financial integration may also have an impact on financial stability, although its direction is not clear. On the one hand, a larger and more diversified financial system will be better able to absorb economic shocks than financial systems in individual countries. The process of financial market integration facilitates consumption-smoothing and risk-sharing opportunities. Integration allows households to hold more diversified equity portfolios and, in particular, to diversify the portion of risk that arises from country-specific shocks. Furthermore, integration spurs the efficiency of financial intermediaries and markets in countries where the financial system is more backward and more heavily regulated, fostering the growth of domestic financial markets and the entry of foreign banks, and improving access to credit for households. As a result, country-specific shocks have a smaller effect on consumption when international financial markets are integrated, since they can be diversified away by borrowing abroad or holding foreign assets. At the same time, easier access to credit helps domestic borrowers to buffer specific shocks to their incomes (Jappelli and Pistaferri, 2011).

On the other hand, financial integration may also increase the risk of cross-border contagion as the recent crises have shown (ECB, 2011). Economic shocks will spread more easily and rapidly in an integrated financial system.

Financial integration may also affect the structure of the financial system, which in turn may have implications for financial stability. Although financial integration will bring about an improvement in the supply of finance in the less financially developed markets and an increase in the size of local financial markets, financial integration does not imply that the financial structures of the countries concerned will converge. As pointed out by Guiso *et al.* (2004), it is possible that the most financially developed countries will share the services provided by their financial system with the other integrating countries. The economies of scale and scope may fuel the expansion of the established intermediaries and markets of the more developed markets. For instance, banks of more developed countries may provide cross-border loans to the firms of less advanced countries, so that the additional provision of credit will not show up in the private domestic credit of the latter countries. Likewise, firms of less financially developed countries can decide to get their shares listed on foreign stock exchanges. Pagano *et al.* (2001) identify a variety of reasons for doing so: overcoming equity rationing in the domestic market, reducing their cost of capital by accessing a more liquid market, and signalling their quality by accepting the scrutiny of more informed investors or the rules of a better corporate governance system. Cross-border bank lending and listing at foreign stock exchanges implies that quantitative indicators of the financial structure remain different.

This discussion implies that the size of the financial market of a given country may no longer be a good indicator of its degree of financial development (Guiso *et al.*, 2004). Distance and geographical segmentation become less important in financially integrated markets. In fact, in a fully integrated market, only the total size of the financial market of the integrating area matters as firms of a given country may have equal access to financial services of all other countries even if their domestic financial sector (scaled by GDP) differs from that in other countries. So differences in the size of local financial markets cannot be exploited to identify the link between financial development and economic growth if countries are perfectly financially integrated (Guiso *et al.*, 2004).

6.5 Conclusions

This chapter defines financial integration as a situation without frictions that discriminate between economic agents in their access to – and their investment of – capital on the basis of their country. Market forces are an important driver of financial integration. Competition can initiate the elimination of segmentation between national markets, resulting in lower prices. Collective action by trade associations is also driving integration. The setting of reference rates, such as the overnight rate (EONIA) and the interbank rate (EURIBOR), is an example of collective action. Finally, public authorities can foster integration. The establishment of an integrated large-value payment system (TARGET) by the ECB was crucial to create a single money market. Likewise, the European Commission's Financial Services Action Plan contributed to completing the internal market for financial services.

There are different categories of financial integration measures. Price-based measures are widely used to identify differences in returns caused by the geographic origin of the assets. While price-based indicators are the most direct measure of financial integration, they can be applied only to relatively homogeneous assets. Financial assets tend to differ in credit risk (corporate bonds) or business risk (equities). News-based measures assume that in an integrated market, only common or global news will move prices. Local news has little impact on a geographically diversified portfolio. Quantity-based measures examine cross-border activities. More cross-border business is an indicator of increased integration.

Examining the integration of Europe's financial markets, it is found that the money market and the government bond market were fully integrated before the financial crisis. The corporate bond market also appeared to be quite well integrated. Equity market integration is more difficult to assess. The empirical evidence suggests a rising degree of integration of equity markets. Due to the financial crisis and the euro crisis, the integration of financial markets seems to have reached a standstill and has in some cases, such as money and sovereign bond markets, been reversed. More recently, indicators suggest an improvement but in most market segments a relatively high degree of fragmentation still remains at the time of writing. In many market segments, financial integration has not yet returned to pre-crisis levels.

Finally, financial integration enables better risk sharing and better allocation of capital. The result is a more efficient and competitive financial system that promotes economic growth. There is also a downside to financial integration. While a well-diversified financial system can better absorb economic shocks, these shocks can also spread more easily in an integrated financial system. It is therefore important that financial stability policies stay in tune with advances in financial integration (see Chapter 13).

Notes

1. In analysing other segments of the bond market, like the corporate bond market, one cannot directly analyse yield differentials relative to a benchmark to assess integration. Corporate bonds are generally not homogeneous enough to allow easy comparison as they differ in their cash-flow structure, liquidity, sector, and, most importantly, credit rating. See Baele *et al.* (2004, 2008) for various price-based measures to assess the integration of the corporate bond market.
2. This box heavily draws on Edison *et al.* (2002).

Suggested Reading

Baele, L., A. Ferrando, P. Hördahl, E. Krylova, and C. Monnet (2008), Measuring European Financial Integration, in: X. Freixas, P. Hartmann, and C. Mayer (eds.), *Handbook of European Financial Markets and Institutions*, Oxford University Press, 165–194.

Enoch, C., L. Everaert, T. Tressel, and J. Zhou (eds.) (2014), *From Fragmentation to Financial Integration in Europe*, IMF, Washington.

Guiso, L., T. Jappelli, M. Padula, and M. Pagano (2004), Financial Market Integration and Economic Growth in the EU, *Economic Policy*, 524–577.

References

Abiad, A., D. Leigh and A. Mody (2007), International Finance and Income Convergence: Europe is Different, IMF Working Paper 07/64.

Adam, K., T. Jappelli, A. M. Menichini, M. Padula, and M. Pagano (2002), Analyse, Compare, and Apply Alternative Indicators and Monitoring Methodologies to Measure the Evolution of Capital Market Integration in the European Union, Report to the European Commission, EC, Brussels.

Adjaouté, K. and J.-P. Danthine (2003), European Financial Integration and Equity Returns: A Theory-Based Assessment, in: V. Gaspar *et al.* (eds.), *The Transformation of the European Financial System*, ECB, Frankfurt.

Baele, L., A. Ferrando, P. Hördahl, E. Krylova, and C. Monnet (2004), Measuring Financial Integration in the Euro Area, ECB Occasional Paper 14.

(2008), Measuring European Financial Integration, in: X. Freixas, P. Hartmann, and C. Mayer (eds.), *Handbook of European Financial Markets and Institutions*, Oxford University Press, 165–194.

Edison, H. J., R. Levine, L. Ricci, and T. Sløk (2002), International Financial Integration and Economic Growth, *Journal of International Money and Finance*, **21**(6), 749–776.

European Central Bank (2003), The Integration of Europe's Financial Markets, *Monthly Bulletin*, October, 53–56.

(2011), *Financial Integration in Europe*, ECB, Frankfurt.

(2014), *Financial Integration in Europe*, ECB, Frankfurt.

European Commission (2006), Commission Staff Working Document Addressed to the European Parliament and to the Council on the Impact of Regulation (EC) No. 2560/2001 on Bank Charges for National Payments, EC, Brussels.

(2014), *European Financial Stability and Integration*, EC, Brussels.

Guiso, L., T. Jappelli, M. Padula, and M. Pagano (2004), Financial Market Integration and Economic Growth in the EU, *Economic Policy*, 524–577.

Hardouvelis, G. A., D. Malliaropulos, and R. Priestley (2006), EMU and European Stock Market Integration, *Journal of Business*, **79**(1), 365–392.

Jappelli, T. and L. Pistaferri (2011), Financial Integration and Consumption Smoothing, *The Economic Journal*, **121**, 678–706.

Lane, P. R. and G. M. Milesi-Ferretti (2001), The External Wealth of Nations: Measures of Foreign Assets and Liabilities in Industrial and Developing Countries, *Journal of International Economics*, **55**, 263–294.

Pagano, M., O. Randl, A. Roëll, and J. Zechne (2001). What Makes Stock Exchanges Succeed? Evidence from Cross-Listing Decisions, *European Economic Review*, **45**, 770–782.

Pukthuanthong, K. and R. Roll (2009), Global Market Integration: An Alternative Measure and its Application, *Journal of Financial Economics*, **94**(2), 214–232.

Quinn, D. (1997), The Correlates of Change in International Financial Regulation, *American Political Science Review*, **91**, 531–551.

Wolswijk, G. and J. de Haan (2005), Government Debt Management in the Euro Area: Recent Theoretical Developments and Changes in Practices, ECB Occasional Paper 25.

CHAPTER

7

Financial Infrastructures

OVERVIEW

This chapter discusses the payment and post-trading (i.e. securities clearing and settlement) systems in the EU. Over the past decade, the volume and value of transactions that are processed via these systems have grown tremendously. Stable and efficient payment and post-trading systems have become of great importance for the operation of financial markets and the economy in general. Up to now, these infrastructures have been very fragmented and competition is limited.

This chapter starts by examining the different elements of payment and post-trading systems. A distinction is made between retail and wholesale payment systems. Given the growing importance of card-based retail payment systems, the main focus will be on the set-up of the existing card schemes. Furthermore, the different steps of the post-trading process, which arranges the transfer of ownership and the payment between buyers and sellers in security markets, will be discussed. Finally, the role of central banks in the regulation and oversight of payment and settlement systems will be clarified.

The second part of the chapter gives an overview of the economic features of payment and securities market infrastructures. These infrastructures are characterised by economies of scale and scope, and network externalities. Understanding these characteristics should enable the reader to better comprehend (future) developments within the EU payment and security market infrastructures.

The third part of this chapter describes the current situation in the payment and post-trading industry and recent initiatives to promote further integration, and addresses weaknesses exposed by the financial crisis.

LEARNING OBJECTIVES

After you have studied this chapter, you should be able to:

- define what a payment system is
- explain the difference between wholesale and retail payment systems
- describe the various steps of the post-trading process
- understand the economic characteristics of payment and securities market infrastructures, and explain how these characteristics influence the EU market structure
- assess the extent to which the different elements of the EU financial infrastructure are integrated
- understand the growing importance of central counterparties (CCPs) and the related concentration risk.

7.1 Payment systems and post-trading services

Payment systems

A *payment* is a transfer of money between economic actors. This transfer can take place, for example, between a consumer and a merchant to pay for delivered goods or services using cash and non-cash money. Cash payments require no systems for settlement between economic actors. Settlement is immediately final when bank notes or coins are handed over. This is different for non-cash payments, such as a transfer from a bank account. In order to settle a transaction, one bank account has to be debited and another has to be credited. Different systems are in place to make sure that the non-cash transfer is completed in a safe and efficient manner. If the transaction takes place between accounts held at the same bank, the bank's internal administrative system can settle the transaction. In general, however, economic agents hold accounts at different banks and therefore non-cash payments require cooperation between banks. A *payment system* can be defined as a combination of technical, legal, and commercial instruments, rules, and procedures that ensure the transfer of money between banks. A distinction can be made between (1) retail payment systems and (2) wholesale payment systems.

Retail payment systems

Retail payment systems are used for the transaction, clearing, and settlement of relatively low-value and non-time-critical payments initiated through payment instruments such as cheques, credit transfers, direct debits, and payment cards (BIS, 2001). Retail payments are generally made in large numbers (*mass payments*) by many economic actors and typically relate to the purchase of goods and services in both the consumer and business sectors (BIS, 2002a). Moreover, retail payments are made using a wide range of payment instruments and in varied contexts. Generally, private sector systems are used for the transaction process and the clearing of retail payments.

Each retail payment system consists of:

- payment instruments used to initiate and direct the transfer of money between the accounts of the payer and the payee (see Box 7.1 for an overview of the main payment instruments available);
- payment infrastructures for transacting and clearing payment instruments, processing and communicating payment information, and transferring payment information between the paying and receiving institutions;
- financial institutions that provide payment accounts, instruments, and services to consumers, and organisations that operate payment transaction, clearing, and settlement service networks for those financial institutions;
- market arrangements (or payment schemes) such as conventions, regulations, and contracts for producing, pricing, delivering, and acquiring the various payment instruments and services in order to maintain a minimum level of efficiency and security between all payment service providers in a market. A *payment scheme* is the set of interbank rules, standards, and practices for the provision or operation of specific payment instruments. In a more practical sense, the scheme defines the characteristics of a specific payment instrument, e.g. the authorisation procedures, the fee structure, and the maximum time frame within which a payment is processed, thereby laying down the rules with which all participating payment service providers have to comply. These rules ensure predictability, security, and efficiency in the provision of the given payment instrument;
- laws, standards, rules, and procedures set by legislators, courts, and regulators that define and govern the mechanics of the payment process and the conduct of payment service markets in order to make payment service providers meet public policy goals (BIS, 2006).

A payment can start with a transaction initiated by the payer (*push transaction*) or initiated by the payee (*pull transaction*) and ends at the moment when the payee has received the agreed amount of money in good order. Depending on the actual payment instrument and the organisation of the banking sector, the payment instruction travels through one or more of the following: from an entry bank (paying/receiving bank or branch) to a settlement bank (bank head office or correspondent bank) and then to a clearinghouse or processing centre (see Figure 7.1). The latter is a central processing mechanism through which financial institutions agree to exchange payment instructions. Settlement takes place at a designated time based on the rules and procedures of the clearinghouse (see also the next section on wholesale payment systems). In most cases the actual settlement of the payment takes place at the central bank (or in some cases a private entity) where the respective settlement banks have their accounts. The distribution of the payment to the payee completes the payment process. *Payment finality*, i.e. the guarantee of a payment to the payee, is critical in this respect.

Box 7.1 Core payment instruments

Credit transfers: a payment initiated by the payer. The latter sends a payment instruction to his/her bank. The bank debits the payer's account and advises the receiver's bank to credit the beneficiary's account. This can happen through different channels and via intermediaries.

Direct debit: a payment initiated by the creditor, who sends the instructions to collect money via his/her bank or via a central processing entity (automated clearinghouse) to the debtor's bank(s). Direct debits are often used for recurring payments, like those for utilities. They require a pre-authorisation ('mandate') by the payer. Direct debits are also used for one-off payments in which case the payer authorises an individual payment.

Payment card: three main types of card payment instruments can be distinguished: (1) *debit cards*, which allow the cardholder to charge purchases directly and individually to an account; (2) *credit cards*, which allow purchases within a certain credit limit. The balance is settled in full or partly by the end of a specified period. In the latter case the remaining balance is taken as extended credit on which the cardholder must pay interest; and (3) *stored value cards* (or prepaid cards) which allow users to pay merchants with funds transferred in advance to a prepaid account.

Cash: in the euro area, only the ECB has the right to authorise the issue of banknotes. The national central banks in the euro area bring bank notes into circulation by providing them to the banking sector. Banknotes are mainly distributed to the public via ATMs (automated teller machines).

Cheque: a written order from one party (the drawer) to another (the drawee; normally a credit institution) requiring the drawee to pay a specific sum on demand of the drawer or to a third party specified by the drawer.

Source: ECB

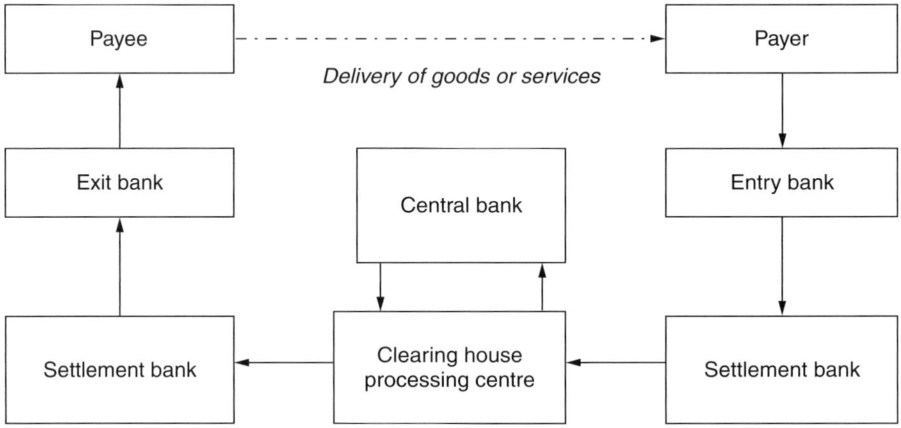

Figure 7.1 The process of initiating and receiving payments (push transaction)
Source: Khiaonarong (2003)

The efficiency of retail payment systems has been enhanced over time by the transition from:

- bank branches towards ATMs in cash distribution;
- paper-based payments to electronic payment systems;
- manual processing of payments to automated end-to-end processing. The latter is also referred to as straight-through processing (STP).

Strengthening the efficiency of these systems is essential as the costs of retail payments to society are substantial. The ECB (2012) has examined the social and private costs of different payment instruments within 13 EU countries,[1] showing that the costs to society of providing retail payment services are on average nearly 1 per cent of GDP. Table 7.1 summarises the average social costs per payment instrument. Cash payments have the lowest social costs of €0.42, followed by debit cards with €0.70 per transaction. In other words, on average cash transactions seem to be the cheapest among all payment instruments. This does not necessarily mean that cash is the most cost-effective payment instrument, because low unit costs may be due to the high volume of cash payments. In the Netherlands, for example, debit card payments have become less costly than cash payments (Jonker, 2013). In 2012 an average cash payment there cost €0.44, whereas an average debit card payment cost €0.30. Between 2002 and 2012, the number of debit card payments more than doubled to 2.5 billion, while cash usage declined to 3.75 billion payments. As a result of the changing payment behaviour of the Dutch, the total costs of cash and debit card payments to society declined by

Table 7.1 Unit social costs and social costs per euro of sales of retail payment instruments (in €, 2009 figures)

Measure	Cash	Cheque	Cards	Debit cards	Credit cards	Direct debits	Credit transfers
			Unit social costs				
Minimum	0.13	2.39	0.22	0.18	0.48	0.14	0.30
Median	0.39	3.46	0.63	0.45	1.97	1.14	1.01
Maximum	0.78	6.10	8.07	3.40	8.65	2.49	12.07
Average	0.41	3.86	1.34	0.81	2.79	1.07	2.22
Weighted average	0.42	3.55	0.99	0.70	2.39	1.27	1.92
			Social costs per €1 of sale				
Minimum	0.013	0.000	0.008	0.008	0.018	0.002	0.000
Median	0.020	0.002	0.016	0.012	0.030	0.004	0.002
Maximum	0.034	0.012	0.081	0.035	0.137	0.011	0.006
Average	0.023	0.004	0.024	0.017	0.052	0.005	0.002
Weighted average	0.023	0.002	0.017	0.014	0.034	0.004	0.002

Source: ECB (2012). Countries included in the sample are Denmark, Estonia, Finland, Greece, Hungary, Ireland, Italy, Latvia, Netherlands, Portugal, Romania, Spain, and Sweden.

10 per cent from over €2.6 billion in 2002 to less than €2.4 billion in 2012. Relative to GDP, the social costs dropped from 0.57 per cent to 0.40 per cent of GDP.

The second part of Table 7.1 provides the results of the social costs per euro of sales (total social costs divided by total sales). It shows that cheques, credit transfers, and direct debits score lowest. This is not surprising, as these payment instruments are mostly used for highly denominated transaction values.

Table 7.2 shows the number of transactions per payment instrument in 13 EU countries as a percentage of the total market. In general, the usage of retail payment instruments differs quite substantially across countries. For example, a country's proportion of cash usage can range from a relatively low 27 per cent (Sweden) up to 95 per cent (Greece and Romania). It is also interesting to see that the usage and adoption of card payments is very asymmetric across European countries, with a maximum of 44 per cent (Denmark) and a minimum of 1.5 per cent (Romania). On average, cash is still the most frequently used retail payment instrument.

With nearly 40 billion payments in 2012, cards have become the most widely used cashless payment instrument in the European Union (ECB, 2014a). As illustrated in Figure 7.2, in the period from 2000

Table 7.2 Market share of retail payment instruments in terms of volume (in %, 2009 figures)

Country	Cash	Cheque	Cards	Debit cards	Credit cards	Direct debits	Credit transfers	Other	Overall
Denmark	34.85	0.43	44.03	41.16	2.87	7.90	12.79	0.00	100.00
Estonia	48.88	0.00	29.29	26.06	3.23	3.52	18.31	0.00	100.00
Finland	38.82	0.02	31.30	29.07	2.23	2.92	26.88	0.05	100.00
Greece	94.99	0.70	2.28	0.26	2.02	0.39	1.51	0.13	100.00
Hungary	76.10	n.a.	5.20	4.48	0.72	1.92	16.40	0.38	100.00
Ireland	66.39	4.94	15.70	10.39	5.31	5.39	7.57	0.00	100.00
Italy	82.66	1.47	6.45	3.95	2.49	2.52	5.28	1.62	100.00
Latvia	77.52	0.00	9.85	7.77	2.08	0.46	11.97	0.47	100.00
Netherlands	47.73	n.a.	21.56	20.62	0.93	13.26	15.60	1.85	100.00
Portugal	60.65	3.51	25.96	22.02	3.94	5.40	4.40	0.07	100.00
Romania	94.88	0.16	1.54	1.25	0.29	0.06	3.35	0.00	100.00
Spain	77.86	0.45	8.45	3.79	4.66	9.69	3.22	0.33	100.00
Sweden	26.64	0.02	39.63	34.45	5.18	6.21	23.40	4.10	100.00
Weighted average	*69.12*	*0.95*	*14.34*	*11.34*	*3.00*	*5.99*	*8.49*	*1.11*	*100.00*
EU27 weighted average	*64.57*	*2.50*	*13.51*	*11.61*	*1.90*	*8.74*	*9.63*	*1.06*	*100.00*

Source: ECB (2012)

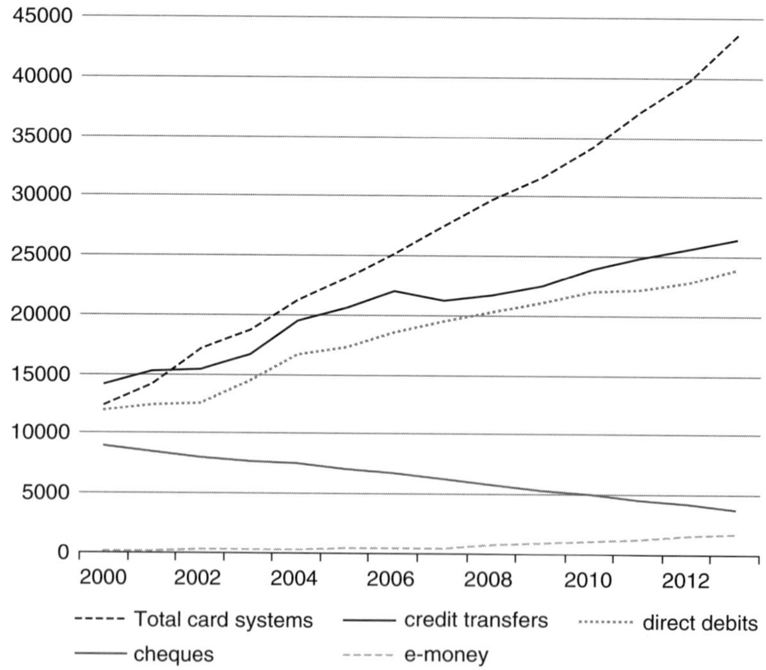

Figure 7.2 Use of payment instruments in the EU, 2000–2012 (transactions in € millions)
Source: ECB (2014a)

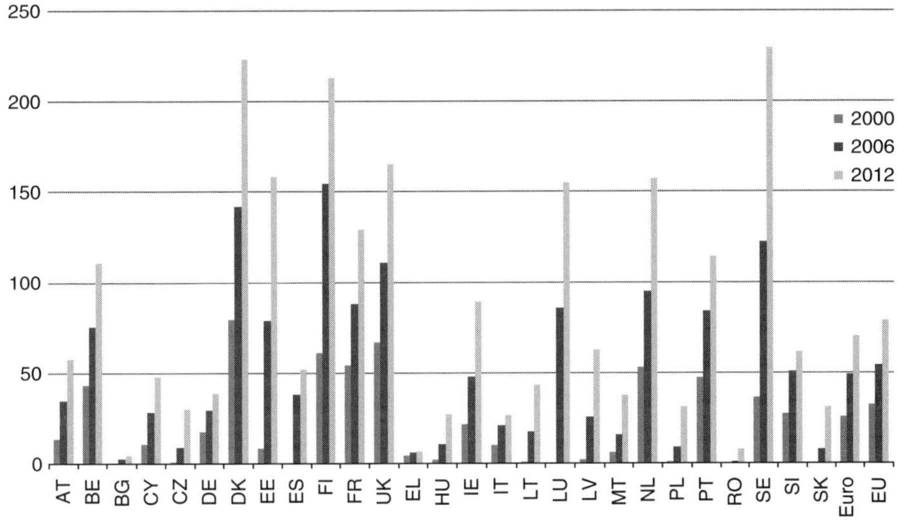

Figure 7.3 Number of card payments per inhabitant and per year, 2000–2012
Source: ECB (2014a)

to 2012, card payments considerably outperformed direct debits and credit transfers with a growth rate of more than 10 per cent (compared to approximately 5 per cent for credit transfers and/or direct debits). As shown in Table 7.2, cash still dominates in terms of the number of payments at the physical point of sale in almost all countries of the EU. However, cards, notably debit cards, have been gaining ground and are becoming more and more important for day-to-day transactions.

There are large variations with respect to card usage across EU Member States (ECB, 2014a). The number of payments made per year and per inhabitant ranged from 4.5 (Bulgaria) to 230.1 (Sweden), while the corresponding annual transaction values ranged between €189 (Bulgaria) and €12,004 (Luxembourg). Even within the euro area, a large discrepancy can be observed, with cards most frequently used in Finland, Estonia, Luxembourg, and the Netherlands. In Greece, Italy, Slovakia, and Germany card payments are least popular, with growth rates for the number of card payments per capita over the period of 12 years (2000–2012) being well below the euro-area average of 273 per cent over this period. Some of the highest growth rates in the use of card payments have been recorded in countries that have adopted the euro more recently.

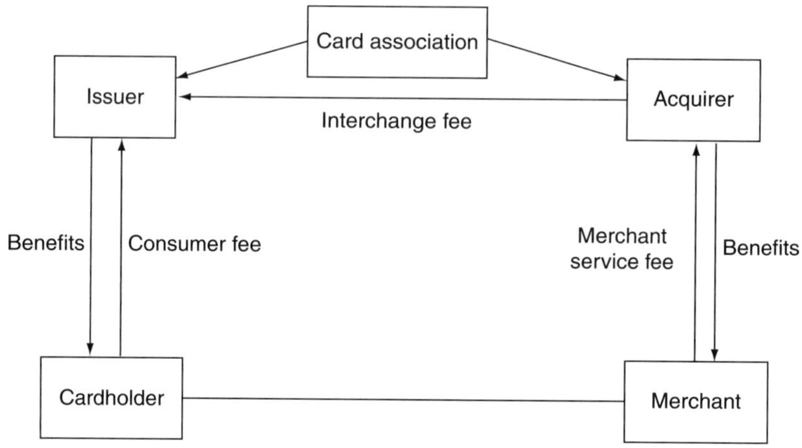

Figure 7.4 Four-party payment scheme
Source: Harper *et al.* (2006)

Card-based payment systems

Given the growing importance of card-based payment systems, this specific means of payment will be briefly explained. In principle, each debit or credit card payment involves the following four parties:

- the *cardholder*: the person who has received the payment card from the issuer and uses the card for payment of goods and services;
- the *issuer*: the payment service provider that issues the payment card to the cardholder;
- the *merchant*: the person accepting the card payment in return for goods or services;
- the *acquirer*: the payment service provider that provides payment services to the merchant.

Moreover, interbank payment arrangements are in place for executing funds transfers between the two intermediaries. There are different arrangements to organise the processing of a card payment. Figure 7.4 depicts a *four-party payment scheme* (cardholder – issuer – acquirer – merchant). Such a scheme (as used, for instance, by Visa and Mastercard) is often referred to as 'open', as the issuer and acquirer can be any financial institution. A payment scheme where issuing and acquiring is performed by the same payment service provider (as used, for instance, by Diners Club and American Express) is referred to as a *three-party scheme* (cardholder – payment service provider – merchant). This is shown in Figure 7.5. As in a three-party scheme the issuer

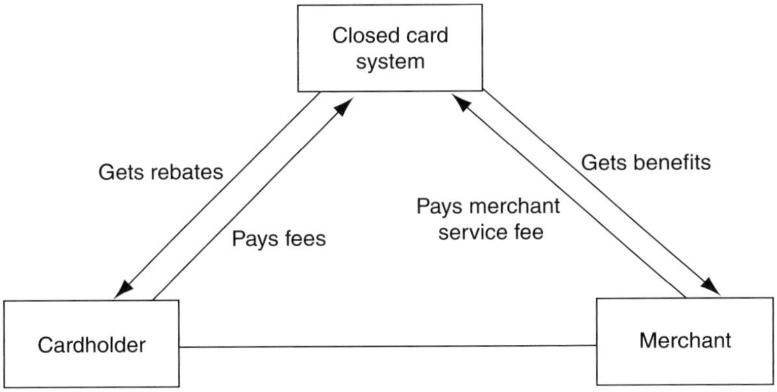

Figure 7.5 Three-party payment scheme
Source: Harper *et al.* (2006)

and acquirer are the same payment service provider, it is also referred to as a 'closed' system.

Card schemes operate under a rather controversial construction, which is also the subject of several regulatory and antitrust investigations, i.e. the interchange and merchant service fees. The *interchange fee* is a fee paid by an acquiring institution to an issuing institution for each payment card transaction at the point of sale of a merchant. The *merchant service fee* is the fee paid for each transaction by a merchant to an acquirer who processes the merchant's transaction through the network and obtains the funds from the cardholder's bank (European Commission, 2007). In a four-party card scheme, the merchant finally receives the amount of the transaction, minus the merchant fee.

The usage of interchange or merchant service fees may raise several concerns. First, these fees may be seen as a collective agreement between competitors that distorts competition in the market for payment cards. Second, the non-transparent pricing of card payments creates hardly any incentive to make use of more efficient payment instruments. Third, as merchants adjust their prices for goods and services for these fees, cross-subsidisation occurs, i.e. consumers who make use of other (more efficient) means of payment subsidise the use of expensive (credit) cards.

Wholesale payment systems

Through *wholesale payment systems* large-value and/or time-critical funds transfers are made between financial institutions within the system (for their own account or for their customers). Although no minimum value is set for these payments, the average value of payments passed through such systems is normally relatively high (BIS, 2001). For a long time, corresponding banking played an important role in the processing of large-value payments, notably foreign currency payments. A *correspondent banking payment* is a payment between two banks that is made through an intermediary, i.e. the correspondent bank. Since the introduction of the euro, there has been a significant decline in corresponding banking systems. Central infrastructure payments are, however, becoming more and more important. In *real-time gross settlement (RTGS) systems*, each payment is immediately settled on a gross basis. The fact that each payment is processed on an individual basis at the time it is received (rather than at a later stage) enhances the stability of the system. TARGET (Trans-European Automated Real-Time Gross Settlement Express Transfer System) is the most important central infrastructure payment system for real-time processing of cross-border transfers throughout the EU. It was built by linking together the different RTGS structures that existed at the national level and settles payments related to monetary policy operations, interbank and customer payments, and payments relating to the operations of all large-value net settlement systems and other financial market infrastructures handling the euro (such as securities settlement systems or central counterparties). TARGET was launched in 1999 to: (1) provide a safe and reliable mechanism for the settlement of euro payments, (2) increase the efficiency of cross-border payments in euros, and (3) serve the needs of the monetary policy of the ECB and to promote the integration of the euro money market. The full integration of the large-value payment systems has been instrumental in achieving this result.

In 2008, the Eurosystem, i.e. the ECB and the National Central Banks of the countries in the euro area, launched the latest version of TARGET, which is referred to as TARGET2. It offers a centralised Single Shared Platform (SSP) to process all payments, which is jointly operated by the Deutsche Bundesbank, the Banque de France, and the Banca d'Italia, on behalf of the entire Eurosystem. In 2013, TARGET2 processed 92.6 million payments, with a total value of €493 trillion. This translates into a daily average of 363,099 payments, with an average daily value of €1.9 billion. TARGET2 is the most important RTGS in the EU and one of the three largest wholesale payment systems in the world, alongside Fedwire in the United States and Continuous Linked Settlement (CLS), the international system for settling foreign exchange transactions (see Figure 7.6).

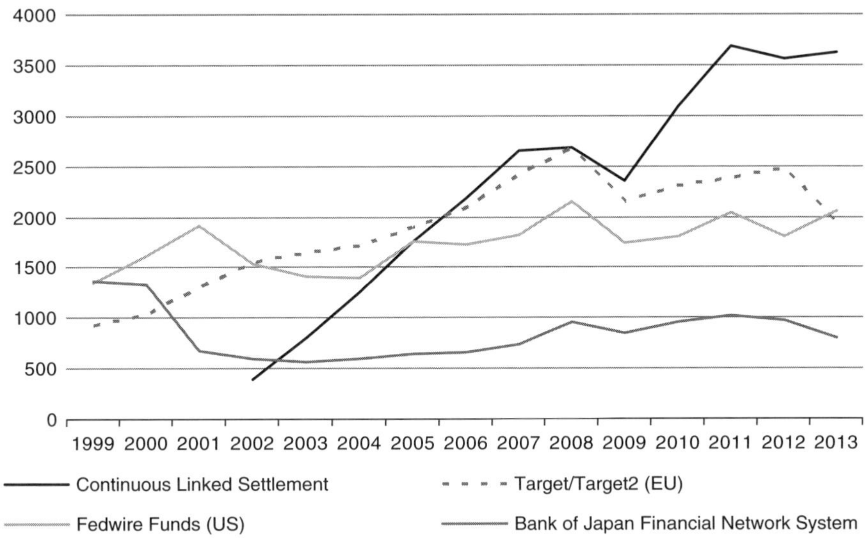

Figure 7.6 Major large-value payments systems in the world (average daily turnover in € billions)
Source: ECB (2014b)

The largest *net settlement system* in Europe is EURO1, a private multilateral, large-value payment system for euro payments established by more than 60 major European banks. This system processes credit transfers and direct debits throughout the day and balances are settled at close of business via a settlement account at the ECB.

Post-trading services

The smooth functioning of and confidence in securities markets depends, among other things, on the efficiency and reliability of their infrastructure. In particular, it is crucial that the transfer of ownership from the seller to the buyer in exchange for a payment takes place in a safe and efficient manner (Kazarian, 2006). In essence, the clearing and settlement or *post-trading process* provides for the transfer of ownership and payment between buyers and sellers in a security market.

The post-trading process begins when the actual securities trade has been executed. The subsequent securities settlement process encompasses a number of complementary steps and actions. Figure 7.7 shows that the post-trading process can be described in terms of four main activities (Giovannini Group, 2001):

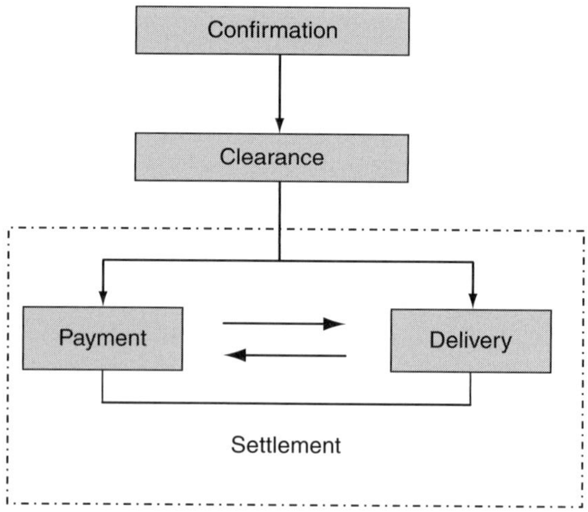

Figure 7.7 Clearing and settlement of a securities trade
Source: Giovannini Group (2001)

- confirmation of terms of the trade as agreed upon by the buyer and the seller;
- clearance, by which the respective obligations of the buyer and seller are established;
- delivery, requiring the transfer of the securities from the seller to the buyer;
- payment, requiring the transfer of funds from the buyer to the seller.

Figure 7.7 shows that the post-trading process starts with the confirmation of the terms of the securities transaction. This can be done either directly between the buyer and the seller ('over-the-counter' or OTC) or indirectly through the securities exchange or a clearing agent. In the end, the respective parties should clearly know what securities are bought or sold and at what price.

The next step is the clearing of the obligation of the counterparties resulting from the matching process. Clearance of a securities transaction establishes the respective obligations of the buyer and the seller and may be achieved on a gross (trade-for-trade) or a net basis (offsetting of mutual obligations). The latter reduces the number of actual transfers. Clearance services can be provided by a clearinghouse, a national central securities depository (CSD), or an international central securities depository (ICSD).[2] The latter two also hold securities and allow them to be processed by book entry (rather than by physical movement of the securities between buyers and sellers).

Securities markets can also make use of *central counterparties* (CCPs), which are entities that interpose themselves between the buyers and the sellers of securities, i.e. buyers and sellers interact indirectly via the CCP. These entities can also offer netting arrangements, which facilitate the management of securities and payment transfers.[3]

The subsequent step is the *settlement* process, which involves the delivery of the securities and the payment of funds between buyers and sellers. The payment is usually made via a banking or payment system, while the delivery of securities is typically carried out in a CSD or an ICSD. According to the BIS (1992), the largest financial risks in securities clearance and settlement occur during the settlement process, especially when no mechanism exists to ensure that delivery occurs if – and only if – payment occurs. Without such a mechanism counterparties are exposed to *principal risk*, i.e. the risk that the seller of a security delivers but does not receive payment or that the buyer of a security makes a payment but does not receive the securities. A securities transaction is settled once the securities are delivered to the buyer and the seller has received the payment. However, formal registration of the transfer of ownership by a CSD often is needed to assure settlement.

Role of the Eurosystem

The smooth functioning of payment and security settlement systems is crucial for:

- a sound currency, i.e. stable and efficient payment systems are an essential condition for maintaining trust in the value of money;
- the conduct of monetary policy, as these systems play an important role in monetary policy operations;
- the functioning of financial markets, i.e. in the absence of a stable and efficient payment infrastructure, financial markets would not be able to process the current volume and value of transactions;
- the maintenance of financial stability, i.e. problems in financial institutions can manifest themselves in payment or security settlement systems. Moreover, these systems can act as a channel for transmitting problems from one institution to another.

For all these reasons, central banks have an interest in the design and management of payment and security settlement systems. The Eurosystem has the statutory task of promoting the smooth operation of payment and settlement systems. It fulfils this task by:

- providing payment and securities settlement facilities: the Eurosystem runs a settlement system for large-value payments in euros (TARGET2) and thereby functions as banker to the banks. The latter means that banks hold funds on their account at the central bank, and payments between banks are made by debiting and crediting central bank accounts. Moreover, the Eurosystem is working on Target2-Securities (T2S), one of the largest infrastructure projects launched in Europe thus far. T2S is scheduled to start in June 2015 and will improve the post-trading infrastructure in Europe by providing a single platform for securities settlement in central bank money. As such, T2S will substantially contribute to financial integration in Europe;
- overseeing the euro payment and settlement systems: the Eurosystem applies internationally agreed standards to ensure the soundness and efficiency of systems handling euro transactions. It also assesses the continuous compliance of euro payment and settlement systems with these standards;
- overseeing compliance with the standards for securities clearing and settlement systems;
- ensuring an integrated regulatory and oversight framework for securities settlement systems;
- acting as a catalyst for change: the Eurosystem promotes efficiency in payment systems and securities markets by encouraging the removal of barriers towards integration.

7.2 Economic features of payment and securities market infrastructures

Payment and securities market infrastructures are characterised by economies of scale and scope and network externalities.

Economies of scale arise when the cost per unit falls as output increases. This effect occurs when it is possible to spread fixed costs over a higher output. Schmiedel and Schönenberg (2005) argue that economies of scale are usually a result of the need for service providers to create a 'critical mass' of customers in order to reap the benefit of sizeable investments in information technology and communication networks. If securities infrastructure providers are successful in attracting a significant number of issuers and participants, these set-up costs may be spread over a wider number of transactions. Similarly, there are strong economies of scale in

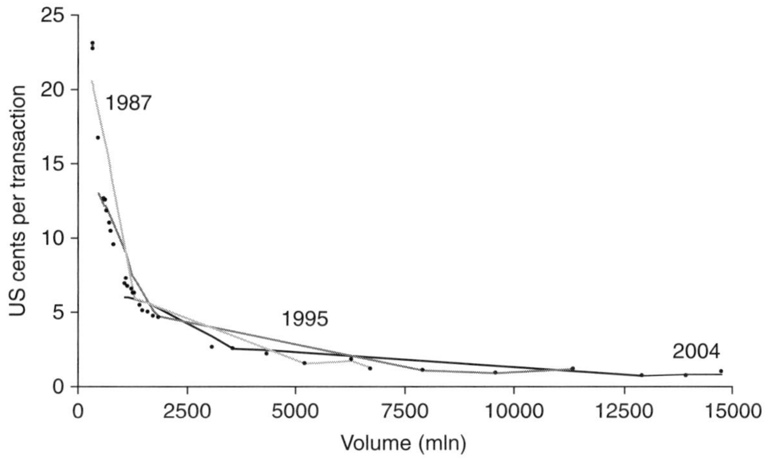

Figure 7.8 Economies of scale in the payment market
Source: Bolt (2007)

the production of payment services. In a European cross-country study, Humphrey *et al.* (2003) find that costs increase by 2 per cent when volumes rise by 10 per cent. Bolt and Humphrey (2007) estimate payment scale economies using a panel of payment and banking data for 11 European countries over 18 years. Their results show that doubling of payment volume would increase total costs by only 27 per cent. Figure 7.8 shows how unit payment costs vary with the total number of payment transactions.[4] The figure clearly shows that the costs of payments decline as the volume of payments that are processed increases.

Economies of scope refer to the reduction of the per-unit costs resulting from the production of a wider variety of goods and services (i.e. when it is cheaper to produce good A and good B together rather than separately). So, integrated financial infrastructures can develop new products and services at a lower unit cost. A precondition for economies of scope is that it is possible to share (certain) input factors for the production of different goods and services.

Economies of scope for CSDs and CCPs can stem from extending the number of financial instruments or trading platforms for which they provide services. Moreover, there is a strong complementary relationship between the various components of securities settlement (Kazarian, 2006). This entails that economies of scope can be obtained by integration along the value chain of a securities transaction, i.e. by combining trading, clearing, and settlement into one firm. Such a supplier can offer its services at lower cost than different suppliers providing these services separately. A good example of such a vertically integrated entity (or 'silo') is Deutsche Börse. Serifsoy and Weiβ (2007) argue that one of the adverse effects of vertical integration is the leverage of a (natural) monopoly from one stage of the value chain upstream or downstream to other stages. An integrated supplier may cross-subsidise its trading costs – and thereby attract customers from other platforms – through its monopoly profits on the clearing and settlement stage, or vice versa. It may also foreclose the market for competitors as users can be forced to 'buy' another service from the same institution.

As for payment systems, economies of scope may exist when the system handles more than one type of payment instrument or service. This allows the operator of the system to spread out the fixed cost of the system over a wider range of payment instruments.

Generally, the demand for payment services is largely inelastic, as payments in themselves do not generate value. A payment is made because of the purchase of a good or a service or to pay off a debt or a financial obligation. Payment services are therefore a convenience good rather than a primary good. However, payment service users may be (very) sensitive to relative payment prices (i.e. price differences between individual payment instruments).

Network externalities are another important economic feature of market infrastructures. A *network* can be defined as a large system consisting of many similar (or complementary) parts that are connected to allow movement or communication between the parts or between the parts and a centre. The addition of a new participant in a network can increase the value of the network for all participants. This means that the value of the services and products offered to the participants depends on the number of other participants purchasing the same services and products (*network externalities*). As an example, consider a simple network consisting of a central junction S and side-branches A, B, C, and D, as shown in Figure 7.9 (based on Economides, 1993). The goods in this network are composite goods, each comprising two complementary components – for example, ASB is comprised of the complements AS and SB. Imagine that the network would consist of the three side-branches A, B, and C. In this case the network would create six products (i.e. ASB, ASC, BSA, BSC, CSA, and CSB). Economides (1993) shows that the addition of a new side-branch to a network composed of n side-branches creates $2n$ new products. So the addition of another side-branch, say D, creates six new products. This is an economy of scope in consumption that

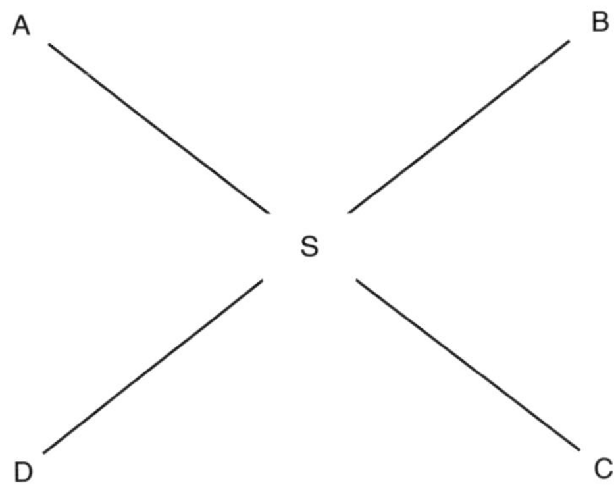

Figure 7.9 Simple network consisting of four side-branches

is called a *network externality*. Network externalities can be found in a variety of industries, such as telecommunications, airlines, railroads, etc. (Shy, 2001). The externality directly increases consumer utility through the provision of new goods, and it may also affect consumers indirectly through price decreases.

Financial markets exhibit positive size externalities as increasing the size of an exchange market increases the expected utility of all participants. Higher participation of traders on both sides of the market decreases the variance of the expected market price and increases the expected utility of risk-averse traders. *Ceteris paribus*, higher liquidity increases traders' utility. Thus, financial exchange markets exhibit network externalities (Economides, 1996).

Payment and securities market infrastructures also have characteristics of network industries, as the benefits to one market participant using a specific platform or system increase when another participant also chooses to do business in that network. The nature of these networks creates scope for formal cooperation among market players. The European Commission (2007) argues that certain types of cooperation (e.g. creating and operating common standards and platforms) may be necessary to generate efficiencies. However, cooperation extending to strategies, pricing, or selling policies could lead to collusion and limit competition and/or exclude third parties.

Networks can be *one-sided* or *two-sided*. A market is two-sided if the platform or system can affect the volume of transactions by charging more to one side of the market and reducing the price paid by the other side by an equal amount. In other words, the price structure matters, and platforms

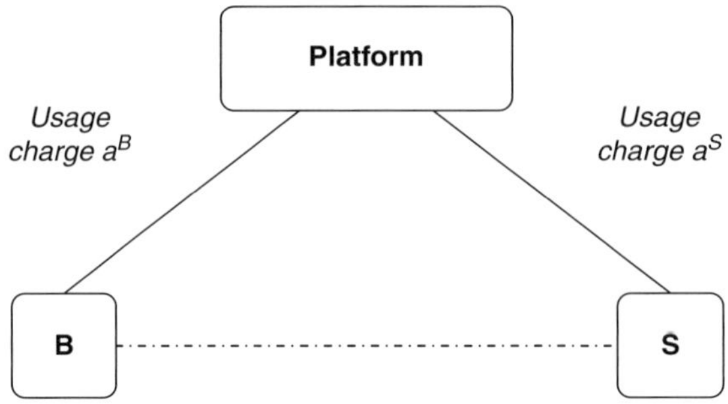

Figure 7.10 Two-sided market
Source: Rochet and Tirole (2006)

must design it so as to bring both sides on board (see Rochet and Tirole, 2006). To explain this further, consider a platform charging per-transaction charges a^B and a^S to the buyer and the seller side, respectively. The market for interactions between the two sides is one-sided if the volume V of transactions realised on the platform depends only on the aggregate price level $a = a^B + a^S$, i.e. V is insensitive to reallocations of this price between the buyer and the seller. However, if V varies with a^B while a is kept constant, the market is said to be two-sided (see Figure 7.10). Generally, payment and security settlement systems are two-sided markets. For example, Figures 7.4 and 7.5 show that the market for payment cards is two-sided, i.e. one side of the market is subsidising the other. This subsidy is made up of the *interchange* and *merchant fee*, which is paid by the acquiring to the issuing bank. Ultimately, these fees raise the price the merchant pays for a card transaction, while they reduce the price for the cardholder, thereby increasing the willingness of the cardholder to make use of a payment card. As a result, the volume of transactions within the card network is higher than would be the case if the cardholder would face higher (visible) costs.

While historically these platforms developed to ensure efficient cooperation in terms of standards and practices, and to share cost between suppliers, over time they created the opportunity to exploit the least elastic side of the market (the merchants originally). At a certain phase, however, the elasticity in the market may shift and it could well be necessary to shift the 'taxation'. This often leads to heavily 'skewed' prices in two-sided markets where the consumer pays a zero fee while the merchant pays a high fee (Bolt and Tieman, 2007).

The presence of network externalities often leads to oligopolies or monopolistic markets. This does not necessarily have to be a problem, as the marginal social benefits from network expansion may be larger than the benefits of having a perfectly competitive market. Perfect competition will generally lead to a network that is too small compared to the socially optimal size. However, given their dominance in certain markets, in practice network providers may be tempted to abuse their economic position and charge monopoly prices, leading to greater inefficiency than under perfect competition.

Finally, network industries are often characterised by *switching costs*, i.e. customers face substantial costs when they want to switch from one network provider to the other. In some situations, high switching costs may 'lock in' users and prevent them from switching to another network. As a consequence, high switching costs may obstruct innovation as users are prevented from making use of new and more efficient services.

7.3 Integration of financial market infrastructures

Given the opportunities to benefit from economies of scale and scope, one would expect substantial consolidation in the EU markets for payment and security settlement services. However, despite the Single Market initiative and the introduction of the euro, the internal market for (retail) payment and post-trading services remains relatively fragmented. This section examines the current state of affairs in the payment and post-trading industry, highlights recent initiatives to promote further integration, and addresses weaknesses exposed by the financial crisis.

Large-value payment systems

The integration of EU large-value payment systems (LVPSs) has been quite remarkable. Before the introduction of the euro in January 1999, LVPSs were organised domestically and almost all cross-border payments were made via correspondent banks. The latter means that banks (or other payment service providers) had individual arrangements under which one bank provided payment and other services to another bank (mostly on a cross-border basis), holding accounts at each other. These correspondent bank arrangements enabled financial institutions to operate cross-border payments without having a foreign branch or subsidiary.

This setting changed substantially in response to the launch of the euro, when the ESCB established TARGET, thereby connecting the existing domestic LVPSs and the ECB payment mechanism. Moreover, private banks introduced EURO1, a high-value payment system for cross-border and domestic transactions in euros between 60 participating banks operating in the European Union. In 2013, TARGET2 had a market share of 91 per cent by value and 59 per cent by number of payments processed in the two large-value payment systems in euro, with the remainder being accounted for by EURO1.

Another important global LVPS is the Continuous Linked Settlement (CLS) system for foreign exchange transactions. This specialised system, based in New York, provides global multi-currency settlement services for foreign exchange transactions, using a payment-versus-payment (PvP) mechanism (i.e. a foreign exchange operation is settled only if both counter-parties simultaneously have a sufficient position in the currency they are selling). PvP has been introduced to prevent the Herstatt risk (or foreign exchange settlement or cross-currency settlement risk). The term *Herstatt risk* refers to the failure of Bankhaus Herstatt in 1974 as a result of incomplete settlement of foreign exchange transactions (see Box 7.2).

Box 7.2 The Herstatt crisis

On 26 June 1974, the German authorities closed Bankhaus Herstatt, a medium-sized bank that was very active in foreign exchange markets. On that day, some of Herstatt's counter-parties had irrevocably paid large amounts of D-Marks to the bank but not yet received dollars in exchange, as the US financial markets had just opened for the day. Herstatt's closure started a chain reaction that disrupted payment and settlement systems. Its New York correspondent bank suspended all US-dollar payments from the German bank's account. Banks that had paid D-Marks to Herstatt earlier that day therefore became fully exposed to the value of those transactions. Other banks in New York refused to make payments on their own account or for their customers until they had confirmation that their counter value had been received. These disruptions were propagated further through the multilateral net settlement system used in New York. Over the next three days, the amount of gross funds transferred by this system declined by an estimated 60 per cent. Bankhaus Herstatt's closure was the first and most dramatic case of a bank failure where incomplete settlement of foreign exchange transactions caused severe problems in payment and settlement systems. Several other episodes occurred in the 1990s but they were less disruptive.

Source: BIS (2002b)

Retail payment systems

For retail payments, the EU still consists of 28 heterogeneous payment areas instead of one single payment market. According to Salo (2006), there are two important explanations for this. First, path dependence can explain the slow change of national payment habits. All national payment systems have their own membership criteria, standards, and practices. Second, a critical mass of network facilities plays a crucial role in the start-up and growth of a network. Over time, national systems have been optimised to satisfy national-user preferences in the most efficient way. Since most payments take place nationally this is a very efficient outcome, but it prevents reaping European-scale benefits. Substituting the existing national systems with one European system does not only run the risk of not being able to satisfy all user requirements, it also means that substantial investments have to be made.

This characteristic of networks can present a barrier to entry for new payment service providers. In fact, the start-up problem can be seen as a chicken-and-egg problem: consumers are not interested in purchasing the good or service when the installed base is too small, and the installed base is too small, because an insufficiently small number of consumers have purchased the good or service (Economides and Himmelberg, 1995).

For now, the way in which cross-border retail transactions are settled varies widely across countries and types of institutions (Freixas and Holthausen, 2008). The first pan-European automated clearinghouse (PE-ACH) for retail payments is the STEP 2 system, which the Euro Banking Association launched in 2003. Payments may be settled on a bilateral basis between national clearinghouses. In case the payee and payer have an account with the same cross-border financial group, the payment may also be settled in house.

The current fragmentation upholds the inefficiency of some payment systems within the EU, with substantial differences in direct prices for payment services between EU Member States. The relatively low aggregated costs of payment services in, for example, the Benelux and Scandinavian countries are closely related to the relatively high usage of more efficient electronic payment instruments. At the national level, authorities have tried to minimise the cost of the payment system. This can be done by reducing the use of cash (the processing of which is very costly, particularly for banks) and by substituting paper-based payment instruments with electronic payments that can be automated from end to end.

For the period 1995–2011, the ECB (2013) finds that there is some evidence of convergence for most payment instruments in Europe. This suggests that the cross-country dispersion of the use of payment instruments has declined over time, notably since the introduction of the single currency. It should, however, be noted that payment behaviours are slow to change, and the differences in payment habits across Europe remain significant. The single market for European retail payments has therefore not yet fully materialised and neither have its benefits.

On various occasions the European Commission has stressed that there are a number of competition concerns in the markets for payment cards and payment systems. Markets in many Member States are highly concentrated. Even though high concentration does not necessarily imply lack of competition, barriers to new entry exist especially in the market for payment cards where market parties charge high card fees.

There are large variations in merchant fees across the EU. For example, firms in Member States with high fees have to pay banks three or four times more of their revenue from card sales than those in Member States with low fees. There are also large variations in interchange fees between banks across the EU, which may not be passed on fully in lower fees for cardholders.

High and sustained profitability (particularly in card issuing) suggests that banks in some Member States enjoy significant market power and can impose high card fees on firms and consumers. Furthermore, some rules and practices of market parties weaken competition at the retail level. Finally, the technical standards diverge across the EU, which may prevent many service providers from operating efficiently on a pan-EU scale.

These findings suggest that there is a need to address several barriers in order to strengthen competition in the EU retail payment market: technical, commercial, and legal barriers. It is crucial that common technical standards are developed and business models need to be aligned. As it is not clear to what extent market forces will initiate these changes, there may be a role for the European Commission to interfere and improve competition in the retail payment market through new legislative proposals. As for the commercial barriers, section 7.1 has shown that there are still substantial differences between user preferences and pricing structures in Europe. The adoption of the Payment Services Directive (PSD) in 2007 created the legal foundation for an EU-wide single market for payments. The fragmentation of retail payment infrastructures is being addressed in the context of the Single Euro Payments Area (SEPA) project. In SEPA, payment systems and infrastructures are expected to establish Europe-wide reach and become pan-European (see next section for further information). To contribute to this, the European Commission adopted an additional legislative package in the field of the EU payments framework in 2013. This package proposes a revised Payments Services Directive (PSD2) and a Regulation on Multilateral Interchange Fees (MIFs).

Single Euro Payments Area

For retail payment systems, the introduction of the Single Euro Payments Area (SEPA) has the potential to remove a number of barriers discussed in the previous section. SEPA is a market-led initiative that aims to ensure that there are no longer any differences between national and cross-border payments within the euro area. It should give payment service providers the opportunity to benefit from economies of scale and scope. SEPA is not merely aimed at improving the processing efficiency of the modest volumes of cross-border payments (EPC, 2006). It will lead to a major changeover of national payment markets in the euro area, as it will introduce new, common business rules and technical standards. Consequently, all electronic payments will be affected and existing national credit transfers, direct debits, and card payments will be phased out and gradually migrate to interoperable formats and processes. Since 2008, the new SEPA payment instruments (credit transfers, direct debits, and cards) have operated alongside existing national processes. After the full transition, purely national payment instruments will no longer exist. Since 1 August 2014 this is the case for credit transfers and direct debits in the euro area. The migration in the euro area was characterised by a 'big bang', as shown in Figure 7.11, especially in some countries and especially concerning direct debits. Every month more than 2 billion payments will now flow across the euro area in new standardised SEPA formats. This allows both consumers and businesses to use a single bank account for all euro credit transfers and direct debits in Europe.

Next to this, the European banking community has defined a framework for the clearing and settlement of payments in SEPA. The framework defines the principles that infrastructure providers must comply with to ensure that they can process SEPA credit transfers and direct debits. As part of the integration process, some clearing and settlement mechanisms for retail payments have taken steps to become pan-European service providers by expanding their service-offering to non-domestic participants and/or by enlarging reachability for their participants by entering into interoperability agreements with other clearing and settlement

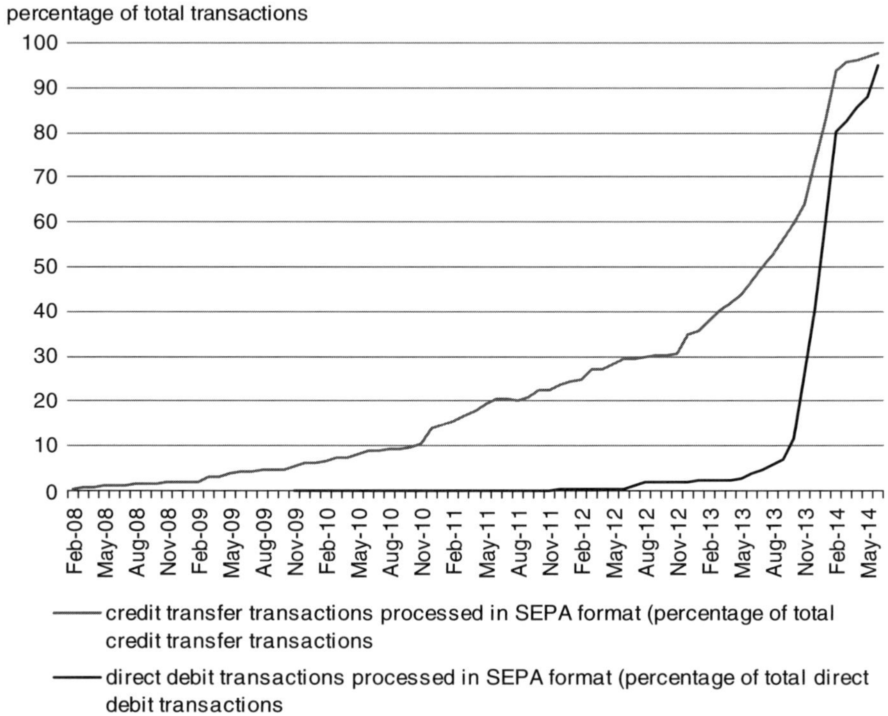

Figure 7.11 Credit transfer and direct debit transactions processed in SEPA format in the euro area, 2000–2012 (percentage of total transactions)
Source: ECB (2014c)

mechanisms. It is expected that the links established under these interoperability agreements will be further deployed after full SEPA migration.

Post-trading industry

As discussed in the previous section, CSDs/CCPs are characterised by economies of scale, economies of scope, and network effects. In principle, these characteristics are compatible with perfectly contestable markets (Schulze and Baur, 2006). However, investments made by CSDs/CCPs, both in human and technical capital, are very specific and therefore not easily recoverable. Moreover, users face substantial switching costs when changing CSDs/CCPs. Consequently, the national markets for post-trading services are far from being perfectly contestable. The EU post-trading industry has evolved into nationally based systems that tend to be monopolistic, i.e. all trades in a given type of security are cleared and settled by a single national

Table 7.3 Studies examining post-trading costs per transaction for users

	EU cross-border	US	Ratio	EU domestic	US	Ratio
Lannoo and Levin (2001)	3.10	0.40	7.75	1.74	0.40	4.35
LSE/OXERA (2002)	3.41	0.53	6.43	2.04	0.53	3.85
Giovannini Group (2001)	2.86	0.46	6.22	1.49	0.46	3.24
NERA (2004)	n.a.	n.a.	n.a.	0.10–0.65	0.10	1.00–6.50
DBG (2005)	n.a.	n.a.	n.a.	0.30–0.60	0.10	1.50–3.00

Source: Schulze and Baur (2006)

entity. This had also resulted in high cost of cross-border settlement and complex settlement procedures, which entail a high level of risk.

Several studies have compared the post-trading costs of domestic versus cross-border transactions, as well as the costs of a domestic transaction in the EU and those in the US. Table 7.3 shows that these studies generally conclude that cross-border prices and costs are considerably higher than the corresponding costs and prices for domestic transactions. The studies by NERA Economic Consulting (2004) and Deutsche Börse Group (2005) also conclude that the costs of domestic transactions differ significantly among Member States. Moreover, post-trading costs per transaction in the EU are substantially higher than in the US.

The Giovannini Group (2001) concluded that fragmentation in the EU clearing and settlement infrastructure significantly complicates the post-trade processing of cross-border securities transactions relative to domestic transactions. Complications arise because of the need to access many national systems, whereby differences in technical requirements/market practices, tax regimes, and legal systems act as barriers to the efficient and safe delivery of post-trading services. The inefficiency that is created by these barriers is reflected in higher costs to pan-EU investors and is inconsistent with the objective of creating a truly integrated EU financial system.

Integration of national systems may bring about various benefits. Among other things, opportunities to exploit economies of scale and scope and increased competition have the potential to lower the cost of post-trading activities and lead to a more efficient allocation of capital, thereby furthering economic growth (see Chapter 1). According to Schulze and Baur (2006), a more efficient EU post-trading system, leading to a lowering of transaction costs of 7–18 per cent, could result in a higher level of GDP (on average between 0.2 and 0.6 per cent).

Post-trading process: TARGET2-Securities and Central Securities Depositories

While generally safe and efficient within national borders, settlement across borders presents higher risks and costs for investors than domestic operations (European Commission, 2014). Meanwhile, the importance of cross-border transactions in Europe continues to increase, accelerated by the launch of T2S. For a long time, each CSD settled according to its own technical set-up and in line with national legal requirements. As a result, interaction between national CSDs was inefficient and costly. T2S therefore provides all CSDs with a single platform for security settlement in Europe. With T2S, interaction between CSDs occurs on a harmonised basis. It makes cross-border settlement identical to domestic settlement, in terms of cost, technical processing, and efficiency. A single set of rules, standards, and tariffs apply to all transactions in Europe, thereby reducing complexity and contributing to financial integration.

Against this background, the CSD Regulation aims to harmonise both the timing and conduct of securities settlement in Europe and the rules governing CSDs. For the first time, it creates a common EU framework for the regulation, authorisation, and supervision of CSDs.

Post-trading: central derivatives clearing

The financial crisis made it clear that the increased use of derivatives had made the financial system more interconnected and less transparent. Before the crisis, most derivatives contracts were non-standardised and therefore highly illiquid. As these were bilateral contracts, the market was strongly interconnected, but also lacked transparency. With some transactions, no collateral was exchanged, leading to a high counterparty risk. Accordingly, when the financial crisis erupted, there was great uncertainty among market participants and policy makers about the risks to which institutions and the financial system were exposed (DNB, 2014).

Therefore, efforts were undertaken at the international level (G20/FSB) to increase the transparency of the derivatives market and reduce counterparty risks. In Europe, these policy initiatives have been incorporated into the European Market Infrastructure Regulation (EMIR, 648/2012/EU), the Directive on Markets in Financial Instruments repealing Directive 2004/39/EC (MiFID II, 2014/65/EC), and the Capital Requirements Regulation (CRR, 575/2013/EU).

The reforms promote central clearing of derivatives and mandatory provision of collateral. Transparency is increased through central clearing of derivatives and through mandatory registration of transactions in trade repositories. In order to encourage clearing via CCPs, bilaterally cleared contracts are required to meet higher capital requirements than centrally cleared contracts. Moreover, central clearing is mandatory for standardised derivatives.

While tackling some problems in post-trading, these reforms also create new risks within the financial system, notably concentration risk. This is related to the central role CCPs play as intermediaries in transactions between parties (see Figure 7.12) and the fact that mandatory central clearing of standardised contracts increases the risk for financial institutions due to rising exposures to CCPs and general clearing members. Moreover, it is likely that, in the near future, the majority of central clearing transactions will be performed by a few large CCPs because of the resulting economies of scale and network effects. These concentration risks place high demands on the risk management and resilience of CCPs. Moreover, as a CCP's bankruptcy can never be entirely ruled out, it is important to reduce the impact of such an event on financial markets. It is therefore important to ensure that a CCP can be resolved in an orderly manner in the event of bankruptcy. Work is currently underway to define international standards for a recovery and resolution framework for CCPs and other market infrastructures. Such standards are vital to ensure the orderly resolution should a CCP default (DNB, 2014).

7.4 Conclusions

Payment systems are composed of instruments, procedures, and transfer systems that ensure the transfer of money from one economic actor to the other. Relatively low-value and non-urgent mass payments are processed through retail payment systems, while wholesale payment systems process large-value and/or high-priority payments between financial institutions.

In securities markets, the clearing and settlement (or post-trading) process provides for the transfer of ownership and payment between buyers and sellers of securities. This process can be divided into four main activities: (1) the confirmation of terms of the trade as agreed by the buyer and the seller, (2) clearance, by which the respective obligations of the buyer and

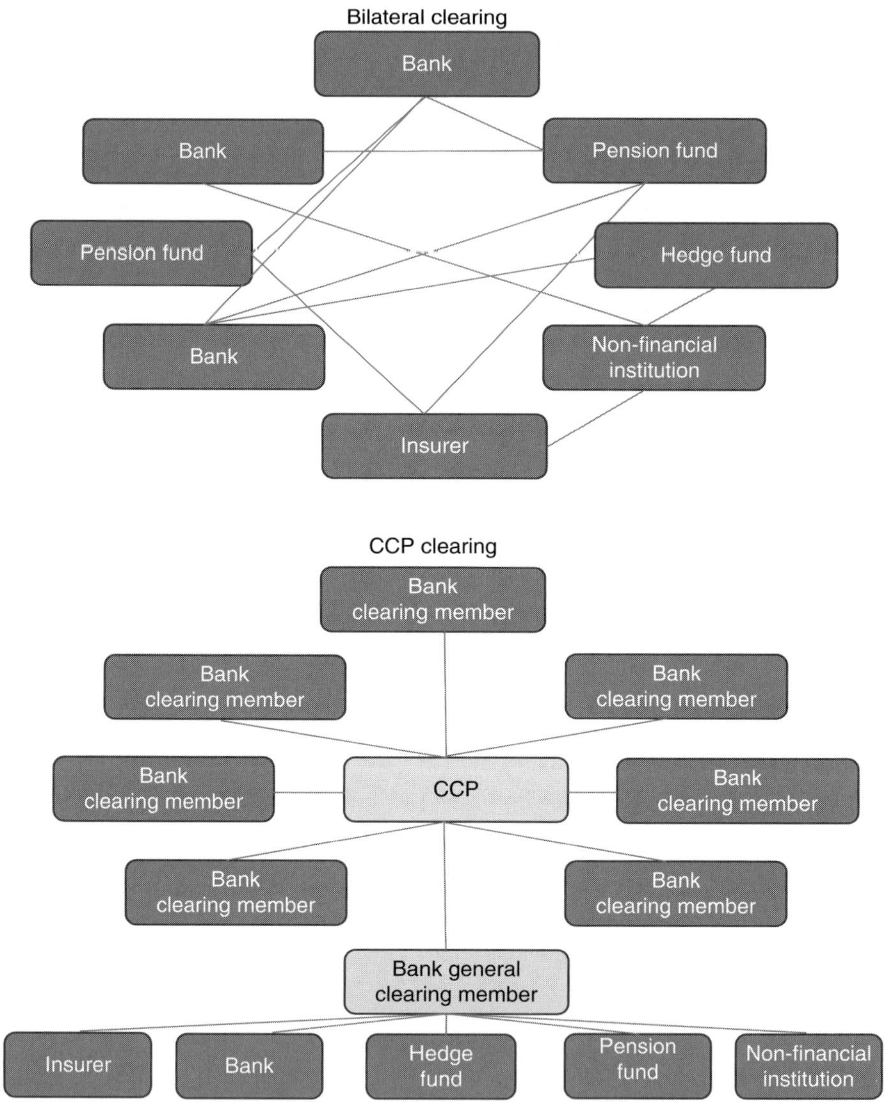

Figure 7.12 CCPs play a key role in derivatives market
Note: many financial institutions do not have direct access to a CCP and therefore use a general clearing member, a bank with direct access to the CCP that conducts transactions for third parties. A bank that exclusively uses its direct access to clear its own derivatives portfolio is known as a clearing member.
Source: DNB (2014)

seller are established, (3) the transfer of the securities from the seller to the buyer, and (4) the transfer of funds from the buyer to the seller.

Payment and securities market infrastructures are characterised by economies of scale and scope, and network externalities. This means that the average costs of payment and post-trading services may fall considerably when the current fragmentation of EU financial infrastructures is overcome. In this respect, the introduction of SEPA should allow providers of payment services to benefit from economies of scale and scope, thereby increasing overall economic efficiency.

The integration of EU large-value payment systems has been quite remarkable, while retail payment systems and post-trading processes have been lagging behind. Different initiatives have been launched to remove existing barriers for integration in these markets and address problems exposed by the financial crisis. However, these reforms also create new risks, notably concentration risk due to the growing importance of central counterparties (CCPs).

Notes

1. Denmark, Estonia, Finland, Greece, Hungary, Ireland, Italy, Latvia, Netherlands, Portugal, Romania, Spain, and Sweden. It should be noted that the ECB study provides a snapshot of the social and private cost situation in 2009.
2. Examples of ICSDs are Euroclear and Clearstream International.
3. Netting can be carried out on either a bilateral or a multilateral basis. While bilateral netting is an arrangement between only two parties to net their bilateral obligations, multilateral netting is arithmetically achieved by summing each participant's bilateral net positions with those of the other participants to arrive at a multilateral net position vis-à-vis all other participants (Kazarian, 2006).
4. Although the curves in Figure 7.8 are not average costs curves, they give a fair reflection of how payment unit costs change with payment volume. The curves refer to estimates for three different years.

Suggested Reading

De Nederlandsche Bank (2014), Systemic Risks Through Central Derivatives Clearing, *Overview of Financial Stability – Spring 2014*, DNB, Amsterdam.

Summers, B. (ed.) (2012), *Payment Systems: Design, Governance and Oversight*, Central Banking Publications, London.

References

Bank for International Settlements (1992), *Delivery Versus Payment in Securities Settlement Systems*, BIS, Basel.

(2001), *BIS Glossary No. 7*, BIS, Basel.

(2002a), *Policy Issues for Central Banks in Retail Payments*, BIS, Basel.

(2002b), *BIS Quarterly Review December 2002 – International Banking and Financial Market Developments*, BIS, Basel.

(2006), *General Guidance for National Payment System Development*, BIS, Basel.

Bolt, W. (2007), Retail Payments and Card Use in the Netherlands: Pricing, Scale, and Antitrust, *Competition Policy International*, **3**(1), 257–270.

Bolt, W. and D. Humphrey (2007), Payment network scale economies, SEPA, and cash replacement, *Review of Network Economics*, **6**(4), 453–473.

Bolt, W. and A. Tieman (2007), Heavily skewed pricing in two-sided market, *International Journal of Industrial Organisation*, **26**(5), 1250–1255.

De Nederlandsche Bank (2014), Systemic Risks Through Central Derivatives Clearing, *Overview of Financial Stability – Spring 2014*, DNB, Amsterdam.

Deutsche Börse Group (2005), The European Post-Trade Market – An Introduction, White Paper.

Economides, N. (1993), Network Economics with Application to Finance, *Financial Markets, Institutions & Instruments*, **2**(5), 89–97.

(1996), The Economics of Networks, *International Journal of Industrial Organization*, **16**(4), 673–699.

Economides, N. and C. Himmelberg (1995), Critical Mass and Network Evolution in Telecommunications, in: G. Brock (ed.), *Toward a Comprehensive Telecommunications Industry: Selected Papers from the 1994 Telecommunications Policy Research Conference*, Lawrence Erlbaum Associates, New Jersey.

European Central Bank (2006), Speech by J.-M. Godeffroy: 'Ten Frequently Asked Questions About TARGET2-Securities' on 20 September 2006 at the British Bankers Association, London. Available at: www.ecb.int/paym/t2s/defining/outgoing/html/10faq.en.html (accessed 13 February 2012).

(2010), *A Single Currency – An Integrated Market Infrastructure* (T2, T2S, CCBM2, SEPA), ECB, Frankfurt am Main.

(2012), The Social and Private Costs of Retail Payment Instruments – A European Perspective, ECB Occasional Paper 137, ECB, Frankfurt am Main.

(2013), Convergence in European Retail Payments, ECB Occasional Paper 147, ECB, Frankfurt am Main.

(2014a), *Card Payments in Europe – A Revised Focus on SEPA for Cards*, ECB, Frankfurt am Main.

(2014b), *Target Annual Report 2013*, ECB, Frankfurt am Main.

(2014c), *Financial Integration in Europe*, ECB, Frankfurt am Main.

European Commission (2005), Annex to the Proposal for a Directive of the European Parliament and of the Council on Payment Services in the Internal Market – Impact Assessment, EC, Brussels.

(2007), *Report on the Retail Sector Inquiry*, EC, Brussels.

(2010), *Commission Proposal on OTC Derivatives and Market Infrastructures*, EC, Brussels.
(2013), *Frequently Asked Questions on CCP Issues*, EC, Brussels.

European Payment Council (2006), *Making SEPA a Reality – Implementing the Single Euro Payments Area*, EPC, Brussels.

Freixas, X. and C. Holthausen (2008), European Integration of Payment Systems, in: X. Freixas, P. Hartmann, and C. Mayer (eds.), *Handbook of European Financial Markets and Institutions*, Oxford University Press, 436–450.

Giovannini, A., J. Berrigan, and D. Russo (2008), Post-trading Services and European Securities Markets, in: X. Freixas, P. Hartmann, and C. Mayer (eds.), *Handbook of European Financial Markets and Institutions*, Oxford University Press, 540–567.

Giovannini Group (2001), *Cross-Border Clearing and Settlement Arrangements in the European Union*, Brussels, November.

Harper, I., S. Rimes, and C. Malam (2006), The Development of Electronic Payment Systems, in: R. Cooper, G. Madden, A. Lloyd, and M. Schipp (eds.), *The Economics of Online Markets and ICT Networks*, Springer, New York, 25–40.

Humphrey, D. B., M. Willesson, T. Lindblom, and G. Bergendahl (2003), What Does It Cost to Make a Payment?, *Review of Network Economics*, June, 159–174.

Jonker, N. (2013), Social Costs of POS Payments in the Netherlands 2002–2012: Efficiency Gains from Increased Debit Card Usage, *DNB Occasional Studies*, **11**(2).

Kazarian, E. G. (2006), Integration of the Securities Market Infrastructure in the European Union: Policy and Regulatory Issues, IMF Working Paper 06/241.

Khiaonarong, T. (2003), Payment Systems Efficiency, Policy Approaches, and the Role of the Central Bank, Bank of Finland Discussion Paper 1.

Lannoo, K. and M. Levin (2001), The Securities Settlement Industry in the EU – Structure, Costs and the Way Forward, CEPS Research Report.

London Stock Exchange/Oxera (2002), Clearing and Settlement in Europe – Response to the first report of the Giovannini Group.

NERA Economic Consulting (2004), The Direct Costs of Clearing and Settlement: An EU–US Comparison, City Research Series 1.

Rochet, J.-C. and J. Tirole (2006), Two-Sided Markets: A Progress Report, *The RAND Journal of Economics*, **35**(3), 645–667.

Salo, S. (2006), Promoting Integration of European Retail Payment Systems: Role of Competition, Cooperation and Regulation, paper presented at the SUERF Seminar The Adoption of the Euro in New Member States: Challenges and Vulnerabilities on the Last Stretch, Malta, 4 May.

Schmiedel, H. and A. Schönenberg (2005), Integration of Securities Market Infrastructure in the Euro Area, European Central Bank Occasional Paper 33.

Schulze, N. and D. Baur (2006), Annex II of Economic Impact Study on Clearing and Settlement, EC, Brussels. Available at: http://ec.europa.eu/internal_market/financialmarkets/docs/clearing/draft/annex_2_En.pdf (accessed 13 February 2012).

Serifsoy, B. and M. Weiß (2007), Settling for Efficiency – A Framework for the European Securities Transaction Industry, *Journal of Banking and Finance*, **31**, 3034–3057.

Shy, O. (2001), *The Economics of Network Industries*, Cambridge University Press, New York.

CHAPTER

8

Financial Innovation

OVERVIEW

The financial sector performs two main functions: (1) reducing information and transaction costs, and (2) facilitating the trading, diversification, and management of risk. Financial innovation ensures that the financial system can provide these functions more efficiently. Financial innovation is the act of creating and then popularising new financial instruments, as well as new financial technologies, institutions, and markets. As such, financial innovation can play an important role in fostering growth and economic prosperity. At the same time, financial innovations have been blamed for their role in the recent financial crisis. This chapter discusses the causes and consequences of financial innovation.

Two important drivers of financial innovation are regulation and deregulation, and technological advances. Regulation may forbid or otherwise restrain financial innovation so that deregulation may spur innovation. At the same time, several innovations have been the results of attempts to circumvent regulation. Technological advances made new instruments possible. The credit card is a good example of financial innovation driven by technological advance, including improvements in communications, data management, and credit scoring.

Financial innovations may improve payments, offer new savings and investment opportunities, and may increase risk sharing. The first part of this chapter examines the causes and consequences of financial innovation, while the second part analyses the pros and cons of financial innovation. This chapter also zooms in on the risks of financial innovation by offering two case studies. One of these case studies is about securitisation of subprime mortgages. Credit rating agencies (CRAs) play an important role in securitisations. This chapter therefore explains the recent debate about CRAs and outlines the recently introduced regulation of CRAs in Europe. The final part discusses the developments within the shadow banking sector.

LEARNING OBJECTIVES

After you have studied this chapter, you should be able to:

- explain the causes and consequences of financial innovation
- understand the advantages and disadvantages of financial innovation
- explain the risks of financial innovation and the impact on financial fragility
- understand the role of credit rating agencies
- understand the role and risks of the shadow banking system.

8.1 Financial innovation: causes and consequences

Financial innovation is the act of creating and then popularising new financial instruments, as well as new financial technologies, institutions, and markets. Financial innovations are sometimes divided into product or process innovations. Product innovations are exemplified by new derivative contracts, new corporate securities, or new forms of pooled investment products, while process improvements are typified by new means of distributing securities, processing transactions, or pricing transactions. In practice, however, this differentiation is not clear, because process and product innovations are often linked (Lerner and Tufano, 2011).

Financial innovation differs from other types of new product development in several ways (Lerner and Tufano, 2011). First, the financial system is highly interconnected. As a result, a financial innovation is likely to generate a complex web of externalities, both positive and negative. Therefore, assessing the social consequences of financial innovation can be very challenging. Second, financial innovations are very dynamic. As an innovation diffuses from pioneering adopters to more general users, these products frequently change in their underlying structure, the way that they are marketed, and how they are used. These transformations mean that the consequences of an innovation may change over time. Finally, many forms of innovation, such as pharmaceuticals, are subject to regulation. But the regulation of new financial products and services is particularly complex. This may ultimately lead to a cat-and-mouse game between the regulator and the industry, with several rounds of reregulation.

As explained in Chapter 1, the financial sector performs two main functions: (1) reducing information and transaction costs, and (2) facilitating the trading, diversification, and management of risk. Financial innovations enhance the efficiency of the financial system to provide these functions better. For instance, they provide households with new choices for investment and consumption and reduce the costs of raising and deploying funds. Similarly, financial innovations may enable firms to raise capital in larger amounts and at a lower cost than they could otherwise. At the same time, financial innovations have been blamed for the recent crisis (see Chapter 2). In one of his columns in the *New York Times*, Nobel Prize laureate Paul Krugman (2007) writes:

> [T]he innovations of recent years – the alphabet soup of C.D.O.s and S.I.V.s, R.M.B.S. and A.B.C.P. – were sold on false pretences. They were promoted as ways to spread risk, making investment safer. What they did instead – aside from making their creators a lot of money, which they didn't have to repay when it all went bust – was to spread confusion, luring investors into taking on more risk than they realised.

This section reviews the literature on financial innovation, mainly drawing on Lerner and Tufano (2011) and Litan (2010). We focus on the consequences of financial innovation, but will first briefly dwell upon the causes of financial innovation.

Causes of financial innovation

Where does financial innovation come from? Generally, financial innovation is driven by investor demand for a particular set of cash flows. Intermediaries recognise this demand and engineer securities with the desired characteristics. By splitting up or combining cash flows of existing securities, the intermediaries can create profits for themselves and may increase social welfare (Lerner and Tufano, 2011). In the model of financial innovation of Gennaioli *et al.* (2012), a financial innovation can address the demand for clients for a particular set of cash flows and thus be socially beneficial. But these authors suggest that these investors may systematically underestimate the risks associated with these new products' cash flows. Once the investors suddenly realise these risks, there will be an exodus back to traditional, safer products. In this way, financial innovation can add to the fragility of the overall financial system.

Two particularly important drivers of innovation have been financial regulation and technological change. Regulation is one of the main drivers of financial innovation. This can be illustrated by the differences in the development of so-called *Exchange Traded Funds* (ETFs) between the US and Europe that will be explained in more detail in section 8.3. ETFs are investment vehicles that track an index (e.g. S&P 500). Whereas in Europe synthetic ETFs have developed very rapidly, in the US physical ETFs are dominant. *Physical ETFs* replicate the index by simply reconstituting the basket of physical securities underlying the index. *Synthetic ETFs* obtain the desired return through entering into an asset swap instead of replicating the index physically. One of the main factors explaining the difference between the US and Europe is difference in regulation. In Europe, regulators take a more liberal stance on the use of derivatives in investment funds. In contrast, the US regulator has adopted a more conservative approach, limiting de facto the development of synthetic ETFs (FSB, 2011).

However, generally the relationship between financial innovation and regulation is complex. Innovators look for opportunities that exploit regulatory gaps. A good example is that bank capital rules have encouraged banks to use off-balance sheet vehicles (see Chapter 2). So regulation may give rise to certain innovations, but then regulators frequently 'catch up' with the products, in a cat-and-mouse process. Under the new bank capital rules, opportunities for banks for using off-balance sheet vehicles have recently been limited. However, even a well-staffed regulatory agency is up against a world of potential entrepreneurs and innovators. Inevitably, regulation will therefore tend to react to innovations with a lag (Lerner and Tufano, 2011).

On the technological front, advances in information technology made the low-cost collection, processing, and dissemination of household and business financial data possible. This, in turn, allows for ever-faster evaluation of creditworthiness, identification of prospective borrowers, and management of existing accounts. A good example of how this may lead to financial innovation is the credit card (Bernanke, 2009). From the consumer's perspective, credit cards provide convenience, facilitate recordkeeping, and offer security from loss.

Consequences of financial innovation

Financial innovations may improve payments, offer new savings and investment opportunities, and may increase risk sharing. Drawing on Litan (2010), we will illustrate these consequences of financial innovation in turn. While most financial products described below are analysed throughout the book (e.g. derivatives in Chapter 5, payments in Chapter 7, and investments in Chapter 9), they are here analysed from the perspective of innovating the functions of the financial system.

Financial innovations: payments

Although the invention of the ATM machine was revolutionary, it was the advent of the networked ATM more than the machine itself that proved to be most useful for consumers. Once ATMs were networked, bank customers were free from not only having to wait in line at a bank, but in fact could get money any time across a wide geographical area. Clearly, ATMs have broadened access to financial services and been a major source of convenience for consumers. Moreover, by eliminating the need for tellers to dispense cash or take deposits, ATMs also have clearly improved productivity in the banking sector.

Another example of an innovation that has made payments easier are credit cards. They not only have become a means of payment, but also a source of credit. More recently, credit cards (along with newer forms of payment, such as PayPal, which are linked to credit cards) have found another use as an important form of payment for online purchases. They permit consumers both to pay and to borrow at the same time and enable consumers to pay without cash, and thus to reduce trips to the bank and/ or ATMs. They also offer a safer way to pay for things than money (which can be stolen).

Debit cards – which automatically deduct a customer's payment at a retail establishment from his or her bank account – are a natural outgrowth of both ATMs and credit cards. After the debit feature was added to ATM cards and as more merchants accepted debit transactions, debit cards grew in popularity.

The Internet has drastically changed the way consumers and businesses buy, and pay for, goods and services. Internet banking has enabled consumers to make payments or use other banking services anywhere in the world, at any moment. In addition, mobile and contactless payments are starting to take off, providing customers with new means of payments. Moreover, in some cases virtual communities have created and circulated their own currency for exchanging the goods and services, thereby providing a new medium of exchange and a unit of account.

Some of these innovations focus on making payments more accessible to a wider range of uses – such as mobile phone payments – while still relying on a trusted central entity. More recent innovations – such as Bitcoin – have introduced a fundamentally different decentralised structure to payment systems by relying on cryptography rather than a central authority (Ali *et al.*, 2014). Users can trade digital currencies with each other in exchange for traditional currency or goods and services without the need for any third party (like a bank). And their creation is not controlled by any central bank. While the latter element has attracted much attention, the distributed ledger underlying these digital currencies is a significant innovation. With conventional bank deposits, banks hold the digital record and are entrusted to ensure its validity. With digital currencies, by contrast, the ledger containing the record of all transactions by all users is publicly available to all. Rather than requiring users to have trust in special institutions, reliance is placed on the network and the rules established to reliably change the ledger.

At the moment, the adoption of digital currencies like Bitcoin appears to be driven by three factors (Ali *et al.*, 2014): (1) ideology, as the digital currency is expressly designed to avoid any central control and to minimise the degree of trust that participants need to place in any third party, (2) financial return, as digital currencies have become viewed by some as an asset class for financial investment, driven by an interaction between the schemes' planned fixed supplies and their increasing publicity, and (3) the pursuit of lower transaction fees compared to existing electronic retail payment systems or international transfers.

Table 8.1 provides an overview of recent innovations in payment technologies and some of their characteristics.

Table 8.1 Recent innovations in payment technologies

Category	Description	New payment system	New currency
Wrappers	Wrappers services are aimed at improving the user interface and accessibility of existing payment systems. Examples include Google Wallet, Apple Pay, and Paym.	No	No
Mobile money	These schemes provide for money to be stored as credits on a smart card or a system-provider's book.	Yes	No
Credits and local currencies	Credits schemes in which private companies accept money in exchange for an alternative account which can be spent on a particular platform, such as within an online game. Local currencies, such as the Bristol Pund, enable people to exchange national currencies for a local equivalent which can be spent in a specific geographical area.	No	Yes
Digital currencies	Digital currencies, like Bitcoin, which incorporate both a new decentralised payments system and a new currency.	Yes	Yes

Source: Ali *et al.* (2014)

Financial innovations: savings and investments

Over the last four decades there has been a proliferation of new ways to save, like *mutual funds*. Mutual funds pool the savings of many small investors by selling them shares in the fund and using the proceeds to buy equity, bonds, money market instruments, or other securities. Mutual funds allow investors to buy or redeem shares on a daily basis at net asset value (NAV) that is calculated by dividing the fund's assets minus liabilities by the number of shares outstanding. This is usually calculated at the end of every trading day. There is a difference between *open-end* and *closed-end funds*. The shares of closed-end funds are listed on a stock exchange. Investors cannot sell their shares back to the fund as they can with an open-end fund, but must sell their shares in the market. The price they receive may be significantly different from NAV. It may be at a 'premium', i.e. higher than net asset value, or, more commonly, at a 'discount', i.e. lower than net asset value. Open-end mutual funds have two advantages that contributed to the growth of mutual funds. First, as the fund agreed to redeem shares at any time, they are very liquid. Second, the open-end character allows the fund to grow as long as investors are willing to put money into the fund.

No doubt, mutual funds are one of the most successful financial innovations of the twentieth century, based on their growth rates, adoption rates, fraction of capital intermediated in the economy, or importance to household balance sheets (Lerner and Tufano, 2011).

One particular type of mutual funds are *money market funds* (MMFs). A money market fund is a fixed-income mutual fund that invests in debt securities which are characterised by their short maturities and minimal credit risk. They gave ordinary people access to interest-bearing short-term assets that even had transaction-like features (one could write a cheque on them). MMFs came into being because of regulatory restrictions. In several countries banks were prohibited from paying interest on checking accounts. In addition, money market instruments can generally only be bought in large amounts. MMFs ingeniously avoided these restrictions and limitations by buying large batches of money market instruments and then sold shares to investors who could buy in with a limited amount of money. In Europe, MMFs are an important source of short-term financing for financial institutions, corporates, and governments. Around 22 per cent of short-term debt securities issued either by governments or by the corporate sector are held by MMFs. MMFs hold 38 per cent of short-term debt issued by the EU banking sector. MMFs in Europe manage assets of around €1 trillion (European Commission, 2014).

Innovation also occurred in various kinds of financial limited partnerships: hedge funds, private equity funds, and venture capital funds. *Hedge funds* use investors' money to borrow still more money, and to make leveraged investments of various kinds, all in an effort to achieve for the investors a superior return adjusted for risk. The funds they use stem from so-called 'sophisticated investors' – wealthy individuals or institutions (pension funds or endowments). Hedge funds are like mutual funds, in that they place investors' money in markets for liquid financial instruments (stocks, bonds, derivatives). The liquid nature of their investments distinguishes hedge funds from *private equity funds*, which tend to buy large or controlling interests in companies, and to hold these positions for sale after several years. Today's typical private equity fund evolved from the leveraged buyout partnerships that were all the rage in the 1980s, and is still typically financed heavily with debt. According to Litan (2010), there is probably no more iconic financial innovation over the last four decades that has helped improve the allocation of savings towards productive investment than the rise of *venture capital funds*. The venture capital fund makes money by investing in young or emerging firms which usually have a novel technology or business model in high-technology industries. As these firms often have a limited operating history, they cannot raise capital in the public markets and are unable to secure a bank loan.

One important financial innovation in the last two decades is the introduction of government bonds whose principal amounts are indexed to inflation. Such bonds were first sold by the British government in the 1980s; later also other governments have issued these instruments. Until such bonds were offered, investors had no (relatively) safe instrument that offered a hedge against inflation.

Financial innovations: risk sharing

A considerable portion of financial innovation over the past decades has come from the use of derivatives, which are financial contracts whose value is derived from some underlying asset. These assets can include equities, bonds, exchange rates, commodities, and residential and commercial mortgages. The more common forms of these contracts include options, forwards/futures, and swaps. The benefits of derivatives relate to:

(1) hedging and risk management;
(2) price discovery; and
(3) enhancement of liquidity.

As documented in Figure 5.10, the total value of derivatives in the EU amounted to €1.4 trillion in 2013.

An innovation that is used overwhelmingly as a way of reallocating financial risks is the 'swap' arrangement. A swap is a contract arranging an exchange of cash flows between two parties. An *interest rate swap* involves the exchange of loan payments with a fixed rate of interest for another payment stream defined by a floating rate of interest. A *currency swap* involves the exchange of payments in different currencies (where both interest rates could be fixed, both variable, or one fixed and the other variable). Parties enter in such arrangements because they want to reduce or change their risk exposure from the assets on their balance sheets. Swaps enable them to do this without actually having to sell the underlying assets (Litan, 2010).

A more recent innovation is the *credit default swap* (CDS). It is an insurance instrument: the purchaser of a CDS receives money upon some defined event of default on a loan or a bond. The CDS market has become dominated by a handful of major banks, which use these instruments to hedge against the default of their borrowers, thereby reducing the amount of capital they are required to hold. Banks also trade these instruments among one other, for their own account or on behalf of customers who want to hedge against the possibility that their supplier or borrower might default, or speculate on this outcome.

A potential future innovation is *home equity insurance.* Shiller and Weiss (1999) have proposed insurance policies to enable individuals to protect themselves against the risks of declines in the prices of their homes, often people's most important asset. The risk of decline in the market value of homes is far greater than the risk of fire or other physical disaster; the potential significance of an insurance industry that protects market value of homes is much larger than that of the existing homeowner's property insurance industry. One predicate for this market is the creation of the Case–Shiller price index for real estate in major metropolitan areas of the US.

8.2 Pros and cons of financial innovation

In the aftermath of the 2007–2009 financial crisis, financial innovation has become controversial. Litan (2010) argues that there is a mix between good and bad financial innovations, although on balance he finds more good ones than bad ones. Individually and collectively, these innovations have improved access to credit, made life more convenient, and in some cases probably allowed the economy to grow faster. But some innovations, such as collateralised debt obligations (CDOs) and structured investment vehicles (SIVs) were poorly designed, while others, such as credit default swaps (CDSs) and adjustable rate mortgages, were misused and contributed to the financial crisis and/or amplified the downturn in the economy when it started.

Litan (2010) analyses the net impact of recent financial innovations, using three criteria:

(1) access to finance;
(2) convenience for users of financial services; and
(3) performance of productivity or total output.

This approach allows an impartial assessment of financial innovations. The fact that many financial innovations have been designed to get around financial regulation does not automatically make them bad. Indeed the opposite is true if the regulations are impeding productive activity. Some financial innovations have been useful for this purpose (Litan, 2010). Table 8.2 presents the net impact for financial products classified according to the different functions of finance (i.e. payments, saving, investment, risk bearing).

Most new financial products score positively on the criteria in Table 8.1. On the payments side, financial innovations have helped to move away from cash. On the saving side, new products offer more convenient, safer, and potentially rewarding ways of savings. According to Litan (2010), the net impact of money market funds (MMFs) on GDP is neutral, as it is not clear that MMFs benefit the economy. Hedge funds and private equity are organised as financial limited partnerships, and are therefore difficult to access for the mass. Private equity has a positive impact on economic growth. A typical private equity firm holds most of its investments longer than five years. While on average jobs fall at private equity-controlled firms during the first two years after they are acquired, employment grows thereafter. Moreover, private equity-controlled firms are good at controlling costs. Litan (2010) concludes that private equity contributes positively to productivity.

Moving to investment, credit scoring has improved banks' ability to assess credit risk. This allowed banks to price risk by reflecting it in the risk premium in the interest rate. Credit scoring has facilitated the extension of personal credit and credit to small businesses. While adjustable rate mortgages increase access to mortgages, they also add to the increase in overall household debt. In addition, underwriting standards on these mortgages were lapsing preceding

Table 8.2 Net impact of recent financial innovations

	Access	Convenience	Productivity/GDP
Payments			
ATMs	++	++	+
Credit card expansion	++	++	+
Debit cards	++	++	+
Saving			
Money market funds	++	++	0
Exchange traded funds	+	+	0/+
Hedge funds	0	0	0/+
Private equity	0	0	+
Investment			
Credit scoring	++	++	0
Adjustable rate mortgages	++	+	–/ –
Asset-backed securities	++	++	–/+
CDOs*	++	++	–
SIVs*	++	++	–
Rise of venture capital	++	++	++ (but future not clear)
Risk bearing			
Options/futures exchanges	++	+	+/++
Interest/currency swaps	++	++	+/++
Credit default swaps	++	+	+

Notes: * The positive scores here were temporary.
Source: Litan (2010)

the financial crisis. CDOs and SIVs permitted subprime mortgages to be originated and sold to investors, who did not fully appreciate the risks (see Chapter 2). This securitised mortgage credit allowed access and convenience to individuals who previously would not qualify for a regular mortgage. Cheap mortgage finance helped fuel the housing boom. The overall impact of the housing boom-bust is negative on GDP. Venture capital has helped to improve the allocation of savings to productive start-ups, which have no access to bank loans or equity markets. So far, venture capital has financed the launch of famous companies, such as Google and Amazon, at an early stage. But venture capital investment is cyclical. In the aftermath of the financial crisis, the contribution of venture capital has dropped significantly.

Finally, derivatives help to spread or allocate risk to those most willing and able to bear it. Derivatives thus allow market participants and traders to manage their risks as well as to take positions. Putting aside the opportunities for traders and market makers in those instruments, derivatives enable firms producing real things in the economy to hedge risks, e.g. to lock in the price of oil, or the price they receive for their products, or to hedge against fluctuations in interest rates or currencies (Litan, 2010). Firms can thus reduce various financial risks to their businesses. This reduction risk may in turn lower their cost of capital. But it is important that firms have the financial skillls to understand the risk profile of derivatives. Otherwise derivatives may introduce unintended risks to their business.

Financial innovation and financial fragility

Financial innovation can turn into financial fragility. Some recent episodes of financial innovation share a common pattern (Gennaioli *et al.*, 2012). It begins with a strong demand from investors for a particular, often safe, stream of cash flows. Some traditional securities in the market offer this pattern, but investors demand more, causing prices to rise. In response to demand, financial intermediaries create new securities offering the sought-after pattern of cash flows, usually by carving out of existing securities that are more risky. By virtue of diversification, tranching, insurance, and other forms of financial engineering, the new securities are believed by the investors, and often by the intermediaries themselves, to be good substitutes for the traditional ones. They are consequently issued and bought in great volumes.

At some point, news reveals that the new securities are vulnerable to some neglected risks, and in particular are not good substitutes for the traditional securities. Both investors and intermediaries are surprised by the news, and investors sell these false substitute securities, moving back to the traditional securities with the cash flows they seek. As investors fly for safety, financial institutions are stuck holding the supply of the new securities. The prices of traditional securities rise while those of the new ones fall sharply, leading to financial fragility.

A recent example is the securitisation of subprime mortgages, which is discussed in section 8.3. Another example is the rise of money market funds (MMFs). The innovation of prime MMFs has arguably created much instability by giving investors the expectation of getting their money back on demand at par, even though it is invested in securities that are far from riskless. Gennaioli *et al.* (2012) suggest that it might be better to help investors form more realistic expectations by mandating that these funds be marked to market. With more realistic expectations of net asset value fluctuations, breaking the buck (i.e. suspending or stopping the return of money on demand at par) would no longer be a dramatic event that sparks a run on these funds and creates financial fragility.

When some risks are neglected, securities are over-issued. The reason is that neglected risks need not be laid off on intermediaries or other parties when manufacturing new securities. Investors thus end up bearing risk without recognising that they are doing so. Markets in new securities are fragile. A small piece of data that brings to investors' minds the previously unattended risks catches them by surprise, causes them to drastically revise their valuations of new securities, and to sell them in the market. The problem is more severe precisely because new securities have been over-issued.

Holmstrom (2010) illustrates the fragility of debt securities. As long as the value of the (underlying) assets is well above the default boundary (see Figure 8.1), the debt securities are perceived to be 'safe'. The value of securities is insensitive to new information. As Holmstrom (2010) puts it, 'the debt securities are fully liquid [in the information-insensitive region], there are no questions asked about the solvency'. Examples of such 'safe' securities are banknotes, US Treasuries, bank deposits, MMFs, and CDOs (prior to the emerging problems with subprime mortgages). Low volatility of the underlying collateral, such as mortgages, enhances the perceived safety. Once the assessment of the asset value drops towards the information-sensitive region in Figure 8.1 due to new information (on neglected risks),

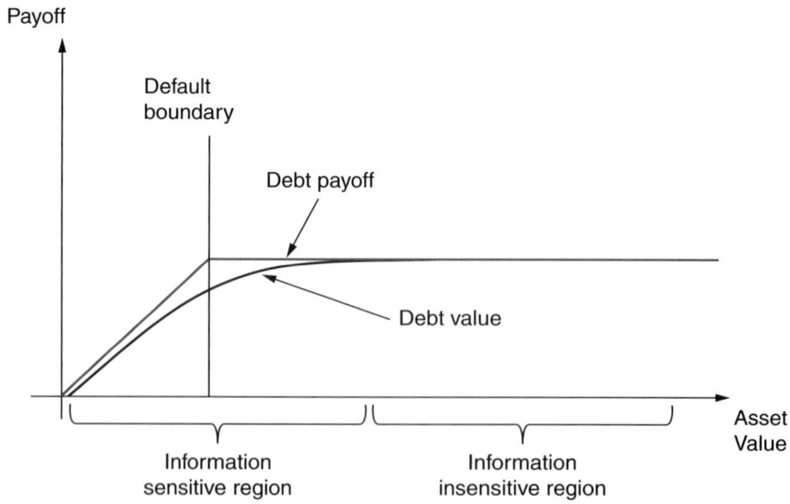

Figure 8.1 Debt and information sensitivity
Source: Holmstrom (2010)

fragility comes into play. The safety of the debt securities starts to be questioned, and investors start to sell them off causing a drop in the value of these debt securities.

Gai *et al.* (2008) suggest that financial innovation and greater macroeconomic stability may have made financial crises in developed countries less likely than in the past. But should a crisis occur, its impact could be greater than was previously the case. Macroeconomic volatility is generally higher in developing countries than in advanced economies, but maximum loan-to-value ratios are invariably lower. Crises in emerging market economies should therefore be more frequent, but less severe than in developed countries. Hoggarth *et al.* (2002) find empirical evidence showing that crises in developed countries do indeed tend to be more costly than those in emerging market economies. While recent innovations have done damage, Box 8.1 suggests that the long-run story is that financial innovation is essential for economic growth.

Box 8.1 Financial innovation and long-run economic growth

According to Levine (2011), financial innovation is essential for growth. As firms become more complex, screening and monitoring firms becomes more difficult. Therefore, without corresponding innovations in finance that match the increases in complexity associated with economic growth, the quality of financial services diminishes, slowing economic growth. Several examples from history illustrate the crucial role of financial innovation in sustaining economic growth. Take the financial impediments to railroad expansion in the nineteenth century in the US. The novelty and complexity of railroads made pre-existing financial systems ineffective at screening and monitoring them. As only local investors with close ties to those operating the railroad provided capital for railroads during the early decades of this new technology, limited finance restricted growth. So financiers innovated. Specialised financiers and investment banks emerged to mobilise capital from individuals, to screen and invest in railroads, and to monitor the use of those investments. Based on their expertise and reputation, these investment banks mobilised funds from wealthy investors, evaluated proposals from railroads, allocated capital, and governed the operations of railroad companies for investors.

Another example provided by Levine (2011) is the information technology revolution of the twentieth century. As nascent high-tech information and communication firms struggled to emerge in the 1970s and 1980s, traditional commercial banks were reluctant to finance them because these new firms did not yet generate sufficient cash flows to cover loan payments. Furthermore, these firms were run by scientists with little experience in operating profitable companies. Conventional debt and equity markets were also wary

Box 8.1 (cont.)

because the technologies were too complex for investors to evaluate. Again, financiers innovated. Venture capital firms arose to screen entrepreneurs and provide technical, managerial, and financial advice to new high-technology firms. In many cases, venture capitalists had become wealthy through their own successful high-tech innovations, which provided a basis of expertise for evaluating and guiding new entrepreneurs. Venture capitalists typically took large, private equity stakes that established a long-term commitment to the enterprise, and they generally became active investors, taking seats on the board of directors and helping to solve managerial and financial problems.

A final example is the biotechnology revolution of the twenty-first century. Screening biotech firms is difficult because of the scientific breadth of biotechnologies, which frequently require inputs from biologists, chemists, geneticists, engineers, bioroboticists, as well as experts on the myriad of laws, regulations, and commercial barriers associated with successfully bringing new medical products to market. It was unfeasible to house all of this expertise in banks or venture capital firms. Yet again, financiers innovated. They formed new financial partnerships with the one kind of organisation with the breadth of skills to screen biotech firms – large pharmaceutical companies. Pharmaceutical companies employ, or are in regular contact with, a large assortment of scientists and engineers, have close connections with those delivering medical products to customers, and employ lawyers versed in drug regulations. According to Levine (2011), improvements in diagnostic and surgical procedures, prosthetic devices, parasite-resistant crops, and other innovations linked to biotechnology would almost certainly be occurring at a far slower pace without financial innovation.

Source: Levine (2011)

8.3 Risks of financial innovation: two case studies

This section offers two case studies of financial innovation: first, one particular form of mutual funds, the so-called exchange traded funds, and second, the securitisation of subprime mortgages. We zoom in on the risks of these innovations.

Exchange traded funds

ETFs are one of the more successful financial innovations in recent decades. *Exchange traded funds* (ETFs) are investment vehicles that track an index (e.g. S&P 500), trade continuously on exchanges, and are redeemable daily. So they offer low-cost diversification and liquidity and tradability. As there is a direct link between the security and its underlying components, ETFs do not require fund managers to choose securities. As a result, ETFs tend to have lower fees than other mutual funds. Like mutual funds, ETFs come in two forms: (1) unit investment trusts, which are like closed-end mutual funds in that they have a fixed number of shares, and (2) open-ended ETFs, which issue new shares as more investors want to invest in them. Most ETFs are listed on US and European exchanges, but they provide exposure to a much more diverse range of markets. For example, two of the three largest ETFs track emerging market indices. Since ETFs are traded on an exchange, investors can buy them as long as the exchange is open rather than being able to buy them only at the close of the market each day, as is the case with mutual funds. As ETFs are like stocks, investors must pay brokerage fees to purchase them and they must be purchased in a fixed number of shares (typically in round lots of a hundred). The industry is highly concentrated. The three top providers, iShares (part of BlackRock), State Street (which uses the Spider brand for all its funds), and Vanguard, control almost 70 per cent of assets (The Economist, 2013).

There are two types of ETFs. *Physical ETFs* replicate the index by simply reconstituting the basket of physical securities underlying the index (e.g. the basket of S&P 500 stocks) with appropriate weights. They are the dominant form of ETF, especially in the US, and are mainly provided by large independent asset managers. *Synthetic ETFs* obtain the desired return through entering into an asset swap, i.e. an OTC derivative, instead of replicating the index physically. They have developed very rapidly in Europe to reach 45 per cent of that market (FSB, 2011). They are typically provided by asset management arms of banks. According to the FSB (2011), one factor supporting their growth resides in the synergies created within banking groups if the derivative trading desk acts as swap counterparty to the asset management arm providing the ETF. Another factor is the more liberal stance of European regulation on the use of derivatives in investment funds, while the US regulator has adopted a more conservative approach, limiting de facto the development of synthetic ETFs.

In a synthetic ETF (see Figure 8.3), the provider (typically a bank) sells ETF shares to investors in exchange for cash, which is then invested in a collateral basket, the return of which is swapped by the derivatives desk of the same bank for the return of an index. Since the swap counterparty is typically the bank also acting as ETF provider, investors may be exposed if the bank

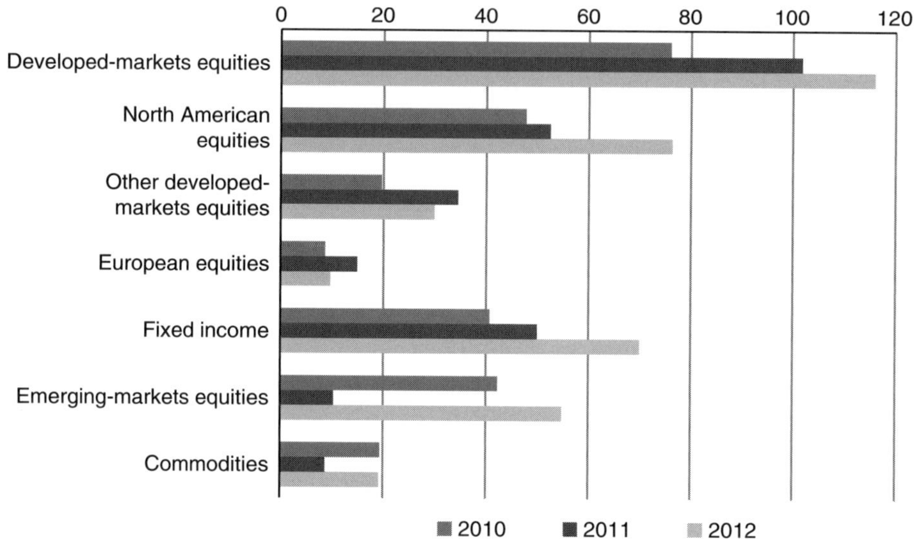

Figure 8.2 The ETF market: net flows by asset, 2010–2012 ($ billion)
Source: BlackRock

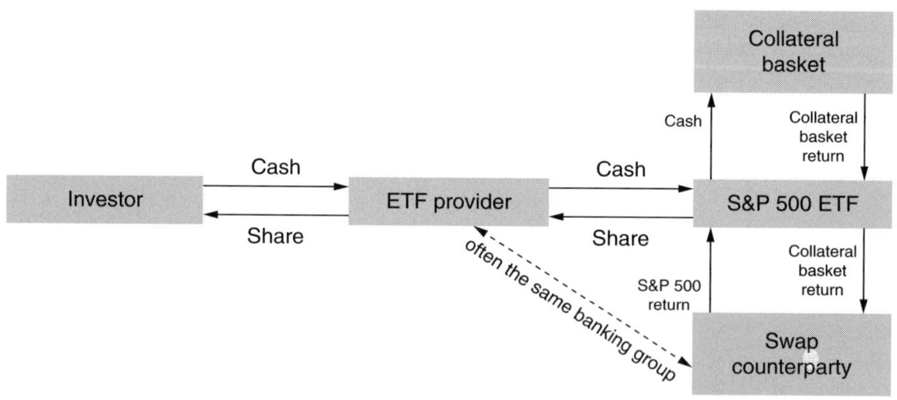

Figure 8.3 Simplified functioning of a synthetic ETF on the S&P 500
Source: FSB (2011)

defaults. Therefore, problems at those banks that are most active in swap-based ETFs may constitute a powerful source of contagion and systemic risk. As there is no requirement for the collateral composition to match the assets of the tracked index, the synthetic ETF creation process may be driven by the possibility for the bank to raise funding against an illiquid portfolio that cannot otherwise be financed in the repo market (FSB, 2011).

Securitisation of subprime mortgages

Until the financial crisis, the benefits of securitisation had been unquestioned. Securitisation is the technology which encouraged unbundling of the production processes for many credit services, permitting separate financial institutions to originate, service, fund, and assume the credit or market risks of a portfolio of loans or other assets (Greenspan, 1997). Numerous types of assets were routinely securitised, including residential mortgages, commercial mortgages, auto loans, and credit card loans. By bundling illiquid loans into packages on which securities could be issued, securitisation was thought to considerably expand the supply of funds available for lending and to distribute the risks of lending throughout the financial system.

As pointed out by Litan (2010), the main reason that securitisation now has a bad name is because of the financial mutation known as the collateralised debt obligations (CDOs). CDOs permitted subprime mortgages to be originated and sold to investors because of an innovation in the way investors were paid. Subprime is lending to individuals with a high level of default risk, because they have a low income or a less than perfect credit history relative to the standards of 'prime' borrowers. The share of subprime in origination of all mortgages rose steadily between 2001 and 2006, from 7.2 to 20.1 per cent. When housing prices started declining while interest increased, losses on these loans rapidly increased. According to recent estimates, these losses amounted to $1.4 trillion in the course of 2008. Although these losses were huge, their magnitude was by no means unprecedented – the losses from the dotcom crash wiped out $5 trillion in the market value of technology companies between March 2000 and October 2002.

What led to the subsequent financial turmoil was the securitisation of these mortgages. Instead of passing through the principal and interest payments made on the underlying mortgages directly to all holders of the securities, as was common for MBSs, the CDO divides securities purchasers into groups or 'tranches' with different risks. The CDO structures a 'waterfall' of payments that flows first to the most risk-averse investors, and then in stages, to investors with higher risk appetites. To provide additional comfort to investors, especially those in the first tranche, insurance is often arranged via, for instance, credit default swaps (CDSs). By structuring the payments in a waterfall-like fashion and layering them with insurance, issuers of CDOs were able to take subprime mortgages that otherwise separately would have received low ratings by the ratings agencies, and to repurpose them into higher-rated securities, whose first tranche even typically received an AAA rating. CDOs were often purchased at market value by off-balance sheet vehicles.

As pointed out by Gorton (2008), when the housing price bubble burst, this chain of securities, derivatives, and off-balance sheet vehicles was so complicated that most investors could not determine the location and size of the risks. For CDO investors and investors in other financial instruments that have CDO tranches in their portfolios, it was impossible to penetrate the chain backwards and value the chain based on the underlying mortgages, i.e. information was lost because of the difficulty of penetrating to the core assets. In a similar fashion, it was impossible for those at the start of the chain to use their information to value the chain 'upwards'. So due to the complexity of the financial instruments that were sold, it was unclear who was actually affected by losses on these instruments and to what extent.

8.4 Credit rating agencies

Functions

Since John Moody started in 1909 with a small rating book, the rating business has developed into a multi-billion-dollar industry. Credit rating agencies (CRAs) play an important role in financial markets through the production of credit risk information and its distribution to market participants. CRAs assess credit risk of borrowers (governments, financial, and non-financial firms) by providing credit ratings. A *credit rating* can be defined as an opinion regarding the creditworthiness of an entity, a debt, or financial obligation, debt security, preferred share, or other financial instrument, or of an issuer of such a debt or financial obligation, debt security, preferred share, or other financial instrument, issued using an established and defined ranking system of rating categories. A rating only refers to the credit risk; other risks, like market risk (the risk due to unfavourable movements in market prices) or liquidity risk (the risk that a given security or asset cannot be traded quickly enough in the market to prevent a loss), are not covered.

CRAs essentially provide two services. First, they offer an independent assessment of the ability of issuers to meet their debt obligations, thereby providing 'information services' that reduce information costs, increase the pool of potential borrowers, and promote liquid markets. Second, they offer 'monitoring services' through which they influence issuers to take corrective actions to avert downgrades via 'watch' procedures.

CRAs have come under attack due to their role in the recent financial crisis. According to many observers, CRAs underestimated the credit risk associated with structured credit products. For instance, more than three-quarters of all private residential mortgage-backed securities issued in the United States from 2005 to 2007 that were rated AAA by Standard & Poor's are now rated below BBB–, i.e. below investment grade (IMF, 2010).

According to the Financial Stability Forum (2008), poor credit assessments of complex structured credit products by CRAs contributed to both the build-up and the unfolding of the financial crisis. With the benefit of hindsight, it is widely believed that CRAs assigned high ratings to complex structured subprime debt based on inadequate historical data and in some cases flawed models. Structured credit products are designed to take advantage of different risk preferences of investors. They are therefore structured for each tranche to achieve a particular credit rating. CRAs generally give these first tranches the highest ratings possible. If during this structuring process CRAs discuss with issuers the rating implications of particular structures, there is a clear potential for conflicts of interest. These conflicts are exacerbated when CRAs also sell consulting services to entities that purchase ratings. Investors have arguably over-relied on CRA ratings, not realising that an AAA rating of a structured instrument is very different from an AAA rating of, say, a government bond.

CRAs have also come under fire for their sovereign rating activities. CRAs were condemned for exacerbating the recent European debt crisis when they downgraded the countries in the midst of the financial turmoil, thereby exacerbating the fiscal problems of countries like Greece, Ireland, Portugal, and Spain. According to Barroso (2010), the then-President of the European Commission, 'ratings appear to be too cyclical, too reliant on the general market mood rather than on fundamentals – regardless of whether market mood is too optimistic or too pessimistic'.

There are around 150 CRAs, but the three largest competitors share roughly 95 per cent of the market. Standard & Poor's Ratings Services and Moody's Investors Service each have 40 per cent of the market while Fitch Ratings holds 15 per cent (White, 2010). While most CRAs are regional or product-type specialists, the three biggest players are truly global and broad in their product coverage. What is more, the sovereign rating coverage of the big three dwarfs that of other CRAs. As of 30 July 2010, Standard & Poor's rated 125 sovereigns, Moody's 110, and Fitch 107 (IMF, 2010).

Credit ratings are expressed on a scale of letters and figures (see Figure 8.4). The Standard & Poor's rating scale is, for example, as follows: AAA (highest

Interpretation	Fitch and S&P	Moody's
Highest quality	AAA	Aaa
High quality	AA+	Aa1
	AA	Aa2
	AA–	Aa3
Strong payment capacity	A+	A1
	A	A2
	A–	A3
Adequate payment capacity	BBB+	Baa1
	BBB	Baa2
	BBB–	Baa3
Likely to fulfill obligations ongoing uncertainty	BB+	Ba1
	BB	Ba2
	BB–	Ba3
High-risk obligations	B+	B1
	B	B2
	B–	B3
Vulnerable to default	CCC+	Caa1
	CCC	Caa2
	CCC–	Caa3
Near or in bankruptcy or default	CC	Ca
	C	C
	D	D

Figure 8.4 Credit ratings
Source: IMF (2010)

rating), AA, A, BBB, BB, B, CCC, CC, C, D (lowest rating). Modifiers are attached to further distinguish ratings within classification. Whereas Fitch and Standard & Poor's use pluses and minuses, Moody's uses numbers. CRAs typically signal in advance their intention to consider rating changes, using 'outlooks' and rating reviews (so-called 'watchlists'). Whereas outlooks represent agencies' opinions on the development of a credit rating over the medium term, watchlists focus on a much shorter time horizon – three months, on average. The watch and outlook procedures are considered to be generally strong predictors of rating changes relative to other public data.

Sovereign credit ratings are an assessment by rating agencies of a government's ability and willingness to repay its public debt both in principal and in interests on time. These ratings are thus forward-looking qualitative measures of the probability of default. Figure 8.5 shows that the three major CRAs publish credit ratings for a high and increasing number of sovereigns.

Ratings play a crucial role in financial markets as investors use them to evaluate the credit risk of financial instruments. The assessment of these instruments requires specific knowledge and is highly time-consuming,

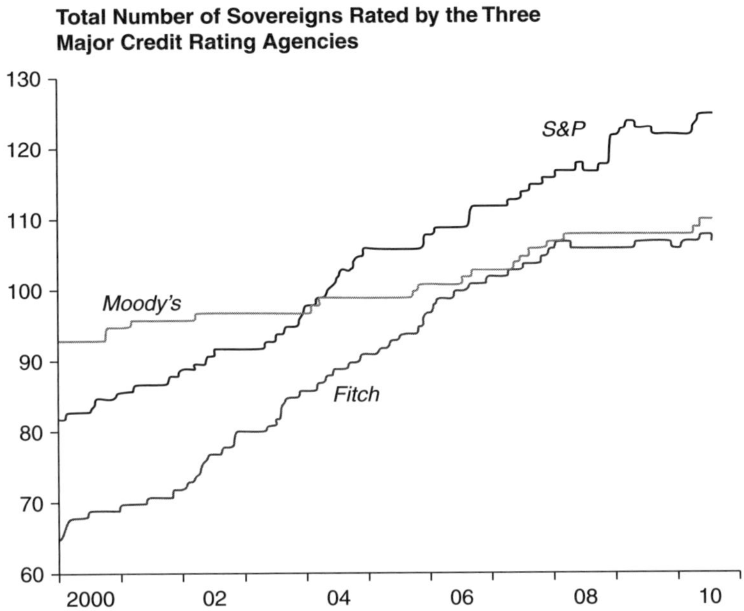

Figure 8.5 Total number of sovereigns rated by the big three CRAs
Source: IMF (2010)

making it attractive for individual investors to rely on the rating of the CRAs. The ratings have an important influence on the interest rate that borrowers have to pay. A downgrading generally leads quickly to a higher interest rate on loans. Portfolio manager performance is often benchmarked against standard indices that are usually constructed on the basis of credit ratings. This implies that a downgrade to below the investment-grade threshold (i.e. BBB-) often triggers immediate liquidation.

CRAs are mainly financed on the basis of an issuer-based compensation scheme, meaning that the agencies are paid by the issuers of these instruments to publish a rating. This may give agencies an incentive to overstate the creditworthiness of a particular product in order to build a good relationship with the issuer, thereby creating a conflict of interest. On the other hand, CRAs must safeguard their credibility with investors as their ratings would otherwise be of no value in the market. Yet, it is doubtful whether the potential loss of reputation sufficiently restrains CRAs and can indeed function as an effective form of sanction. CRAs may be manipulated by issuers which shop for a rating.

Regulating CRAs

Until recently, CRAs were mainly governed by the 'Code for Conduct Fundamentals for Credit Rating Agencies' of the International Organisation of Securities Commissions (IOSCO), which sets international standards for security markets. The IOSCO code has been updated in the wake of the global financial crisis. However, this code is based on voluntary compliance and lacks enforcement mechanisms (self-regulation). CRAs were supposed to follow the code or explain why they did not do so (comply or explain). In the wake of the financial crisis, the EU has introduced regulation for CRAs, focusing on registration, enhanced oversight, and transparency. While the European Commission considers the revised IOSCO code to be 'the global benchmark', it maintained that its substance had to be made more specific, to make it easier to apply in practice, and more efficient. Therefore, Regulation on Credit Rating Agencies (1060/2009/EC), which has been changed twice (by Regulation 513/2011 and Regulation 462/2013), determines that CRAs are supervised (see de Haan and Amtenbrink (2012) for details).

The European Securities and Markets Authority (ESMA) is, among other things, responsible for the registration and ongoing supervision of registered credit rating agencies. ESMA is an independent EU Authority that contributes to safeguarding the stability of the European Union's financial system by ensuring the integrity, transparency, efficiency, and orderly functioning of securities markets, as well as enhancing investor protection (see Chapter 12).

Under the EU Regulations, ratings for structured finance instruments must ensure that those credit rating categories that are attributed to structured finance instruments are clearly differentiated using a symbol, which distinguishes them from rating categories used for any other entities, financial instruments, or financial obligations. This should make it clear to investors that the ratings of structured finance instruments are different from the ratings of other financial instruments. CRAs are also obliged to disclose the methodologies, models, and key rating assumptions such as mathematical or correlation assumptions used in their credit rating activities as well as their material changes.

CRAs are obliged to disclose conflicts of interest in a complete, timely, clear, concise, specific, and prominent manner and record all significant threats to the rating agency's independence or that of its employees involved in the credit rating process, together with the safeguards applied to mitigate those threats. For instance, the administrative or supervisory board of a CRA must include at least one-third, but no less than two non-executive members who are independent with a non-renewable term in office not exceeding five years. At the same time, CRAs may no longer provide consultancy or advisory services to the rated entity or a related third party. Compensation arrangements of employees involved in the rating process may not be contingent on the amount of revenue that the CRA derives from the rated entities or related third parties to which the analyst or persons approving the credit ratings provide services.

Critics of the European Regulation argue that serious monitoring of the performance of CRAs is lacking. Goodhart (2009) has argued in favour of an independent institution, a CRA Assessment Centre (CRAAC), whose only task would be to assess the accuracy of CRA estimates and to publish comparative studies of such accuracy. All CRAs in all countries should be required to place with CRAAC a record of each product rated and a measure of the uncertainty of this rating. This might help competition as investors want forecast accuracy. At present, they have no simple or straightforward way of checking this, and therefore fall back on reliance on brand names, which reinforces oligopoly. At the same time, more competition may not lead to more reliable ratings, as more suppliers may give more opportunities for rating shopping. This is illustrated by a study of Becker and Milbourn (2010), who examine how the quality of ratings issued by Standard & Poor's and Moody's responded to the new competition presented by Fitch. These authors find that the ratings issued by Standard & Poor's and Moody's rose as competition increased, while the ratings are less informative about the value of bonds when raters faced more competition. Finally, the ability of firm level ratings to predict default became lower when Fitch got a higher market share.

8.5 Shadow banking

The shadow banking system can broadly be described as credit intermediation involving entities and activities outside the regular banking system (see Figure 8.6). Shadow banking comprises a chain of interconnected financial intermediaries that conduct either all three or any one of the classic banking functions, i.e. maturity, credit, and liquidity transformation, but without access to the explicit public safety nets of the deposit guarantee schemes and/or the central bank emergency liquidity assistance programmes (European Commission, 2014). It includes, for instance, Money Market Funds, hedge funds, and financial vehicle corporations. Different processes are carried out in the various parts of the chain, such as securitisation and the creation of structured products geared to a specific investor risk profile.

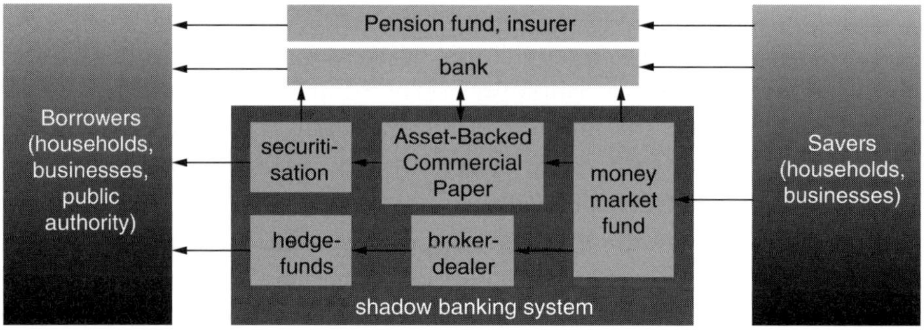

Figure 8.6 Shadow banking in the credit intermediation system
Source: Turner (2012)

Banks, insurers, and pension funds are by definition not part of the shadow banking system, but do interact with it. For example, banks are generally the originators of loans to the public, which are then securitised; institutional investors are in turn important buyers of securitised products. The opportunities for shadow banking have increased substantially in recent decades as financial flows have become less tied to national borders and specific sectors. Financial innovation is one of the drivers of this process, but so are supervisory and tax arbitrage (Broos *et al.*, 2012).

The shadow banking system provides a number of benefits, and hence constitutes a useful part of the financial system (Ghosh *et al.*, 2012). For example, shadow banks provide alternatives to bank deposits for large investors. Specialisation enables them to channel resources towards specific needs more efficiently. Moreover, shadow banks provide alternative funding for the real economy, for example by facilitating credit extension to certain sectors that might otherwise not have access to credit. Shadow banks can also provide funding and risk diversification as well as providing investors and banks with a range of tools for liquidity, maturity, and credit risk management.

At the same time, shadow banking activities can be an important source of systemic risk. The primary risks include (Ghosh *et al.*, 2012):

- The potential for excess leverage and amplification of procyclicality. Activities in the shadow banking system can be highly leveraged, including through securities financing transactions (SFTs) that entail a temporary transfer of securities by a lender to a borrower on a collateralised basis (see below). This can facilitate high levels of leverage since these assets can subsequently be used as collateral to raise more funds, which can then be used to buy more assets that in turn can be used as collateral to raise more funds, hence amplifying procyclicality.

- Instability of wholesale funding and potential for a 'modern-style bank run'. The shadow banking system relies on wholesale funding, which is not directly or permanently supported by any official safety net (such as a deposit guarantee scheme and access to central banks as lenders of last resort). Shadow banks undertake significant maturity and liquidity transformations, and many, if not most, fund themselves through short-term or callable deposit-like liabilities. This can expose the system to a 'run' or sudden, large-scale withdrawals by clients of their funds, undermining the wider financial system.
- Transmission of systemic risk. Shadow banking activities are often linked to the regular banking system through a complex web of interconnections. Commercial banks are often part of the shadow banking chain, or provide explicit or implicit support to the shadow banking entities to enable maturity and liquidity transformation. Also, banks often invest in financial products of shadow banks, alongside other providers of funds, such as consumers and corporations. The failure of an institution in the shadow banking sector could then generate significant contagion and affect the overall financial system stability.
- Regulatory arbitrage and circumvention. Shadow banking activities could be used to circumvent the tighter regulations imposed on banking institutions. Provided that shadow banks are not subject to a similar set of regulations and oversight, the tightening of the regulation of risky banking activities could push such activities from the regulated banking system toward less- or unregulated shadow banks, and could even generate systemically important non-bank financial institutions.

Not surprisingly, shadow banking is high on the international policy agenda, with the Financial Stability Board (FSB) playing a leading role. For the moment, a key objective is to get a better understanding of the shadow banking system and the associated vulnerabilities, and to monitor the system. Efforts are also underway to make risks more manageable, for example by tightening regulations for specific entities such as money market funds, or activities such as securitisation and securities lending. The financial system can also be strengthened indirectly, for example, by better protecting banks against risks in the shadow banking system through the existing supervision framework (Broos *et al.*, 2012).

In order to get a better understanding of developments within the shadow banking sector, the FSB looks at developments of 'Other Financial Intermediaries' (OFIs). The latter includes all financial institutions except for banks, insurers, and pension funds. An advantage of this particular measure

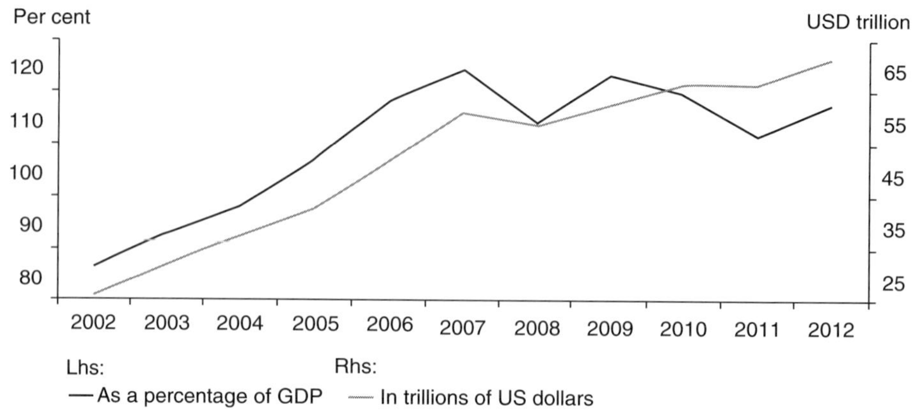

Figure 8.7 Assets of non-bank financial intermediaries, 2002–2012
Source: FSB (2013)

is that it can be easily compared and aggregated across countries. Disadvantage is that it includes various institutions that are actually not shadow banks, thereby blurring the picture somewhat.

Based on the OFIs measure, global non-bank financial intermediation grew by $5 trillion in 2012 to reach $71 trillion in 2012 (see Figure 8.7). Moreover, globally OFI assets represent on average about 24 per cent of total financial assets, about half of banking system assets, and 117 per cent of GDP. These patterns have been relatively stable since the crisis. By absolute size, advanced economies remain the ones with the largest non-bank financial systems (see Figure 8.8). The US had the largest system of non-bank financial intermediation at the end of 2012 with assets of $26 trillion, followed by the euro area ($22 trillion), the UK ($9 trillion), and Japan ($4 trillion).

Curtailing the generation of systemic risks in the shadow banking sector is an important regulatory driver. The European Commission has already implemented, or is in the process of implementing, a number of measures to provide a better framework for these risks, such as harmonised rules applying to hedge fund activity via the Alternative Investment Fund Managers Directive (AIFMD, 2011/61/EU) as well as proposals to improve the transparency of securities financing transactions and new rules on money market funds.

Alternative Investment Funds (AIFs) contain different investment funds. AIFs invest in a wide variety of asset types and employ very different investment strategies. *Inter alia*, hedge funds, private equity funds, infrastructure funds, commodity funds, real estate funds, or other special funds can all

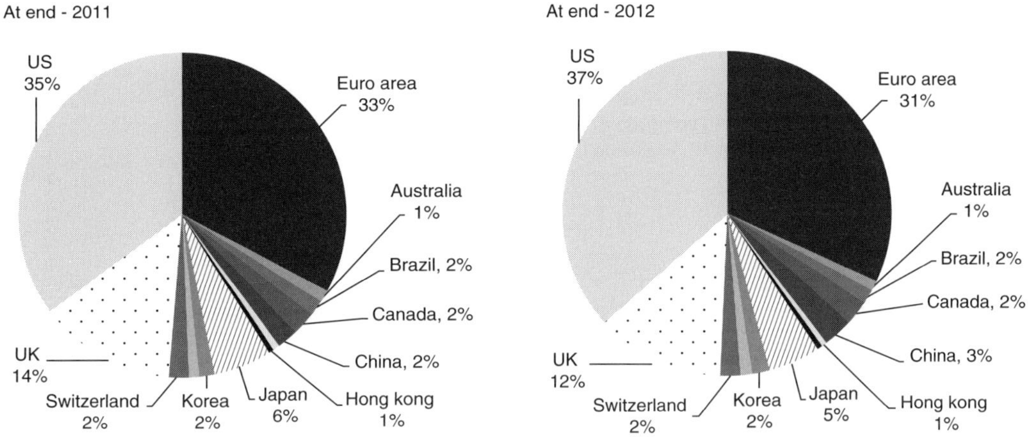

Figure 8.8 Share of assets of non-bank financial intermediaries
Source: FSB (2013)

be classified as AIFs. The AIF sector is estimated to represent around €2.5 trillion in assets. The AIFMD makes all AIF managers subject to appropriate authorisation and registration requirements, allows monitoring of macro- and microprudential risks, and introduces several investor protection tools (European Commission, 2014).

Securities financing transactions (SFTs) are transactions that use assets belonging to the counterparty to obtain funding from or to lend them out to another entity. In practice, this includes lending or borrowing of securities and commodities repurchase (repo) or reverse repurchase transactions, or buy-sell back or sell-buy back transactions. SFTs are used by almost all actors in the financial system, be they banks, securities dealers, insurance companies, pension funds, or investment funds. To ensure that regulators have access to the information, the proposed Regulation on the reporting and transparency of Securities Financing Transactions requires that all SFTs are reported to a trade repository, or, if that is not possible, directly to the European Securities and Markets Authority (ESMA). In order to ensure that investors have sufficient information over the use of SFTs, the proposal requires periodical reports and fund's pre-investment documents, such as the prospectus, to include detailed information on the use of those SFTs by fund managers.

Under the proposed MMF regulation, MMFs should have adequate liquidity to face investor's redemption requests. The proposal also aims to ensure that the portfolio of MMFs is of appropriate duration and sufficient quality.

The Commission proposal likewise introduces an obligation that MMFs gradually establish a capital buffer amounting to 3 per cent of the MMF's Net Asset Value (NAV). The proposed new rules are expected to enter into force in 2015 (European Commission, 2014).

8.6 Conclusions

Financial innovation is the act of creating and then popularising new financial instruments, as well as new financial technologies, institutions, and markets. Generally, financial innovation is driven by investor demand for a particular set of cash flows; financial regulation (e.g. opportunities to exploit regulatory gaps) or technological change. Financial innovations may improve payments, offer new savings and investment opportunities, and may increase risk sharing. Financial innovation can however also add to the fragility of the overall financial system.

In the aftermath of the 2007–2009 financial crisis, financial innovation has become controversial. While most innovations seem to have improved access to credit, made life more convenient, and in some cases even allowed the economy to grow faster, some innovations, such as collateralised debt obligations (CDOs) and structured investment vehicles (SIVs) were poorly designed, while others, such as credit default swaps (CDSs) and adjustable rate mortgages, were misused and contributed to the financial crisis and/or amplified the downturn in the economy when it started. Moreover, although financial innovation and greater macroeconomic stability may have made financial crises in developed countries less likely, it seems that innovations have made their impact greater than was previously the case.

Credit rating agencies (CRAs) play an important role in financial markets through the production of credit risk information on financial instruments (including new instruments) and its distribution to market participants. However, CRAs received heavy criticism over the past years due to: (1) the conflicts of interests inherent to their business model, (2) their role in the recent financial crisis, i.e. by underestimating the credit risk associated with structured credit products, and (3) their sovereign rating activities, i.e. when downgrading various EU Member States in the midst of the financial crisis, thereby exacerbating the fiscal problems of these countries.

The crisis has shown that the shadow banking sector can give rise to systemic risks. The increased complexity of financial instruments and entities involved has made the financial system less transparent. Moreover, the fact that parts of the shadow banking sector remain unregulated makes it difficult to spot and address emerging risks. The shadow banking system will continue to exploit new developments and policy initiatives. Moreover, stricter prudential requirements for banks (e.g. Basel III) provide incentives to move business to the shadow banking sector. It is therefore important to continue to closely monitor the shadow banking system and strengthen the regulatory and supervisory framework where needed.

Suggested Reading

Ali, R., J. Barrdear, R. Clews, and J. Southgate (2014), The Economics of Digital Currencies, *Quarterly Bulletin 2014 Q3*, Bank of England, London.

Gennaioli, N., A. Shleifer, and R. Vishny (2012), Neglected Risks, Financial Innovation, and Financial Fragility, *Journal of Financial Economics*, **104**, 452–468.

Lerner, J. and P. Tufano (2011), The Consequences of Financial Innovation: A Counterfactual Research Agenda, NBER Working Paper 16780.

Litan, R. (2010), In Defense of Much, But Not All, Financial Innovation, Wharton Financial Institutions Center Working Paper 2010–06.

References

Ali, R., J. Barrdear, R. Clews, and J. Southgate (2014), Innovations in Payment Technologies and the Emergence of Digital Currencies, *Quarterly Bulletin 2014 Q3*, Bank of England, London.

Barroso, J. M. Durão (2010), Statement to the European Parliament prior to the meeting of the Heads of State and Government of the Euro Area, European Parliament Plenary, Brussels, 5 May.

Becker, B. and T. Milbourn (2010), How Did Increased Competition Affect Credit Ratings? Available at: www.hbs.edu/research/pdf/09–051.pdf (accessed 13 February 2012).

Bernanke, B. (2009), Financial Innovation and Consumer Protection, At the Federal Reserve System's Sixth Biennial Community Affairs Research Conference, Washington DC, 17 April.

Broos, M., K. Carlier, J. Kakes, and E. Klaaijsen (2012), Shadow Banking: An Exploratory Study for the Netherlands, *DNB Occasional Studies*, **10**(5), DNB, Amsterdam.

de Haan, J. and F. Amtenbrink (2012), Taming the Beast? New European Regulation for Credit Rating Agencies,*Zeitschrift für Staats- und Europawissenschaften (ZSE)* [Journal for Comparative Government and European Policy], **4**, 433–458.

The Economist (2013), Twenty Years Young. The Anniversary of a Successful Financial Innovation, 26 January, 2013.

European Commission (2014), *Economic Review of the Financial Regulation Agenda*, EC, Brussels.

Financial Stability Board (2011), Potential Financial Stability Issues Arising from Recent Trends in Exchange-Traded Funds (ETFs), 12 April.

(2013), *Global Shadow Banking Monitoring Report 2013*, FSB, Basel.

Financial Stability Forum (2008), *Report of the Financial Stability Forum on Enhancing Market and Institutional Resilience*, 7 April, available at: www.fsforum.org/publications/r_0804.pdf (accessed 13 February 2012).

Gai, P., S. Kapadia, S. Millard, and A. Perez (2008), Financial Innovation, Macroeconomic Stability and Systemic Crises, *Economic Journal*, **118**, 401–426.

Gennaioli, N., A. Shleifer, and R. Vishny (2012), Neglected Risks, Financial Innovation, and Financial Fragility, *Journal of Financial Economics*, **104**, 452–468.

Ghosh, S., I. Gonzales del Mazo, and I. Öther-Robe (2012), Chasing the Shadows: How Significant Is Shadow Banking in Emerging Markets?, *Economic Premise*, 88, World Bank, Washington, DC.

Goodhart, C. (2009), *The Regulatory Response to the Financial Crisis*, Edward Elgar, Cheltenham.

Gorton, G. (2008), The Subprime Panic+, Yale International Center for Finance Working Paper 08–25.

Greenspan, A. (1997), Remarks by the Chairman of the Board of Governors of the US Federal Reserve System, Mr Alan Greenspan, at the Conference on Bank Structure and Competition of the Federal Reserve Bank of Chicago.

Hoggarth, G., R. Reis, and V. Saporta (2002), Costs of Banking System Instability: Some Empirical Evidence, *Journal of Banking and Finance*, **26**, 825–855.

Holmstrom, B. (2010), Comments on 'The Credit Rating Crisis', *NBER Macroeconomics Annual*, **24**(1), 215–222.

IMF (2010), The Uses and Abuses of Sovereign Credit Ratings, Chapter 3 in the 2010 IMF Global Financial Stability Report.

Krugman, P. (2007), Innovating Our Way to Financial Crisis, *New York Times*, 3 December.

Lerner, J. and P. Tufano (2011), The Consequences of Financial Innovation: A Counterfactual Research Agenda, NBER Working Paper 16780.

Levine, R. (2011), Finance, Long-run Growth, and Economic Opportunity, in: T. Beck (ed.), *The Future of Banking*, A VoxEU.org eBook, CEPR, London.

Litan, R. (2010), In Defense of Much, But Not All, Financial Innovation, Wharton Financial Institutions Center Working Paper 2010–06.

Shiller, R. and A. Weiss (1999), Home Equity Insurance, *Journal of Real Estate Finance and Economics* **19**, 21–47.

Turner, A. (2012), Securitisation, *Shadow Banking and the Value of Financial Innovation*, Financial Services Authority, London.

White, L. J. (2010), The Credit Rating Agencies, *Journal of Economic Perspectives*, **24**, 211–226.

Part III

Financial Institutions

CHAPTER

9

The Role of Institutional Investors

OVERVIEW

Over the last decades, the intermediation of financial assets has gradually shifted from banks towards institutional investors, such as pension funds, insurance companies, and mutual funds. In this process of re-intermediation, the assets of institutional investors of the EU-15 countries tripled from 49 per cent of GDP in 1990 to 165 per cent in 2012.

This chapter starts off with an overview of the growth of institutional investors over the last two decades. The development of the main types of institutional investors is documented. There is a small group of countries with large-scale funded pensions (Denmark, Ireland, the Netherlands, and the United Kingdom). Other countries rely more on life insurance and mutual funds. New types of institutional investment, such as hedge funds and private equity, are also discussed.

Both the demand side (growing investments by pension funds to cater for ageing, and by mutual funds to accommodate wealth accumulation of households) and the supply side (shift from bank-financing to market-financing) point to further growth of institutional investment. There is no substantial institutional investment yet in the new EU Member States, but institutional investors in these countries are expected to grow in line with economic development.

This chapter also analyses the impact of institutional investors on the functioning of the financial system. Institutional investors are pooling funds and transferring economic resources over different asset classes and countries. They also transfer resources over time. Moreover, they increase the efficiency of the financial system.

One would expect institutional investors to invest according to the principles of finance theory as implied by the international version of the Capital Asset Pricing Model (CAPM). This theory shows the gains of international diversification. However, there is a home bias in investments of institutional investors. Still, this bias declined from 1997 to 2012, especially in the countries in the euro area, a trend which can be attributed to the introduction of the euro. With the elimination of exchange-rate risk, investors based in the euro area have reallocated part of their portfolio from their home country to the wider euro area.

LEARNING OBJECTIVES

After you have studied this chapter, you should be able to:

- describe the different types of institutional investors and their functions
- understand the growth of institutional investment and the factors that explain this growth
- explain the theory of international diversification
- assess the home bias of institutional investments and the change in the home bias following the introduction of the euro.

9.1 Different types of institutional investors

This section describes the main types of institutional investors in the EU and their role in the EU financial system. *Institutional investors* are specialised financial institutions that manage collectively savings of small investors (Davis and Steil, 2001). The size of institutional investors differs across countries. Most countries in southern Europe are characterised by low institutional saving, while the role of institutional investors in north-western Europe is more important. The three most important categories of institutional investors are pension funds, insurance companies, and mutual funds. Table 9.1 illustrates the role of these institutional investors in the EU. For comparative purposes, Switzerland and the US are also included in this table.

Pension funds

Pension funds collect, pool, and invest funds contributed by sponsors (employers) and beneficiaries (employees and their family members) to provide for the future pension entitlements of beneficiaries.

In the EU, pay-as-you-go (PAYG) pensions are common to provide for some basic pension level (first tier). This system is not funded but based upon solidarity between generations, as the working generation has to pay for the pensions of the retired generation. Some countries have accumulated major pension assets, which provide beneficiaries with an additional pension (second tier). These funded pensions can be based on defined benefit or defined contribution (Davis and Steil, 2001 and Feldstein and Siebert, 2002). *Defined benefit (DB) funds* offer employees a guaranteed rate of return (the risk is

Table 9.1 Assets of different types of institutional investors (% of GDP), 2012

	Pension funds	Life insurance companies	Mutual funds	Total
Austria	5	35	49	89
Belgium	5	69	23	97
Bulgaria	7	7	1	15
Cyprus	n.a.	69	12	81
Czech Republic	7	11	5	24
Denmark	34	98	91	223
Estonia	9	5	3	17
Finland	3	29	35	67
France	0	102	53	155
Germany	6	44	51	101
Greece	0	8	3	11
Hungary	4	8	8	21
Ireland	40	141	622	803
Italy	2	34	14	50
Latvia	1	2	1	4
Lithuania	4	3	1	8
Luxembourg	3	325	5,675	6,002
Malta	0	29	210	239
Netherlands	168	78	98	344
Poland	17	9	10	36
Portugal	9	32	17	58
Romania	2	3	5	10
Slovakia	10	10	5	24
Slovenia	5	18	5	28
Spain	9	27	14	50
Sweden	9	87	49	146
United Kingdom	92	94	49	236
EU-15	28	66	72	165
NMS-12	10	10	8	28
EU-27	27	61	67	155
Switzerland	114	90	82	286
United States	75	42	80	197

Notes: EU-15, NMS-12, and EU-27 are calculated as a weighted average; n.a. means not available.

Source: ECB, OECD

borne by the employer), while the returns of *defined contribution (DC) funds* are solely determined by the market (the risk is borne by the employees). DC plans have gained popularity in recent years, as employers have sought to minimise the risk of their obligations, while employees desire funds that are readily transferable if they move from one job to another. A hybrid is the *collective defined contribution* (CDC) pension. This does not guarantee a certain return by the company, but employees are able to save collectively for their pension via their employer and to pool risks.

The role of pension funds in the financial system differs across countries. In countries with large pension assets (relative to GDP), such as the Netherlands, Switzerland, the UK, and the US, pension funds are an important vehicle for collective saving for retirement purposes (see Table 9.2). Pension funds in these countries are among the largest investors, with assets under management worth billions of euros (for example, the Dutch civil servants' pension fund ABP; see Box 9.1). Historically, some large EU countries (like Germany, France, and Italy) have relied on other forms of retirement funding. The lack of a funded pension system in these countries directed households towards life insurances and mutual funds.

Since early withdrawal of funds is usually restricted or forbidden, a pension fund has long-term liabilities resulting in a long-term oriented investment strategy. This allows a pension fund to hold high-risk/return instruments (for example, investments in commodities, hedge funds, and private equity). Clients of a pension fund have no (direct) influence on the investment process of the fund but are protected by regulation, since pension funds have to comply with the 'prudent person' rule (they should, for example, diversify their portfolios). Moreover, pension funds are under the scrutiny of financial supervisors (see Chapter 12). Table 9.2 shows the growth of pension fund assets from 2001 to 2012. The years 2007 and 2009 are also highlighted to see the impact of the financial crisis in 2007–2009.

Insurance companies

Life insurance companies offer a mix of long-term saving and insurance products. Historically, life insurance companies provided insurance for dependants against the risk of death, but life insurers increasingly also offer long-term saving products. Pension funds and life insurance companies therefore often have close ties. Life insurance companies offer annuities for guaranteeing pension benefits as well as guaranteed investment contracts that may be purchased by pension funds. *Non-life insurance companies*

Table 9.2 Assets of pension funds (in € billion and % of GDP), 2001–2012

	2001		2007		2009		2012	
	euro	%	euro	%	euro	%	euro	%
Austria	8	4	13	5	14	5	16	5
Belgium	14	6	14	4	14	4	18	5
Bulgaria	n.a.	n.a.	1	4	2	5	3	7
Cyprus	n.a.	n.a.	n.a.	n.a.	n.a.	n.a.	n.a.	n.a.
Czech Republic	2	3	6	5	8	6	11	7
Denmark	42	23	61	27	65	29	82	34
Estonia	0	0	1	5	1	7	2	9
Finland	0	0	0	0	5	3	6	3
France	0	0	2	0	4	0	6	0
Germany	74	4	112	5	126	5	168	6
Greece	0	0	0	0	0	0	0	0
Hungary	3	4	11	11	13	14	4	4
Ireland	51	44	87	46	69	42	66	40
Italy	10	1	26	2	26	2	34	2
Latvia	0	0	0	0	0	1	0	1
Lithuania	0	0	1	2	1	4	1	4
Luxembourg	n.a.	n.a.	0	1	0	1	1	3
Malta	0	0	0	0	0	0	0	0
Netherlands	451	101	763	134	745	130	1,007	168
Poland	6	3	39	13	42	13	65	17
Portugal	15	11	22	13	22	13	15	9
Romania	n.a.	n.a.	0	0	1	1	2	2
Slovakia	n.a.	n.a.	2	4	4	6	7	10
Slovenia	0	1	1	3	1	4	2	5
Spain	45	7	88	8	86	8	88	9
Sweden	59	24	29	8	27	9	39	9
United Kingdom	1,180	74	1,488	72	1,265	80	1,786	92
EU-15	1,949	22	2,705	23	2,467	23	3,332	28
NMS-12	10	3	63	7	73	8	97	10
EU-27	1,959	21	2,768	22	2,540	22	3,429	27

Notes: EU-15, NMS-12, and EU-27 are calculated as a weighted average; n.a. means not available.
Source: ECB

protect against risks such as accidents, illness, theft, and fire. As the asset base of life insurance is far larger than that of non-life insurance, the remainder of this section focuses on life insurance.

All EU-15 countries (except for Greece) have significant life insurance assets relative to GDP. Table 9.3 indicates that life insurance assets are

Box 9.1 ABP

The ABP (Algemeen Burgerlijk Pensioenfonds) is the Dutch pension fund for employers and employees of the government and the educational sector. It was founded by the government in 1922 and privatised in 1996. ABP provides its 2.8 million customers (employees, former employees, pensioners) with income security against pension, disability, and death.

ABP is the third largest pension fund in the world with around €360 billion of assets at the end of 2013. Given its objective to guarantee an adequate pension at all times at the lowest possible premiums, ABP's investment policy is geared towards a long-term risk-return profile. Diversification is a key element of that policy. The investment mix consists of 65 per cent in equities and alternative investments, such as real estate, private equity, and commodities, and 35 per cent in bonds. Over time, the share of equities and alternative investments has increased (see Figure 9.1). The geographical mix consists of 12 per cent of assets in the Netherlands, 41 per cent in the rest of Europe, and 47 per cent in the rest of the world.

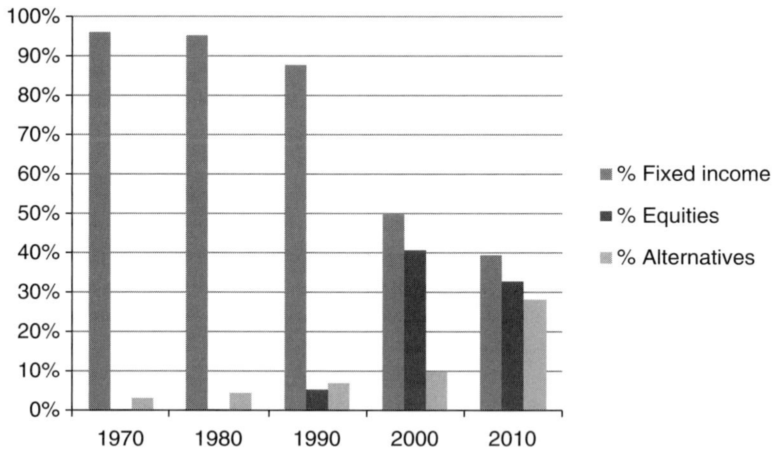

Figure 9.1 Portfolio of ABP (% share), 1970–2010
Source: ABP

concentrated in the UK, France, and Germany. The Netherlands and Italy also have a large life insurance industry. Life insurance companies function as retirement saving vehicles in countries with a weak pension sector (such as Belgium, France, Germany, and Italy). As life insurance companies offer a diverse range of products, they have different kinds of liabilities, which allows

Table 9.3 Assets of insurance companies (in € billion and % of GDP), 2001–2012

	2001		2007		2009		2012	
	euro	%	euro	%	euro	%	euro	%
Austria	58	27	88	32	98	35	108	35
Belgium	116	45	217	65	220	65	261	69
Bulgaria	n.a.	n.a.	1	4	2	6	3	7
Cyprus	2	18	n.a.	n.a.	10	60	12	69
Czech Republic	5	8	12	9	14	10	17	11
Denmark	97	54	163	72	183	82	241	98
Estonia	0	3	1	5	1	5	1	5
Finland	32	23	53	30	48	28	56	29
France	837	56	1,374	72	1,760	93	2,072	102
Germany	943	45	1,109	46	1,164	49	1,186	44
Greece	12	9	20	9	16	7	15	8
Hungary	3	6	9	8	8	9	8	8
Ireland	56	48	163	86	204	126	231	141
Italy	307	25	540	35	542	36	536	34
Latvia	0	2	1	2	1	3	1	2
Lithuania	0	1	1	3	1	4	1	3
Luxembourg	29	127	61	161	101	284	140	325
Malta	1	12	1	25	2	27	2	29
Netherlands	297	66	362	64	385	67	468	78
Poland	13	6	33	10	29	9	35	9
Portugal	27	21	53	31	58	34	53	32
Romania	n.a.	n.a.	2	1	3	3	4	3
Slovakia	1	6	5	9	6	10	7	10
Slovenia	1	6	4	12	5	15	6	18
Spain	149	22	243	23	262	25	276	27
Sweden	0	0	276	82	251	86	356	87
United Kingdom	1,740	109	2,098	102	1,634	103	1,821	94
EU-15	4,699	52	6,820	59	6,925	64	7,821	66
NMS-12	27	6	69	8	82	9	96	10
EU-27	4,726	50	6,889	56	7,007	60	7,917	61

Notes: EU-15, NMS-12, and EU-27 are calculated as a weighted average; n.a. means not available.
Source: ECB

them a certain degree of diversification. Life insurance companies sell their products in a competitive market and compete both with each other and with pension funds and mutual funds. As a result, life companies may have a strong incentive for risk taking on the asset side.

From a customer point of view, the economic function of life insurance companies is (next to insurance for dependants) the provision of customised saving schemes. Saving and investing via life insurance is aimed not only at retirement but also at other long-term saving objectives (like the education of siblings), which makes them not only a substitute but also a supplement to pensions. While pension schemes are more standardised, life insurance products can be tailored towards the needs of an individual. But this advantage comes at a price. The transaction and marketing costs of life policies are far higher than the costs of pension contracts.

Mutual funds

The mutual fund industry is among the most successful financial innovations (Khorana *et al.*, 2005). *Mutual funds* are investment vehicles whose underlying assets are identifiable and are marked to market on a regular (usually daily) basis. Moreover, the specific assets of the fund can be created or redeemed upon demand. Mutual funds contractually link investors' claims to the underlying asset. Investors can easily enter and exit the fund and pay or receive current market prices for their investments. Investors in mutual funds are residual claimants and bear all the risk of the fund.

The primary role of mutual funds is the pooling of funds. In contrast to pension funds, they do not necessarily transfer these funds over time. Many investors in mutual funds have a relatively short investment horizon, so the mutual fund is not specifically intended for retirement saving. The size of mutual funds differs sharply, ranging from small, specialised funds to major players like Fidelity Investments and Vanguard (having each about $2,000 billion of assets under management in 2014). These larger funds also have important stakes in companies, which makes them prominent players in corporate governance.

Investors choose a fund with a specific investment objective (for instance, a bond fund, an equity fund, or an emerging market fund). The asset allocation of the fund is generally fixed by the prospectus, while the security selection process is either active or passive. Active asset managers try to 'beat the market' by picking stocks that they consider good investments. Passive funds 'track' the index and do not deviate from the market benchmark. They generally incur lower transaction costs and have lower investment fees.

Table 9.4 illustrates the growth of mutual funds between 2001 and 2012. Luxembourg and Ireland are outliers due to a favourable tax treatment of these funds. Remarkable is the large size of mutual fund investment in France

Table 9.4 Assets of mutual funds (in € billion and % of GDP), 2001–2012

	2001		2007		2009		2012	
	euro	%	euro	%	euro	%	euro	%
Austria	98	45	161	59	141	51	150	49
Belgium	87	34	118	35	94	28	87	23
Bulgaria	n.a.	n.a.	1	2	0	1	1	1
Cyprus	n.a.	n.a.	1	8	1	8	2	12
Czech Republic	3	4	4	3	4	3	8	5
Denmark	38	21	137	60	116	52	224	91
Estonia	0	1	1	8	1	4	1	3
Finland	12	9	49	27	43	25	67	35
France	649	43	1,201	63	1,013	54	1,068	53
Germany	794	38	1,054	43	1,060	45	1,350	51
Greece	17	13	15	6	8	3	5	3
Hungary	3	5	10	9	8	8	8	8
Ireland	182	155	516	272	459	283	1,019	622
Italy	395	32	291	19	225	15	216	14
Latvia	0	0	0	1	0	1	0	1
Lithuania	0	0	0	1	0	0	0	1
Luxembourg	854	3,779	1,933	5,156	1,694	4,757	2,434	5,675
Malta	1	12	1	22	7	109	15	210
Netherlands	112	25	100	18	456	80	587	98
Poland	3	2	37	12	23	7	38	10
Portugal	26	20	40	23	33	20	28	17
Romania	n.a.	n.a.	4	3	2	2	7	5
Slovakia	n.a.	n.a.	2	4	2	3	4	5
Slovenia	3	11	4	12	2	6	2	5
Spain	158	23	299	28	194	18	148	14
Sweden	87	35	156	46	141	48	200	49
United Kingdom	362	23	684	33	627	39	954	49
EU-15	3,871	43	6,753	59	6,303	58	8,538	72
NMS-12	12	3	66	8	49	6	85	8
EU-27	3,883	41	6,819	55	6,352	54	8,623	67

Notes: Mutual fund data includes both UCITS (equity, bonds, balanced, money market, funds of funds, and other UCITS funds) and non-UCITS (real estate funds, special funds, and other non-UCITS). UCITS are collective investment schemes, which can operate freely throughout the EU on the basis of a single authorisation (see Chapter 12). EU-15, NMS-12, and EU-27 are calculated as a weighted average; n.a. means not available.

Source: ECB

and Germany. The new Member States have the smallest mutual fund market size relative to GDP. Also, in Italy and Spain this market is small.

Special types of institutional investors

In addition to the three main types of institutional investors described above, two other important institutional asset managers are hedge funds and private equity investors. During the last decade, they have gained popularity as they offer opportunities to diversify risk and increase expected returns.

Originally, *hedge funds* were eclectic investment pools, typically organised as private partnerships and often located offshore for tax and regulatory reasons. Since they operate through private placements and restrict share ownership to wealthy individuals and institutions, most disclosure and regulation requirements that apply to mutual funds and banks do not apply to hedge funds. Funds legally domiciled outside the main financial market countries are generally subject to even fewer regulations. Hedge-fund managers, who are paid on a fee-for-performance basis, are free to use a variety of investment techniques, including short positions and leverage, to raise returns and limit the investment risks. In contrast to investment funds, hedge funds concentrate more on absolute than on relative returns. The primary aim of most hedge funds used to be to reduce volatility and risk while attempting to deliver positive returns under all market conditions ('hedging'). However, the investment strategy of many funds has become more risky over the last decade, including the use of leverage. The aggressive investment style of some hedge funds can land them in financial trouble, as the bailout of the hedge fund LTCM in 1998 illustrates (see Box 9.2).

Box 9.2 The LTCM crisis

The hedge fund Long-Term Capital Management (LTCM) was founded in 1994. Its Board of Directors included Nobel Prize winners Myron Scholes and Robert Merton. The core strategy of LTCM was convergence trades, trying to take advantage of small differences in prices among closely related securities (Jorion, 2000). Compare, for example, a less liquid (called off-the-run) Treasury bond yielding 6.1 per cent versus 6.0 per cent for the more recently issued (called on-the-run) Treasury bond. The yield spread represents some compensation for the liquidity risk. Over a year, a trade that is long off-the-run and short on-the-run would generate a return of 10 basis points. The

Box 9.2 (cont.)

key is that eventually the two bonds converge to the same value at maturity. LTCM used this strategy in a variety of markets, such as spreads on different government bonds, mortgage-backed versus government securities, high-yielding versus low-yielding European bonds, equity pairs (stocks with different share classes), and so on. Most of the time, these trades should be profitable except for default or market disruption.

Such strategies generate tiny profits, so that leverage has to be used to create attractive returns. At the time of the crisis in 1998, LTCM had borrowed $125 billion compared with equity of $5 billion. This led to a *leverage ratio L*, defined as debt to equity, of 25. The following equation illustrates the impact of leverage: $r_{equity} = r_{assets} + L(r_{assets} - r_{debt})$. When the return on assets r_{assets} is higher than the return on debt r_{debt}, a large leverage would generate a high return on equity r_{equity}. But when the return on assets drops below that on debt, a large leverage would generate sizeable losses.

Initially, this strategy was very productive, with annual profits of almost 40 per cent. But losses occurred due to the Russian financial crisis in August 1998 when the Russian government defaulted on its bonds. Panicking investors sold Japanese and European bonds to buy US Treasury bonds. The profits that were supposed to occur as the value of these bonds converged became huge losses as the value of the bonds diverged. LTCM's equity capital dropped to around $600 million. The Federal Reserve Bank of New York organised a bailout of $3.6 billion by major creditors (14 leading investment banks) to avoid more collapses, without committing its own money. In return, the participating banks got a 90 per cent share in the fund. The fear was that there would be a chain reaction as LTCM liquidated its securities to cover its debt, leading to a drop in prices, which would force other companies to liquidate their own debt, creating a vicious cycle. The total losses amounted to $4.6 billion. After the bailout, the panic abated and the positions formerly held by LTCM were eventually even liquidated at a small profit to the bailers (Jorion, 2000). LTCM closed its books in 2000.

Critics have pointed out that this bailout increased moral hazard problems as financial institutions could take more risks because they suffer less in case of failure (Kho *et al.*, 2000). While central bankers typically argue that a bailout is necessary to prevent contagion and systemic threats, academics stress moral hazard. Furfine (2006) has estimated the potential costs of the Fed's intervention by examining the rates for interbank borrowing of large banks. The spreads on interbank borrowing go down if the market believes that these banks are 'too big to fail'.

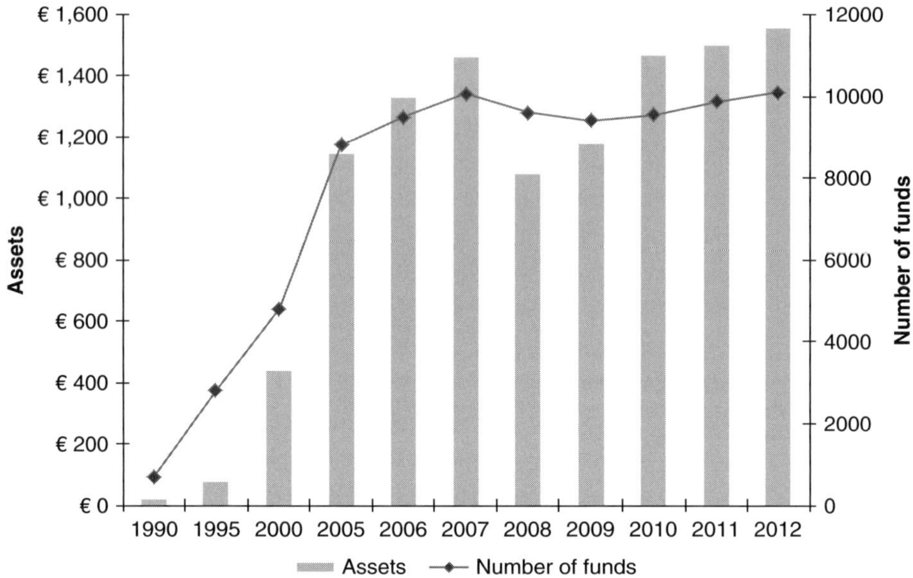

Figure 9.2 Global hedge funds market (number of funds and assets in € billion), 1990–2012
Source: TheCityUK (2013)

Figure 9.2 illustrates the enormous growth of the hedge-fund industry. While there was a strong decline during the financial crisis in 2008, it is estimated that hedge funds in total managed around €1,600 billion in 2012. Total investment positions of hedge funds are even bigger as they can leverage their assets through borrowing money and through the use of derivatives, short positions, and structured securities. The growth of the hedge-fund industry was initially driven by investments by wealthy individuals and institutions looking for higher returns. However, during the last decade small investors have been able to invest via *funds of hedge funds*, which are investment funds that invest solely in hedge funds. Also, pension funds invest in hedge funds and funds of funds, as illustrated in Figure 9.3.

The distinctions between hedge funds and other types of funds are blurring. Hedge funds are characterised as unregulated private funds that can take on significant leverage and employ complex trading strategies using derivatives or other new financial instruments. Although private equity funds are usually not considered hedge funds, they are also typically unregulated and often use leverage for their investments. However, new regulations for hedge funds and private equity were introduced in the aftermath of the financial crisis (see Chapter 12). Traditional asset managers also increasingly

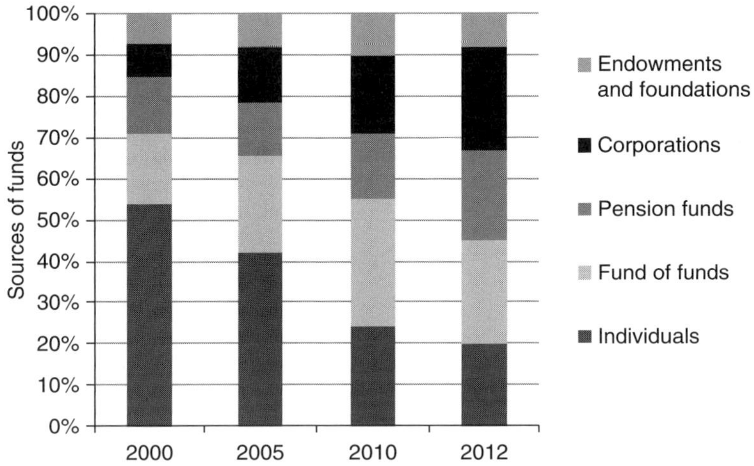

Figure 9.3 Hedge funds' sources of capital (% of total funds), 2000–2012
Source: TheCityUK (2013)

use derivatives or invest in structured securities that allow them to take leveraged or short positions.

In general, hedge funds provide liquidity and absorb risk. Moreover, due to their innovative trading strategies, they also play a role in financial innovation (see Chapter 8). Hedge funds thus improve the efficiency of the financial system. At the same time, they have the potential to amplify market price fluctuations if their investment behaviour becomes one-sided or if they concentrate on specific markets, in particular small-sized and low-liquidity markets. Hedge funds fall under the Alternative Investment Fund (AIF) Managers Directive (AIFMD). This European Directive makes all AIF managers subject to appropriate authorisation and registration requirements, allows monitoring of macro- and microprudential risks, and introduces several investor protection tools (European Commission, 2014).

Private equity investors invest in non-public companies and often finance these investments with a significant amount of debt, up to 90 per cent in the case of a leveraged buyout. By means of investment funds, which are open to certain institutions and wealthy individuals, they invest in companies and aim at annual returns of 20–25 per cent. This makes them attractive for institutional investors also. Some institutional investors invest in private equity by means of their own private equity branch. An example is AlpInvest, a private equity company owned until recently by two Dutch pension funds (ABP and PGGM, the Dutch pension fund for the healthcare and social work sector). In 2011 AlpInvest was sold to the Carlyle Group.

Table 9.5 The most important countries with private equity investments (€ billion and %) in 2011

	Total investment value	Market share	As % of GDP
United States	86.6	46%	0.8%
United Kingdom	23.2	12%	1.3%
China	15.5	8%	0.3%
France	10.0	5%	0.5%
India	7.7	4%	0.6%
Germany	4.6	2%	0.2%
Others	42.5	22%	–
Total	190.1	100%	–

Source: TheCityUK (2012)

Table 9.5 illustrates that the US and the UK have the biggest private equity markets, while China has rapidly increased towards the third biggest market. Relative to GDP, private equity markets are small. Still, these markets are growing rapidly, driven by the demand for risky assets and exposure to the non-public market. Private equity funds have become an important source of funds for start-up firms, private middle-market firms, firms in financial distress, and public firms seeking buyout financing (Smit, 2003).

Differences among institutional investors

Institutional investors differ from each other along three dimensions. First, the client base of the investor can be captive or can be determined via the market. In continental Europe, defined benefit pension funds often have a captive client base, as most employers use only one fund. In contrast, mutual funds must compete for clientele by means of low fees and/or an excellent track record.

Second, the investment horizon of institutional investors differs sharply. While pension funds have a very long investment horizon, mutual funds can have short-term investment objectives.

Third, the asset-allocation process differs across institutional investors. Mutual funds mainly focus on security selection or 'stock picking' and individual investors select the mutual fund that best matches with their risk preferences. Pension funds and life insurance companies take investment decisions concerning the percentage of equity and bonds in their portfolios, and diversify the risks within these asset classes. Figure 9.4 illustrates these differences.

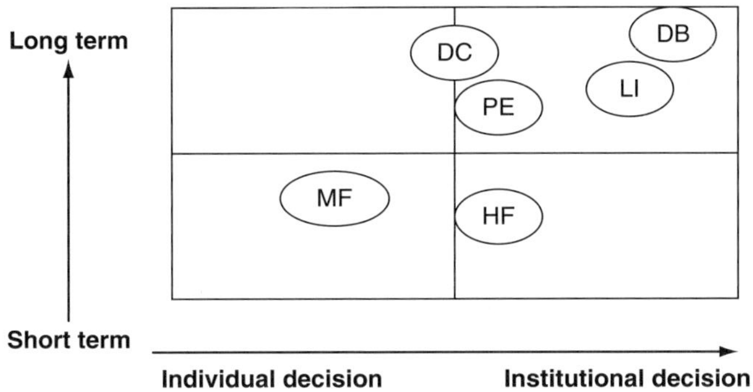

Figure 9.4 Investment horizon and decision power about asset allocation
Note: MF = mutual fund; DC = defined contribution pension scheme; DB = defined benefit pension scheme; LI = life insurance company; PE = private equity; HF = hedge fund.

9.2 The growth of institutional investors

Re-intermediation

Institutional investors have made banks less important as intermediaries of financial assets, a development which Rajan (2007) calls '*re-intermediation*' (see Table 9.6). Also, in countries with a bank-dominated financial system, like France, Germany and Italy, the role of institutional investors has increased. This is mainly due to the growth of the mutual fund industry. Nevertheless, the largest EU countries are still mainly bank-oriented. Outside Europe, institutional investors are more important financial intermediaries. The US is the prime example, where institutional claims are twice as large as bank claims. As Box 9.3 explains, re-intermediation is less important in the new EU Member States, as the role of institutional investors in those countries is currently rather limited.

Table 9.7 illustrates that the total claims of institutional investors in the EU-15 have increased enormously over the last two decades. The weighted average of assets to GDP rose from 49 per cent in 1990 to 165 per cent in 2012. In the US, institutional investment shows a similar trend, with an increase from 80 per cent of GDP in 1990 to 197 per cent in 2012. When the global stock markets tumbled after the Internet bubble in 2000 and the financial crisis in 2008, the assets of institutional investors declined sharply. The turmoil on the global financial markets reveals the vulnerability of institutional investors (with equity investments of up to 50 per cent of their portfolio) to such downward

Table 9.6 Bank and institutional intermediation ratios (in % of intermediated claims), 1970–2010

		1970	1980	1990	2000	2010	Δ 1970–2010
France	*Bank*	95	94	81	71	71	**–24**
	Institutional	5	6	19	29	29	**24**
Germany	*Bank*	89	88	83	76	72	**–17**
	Institutional	11	12	17	24	28	**17**
Italy	*Bank*	94	95	90	72	81	**–13**
	Institutional	6	5	10	28	19	**13**
United	*Bank*	67	71	63	60	73	**6**
Kingdom	*Institutional*	33	29	37	40	27	**–6**
EU4	***Bank***	**86**	**87**	**79**	**70**	**74**	**–12**
	Institutional	**14**	**13**	**21**	**30**	**26**	**12**
Canada	*Bank*	66	74	64	55	56	**–10**
	Institutional	34	26	36	45	44	**10**
Japan	*Bank*	82	78	70	60	51	**–31**
	Institutional	18	22	30	40	49	**31**
United States	*Bank*	65	65	51	43	33	**–32**
	Institutional	35	35	49	57	67	**32**
G7	***Bank***	**80**	**81**	**72**	**62**	**62**	**–18**
	Institutional	**20**	**19**	**28**	**38**	**38**	**18**

Notes: The intermediation ratio measures the share of the financial claims of banks and institutional investors as a percentage of total intermediated claims. The sum of bank and institutional ratios add up to 100. Data for other EU Member States and time periods are not available, but the objective of this table is to show the shift from bank to institutional intermediation.
Source: Updated from Davis (2003)

market pressures. Nevertheless, institutional investors are long-term investors that tend to keep their equity holdings more or less constant. They recover earlier losses when equity markets bounce back.

Drivers of growth of institutional investment

The growth of institutional investment can be explained by supply and demand factors. Institutional investors have become more efficient in their function as a financial intermediary, while households have an enhanced need for services provided by institutional investors. Institutional investors are well placed to perform the key functions of the financial system as identified in Chapter 1, i.e. trade, manage, and diversify risk, and reduce information and trading costs.

Box 9.3 Institutional investment in the new EU Member States

Institutional investment can be seen as a luxury good. The most basic financial needs of households are the use of currency (coins and banknotes) and bank services (depositing and lending). Only when their income is increasing do households start to buy insurance and to save for retirement. This relationship is presented in Figure 9.5. Institutional investment starts to develop at a GDP per capita of around €15,000 and becomes meaningful beyond levels of €20,000. Currently, the new EU Member States (as well as Greece and Portugal, which entered the EU in the 1980s) have a very small institutional sector, but institutional investment in these countries is expected to grow in line with economic development.

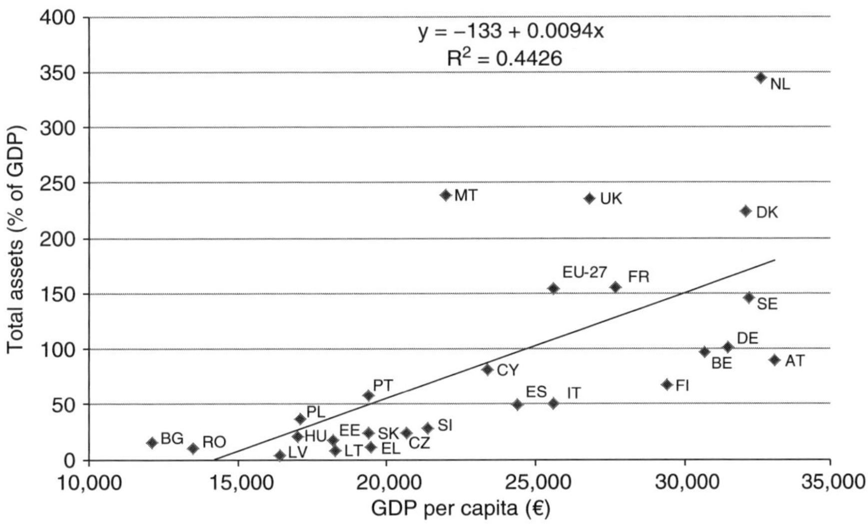

Figure 9.5 Institutional investment and economic development, 2012
Note: Total assets of institutional investment are defined as the assets of pension funds, insurance companies, and mutual funds. Ireland and Luxembourg are excluded, as they attract mutual funds from other countries due to a favourable tax regime.
Source: Own calculations based on ECB and Eurostat data

Supply-side factors

Institutional investors are pooling funds from individual households. Due to economies of scale, they are able to invest these funds more efficiently than individuals. Moreover, institutional investors are able to invest in assets that are indivisible (such as property) and therefore often not available to small

Table 9.7 Assets of institutional investors (% of GDP), 1990–2012

	1990	1995	2000	2005	2010	2012
Austria	22	35	71	99	94	89
Belgium	40	41	83	101	100	97
Denmark	53	69	103	149	189	223
Finland	6	16	43	52	62	67
France	49	76	127	120	154	155
Germany	34	45	81	98	99	101
Greece	1	12	32	20	10	11
Ireland	n.a.	53	199	366	598	803
Italy	12	26	63	61	51	50
Luxembourg	790	2,017	4,084	4,853	5,750	6,002
Netherlands	120	151	199	209	293	344
Portugal	8	35	52	65	64	58
Spain	n.a.	43	59	60	50	50
Sweden	47	65	109	157	152	146
United Kingdom	105	167	213	209	234	236
EU-15	49	73	125	137	155	165
Switzerland	107	141	224	248	282	286
United States	80	122	177	185	194	197

Notes: EU-15 is calculated as a weighted average; n.a. means not available.
Source: ECB, OECD

investors. So, institutional investors provide diversified portfolios at low cost to households. For instance, a mutual fund requires a low level of minimum investment and offers households the possibility to invest in a diversified way. Costs of asset management are low as they are shared among many households, so that institutional investors offer an attractive risk-return profile.

Because of their policy to hedge exposure and to diversify their investments, institutional investors are increasingly using derivatives. Many of the new risk-management tools have been developed especially for institutional investors, increasing the efficiency of the financial system. Furthermore, when institutional investors adopt more active trading policies, they enhance the liquidity of markets, leading to higher efficiency and lower transaction costs. According to Davis (2003, p. 21), 'by demanding liquidity, institutional investors help to generate it'.

With respect to corporate governance, institutional investors have more 'bargaining power' than individual investors as they are often important shareholders in companies. However, the different types of institutional investors are not equally active in corporate governance. Gillan and Starks (2003) distinguish between pressure-sensitive and insensitive institutional investors. Pressure-sensitive investors are bankers and insurers who care about current or potential business relations with corporations in which they invest. They are more passive institutions. Pension funds and mutual funds are not sensitive to pressure and therefore are more active institutions. In particular, public pension funds are the pioneers in active corporate governance. Well-known examples are Hermes (the UK postal pension fund), CalPERS (California Public Employees' Retirement System), and ABP (see Box 9.1). More recently, hedge funds have become aggressive players in corporate governance.

Also, deregulation has spurred the development of institutional investors. For example, fees have been reduced and institutional investors have more freedom to investment internationally and to distribute their products to a wider public. Deregulation has also stimulated competition among asset management institutions, which has lowered costs for the end-user, i.e. households. The European Commission plays a crucial role in regulatory issues concerning institutional investors. Because of the ageing problems that the EU Member States face (see below), the Commission urged countries to reform their pension schemes. At the same time, the Commission proposed a number of directives that would impose severe restrictions on pension funds and life insurance companies ('quantitative portfolio regulations'). After lengthy negotiations between the Commission, the Member States, and the pension funds, a Pension Directive was adopted in 2003 to stimulate the single European market for pension funds. This directive promotes prudential investing of pension funds applied to the portfolio as a whole rather than to individual investments (the 'prudent person' principle). No quantitative restrictions have been imposed on the portfolio composition of EU pension funds. EU pension funds are thus able to optimise their risk-return profile (see section 9.3 on international diversification).[1]

In contrast, insurance companies do face certain regulatory restrictions. The percentage of equity as well as the percentage of foreign assets in their portfolio is restricted. The new regulatory framework for the insurance industry, Solvency II, removes most of these restrictions, which would be advantageous for the proper development of institutional investments in the EU. Solvency II is due to be implemented in January 2016. Chapter 12 explains the regulatory framework for financial institutions in Europe.

The final supply-side factor furthering the development of institutional investors consists of fiscal advantages. Pension funds benefit from deferred taxation (contributions and investment returns are not taxed, but payouts are taxed). Life insurance contributions also often benefit from deferred taxation, while mutual funds enjoy a favourable tax regime in some EU countries (such as Luxembourg and Ireland).

Demand-side factors

Demand-side factors also play an important role in explaining the vast growth of institutional investment. The need for saving via institutional investors is linked to the level of social security benefits to which households are entitled. Institutional investment is stimulated when social security provides only a minimum level of income after retirement. In that case, the remaining part of income is provided via some kind of institutional saving.

The demand for institutional savings is mainly fuelled by demographic developments. Figure 9.6 shows that the EU population is ageing. The need to save for retirement is thus increasing. Saving for retirement is done primarily via institutional investors. Which institutions benefit most from these demographic developments depends on the country-specific situation. In countries where pension funds are well established, like the Netherlands and the UK, retirement saving primarily takes place via pension funds. Employees in France, where pension funds are practically non-existent, save for their retirement via life insurance companies and mutual funds.

Demographic projections for the EU indicate that by 2050 the dependency ratio will be double that of today, moving from around 25 in 2010 to 50 in 2050. Note that the dependency ratios of the new and old Member States are

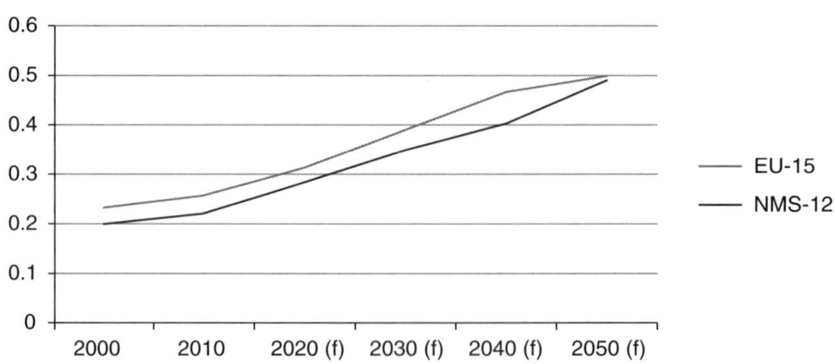

Figure 9.6 Dependency ratio: actual figures and forecasts, 2000–2050
Notes: EU-15 and NMS-12 are unweighted averages; (f) means forecast.
Source: Eurostat

converging. The *dependency ratio* is equal to the number of elderly persons of an age when they are generally economically inactive (aged 65 and over) divided by the number of persons of working age (from 15 to 64), expressed as a percentage. The increase in the dependency ratio can be explained by a decline in the fertility rates and increased life expectancy in the EU. Total fertility rates have declined dramatically over the past decades, falling from an average of 2.7 children per woman of child-bearing age in 1970 to 1.6 in 2012. At the same time, life expectancy in the EU-15 increased from 71 years in 1970 to 80.3 years in 2012. It is expected to increase further. To alleviate the impact on the working population and the budget position, Member States have started to increase the retirement age beyond the standard age of 65 years. It is expected that retirement age will rise in line with life expectancy.

Finally, over the last two decades European households have become wealthier, which has resulted in an increase in their investment horizon. These household investors bother less about the liquidity of their investments, as they are better positioned to absorb liquidity shocks. Less liquid investments offer a higher return. So wealthier households will search for the highest risk-return profile in the medium to long run. This means a shift from the traditional savings accounts (which can often be withdrawn on demand) towards long-term investments. However, most retail investors are risk averse and do not feel very comfortable with making investment decisions. So investing via institutional investors instead of direct investment will be more convenient.

9.3 Portfolio theory and international diversification

Portfolio theory

According to the international version of the CAPM, investors should hold an internationally diversified portfolio since such a portfolio maximises returns given a certain risk profile. This can be explained by Figure 9.7 which plots the mean and standard deviation of annualised monthly returns from January 1980 to December 2005 for two different equity portfolios. The first is the MSCI (Morgan Stanley Capital International) USA Index, which is a proxy for the American stock market. The second is based on the MSCI Europe Index, which is a proxy for the European stock market. Moving along the curve from 100 per cent US stocks to 100 per cent European stocks, the line plots the mean returns and standard deviations. This is a simplified version of the so-called *efficient frontier*, i.e. the portfolio with the minimum standard deviation for a given return.

The mean of the MSCI USA is lower than portfolio C, which has the same standard deviation but includes a fraction of European stocks. In fact, as long as investors prefer higher returns and lower variance, the minimum-variance portfolio at point B (with 40 per cent European equity) is preferable to a portfolio consisting of US shares only. However, as will be explained in more detail in the next section, American investors hold only 7 per cent of European stocks in their equity portfolio, which is indicated by point A.

Figure 9.7 illustrates that it is beneficial for investors to diversify geographically. The formal international CAPM can be derived from the standard mean-variance framework modified to include foreign securities (Lewis, 1999). In the mean-variance framework, investors optimise their portfolio by increasing their return (i.e. the mean of their wealth) and decreasing their risk (i.e. the variance of their wealth). By introducing foreign stocks, investors have to choose the optimal mix of domestic and foreign stocks in their portfolio. Box 9.4 presents the international CAPM derived by Lewis.

International diversification

When investors diversify their portfolio internationally, they can generate an extra return and/or reduce risk. Lewis (1999) calculates that an American

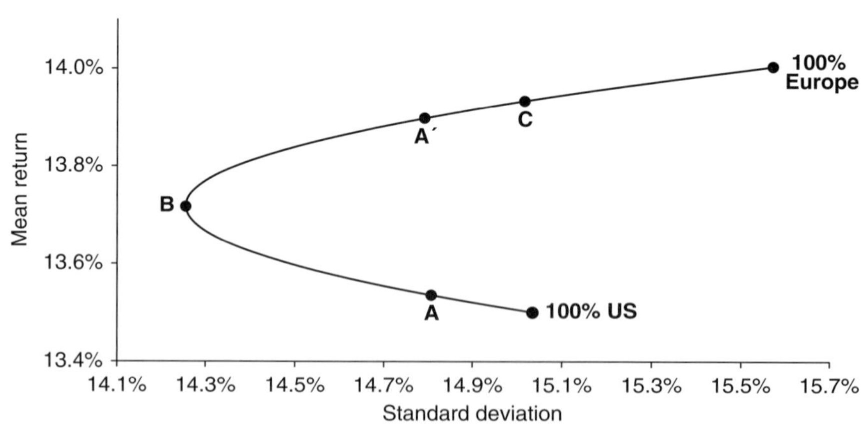

Figure 9.7 The simplified efficient frontier for US and European equities

Note: This graph is based on returns from the MSCI USA Index and MSCI Europe Index over the period 1980–2005.

Source: Schoenmaker and Bosch (2008)

Box 9.4 The international CAPM

Suppose that domestic investors have access to two risky assets, a domestic and a foreign stock. The domestic investor chooses the proportion of his wealth portfolio held in foreign stocks, x (with $0 < x < 1$). The investor's objective is to increase mean wealth, $E(W_1)$, and decrease the variability of wealth, $\text{var}(W_1)$. His objective function is given by:

$$\max \qquad V = V\Big(E(W_1), \text{var}(W_1)\Big) \tag{9.1}$$

$$\text{subject to} \qquad V_1 > 0,\ V_2 < 0 \tag{9.2}$$

where W_1 = next-period wealth, and E = the expected value conditional upon information known at time 0. V_1 is the partial derivative of V with respect to the first term, and V_2 with respect to the second term. The one-period return is a combination of the foreign return earned on the fraction of foreign stocks, denoted by x, and the domestic return earned on the fraction of domestic stocks, denoted by $(1 - x)$, and is given by:

$$\begin{aligned} W_1 &= W_0\Big(1 + X \cdot r^f + (1 - X) \cdot r^h\Big) \\ &= W_0\Big(1 + X \cdot (r^f - r^h) + r^h\Big) \end{aligned} \tag{9.3}$$

where W_0 = current wealth, r^f = foreign return, and r^h = domestic return. The variance of the one-period return is given by:

$$\begin{aligned} \text{var}(W_1) &= \text{var}\Big(W_0\Big(1 + X \cdot (r^f - r^h) + r^h\Big)\Big) \\ &= W_0^2 \text{var}\Big(1 + X \cdot (r^f - r^h) + r^h\Big) \\ &= W_0^2\Big(X^2 \text{var}(r^f - r^h) + 2 \cdot X \cdot (\rho_{fh} \cdot \sigma_f \cdot \sigma_h - \sigma_h^2) + \sigma_h^2\Big) \end{aligned} \tag{9.4}$$

where $\sigma_h^2 = \text{var}(r^h)$ = the variance of the domestic stock return, $\sigma_f^2 = \text{var}(r^f)$ = the variance of the foreign stock return to the domestic investor, and $\sigma_{fh} = \rho_{fh} \cdot \sigma_f \cdot \sigma_h = \text{cov}(r^f, r^h)$ = where the covariance between the domestic and foreign returns. The optimal fraction of foreign stock x^* can be calculated by deriving the first-order condition of the objective function V. The first-order condition is given by:

$$\frac{\delta V}{\delta x} = V_1 \cdot W_0 \cdot (r^f - r^h) + V_2 \cdot W_0^2 \cdot \Big(2 \cdot x \cdot \text{var}(r^f - r^h) + 2 \cdot \sigma_{fh} - 2 \cdot \sigma_h^2\Big) = 0 \tag{9.5}$$

Box 9.4 (cont.)

Dividing by W_0 and arranging terms leads directly to:

$$x^* = \frac{r^f - r^h}{\text{var}(r^f - r^h)} \cdot \frac{-V_1}{2 \cdot V_2 \cdot W_0} + \frac{\sigma_h^2 - \sigma_{fh}}{\text{var}(r^f - r^h)}$$

$$= \frac{(r^f - r^h)/\gamma}{\text{var}(r^f - r^h)} + \frac{\sigma_h^2 - \sigma_{fh}}{\text{var}(r^f - r^h)} \qquad (9.6)$$

where γ is the parameter of risk aversion $\frac{-2 \cdot V_2 \cdot W_0}{V_1}$. The interpretation of the demand function for foreign stock is straightforward. The first term on the right-hand side of equation 9.6 represents the demand arising from higher-potential returns from the foreign stock. The lower the risk aversion, γ, the greater the response of demand to higher expected returns. However, as γ increases, the importance of relative returns across countries declines. In the limiting case when γ equals infinity, i.e. investors are infinitely risk averse, the first term disappears. The demand for foreign stock then reduces to the second term, i.e. the portfolio share that minimises the variance of the wealth portfolio. This portfolio is illustrated by point B in Figure 9.7. Thus, in general, the demand for foreign stock depends on a combination of the risky portfolio share given by the first term and the minimum-variance portfolio given by the second term.

Source: Lewis (1999)

investor can generate an extra return of about 50 basis points per year while also decreasing risk (moving to point B in Figure 9.7), or 80 basis points per year with no change in risk (moving to point A′ in Figure 9.7). Empirical evidence for European investors shows an even stronger effect. Schröder (2003) finds that a British investor, holding the optimal portfolio of 80 per cent non-domestic assets instead of a portfolio of 20 per cent non-domestic assets, generates an extra return of 2.2 per cent per year. A German investor, holding the optimal portfolio, generates an extra return of 3 per cent per year. The excess return for European investors is larger than for American investors because the US market is very large so there is less upside potential from investing in foreign markets.

By the same token, international diversification reduces the cost of capital (Stulz, 1999). The expected return that investors require for investing in equity to compensate them for risk generally falls, resulting in lower cost of capital for companies.

The international CAPM is derived under the assumption that capital markets are perfect. Perfect capital markets imply a world without any barriers.

However, several barriers may hamper international capital flows (Karolyi and Stulz, 2003). First, there are traditional barriers including capital controls and trading costs. While capital controls have been abolished in the EU over the past three decades (see Chapter 3), cross-border trading costs are still higher than domestic trading costs (see Chapter 7 on cross-border trading costs in the EU). Second, barriers can be related to different expectations about stock returns, volatilities, and covariances. In particular, investors can be more uncertain about the expected returns of foreign stock. An important risk in the cross-border setting is exchange-rate risk. The degree of risk aversion is captured by γ in equation 9.6. Finally, barriers can emerge from differences in information between local and foreign investors. According to the 'corporate insider theory', it is not possible for the home bias to fall sharply if it is optimal for insiders to have large ownership stakes in corporations in a specific country and foreign investors are not corporate insiders (Stulz, 2005). The existence of insider ownership thus limits the holdings of foreign investors.

The increasing importance of institutional investors may reduce the home bias. As professional parties, they may have better means to overcome the barriers to international investment. They employ, for example, analysts who can reduce the information asymmetries. Furthermore, due to their size, they can negotiate lower tariffs for large (cross-border) deals. Section 9.4 produces some empirical evidence on the impact of institutional investors on the home bias.

9.4 The home bias in European investment

Measuring the home bias

A *home bias* exists when investors underweight foreign assets in their portfolio while this might not be optimal from a diversification point of view. There is robust evidence across a large range of countries for the existence of such a home bias (Chan *et al.*, 2005). This section analyses to what extent (institutional) investors in Europe diversify their investments geographically. By comparing the levels of the home bias between 1997 and 2012, it is possible to analyse whether the home bias has declined over time. Two periods are distinguished: the start of EMU (1997–2004) and the financial crisis (2004–2012). In the first period the home bias may have decreased, as exchange rate risk is eliminated for the euro-area countries. In the second period the home bias may have increased, as financial market turmoil may induce investors to withdraw their foreign investments to their home market, which they know best.

To derive the home bias, the international CAPM is used. The optimal portfolio with no bias can be calculated under strict assumptions (Elton *et al.*, 2007). In the international setting, these assumptions include fully integrated capital markets and purchasing-power parity. Fully integrated capital markets imply that investors can buy and sell securities in foreign markets without any restrictions or extra transaction costs. Under purchasing-power parity the long-run equilibrium exchange rates of currencies are equal to the currencies' purchasing power. It is based on the law of one price, which means that identical goods (including securities) in different markets must have the same price. When purchasing-power parity holds, exchange-rate risk is no longer relevant. If there are homogeneous expectations, all investors select the same optimal portfolio. Equilibrium in the international setting is achieved when all investors hold the world market portfolio in which each country portfolio is weighted by its market capitalisation.

The equity home bias, labelled EHB_i, is measured as one minus the *foreign asset acceptance ratio* which measures the extent to which the share of foreign assets in the portfolio of country *i* diverges from the relative share of foreign assets in the total world market portfolio (Ahearne *et al.*, 2004). The home bias is higher, the more the foreign asset acceptance ratio is below unity. The equity home bias is given by:

$$EHB_i = 1 - \frac{Foreign\ Equity_i}{Foreign\ Equity\ to\ Total\ Market_i} \tag{9.7}$$

in which $Foreign\ Equity_i$ = share of country *i*'s holdings of foreign equity in country *i*'s total equity portfolio (1 – share of domestic equity); $Foreign\ Equity\ to\ Total\ Market_i$ = the share of foreign equity in the world portfolio available to country *i* (1 – share of country *i* in the total market capitalisation). The country portfolio is calculated as the domestic market capitalisation plus foreign equity holdings minus foreign owners of domestic equity.

Equation 9.7 measures to what extent domestic equity is overweighed compared with foreign equity in the investment portfolio. *EHB* will be equal to 0 if investors show no preference for equity issued domestically. If domestic investors have a preference for domestic equity, the ratio will be between 0 and 1. The home bias formula can be illustrated as follows. Country *i* investors allocate 15 per cent of their portfolio to foreign equity, while the total world market portfolio comprises 75 per cent of foreign equity and 25 per cent of domestic equity. Country *i* investors thus exploit international diversification to only one-fifth (15/75) and thus have a home bias of 0.8. EHB_i is 1.0 if domestic investors invest 100 per cent of their equity portfolio domestically. In a similar vein, the preference of investors for domestic debt securities can be measured. This home bias measure for bonds is BHB_i.

Next, the *regional bias* can be measured. The question is whether European investors show a preference for European securities in their foreign securities portfolio in comparison with US securities. Within the part of the investment portfolio that is invested in foreign equity and bonds, EU investors should, according to the international CAPM, show no preference for either European or US equities and bonds.

Similar to the analysis of the domestic home bias, it can be tested whether European investors have a bias towards European equities and bonds. The regional bias for European investors is measured as one minus the US asset acceptance ratio. This ratio measures the extent to which the share of US assets in the foreign equity portfolio of country i diverges from the relative share of US assets in the total foreign market portfolio. The regional bias for equities is given by:

$$REB_i = 1 - \frac{US\ Equity_i}{US\ Equity\ to\ Foreign\ Market\ Portfolio_i} \qquad (9.8)$$

in which $US\ Equity_i$ = share of country i's holdings of US equity in country i's total foreign equity portfolio (1 – share of EU equity in foreign portfolio); $US\ Equity\ to\ Foreign\ Market\ Portfolio_i$ = share of US equity in the foreign-equity portfolio which is available for country i. The available foreign portfolio for country i is total domestic market capitalisation of EU and US minus domestic market capitalisation of country i.

The foreign market portfolio differs per country. For example, as the UK comprises a large part of total EU equity, the foreign equity portfolio for the UK is smaller than that of other countries. The same applies to the foreign bond portfolio. It is expected that the regional bond bias (RBB) is higher than the regional equity bias (REB) for the countries in the euro area, because there is no exchange rate risk involved, and international diversification of bonds primarily focuses on credit risk diversification.

Evidence on the home bias

Some earlier empirical studies measure the development of the home bias in the EU-15 after the introduction of the euro in 1999 (De Santis and Gérard, 2009; Schoenmaker and Bosch, 2008). These studies show a large

Table 9.8 Equity and bond home bias, 1997–2012

	Equity home bias					Bond home bias				
	1997	2004	2012	Δ 97–04	Δ 04–12	1997	2004	2012	Δ 97–04	Δ 04–12
Austria	0.81	0.67	0.65	−0.14	−0.02	0.81	0.66	0.75	−0.14	0.08
Belgium	0.86	0.72	0.74	−0.14	0.02	0.82	0.58	0.67	−0.24	0.09
Denmark	0.83	0.73	0.63	−0.10	−0.11	0.91	0.87	0.87	−0.04	0.00
Finland	0.96	0.75	0.61	−0.21	−0.14	0.93	0.60	0.61	−0.33	0.01
France	0.90	0.79	0.79	−0.11	0.01	0.87	0.69	0.76	−0.18	0.07
Germany	1.00	0.77	0.80	−0.23	0.03	1.00	0.80	0.73	−0.20	−0.07
Greece	1.00	0.97	0.98	−0.03	0.01	1.00	0.83	0.86	−0.17	0.03
Italy	0.89	0.84	0.78	−0.04	−0.07	0.93	0.84	0.91	−0.10	0.07
Netherlands	0.77	0.44	0.49	−0.33	0.05	0.75	0.61	0.70	−0.14	0.09
Poland	1.00	0.99	0.99	−0.01	0.00	n/a	0.99	1.00	n/a	0.00
Portugal	0.94	0.86	0.80	−0.09	−0.06	0.87	0.67	0.84	−0.20	0 17
Spain	0.95	0.93	0.94	−0.02	0.02	0.95	0.68	0.93	−0.26	0.24
Sweden	0.87	0.73	0.70	−0.14	−0.03	n/a	0.83	0.88	n/a	0.05
United Kingdom	0.84	0.80	0.76	−0.04	−0.04	0.73	0.78	0.82	0.05	0.03
United States	0.84	0.82	0.75	−0.02	−0.06	0.95	0.96	0.96	0.01	0.00
EU-14	0.85	0.77	0.75	−0.08	−0.03	0.84	0.73	0.82	−0.10	0.08
Euro area	0.86	0.76	0.74	−0.10	−0.02	0.87	0.70	0.81	−0.17	0.11
Non-euro area	0.84	0.79	0.75	−0.06	−0.04	0.76	0.80	0.83	0.04	0.03

Note: EU-14, euro, and non-euro area are calculated as a weighted average; n.a. means not available.
Source: Schoenmaker and Soeter (2014)

decrease in the home bias and an increase in the regional bias for the euro-area countries. Updating these earlier studies, Schoenmaker and Soeter (2014) examine the home bias for the original EU-15. Luxembourg and Ireland are excluded as they attract large amounts of foreign investment due to favourable tax policies, while the largest new Member State Poland is added to the dataset.

Table 9.8 gives an overview of the equity and bond home bias in 1997, 2004, and 2012.[2] All countries experienced a sharp decline of the EHB from 1997 to 2004. The Netherlands has the lowest home bias (0.44 in 2004); it also had the largest decline from 1997 to 2004. The low home bias in the Netherlands reflects the large proportion of institutional investors, in particular pension funds, that tend to invest in a professional way applying international diversification. Rubbaniy *et al.* (2014) find a large decrease in the home bias of pension funds' investments in equities and bonds after the introduction of the euro. The southern European countries have a bias around 0.90 and the new Member State, Poland, also has a very high home bias of 0.99. The equity home bias in the UK and the US decreased slightly from 1997 to 2004 but was still relatively high (0.80 and 0.82, respectively).

The weighted average bias for the EU-14 declined by 0.08 from 1997 to 2004. It is interesting that the EU bias has decreased after the introduction of the euro, without a significant change of the US bias over this period. While the weighted-average bias for the countries in the euro area was higher in 1997 than the bias of the non-euro countries, the bias for the countries in the euro area decreased by 0.10 from 1997 to 2004 compared with 0.06 for the non-euro countries.

There is a small decrease in the EHB for all countries from 2004 to 2012. So there is no evidence of a clawing back of equity investments to the home country after the financial crisis.

Table 9.8 also illustrates that the BHB has declined in all euro-area countries in the sample, and this reduction is in general larger than that of the EHB. This can be attributed to the introduction of the euro. In 2004, the BHB is the lowest for Belgium (0.58), followed by Finland and the Netherlands. Denmark, Sweden, Greece, Italy, and Poland still exhibit a large BHB relative to the other EU Member States. Non-euro-area countries in the sample experienced an increase in 2004.

The US has an exceptionally high BHB at 0.96. It can be concluded that US investors are very domestically focused within their long-term debt portfolios, and allocate only a small percentage of their bond portfolio to EU bonds. This is partly in line with theory. As the US economy is very large, there is more scope for US investors to diversify credit risk domestically without incurring exchange-rate risk.

But there is an increase in the BHB in the 2004–2012 period. The financial crisis and the subsequent euro crisis have led to an increase in the home bias (except for Germany). So, foreign investors fled the crisis-stricken countries (Greece, Ireland, Portugal, Spain, and Italy) and invested at home. Domestic investors in the latter had to pick up these bonds, also increasing the home bias in the distressed countries.

As illustrated above, all countries in the sample exhibit a home bias towards domestic equities and bonds. Within the portfolio of foreign securities of the 15 countries in the sample, a distinction can be made between investments in European and US securities. If the home bias puzzle is mainly a geographical phenomenon, this implies that within their foreign portfolio European investors give too much importance to European securities.

Table 9.9 reports the regional bias for equities and bonds. Investors in all European countries in the sample overweigh European relative to US equities.

Table 9.9 Regional equity and bond bias of European investors, 1997–2012

	Regional bias towards EU-14 equities					Regional bias towards EU-14 bonds				
	1997	2004	2012	Δ 97–04	Δ 04–12	1997	2004	2012	Δ 97–04	Δ 04–12
Austria	0.55	0.57	0.72	0.02	0.16	0.63	0.85	0.83	0.21	–0.02
Belgium	0.70	0.76	0.73	0.06	–0.03	0.65	0.90	0.88	0.25	–0.02
Denmark	0.59	0.40	0.14	–0.19	–0.25	0.71	0.62	0.68	–0.09	0.06
Finland	0.70	0.73	0.54	0.03	–0.19	0.72	0.89	0.91	0.17	0.02
France	0.49	0.74	0.73	0.24	–0.01	0.71	0.78	0.82	0.08	0.04
Germany	n/a	0.62	0.56	n/a	–0.06	n/a	0.86	0.84	–0.14	–0.02
Greece	n/a	0.24	0.25	n/a	0.01	n/a	0.80	0.94	–0.20	0.14
Italy	0.54	0.52	0.71	–0.02	0.19	0.56	0.73	0.78	0.17	0.06
Netherlands	0.27	0.11	0.12	–0.15	0.00	0.79	0.73	0.74	–0.06	0.02
Poland	n/a	n/a	n/a	n/a	n/a	n/a	n/a	n/a	n/a	n/a
Portugal	0.34	0.80	0.63	0.46	–0.17	0.53	0.83	0.87	0.30	0.04
Spain	0.35	0.73	0.73	0.38	0.00	0.83	0.81	0.87	–0.02	0.06
Sweden	0.28	0.24	0.31	–0.04	0.07	0.43	0.54	0.62	0.11	0.08
United Kingdom	0.47	0.37	0.15	–0.10	–0.22	0.42	0.33	0.38	–0.09	0.05
EU-14	0.44	0.47	0.38	0.03	–0.09	0.66	0.74	0.76	0.08	0.01
Euro area	0.43	0.53	0.49	0.10	–0.04	0.69	0.80	0.82	0.11	0.02
Non-euro area	0.46	0.38	0.24	–0.08	–0.14	0.44	0.42	0.46	–0.02	0.04

Notes: EU-14, euro, and non-euro area are calculated as a weighted average; n.a. means not available.
Source: Schoenmaker and Soeter (2014)

This means that the home bias also persists on a regional level. The weighted average REB for the EU-14 increased from 1997 to 2004. The split between countries inside and outside the euro area identifies an interesting pattern. The REB increased by 0.10 for the euro countries, while the bias declined by 0.08 for the non-euro countries.

The Netherlands has the lowest REB of the EU-14 countries (0.11 in 2004), followed by Sweden and Greece. Belgium, France, Spain, Austria, and Italy show a high preference for European equities in their foreign- investment portfolios. It is remarkable that the bias of Portugal, Spain, and France increased strongly from 1997 to 2004. Investors in these countries evidently moved to a euro-area investment strategy and thereby reduced their foreign (US) equity holdings. The 2004–2012 period indicates a reversal of the regional bias. Nevertheless, the REB for the euro countries in 2012 is higher than in 1997.

Table 9.9 also reports that the RBB for the EU-14 countries increased from 1997 to 2004. The increase in the RBB was driven by the euro-area countries.

The RBB increased by 0.11 for the countries in the euro area and declined by 0.02 for those outside. The absolute value of the bias in 2004 was almost twice as large for the euro countries (0.80 vs. 0.42). Denmark, Sweden, and the UK (which are all non-euro countries) have a low RBB. It can be concluded that for the euro-area countries the decline in the BHB is caused by a shift from domestic towards EU-14 bonds, and not to US bonds. These countries diversify the credit risk of the bond portfolio to a significant extent, but within the EU. The interest rate risk is hedged by investing primarily in EU bonds, which have interest rates that are almost identical (euro area) or linked (non-euro area) to domestic rates. Moreover, exchange-rate risk is largely eliminated. The subsequent 2004–2012 period shows a very small increase in the RBB.

The international diversification strategy of institutional investors is graphically illustrated in Figures 9.8–9.11. Data for 1997, 2004, and 2012 are compared for four regions: the US, the EU-14, the ten euro countries within the EU-14, and the four non-euro countries within the EU-14. Figures 9.8 and 9.9 illustrate that the decline in the home bias is larger for the EU than for the US. Within the EU-14 countries, the ten euro countries show a larger decline in the home bias than the four non-euro countries.

While the equity and bond home bias in the euro area have declined faster than in the non-euro countries (Figures 9.8 and 9.9), the reverse is true for

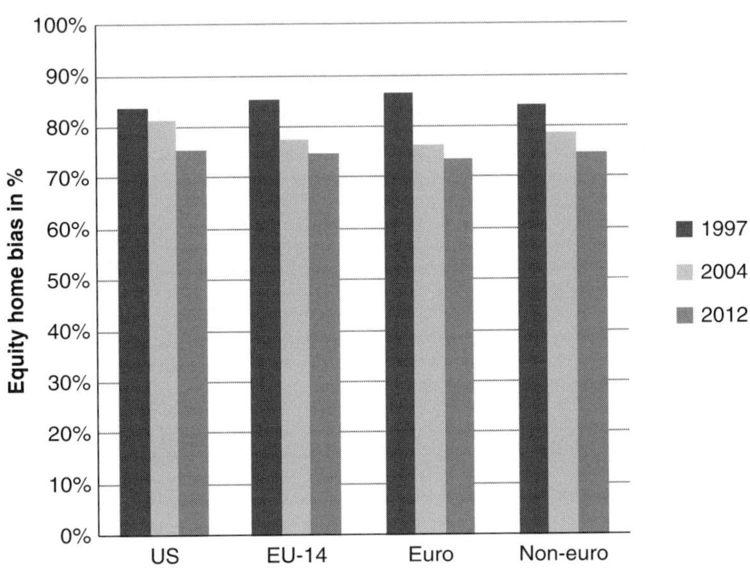

Figure 9.8 Equity home bias per region, 1997 vs. 2012

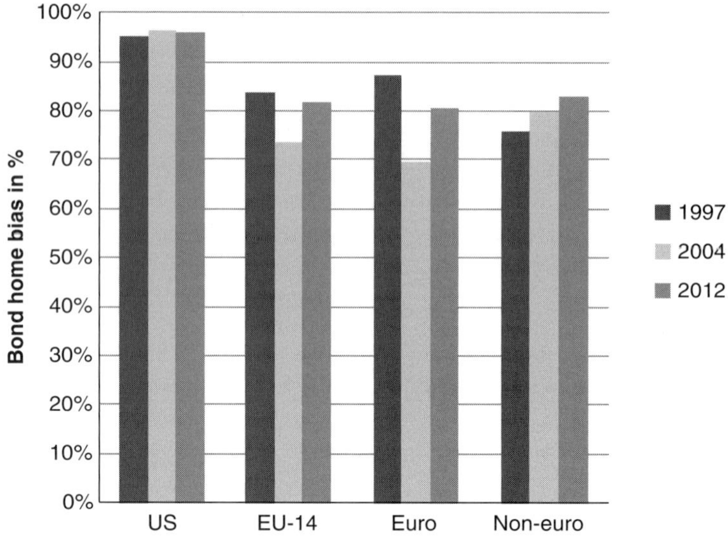

Figure 9.9 Bond home bias per region, 1997 vs. 2012

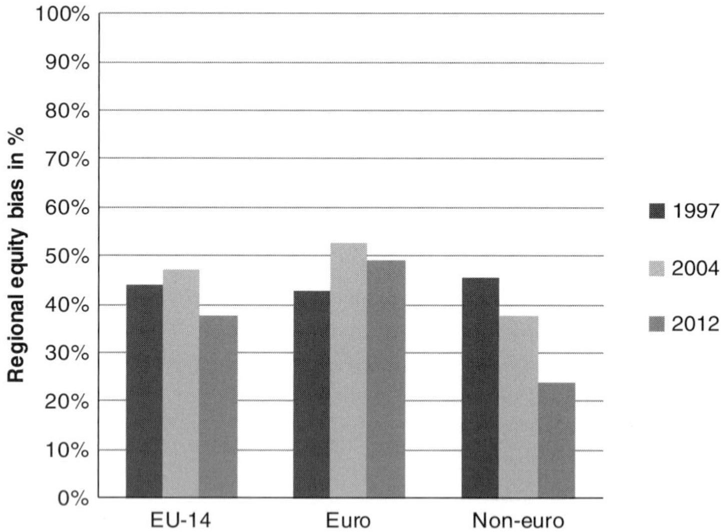

Figure 9.10 Regional equity bias per region, 1997 vs. 2012

the regional bias (Figures 9.10 and 9.11). In fact, this bias has increased for both equity and bonds in the euro area, but has decreased on average for the four non-euro countries. These results are consistent with the theory of economic integration. Since the introduction of the euro in 1999, investors in the euro countries have allocated a larger part of their portfolio to foreign

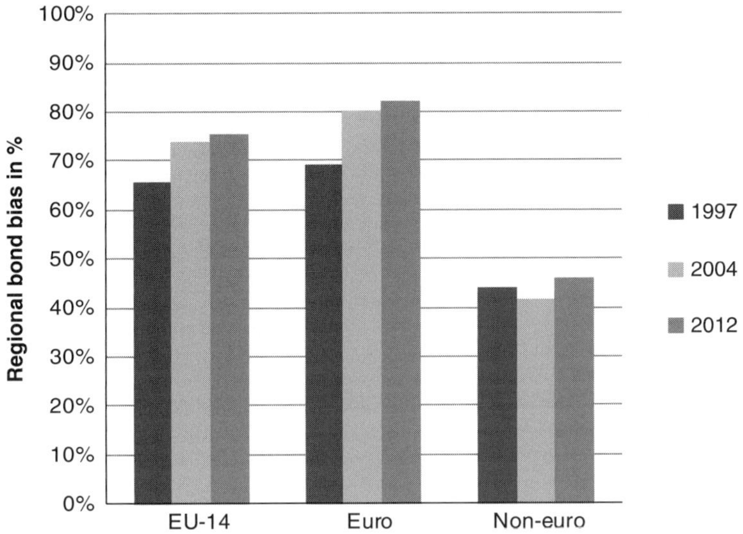

Figure 9.11 Regional bond bias per region, 1997 vs. 2012

assets than have non-euro countries and the US. At the same time, the regional bias of the euro area has increased, as investors in euro countries have invested their foreign assets mainly in their own region. Investors based in the euro area have thus shifted from a country-based investing strategy towards a sector-based strategy. So there is a 'euro effect' as the euro has caused a decrease of the home bias but an increase of the regional bias. The regional bias decreased for the non-euro countries, which means that they partly shifted their foreign assets towards US assets compared with EU assets.

Explaining the home bias

If the gains of international diversification are positive and significant, why do (institutional) investors not hold the theoretically optimal portfolio? Table 9.10 explains which factors influence the size of the equity home bias.

The first factor is the ratio of total exports to GDP. This is a proxy for 'trade'. Investors in countries with a large export-to-GDP ratio have a lower need for international diversification, as the companies in these countries are already diversifying via their international business. However, this ratio could also be a proxy for the mindset of investors in a country indicating the openness of that country. If companies tend to do business abroad and diversify their business geographically, investors could act in the same manner.

Table 9.10 Determinants of the equity home bias (OLS regression)

Independent variables	Expected sign	Coefficient	*t*-value
Constant		0.915***	17.3
Export	+/–	–0.324***	3.9
Institutional	–	–0.146**	2.4
Insider	+	0.127	1.3
Market cap	+	0.159*	2.0
N		42	
Adj. R^2		0.69	
F-statistic		16.25	

Notes: OLS panel regression using EHB_i as the dependent variable. Data for 1997, 2002, and 2004 for the EU-13 and the US are used for this analysis. Period-specific fixed effects are included in the regression.
(***), (**), (*) indicate statistical significance at the 1 per cent, 5 per cent, and 10 per cent levels, respectively.
Source: Schoenmaker and Bosch (2008)

Table 9.10 reports that export to GDP has a significant negative effect on the home bias. This supports the theory that countries with relatively large trade volumes can be considered as more 'open' and have a lower bias due to the *openness effect*. The domestic companies in these countries have significant exposure to the world market due to their level of international trade.

However, investors in these countries are subject to a lower EHB, as they also tend to 'trade' (invest) internationally.

The second factor is the size of the institutional sector. Table 9.10 shows that the relative size of the institutional sector has a negative and significant effect on the home bias. Countries in which institutional investors manage a larger part of the financial assets exhibit larger international diversification. Indeed, this finding indicates that institutional investors, as professional asset managers, are subject to a lower home bias than non-financial corporations or households. This is the *professionalism effect*.

The third factor is the percentage of shares held by corporate insiders. Insider ownership is expected to increase the home bias in two ways. First, domestic investors hold shares that foreign investors cannot own. Second, domestic investors allocate a lower amount to foreign equity, as they have locked up a part of their portfolio in domestic assets. It should be noted, however, that the theory concerning insider ownership is developed to explain the bias towards a country (Stulz, 2005), but not necessarily the home bias of a country itself. The share of corporate insiders is the only variable that is not significant in Table 9.10, although it has the expected positive sign.

The fourth factor is the size of the domestic stock market to GDP. Table 9.10 illustrates that the relative size of the domestic stock market has a positive and significant effect on the home bias. Thus, investors are more domestically oriented if their domestic stock market is well developed. This indicates that investors are subject to the *availability effect*, which means that investors are more eager to invest in domestic assets when these domestic assets are readily available.

Finally, behavourial approaches may also explain the home bias. Behavioural finance draws upon psychological effects of individual behaviour. Huberman (2001), for example, argues that familiarity with domestic companies makes it easier for investors to invest in domestic equity. Campbell and Kräussl (2007) find that investors concerned with downside risk tend to hold a larger proportion of their portfolio in domestic equity, due to the greater downside risk from investing abroad.

9.5 Conclusions

The institutionalisation of the investment process, where professional market investors manage private savings, is a global trend. This chapter distinguishes three main types of institutional investors: pension funds, life insurance companies, and mutual funds. Both the demand side (growing investments by pension funds to cater for ageing and by mutual funds to accommodate wealth accumulation of households) and the supply side (shift from bank-financed companies to market-financed companies via equity and bonds) point to future growth of institutional investment.

As in many other financial sectors, distinctions between types of institutional investors are blurring. Mutual funds, in particular, are being used as a vehicle for retirement saving and are a specific asset class for pension funds. Private equity and hedge funds are alternative investments, which are increasingly added to the portfolio of pension funds. Insurance companies launch their own investment funds and are widely involved in pension provision, provision of annuities, and guaranteed investment contracts for pension funds, while also performing asset management for pension funds.

Institutional investors play an important role in monitoring companies in which they invest. This promotes good corporate governance. As dominant investors, institutional investors have the clout to influence the management of companies.

Finance theory suggests that investors should aim for international diversification of their investment portfolio to maximise returns given a certain risk profile. Nevertheless, there is a strong home bias in equity and bond portfolios. This chapter shows that the increasing professionalism of institutional investors (compared with individual investors) has led to a decline in the home bias in Europe. The elimination of exchange-rate risk following the introduction of the euro has led to a further decline of the home bias in the euro area. However, the financial crisis and the subsequent euro crisis have led to an increase in the bond home bias, but not in the equity home bias.

Notes

1. Davis and Steil (2001) discuss the two main approaches, namely '*prudent person rules*', which enjoin portfolio diversification and broad asset-liability matching, and '*quantitative portfolio regulations*', which limit holdings of certain types of asset within the portfolio. Both seek to ensure adequate portfolio diversification and liquidity of the asset portfolio, but in different ways.
2. Data concerning foreign equity and bond holdings are extracted from a country-level dataset of the IMF, the Coordinated Portfolio Investment Survey (CPIS). Luxembourg and Ireland are excluded from the EU-15 as they attract large amounts of foreign investment due to favourable tax policies, while Poland and the US are added to the dataset. This results in a sample of 15 countries. A proxy for the world market portfolio is the domestic market capitalisation of the EU-14 and the US. In this way, we analyse to what extent the EU-14 countries and the US overweight domestic equity in their portfolio compared with foreign equity.

Suggested Reading

Davis, E. P. and B. Steil (2001), *Institutional Investors*, MIT Press, Cambridge (MA).

Elton, E. J., M. J. Gruber, S. J. Brown, and W. M. Goetzmann (2007), *Modern Portfolio Theory and Investment Analysis*, 7th edition, John Wiley & Sons, New York.

Feldstein, M. S. and H. Siebert (eds.) (2002), *Social Security Pension Reform in Europe*, University of Chicago Press.

Gillan, S. L. and L. T. Starks (2003), Corporate Governance, Corporate Ownership, and the Role of Institutional Investors: A Global Perspective, *Journal of Applied Finance*, **13**, 4–22.

Lewis, K. K. (1999), Trying to Explain Home Bias in Equities and Consumption, *Journal of Economic Literature*, **37**, 571–608.

References

Ahearne, A. B., W. Griever, and F. Warnock (2004), Information Costs and the Home Bias, *Journal of International Economics*, **62**, 313–336.

Campbell, R. A. and R. Kräussl (2007), Revisiting the Home Bias Puzzle: Downside Equity Risk, *Journal of International Money and Finance*, **26**, 1239–1260.

Chan, K., M. V. Covrig, and L. K. Ng (2005), What Determines the Domestic Bias and Foreign Bias? Evidence from Mutual Fund Equity Allocations Worldwide, *Journal of Finance*, **60**, 1495–1534.

Davis, E. P. (2003), Institutional Investors, Financial Market Efficiency and Stability, The Pensions Institute (London) Working Paper PI-0303.

Davis, E. P. and B. Steil (2001), *Institutional Investors*, MIT Press, Cambridge (MA).

De Santis, R. A. and B. Gérard (2009), International Portfolio Reallocation: Diversification Benefits and European Monetary Union, *European Economic Review*, **53**, 1010–1027.

Elton, E. J., M. J. Gruber, S. J. Brown, and W. M. Goetzmann (2007), *Modern Portfolio Theory and Investment Analysis*, 7th edition, John Wiley & Sons, New York.

European Commission (2014), *European Financial Stability and Integration*, EC, Brussels.

European Fund and Asset Management Association (2005), *Trends in European Investment Funds*, EFAMA, Brussels.

Feldstein, M. S. and H. Siebert (eds.) (2002), *Social Security Pension Reform in Europe*, University of Chicago Press.

Financial Stability Forum (2007), *Update of the FSF Report on Highly Leveraged Institutions*, FSF, Basel.

Furfine, C. (2006), The Costs and Benefits of Moral Suasion: Evidence from the Rescue of Long-Term Capital Management, *Journal of Business*, **79**, 593–622.

Gillan, S. L. and L. T. Starks (2003), Corporate Governance, Corporate Ownership, and the Role of Institutional Investors: A Global Perspective, *Journal of Applied Finance*, **13**, 4–22.

Hedge Fund Standards Board (2008), *Best Practice Standards*, HFSB, London.

Huberman, G. (2001), Familiarity Breeds Investment, *Review of Financial Studies*, **14**, 659–680.

Jorion, P. (2000), Risk Management Lessons from Long-Term Capital Management, *European Financial Management*, **6**, 277–300.

Karolyi, G. A. and R. M. Stulz (2003), Are Financial Assets Priced Locally or Globally?, in: G. M. Constantinides, M. Harris, and R. M. Stulz (eds.), *The Handbook of the Economics of Finance*, Elsevier, Amsterdam, 975–1020.

Kho, B. C., D. Lee, and R. M. Stulz (2000), US Banks, Crises, and Bailouts: From Mexico to LTCM, *American Economic Review*, **90**, 28–31.

Khorana, A., H. Servaes, and P. Tufano (2005), Explaining the Size of the Mutual Fund Industry Around the World, *Journal of Financial Economics*, **78**, 145–185.

Lewis, K. K. (1999), Trying to Explain Home Bias in Equities and Consumption, *Journal of Economic Literature*, **37**, 571–608.

Organisation for Economic Co-operation and Development (2003), *Institutional Investors Statistical Yearbook*, OECD, Paris.

Rajan, R. G. (2007), Benign Financial Conditions, Asset Management, and Political Risks: Trying to Make Sense of our Times, in: D. D. Evanoff, G. G. Kaufman, and J. R. LaBrosse (eds.), *International Financial Stability: Global Banking and National Regulation*, World Scientific Publishing, Singapore, 19–28.

Rubbaniy, G, I. van Lelyveld, and W. Verschoor (2014), Home Bias and Dutch Pension Funds' Investment Behavior, *European Journal of Finance*, **20**(1), 978–993.

Schoenmaker, D. and T. Bosch (2008), Is the Home Bias in Equities and Bonds Declining in Europe?, *Investment Management and Financial Innovations*, **5**, 90–102.

Schoenmaker, D. and C. Soeter (2014), New Evidence on the Home Bias in European Investment, Duisenberg School of Finance Policy Brief 34.

Schröder, M. (2003), Benefits of Diversification and Integration for International Equity and Bond Portfolios, ZEW Economic Studies 19, Heidelberg.

Smit, H. T. J. (2003), The Economics of Private Equity, ERIM (Erasmus University, Rotterdam) Report Series EIA-2002-13.

Stulz, R. M. (1999), Globalisation of Equity Markets and the Cost of Capital, NBER Working Paper 7021.

(2005), The Limits of Financial Globalisation, *Journal of Finance*, **60**, 1595–1638.

TheCityUK (2012), *Private Equity*, London.

(2013), *Hedge Funds*, London.

CHAPTER

10

European Banks

OVERVIEW

The traditional business of banking is the provision of long-term loans that are funded by short-term deposits. Banks have a comparative advantage against other financial institutions in providing liquidity. They have also developed technologies to screen and monitor borrowers in order to reduce asymmetric information between the lender and the borrower. These liquidity-providing and monitoring functions also give banks a key position in modern capital-market transactions, such as underwriting, trading, and derivatives transactions.

Risk is fundamental to the business of banking. Progress in information technology in combination with demands by supervisors has spurred the development of advanced risk-management models. This, in turn, has prompted the centralisation and integration of some management functions such as risk management, treasury operations, compliance, and auditing. This integrated approach to risk management aims to ensure a comprehensive and systematic approach to risk-related decisions throughout the banking group. Moreover, banks with an integrated risk-management unit can exploit diversification opportunities at the group level.

The European banking market is made up of 28 national banking systems. Each national banking system has its own characteristics, such as the number of banks, the level of concentration, and the intensity of competition. Some banking systems are highly concentrated, but this does not necessarily lead to a lack of competition. An important condition for competitive pressure is that the market is open to new entry (contestability). The European Commission therefore promotes the removal of remaining obstacles to cross-border mergers and acquisitions.

Domestic banking mergers used to be very common, while more recently the frequency of cross-border mergers has increased. While it is not possible yet to speak of an integrated banking market, the level of cross-border penetration has gradually increased. The Banking Union will foster the change from the 19 national banking systems of the euro countries into an integrated banking union landscape.

LEARNING OBJECTIVES

After you have studied this chapter, you should be able to:

- explain the role of banks as liquidity providers to the economy
- explain the role of banks in screening and monitoring (potential) borrowers
- explain the use of risk-management models by modern banks and the centralisation of the risk-management function
- explain the dynamics of domestic and cross-border mergers and acquisitions in banking
- understand the dynamics of the Banking Union landscape.

10.1 Theory of banking

Drivers of bank profitability

Banks perform multiple functions. The traditional business of banks is lending. Before a bank grants a loan, it screens the creditworthiness of a potential borrower. After the loan is granted, a bank monitors whether the borrower takes excessive risks. The lending business generates income for banks. As loans are funded with deposits, the difference (or spread) between the lending and borrowing rate determines a bank's profitability. Banks also make profits through various fee-earning activities, like capital-market transactions, such as underwriting and trading, and derivatives transactions. Banks use modern risk-management models to measure and control the risks arising from these transactions. These risk-management models are built on the monitoring technology that banks use in their lending business.

Lending business

Banks take deposits from the public and grant loans on their own account. These loans are typically held to maturity (the 'originate and hold' model). Banks are thus engaged in the transformation of liquid deposits into illiquid loans. The intermediation function of banks can be explained using a simple balance sheet (see Figure 10.1). On the liability side, banks fund themselves with many small deposits D from the public. The effective deposit rate r_D includes both the explicit interest paid and the cost

Bank	
Reserves (*R*)	Equity (*E*)
Loans (*L*)	Deposits (*D*)

Figure 10.1 Simplified balance sheet of a bank

of free services (for example, free access to ATMs). While deposits are redeemable on demand, depositors usually do not ask for their money back at the same time. Banks therefore hold only a fraction of these deposits in the form of liquid reserves R that consist of balances with the central bank or readily tradable assets, such as Treasury securities, that pay the risk-free rate r_F.

Banks provide loans L. The expected loan rate r_L is different from the contracted rate on loans, as some borrowers default on their loan. Assuming a risk-neutral bank, the difference between the contracted loan rate r_C and the expected loan rate r_L is given by:

$$E(1 + r_C) = (1 + r_C) \cdot (1 + p) + (1 + r_C) \cdot p \cdot \gamma = 1 + r_L \tag{10.1}$$

where p is the probability of default and γ the recovery rate (the fraction of the principal and interest recovered in case of default). Equation 10.1 can be illustrated with a simple example. Assume a contracted loan rate of 9 per cent, a probability of default of 5 per cent and a recovery rate of 80 per cent. The expected loan rate is 7.91 per cent, calculated as (1.09 * 0.95) + (1.09 * .05 * 0.8) = 1.0791.

The bank's profit π is the interest margin net of cost C and is given by:

$$\pi = L \cdot r_L + R \cdot r_F - D \cdot r_D - C \tag{10.2}$$

An important determinant of bank profitability is the risk premium RP, i.e. the difference between the contracted loan rate and the risk-free rate (r_C – r_F). The risk premium covers the expected loan losses (that are a function of the probability of default p and the recovery rate γ), the cost of the loan business, and the reward for risk taking on the loans.

Fee-based business

Banks also make profits from fee-earning activities. These off-balance sheet activities are related to the traditional loan business and include securitisation of assets (see Chapter 1), credit lines, and guarantees, such as letters of credit. Off-balance sheet activities also encompass derivative transactions, such as forwards, options, and swaps. Nowadays, large banks are the key players in the derivatives markets.

Asset securitisation involves the sale of income-generating financial assets (such as mortgages, car loans, trade receivables, credit card receivables, and leases) by a bank, the originator of the financial assets, to a *special purpose vehicle* (SPV). The SPV finances the purchase of these financial assets by the issue of commercial paper, which is secured by those assets (see Chapter 8). Banks can thus liquefy their illiquid loans. The resulting 'originate and distribute' model separates the functions of granting loans and funding loans. When loans on their balance sheet are securitised, banks can provide new loans.

Finally, banks are increasingly involved in fee-earning capital-market and asset management activities. European banks deliver services like underwriting securities, advising on mergers and acquisitions (M&As), and managing assets. In this way, they have recovered part of the business lost due to dis-intermediation (see Chapter 9). Non-interest income of banks in the EU amounts to 40 per cent of total income (ECB, 2010).

Banks as liquidity providers

Banks have an advantage compared with other financial institutions in providing liquidity. This advantage is rooted in the structure of the banking system (Garber and Weisbrod, 1990). First, under normal circumstances there is an active and deep interbank market in which banks trade their liquidity surpluses and deficits so that liquidity shocks at individual banks can easily be offset. A bank with a surplus lends to a bank with a deficit, and vice versa. As shown in Chapter 5, the euro interbank market has worked smoothly from the first day of EMU until the crisis. Money market rates quickly converged to a single euro-wide money market rate. TARGET2 (the wholesale payment system of the National Central Banks and the European Central Bank) provide the infrastructure for transferring funds in real time (see Chapter 7).

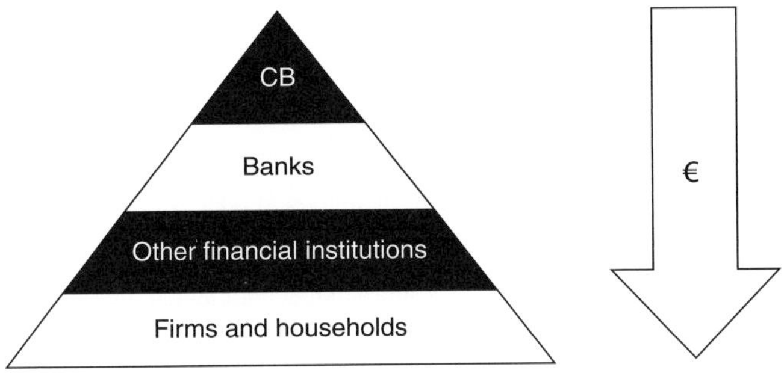

Figure 10.2 Liquidity pyramid of the economy
Note: CB = central bank. In this liquidity pyramid, the central bank provides liquidity to the banking system. Banks in turn provide liquidity to other financial institutions. Banks also provide liquidity to firms and households.

Second, aggregate liquidity shocks are smoothed by the central bank. A central bank conducts open market operations to inject (withdraw) liquidity in the money market if there is an aggregate shortage (surplus). Banks are the usual counterparties of the central bank in these open market operations. If an individual bank cannot square its position at the end of the day, it can use facilities offered by the central bank. To stimulate banks to do their business as much as possible on the money market, the rates for these standing facilities are slightly off-market. At the time of writing, the ECB's deposit rate is, for example, 0.25 per cent below the official refinancing rate for open market operations and the marginal lending rate is 0.25 per cent above the official refinancing rate (see Chapter 4).

These features of the banking system enable banks to provide liquidity to other financial institutions if and when needed. More importantly, they are also the main provider of liquidity to households and firms. The liquidity pyramid in Figure 10.2 illustrates these relationships. The central bank is at the top of the pyramid, as it can create liquidity without limit by expanding its balance sheet (granting loans and taking deposits). As explained above, the central bank only provides liquidity to banks that in turn provide liquidity to the rest of the financial system and to households and firms. Especially during crises it is important that central banks act swiftly to provide liquidity. However, banks also play a crucial role under these circumstances, as the examples presented in Box 10.1 illustrate.

During the financial crisis, liquidity became available only for banks against collateral either in private repo operations, by issuing secured bonds, or by pledging assets in the central bank. As a consequence, a significant proportion of banks' assets became encumbered. Notably in

Box 10.1 Liquidity management during crises

On 19 October 1987 the US stock market crashed, with the S&P 500 stock market index falling about 20 per cent. The crash showed the vulnerability of the trading systems, as they were not capable of processing so many transactions at once. Uncertainty about information contributed to a pull-back by investors from the market. Another factor contributing to the crash were *margin calls* to securities traders that accompanied the large price changes. When securities traders buy securities with borrowed money, they have to deposit a margin with the clearinghouse to cover the credit risk of the clearinghouse. As the value of securities declined, the clearinghouse called for extra margin. While necessary to protect the solvency of the clearinghouse processing the trades, the size of the margin calls reduced market liquidity as securities traders had drawn on their working capital to meet these margin calls and subsequently had difficulties in continuing trading. The Federal Reserve stepped in by providing highly visible liquidity support through massive open market operations. More importantly, the Federal Reserve also encouraged banks to extend liquidity support to securities traders (brokers and dealers). The extension of credit by banks to securities firms was key to their ability to meet their clearing and settlement obligations and to continue to operate in these markets.

Another example was the subprime mortgage market crisis in the summer of 2007. Many banks, including various large banks, such as Goldman Sachs, City Group, and Merrill Lynch, announced large losses due to this crisis. As it was unclear to what extent banks were exposed to these risks, banks were reluctant to provide short-term loans to each other. The ECB and the Federal Reserve therefore stepped in and provided massive liquidity support. The Bank of England (BoE), however, initially remained on the sidelines. On 12 September 2007 BoE governor Mervyn King said the Bank of England would be prepared to provide emergency loans to any bank that ran into short-term difficulties as a result of temporary market conditions. But he appeared to rule out following the lead of the ECB and the US Federal Reserve in pumping huge sums into the banking system to ease the liquidity drought. On 13 September, British bank Northern Rock, the country's fifth largest mortgage lender, applied to the BoE for emergency funds caused by liquidity problems. Concerned customers withdrew an estimated £2 billion in just three days; this was the first run on a British bank in more than a century. On 17 September, Chancellor Alistair Darling intervened to try to end the crisis by agreeing to guarantee all deposits held by Northern Rock.

peripheral euro-area countries banks increased their asset encumbrance due to central bank lending. However, banks from some core countries and non-euro-area countries also have significant levels of asset encumbrance, although mainly in the form of covered bonds (see Figure 10.3).

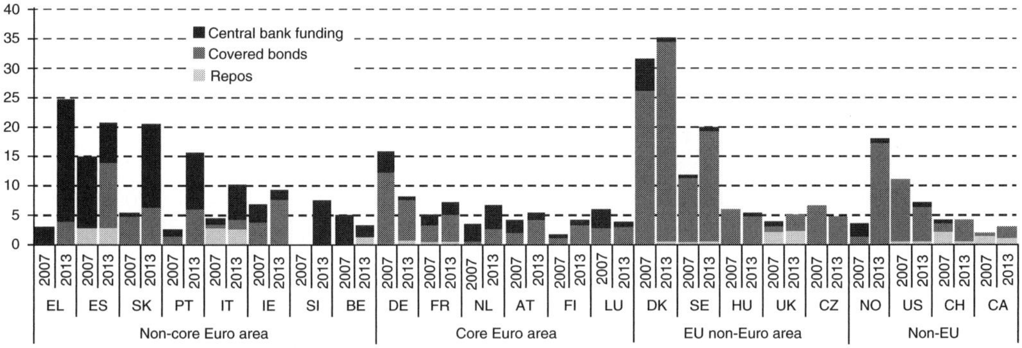

Note: Covered bonds include asset-backed securities.

Figure 10.3 Asset encumbrance (percentage of assets)
Source: European Commission (2014)

Banks as delegated monitor

Asymmetric information lies at the core of banking. A borrower has private information on the cash flow of an investment project, which is unobservable to outside lenders. Banks therefore monitor (potential) clients. Monitoring is defined here in a broad sense (Freixas and Rochet, 2008) as:

- screening projects ex ante (adverse selection);
- preventing opportunistic behaviour of the borrower during the project (moral hazard);
- auditing a borrower who fails to meet its contractual obligation (costly state verification).

Banks have a comparative advantage in monitoring (potential) borrowers if the following conditions are met (Diamond, 1984). First, a bank can develop economies of scale in monitoring by financing many investment projects. Second, the capacity of individual lenders is small compared to the size of many investment projects so that each project needs several lenders who would then need to monitor the borrowers. Finally, the costs of delegating this monitoring to a bank are small. Box 10.2 presents the Diamond model of delegated monitoring that shows that under these conditions it is efficient to delegate monitoring to a bank.

When the number of borrowers is large, it is efficient to delegate monitoring to one party. In the model shown in Box 10.2, a bank emerges as the delegated monitor for all lenders. Another party to whom lenders may delegate monitoring is a credit rating agency. A *credit rating agency* assigns credit ratings to firms and governments that issue debt obligations, such as

Box 10.2 When is it optimal to delegate monitoring to banks?*

Consider n identical borrowers who need funds for their investment projects. Each investment requires one unit of account and the returns of the investment are identically independently distributed. The cash flow $\tilde{y}$ that a borrower obtains from his investment is unobservable for lenders. The asymmetric information regarding the cash flow gives rise to moral hazard, which can be solved either by monitoring the firm at a cost K or by signing a debt contract with a cost C (in case of insufficient cash flow). It is assumed that monitoring is more efficient than using the debt contract: $K < C$. The next assumption is that each lender has only $\frac{1}{m}$ available for investment (i.e. lenders have a small capacity to lend). So each project needs m lenders. If small lenders provide the funds needed for the investment (direct lending), the total costs of monitoring all projects by all borrowers would amount to $n \cdot m \cdot K$.

Next, a bank is introduced. Facing the same trade-off between monitoring or signing debt contracts, the bank will also choose to monitor borrowers since $K < C$. The bank emerges as a delegated monitor, which monitors the borrowers on behalf of lenders. But who will monitor the bank? It is very costly for all lenders to monitor the bank. The solution is that the bank offers a debt contract (deposit). The lender is promised a nominal amount $\frac{r_D}{m}$ in return for a deposit $\frac{1}{m}$. The bank is liquidated if its announced cash flow $\tilde{z}$ falls below the total sum promised to depositors $n \cdot r_D$. Now, a mechanism is needed to ensure that a bank will truthfully reveal the realised cash flow $\tilde{z} = \sum_{i=1}^{n} \tilde{y}_i - n.K$. The threat of an audit in case of failure at a cost is used to make the contract incentive compatible.

Suppose that depositors are risk neutral and have access to outside investments with a return of r. The equilibrium repayment on deposits r_D is then determined by:

$$E\left[\min\left(\sum_{i=1}^{n} \tilde{y}_i - n \cdot K, n \cdot r_D\right)\right] = n \cdot r \qquad (10.3)$$

Equation 10.3 shows that the return r is equal to the minimum of the expected cash flow of the project minus monitoring costs and the expected unit return on deposits. In equilibrium, the expected unit return on deposits r_D equals r. Next, the total cost of delegation C_n is equal to the expectation of a costly audit in case of failure:

$$C_n = E\left[\max\left(n \cdot r_D + n \cdot K - \sum_{i=1}^{n} \tilde{y}_i, 0\right)\right] \qquad (10.4)$$

Delegated monitoring is more efficient than direct lending if the combined cost of monitoring by the bank and delegation is lower than the cost of monitoring by all lenders:

$$n \cdot K + C_n < n \cdot m \cdot K \qquad (10.5)$$

Box 10.2 (cont.)

Dividing by n gives:

$$K + \frac{C_n}{n} < m \cdot K \tag{10.6}$$

Since $m > 1$, monitoring by bank is less costly than monitoring by all lenders if $\frac{C_n}{n}$ goes to zero when n goes to infinity. Dividing equations (10.3) and (10.4) by n produces:

$$E\left[\min\left(\frac{1}{n}\sum_{i=1}^{n}\widetilde{y}_i - K, r_D\right)\right] = r \tag{10.7}$$

and

$$\frac{C_n}{n} = E\left[\max\left(r_D + K - \frac{1}{n}\sum_{i=1}^{n}\widetilde{y}_i, 0\right)\right] \tag{10.8}$$

According to the law of large numbers, $\frac{1}{n}\sum_{i=1}^{n}\widetilde{y}_i$ converges to $E(\widetilde{y})$. Since $E(\widetilde{y})>K+r$, equation (10.7) shows that $r_D = r$ when n goes to infinity. Substituting these results into equation (10.8) yields:

$$\lim_n \frac{C_n}{n} = \max\left(r + K - E(\widetilde{y}), 0\right) = 0 \tag{10.9}$$

So, the cost of delegation goes to zero when n goes to infinity.

Source: Freixas and Rochet (2008)

bonds (see Chapter 8).[1] A credit rating measures the creditworthiness of a firm. It basically looks at the firm's ability to pay back a loan, which can be derived from observing the firm's cash flows. The resulting credit rating affects the interest rate charged for the bonds.

What determines the choice between direct and intermediated lending? In practice, direct lending in the form of issuing bonds at the capital market is less expensive than bank lending. So only those firms that cannot issue direct debt on financial markets will request bank lending (Freixas and Rochet, 2008). When the uncertainty about the firm's cash flows is relatively small (i.e. the asymmetric information between the firm and the lenders is limited), the firm can borrow on the market. As the uncertainty increases, banks come into play as they have more possibilities than credit rating agencies to ask for information and to intervene when necessary. When the uncertainty becomes too large, a firm cannot obtain finance. The resulting equilibrium is that large, well-capitalised firms with a track record of published annual reports finance themselves directly, while smaller, new firms have to turn to banks.

10.2 The use of risk-management models

Risk taking is fundamental to the business of banking. Only by taking calculated financial risks can a bank earn a rate above the risk-free rate of return. Banks unbundle and bundle financial risks. First, risks are decomposed so that they can be managed one by one. For example, the risk on a bank loan with a fixed interest rate can be separated into interest rate risk (i.e. the risk of loss because of rising interest rates) and credit risk (i.e. the risk of loss because of a default by a borrower). The bank can separately manage the interest rate risk (e.g. by buying an interest rate derivative with the same maturity as the bank loan) and the credit risk (e.g. by requiring collateral from the borrower). Next, risks are aggregated to reap the benefits of diversification. An example is a diversified portfolio of loans to companies from different sectors and/or geographic regions. The traditional role of banks in monitoring credit risk has evolved towards the use of advanced models to measure and manage risk. Risk management has been broadened from credit risk to market risk (i.e. the risk of loss because of unfavourable movements in market prices) and operational risk (i.e. the risk of loss from inadequate or failed internal processes, people or systems, or from external events). Progress in information technology has facilitated the development of risk-management models, which rely on statistical methods to process financial data. The financial services sector is one of the most IT-intensive industries (Berger, 2003).

Modern risk management

The main risk types for a bank are credit risk, market risk, and operational risk. The concept of economic capital can be used for measuring different risks in a comparable way. *Economic capital* is defined as the amount of capital a bank needs in order to be able to absorb losses over a certain time interval with a certain confidence level. Banks usually choose a time horizon of one year. The confidence interval depends on the bank's objectives.

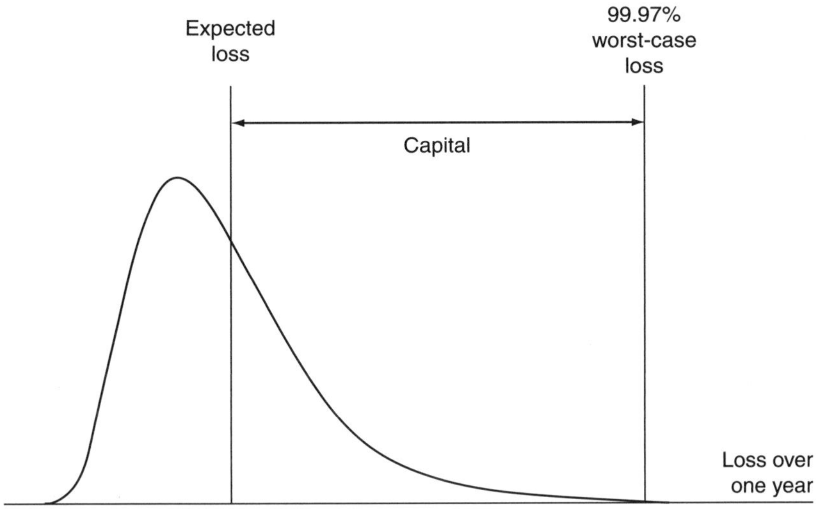

Figure 10.4 Economic capital of an AA-rated bank
Source: Hull (2009)

A common objective for a large international bank is to maintain an AA credit rating (Hull, 2009). Companies rated AA have a one-year probability of default of 0.03 per cent. This results in a confidence level of 99.97 per cent. Figure 10.4 illustrates the calculation of economic capital.

Economic capital can be used to calculate the *risk adjusted return on capital* (RAROC) that is given by:

$$\text{RAROC} = \frac{\text{Revenues} - \text{Costs} - \text{Expected Losses}}{\text{Economic Capital}} = \frac{\pi}{E} \qquad (10.10)$$

Both the numerator and the denominator are adjusted for risk in the RAROC formula. This is an improvement compared with the widely used standard *return on equity measure* (ROE), defined as earned profit divided by available equity. An example can illustrate the working of RAROC. An AA-rated bank estimates its expected losses as 1 per cent of outstanding loans per year on average. The worst-case loss at 99.97 per cent confidence is 4 per cent of outstanding loans. So the economic capital for €100 of loans is €3 (the difference between worst-case loss and expected loss). The numerator starts with the revenues: the spread between the promised loan rate and the risk-free rate is 2.20 per cent. The costs of the bank amount to 0.75 per cent of the loan. So RAROC is $\frac{2.20-0.75-1.00}{3.00} = 15$ per cent.

RAROC has emerged as the leading methodology for large banks (as well as other financial institutions, such as insurance companies) to measure and manage risk. The use of internal risk models has been stimulated by supervisors allowing banks to use their internal models to calculate capital requirements (see Chapter 12 for the Basel capital adequacy rules). Within the RAROC framework, banks first calculate the risk for credit, market, and operational risk and then aggregate the different risk types for the whole bank. To assess the overall risk profile of the bank, correlations across risk types have to be taken into account (Van Lelyveld, 2006).

The first type of risk is credit risk. *Credit risk* is defined as the risk of loss because of the failure of a counterparty to perform according to the contractual arrangement, for instance due to a default by a borrower.[2] In a modern bank, counterparties include not only the traditional counterparties on loans (borrowers) but also counterparties in derivatives transactions and in payment and settlement systems. Diversification is an important tool to manage credit risk. By lending to companies from different sectors, banks can diversify away the sectoral exposures in their loan portfolio. Similarly, international expansion would reduce the business-cycle risk. As long as business cycles across euro area countries are not fully synchronised, there is scope for diversification within Europe. Clearly, geographic (and sectoral) diversification would not protect a bank against a worldwide economic downturn. A second tool to manage credit risk is monitoring counterparties.

The typical time horizon for credit risk is one year. This type of risk thus fits nicely into economic capital models that also use the one-year horizon. Figure 10.5 gives the loss distribution for credit risk. Its shape is quite skewed, as the vast majority of counterparties will repay (almost) in full and only a minority default (partly) on their payment obligation.

The second type of risk is market risk. *Market risk* is the risk of loss because of unfavourable movements in market prices like interest rates, foreign exchange rates, equity prices, and commodity prices. Market risk relates primarily to a bank's trading portfolio and focuses on changes in market value. Losses due to market risk materialise when an adverse price movement causes the mark-to-market valuation of a trading position to decline. Banks typically manage their trading portfolio within a Value-at-Risk framework (VaR) with a ten-day time horizon (see Box 10.3). The rationale is that a bank can close its position (e.g. selling a security or taking an opposite position in a new derivative transaction) within ten business days. Under

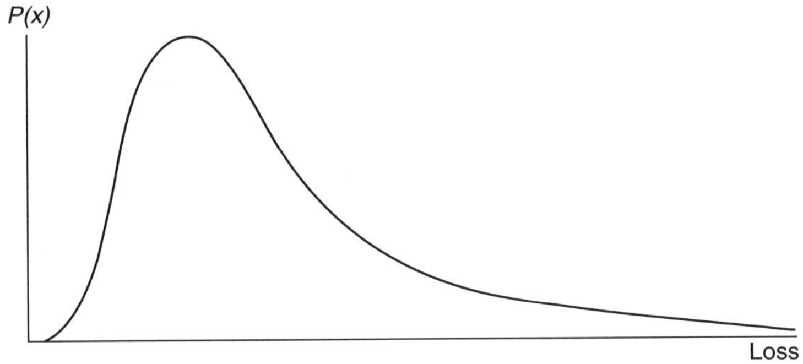

Figure 10.5 Loss distribution for credit risk

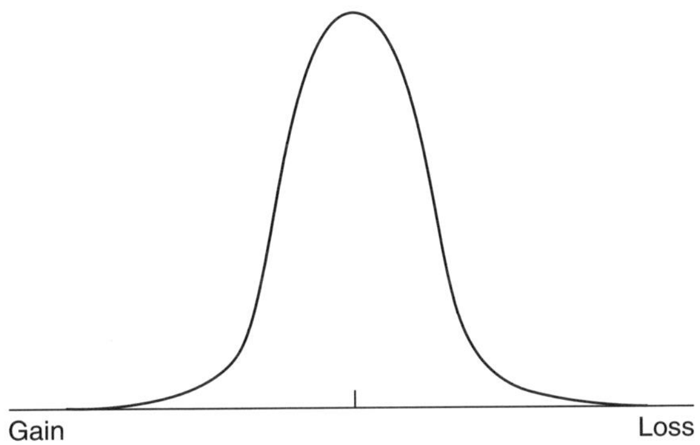

Figure 10.6 Loss distribution for market risk

certain assumptions, the standard deviation of ten-day losses can be translated to the one-year horizon of economic capital models.[3]

A specific market risk occurs when assets and liabilities in the balance sheet are not matched. This risk is labelled *asset and liability management* (ALM) risk. The ALM risk of banks refers to the interest rate risk in the banking book, where long-term assets (loans) are funded by short-term liabilities (deposits). Insurance companies face the opposite problem: their liabilities typically have a longer maturity than assets (see Chapter 11).

The loss distribution for market risk is very different from that for credit risk. Figure 10.6 shows that the loss distribution for market risk is symmetrical. A good example is the price of equity. According to the efficient market hypothesis, all available information (including information on the future prospects of a company) is reflected in the equity price of a company. So today's stock price is the best predictor of tomorrow's stock price. The stock

Box 10.3 Value-at-Risk

A primary tool for measuring market risk is the *Value-at-Risk methodology*. The VaR measure summarises the expected maximum loss (i.e. Value-at-Risk) over a target horizon of N days within a given confidence interval of *X* per cent. As will be discussed in Chapter 12, the Basel capital framework calculates capital for a bank's trading book using the VaR measure with $N = 10$ and $X = 99\%$. This means that the bank is 99 per cent certain that the loss level over 10 days will not exceed the VaR measure. So only in 1 out of 100 trading days is the bank's loss expected to exceed the VaR measure.

The main advantage is that the risk of a portfolio comprising various financial assets is contained in a single measure, the VaR measure. Figure 10.7 illustrates VaR for the situation where the change in the value of a portfolio is approximately normally distributed. The basic VaR methodology assumes a normal (bell-shaped) distribution of returns. However, the returns on financial assets are non-normal with heavy tails (Daníelsson, 2011). So VaR underestimates the market risk of a portfolio. Extreme value theory, which uses extreme values (e.g. one-day losses of 5 per cent or larger) to measure the tails of a distribution more accurately, is typically applied to get a better estimation of the downside risk of a portfolio of assets. Alternatively, banks can complement the VaR methodology with stress-test scenarios to get a better picture of potential losses.

Source: Hull (2009)

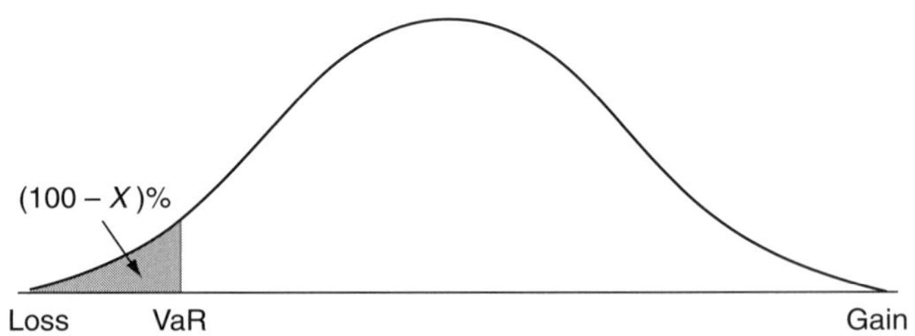

Figure 10.7 Calculation of VaR with a confidence level of X%
Source: Hull (2009)

price will move only with the arrival of new information, which appears randomly. The stock price follows a random walk with equal likelihood of upward and downward movements.

Operational risk has become part of risk management. *Operational risk* is defined as the risk of loss from inadequate or failed internal processes, people or systems, or from external events. A famous example of operational risk is the failure of Barings Bank in 1995. Nick Leeson, a trader for Barings in Singapore, made money by arbitraging between the Nikkei 225 futures on the Singapore and the Osaka exchanges. Barings had no effective risk limits in place and Nick Leeson could build up large positions. When the market moved against Leeson, Barings' total loss was close to $1 billion (Hull, 2009). A more recent example was the rogue trader scandal at Société Générale (SocGen) that cost the bank €4.9 billion. Jérôme Kerviel, a junior trader at SocGen, secretly built up huge and risky positions in the derivatives market. He was taking greater and greater risks over a period dating back to March 2007 for large amounts and to 2005 for smaller amounts. SocGen only discovered the fraud between 18 and 20 January 2008. Unwinding the positions over the subsequent three days cost the bank billions. The variety of concealment techniques used, a lack of systematic checks by staff when warning flags were raised, and shortcomings in the control systems all contributed to the late discovery of Kerviel's activities.

Other examples of operational risk are IT failures, judicial settlements, or terrorist attacks. The Barings and SocGen examples illustrate that operational risk can interact with credit and market risk. When a trader exceeds limits, losses result only if the market moves against the trader. Figure 10.8 provides the loss distribution for operational risk. The loss distribution is very skewed, even more skewed than the credit risk loss distribution. Most of the time, operational losses are modest, but occasionally they are very large.

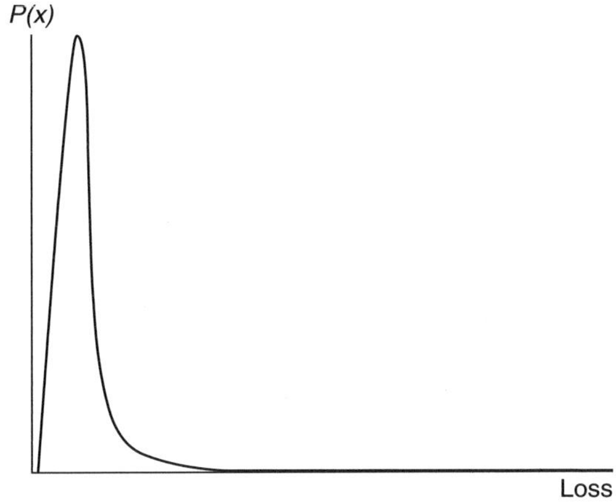

Figure 10.8 Loss distribution for operational risk

A recent form of operational risk is judicial settlements. French bank BNP Paribas, for example, has pleaded guilty to two criminal charges and agreed to pay €6.6 billion to resolve accusations that it violated US sanctions against Sudan, Cuba, and Iran. This was a severe punishment through which US policy makers wanted to send a clear message to other financial institutions around the world. Under its new strategy, the US Department of Justice tries to snare more major banks for possible money laundering or sanctions violations. Another example is that several major international banks paid large settlements for their involvement in the Libor fraud. The Libor scandal refers to fraudulent actions connected to *LIBOR* (London Interbank Offered Rate), which is an average interest rate calculated through submissions of interest rates by major banks in London. It was discovered that some banks were falsely inflating or deflating their rates so as to profit from trades, or to signal creditworthiness. Libor underpins the lending and derivatives markets.

There are severe shortcomings in the use of internal risk management models, such as RAROC, for calculating regulatory capital. Risk management models focus on day-to-day risk and not on tail risks (Danielsson, 2013). These models are typically based on the normal distribution and assume that risks are independent (i.e. no correlation) and exogenous. The financial crisis showed that tail events can and do happen. Extreme value theory, which deviates from the normal distribution, can be used to assess tail events. Moreover, most markets went down at the same time, showing high correlation of risks. The unfolding of the financial crisis also highlighted the endogenous nature of risk. Endogenous risk refers to the risk from shocks that are generated and amplified within the system. It stands in contrast to exogenous risk, which refers to shocks that arrive from outside the system. Financial markets are subject to both types of risk. However, the greatest damage is done by risk of the endogenous kind (Danielsson, 2013).

In response to these shortfalls, regulators are increasingly demanding the use of stress tests to assess the impact of various severe scenarios on a bank's regulatory capital. The US authorities have initiated system-wide stress tests in 2009. Following the US example, the European Banking Authority (EBA) has conducted several stress tests of the European banking system. In *stress tests* the implications for individual banks' financial positions under several macroeconomic scenarios are examined, taking the banks' exposures and business models into account. However, these tests were criticised as some banks which passed the test soon thereafter got into trouble. With the advance to Banking Union, EBA and the ECB have conducted a more demanding stress test as part of the comprehensive assessment (see Chapter 12).

While credit, market, and operational risk can threaten their solvency (and are therefore incorporated in the economic capital calculation), banks also incur liquidity risk. *Liquidity risk* arises when a bank has insufficient liquid resources to meet a surge in liquidity demand. (In Chapter 5, *market liquidity* is discussed and defined as the ease with which an investor can sell or buy a security immediately at a price close to the fair price.) The classical case of a surge in liquidity demand for a bank is the sudden withdrawal of deposits. Banks manage their liquid resources in two ways. The first way is maintaining a pool of liquid assets. Reserves at the central bank are the most liquid assets but generate a relatively low return. Other liquid assets are government bonds, which can be easily sold. But a bank typically holds only a fraction of its demand deposits in liquid assets. The remainder is invested in illiquid, but high-return, assets such as loans. These assets can be liquidated immediately only at low prices.

The second way banks can manage liquidity risk is by preserving a diversified funding base (also referred to as *funding liquidity*). As explained in section 10.1, banks can fund themselves in the interbank market. As long as banks have sufficient confidence in each other, a bank is able to borrow from other banks. Trust is therefore the most important 'asset' for a bank. When a bank loses the trust of other banks, it will face liquidity problems and possibly even failure. A case in point is the failure of Continental Illinois Bank in May 1984. This bank experienced funding difficulties in domestic markets and Continental therefore had to turn to more expensive Eurodollar deposits in London. Rumours that Continental was on the verge of bankruptcy resulted in a run on Continental's wholesale deposits by both domestic and foreign banks.

Centralisation of risk management

The organisational structure of international banks is moving from the traditional country model to a business-line model with integration and centralisation of key management functions (Schoenmaker and Oosterloo, 2008). These management functions comprise risk management, internal controls, treasury operations (including liquidity management and funding), compliance, and auditing. One of the most notable advances in risk management is the growing emphasis on developing a firm-wide assessment of risk. Such an integrated approach to risk management aims to ensure a comprehensive and systematic approach to risk-related decisions throughout the financial group. It allows senior management to have a full picture of the group's overall risk profile. RAROC provides the methodology to compare and aggregate different risks.

Moreover, financial groups with a centralised risk management unit in place could reap economies of scale in risk management. Nevertheless, these centralised systems still rely on local branches and subsidiaries for local market data. The potential capital reductions that can be achieved by applying the advanced approaches of the Basel framework (see Chapter 12) encourage banking groups to organise their risk management more centrally. A well-constructed risk and capital management framework can deliver significant benefits and substantially strengthen the competitive position of financial groups. The emergence of so-called chief risk officers (CROs) at the headquarters of large financial groups illustrates this trend towards centralisation.

The dominant approach among large international financial institutions is to adopt a 'hub and spoke' organisational model (Kuritzkes *et al.*, 2003). The spokes are responsible for risk management within business lines, while the hub provides centralised oversight of risk and capital at the group level. Activities at the spoke include the credit function within a bank, as local managers are familiar with the local conditions, such as the business cycle relevant for credit risk in a country. Moreover, aggregation across risk factors within a business line also typically takes place in the spokes.

While the hub is dependent on risk reporting from the spokes, in many cases it is also responsible for overseeing the development of an integrated economic capital framework (such as RAROC) that is then implemented within the spokes. The specific roles of the hub vary, but tend to include assuming responsibility for group-level risk reporting, participating in decisions about group capital structure, funding practices, and target debt rating, acting as liaison with regulators and rating agencies, and advising on major risk transfer transactions, such as collateralised loan obligations and securitisations.

10.3 The European banking system

Banking markets across Europe

The banking markets of most EU Member States are dominated by domestic banks. One way to assess the presence of foreign banks is *cross-border*

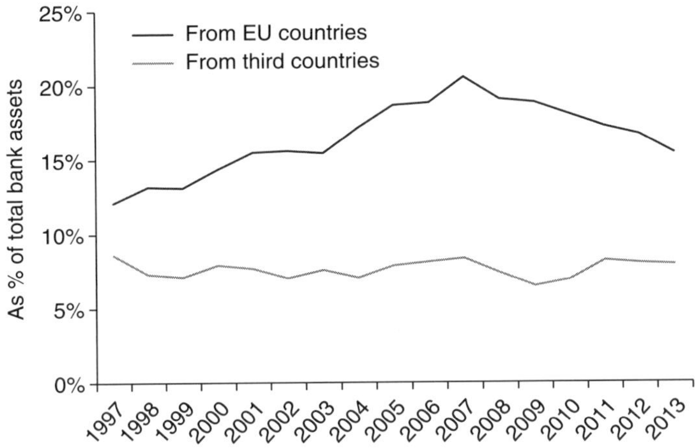

Figure 10.9 Cross-border penetration in European banking (%), 1997–2013
Note: Share of assets from other EU countries and third countries measured as a percentage of total banking assets. The share is calculated for the EU-28.
Source: Schoenmaker (2014)

penetration. This measure is defined as the assets of banks from other EU Member States (or third countries) as a percentage of the country's total banking assets. Average cross-border penetration in the EU gradually increased from 12 per cent in 1997 to 21 per cent in 2007 (Figure 10.9). After the financial crisis, it fell back to 15 per cent in 2013. Cross-border penetration from third countries was 8 per cent in 2013. However, the degree of cross-border penetration is very uneven across the EU Member States, as Table 10.1 shows. While the banking systems of the new Member States are dominated by banks from other EU countries (with a penetration rate of 61 per cent), average cross-border penetration in the EU-15 is only 14 per cent. With 63 per cent, Luxembourg has a high cross-border penetration (reflecting the country's favourable tax regime), while the corresponding figures for France, Germany, the Netherlands, Spain, and Sweden are 10 per cent or less.

Table 10.1 also shows that the penetration by banks from third countries is well below 15 per cent for all EU Member States, except for the UK where it stands at 28 per cent, illustrating London's position as a major international financial centre. Most banking business in London is focused on large firms (i.e. wholesale). There is much evidence suggesting that EU wholesale banking markets are highly integrated, in contrast to retail banking, i.e. banking services delivered to consumers and SMEs (see Box 10.4).

Table 10.1 Cross-border penetration in EU Member States, 2013

	(1) Number of banks	(2) Total banking assets (in € billion)	(3) Assets of domestic banks (in % of (2))	(4) Assets of banks from other EU countries (in % of (2))	(5) Assets of banks from third countries (in % of (2))
Austria	731	915	76	17	7
Belgium	103	1,021	34	51	15
Bulgaria	30	47	28	69	3
Croatia	32	57	n.a.	n.a.	n.a.
Cyprus	101	90	71	13	16
Czech Republic	56	191	6	93	1
Denmark	161	1,047	81	18	1
Estonia	31	20	2	92	6
Finland	303	522	34	65	1
France	623	7,565	91	8	1
Germany	1,842	7,525	89	10	1
Greece	40	407	97	3	0
Hungary	189	111	48	48	4
Ireland	458	972	61	29	10
Italy	694	4,039	87	12	1
Latvia	63	29	40	45	15
Lithuania	91	24	27	73	0
Luxembourg	147	843	22	63	15
Malta	27	50	62	25	13
Netherlands	253	2,250	92	6	2
Poland	691	362	34	59	7
Portugal	151	513	80	19	1
Romania	39	91	30	70	0
Slovakia	28	61	4	96	0
Slovenia	23	46	69	31	0
Spain	290	3,143	92	7	1
Sweden	168	1,212	91	8	1
United Kingdom	358	8,889	56	16	28
EU-15	6,322	40,863	78	14	8
NMS-13	1,401	1,180	34	61	5
EU-28	7,723	42,043	77	15	8

Notes: Share of business from domestic banks, share of business of banks from other EU countries, and share of business of banks from third countries are measured as a percentage of the total banking assets in a country. The shares add up to 100 per cent. Figures are for 2013. EU-15, NMS-13, and EU-28 are calculated as a weighted average (weighted according to assets).
Source: ECB

Box 10.4 Banking market integration

According to Dermine (2006), the 'law of one price', which represents the theoretical benchmark for integrated markets, is unlikely to hold in retail banking markets for various reasons. First, trust and confidence are important in these markets. Customers want to be sure that their money is in safe hands. Knowledge of the respective bank, the national legal system, language, cultural preferences, and geographical proximity may lead to a preference for a domestic bank, i.e. there are differentiated products. Second, retail customers generally buy a package of financial services from the same bank, rather than individual services. Therefore, the 'law of one price' may hold for the bundle of services, but not necessarily for each individual service. Third, asymmetric information in lending is quite important, and local knowledge can help to reduce this information asymmetry. Local banks may therefore be in a better position to lend to SMEs than foreign banks. Fourth, the 'law of one price' assumes the absence of transportation costs and regulatory barriers. But differences in legislation, like tax and consumer-protection rules, may create substantial barriers for foreign bank entry.

Still, there is evidence that EU retail banking markets also have become more integrated until the crisis. However, as Figure 10.10 shows, more recently the standard deviation of bank loans to non-financial corporations has increased. Only after the summer of 2012 did the dispersion decline. As Figure 10.10 shows, the smallest loans have the highest dispersion in interest rates. As these very small loans are typically used by small- and medium-sized enterprises (SMEs), the fragmentation appears to affect these companies even more than larger companies.

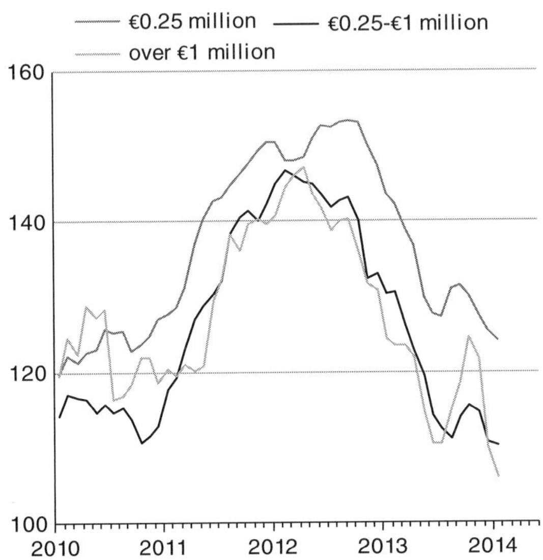

Figure 10.10 Cross-country standard deviation of interest rates on bank loans to non-financial corporations, 2010–2013
Source: ECB

Most small customers receive their financial services from domestic suppliers, and the range and terms under which products are available differ substantially across the EU Member States.

In 2013, there were slightly more than 7,700 banks in the EU. These banks can be segmented into three groups. The first, very large, group of banks consists of small banks operating in a region of a country. In particular, Germany and Austria have many small savings and cooperative banks, most of which have assets of less than €2 billion. About 20 per cent of German banks belong to public savings groups and about 60 per cent to the cooperative banking sector (Hackethal, 2004). The second group consists of medium-sized banks with assets ranging from €2 to €100 billion. These banks often operate on a country-wide scale. The third group are the large banks having assets up to €2,000 billion; they usually do a significant part of their business abroad.

Table 10.2 shows the biggest 30 banks in Europe, representing nearly half of the assets of the European banking system. Schoenmaker (2014) splits large banks in four categories, depending on the composition of their assets. A global bank has less than 50 per cent of its assets in the home country and the majority of its international assets in the rest of the world. These banks include HSBC, Barclays, and Standard Chartered from the UK, Deutsche Bank from Germany, and Credit Suisse and UBS from Switzerland.

A European bank has less than 50 per cent of its assets in the home country and the majority of its international assets in the rest of Europe. Some European banks focus on a specific region in the EU. The Nordea Group, for example, primarily operates in the Nordic countries. Other European banks operate Europe-wide; examples include BNP Paribas, UniCredit, and ING.

A semi-international bank has between 50 and 75 per cent of its assets in the home country. Examples are RBS from the UK, BBVA from Spain, Commerzbank from Germany, and KBC from Belgium.

Finally, a domestic bank has 75 per cent or more of its assets in the home country. Examples include Crédit Agricole in France, the Rabobank in the Netherlands, and the Lloyds Banking Group in the UK.

International comparison

Turning to international banking, the geographical segmentation of large banks on the other continents, the Americas and the Asia-Pacific, can be compared with the geographical spread of the large European banks.

Table 10.2 Biggest 30 banks in Europe in 2013

Banking groups	(1) Capital strength[a] (in € billion)	(2) Total assets (in € billion)	(3) Business in home country (as % of (2))	(4) Business in rest of EU (as % of (2))	(5) Business in rest of world (as % of (2))
Global banks[b]					
1. HSBC (UK)	115	1,937	37	11	52
2. Barclays (UK)	67	1,568	36	26	38
3. Deutsche Bank (Germany)	51	1,612	28	30	42
4. Credit Suisse (Switzerland)	37	710	23	22	55
5. UBS (Switzerland)	35	821	33	25	42
6. Standard Chartered (UK)	31	489	16	5	79
European banks[c]					
1. BNP Paribas (France)	72	1,800	34	44	22
2. Santander (Spain)	61	1,116	29	41	30
3. UniCredit (Italy)	43	846	40	59	1
4. ING (Netherlands)	38	788	38	48	14
5. Nordea (Sweden)	24	631	24	75	1
6. Danske Bank (Denmark)	22	432	48	51	1
Semi-international banks[d]					
1. Royal Bank of Scotland (UK)	60	1,228	61	16	23
2. BBVA (Spain)	40	583	51	9	40
3. Commerzbank (Germany)	26	550	51	33	16
4. DNB Group (Norway)	16	285	74	18	8
5. KBC (Belgium)	14	241	53	45	3
6. SEB Bank (Sweden)	12	280	63	34	3
Domestic banks[e]					
1. Crédit Agricole (France)	63	1,707	81	11	8
2. Groupe BPCE (France)	47	1,124	77	11	12
3. Lloyds Banking Group (UK)	46	1,012	82	12	6

Table 10.2 (cont.)

Banking groups	(1) Capital strength[a] (in € billion)	(2) Total assets (in € billion)	(3) Business in home country (as % of (2))	(4) Business in rest of EU (as % of (2))	(5) Business in rest of world (as % of (2))
4. Société Générale (France)	41	1,235	76	13	11
5. Rabobank (Netherlands)	35	674	76	6	18
6. Intesa Sanpaolo (Italy)	34	626	86	12	2
7. Crédit Mutuel (France)	30	659	84	11	5
8. La Caixa Group (Spain)	18	351	91	7	2
9. ABN AMRO (Netherlands)	17	372	80	13	7
10. Landesbank Baden-Württemberg (Germany)	15	274	75	18	7
11. DZ Bank (Germany)	14	387	75	19	6
12. Bayerische Landesbank (Germany)	14	256	75	18	7
Top 30 European banks	1,135	24,592	53	24	23

Notes:

[a] Top 30 banks a reselected on the basis of capital strength (Tier 1 capital (see Chapter 12) as published in *The Banker*).

[b] Global banks: less than 50 per cent of assets in the home country and the majority of their international assets in the rest of the world.

[c] European banks: less than 50 per cent of assets in the home country and the majority of their international assets in the rest of Europe.

[d] Semi-international banks: between 50 and 75 per cent of assets in the home country.

[e] Domestic banks: 75 per cent or more of assets in the home country.

Source: Schoenmaker (2014)

Table 10.3 Development of international banking by continent, 2000–2011

	2000			2004			2008			2011		
Continent	h	r	w	h	r	w	h	r	w	h	r	w
Europe	55	20	25	54	22	24	51	21	28	53	23	24
Americas	77	8	15	78	9	13	73	9	18	70	11	19
Asia-Pacific	80	6	14	86	4	10	82	7	11	87	5	8

Notes: Share of business in home country (h), rest of the region (r), and rest of the world (w) of the top banks by continent. The top 30 banks for Europe; the top 15 banks for Americas and Asia-Pacific. The shares add up to 100 per cent.
Source: Schoenmaker (2013)

Table 10.3 shows that European banks are the most international, with close to 50 per cent of business abroad. This may be due to the integrated European banking market. But even when looking at the business outside the region, European banks are the most international with 24 per cent of business in the rest of the world. The American banks are catching up; their business in the rest of the world rose from 15 per cent in 2000 to 19 per cent in 2011.

The picture is very different for the Asian-Pacific banks. They used to have a very domestic orientation (Schoenmaker, 2013), which has been reinforced over the last years. Business in the rest of the world has declined from 14 per cent in 2000 to 8 per cent in 2011. The composition of the large Asian-Pacific banks is shifting from the major Japanese banks to the major Chinese banks. The Chinese banks have an even stronger domestic orientation than the Japanese banks.

Domestic and cross-border mergers and acquisitions

Mergers and acquisitions (M&As) have changed and will continue to change the European banking markets. It was widely expected that the Single Market initiative (see Chapter 3) would ease the path for cross-border M&As. Instead, banks prepared themselves for the Single Market by merging with other domestic banks. Cross-border mergers increased only after the start of EMU (see Figure 10.11).

Boot (1999) argues that domestic banks in Europe were often protected as they were regarded as national flagships. A fundamental belief that national financial institutions should not be controlled by foreigners prevented almost any cross-border merger up to the late

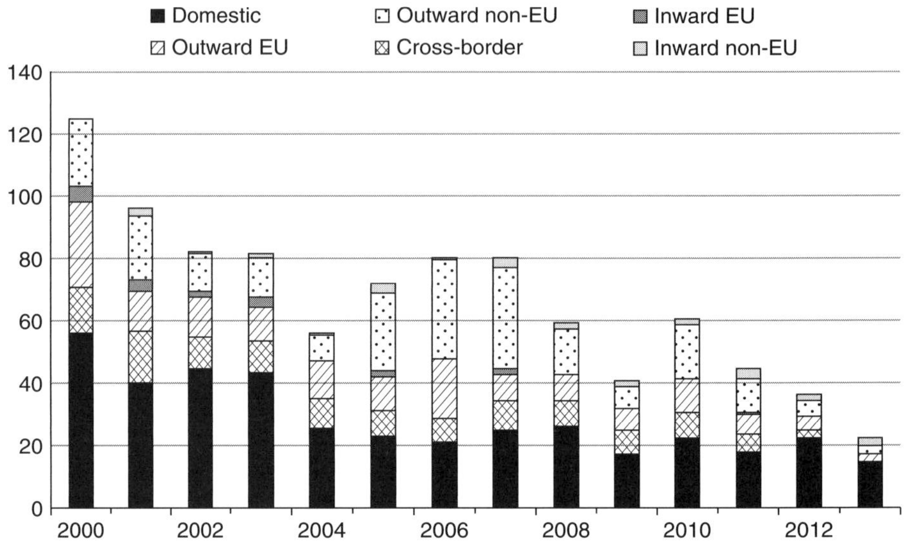

Figure 10.11 Banking M&As in Europe (value of completed deals, € billion), 2000–2013
Source: Dealogic M&A

1990s. The shift towards cross-border deals reflected high concentration in national banking systems. Some national banking systems had become so concentrated that further domestic mergers would be blocked by the competition authorities. In principle, the European Commission (DG Competition) permits mergers up to the threshold of 2,000 for the Herfindahl Index (see below). Several countries are close to, or even above, this threshold.

As the potential for domestic mergers is increasingly exhausted, the number of cross-border bank mergers increased until the financial crisis affected Europe. While early cross-border mergers in the 1990s created regional banks, such as Fortis in the Benelux countries and Nordea in Scandinavia, recent mergers are more widely spread across Europe. Examples are the takeover of Abbey National (UK) by Banco Santander (Spain) in 2004 and the takeover of Bank Austria Credit Anstalt (Austria) and HypoVereinsbank (Germany) by UniCredit (Italy) in 2005. However, as Figure 10.11 illustrates, the transaction value of M&A activity has decreased sharply since 2007. The peak in transaction values in 2007 reflected the merger of the Italian banks Sanpaolo IMI and Banca Intesa and the acquisition of ABN Amro by the consortium of Royal Bank of Scotland (UK), Fortis (Belgium), and Banco Santander (Spain), which resulted in the split of ABN

AMRO into three parts. Already seen as having paid too high a price, both Fortis and RBS were among the first large European banks to be affected by the crisis in 2008. After the demise of Fortis, Fortis Netherlands and the Dutch part of ABN AMRO were nationalised and merged into a new bank named again ABN AMRO. BNP Paribas took over the remainder of Fortis (mainly the Belgian and Luxembourg parts). Important domestic deals include the acquisition of Dresdner Bank by Commerzbank and HBOS by Lloyds TSB in 2008.

Important drivers of cross-border mergers are geographic diversification and a potential efficiency improvement (see Box 10.5 for further details). A good example was the takeover of Abbey National by Banco Santander. The former had strategic problems as it was venturing into corporate banking without success and used outdated IT systems. The inefficiency of Abbey National was illustrated by a high cost-to-income ratio of 83 per cent and a negative return on equity of 10 per cent. In contrast, Santander had developed a new payment technology and had a cost-to-income ratio of 63 per cent. After the takeover, Santander successfully introduced this technology with new management at Abbey National to improve efficiency; in 2006, Abbey's cost-to-income ratio was 56 per cent.

From 2008 to 2012, the overall value of M&A deals decreased fourfold to just €10 billion. Significantly, no large cross-border (intra-euro-area) transaction or transaction with a buyer from another EU country (inward EU) took place in 2012 and 2013. The M&A activity involving non-EU acquirers also remained subdued. Likewise, the value of outward transactions of euro-area banks (with these banks as acquirers) in Eastern Europe decreased considerably from the levels observed in 2008–2011 (ECB, 2013).

Market structure and competition

Table 10.4 shows some indicators of the structure of the EU banking sector. Between 1997 and 2013 the total number of banks in the EU decreased from 12,213 to 7,723, i.e. a reduction of almost 40 per cent. The trend in the US is similar. The number of US banks dropped from 10,927 in 1997 to 6,813 in 2013. Due to the decline in the number of credit institutions the concentration in the national banking markets has increased. Table 10.4 presents two concentration measures: the market share of the biggest five banks (CR5) and the Herfindahl Index, which is defined as the sum of the squares of the market shares of all banks in the

Box 10.5 The economics and performance of M&As

The classical motive for M&As in financial services is market extension (Walter, 2004). By merging with or acquiring another bank, it becomes possible to expand geographically into markets in which the acquiring bank has been absent or weak. The risk profile of the bank may be improved to the extent that business is spread across different macroeconomic environments. Or the bank wants to broaden its product range or client coverage because it sees profit opportunities that may be complementary to what it is already doing (see Chapter 11 for the expansion of banks into insurance activities). Other motives are that the acquiring bank may aim for more market power, thereby imposing better pricing conditions on customers, or may aim for a too-big-to-fail status as that may offer (implicit) government protection.

A key issue is whether economies of scale exist in banking. In an information- and distribution-intensive industry with high fixed costs such as financial services, there may be potential for scale economies. In particular, domestic mergers offer scope for cost synergies, as overlapping branch networks can be rationalised. But there is also potential for diseconomies of scale attributable to disproportionate increases in administrative overheads or management of complexity. Until recently, most research did not yield strong support for economies of scale banking. However, more recent studies report strong evidence for scale economies. For instance, Hughes and Mester (2013) find positive scale economies for even the largest institutions.

Campa and Hernando (2006) examine the performance record of mergers and acquisitions in the European financial industry. Merger announcements imply positive excess returns to shareholders of the target company (the takeover premium), while the returns to shareholders of the acquiring firms are essentially zero around announcement. One year after the announcement, excess returns are not significantly different from zero for both targets and acquirers. Campa and Hernando (2006) also provide evidence on the operating performance. M&As usually involve target banks with lower operating performance than the average bank. The M&A transactions result in significant improvements in the target bank's performance beginning on average two years after the transaction is completed.

Beltratti and Paladino (2013) focus on acquisitions in the banking sector in the EU that have been completed or terminated over the period 2007–2010. They report that abnormal returns for bank acquirers are zero on average at the announcement but positive after completion. Abnormal returns are larger for more efficient banks and for banks with higher profitability and with less leverage.

Table 10.4 Market structure indicators, 1997 and 2013

	Size		Concentration				Competition
	Number of banks		CR5 (in %)[a]		Herfindahl Index[b]		H-statistic
	1997	2013	1997	2013	1997	2013	1990–2005
Austria	928	731	44	37	515	405	0.07
Belgium	131	103	54	64	699	979	0.54
Bulgaria	35[c]	30	52[c]	50	721[c]	730	n.a.
Croatia	n.a.	32	n.a.	73	n.a.	1,384	n.a.
Cyprus	623	101	92	63	2,747	1,486	–0.11
Czech Republic	50	56	67	63	2,533	999	0.77
Denmark	213	161	70	68	1,431	1,160	0.30
Estonia	12	31	83	90	4,312	2,483	0.47
Finland	348	303	88	84	2,150	3,080	–0.24
France	1,258	623	40	46	449	551	0.58
Germany	3,420	1,842	17	31	114	266	0.65
Greece	55	40	56	94	885	2,136	0.47
Hungary	286	189	53	52	2,101	836	0.16
Ireland	71	458	41	48	500	674	1.11
Italy	909	694	25	40	201	406	0.08
Latvia	37	63	51	64	1,450	1,037	0.57
Lithuania	37	91	84	87	2,972	1,892	0.45
Luxembourg	215	147	23	34	210	357	0.31
Malta	29	27	98	77	4,411	1,458	0.72
Netherlands	648	253	79	84	1,654	2,104	0.80
Poland	1,378	691	46	45	859	586	0.10
Portugal	238	151	46	71	577	1,196	–0.14
Romania	39[c]	39	55[c]	54	1,251[c]	821	0.63
Slovakia	29	28	63	70	2,643	1,215	0.26
Slovenia	34	23	62	57	2,314	1,045	0.38
Spain	416	290	32	56	285	757	0.87
Sweden	237	168	58	58	830	876	0.48
United Kingdom	537	358	24	44	208	525	0.76
EU-15[d]	9,624	6,322	34	47	406	668	0.59
NMS-13[d]	2,589	1,401	63	57	1,985	965	0.31
EU-28[d]	12,213	7,723	35	48	445	676	0.59

Notes:

[a] CR5 is the share of the five largest banks, measured as a percentage of total assets.

[b] The Herfindahl Index is calculated as the sum of the squares of all the banks' market shares according to total assets, and rescaled from 0 to 10,000.

[c] The figure is for 2003.

[d] EU-15, NMS-13, and EU-28 are calculated as a weighted average (weighted according to assets). n.a. means not available.

Source: Number of banks and concentration from ECB and Allen *et al.* (2006); competition from Bikker *et al.* (2006)

sector ($HI = \sum_{i=1}^{n} s_i^2$, where s_i is the market share of bank i). While the CR5 ratio is easily measurable, it does not take into account the remaining banks in the industry in contrast to the Herfindahl Index. The latter ranges between $1/n$ and 1, reaching its lowest value, the reciprocal of the number of banks (n), when all banks in a market are of equal size, and reaching unity in the case of monopoly. The index as published by the ECB has been rescaled and ranges between 0 and 10,000.

Table 10.4 shows that there are substantial concentration differences across the EU. In Austria, France, Germany, Ireland, Italy, Luxembourg, Poland, and the United Kingdom the concentration ratios in the banking markets are relatively low. The highest concentration ratios can be found in Estonia, Finland, Greece, Lithuania, Malta, and the Netherlands.[4] From 1997 to 2013, the concentration ratios in the NMS-13 have gradually declined towards the level of the EU-15.

Another important feature of markets is the degree of competition. Panzar and Rosse (1977) have constructed a measure of competition, the so-called *H-statistic*, that is defined as the sum of the factor price elasticities of interest revenue with respect to borrowed capital, labour and physical capital. The value of H can be interpreted as follows. In case of a monopoly, H is lower than or equal to zero. This also applies to an oligopolistic market with cartels or complete imitation of each other's behaviour. A value of H between zero and one indicates monopolistic competition. A value equivalent to one points to perfect competition, as each change in input prices leads to a comparable change in output prices. The results of Bikker *et al.* (2006) as shown in Table 10.4 suggest that there is strong competition (i.e. values of H above 0.75) in the banking sectors of the Czech Republic, Ireland, the Netherlands, Spain, and the United Kingdom. France, Germany, Malta, and Romania have an intermediate level of competition (H around 0.60), while banking competition in Austria, Cyprus, Finland, Hungary, Italy, Poland, and Portugal is low.

The *structure-conduct-performance (SCP) paradigm* postulates a connection between market structure, banking behaviour, and profitability. The reasoning is as follows: in markets with a high degree of concentration, firms have more market power, which allows them to set prices above marginal costs and achieve higher profits. While earlier studies find a relationship between concentration and profitability, more recent studies suggest that there is no connection between the two (Claessens and Laeven, 2004; Jansen and De Haan, 2006).

Two alternative theories suggest that concentration does not necessarily reduce market competition. According to the *contestability theory,* a concentrated banking market can still be competitive as long as the entry barriers for potential newcomers are low. According to the *efficiency hypothesis,* the most efficient banks gain market share at the cost of less efficient banks. In other words, high concentration can be a result of fierce competition in a market (Bikker *et al.*, 2006).

Claessens and Laeven (2004) examine the competitiveness of a banking market in a large cross-section of countries and find no evidence that banking system concentration is negatively associated with competitiveness. In fact, they sometimes find evidence that more concentrated banking systems are more competitive.

Concentration is loosely related to bank size. Markets become more concentrated when the number of banks decreases or when the skewness of the size distribution of banks increases (i.e. the number of large banks increases). But the markets in some countries (e.g. Germany and France) have low levels of concentration and large banks. As Bikker *et al.* (2006) point out, large banks may have market power as they are probably in a better position to collude with other banks and may benefit from a more established reputation. Furthermore, they are in a better position than small banks to create new banking products due to economies of scale. Indeed, Bikker *et al.* (2006) report that market power increases with bank size. Their research covers 18,467 banks in 101 countries over a period of 16 years.

10.4 The new Banking Union landscape

The establishment of the Banking Union (BU) creates a sub-market within the EU. It is expected that the BU will become an integrated market, where banks can manage their balance sheet at the aggregate BU level and the ECB conducts supervision with a European perspective. Currently, national supervisors prevent European banks from operating on a European scale, as they informally request banks to lend or invest in the same country as where deposits are collected. Moving to the demand side, it will take some time before consumers regard a bank from elsewhere in the BU as a domestic bank to which they can entrust their money. When that happens a truly integrated retail banking market will emerge. Corporates, especially the larger ones, are expected to adapt faster and select their main banks from across the BU.

Table 10.5 Banking systems across three regions (BU, EU, US), 2013

	Number of banks	Total assets in € billion	Of which: domestic (%)	other EU (%)	third country (%)
BU	5,908	29,982	83	14	2
Non-BU	1,815	12,061	60	19	21
EU	7,723	42,043	77	15	8
US	6,813	11,862	86	–	14

Note: Total banking assets come from the home country, other EU countries, and third countries (i.e. outside the EU or the US). The three components add up to 100 per cent.
Source: Table 10.1 for European banks and Federal Reserve, FDIC, and Flow of Funds for US banks.

The previous section compared the original Member States (EU-15) with the new Member States (NMS-13). This section splits the EU banking system into the BU and the non-BU countries. Table 10.5 indicates that the BU covers about 75 per cent of the total EU banking system. The BU countries have relatively closed banking markets, with assets from other EU countries at 14 per cent and from third countries at 2 per cent. The overall cross-border penetration for the EU is higher, due to the UK with business from third countries at 28 per cent. This highlights the current status of London as international financial centre. Will London continue to service the BU, or will Frankfurt emerge as the financial centre of the BU?

The BU banking system is comparable to that of the US in several ways. The number of banks is about 6,000 (see Table 10.5). The system has a strong domestic orientation at about 85 per cent of all assets. Foreign bank affiliates account for 14 per cent of the US banking system. But there is an important difference. The US banking system has fewer assets, €12 trillion compared to the BU with €30 trillion. The US financial system depends less on bank intermediation and more on capital markets (see Chapter 1). The major banks are also comparable. Figure 10.12 shows the geographical segmentation of the top 20 banks in the three regions (EU, BU, and US). The large BU and US banks have just over 70 per cent of their assets at home (i.e. the BU and the US). The rest of the region (i.e. the rest of Europe and the rest of North and South America) counts for 11 per cent. The rest of the world amounts to about 18 per cent. The large EU banks are more international. They have not only a smaller home base (one country), but also more business in the rest of the world. Examples of major global banks outside the BU are HSBC, Barclays, and Standard Chartered from the UK. Summing

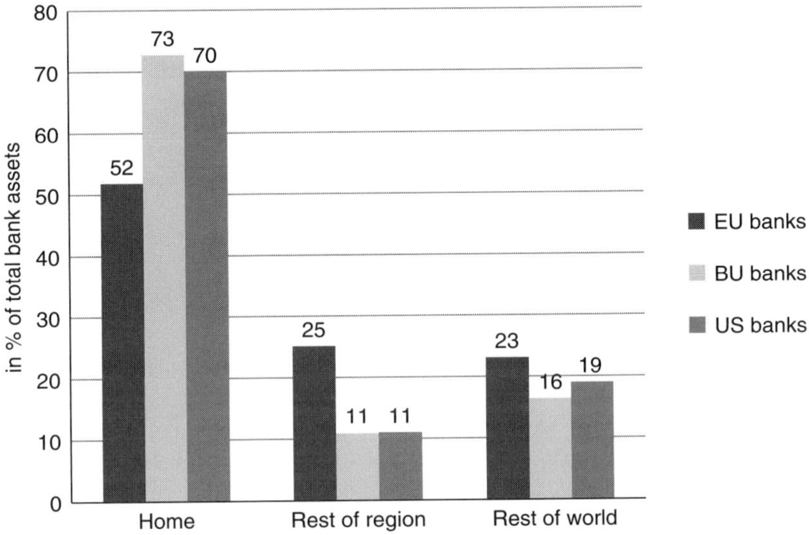

Figure 10.12 Geographic segmentation of top 20 banks in the EU, BU, and US (in %), 2013
Note: Total assets of the top 20 banks are segmented into domestic, rest of the region, and rest of the world.

up, the BU is like the US a relatively closed banking system, with limited inward and outward expansion.

The start of the BU entails a paradigm shift for banks and policy makers. The home market expands for banks from their country to the wider BU. Table 10.6 illustrates the geographic segmentation, splitting a bank's business in the BU, the rest of Europe (i.e. business in the non-BU member states), and the rest of the world. Some of the European banks operating on a regional basis (the second group in Table 10.2) have now become pan-Banking Union banks. BNP Paribas, UniCredit, and ING Bank operate throughout the BU, with 65–80 per cent of their assets in the BU. These banks are comparable with the super-regional banks in the US, such as Bank of America, with a large presence across the whole region. Also the semi-international and domestic banks (the third and fourth group in Table 10.2) have become large players in the BU. The market share of the biggest banks in the BU lingers around 2 to 5 per cent, which is very low. The top 5 banks by market share are four French banks (i.e. Crédit Agricole, BNP, Société Générale, and BPCE) and a German bank (i.e. Deutsche Bank). The market share of the 20 biggest banks amounts to 37 per cent.

Table 10.6 Biggest 20 banks in BU in 2013

Banking Group	Total assets in € bn	Banking Union in %	Rest of Europe in %	Rest of world in %	Market share in %
1. Crédit Agricole	1,707	89	3	8	5.0
2. BNP Paribas	1,800	66	12	22	4.0
3. Société Générale	1,235	82	7	11	3.4
4. Groupe BPCE	1,124	84	4	12	3.1
5. Deutsche Bank	1,612	46	12	42	2.5
6. UniCredit	846	82	17	1	2.3
7. Crédit Mutuel	659	94	1	5	2.1
8. ING Bank	788	76	10	14	2.0
9. Intesa Sanpaolo	626	92	6	2	1.9
10. Rabobank	674	80	2	18	1.8
11. Banco Santander	1,116	34	37	30	1.3
12. Commerzbank	550	63	21	16	1.1
13. DZ Bank	387	87	7	6	1.1
14. La Caixa Group	351	96	2	2	1.1
15. ABN AMRO	372	90	3	7	1.1
16. BBVA	583	57	3	40	1.1
17. Landesbank Baden-Würt.	274	85	8	7	0.8
18. Bayerische Landesbank	256	83	10	7	0.7
19. KBC Group	241	72	26	3	0.6
20. Erste Group	200	56	41	3	0.4
Top 20 banks	15,400	73	11	16	37.4

Note: Total assets are divided in assets in the BU, in rest of Europe, and the rest of the world. A bank's market share is calculated as a bank's assets in the BU divided by total assets in the BU. The top 20 is ranked by market share.
Source: Assets are taken from The Banker (July 2014). Segmentation of assets is calculated by the authors on the basis of annual reports.

Further consolidation within the BU can be expected. The market share of the 5 biggest banks (CR5) in the BU is 18 per cent (Table 10.6). To compare, the CR5 is 47 per cent for the EU-15 countries and 48 per cent for the US. Even in a large country with a dispersed banking system like Germany, the CR5 is over 30 per cent (Table 10.4). The major US banks were formed after the lifting of restrictions on interstate banking by the Riegle-Neal Interstate Banking and Branching Efficiency Act of 1994. Through several mergers and acquisitions, super-regional banks, such as JPMorgan Chase and Bank of America, emerged with a market share of 13 and 11 per cent, respectively.

Finally, an international perspective can be sketched. The Financial Stability Board (FSB) has produced a list of *global systemically important banks*, the so-called G-SIBs (see Chapter 12 for further details). These banks are the large financial players, which can pose a systemic threat to the global financial system (Bertay *et al.*, 2013). Table 10.7 provides an overview of these G-SIBs, which have assets up to €2 trillion. Remarkably, the BU encompasses

Table 10.7 Global systemically important banks (G-SIBs), 2013

	Total assets	World assets rank	Capital surcharge	Home country	Rest of region	Rest of world
Banking groups	in € bn		in %	% of total assets	% of total assets	% of total assets
Global banks						
1. HSBC (UK)	1,937	2	2.5	37	11	52
2. Deutsche Bank (BU)	1,612	10	2.0	46	12	42
3. Barclays (UK)	1,568	11	2.0	36	26	38
4. Citigroup (US)	1,364	13	2.0	40	23	37
5. UBS (Switzerland)	821	23	1.5	33	25	42
6. Credit Suisse (Switzerland)	710	25	1.5	23	22	55
7. Standard Chartered (UK)	489	42	1.0	16	5	79
Regional banks						
1. Banco Santander (BU)	1,116	18	1.0	34	37	30
2. Nordea (Sweden)	631	31	1.0	24	75	1
Semi-international banks						
1. BNP Paribas (BU)	1,800	4	2.0	66	12	22
2. Mitsubishi UFJ Financial Group (Japan)	1,778	5	1.5	66	8	26
3. JPMorgan Chase (US)	1,752	6	2.5	71	2	27
4. Bank of China (China)	1,649	9	1.0	74	16	10
5. Royal Bank of Scotland (UK)	1,228	15	1.5	61	16	23
6. Mizuho Financial Group (Japan)	1,211	16	1.0	75	5	20
7. ING Bank (BU)	788	24	1.0	75	11	14
8. Goldman Sachs (US)	661	29	1.5	53	5	42
9. Morgan Stanley (US)	604	35	1.5	69	7	24
10. BBVA (BU)	583	36	1.0	57	3	40
11. Bank of New York Mellon (US)	271	68	1.0	75	1	24

Table 10.7 (cont.)

Banking groups	Total assets in € bn	World assets rank	Capital surcharge in %	Home country % of total assets	Rest of region % of total assets	Rest of world % of total assets
Domestic banks						
1. ICBC (China)	2,248	1	1.0	94	4	2
2. Crédit Agricole (BU)	1,707	8	1.5	89	3	8
3. Bank of America (US)	1,526	12	1.5	86	2	12
4. Société Générale (BU)	1,235	14	1.0	82	7	11
5. Groupe BPCE (BU)	1,124	17	1.0	84	4	12
6. Sumitomo Mitsui Financial Group (Japan)	1,112	19	1.0	78	7	15
7. Wells Fargo & Co (US)	1,107	20	1.0	95	2	3
8. UniCredit (BU)	846	22	1.0	82	17	1
9. State Street (US)	176	96	1.0	81	17	2
Total G-SIBs	1,160			64	12	24

Notes: The second column presents the assets rank on the basis of the Top 1000 World Banks, as published in The Banker (2014). Total assets are segmented over the home country, the rest of the region, and the rest of the world. Total of G-SIBs is calculated as a weighted average (weighted according to assets).
Source: The list of G-SIBs is from the FSB (2013). Assets are taken from The Banker (July 2014). Segmentation of assets is calculated by the authors based on annual reports.

most of the G-SIBs with 9 out of 29, followed by the US with 8 and the UK with 4. The ECB, as supervisor of the G-SIBs from the BU, is thus a major player together with the Federal Reserve and the Bank of England in international policy making and supervision.

10.5 Conclusions

Banks are key players in the financial system, providing liquidity to other financial institutions and to firms and households. They have also developed technologies to monitor borrowers. Banks have expanded their business from traditional lending to modern capital-market transactions, thereby preserving their role in the financial system.

Banks use advanced models to measure, manage, and price market risk. The use of these advanced models has spurred the centralisation of risk management. While the business is done by the local bank managers who are familiar with the economic environment in which the local business units have to operate, the influence of the head office on the pricing of bank products is increasing. As the financial crisis illustrated shortcomings in risk management models, banks are complementing the models with stress tests.

Cross-border banking had gradually increased to 21 per cent in 2007 and has subsequently fallen back to 15 per cent in 2013. This chapter has documented the emergence of banks that operate Europe-wide. Nevertheless, retail banking markets are still segmented. Customers have a preference to do business with banks they 'know' and thus have a bias towards domestic banks. Cultural differences appear to be more important than regulatory differences. The policy of the European Commission is shifting from harmonising rules (Chapter 12) to ensuring effective competition (Chapter 14) in turn. The Banking Union will change the European banking landscape and may spur retail integration within the Banking Union.

New evidence suggests that concentration does not necessarily reduce market competition. The contestability theory indicates that a banking market is competitive as long as the barriers for potential newcomers are low. Competition policy is important to open national markets: both to promote new entrants within a country and to promote foreign entry through cross-border mergers.

Notes

1. There is, however, an important conflict of interest. Credit rating agencies are paid by the firms and governments whose securities they rate. This conflict is unavoidable due to the free-riding problem, i.e. ratings are valuable only if everybody knows them, but lenders (investors) have no reason to pay for information that is available to everyone else too.
2. A *counterparty* is a legal and financial term. It means a party to a contract.
3. Assuming a normal distribution, the time horizon of the standard deviation can be expanded by multiplying with $\sqrt{t}$. Given that there are 252 business days in the year, the standard deviation of the one-year loss distribution equals the standard deviation of the ten-day loss distribution multiplied by $\sqrt{25.2}$ (Hull, 2009).
4. The European Commission investigates a proposed merger when the (rescaled) Herfindahl Index would pass the threshold of 2,000 after the merger (see Chapter 14).

Suggested Reading

Freixas, X. and J. C. Rochet (2008), *Microeconomics of Banking*, 2nd edition, MIT Press, Cambridge (MA).

Hull, J. C. (2009), *Risk Management and Financial Institutions*, 2nd edition, Pearson Education, Upper Saddle River (NJ).

Schoenmaker, D. (2013), *Governance of International Banking: The Financial Trilemma*, Oxford University Press, New York.

References

Allen, F., L. Bartiloro, and O. Kowalewski (2006), The Financial System of EU 25, in: K. Liebscher, J. Christl, P. Mooslechner, and D. Ritzberger-Griinwald (eds.), *Financial Development, Integration and Stability in Central Eastern and South-Eastern Europe*, Edward Elgar, Cheltenham, 80–104.

Avgouleas, E, C. Goodhart, and D. Schoenmaker (2013), Bank Resolution Plans as a catalyst for global financial reform, *Journal of Financial Stability*, **9**, 210–218.

Beltratti, A. and G. Paladino (2013), Is M&A Different during a Crisis? Evidence from the European Banking Sector, *Journal of Banking and Finance*, **37**, 5394–5405.

Berger, A. N. (2003), The Economic Effects of Technological Progress: Evidence from the Banking Industry, *Journal of Money, Credit, and Banking*, **35**, 141–176.

Bertay, A. C., A. Demirguç-Kunt, and H. Huizinga (2013), Do We Need Big Banks? Evidence on Performance, Strategy and Market Discipline, *Journal of Financial Intermediation*, **22**, 532–558.

Bikker, J. A., L. Spierdijk, and P. Finnie (2006), The Impact of Bank Size on Market Power, DNB Working Paper 120.

Boot, A. W. A. (1999), European Lessons on Consolidation in Banking, *Journal of Banking and Finance*, **23**, 609–613.

Campa, J. M. and I. Hernando (2006), M&As Performance in the European Financial Industry, *Journal of Banking and Finance*, **30**, 3367–3392.

Claessens, S. and L. Laeven (2004), What Drives Bank Competition? Some International Evidence, *Journal of Money, Credit and Banking*, **36**, 563–583.

Daníelsson, J. (2011), *Financial Risk Forecasting*, John Wiley and Sons, New York.

Daníelsson, J. (2013), *Global Financial Systems: Stability and Risk*, Pearson, London.

Dermine, J. (2006), European Banking Integration: Don't Put the Cart before the Horse, *Financial Markets, Institutions & Instruments*, **15**(2), 57–106.

Diamond, D. W. (1984), Financial Intermediation and Delegated Monitoring, *Review of Economic Studies*, **51**, 393–414.

European Central Bank (2004), *Report on EU Banking Structures*, ECB, Frankfurt am Main.

(2010), *EU Banking Sector Stability*, ECB, Frankfurt am Main.

(2013), *Banking Structures Report*, ECB, Frankfurt am Main.

European Commission (2014), *European Financial Stability and Integration Report*, EC, Brussels.

Financial Stability Board (2013), *2013 Update of Group of Global Systemically Important Banks (G-SIBs)*, FSB, Basel.

Freixas, X. and J. C. Rochet (2008), *Microeconomics of Banking*, 2nd edition, MIT Press, Cambridge (MA).

Garber, P. M. and S. R. Weisbrod (1990), Banks in the Market for Liquidity, NBER Working Paper 3381.

Hackethal, A. (2004), German Banks and Banking Structure, in: J. P. Krahnen and R. H. Schmidt (eds.), *The German Financial System*, Oxford University Press, 71–106.

Hughes, J. P. and L. Mester (2013), Who Said Large Banks Don't Experience Scale Economies: Evidence from a Risk-Return Cost Function, *Journal of Financial Intermediation*, **22**, 559–585.

Hull, J. C. (2009), *Risk Management and Financial Institutions*, 2nd edition, Pearson Education, Upper Saddle River (NJ).

Jansen, D. J. and J. de Haan (2006), European Banking Consolidation: Effects on Competition, Profitability, and Efficiency, *Journal of Financial Transformation*, **17**, 61–72.

Kuritzkes, A., T. Schuermann, and S. Weiner (2003), Risk Measurement, Risk Management, and Capital Adequacy in Financial Conglomerates, in: R. Herring and R. Litan (eds.), *Brookings-Wharton Papers on Financial Services: 2003*, Brookings Institution, Washington DC, 141–193.

Panzar, J. C. and J. N. Rosse (1977), Chamberlin vs Robinson: An Empirical Study for Monopoly Rents, Studies in Industry Economics, Research Paper 77, Stanford University.

Schoenmaker, D. (2013), *Governance of International Banking: The Financial Trilemma*, Oxford University Press, New York.

(2014), The Emerging Banking Landscape of the New Banking Union, Duisenberg School of Finance Policy Paper 35.

Schoenmaker, D. and S. Oosterloo (2008), Financial Supervision in Europe: A Proposal for a New Architecture, in: L. Jonung, C. Walkner, and M. Watson (eds.), *Building the Financial Foundations of the Euro – Experiences and Challenges*, Routledge, London, 329–346.

Schoenmaker, D. and C. van Laecke (2006), Current State of Cross-Border Banking, London School of Economics FMG Special Papers 168.

Van Lelyveld, I. (ed.) (2006), Economic Capital Modelling: Concepts, *Measurement and Implementation*, Risk Books, London.

Walter, I. (2004), *Mergers and Acquisitions in Banking and Finance: What Works, What Fails, and Why*, Oxford University Press.

CHAPTER

11

European Insurers and Financial Conglomerates

OVERVIEW

The function of insurance is to protect individuals and firms from adverse events through the pooling of risks. Life insurance protects against premature death, disability, and retirement. Non-life insurance protects against risks such as accidents, illness, theft, and fire. Insurance is a risky business, as insurance companies collect premiums and provide cover for adverse events that may or may not arise somewhere in the future. The pattern of small claims, such as fire or car accidents, is fairly predictable. However, larger accidents or catastrophes (like hurricanes) involve high claims with low probability.

The insurance business is plagued by asymmetric information problems. There is a moral hazard problem when the behaviour of the insured, which can be only partly observed by the insurer, may increase the likelihood that the insurer has to pay. After signing the contract, the insured may behave less cautiously because of the insurance. Another problem is adverse selection. High-risk individuals (for instance, ill people) may seek out more (health) insurance than low-risk persons. The insurer may therefore end up with a pool of relatively high risks. Mechanisms to separate high from low risks are explained in this chapter.

Insurance companies tend to centralise risk management, using internal risk-management models at their headquarters. But there is still a role for local business units to capture factors that are location-specific. The same is true for asset management. As insurance companies are large asset managers, they can profit from economies of scale through the pooling of assets.

Insurance systems vary considerably across Europe. Life insurance is quite prominent in the EU-15, but far less so in the new EU Member States. Non-life insurance is more evenly spread across the EU. With the creation of the European single insurance market, insurers used mergers and acquisitions – at both the national and the European level – to become large enough to act at the European level. While it is still not possible to speak of an integrated insurance market, the level of cross-border insurance has gradually increased.

Finally, the chapter analyses financial conglomerates that combine banking and insurance. These conglomerates have the possibility of cross-selling insurance products through the bank and they may also gain from increased diversification possibilities. Yet it is difficult to manage a complex financial group that runs fairly different lines of business.

LEARNING OBJECTIVES

After you have studied this chapter, you should be able to:

- explain the nature of insurance business
- explain the economics of insurance risk
- explain the use of risk-management models by insurers and the centralisation of the risk-management function
- describe the structure of the European insurance market
- identify the characteristics of financial conglomerates and the role they play in the financial system.

11.1 Theory of insurance

Small vs. large claims insurance

The function of *insurance* is to protect individuals and firms against adverse events. Insurance companies are able to provide this protection through the pooling of individual risks. By combining the risks of various clients in a pool, insurance companies can spread the risks over this (large) group of clients. There are different types of insurance. *Life insurance* protects against premature death, disability, and retirement. While it is difficult to predict the death of an individual, death rates for large populations are fairly stable and therefore easier to predict. Other types of insurance are grouped under the name of *non-life insurance*, which protects against risks such as accidents, theft, and fire. Non-life insurance is sometimes also called property and casualty (P&C) or property and liability (P&L) insurance.

Insurance company	
Assets (A)	Equity (E)
	Technical provisions (TP)

Figure 11.1 Simplified balance sheet of an insurance company

The risk dynamics of non-life insurance are more diverse than those of life insurance. Relatively small accidents (like car accidents) are fairly predictable and can easily be pooled by an insurance company. But larger accidents or catastrophes follow a different pattern: they are low-probability but high-impact events. A good example is Hurricane Katrina in New Orleans in 2005. The risk of such a catastrophe is too big for one insurance company and is therefore divided among different insurance and re-insurance companies.

The intermediation function of insurers can be illustrated with a simple balance sheet (see Figure 11.1). Insurers collect premiums P from clients and make payouts on claims C by these clients when the risk materialises. On the asset side, insurers invest the collected premiums in assets A, which earn a return R_A. On the liability side, insurers make technical provisions TP to cover expected future claims. In addition, insurers maintain a capital buffer E to cover unexpected claims.

Insurers evaluate the risk of prospective clients. If a client is accepted, the insurers have to decide how much coverage a client should receive and how much he should pay for it. The function of an underwriter is to acquire – or to 'write' – business that will bring the insurance company profits. The insurance business is viable only when the collected premiums exceed the payout on claims. When a claim is made, the insurer must determine the extent of the loss. Many insurers employ 'adjusters' who determine the liability of the insurer and the settlement to be made. The *claim ratio* measures the adjusted claims as a ratio to premiums earned, i.e. C/P. A claim ratio of less than 100 per cent means that premiums earned are sufficient to cover claims.

The insurance company also has to cover its expenses *Exp*. The biggest expenses are commissions paid to insurance agents for the acquisition of business. These acquisition costs are very high. To reduce their acquisition costs, insurers are increasingly selling insurance to the public directly (*direct writing*). The insurer must also gather information about potential clients to

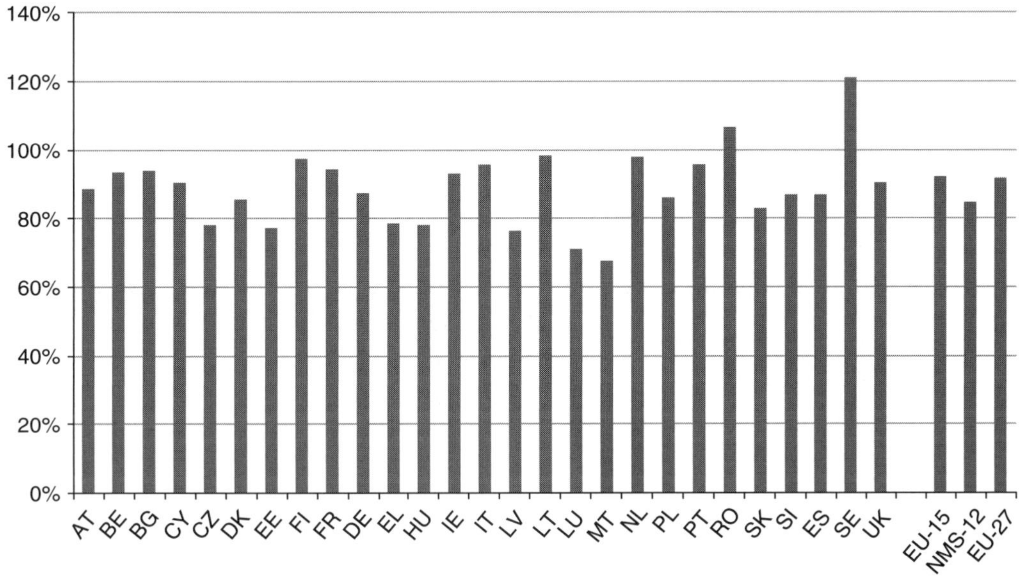

Figure 11.2 Combined ratios across Europe (in %), 2012
Note: Claims and expenses in percentage of premiums.
Source: EIOPA (2013a)

assess the underwriting risk and avoid adverse selection (see below). Finally, insurers incur administrative expenses. The *expense ratio* expresses total expenses relative to premiums earned, i.e. Exp/P.

A common economic measure to assess the profitability of non-life insurers is the combined ratio CR, which expresses claims and expenses relative to premiums earned:

$$CR = C/P + Exp/P = \frac{C + Exp}{P} \tag{11.1}$$

Figure 11.2 shows the combined ratio for various EU Member States. The combined ratios for Romania and Sweden are well above 100 per cent, indicating that the non-life insurance sector in these countries makes a loss. However, investment returns are not included (see below). In the Czech Republic, Estonia, Greece, Hungary, Latvia, Luxembourg, and Malta the combined ratio ranges between 70 per cent and 80 per cent, indicating a healthy profit. The combined ratio of the EU-27 average is 92 per cent. This results in a margin of 8 per cent.

The combined ratio provides an incomplete view of a non-life insurer's profitability. Premiums are invested before payouts are made. Investment returns R_A are therefore an important source of income for insurers. The *profitability* π, as a percentage of premium earned, is equal to the results on claims and expenses (100 – CR) and the investment returns:

$$\pi = 100 - CR + R_A / P = 100 + \frac{R_A - C - Exp}{P} \tag{11.2}$$

Equation 11.2 illustrates that the successful management of an insurance company depends on making adequate investment returns and properly calculating underwriting risks while keeping a lid on acquisition and administrative expenses. This equation can be illustrated with a simple example. Assume a claim ratio of 65 per cent of earned premiums, an expense ratio of 32 per cent, and allocated investment income of 9 per cent. The profit is 12 per cent of earned premiums (100 + 9 – 65 – 32 = 12).

The stochastic properties of large claims are very different from those of small claims. Small claims have a distribution with light tails (e.g. the normal distribution). In a large portfolio, the expected claim size approaches the average claim size according to the law of large numbers. Box 11.1 sets out the mathematics of calculating small claim risks in more detail.

In contrast, large claims are characterised by distributions with heavy tails. Insurance portfolios with heavy-tailed claim sizes are dangerous. Figure 11.4 shows the log-normal distribution, an example of a heavy-tailed distribution. In the tail on the right are events with a low probability but a large impact on the overall claim amount. We need extreme value statistics to model these large claims. The distribution needs to be fitted from a relatively small number of observations (the excesses over high thresholds). Embrechts *et al.* (1997) provide an overview of modelling extreme events.

Large losses are caused not only by nature (natural catastrophes) but also by man (man-made disasters). Table 11.1 provides an overview of the largest catastrophes over the last 40 years. Hurricane Katrina in New Orleans caused an insured loss of €58 billion, while the total loss (insured and uninsured) mounted to over €100 billion. The tsunami, triggered by an earthquake, damaged the nuclear plant at Fukushima (Japan) and caused an insured loss of €27 billion. Hurricane Sandy flooded the southern part of New York with €27 billion of insured losses. The terrorist attack on the Twin Towers and the Pentagon in 2001 led to an insured loss of €19 billion. Europe has

Box 11.1 The mathematics of small claims insurance*

This box abstracts from expenses, investment returns, and dividend payouts and focuses on the premium setting P and the claim process C. The premium setting follows the dynamics of the claim process. The pattern of small claims is different from that of large claims.

The stochastic properties of the small claim-size model can be derived formally following Mikosch (2004). The total size of the claims $C(t)$ is the product of the number of claims $N(t)$ over period t and the size of the claims X_i:

$$C(t) = \sum_{i=1}^{N(t)} X_i, \; t \geq 0 \tag{11.3}$$

where N is independent of the claim size. Both the number of claims and the size of claims are random variables. The claim numbers can often be described as a Poisson process. A Poisson process is a stochastic process, which is used for modelling random events that occur independently of one another. A variable following a homogeneous *Poisson process* has the property that the mean and variance of the distribution are the same. So for N it is possible to write: $\lambda = E(N) = \text{var}(N)$ where λ is the frequency of claims.

Equation (11.3) specifies the realised claims at time t. But an insurer needs to estimate the expected claims at the time of selling an insurance, i.e. $T = 0$. Exploiting the independence of the claim size sequence X_i and the claim number process $N(t)$, the expected total claim amount is given by:

$$E[C(t)] = E\left[E\left(\sum_{i=1}^{N(t)} X_i \middle| N(t)\right)\right] = E[N(t) \cdot E(X_1)] = \lambda \cdot t \cdot E(X_1) \tag{11.4}$$

Equation 11.4 shows that the expected total claim amount grows linearly with t. Using the properties of the Poisson distribution, i.e. $\lambda \cdot t = E[N(t)] = \text{var}(N(t))$, the variance is denoted by:

$$\text{var}\left(C(t)\right) = \lambda \cdot t\left[\text{var}(X_1) + \left(E(X_1)\right)^2\right] = \lambda \cdot t \cdot E(X_1^2) \tag{11.5}$$

An insurer with a large portfolio is interested in the asymptotic behaviour of the total claim amount. Applying the law of large numbers, the mathematical foundation of insurance, the total claim amount is given by:

$$\lim_{t} \frac{C(t)}{t} = \lambda \cdot E(X_1) \tag{11.6}$$

The law of large numbers thus says that the total claim amount is the expected claim amount. Put differently, the number of claims is the average number of claims λ and the claim size is the average claim size $E(X_i)$. But the total claim amount may vary in practice. The risk of insurance is determined by the variance of the claims. The claim amount for a large population follows a normal distribution (i.e. a symmetric, bell-shaped curve).

Box 11.1 (cont.)

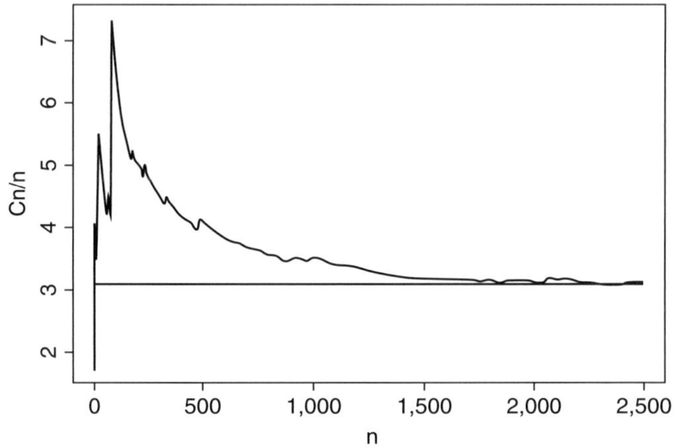

Figure 11.3 The law of large numbers and fire insurance claims
Source: Mikosch (2004)

Figure 11.3 visualises the law of large numbers for a portfolio of Danish fire insurance claims (Mikosch, 2004). The data cover the period 1980–1992 and include about 2,500 observations. Because the sample of fire insurance claims contains very large values, the ratio *Cn/n* converges to $E(X_i)$ very slowly in Figure 11.3.

Next, an insurer needs to set a premium $P(t)$ to cover the claims. As the total claim amount varies, it is necessary to choose a premium by loading the expected claim amount by certain positive number ρ. The premium is given by:

$$P(t) = (1 + \rho) \cdot E[C(t)] \tag{11.7}$$

for some positive number ρ, called the safety loading. It is evident that the insurance business is more on the safe side the larger ρ. The safety loading can thus absorb fluctuations in the claim amount. But an overly large safety loading would make the insurance business less competitive.

The final step is to define the surplus or risk process of the portfolio. Following Mikosch (2004), $E(t)$ is the insurer's capital or equity balance at given time t (see also Figure 11.1) and is given by:

$$E(t) = E(0) + P(t) - C(t),\ t \geq 0 \tag{11.8}$$

where $E(0)$ is initial capital. A large initial capital is needed and reinforced by supervisors (see Box 11.5). When starting an insurance company, the supervisor requires a sufficiently large initial capital buffer to prevent the business from bankruptcy due to many small or a

Box 11.1 (cont.)

few large claims in the first period, before the premium income can balance the losses and the gains.

What is the risk for an insurer with a sufficient capital balance $E(0)$ and a sufficiently prudent premium rate ($\rho > 0$)? First, there may be an upward drift $\delta > 0$ in the claim amount which was not expected by the insurer at the time when setting the premium. The realised claim amount is thus larger than expected: $C(t) = (1 + \delta) \cdot E[C(t)]$. Examples of such a drift are a shorter life expectancy due to a new illness or more car accidents due to an unexpected shift in weather conditions (e.g. strong winters with frozen roads). The insurer will incur losses when $\delta > \rho$ and may go bankrupt when cumulative losses wipe out the capital balance $(\delta - \rho) \cdot E[C(t)] > E(0)$.

Second, the principle of independence may be violated. A case in point is the accumulation of payouts on life policies by ING in the aftermath of the terrorist attack at the Twin Towers in New York on 11 September 2001. While it thought it had an adequate geographical spread of its life portfolio in the New York and New Jersey area, ING appeared to have a large concentration among people working in the Twin Towers.

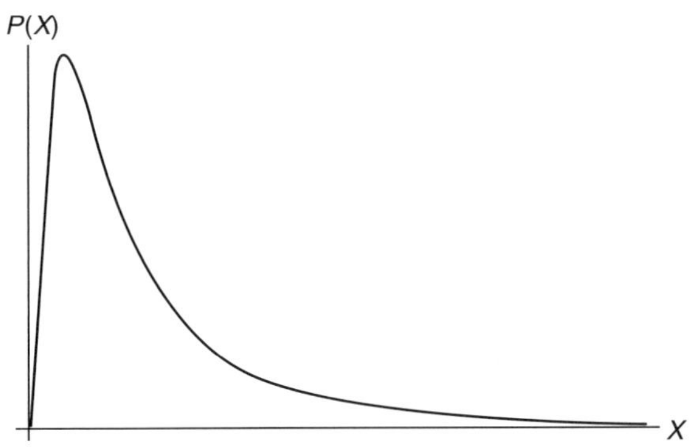

Figure 11.4 Heavy-tailed distribution

experienced several winter storms, such as Daria in 1990 and Lothar in 1999, causing an insured loss of close to €6 billion each. The highest insured losses are suffered in the US, Europe, and Japan due to the higher insurance density in the industrialised countries. Emerging markets generally have a lower insurance density, so that only a small proportion of victims benefit from insurance cover. An example was the tsunami in the Indian Ocean in 2004, which had a death toll of 220,000. Yet this extreme event is not taken up in Table 11.1 as only insured losses are counted.

Re-insurance

Individual insurers cannot bear these large losses on their own – their equity would be wiped out when an extreme event occurs. The risks (and premiums) of catastrophe insurance are therefore shared among insurers (Rejda, 2005). A common mechanism to share insurance risk is *re-insurance*, which is shifting part or all of the insurance originally written by one insurer to another insurer.[1] The insurer that originally writes the business is called the ceding company. The insurer that accepts part or all of the insurance risk from the ceding company is the re-insurer. Finally, the re-insurer may in turn re-insure part or all of the risk with another insurer.

The insurance risk of extreme events is thus sliced in different layers and divided between different insurers. Re-insurance can be designed in different ways. One format is *proportional re-insurance.* The insurer cedes a proportion of the premiums and the risks to a re-insurer. The remainder of the premiums and risks is retained by the ceding insurer (the retention amount). Another format, in particular used for catastrophe insurance, is *excess-of-loss re-insurance.* Losses in excess of a certain limit (i.e. the retention limit) are paid by the re-insurer up to some maximum limit. These amounts are expressed in money amounts. Excess-of-loss contracts allow for tailor-made slicing of the insurance risk. The terrorist attacks on 11 September 2001 show the importance of re-insurance. Re-insurers paid out at least half of the insured losses (Rejda, 2005).

In case of large catastrophes, traditional insurance and re-insurance may not suffice. The financial losses due to, for instance, a large flood can supersede the absorption capacity of individual insurers and re-insurers. Therefore, many countries have a government programme that covers part of the risk (see Box 11.2). However, government involvement gives rise to moral hazard, as private parties may seek to shift the risk to government (Loubergé, 2000; Kessler, 2008). There are several ways to mitigate this undesired effect. First, governments could provide cover for only the top layer of the risk. Private (re-)insurers are then taking the first layers of risk of the catastrophe and have an incentive to take appropriate precautionary measures, thereby reducing moral hazard. Second, governments should

Table 11.1 Catastrophes: the 25 most costly insurance losses, 1970–2013

Insured loss (in € billion, 2013 figures)	Victims (dead and missing)	Date (year)	Event	Country
58.3	1,836	2005	Hurricane Katrina: floods	US, Mexico
27.3	19,135	2011	Earthquake (M 9.0) triggers tsunami	Japan
26.8	237	2012	Hurricane Sandy: storm surge	US (New York)
20.0	43	1992	Hurricane Andrew: floods	US, Bahamas
18.6	2,982	2001	Terror attack on WTC, Pentagon	US
16.6	61	1994	Northridge earthquake (M 6.6)	US
16.5	136	2008	Hurricane Ike: floods	US, Caribbean
12.5	181	2004	Hurricane Ivan: damage to oil rigs	US, Caribbean
12.0	124	2011	Floods caused by monsoon rains	Thailand
11.7	815	2011	Earthquake (M 6.3), aftershocks	New Zealand
11.3	35	2005	Hurricane Wilma: floods	US, Mexico
9.1	34	2005	Hurricane Rita: floods	US, Mexico
8.4	123	2012	Drought in the Corn Belt	US
7.5	24	2004	Hurricane Charley	US, Cuba
7.3	51	1991	Typhoon Mireille	Japan
6.5	71	1989	Hurricane Hugo	US, Puerto Rico
6.4	562	2010	Earthquake (M 8.8) triggers tsunami	Chile
6.3	95	1990	Winter storm Daria	France, UK, Benelux
6.1	110	1999	Winter storm Lothar	Switzerland, UK, France
5.7	354	2011	Severe storms, tornadoes	US (Alabama et al)
5.5	155	2011	Severe storms, tornadoes	US (Missouri et al)
5.2	54	2007	Winter storm Kyrill: floods	Germany, UK, NL
4.8	22	1987	Storm and floods in Europe	France, UK, Netherlands
4.8	38	2004	Hurricane Frances	US, Bahamas
4.5	55	2011	Hurricane Irene, extensive flooding	US

Notes: The losses include property and business interruption, but exclude liability and life-insurance losses. The losses are indexed to 2013.

Source: Sigma No.1, Swiss Re (2014)

Box 11.2 Flood insurance

While flooding affects many people worldwide and often causes serious damage (see Table 11.1), insurance cover for the risk of flooding is not widespread. This box reviews (lack of) insurance solutions in some selected countries.

The oldest insurance scheme is found in the US. The National Flood Insurance Program (NFIP) that was set up in 1968 covers losses through river flooding. The maximum cover for residential buildings/contents is $250,000/100,000. Premiums are high and vary in line with the flood hazard. Prior to the Mississippi floods of 1993, 15–20 per cent of property in exposed areas was insured under NFIP. After the most recent floods, these figures went up markedly. There is no cap on insured losses, as NFIP is government funded.

In France, the insurance market is based on private insurers, but is statutorily regulated. The Caisse Centrale de Réassurance (CCR) is the main re-insurer and is guaranteed by the state. Insurance penetration is practically 100 per cent.

The United Kingdom has only private insurers and no state insurance. Insurance cover is generally included in homeowners' and household contents policies in conjunction with storm cover. Premium rates are often high for storm/flood and are broken down to individual postcodes. Insurance penetration is 95 per cent.

The Netherlands has an enormous loss potential. Some 70 per cent of property is at risk as vast areas lie below sea level (storm surge) and/or can be flooded by the Rhine or the Maas rivers. The Dutch insurers concluded a market agreement in 1965 to exclude flood cover. The result is that the state is expected to pay (partial) compensation in the event of a disaster. An example is the flooding of the Rhine and the Maas in 1995 with an economic loss of €900 million, of which €180 million was paid by the government.

Source: Swiss Re (1998)

charge sufficiently high premiums, thereby pushing the insurance coverage back to the market as much as possible. Private (re-)insurers have a competitive motive to underbid the premium charged by the government. Only when the risk is too high in relation to the premium will private (re-)insurers drop out. In that case the government ends up providing residual coverage for catastrophes.

An alternative to traditional re-insurance and government insurance is securitisation of the risk. A recent example is the catastrophe bond (also known as cat bond). *Cat bonds* are corporate bonds that permit the issuer of the bond to skip or defer scheduled payments if a catastrophic loss beyond a certain threshold occurs. If insurers have built up a portfolio of risks by insuring properties in a region that may be hit by a catastrophe, they could create a special-purpose entity that issues the cat bond. Investors who buy the bond make a healthy return on their investment, unless a catastrophe (like a hurricane or an earthquake) hits the region; in that case, the principal initially paid by the investors is forgiven and is used by the sponsor to pay the claims of policy holders. The bonds pay relatively high interest rates and help institutional investors to diversify their portfolio, because natural disasters occur randomly and are not correlated with the stock market or other common factors (Rejda, 2005).

Asymmetric information

Under the assumption of full information complete insurance is possible at actuarially fair premium rates. But complete coverage is not always available in insurance markets due to asymmetric information (Loubergé, 2000). Insurance is subject to moral hazard when the contract outcome is partly influenced by the behaviour of the insured and the insurer cannot observe, without costs, to which extent reported losses can be attributed to the behaviour of the insured. Complete coverage may not be attainable under moral hazard. This is due to the trade-off between the goal of efficient risk sharing, which is met by allocating the risk to the insurer, and the goal of efficient incentives, which requires leaving the consequences of decisions about care with the decision maker, i.e. the insured.

Insurance is also subject to adverse selection. The ex-ante information asymmetry arises because the insured generally knows more about his risk profile than the insurer. The risk type of the insured cannot be determined ex ante by the insurer; the insurer can only charge the same premium rate based on aggregate risk. The high-risk types are the ones who are most eager to buy insurance, producing an undesirable outcome for the insurer.

While both types of asymmetric information (i.e. moral hazard and adverse selection) may lead to sub-optimal insurance outcomes, this section focuses on adverse selection, which is potentially a serious problem in any type of insurance market. Chapter 10 explains moral hazard in more detail. In a seminal paper, Rothschild and Stiglitz (1976) analyse adverse selection in the insurance market. They model the effect of two types of individuals under asymmetric information (i.e. the insurer does not know the type): the high-risk type H with accident probability P^h and the low-risk type L with

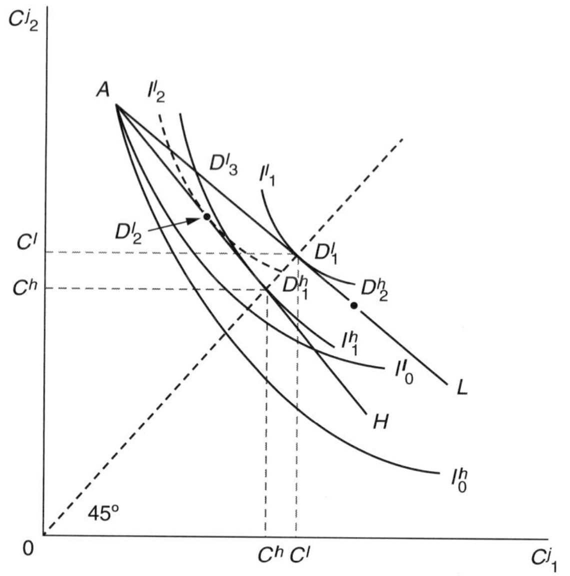

Figure 11.5 The Rothschild–Stiglitz model of the insurance market
Source: Spencer (2000), adapted from Rothschild and Stiglitz (1976)

accident probability P^l. We assume competitive insurance markets so that insurance is offered at actuarially fair premiums, as premiums are competed down to cost price. Following Spencer (2000), we define the premium ratio $B^l = (1 - P^l) / P^l$. If the contract with B^l is offered (represented by the fair-odds line AL in Figure 11.5), the insurer breaks even on the low-risk transactions at point $D_1{}^l$. This is the point of tangency between the budget line AL and the indifference curve of the low-risk individuals $I_1{}^l$. But the insurer loses on contracts with high-risk individuals who move to a point such as D_2^h on the fair-odds line AL. This is the adverse selection effect: high-risk individuals buy more insurance.

On the other hand, if a premium ratio of B^h is offered (represented by the fair-odds line AH), the insurer breaks even on contracts with high-risk clients at point D_1^h. But the insurer makes a profit on low-risk individuals. In this case, the best that the low-risk types can do is to move to a point such as D_2^l. This is the point of tangency between the budget line AH and the indifference curve of the low-risk individuals I_2^l (dashed) which lies between I_1^l.

Neither of these situations is consistent with the assumption of a contestable market. In the second case, another insurer can enter the market and offer a contract just to the left of the point D_3^l on the fair-odds line AL. Because this line lies to the left and below indifference curve I_1^h, the high-risk types will prefer the original contract and remain at D_1^h. However, because D_3^l lies above I_2^l, the new contract will be preferred to the original one by the low-risk individuals. This will give the new entrant all of the low-risk business at an actuarially fair premium (since D_3^l lies along AL, which is actuarially fair for low-risk types). The incumbent will be left with all high-risk individuals at the actuarially fair premium.

In equilibrium, the insurance market offers the two contracts simultaneously and clients self-select. This two-tier contract structure forces the low-risk types to distinguish themselves from the high-risk types in order to gain full insurance at an actuarially fair premium. The low-risk types get partial insurance at a fair premium. In practice, this partial insurance usually takes the form of a 'deductible' (i.e. own risk for the client) which reduces the scale of the compensation by a fixed amount. Alternatively, when losses are variable (rather than the fixed amount here), 'co-insurance' (fractional compensation) can be used. This two-tier market solution with self-selection is known as a *separating equilibrium*.

Box 11.3 provides some numerical examples to illustrate the working of the Rothschild–Stiglitz model. The application of a 'deductible' or 'co-insurance' is one way to separate high- and low-risk individuals. Another mechanism is screening. In the case of health insurance, the insurer can require the potential client to undergo a medical test. The insurer can also offer two contracts: one contract at a low premium for people who pass the medical test and a high premium for people who are not willing to do the test.

Finally, the government can impose compulsory insurance to enforce a pooling equilibrium (Spencer, 2000). It can bring in legislation stating that all individuals should take out full insurance. The compulsion prevents low-risk individuals breaking ranks and taking up a partial insurance offer from a rival insurer. A typical example of such compulsory insurance is health insurance. As part of its social policy, a government may find it desirable that all citizens are fully insured in case of illness at an affordable premium. Without compulsion, low-risk individuals would have partial insurance and high-risk individuals would pay a high premium (the separating equilibrium).

Box 11.3 Some numerical examples with high- and low-risk individuals

The working of the Rothschild–Stiglitz model can be easily illustrated with some numerical examples. The first example is with a relatively small proportion of high-risk individuals, so the insurer is still able to offer a single contract to all insured (high- and low-risk). The case where everybody can be charged the same premium is called a *pooling equilibrium*. Assume two types: healthy people with a low risk of illness at 1/1000 ($p^l = 0.001$) and unhealthy people with a high risk of illness 1/100 ($p^h = 0.01$). The cost of illness is €100,000 per episode. The population comprises 90 per cent healthy people and 10 per cent unhealthy people. Table 11.2 provides the details. The cost of insurance for the healthy is €100 (= 100,000 * 1/1000) and for the unhealthy €1,000 (= 100,000 * 1/100). The average cost is €190 (= 0.90 * 100 + 0.10 * 1,000). If insurance is offered at an actuarially fair premium of €190 for the whole population, both types will buy full insurance as the premium is below their reservation prices of €200, respectively €1,500.

In the second example, the proportion of healthy people is changed to 80 per cent (see Table 11.3). This has an impact on the average cost, which becomes €280 (= 0.80 * 100 + 0.20 * 1,000). Now, healthy people are unwilling to buy insurance at this premium as it is above their reservation price of €200. The pooling equilibrium breaks down; only the unhealthy people will buy insurance. Since the insurer knows that, it will charge a premium of €1,000. The result is that the 80 per cent healthy people are not insured.

In the third example, we assume that the insurer has enough market power to charge premiums above the actuarially fair premium. The figures are shown in Table 11.4. The average premium is €150 (= 0.50 * 100 + 0.50 * 200). Since healthy people are not willing to pay €150, there is again no pooling equilibrium. We now try to set up a separating equilibrium with two policies. The general policy is available for €240. In addition, the insurer offers an insurance policy for €100 to anyone who can pass a medical test, which costs €40. The healthy people will pick up the second contract. They pay €100 for the insurance and €40 for the medical test. Unhealthy people can pass the test only when they bribe the doctor, which is costly (€110). So unhealthy people will take the general policy at a premium of €240 rather than the second policy at a cost of €250 (€100 for the insurance and €150 for the test). This equilibrium with two different contracts and premiums is a separating equilibrium.

Table 11.2 Pooling equilibrium

Type	% of population	Risk of illness	Cost to insure	Willingness to pay
Healthy people	90	1/1000	€100	€200
Unhealthy people	10	1/100	€1,000	€1,500

Box 11.3 (cont.)

Table 11.3 No equilibrium

Type	% of population	Risk of illness	Cost to insure	Willingness to pay
Healthy people	80	1/1000	€100	€200
Unhealthy people	20	1/100	€1,000	€1,500

Table 11.4 Separating equilibrium

Type	% of population	Risk of illnss	Cost to insure	Willingness to pay	Cost of medical test
Healthy people	50	1/1000	€100	€140	€40
Unhealthy people	50	1/500	€200	€250	€150

11.2 The use of risk-management models

While the underwriting of risk is one of their core competencies, insurers are similar to banks when it comes to risk-management systems and practices (Von Bomhard, 2005). In fact, the banking industry imported risk-management skills from the insurance sector and developed them further. Several banking crises, like the financial crisis of 2007–2009 and the Scandinavian banking crisis in the 1990s (see Chapter 2), have underlined the importance of good risk and capital management for banks. Another reason are the similarities between traditional actuarial thinking that prevails in insurance companies and financial economic thinking that prevails in banks. Modern risk management at insurers integrates actuarial techniques and total balance sheet management (see below).

Modern risk management

The main risk types for an insurer are underwriting risk, market risk, credit risk, and operational risk. As explained in Chapter 10, economic capital has emerged as a 'common currency' for risk taking within financial institutions. *Economic capital* is defined as the amount of capital a financial institution needs to absorb losses over a certain time interval with a certain confidence level. Financial institutions usually choose a time horizon of one year.

The risk-adjusted return on capital for an insurer is given by:

$$\text{RAROC} = \frac{\text{Revenues} - \text{Costs} - \text{Expected Claims}}{\text{Economic Capital}} = \frac{\pi}{E} \qquad (11.9)$$

The revenues consist of premiums P and investment returns R_A (see equation 11.2). Both the numerator and the denominator are adjusted for risk in the RAROC formula. RAROC divides profit by economic capital. RAROC can be used to assess past performance, but also to forecast future performance. It can thus be applied to determine whether activities should be discontinued or expanded.

RAROC is emerging as the leading methodology for large financial institutions to measure and manage risk. The use of internal risk models has been stimulated by supervisors, who allow insurers to use their internal models to calculate capital requirements (see Box 11.5 on the new Solvency II capital adequacy rules). Within the RAROC framework, insurers first calculate the risk for each risk type (underwriting, market, credit, and operational risk) and then aggregate these.[2]

The first type of risk is *underwriting risk*. Insurers make provisions for future claims. An unforeseen increase in the size and frequency of claims is a key risk factor for insurers. In life insurance, *longevity risk* is the risk that future trends in survival rates prove to be higher than projected. The payout period on annuities or pension contracts may thus be longer than expected. Insurance premiums to cover underwriting risk tend to follow a cyclical pattern. Several studies (e.g. Niehaus and Terry, 1993) identify the existence of an underwriting cycle in insurance markets. Box 11.4 explores different theories explaining the underwriting cycle.

The second type of risk is *market risk*. A specific market risk occurs when assets and liabilities in the balance sheet are not matched. This risk is labelled *asset and liability management risk*. In insurance companies, ALM risk is very important (Van Lelyveld, 2006). ALM risk increases when there is a significant mismatch between assets and liabilities. For life business, asset durations are generally shorter than liability durations. *Duration* is the effective maturity of an asset or liability. This duration mismatch will primarily cause an interest rate risk, as most assets consist of

Box 11.4 The underwriting cycle

The *underwriting or insurance cycle* is a distinct pattern of upward and downward movements in insurance premiums and their subsequent impact on underwriting profitability. Cyclical patterns, typically running over a period of six to nine years, tend to be particularly pronounced in insurance markets. While both demand and supply of insurance varies over time, variations in supply are the more important. New financial capital can come into a market quickly to increase supply when premiums are high, and also can be withdrawn quickly when returns on insurance are low.

There are several theories explaining the underwriting cycle (see Niehaus and Terry, 1993). The first one is based on fluctuations in profits and assumes a competitive market. If profits are high, some insurers may reduce insurance premiums to attract more clients in expectation of these higher profits. Other insurers, not wishing to lose market share, may then also reduce premiums.

The second theory is founded on the availability and cost of equity capital. There are two main effects when stock markets rise markedly. First, the cost of capital falls for existing and new insurers. Second, rising share prices increase the value of an insurer's asset holdings and thereby also the value of equity. The increased availability and reduced cost of capital increases supply and hence exerts downward pressure on premiums.

The third theory holds that claims rather than capital-market effects are the key cause of underwriting cycles. It supposes that insurers tend to underestimate the potential for large claims when there are no large individual losses or accumulation of losses. However, when a very large loss occurs, premiums rise sharply. A case in point is car insurance. After a few 'soft' winters without frozen roads, the frequency of car accidents seems to be relatively low and premiums may decrease. But after a 'strong' winter with multiple car accidents, premiums tend to rise again. This theory assumes that insurers have a short memory. This theory also supposes that following a major loss, insurers will try to recover some of their losses. Of course, exceptionally large losses or accumulations of loss are likely to be more or less random in their timing, but their effects may appear to be cyclical.

bonds.[3] Insurers also invest in equities and other investments to increase returns. While equities tend to generate a higher return than bonds in the long run (Dimson *et al.*, 2002), they also generate a considerably higher ALM risk. Insurers use advanced models to optimise their risk-return profile. The ability to invest in equities rather than in bonds depends on the size of an insurer's capital buffer. The larger the capital buffer, the more risk (and thus equity investments) the insurer is allowed to take (see Box 11.5 for further details).

The third type of risk is *credit risk*. While banks grant loans, insurers typically invest in traded assets such as bonds. Credit risk is present because the value of bonds may decline as a result of an increase in the perceived likelihood that the issuer will not be able to meet scheduled payments in the future. For most banks, lending activities are typically the main source of credit risk. But a typical insurer attributes only 5–10 per cent of total risk capital to credit risk (Van Lelyveld, 2006).

The fourth type of risk is *operational risk*. This is the risk of loss from inadequate internal processes, people or systems, or from external events. While developments in the insurance industry generally follow those in banking, most insurers model external-event risk separately as an underwriting risk. The insurance industry has its own operational risks. Recently, misselling of investment-linked insurance policies has led to large settlements to policy holders in several countries (e.g. the UK and the Netherlands). In the past, insurers had not always been transparent on the investment costs. Moreover, insurers had not always adequately explained the risks of an investment-linked policy (i.e. that investments may have a negative return) violating duty of care rules (see Chapter 12).

The impact of the various types of risk differs across banking and insurance. The main business of banks is granting loans. Credit risk is the most important risk driver in banking, followed by market and ALM risk. ALM risk is caused by long-term assets funded by short-term deposits. The main risk in life insurance is market risk related to the large asset portfolios. Life insurers collect premiums on life policies, which are invested over a long period. The next type of risk is ALM risk, which is opposite to banking ALM risk. Life insurers typically invest the premiums on their long-term policies in shorter-lived assets. Insurance or underwriting risk is the main risk driver for P&C insurers. Figure 11.6 illustrates the relative importance of the different types of risk.

As explained in Chapter 10, risk-management models have several shortcomings. Given the possibility of large losses in case of natural or man-made disasters, the proper modelling of tail risk is challenging for P&C insurers. Another risk that is difficult to model is longevity. Unanticipated increases in life expectancy have recently posed losses for life insurers, as well as pension funds.

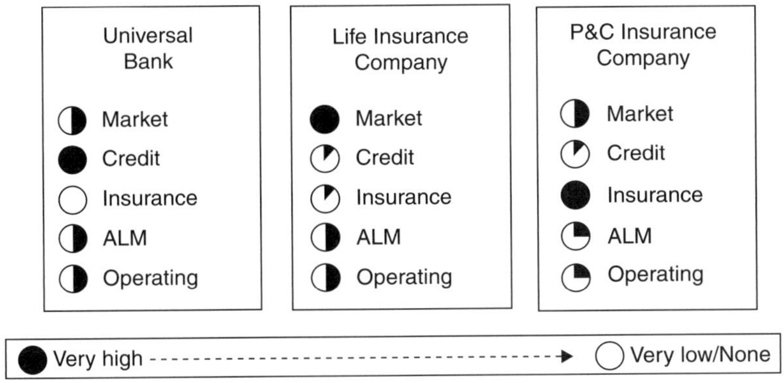

Figure 11.6 The relative role of risk types in banking and insurance
Source: Oliver, Wyman and Company (2001)

Centralisation of risk management

The organisational structure of international financial firms is moving from the traditional country model to a business-line model with integration of key management functions. One of the most notable advances in risk management is the growing emphasis on developing a firm-wide assessment of risk. These integrated approaches to risk management aim to ensure a comprehensive and systematic approach to risk-related decisions throughout the financial firm. Once firms have a centralised risk-management unit in place, they may benefit from economies of scale in risk management. Nevertheless, these centralised systems still rely on local branches and subsidiaries for local market data. The potential capital reductions that can be achieved by applying the advanced approaches of the Basel II framework encourage banking groups to organise their risk management more centrally (see Chapter 10). The same is true for the Solvency II framework for the European insurance industry (Drzik, 2005). Firms that implement a well-constructed risk- and capital-management framework can derive significant near-term business benefits, and substantially strengthen their medium-term competitive position.

Kuritzkes *et al.* (2003) provide evidence that internationally active financial conglomerates are putting in place centralised risk and capital-management units. The dominant approach is to adopt a so-called 'hub and spoke' organisational model. The spokes are responsible for risk management within business lines, while the hub provides centralised oversight of risk and capital at the group level. Activities at the spoke include the credit function within a bank, or the actuarial function within an insurance subsidiary or group, each of which serves the front-line managers for most trading decision-making.

Schoenmaker *et al.* (2008) confirm the shift to a more holistic approach in the European insurance industry. Developments in the field of accounting (for instance, the introduction of International Financial Reporting Standards (IFRS) and the Sarbanes Oxley Act in the US) and in supervision (Solvency II) contribute to the centralisation of risk- and capital-management processes. Moreover, as insurance groups operate in various countries, the need for a coherent policy regarding risk and capital management is increasing. This, in turn, has led to the adoption of chief risk officers (CROs) in large insurance groups.

Hub functions

Applying the hub and spoke model to a sample of large European insurance companies, Schoenmaker *et al.* (2008) identify which functions are executed at the centre (hub) and which functions are performed at the local business units (spokes). The hub accommodates decisions and responsibilities for the group as a whole at a central level in the organisation. Although large insurance groups have a distinct central risk-management framework in place, there are great differences between the responsibilities and actual implementation of these frameworks. In some groups central risk- and capital-management processes are still in their infancy, while in other groups these processes are much more advanced and commonly accepted in the organisation.

All groups use their risk-management framework to get an overview and to monitor the group-wide risk exposure. The majority of the groups also use their risk framework for specifying their risk profile and setting risk management, control, and business-conduct standards for the group's worldwide operations (i.e. 'the rules of the game'). This group-wide risk profile specifies some risk-tolerance levels. Within these boundaries, the local units can act more or less independently. Furthermore, group-wide policies regarding risk management enable a broadly consistent approach to the management of risks at the business-unit level.

The risk-management framework encompasses several bodies with their own specific tasks. On top of the central risk-management framework is the group risk committee at the executive level, with the chief executive officer (CEO) or chief financial officer (CFO) bearing the ultimate responsibility.

This committee is often responsible for setting the strategic guidelines and policies for risk management, for monitoring consolidated risk reports at group level, and for allocating economic capital to various entities of the group. Sometimes groups also have risk committees below the executive level. This may be the case in a financial group with both banking and insurance activities. The group risk committee is then responsible for the group as a whole, while banking and insurance risk committees reporting to the group risk committee are responsible for the risk management in banking and insurance, respectively.

Furthermore, many groups also have central or group risk-management teams. These teams are responsible for the development and implementation of the risk-management framework, for supporting the work of the risk committees, for reporting and reviewing risks, and for recommendations concerning risk methodologies. Many times, these central/group risk-management teams are headed by a CRO who oversees all aspects of the group's risk management and often reports to the CEO or CFO of the group and is present at meetings of the executive board.

Spoke functions

In the spokes, decisions are being taken on the level of the business/country unit. Insurance is very much a local business, with significant differences between the operational environment of the host countries in which the insurance group is active. Specific local knowledge is often required with respect to national rules and regulations (such as fiscal legislation, contracts, social security, consumer protection, or local risks), complicating the steering process at a central level. So a great number of decisions still have to be made by the local business units. In general, the actuary determines the specific risk at the local level. At the group level, these local models are subsequently monitored and assessed. Although the general conditions for determining local risk models are set at the central level, the local units carry the ultimate responsibility for their risk management.

So, despite the emergence of centralised risk management, the risk-management practices of the largest insurance groups are still to a large extent influenced by the risk-management policies of the local business units. Therefore, in general one could say that the 'rules of the game' are being determined at central level in the hub and that the local managers in the spokes determine 'how the game is actually being played' within the margins of these rules. This general principle is summarised in Figure 11.7

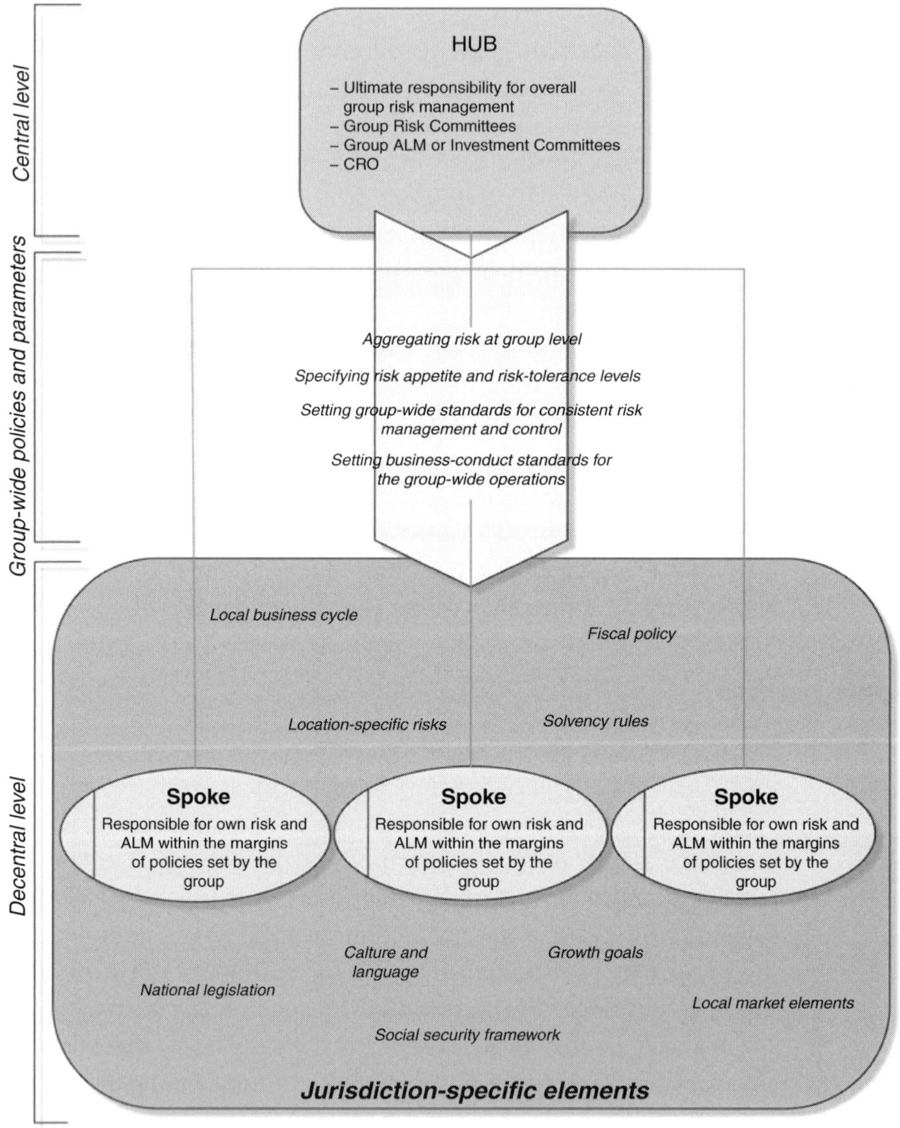

Figure 11.7 Organisation of risk and capital management in insurance groups
Source: Schoenmaker *et al.* (2008)

which gives an overview of the roles and responsibilities for each level of the organisation, whereby the spokes are placed within a field of jurisdiction-specific parameters in order to capture the location-specific factors that influence the business decisions.

11.3 The European insurance system

Insurance markets across Europe

The insurance markets vary significantly across Europe. This is illustrated by differences in the *insurance penetration*, i.e. insurance premiums as a percentage of GDP, which ranges from 1.4 per cent in Romania to 12.5 per cent in the Netherlands (see Table 11.5). There is a large difference between the new Member States of the EU and the EU-15. Whereas the prevalence of life insurance is 4.7 per cent in the EU-15, it amounts to only 1.6 per cent in the NMS-12. Life insurance is basically a savings product for the future, where the payout is linked to somebody's life. Life insurance may be considered as a 'luxury' good: only at high income levels do households start to save for retirement (Focarelli and Pozzolo, 2008).

Non-life insurance is less diverse across Europe. It looks more like a 'necessary' good offering basic protection against accidents, such as car accidents, fire, or illness. Non-life penetration is 3.4 per cent in the EU-15 and 1.7 per cent in the NMS-12. Also, at the country level the differences are less pronounced than for life insurance. The insurance penetration ranges from 1.1 per cent in Lithuania and Romania to 4.1 per cent in Slovenia. The Netherlands, with a non-life penetration ratio of 9.4 per cent, is an outlier as health insurance there has been privatised.

Table 11.6 illustrates the major business lines of non-life insurers. Motor insurance is the largest class of non-life business, but health insurance is catching up. The strong increase of health insurance reflects the privatisation of the healthcare sector in the Netherlands in 2006. Property insurance is increasing as well. Other non-life insurance includes general liability, marine, aviation, and transport insurance.

In 2012, some 3,700 insurance companies operated in the EU. Their number has declined since the creation of the European single market, due to mergers and acquisitions at both the national and the European level. Insurance companies aim for sufficient critical mass to be able to compete effectively at the European level.

The insurance market has a large number of small and medium-sized insurers with a very low market share and a small number of insurance groups with a high market share. The small insurers, with premium income below €10 million, are found in the non-life insurance sector in particular. Some 30 per cent of the smaller insurers are mutual companies (CEA, 2007).

Table 11.5 Insurance penetration in the EU, 2012

	Number of insurers	Total premium income (in € billion)	Insurance penetration (in % of GDP)		
			Total	Life	Non-life
Austria	76	16.3	5.3	2.1	3.2
Belgium	136	32.9	8.8	5.6	3.1
Bulgaria	44	0.8	2.0	0.3	1.7
Cyprus	33	0.9	5.2	2.4	2.8
Czech Republic	53	6.1	4.0	1.9	2.1
Denmark	176	25.0	10.2	7.1	3.1
Estonia	17	0.4	2.4	0.9	1.5
Finland	74	8.5	4.4	2.3	2.1
France	339	177.6	8.7	5.5	3.2
Germany	471	190.3	7.1	3.2	3.9
Greece	74	4.6	2.4	1.1	1.3
Hungary	50	2.6	2.6	1.4	1.2
Ireland	279	13.4	8.2	6.1	2.1
Italy	235	105.6	6.7	4.4	2.3
Latvia	22	0.4	1.9	0.2	1.8
Lithuania	25	0.5	1.6	0.5	1.1
Luxembourg	89	2.0	4.5	2.7	1.9
Malta	59	0.3	4.4	2.4	2.0
Netherlands	214	75.1	12.5	3.2	9.4
Poland	77	15.5	4.1	2.4	1.7
Portugal	79	5.6	3.4	1.3	2.1
Romania	51	1.8	1.4	0.3	1.1
Slovakia	37	2.0	2.8	1.6	1.3
Slovenia	23	1.9	5.5	1.4	4.1
Spain	351	56.7	5.5	2.6	2.9
Sweden	209	18.5	4.5	2.7	1.9
United Kingdom	382	239.9	12.4	9.1	3.3
EU-15	3,184	971.9	8.2	4.7	3.4
NMS-12	491	33.4	3.3	1.6	1.7
EU-27	3,675	1,005.4	7.8	4.5	3.3

Notes: Insurance penetration is measured as premium income as a percentage of GDP. EU-15, NMS-12, and EU-27 are calculated as a weighted average (weighted according to total premium income).
Source: EIOPA (2013a)

Large insurance groups have a premium income ranging from around €5 billion up to €100 billion. Table 11.7 shows the largest 25 insurers in Europe, amounting to half of the premium income of the European insurance market.

Table 11.6 Non-life premium income in the EU (in € billion), 1995–2012

	1995	2000	2005	2010	2012
Motor insurance	78	98	119	124	134
Health insurance	51	66	88	108	113
Property insurance	47	54	74	84	89
Other non-life	48	51	72	111	115
Total non-life	224	269	353	427	451

Source: Insurance Europe (2014)

Table 11.7 Biggest 25 insurance groups in Europe in 2012

Insurance groups	(1) Premium income[a] in (€ billion)	(2) Total assets (in € billion)	(3) Premium income in home country (as % of (1))	(4) Premium income in rest of Europe (as % of (1))	(5) Premium income rest of world (as % of (1))
Global insurers[b]					
1. Zurich Financial Services (Switzerland)	39	310	11	40	49
2. Prudential (UK)	37	380	23	0	77
3. Talanx (Germany)	27	130	35	32	33
4. MAPFRE (Spain)	22	57	37	7	56
5. ING Insurance (Netherlands)	20	340	36	23	41
6. AEGON (Netherlands)	20	366	19	35	46
7. ACE (Switzerland)	22	70	18	0	82
8. Royal & Sun Alliance (UK)	12	28	36	30	34
9. SCOR (France)	10	33	22	20	58
European insurers[c]					
1. AXA (France)	85	762	23	50	27
2. Allianz (Germany)	72	695	25	44	31
3. Generali (Italy)	70	442	29	65	6
4. BNP Paribas Cardif (France)	20	170	32	45	23

Table 11.7 (cont.)

Insurance groups	(1) Premium income[a] in (€ billion)	(2) Total assets (in € billion)	(3) Premium income in home country (as % of (1))	(4) Premium income in rest of Europe (as % of (1))	(5) Premium income rest of world (as % of (1))
5. Swiss Life (Switzerland)	10	126	49	47	4
6. Vienna Insurance Group (Austria)	10	42	43	57	0
Semi-international insurers[d]					
1. Aviva (UK)	28	389	50	34	16
2. Crédit Agricole Assurances (France)	23	291	66	30	4
3. Ageas (Belgium)	10	97	64	33	3
Domestic insurers[e]					
1. Lloyds (UK)	31	81	82	5	13
2. CNP (France)	26	353	81	8	11
3. Achmea (Netherlands)	20	95	94	6	0
4. ERGO (Germany)	17	147	77	18	5
5. Covéa (France)	15	87	89	10	1
6. Groupama (France)	11	88	80	20	0
7. Unipol (Italy)	12	83	100	0	0
Top 25 Insurance Groups	27	226	40	33	27

Notes:

[a] Top 25 insurance groups are selected on the basis of gross written premium in 2012.

[b] Global insurers: less than 50 per cent of premium in the home country and the majority of their international premium in the rest of the world.

[c] European insurers: less than 50 per cent of premium in the home country and the majority of their international premium in the rest of Europe.

[d] Semi-international insurers: between 50 and 75 per cent of premium in the home country.

[e] Domestic insurers: 75 per cent or more of premium in the home country.

Source: Schoenmaker and Sass (2014)

Within the group of large insurance groups, Schoenmaker *et al.* (2008) define insurers as 'domestic' if they receive 75 per cent or more of their premiums in the home country. Examples are CNP in France and Achmea in the Netherlands. A semi-international insurer has between 50 and

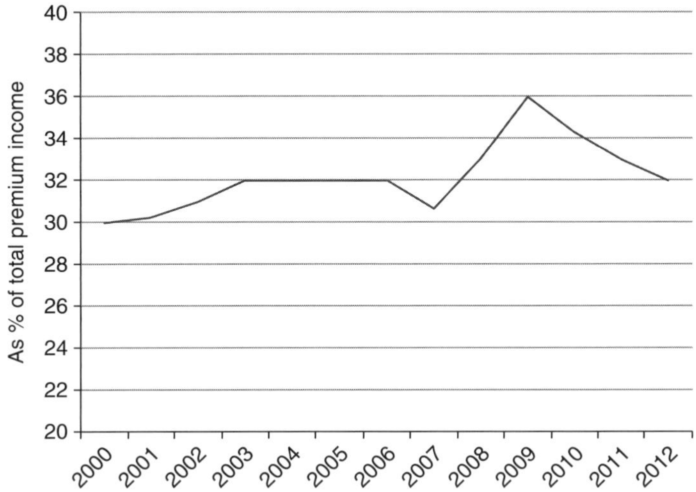

Figure 11.8 Cross-border penetration of top 25 EU insurers (%), 2000–2012
Note: Share of premium income from other EU countries measured as a percentage of total premium income. The share is calculated for the top 25 insurance groups in Europe, which represent more than half of total premium income for the EU-27.
Source: Schoenmaker and Sass (2014)

75 per cent of its premium in the home country. A European insurer has less than 50 per cent of its premium in the home country and the majority of its international premium in the rest of Europe. Some European insurers focus on a specific region within Europe. Others, like Allianz, AXA, and Generali, operate Europe-wide. The remaining international insurers are 'global' insurers operating on a worldwide scale. This group includes Zurich Financial Services and ACE from Switzerland, ING and Aegon from the Netherlands, and Prudential and RSA from the UK.

In order to operate successfully in a foreign market, an insurer needs to know the legislation (e.g. on liability), fiscal treatment, and accident statistics (e.g. the number of car accidents) of that country. As these differ across EU countries, a major effort is required before entry of a foreign market. Cross-border insurance is therefore typically done by large insurance groups. The preferred method of entering a foreign market is through a subsidiary, usually by the acquisition of a local insurer. Figure 11.8 illustrates the cross-border penetration of the top 25 insurers in Europe. The cross-border penetration rose from 30 per cent to 36 per cent between 2000 and 2009 and fell back to 32 per cent in 2012. The corresponding figure for the largest 30 banks in Europe was 24 per cent in 2013 (see Chapter 10). Large insurance

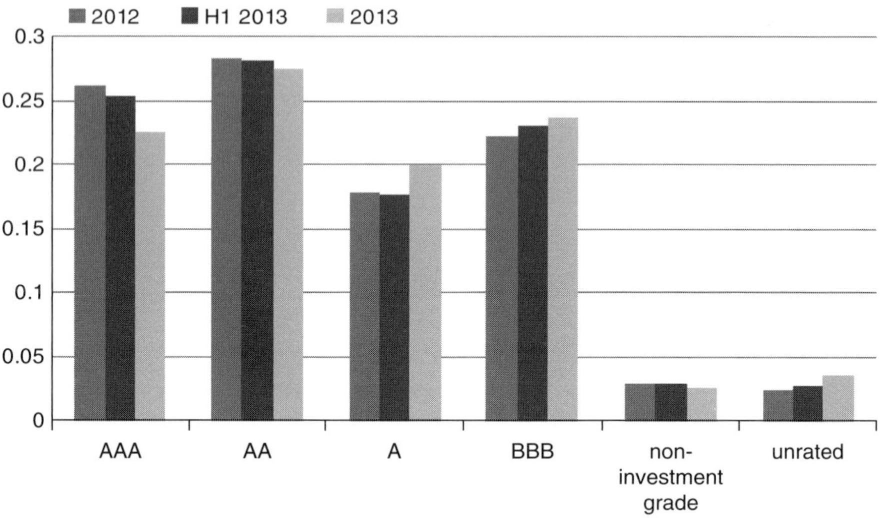

Figure 11.9 Bond investments of selected large euro insurers, 2012–13 (percentage of total bond investments)
Source: ECB (2014)

groups are thus more internationally oriented than their counterparts in banking.

Portfolios

Investment activity of large euro-area insurers is concentrated in government, bank bond and corporate bond markets. Investments in structured credit, equity, and commercial property remained at low levels in 2013 (ECB, 2014). The fixed income portfolio is dominated by highly rated bonds (see Figure 11.9). In that way, insurers limit their credit risk. They also tend to match the maturity of bonds with the maturity of the their long-term liabilities. The demand for high-quality long-term bonds, already a preferred habitat, could strengthen as firms economise on capital charges under the new Solvency II regime (see Box 11.5).

Liability-driven investment strategies thus tend to raise the demand for risk-free long-term assets used for limiting duration gaps without attracting higher risk charges. As this favours government bonds, there is concern about the prospects for corporates, and bank funding in particular, over the medium term. Insurance companies (and pension funds) have continued to reduce their exposure to financial institutions since the crisis.

There are also concerns that the new Solvency II regime drives insurers unilaterally towards government and corporate bonds. Institutional

Box 11.5 Solvency II

On 13 November 2013 the European Parliament, the European Council, and the European Commission reached a political agreement on the so-called Omnibus II Directive. This Directive stipulates that the Solvency II framework will enter into force on 1 January 2016. The Omnibus II Directive makes various changes to the Solvency II Directive (Directive 2009/138/EC), which was adopted as early as 2009. The Omnibus II Directive regulates, among other things, the transitional measures in connection with the introduction of Solvency II and the role of the European Insurance and Occupational Pensions Authority (EIOPA).

The agreement on the Omnibus II Directive implies that the outline of the Solvency II framework has now been established. This will have to be elaborated by the European Commission in secondary legislation.

The key objectives of Solvency II are: (1) Improved consumer protection: it will ensure a uniform and enhanced level of policy holder protection across the EU. A more robust system will give policy holders greater confidence in the products of insurers; (2) Modernised supervision: supervisors will shift their focus from compliance monitoring and capital to evaluating insurers' risk profiles and the quality of their risk-management and governance systems; (3) Furthering EU market integration through the harmonisation of supervisory regimes and increased international competitiveness of EU insurers.

Solvency II is not just about capital. It is a comprehensive programme of regulatory requirements for insurers, covering authorisation, corporate governance, supervisory reporting, public disclosure, and risk assessment and management, as well as solvency and reserving. As in Basel II for Banking, the regime has a three-pillar structure, with each pillar governing a different aspect of the Solvency II requirements. Pillar 1 is designed to ensure that a firm is adequately capitalised to deliver policy holder protection. It provides rules for how insurers should value their liabilities (including the money that gets paid to policy holders in the event of a claim) and assets (such as government bonds, shares, property) that they own. The rules also cover the amount of funds insurers need to hold in reserve to make sure they can pay policy holders' claims (see below). Pillar 2 imposes standards of risk management and governance on firms. Each firm is required to undertake its own forward-looking assessment of its risks, solvency needs, and adequacy of capital resources. Pillar 3 ensures what information insurers report on their business and how it is reported. Some reports are public and anyone can see them; some are privately reported to the financial supervisor. More information allows the public (and the supervisor) to understand more about the businesses that provide insurance to individuals and institutions.

Pillar 1 contains the *solvency capital requirement* (SCR). The SCR is the capital required to ensure that the insurance company will be able to meet its obligations. To be more specific, the SCR is the Value-at-Risk of the basic own funds of a (re)insurance company

Box 11.5 (cont.)

subject to a confidence level of 99.5 per cent over a one-year period. The SCR is calculated using either a standard formula or, with supervisory approval, an internal model. The standard formula is a risk-sensitive framework designed to capture the risks a firm may face and calculate the capital requirements from these risks. The standard formula categorises risks into risk modules for capital purposes; these modules are market risk, credit risk, underwriting risk (life and non-life), and operational risk.

In addition to the SCR capital a *minimum capital requirement* (MCR) must be calculated. The MCR is the Value-at-Risk of the basic own funds of a (re)insurance company subject to a confidence level of 85 per cent over a one-year period. For supervisory purposes, the SCR and MCR can be regarded as 'soft' and 'hard' floors respectively. If an insurer's available resources fall below the SCR, supervisors are required to take action with the aim of restoring the insurer's finances back into the level of the SCR as soon as possible. If, despite supervisory intervention, the available resources of the insurer fall below the MCR, then 'ultimate supervisory action' will be triggered. In other words, the insurer's liabilities will be transferred to another insurer and the licence of the insurer will be withdrawn or the insurer will be closed to new business and its in-force business will be liquidated.

investors, such as insurers and pension funds, are important long-term investors for the real economy. Examples of long-term assets for insurers are (EIOPA, 2013b):

- infrastructure financing and other long-term financing through project bonds, other types of debt, and equity;
- Small and Medium-sized Enterprises (SME) financing through debt and equity;
- Socially Responsible Investments (SRI) and social business financing through debt and equity;
- long-term financing of the real economy through securitisation of debt serving the above mentioned purposes.

Market structure

Between 1994 and 2012 the total number of insurers in the EU decreased from 5,201 to 3,675 (see Table 11.8). This consolidation mainly reflects mergers or acquisitions of small and medium-sized domestic insurers. At the same time, some of the large insurers expanded domestically as well as cross-border.

Table 11.8 Market structure indicators, 1994/95 and 2012

	Size		CR5 (in %)				Competition
	Number of insurers		Life		Non-life		Combined ratio[b]
	1994	2012	1995	2012	1995	2012	2012
Austria	74	76	46	51	54	48	89
Belgium	252	136	64	66	52	61	94
Bulgaria	30	44	n.a.	67	n.a.	58	94
Cyprus	46	33	89	96	36	61	90
Czech Republic	27	53	97	65	93	74	78
Denmark	250	176	57	56	63	72	86
Estonia	15	17	100	100	65	96	77
Finland	57	74	99	92	88	86	97
France	577	339	50	51	41	28	94
Germany	742	471	31	38	23	25	87
Greece	149	74	68	70	39	40	79
Hungary	13	50	93	56	96	78	78
Ireland	122	279	61	84	50	54	93
Italy	265	235	45	46	34	46	96
Latvia	42	22	n.a.	100	n.a.	91	77
Lithuania	35	25	n.a.	47	n.a.	60	98
Luxembourg	76	89	67	51	82	71	71
Malta	24	59	n.a.	100	n.a.	76	68
Netherlands	492	214	68	72	35	42	98
Poland	34	77	100	59	90	67	86
Portugal	87	79	59	59	53	59	95
Romania	39	51	n.a.	75	n.a.	62	107
Slovakia	11	37	98	71	98	89	83
Slovenia	10	23	90	87	95	77	87
Spain	417	351	29	49	20	38	87
Sweden	494	209	74	80	77	77	121
United Kingdom	821	382	29	62	27	35	90
EU-15[c]	4,875	3,184	44	55	33	37	92
NMS-12[c]	326	491	96	64	91	71	85
EU-27[c]	5,201	3,675	44	55	34	38	92

Notes:

[a] CR5 is the share of the five largest life (non-life) insurers, measured as a percentage of total life (non-life) premium.

[b] Combined ratio is measured as claims and expenses in % of premium.

[c] EU-15, NMS-12, and EU-27 are calculated as a weighted average (weighted according to premium) for CR5 and the combined ratio.

n.a. means not available.

Source: EIOPA (2013a)

There are different types of insurance companies. The main model is the limited-liability (or joint-stock) insurance company owned by shareholders, whose liability for losses is restricted to the share capital. The model of mutual insurer, owned by the policy holders, still counts for about 20 per cent of the European market (ACME, 2003). The significance of mutuals is large in some markets, such as France and Germany (about 30 per cent), and small in other markets, like the United Kingdom (about 10 per cent). There is a trend towards 'demutualisation', meaning that mutuals are converted into limited-liability insurance companies.

Again, there are substantial differences between the EU-15 and the NMS-12. First, the number of insurers in the EU-15 is substantially higher than in the NMS-12. This is largely due to the significant number of small insurers in countries, such as France, Germany, and the United Kingdom.

Second, the trend in the number of insurers is different. On average, the number of insurers in the EU-15 declined by about 35 per cent over the 1994–2012 period, while in the NMS-12 the corresponding figure increased by 50 per cent. The change in the number of insurers influences the degree of concentration in the different national insurance markets. Table 11.8 presents the CR5 ratio, which measures the market share of the top five insurers in the insurance industry. The table illustrates that the insurance markets in the NMS-12 are generally more concentrated than the markets in the EU-15. However, there is convergence. The concentration ratios in the EU-15 are increasing towards 40 to 50 per cent, while concentration in the NMS-12 is decreasing towards 60 to 70 per cent.

Overall, life insurance markets are more concentrated than non-life markets. That can be explained by the nature of the product. Life-insurance companies carry closely related (savings) products dependent on life expectancy. By contrast, non-life insurance is an industry with very different business lines (see Table 11.6). Among non-life insurers, there are many mono-liners that underwrite one type of insurance only. These specialised insurers are by definition smaller than multi-liner insurers that combine different business lines.

Measurement of competition in the insurance industry is still underdeveloped. There are no adequate indices of insurance prices that would allow comparison. An alternative approach is to rely on indirect measures, such as profitability (European Commission, 2007). A common economic measure to assess the profitability of non-life insurers is the combined ratio (see section 11.1). However, the use of the combined ratio has two major drawbacks. First, when claims are more likely to arise in the future, the matching principle of accounting is not satisfied. Clients pay, for example, their premium for their insurance in year 1, while the payout on claims may arise only in year 2 or 3. Second, investment returns are not included in the combined ratio. This is an important source of income, as premiums are invested in financial assets that are held until claims are paid.

The combined ratios are reported in the last column of Table 11.8. The figures indicate that the non-life insurance industry is competitive in Europe with a combined ratio of 92 per cent (EU-27) yielding a margin of 8 per cent. The margin is higher in the NMS with a margin of 15 per cent. At the country level, the picture is more diverse. The majority of EU Member States have a combined ratio between 90 per cent and 100 per cent. Some countries (Romania and Sweden) have combined ratios above 100 per cent and make a loss. Finally, a group of countries (Czech Republic, Estonia, Greece, Hungary, Latvia, Luxembourg, and Malta) have combined ratios between 65 per cent and 80 per cent. These ratios suggest a lack of competition, but the results should be interpreted with care and provide only an indication of lack of competition.

Insurance is sold through a variety of distribution channels. A growing share of insurance products is sold directly by employees of an insurance company or directly via the Internet channel (*direct writing*). Internet sales are expected to grow fast, particularly for simple non-life insurance products. Historically, insurance intermediaries in the form of brokers and agents play a dominant role. Brokers are fully independent, specialist insurance intermediaries. They are not tied to any specific insurance company. Insurance agents are typically less independent than insurance brokers. Agents can work exclusively for one insurance company, but may also offer competing products from a wide range of insurers. A final distribution channel is *bancassurance* (the combination of a bank and an insurance company within a financial institution), where insurance products are sold through the bank.

Distribution channels vary significantly across European countries. The distribution of life insurance is mainly driven by bancassurance networks (banking combined with assurance), with the exception of the United Kingdom and Ireland where brokers dominate the distribution of life products (see Figure 11.10). Bulgaria, Slovakia, and Slovenia also show a weaker role for banks. In non-life insurance, insurance products are principally distributed via agents in a large number of countries (Spain, France, Italy, Poland, Portugal, Slovakia, and Slovenia). The broker channel dominates in some other countries (the United Kingdom, Ireland, the Netherlands, and Belgium). The predominance of agents and brokers on almost every market

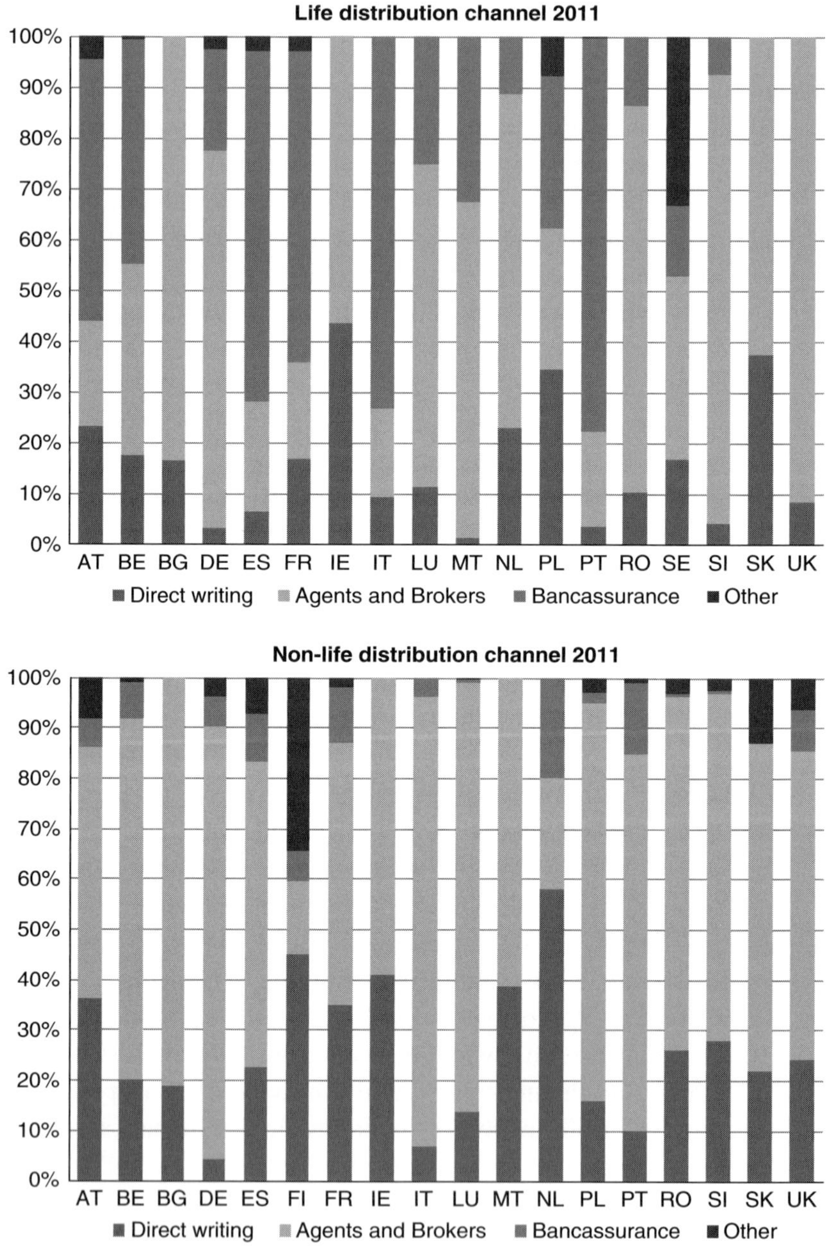

Figure 11.10 Distribution channels in Europe
Source: Insurance Europe (2014)

Table 11.9 Development of international insurance by continent, 2000–2012

	2000			2004			2008			2012		
Continent	h	r	w	h	r	w	h	r	w	h	r	w
Europe	48	30	22	45	34	21	40	34	26	40	33	27
Americas	80	5	15	76	13	11	74	11	15	78	3	19
Asia-Pacific	–	–	–	97	1	2	95	2	3	96	2	2

Notes: Share of gross written premium in home country (h), rest of the region (r), and rest of the world (w) of the top 20 insurers by continent. The shares add up to 100 per cent.
Source: Schoenmaker and Sass (2014)

finds its origin in the preference of the insured to benefit from proximity at the time of the contract and, above all, in the case of a claim. Direct writing is used more for non-life than for life products.

International outlook

Turning to international insurance, the geographical segmentation of large insurers on the other continents, the Americas and the Asia-Pacific, can be compared to the geographical spread of the large European insurers. Table 11.9 shows that European insurers are the most international with 60 per cent of gross written premium abroad. This may be due to the integrated European insurance market. But even when looking at the gross written premium outside the region, European insurers are the most international with 27 per cent of gross written premium in the rest of the world. The American insurers are catching up; their gross written premium in the rest of the world rose from 15 per cent in 2000 to 19 per cent in 2012.

The picture is very different for the Asian-Pacific insurers. They have a very domestic orientation. Combined gross written premium in the rest of the region and the rest of the world is only 4 per cent. Similar to banking, the composition of the large Asian-Pacific insurers is shifting from the major Japanese insurers to the major Chinese insurers (see also Table 11.10). The rise of Chinese financial institutions and the demise of Japanese ones is in line with developments in the respective GDPs. That shows that financial institutions are intrinsically connected with the economy.

Following the Single Market, regional integration is very strong in Europe. That is true both for banking (23 per cent in Table 10.3) and for insurance (33 per cent in Table 11.9). By contrast, regional integration is very weak in the Americas and in the Asia-Pacific. Regional business, in the rest of North

Table 11.10 Global systemically important insurers, 2013

Insurance companies	Total assets in € bn	Gross written premium in € bn	Of which: domestic (%)	region (%)	world (%)
Allianz (Germany)	695	72	25	44	31
AIG (US)	344	29	70	21	9
Aviva (UK)	389	28	50	34	16
AXA (France)	762	85	23	50	27
Generali (Italy)	442	70	29	65	6
MetLife (US)	634	32	65	3	32
Ping An Insurance (China)	143	37	99	1	0
Prudential Financial (US)	205	52	67	0	33
Prudential (UK)	380	37	23	0	77
Total G-SIIs	444	49	44	31	25

Notes: Gross written premium is segmented over the home country, the rest of region, and the rest of world. Total of G-SIIs is calculated as a weighted average (weighted according to gross written premium).
Source: Schoenmaker and Sass (2014)

and South America and the rest of the Asia-Pacific, is very small (compared to business in the rest of the world).

The Financial Stability Board (FSB) has produced a list of *global systemically important insurers*, the so-called G-SIIs. These insurers are the large financial players, which can pose a systemic threat to the global financial system. Weiβ and Mühlnickel (2014) find that insurers that were most exposed to systemic risk were on average larger, relied more heavily on non-policy holder liabilities, and had higher ratios of investment income to net revenues. It appears that firm size is the most important factor. Table 11.10 provides an overview of these G-SIIs, which have assets up to €800 billion. The initial list comprises the major insurance companies, with five insurers from Europe, three from the US, and one from China. The FSB is expected to make a decision on the G-SII status of major reinsurers later in 2015. Comparing the G-SIBs in Chapter 10 and G-SIIs in this chapter, it is clear that the large systemic insurers are smaller in size and in number than the large systemic banks.

11.4 Financial conglomerates

Financial conglomerates combine banking and insurance activities. There are various arguments in favour of financial conglomerates: commercial integration, financial integration, and operational integration. First, commercial integration is related to cross-selling of multiple financial services to clients. The most important form of cross-selling is the provision of insurance services to the bank's customer base. This is called *bancassurance.* Cross-selling can also happen the other way round, when an insurer provides banking services to its clients. This is called *assurfinance.* Sharing of customer databases facilitates cross-selling. Cross-selling generates economies of scope through reduced client information and transaction costs and consequently higher prices and/or transaction volumes for the financial group (Schmid and Walter, 2009).

Second, financial integration is an important driver of financial conglomerates. There is scope for financial diversification as the risk profile of the insurance activities is different from the risk profile of banking activities. These differences in risk profile are analysed in sections 10.2 and 11.2. The question is how stable these diversification benefits are. Diversification is particularly useful in bad times. The normal distribution underestimates the downside risk, since the return series of financial assets have a fat-tailed distribution. Slijkerman *et al.* (2013) apply extreme value theory, which gives a much better description of the downside risk than the normal approximation. For a sample of European financial conglomerates, they find evidence for diversification benefits (see also Box 11.6).

Third, operational integration can produce efficiencies in the back office. Operational integration generates economies of scope. Sharing of joint costs, such as IT platforms, across a diversified range of activities leads to higher levels of operating efficiency (Schmid and Walter, 2009). Another example is joint management of assets across the financial conglomerate.

There are also arguments against financial conglomerates. First, cross-subsidisation across business lines may lead to an inefficient allocation of capital and reduced performance. The profit in banking can be used for less-performing insurance activities, and vice versa. Second, opaque accounts may make it difficult to get a clear picture of the risk profile of financial conglomerates. As financial institutions report on a consolidated basis, it is difficult to detangle balance-sheet items as well as profit-and-loss items between banking and insurance business. This also gives scope for transfer of (risky) assets within a conglomerate (Schmid and Walter, 2009).

These arguments can be summarised under the heading of managerial complexity (Plantin and Rochet, 2007). A financial conglomerate is a portfolio of various business lines which require different expertise and give rise to different risks. It is very demanding to manage such a diversified firm in a

Box 11.6 Functional or geographical diversification?

Financial firms can pursue different diversification strategies. Functional diversification is the combination of different activities, such as banking and insurance. Swiss Re (2007) indicates that Europe has the highest share of financial conglomerates. In particular, the combination of banking and life insurance accounts for more than half of the life-insurance market in Europe. In North America and Asia, the penetration of financial conglomerates is much lower than in Europe. This partly reflects the previously restrictive regulations on combining banking and insurance. In the US, the Gramm-Leach-Bliley Act of 1999 removed barriers between banks and insurance companies. The Japanese bancassurance market was fully liberalised only by the start of 2007.

Geographical diversification aims to spread the activities over different regions. Schoenmaker and Van Laecke (2006) show that geographical diversification of European banks exceeds that of American and Asian banks.

The two effects can be decomposed. Van Lelyveld and Knot (2009) do not find a structural discount for functional diversification, but they report that large financial conglomerates appear to trade at a discount. Functional diversification is thus predominantly value destroying for larger conglomerates. In contrast, Schmid and Walter (2009) report that geographically diversified financial firms trade at a small premium. Geographical diversification is thus value enhancing.

coherent way. The empirical literature finds a significant (both in statistical and economic terms) discount for non-financial conglomerates, i.e. the shares of conglomerates seem to be structurally undervalued. Although one would expect mixed financial conglomerates to be formed mainly to create added value generated by the combination of banking and insurance, this added value has thus far not been transferred to the shareholders. The main arguments for this conglomerate discount are managerial complexity and the lack of focus.

Most studies on financial conglomerates focus on the US. The US definition of a financial conglomerate is a financial institution that is active in at least two of the following areas: commercial banking (lending), investment banking (capital-market transactions), insurance, and asset management. In practice, most financial conglomerates combine commercial and investment banking. Schmid and Walter (2009) and Laeven and Levine (2007) report a substantial and persistent conglomerate discount for US conglomerates. The market values of financial conglomerates that engage in multiple financial activities is about 10 per cent lower than those of comparable financial institutions that specialise in the individual activities.

Van Lelyveld and Knot (2009) focus specifically on the valuation of bank-insurance conglomerates. Using a dataset for 45 financial conglomerates, 45 banks, and 45 insurers, they compare the valuation of the three groups. Van Lelyveld and Knot (2009) do not find a structural diversification discount, but they observe considerable variability of the valuation. Large financial conglomerates face a larger discount, which is consistent with the hypothesis that larger conglomerates have more opportunities for inefficient cross-subsidisation.

On balance, the negative arguments present in financial conglomerates outweigh the positive elements. This is in line with recent market developments of large financial conglomerates. An example from the US is Citigroup, which grew out of a merger between Citicorp (banking) and Travelers (insurance) in 1998. Citigroup has, however, divested most of its insurance underwriting business over the last few years. The Swiss bank, Credit Suisse, formed a financial conglomerate in 1997 with its acquisition of the insurer, Winterthur. However, in 2006, Credit Suisse sold Winterthur to the French insurer AXA. The financial crisis speeded up the process of divestment. The European Commission demanded that, when receiving state aid, large financial groups should be downsized and split up (see Chapter 14). The leading financial Belgian conglomerate Fortis was split on product and geographic lines in 2008. The Dutch banking and insurance parts were separately nationalised by the Dutch government, while the Belgian–Luxembourg banking part was sold to BNP Paribas and the insurance part continued under the name Ageas. In 2013 and 2014, ING separated its banking and insurance business by selling off the insurance parts. Finally, the smallish Dutch conglomerate SNS Reaal was also forced to separate its bank (SNS) and insurer (Reaal) after receiving state aid in 2013.

Financial conglomeration is facilitated by the strong demand for long-term savings products. Growth opportunities in life-insurance and pension products lead to increasing orientation of banks towards these areas. Figure 11.11 indicates that the market share of financial conglomerates in life insurance amounts to 30 per cent in selected countries, where bank-distribution channels are effective. Spain, France, Italy and Portugal, in particular, have large financial conglomerates combining banking and life insurance. Examples are BNP Paribas with BNP Paribas Cardif for insurance, and Crédit Agricole with Crédit Agricole Assurances (see Tables 10.2 and 11.7).

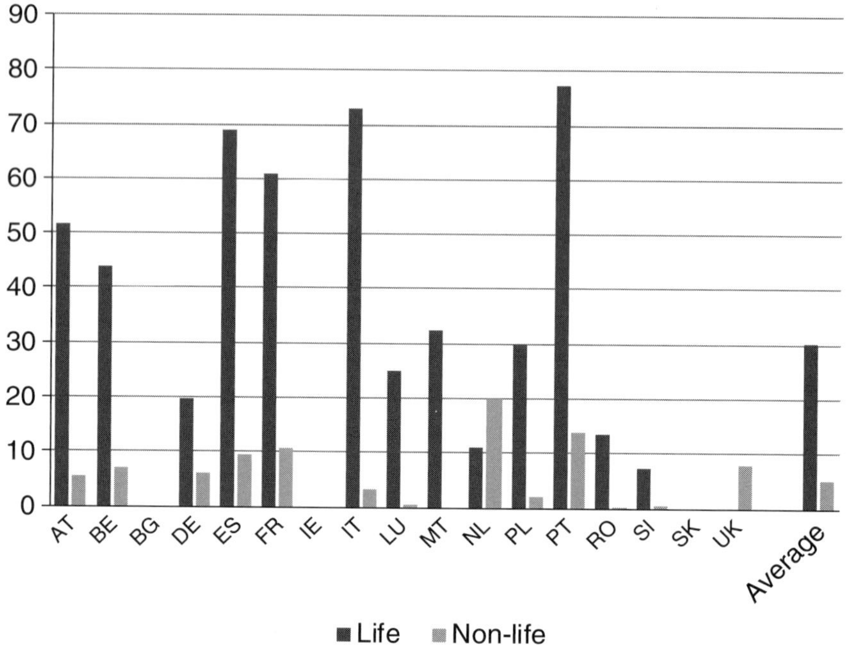

Figure 11.11 Market share of financial conglomerates in insurance (%), 2011
Notes: The bars represent the market share of financial conglomerates in the distribution of life and non-life insurance. Data are not available for all EU-27 countries.
Source: Insurance in Europe (2014)

Penetration in non-life is less pronounced. The market share of financial conglomerates in non-life insurance is only 5 per cent.

11.5 Conclusions

Insurance seeks to protect individuals and firms from adverse events through the pooling of risks. The business lines are very diverse. Non-life insurance includes car, property, and liability insurance, while life insurance provides cover for premature death or retirement. Insurance companies collect premiums today and make payments when adverse events happen in the future. Insurance is thus a risky business. Indeed, risk is the essence of an insurance company. This chapter has shown that the pattern of small claims, such as fire or car accidents, is fairly predictable. But larger accidents or catastrophes (like hurricanes) involve high claims with low probability. The risk of catastrophes is too big for one insurance company and is therefore divided among different insurance and re-insurance companies. Insurance companies tend to centralise risk management using internal risk-management models. Insurers and banks are converging with regard to risk-management systems and practices.

The insurance markets vary considerably across Europe. Life insurance is quite prominent in the EU-15 and can be considered a 'luxury' good. Non-life is more evenly spread across the EU and is regarded as a 'necessary' good. The figures indicate that the level of cross-border insurance has gradually increased. Insurance is sold through a variety of distribution channels. A growing share of insurance products is sold directly through the Internet or by employees of an insurance company. Insurance intermediaries such as brokers and agents play a dominant role, which however is expected to decrease for simple non-life insurances. A final distribution channel for insurance products is 'bancassurance'.

Financial conglomerates combining banking and insurance have emerged in Europe. They cover about 30 per cent of the life insurance and 5 per cent of the non-life insurance markets. An important driver of financial conglomerates is the cross-selling of insurance products to banking customers. Another driver is financial-diversification benefits as the risk profile of banking and insurance activities is quite different. However, this chapter also indicates that it may be difficult for managers to run a diversified firm with different business lines.

Notes

1. Re-insurance is also used for other reasons. First, it can be used to increase an insurer's underwriting capacity. It enables the insurer to pass on part of the risk. Second, it can be used to stabilise profits. It enables the insurer to level out the effects of poor loss performance.
2. To assess the overall risk profile of the insurance company, correlations across risk types should be taken into account, but incorporating diversification effects between risk types is still in the embryonic stage of development (Van Lelyveld, 2006).
3. In addition to interest rate risk, bonds are subject to credit risk. The credit risk of government bonds issued by developed countries is typically very low, while the credit risk of corporate bonds is usually higher.

Suggested Reading

Dionne, G. (ed.) (2000), *Handbook of Insurance*, Kluwer, Dordrecht.

Drzik, J. (2005), At the Crossroads of Change: Risk and Capital Management in the Insurance Industry, *The Geneva Papers on Risk and Insurance – Issues and Practice*, **30**, 72–87.

Mikosch, T. (2004), *Non-Life Insurance Mathematics: An Introduction with Stochastic Processes*, Springer-Verlag, Berlin.

Rees, R. (2008), Insurance and Re-insurance Companies, in: X. Freixas, P. Hartmann, and C. Mayer (eds.), *Handbook of European Financial Markets and Institutions*, Oxford University Press, 414–435.

Van Lelyveld, I. and K. Knot (2009), Do Financial Conglomerates Create or Destroy Value? Evidence for the EU, *Journal of Banking and Finance*, **33**, 2312–2321.

References

Association des Assureurs Coopératifs et Mutualistes Européens (2003), *Valuing Mutuality II*, ACME, Brussels.

Comité Européen des Assurances (2007), *European Insurance in Figures, CEA Statistics*, No. 31, CEA, Brussels.

Dimson, E., P. Marsh, and M. Staunton (2002), *Triumph of the Optimists: 101 Years of Global Investment Returns*, Princeton University Press.

Drzik, J. (2005), At the Crossroads of Change: Risk and Capital Management in the Insurance Industry, *The Geneva Papers on Risk and Insurance – Issues and Practice*, **30**, 72–87.

Embrechts, P., C. Klüppelberg, and T. Mikosch (1997), *Modelling Extremal Events for Insurance and Finance*, Springer, Heidelberg.

European Central Bank (2014), *Financial Stability Review*, May, ECB, Frankfurt am Main.

European Commission (2007), *Business Insurance Sector Inquiry: Interim Report*, EC, Brussels.

European Insurance and Occupational Pensions Supervisors Authority (2013a), *Statistical Annex 2005–2012*, EIOPA, Frankfurt am Main.

European Insurance and Occupational Pensions Supervisors Authority (2013b), *Discussion Paper on Standard Formula Design and Calibration for Certain Long-Term Investments*, EIOPA, Frankfurt am Main.

Focarelli, D. and A. F. Pozzolo (2008), Cross-Border M&As in the Financial Sector: Is Banking Different from Insurance?, *Journal of Banking and Finance*, **32**, 15–29.

Insurance Europe (2014), *European Insurance in Figures*, Insurance Europe, Brussels.

Kessler, D. (2008), Insurance Market Mechanisms and Government Interventions, *Journal of Banking and Finance*, **32**, 4–14.

Kohn, M. (2004), *Financial Institutions and Markets*, 2nd edition, Oxford University Press.

Kuritzkes, A., T. Schuermann, and S. Weiner (2003), Risk Measurement, Risk Management, and Capital Adequacy in Financial Conglomerates, in: R. Herring and R. Litan (eds.), *Brookings-Wharton Papers on Financial Services: 2003*, Brookings Institution, Washington DC, 141–193.

Laeven, L. and R. Levine (2007), Is There a Diversification Discount in Financial Conglomerates?, *Journal of Financial Economics*, **85**, 331–367.

Loubergé, H. (2000), Developments in Risk and Insurance Economics: The Past 25 Years, in G. Dionne (ed.), *Handbook of Insurance*, Kluwer, Dordrecht, 3–33.

Mikosch, T. (2004), *Non-Life Insurance Mathematics: An Introduction with Stochastic Processes*, Springer-Verlag, Berlin.

Niehaus, G. and A. Terry (1993), Evidence on the Time Series Properties of Insurance Premiums and Causes of the Underwriting Cycle, *Journal of Risk and Insurance*, **60**, 466–479.

Oliver, Wyman and Company (2001), *Study on the Risk Profile and Capital Adequacy of Financial Conglomerates*, Oliver, Wyman and Company, London.

Plantin, G. and J.-C. Rochet (2007), *When Insurers Go Bust: An Economic Analysis of the Role and Design of Prudential Regulation*, Princeton University Press.

Rejda, G. E. (2005), *Principles of Risk Management and Insurance*, 9th edition, Addison Wesley, Boston.

Rothschild, M. and J. Stiglitz (1976), Equilibrium in Competitive Insurance Markets: An Essay on the Economics of Imperfect Information, *Quarterly Journal of Economics*, **90**, 629–649.

Schmid, M. M. and I. Walter (2009), Do Financial Conglomerates Create or Destroy Economic Value?, *Journal of Financial Intermediation*, **18**, 193–216.

Schoenmaker, D. and C. van Laecke (2006), *Current State of Cross-Border Banking, FMG Special Papers 168*, London School of Economics, London.

Schoenmaker, D., S. Oosterloo, and O. Winkels (2008), The Emergence of Cross-Border Insurance Groups within Europe with Centralised Risk Management, *Geneva Papers on Risk and Insurance – Issues and Practice*, **33**, 530–546.

Schoenmaker, D. and J. Sass (2014), Cross-border Insurance in Europe, Duisenberg School of Finance Policy Paper 45.

Slijkerman, J. F., D. Schoenmaker, and C. G. de Vries (2013), Systemic Risk and Diversification across Banks and Insurers, *Journal of Banking and Finance*, **37**, 773–785.

Spencer, P. D. (2000), *The Structure and Regulation of Financial Markets*, Oxford University Press.

Swiss Re (1998), *Floods – An Insurable Risk? A Market Survey*, Swiss Re, Zurich.

(2007), Bancassurance: Emerging Trends, Opportunities and Challenges, *Sigma*, 5.

(2014), Natural Catastrophes and Man-Made Disasters in 2013, *Sigma*, 1.

Van Lelyveld, I. (ed.) (2006), *Economic Capital Modelling: Concepts, Measurement and Implementation*, Risk Books, London.

Van Lelyveld, I. and K. Knot (2009), Do Financial Conglomerates Create or Destroy Value? Evidence for the EU, *Journal of Banking and Finance*, **33**, 2312–2321.

Von Bomhard, N. (2005), Risk and Capital Management in Insurance Companies, *The Geneva Papers on Risk and Insurance – Issues and Practice*, **30**, 52–59.

Weiss, G. and J. Mühlnickel (2014), Why Do Some Insurers Become Systemically Relevant?, *Journal of Financial Stability*, **13**, 95–117.

Part IV

Policies for the Financial Sector

CHAPTER

12

Financial Regulation and Supervision

OVERVIEW

This chapter reviews the reasons for regulation and supervision of financial services. Regulation refers to the process of rule making and the legislation underlying the supervisory framework, while supervision refers to monitoring the behaviour of individual firms and enforcing legislation. The case for government intervention is based on market failures. A first market failure is rooted in asymmetric information: financial institutions are generally better informed than their customers. A second market failure is externalities: the failure of a financial institution may affect the stability of the financial system as a whole. A third market failure occurs when certain players in the market exert undue market power.

The chapter discusses financial supervision in more detail, distinguishing between prudential supervision and conduct-of-business supervision. Prudential supervision aims to protect consumers by ensuring the safety and soundness of financial institutions. Conduct-of-business supervision focuses on how financial institutions deal with their customers and how financial institutions behave in markets. For instance, information provisions aim to ensure that consumers get the right information about financial products. In addition, there are guidelines for objective and high-quality advice to protect the interests of customers. Conduct-of-business rules also promote fair and orderly markets.

This chapter also discusses the organisational structure of financial supervision, which is changing as most EU countries are moving from the traditional sector model (with separate banking, securities, and insurance supervisors) towards cross-sector models.

Finally, this chapter discusses financial supervision in the EU. It is questionable whether national-based supervision is an adequate arrangement in an integrating market. The new European supervisory structure and the Banking Union are explained, followed by a discussion of several challenges that supervisors face.

LEARNING OBJECTIVES

After you have studied this chapter, you should be able to:

- explain the main market failures in the financial system and the role of government intervention to remedy these failures
- understand the aims and instruments of prudential supervision
- understand the aims and instruments of conduct-of-business supervision
- describe the various supervisory structures
- understand the Banking Union and the need for European financial supervision in an integrated financial market.

12.1 Rationale for government intervention

Market failure

This section reviews the reasons for regulation and supervision of financial services. Regulation refers to the process of rule making and the legislation underlying the supervisory framework, while supervision refers to monitoring the behaviour of individual firms and enforcing legislation. The case for government intervention is based on market failures. A *market failure* occurs when the private sector if left to itself (i.e. without government intervention) would produce a sub-optimal outcome. Goodhart *et al.* (1998) identify three main reasons for government intervention in the financial sector:

1. *Asymmetric information*: customers are less informed than financial institutions. Financial supervision aims to protect customers against this information asymmetry. This chapter analyses how this can be done.
2. *Externalities*: the failure of a financial institution may affect the stability of the financial system. Systemic supervision aims to foster financial stability and to contain the effects of systemic failure. Chapter 13 discusses policies aimed at maintaining financial stability.
3. *Market power*: financial institutions or financial infrastructures, such as payment systems, may exert undue market power. Competition policy aims to protect consumers against monopolistic exploitation. Chapter 14 examines this topic.

Asymmetric information arises in two cases. First, customers are generally unable to properly assess the safety and soundness of a financial institution, because that requires extensive effort and technical knowledge. Establishing some sort of oversight may be needed, as financial institutions have an incentive to take too much risk. This is because high-risk investments generally bring in more revenues that accrue to the institution, while in case of failure a substantial part of the losses will be borne by the depositors. The information asymmetry creates problems of adverse selection (a riskier financial institution may make a more attractive offer to potential customers) as well as moral hazard (a financial institution may increase its risk after it has collected funds from customers). Prudential supervision aims to protect customers by ensuring the soundness of financial institutions. Moreover, governments provide direct protection to depositors through deposit guarantee schemes with a cover of €100,000 in the EU (see Chapter 3). However, a government safety net may provide banks with an even stronger incentive for risky behaviour. Prudential supervision is thus also needed to counter this incentive by ensuring the banks' soundness (Mishkin, 2000). Section 12.2 discusses prudential supervision in more detail.

Second, customers may not be in a position to assess properly the behaviour of a financial institution. This problem is common in professional services (Goodhart *et al.*, 1998). In most cases, private-sector mechanisms are used to mitigate this principal-agent problem. A disciplinary body of a privately run medical association can, for example, expel a member when it finds that this member has (repeatedly) failed to meet the minimum standards of the medical profession. Why, then, is government supervision of financial services needed? An important explanation draws on the fiduciary nature of financial services. A customer hands over his money today, while the service is rendered in the (sometimes far) future. For example, only after retirement does it become clear whether the advised pension savings scheme is appropriate to meet the financial needs of the retirees. Moreover, the amount of money at risk is typically larger in financial services than in other professional services. Conduct-of-business supervision focuses on how financial institutions conduct business with their customers and how they behave in markets. Section 12.3 discusses conduct-of-business rules to mitigate the behaviour of financial institutions.

The second market failure that may give rise to government regulation is externalities. There is a risk that a sound financial institution may fail when another financial institution goes bankrupt (spillover effects). This externality is not incorporated in the decision making of the financial institution. The social costs of the failure of a financial institution thus exceed the private costs. In particular, banks are subject to spillover effects as their balance sheet contains illiquid assets financed by redeemable deposits. When rumours about the quality of a bank's assets spread, depositors may withdraw their deposits. The liquidity and subsequently the solvency of a bank will be threatened when it has to liquidate its assets at fire sale prices (i.e. prices well below prices under normal market conditions). The failure of multiple banks may lead to a banking crisis. Macroprudential supervision aims to foster financial stability and to contain the effects of systemic failure. The task of maintaining financial stability is usually assigned to a country's central bank. Chapter 13 explains in more detail why the financial system (and especially the banking sector) is more susceptible to systemic risk than other economic sectors and discusses the role of the central bank to contain systemic risk.

The third market failure is related to market power. In a monopoly (only one firm) or an oligopoly (a few firms which may collude), firms can raise and maintain prices above the level that would prevail under (perfect) competition. The exercise of market power by firms is to the detriment of consumers who face higher prices and less choice of products or services. Lack of competition occurs in many economic sectors. In the financial sector, economies of scale (incentive for mergers) and network economies (e.g. in payment systems, see Chapter 7) or stock exchanges (see Chapter 5)) may reduce competition. Competition policy aims to ensure effective competition by taking a strong line against price fixing, market-sharing cartels, abuse of dominant market positions, and anti-competitive mergers. Chapter 14 explains the EU competition policy for the financial sector.

Government failure

Government failure is the public sector analogy to market failure and occurs when government intervention causes a less efficient allocation of goods and resources than would occur without that intervention. There is thus a need to weigh problems of government failure against those due to market failure (Besley, 2007). There are various consequences of government intervention. First, government-induced protection may have a detrimental impact on incentives for consumers. Why should consumers be careful if they are protected against possible negative outcomes of their actions? Second, government regulation may lead to bureaucracy ('red tape') restricting the activities of financial institutions. Moreover, as supervisory agencies need information they generally have a more or less elaborate system of supervisory reporting in place which puts an administrative burden on the sector.

Some academics consider government failure a bigger problem than market failure. For instance, adherents of free banking challenge the justification for any form of government regulation of the financial system, arguing that there is nothing special about financial services that should make this sector an exception to the general rule of free trade (see, for instance, Dowd, 1996). In their view, a policy of *laissez-faire* for the financial sector is optimal as government intervention undermines the market forces that make the financial system safe. Other academics favour limited government intervention. For instance, Benston and Kaufman (1996) argue for some minimum prudential standards (in particular capital requirements) to counter externalities, but beyond these standards there is no special need for protection of customers. However, most academics and policy makers consider independence of financial supervisors a more adequate response to minimise distortive political interventions (see Box 12.1)

Box 12.1 Supervisory independence

According to Quintyn and Taylor (2003), in almost all of the systemic financial sector crises of the 1990s, political interference in the supervisory process was a major factor contributing to the weakening of banks in the run-up to the crisis. There are several reasons why independence of supervisors from political interference may be beneficial for maintaining financial stability. Independence may help to overcome an *inaction bias*. As pointed out by Quintyn and Taylor (2003), the incentives for politicians to rescue failing banks are similar to those for inaction in the face of inflation. The decision to close a failing bank is usually unpopular as costs must be incurred in the short term in order to make long-term gains, which makes forbearance an attractive option (see Box 12.2). Another explanation for the inaction bias is uncertainty, which causes a tendency for policy makers to prefer to make a type-1 mistake (in other words, incorrectly assuming that things will work out well) than a type-2 mistake (incorrectly assuming that things will go wrong). Furthermore, politicians eager to avoid a necessary closure may therefore be tempted to pressure supervisors to organise a bailout or to excuse the failing bank from regulatory requirements, even at the risk of worsening the problem and increasing the long-term costs of resolving it.

Another reason why independence of the financial supervisor may be beneficial is that there are multiple values and interests at stake in financial market regulation. Politicians may, for instance, want to boost the position of the national financial industry, pressuring the supervisor for a lenient approach towards national financial firms (Pagliari, 2012).

Box 12.1 (cont.)

Essentially this argument in favour of supervisory independence is comparable to that relating to monetary decisions. The independent status is important as a means of ensuring that the authority is at all times able to take the required action. However, there is also the risk that an independent agency might pursue an agenda of its own, going against the wishes of the political majority. This points to the need for proper forms of transparency and accountability (see section 12.5).

12.2 Microprudential supervision

For a long time, the regulatory system in the EU was based on the principle of home-country control combined with minimum standards set out in directives and mutual recognition. Directives are addressed to national authorities, which must subsequently take action to implement them in national legislation (see Chapter 3). This gives rise to national interpretations and the use of national discretion, which hinders full regulatory harmonisation. The increased use of regulations, which are directly applicable across the EU, aims to address such inconsistencies and deliver a single set of harmonised prudential rules which institutions throughout the EU must respect. This is generally referred to as the Single Rulebook.

Within the EU, a financial institution is authorised and supervised in its home country and can expand throughout the EU by offering cross-border services in other EU Member States or establishing branches in these countries without additional supervision by host-country authorities (*home-country control*). The host country has to recognise supervision from the home-country authorities (*mutual recognition*), as minimum requirements for prudential supervision have been laid down in the respective EU Directives (*minimum standards*). However, financial institutions also operate through subsidiaries (separate legal entities) in other countries for reasons of taxation and limited liability (Dermine, 2006). These subsidiaries are separately licensed and supervised by the host-country authorities. Within the Banking Union, the ECB is responsible for granting and, where necessary, withdrawing the authorisation of credit institutions.

According to Lastra (2006), *microprudential supervision* can be understood as a process with four stages:

1. Licensing, authorisation, or chartering of financial institutions (i.e. the entry into the business). The objective of this stage is to establish whether a person is fit and proper, i.e. before a person may obtain a licence, supervisors determine a person's integrity, honesty, reputation, and capability to manage a financial services provider. In this respect, the Basel core principles for effective banking supervision state that 'the licensing process at a minimum should consist of an assessment of the ownership structure and governance of the bank and its wider group, including the fitness and propriety of Board Members and senior management, its strategic and operating plan, internal controls and risk management, and its projected financial condition, including its capital base' (BIS, 2006).
2. The ongoing monitoring of the health of financial institutions and the financial system, in particular the asset quality, capital adequacy, liquidity, large exposures, management, internal controls, and earnings. Supervision is exercised through a broad range of instruments, including off-site and on-site examinations (or inspections), auditing (internal unpublished audit and external published audits), analysis of statistical requirements, and internal controls. In case of distress in financial institutions, the supervisory authorities have to act. Box 12.2 discusses two different reactions to distress.
3. Sanctioning or imposition of penalties in case of non-compliance with the law, fraud, bad management, or other types of wrongdoing.
4. Crisis management, which comprises lender of last resort, deposit insurance, and insolvency proceedings (see Chapter 13 for an in-depth discussion of crisis management).

Box 12.2 Forbearance versus prompt corrective action

Once a supervisory authority finds out that a financial institution is in distress there are two possible ways to react. The supervisor can intervene and resolve the distressed institution by requiring capital injections, the sale of assets, a merger with a sound institution, or liquidation once the regulatory capital ratio falls below a predetermined threshold. Alternatively, the supervisor can choose to allow the distressed financial institution to continue operation even though it is unable to meet the minimum regulatory requirements. The first response is generally called *prompt corrective action* (PCA), while the second type of response is referred to as *forbearance*. PCA has been prescribed in the US in the 1991 Federal Deposit Insurance Corporation Improvement Act (FDICIA). Forbearance may dilute banks' incentives to behave prudently and induce undue liquidity support.

Box 12.2 (cont.)

In view of the emergence of large cross-border banking groups, the European Shadow Financial Regulatory Committee (2005) advocates the implementation of a system of PCA in Europe as well. These procedures would reduce the likelihood of a sudden banking crisis and contribute to host-country supervisors' trust in home-country supervisors.

Nieto and Wall (2007) identify three important aspects of the philosophy underlying PCA: (1) the primary focus of banking supervisory authorities should be on protecting the deposit-insurance fund and minimising government losses; (2) banking supervisors should have a clear set of required actions to be taken as a bank becomes progressively more undercapitalised; and (3) any undercapitalised bank should be closed before the economic value of its capital becomes negative. Moreover, the authors identify several institutional prerequisites for PCA: supervisory independence and accountability, adequate authority, accurate and timely information, and adequate resolution procedures.

According to the BIS (1997), banks face the following key risks (see Chapter 10 for an in-depth discussion):

- *credit risk*: the risk of a loss because of the failure of a counterparty to perform according to a contractual arrangement, for instance due to a default by a borrower;
- *country risk*: the risks associated with the economic, social, and political environments of the borrower's home country;
- *market risk*: the risk due to unfavourable movements in market prices;
- *interest rate risk*: the risk related to unfavourable movements in interest rates. This risk impacts both the earnings of a bank and the economic value of its assets, liabilities, and off-balance sheet instruments;
- *liquidity risk*: this risk arises when a bank has insufficient liquid resources to meet a surge in liquidity demand. In extreme cases, insufficient liquidity can lead to the insolvency of a bank;
- *operational risk*: the risk of loss from inadequate or failed internal processes, people or systems, or from external events;[1]
- *legal risk*: risks stemming from inadequate or incorrect legal advice, changes in laws affecting the bank, new types of transactions, etc.;
- *reputational risk*: this may arise from operational failures, failure to comply with relevant laws and regulations, or other sources. Reputational risk is particularly damaging as confidence is elementary in banking.

Capital and liquidity requirements

In order to cover the risks mentioned above, banks are required to hold a minimum level of own financial resources, i.e. *capital*. These capital requirements serve as a buffer against unexpected losses, thereby protecting depositors and the overall stability of the financial system. The challenge is to determine how much capital banks need to hold in order to ensure that they are sufficiently capitalised.[2] If capital levels are too low, banks may be unable to absorb potential losses.

The Basel Committee on Banking Supervision (BCBS) is the primary global standard-setter for the prudential regulation of banks and provides an international forum for cooperation on banking supervisory matters (see Box 3.5). The Basel standards have subsequently been implemented in European and national legislation. The 1988 Basel I Accord presented the first set of global standards for bank capital adequacy, aimed at establishing a minimum base of own funds in every bank. Basel I required banks to ensure that 8 per cent of the risk-weighted assets on the balance sheet are backed by own funds in order to absorb losses that could not be absorbed by its creditors. The aim of *risk-weighted assets* (RWAs) is to move from a static capital requirement to a requirement based on the riskiness of a bank's asset classes *i*. Risk weights range from 0 per cent for assets that are deemed the 'safest' to a 100 per cent for the riskiest assets. For example, EU authorities allow for a zero risk weight being applied to EU sovereign exposures. The risk-weighted capital ratio (RWCR) is:

$$RWCR = \frac{Capital}{Risk\ Weighted\ Assets} = \frac{Capital}{\sum_{i=1}^{n} Risk\ Weight_i * Asset\ Class_i} \geq 8\% \tag{12.1}$$

Its successor, the Basel II Accord, tried to create a better link between minimum regulatory capital and risk, as well as enhancing market discipline. The Basel II framework has a three-pillar structure:

- The first pillar covers the minimum capital requirements for credit risk, operational risk, and market risk. Unlike the Basel I accord, where capital requirements were specified in detail by supervisors, Basel II allowed banks to use their internal risk-management models for the calculation of the required amount of capital. Because of the use of internal ratings calculated by individual banks, similar capital ratios may reflect a very different risk measurement.
- The second pillar (supervisory review) entails supervisory authorities examining the activities and risk profile of the bank in order to see whether

there is a need for banks to hold additional capital (on top of the level of capital calculated under Pillar 1).

- The third pillar aims at enhancing market discipline by increasing the transparency of the amount and composition of a bank's capital relative to its risk profile, thereby introducing incentives for banks to conduct their business in a safe, sound, and efficient manner.

Despite these efforts, the financial crisis of 2007–2009 revealed serious weaknesses in the way banks had been operating as well as the way in which their operations were regulated and supervised:

(1) Banks held too little capital and the capital they held was of poor quality and in effect not able to cover the losses banks were facing.
(2) Banks were not holding enough liquid funds and so faced a shortage of cash when they needed it most.
(3) Banks took on too many assets compared to their capital (i.e. banks were highly 'leveraged'). When the crisis hit, many of these assets fell in value. When banks tried to sell these assets at the same time, prices fell further and this contributed to making the crisis worse.

Against this background, the Basel Committee developed new international minimum standards on bank capital adequacy (Basel III). Within the EU, Basel III has been implemented through the Capital Requirements Regulation (CRR) and the Capital Requirements Directive IV (CRD IV). This package of legislation, which applies as of 1 January 2014, introduces both capital reforms and new liquidity standards.[3]

CRR/CRD IV aims to increase the quality of eligible capital. The financial crisis showed that in some cases capital was of poor quality and not available to absorb losses as they materialised. A key aspect of CRR/CRD IV is a stricter definition of capital. Capital comes in different forms that serve different purposes. There are two types of capital:

- *Going concern capital*: this allows an institution to continue its activities and helps to prevent insolvency. Tier 1 capital is considered to be the going concern capital. The purest form is Common Equity Tier 1 (CET1) capital.
- *Gone concern capital*: this helps to ensure that depositors and senior creditors can be repaid if the institution fails. This category of capital includes hybrid capital and subordinated debt. Gone concern capital is named Tier 2 capital.

Tier 1 capital is seen as the best form of capital, with CET1 instruments, mainly common shares and retained earnings, being the predominant form of Tier 1 capital. Tier 2 capital is known as supplementary capital. The latter consists of undisclosed reserves, revaluation reserves, general provisions, hybrid instruments, and subordinated debt.

Previously, banks had to hold total capital of at least 8 per cent of RWAs. This percentage has not been changed under CRR/CRD IV. However, the minimum requirement for CET1 capital has been increased from 2 per cent to 4.5 per cent, while total Tier 1 capital should be 6 per cent. Tier 2 capital should be at least 2 per cent. Furthermore, several new buffers have been introduced (see Box 12.3).

Box 12.3 Capital buffers in CRR/CRD IV

Capital conservation buffer

The capital conservation buffer is a capital buffer of 2.5 per cent of total exposures of a bank that needs to be met with an additional amount of the highest quality of capital (i.e. CET1 capital). It sits on top of the 4.5 per cent CET1 capital requirement. As its name indicates, the buffer's objective is to conserve a bank's capital. When a bank breaches the buffer, i.e. when its CET1 capital ratio falls below 7 per cent, automatic safeguards kick in and limit the amount of dividend and bonus payments a bank can make. The further the bank 'eats' into the buffer, the stricter the limits become. This prevents the bank's capital from being further eroded by such payments.

Countercyclical buffer

The purpose of the countercyclical buffer is to counteract the effects of the economic cycle on banks' lending activity, thus making the supply of credit less volatile and possibly even reduce the probability of credit bubbles or crunches. In good times, i.e. where an economy is booming and credit growth is strong, it requires a bank to have an additional amount of CET1 capital between 0 and 2.5 per cent. This prevents the credit from becoming too cheap so that banks lend too much. If a bank does not have enough capital to fill this buffer, the same restrictions as in the case of the capital conservation buffer kick in. When the economic cycle turns, and economic activity slows down or even contracts, this buffer can be 'released' (i.e. the bank is no longer required to have the additional capital). This allows the bank to keep lending to the real economy or at least reduce its lending by less than would otherwise be the case.

Box 12.3 (cont.)

Global systemic institution buffer

CRD IV includes a mandatory systemic risk buffer of CET1 capital for banks that are identified by the relevant authority as globally systemically important. The identification criteria and the allocation into categories of systemic importance are in conformity with the G-20 agreed G-SIFI criteria and include size, cross border activities, and interconnectedness (see Chapters 10 and 13). The mandatory surcharge will be between 1 and 3.5 per cent CET1 of RWAs, will need to be met with CET1 capital, and will apply from 1 January 2016 onwards.

Other systemically important institutions buffer

CRD IV provides for a supervisory option for a buffer on 'other' systemically important institutions (O-SIIs). This includes domestically important institutions as well as EU-important institutions. In order to prevent adverse impacts on the internal market there is framing in the form of the criteria used to identify O-SIIs, a notification/justification procedure, and an upper limit to the size of the buffer (2 per cent of RWAs).

Systemic risk buffer

Each Member State may introduce a Systemic Risk Buffer of CET1 for the financial sector or one or more subsets of the sector, in order to prevent and mitigate long-term non-cyclical systemic or macro-prudential risks with the potential of serious negative consequences to the financial system and the real economy in a specific Member State. From 2015 onwards and for buffer rates between 3 and 5 per cent the Member States setting the buffer will have to notify the European Commission, the EBA (see below), and the ESRB (see Chapter 13). The Commission will provide an opinion on the measure decided and if this opinion is negative, the Member States will have to 'comply or explain'. Buffer rates above 5 per cent will need to be authorised by the Commission through an implementing act, taking into account the opinions provided by the ESRB and by the EBA.

Source: European Commission (2013)

In addition, a minimum *leverage ratio*, i.e. the ratio between a bank's non-risk-weigthed assets and its Tier 1 capital, has been introduced as a supplementary measure to the risk-based framework of Basel II. The leverage ratio (LR) is defined as follows:

$$LR = \frac{Tier\ 1\ capital}{Total\ Assets} = \frac{Tier\ 1\ capital}{\sum_{i=1}^{n} Asset\ Class_i} \geq 3\% \tag{12.2}$$

The leverage ratio is intended to be a hard backstop against the risk-based capital requirements (Equation 12.1) and is also designed to constrain excess leverage, which was common among many banks before the crisis. The capital measure is made up of Tier 1 capital and is currently set at a minimum of 3 per cent. It was, however, agreed that data and experience must be gathered before an effective leverage ratio can be introduced as a binding requirement in each jurisdiction.

Figure 12.1 presents an overview of the new capital framework, including the new capital buffers.

Basle III also introduced two new liquidity measures:

- The Liquidity Coverage Ratio (LCR), which requires banks to have enough cash (or cash equivalent securities) to meet net cash outflows over a short (30-day) period of acute stress. The LCR is defined as follows:

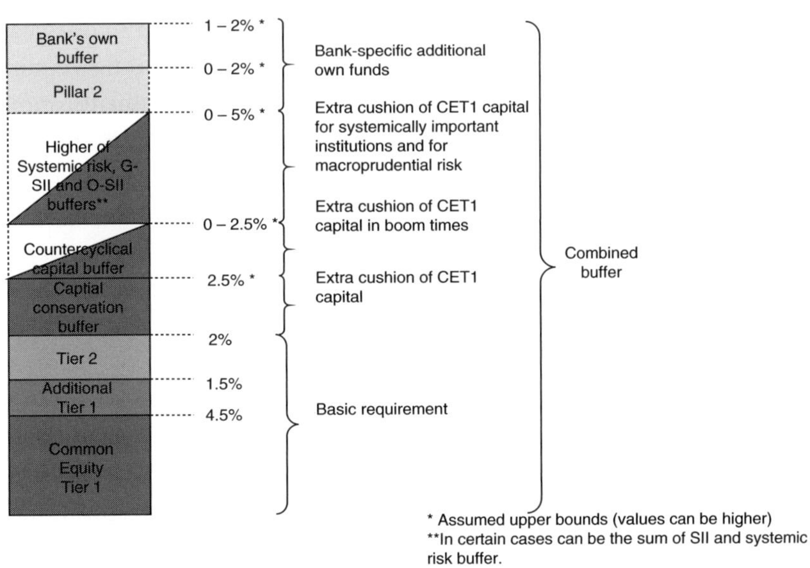

Figure 12.1 CCR/CRD IV capital framework
Source: European Commission (2013)

$$LCR = \frac{High\ quality\ liquid\ assets}{Total\ net\ cash\ outflows\ over\ 30\text{-}day\ period} \geq 100\% \qquad (12.3)$$

The LCR aims to ensure that sufficient high-quality liquid assets (HQLA) are available so that a bank can survive for one month in case of a stress scenario. Assets are considered to be HQLA if they can be easily and immediately converted into cash at little or no loss of value. This requires that an asset is considered relatively safe and there is low correlation with risky assets. Moreover, the market for these assets should be well developed and sizable, and prices should be relatively stable. Depending on the precise characteristics of HQLA, these assets are divided into Level 1 and Level 2 assets. Level 1 assets can be included without limit, while Level 2 assets can only comprise 40 per cent of the stock. In order to take account of possible liquidity impediments, Level 2 assets are subject to haircuts.

- The Net Stable Funding Ratio (NSFR), which requires banks to have sufficient available stable funding (ASF) which can support operations over at least a one-year period of less severe stress. The NSFR is defined as follows:

$$NSFR = \frac{Available\ stable\ funding\ over\ 1\ year\ period}{Required\ stable\ funding\ over\ 1\ year\ period} \geq 100\% \qquad (12.4)$$

ASF is funding on which banks can rely for a period of one year or longer. An example is Tier 1 and Tier 2 capital. The funding requirement of a specific asset is determined by its marketability, maturity, and duration of encumbrance. The NSFR aims to limit over-reliance on short-term wholesale funding during times of buoyant market liquidity and encourage better assessment of liquidity risk across all on- and off-balance sheet items.

The LCR will be phased-in, with full implementation in 2018. However, Member States may require LCR levels up to 100 per cent before the LCR is fully introduced in 2018.

In a stressed situation, a financial institution may be forced to make use of its liquid assets so that its LCR ratio falls below the required level. Under the Regulation, this institution is then required to immediately notify the supervisory authorities and submit a plan for the timely restoration of the LCR ratio to the required level.

The NSFR is not yet included in EU legislation. The European Commission will prepare a legislative proposal by 31 December 2016. The

CRR however already establishes the general rule that institutions shall ensure that long-term obligations are adequately met with a diversity of stable funding requirements under both normal and stressed conditions.

In Europe, a somewhat similar system for regulatory capital has been introduced for insurance companies as well. The so-called Solvency II Directive (2009/138/EC) establishes (more) sophisticated solvency requirements for insurers, in order to guarantee that they have sufficient capital to withstand adverse events, such as floods, storms, or major catastrophes. This will help to increase their financial soundness. The Solvency II Directive draws on the experiences from banking and follows the three-pillar approach of the Capital Requirements Directive (see Box 11.5).

Basel III criticism

Critics argue that Basel III has two major flaws (Admati and Hellwig, 2013). First, its equity requirements are considered too low. The appropriate level of equity depends on the ability of the banking system to absorb losses under stress, while continuing critical banking functions. Second, for the most part the required equity is related not to a bank's total assets, but to the RWAs. However, it can make quite a difference whether the minimum capital requirements relate to the total assets of a bank or to its RWAs. For example, the roughly €55 billion in equity that Deutsche Bank had on its reported balance sheet at the start of 2011 represented more than 14 per cent of the bank's RWAs of €381 billion, but only 2.5 per cent of the bank's total assets of €2.2 trillion. Figure 12.2 shows the evolution of average risk weights over time: for major global firms, the average risk weights fell almost continuously from 70 per cent in 1993 to below 40 per cent at the start of 2008. The financial crisis made it painfully clear that the pre-crisis fall in average risk weights did not represent a systematic reduction in risk within the banking system. As a result, some regulators, banks, and market participants have expressed doubts about the complexity, adequacy, consistency, transparency, and comparability of risk-weighted capital (Le Leslé and Avramova, 2012 and Haldane, 2012).

The idea behind risk weighting is that if the assets which a bank holds are less risky, less equity may be needed for the bank to absorb potential losses. Within the process of calculating RWAs banks are allowed to use their own internal measures for key drivers of risk and determine their own estimates of probabilities of default. According to some, this leads to an underestimation of risk, as banks try to maximise their *return on equity* (ROE) by managing their RWAs down, for example, by concentrating on investments that are treated as

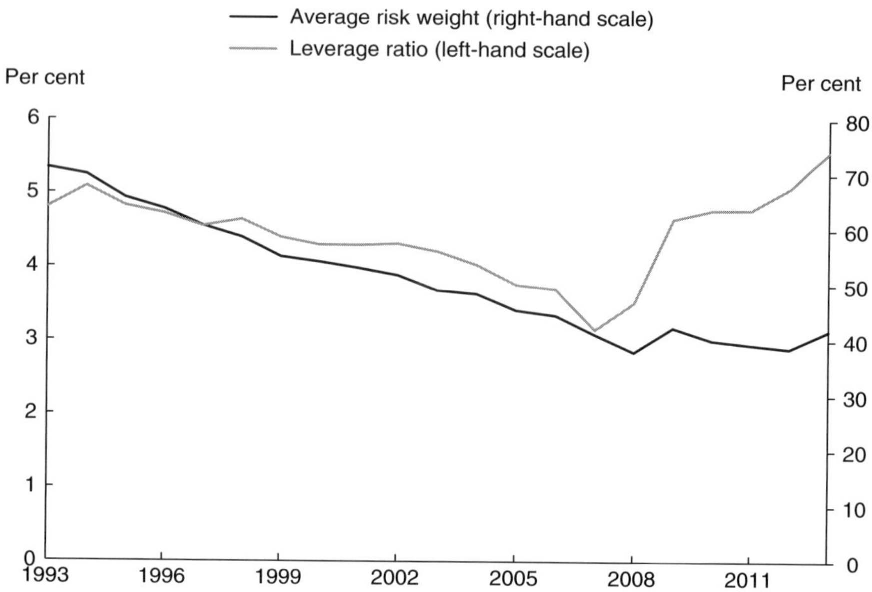

Figure 12.2 Average risk weights and leverage ratio of large banks
Source: Bank of England (2014). The sample includes Bank of America, Barclays, BNP Paribas, BNY Mellon, Citigroup, Commerzbank, Deutsche Bank, HSBC, ING, JPM, LBG, RBS, Santander, State Street, UBS, UniCredit, and Wells Fargo.

safe, such as sovereign exposures (see below), or by using derivatives to shift risks off their balance sheet. It is also argued that RWAs are subjective and vary from one bank to the other, thereby making it difficult to compare capital ratios. The new Basel III leverage ratio can serve as an important backstop to risk-based ratios. Figure 12.2 shows that after a gradual, but persistent, decline from 1993 to 2007, the leverage ratio increased after the crisis from 3.1 per cent in 2007 to 5.5 per cent in 2013. As such, the leverage ratio is particularly suited to providing greater resilience against events which are not foreseeable by risk models and not foreseen by stress tests. In stress tests, the implications for banks' financial position under several macroeconomic scenarios are examined, taking the banks' exposures and business model into account. While it has been argued that the leverage ratio sometimes performs better at predicting failure than risk-weighted capital ratios, it is clear that some banks that failed during the financial crisis were not highly leveraged. Moreover, the leverage ratio in itself creates incentives to invest in high-risk assets, as the capital requirement for low- and high-risk assets is the same. It is therefore argued that capital adequacy assessment should rely on a combination of capital metrics (Le Leslé and Avramova, 2012).

A related issue is the regulatory treatment of sovereign exposures. Within the Basel III framework, the status of sovereign exposures as the lowest-risk assets has been maintained and the EU legislative framework provides for risk weights of zero for EU sovereign exposures. However, the euro crisis has shown that sovereign exposures can carry significant risk (see Chapter 2), which could lead to a more critical stance with respect to the adequacy of the regulatory framework on sovereign risks. In addition to risk weights, limits on large exposures could be useful to contain the risk of sovereign debt for a bank, as some banks tend to invest heavily in sovereign bonds of their home country.

12.3 Conduct-of-business supervision

Conduct-of-business supervision focuses on how financial institutions conduct business with their customers and how they behave in markets, by prescribing rules about appropriate behaviour and monitoring behaviour that can be harmful to customers and to the functioning of markets. It is a relatively new activity, which became prominent after the liberalisation of financial markets. In the Big Bang in 1986, fixed commissions for trading at the London Stock Exchange were abolished. The Big Bang was the start of a process of liberalising financial markets across Europe. Liberalisation promotes entry of new players and may thereby lead to a wider choice of products and services (at lower prices). Conduct-of-business rules ensure a fair treatment of, in particular, retail customers in these liberalised markets.

The focus of conduct-of-business regulation is on the activities of financial institutions. The dividing lines between the sub-sectors of banking, insurance, and securities are blurring; the same type of product is increasingly offered by different financial institutions. Merton (1995) proposes a functional approach towards regulation to prevent regulatory arbitrage between different types of financial institutions. So, in his view the same conduct-of-business rules should apply to whoever (a bank, an insurer, or an investment firm) is offering, for example, long-term savings products to retail customers.

Protecting retail customers

Conduct-of-business rules protecting retail customers comprise the following elements (Llewellyn, 1999):[4]

- mandatory information provisions;
- objective and high-quality advice;
- duty of care.

Mandatory information provisions ensure that customers get the right information at the right time. Selecting an inappropriate product can have adverse consequences for retail customers and an important safeguard against this is proper disclosure and sufficient information (*transparency*). Good information helps customers to understand the key features of a financial product, including the risks, potential returns, and costs. Mandatory information provisions specify the (minimum) information needed to understand products. These provisions also require financial institutions to present this information in a consistent format to compare products.

Developing customers' literacy in financial matters is becoming increasingly important, as individuals take many decisions affecting their financial security and capital markets have become more accessible to consumers. The European Commission (2007) reports that international surveys demonstrate a low level of understanding of financial matters on the part of customers. There is a strong correlation between low levels of financial literacy and the ability to make appropriate financial decisions. Customers with poor financial literacy find it hard to understand and make use of the information they receive when purchasing financial services.

Conduct-of-business rules can also give guidelines for the quality and objectivity of advice. Providing advice is distinct from providing information. Whilst information merely describes the (essential) characteristics of a product or service, *advice* implies a recommendation to a given customer to opt for a specific product. A financial institution must take steps to ensure that a recommendation is suitable for its customer. This can, for example, be done by making a customer's profile containing information about the customer's knowledge and experience relevant to the specific type of financial product, financial situation, and investment objectives. When advice is given, it should be objective, based on the profile of the customer, and commensurate with the complexity of the products and the risks involved. The requirement of objectivity aims to minimise potential conflicts of interests when financial institutions are better informed than customers. Customers in some countries rely on independent advice to make appropriate decisions.

More generally, financial institutions have a duty of care towards their customers. A *duty of care* is an obligation imposed on financial institutions requiring that they adhere to a reasonable standard of care while dealing with customers. It aims to enhance responsible behaviour of financial institutions. A financial institution breaches its duty of care when it sells, for example, a high-risk investment product to a customer who cannot afford to bear the financial risk (e.g. a low-income household with limited savings). Figure 12.3

TYPE OF PRODUCT	COUNTRY
Highly (and increasingly) complex products, such as structured products	Belgium, Denmark, Estonia, Germany, Italy, Latve, Spain
Complex hedging products designed to protect borrowers on flexible rate mortagages	Latvia, Spain
Self-certified and interest only mortgages	UK
Mortgage insurance products	Poland
Loans to individuals that are exposed to exchange rate risks, the extent of which is often unknown to the consumer	France, Hungary
Unregulated collective investment schemes, which invest in assets that are not always traded in established markets are therefore difficult to value. They may be highly illiquid, and have risks to capital that are generally opaque	UK, Germany
Units in funds based on hedging strategies	Belgium
Product wrapping which prevents consumers from comparing features, prices and charges and thus from making well-informed investment decisions	Finland
Banks placing financial instruments such as hybrid products with their own retail clients, where the risks were in some cases not disclosed of sufficiently explained and some consumers claim that they were given the impression that the investment was a protected deposit	Spain, UK
Insurance products linked to complex underlying structures	France
Expensive and opaque unit-linked insurance and pension products	Netherlands

Figure 12.3 Retail misselling of financial products across the EU
Source: European Commission (2014b)

provides an overview of actual or suspected misselling to retail customers provided by the European Commission (2014b).

To sum up, on the one hand conduct-of-business rules require proper information provision (transparency) to (potential) customers. This should enable customers to take better decisions. On the other hand conduct-of-business rules set minimum standards for advice and introduce a duty of care for financial institutions. The challenge for policy makers is to find the right balance between empowering customers by providing information and education (fostering financial literacy) and protecting customers by setting minimum standards for financial institutions' behaviour.

Since conduct-of-business rules are relatively new, they are not (yet) applied to all financial activities at the level of the EU. Until recently, rules for consumer credit and mortgage credit were largely left to the national authorities. The Directive on Consumer Credit (2008/48/ EC) focuses on transparency and consumer rights. It provides for a comprehensible set of information to be given to consumers before the contract is concluded and also as part of the credit agreement. In order to enhance the comparability of different offers and to make the information better understandable, the pre-contractual information needs to be supplied in a standardised form, e.g. using the Annual Percentage Rate of Charge, which is a single figure, harmonised at EU level, representing the cost of the credit.

In the insurance markets, intermediaries play a vital role in selling insurance products. They also play a role in protecting the interests of insurance customers, primarily by offering them advice and assistance and by analysing their specific needs. At the same time, insurance intermediaries face incentives to sell products on which they earn a high commission, while these products are not always suitable for the customer. The Insurance Mediation Directive (2002/92/EC) contains rules to ensure a high level of professionalism and competence among insurance intermediaries whilst guaranteeing a high level of protection of customers' interests. In 2012 the Commission adopted a proposal for a revision of the Insurance Mediation Directive (IMD 2). The goal of the Commission's proposal is to upgrade consumer protection in the insurance sector by creating common standards across insurance sales and ensuring proper advice.

EU rules are most advanced in the field of securities. The Markets in Financial Instruments Directive (MiFID; 2004/39/EC), which replaced the Investment Services Directive (93/22/EEC), comprises a comprehensive set of operating conditions applicable to both banks and investment firms that regulates the relationship between these firms and their clients. This framework consists of a set of conduct-of-business, best-execution, and client-order-handling rules, as well as inducements and conflicts-of-interest provisions. Specific attention is paid to retail clients for whom a specific regime has been established, which entails reinforced fiduciary duties upon the firm. As of January 2017 the Directive on Markets in Financial Instruments repealing Directive 2004/39/EC (MiFID II; 2014/65/EU) and the Regulation on Markets in Financial Instruments (MiFIR; 600/2014/EU) will apply. With respect to the protection of retail investors, investment firms

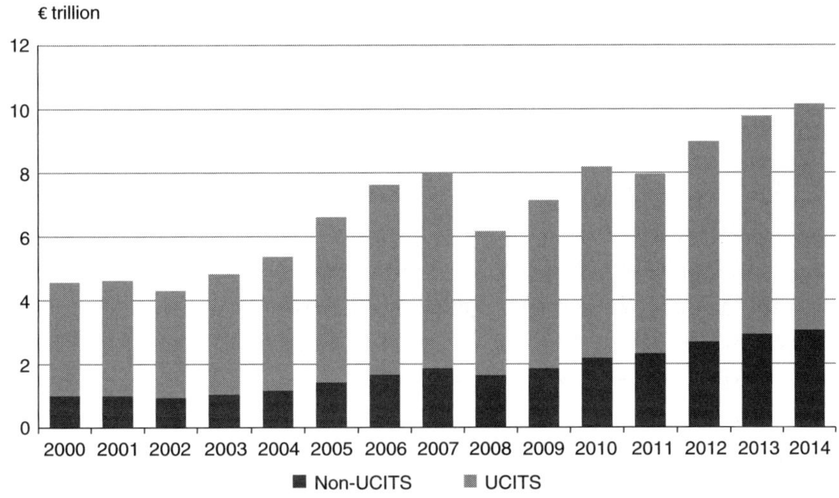

Figure 12.4 Assets of European investment funds (€trillion), 2000–2014
Source: European Fund and Asset Management Association

will have to meet stricter standards to ensure that investors can trust that they are being offered products which are suitable to them and that their assets are well protected. Investors will also be able to rely on independent and neutral advice and fee and remuneration structures must not conflict with this requirement.

Another set of EU rules in the investment-services field is contained in the Undertakings for Collective Investments in Transferable Securities Directive (2009/65/EC). This Directive allows Undertakings for Collective Investments in Transferable Securities (UCITS) to operate freely throughout the EU on the basis of a single authorisation. A collective investment fund may apply for UCITS status in order to allow EU-wide marketing. Figure 12.4 illustrates that the vast majority of European investment funds are operating under a UCITS licence. In 2014, investments in UCITS amounted to €7 trillion, while non-UCITS totalled €3 trillion. In 2009 the European Commission completed a programme of improvements to the earlier UCITS Directive of 2001. These improvements aim at establishing a new standardised and harmonised disclosure document designed to empower investors to take more effective investment decisions as well as strengthening the rules for the conduct of UCITS management companies, including the prevention, management, and disclosure of conflicts of interest. In 2014 Directive 2014/91/EU was adopted, amending Directive 2009/65/EC. This new directive introduces new rules on UCITS depositaries, such as the entities eligible to assume this role, their tasks, delegation arrangements, and the depositaries' liability as well as general remuneration principles that apply to fund managers.

Market functioning

Conduct-of-business regulation promoting fair and orderly markets contains the following elements:

- transparency of trading;
- prohibition of insider trading and market manipulation;
- information requirements for issuers, including prospectus and financial reporting, and for shareholders.

Rules on the *transparency of trading* require disclosure of quotes, i.e. prices at which traders are prepared to sell or buy securities, and of prices at which trades have taken place. Potential investors can only analyse and compare trading conditions for securities when quotes (pre-trade transparency) are published. Post-trade transparency is also important to get timely insight into the movement of prices. The transparency requirements seek to achieve an adequate price-formation process, to ensure best execution and to provide for a level playing field between the different types of trade venue (see also Box 5.2).

Insider trading and market manipulation undermine the proper functioning and integrity of markets. *Insider-trading rules* put a ban on trading with inside information, i.e. material information on the firm that has not yet been made public. The use of this information by insiders, such as management or employees, may influence the price of the firm's securities. To speed up the release of new information (and thus reduce the potential for insider trading), insider-trading rules require listed firms to disclose inside information as soon as possible. It thus promotes transparency and equal treatment of investors. *Market-manipulation rules* prohibit the spread of rumours to influence (i.e. 'manipulate') the price of a security.

Firms that issue securities are required to publish information on a regular basis. First, firms have to publish a prospectus when they are issuing securities. A *prospectus* commonly provides investors with material information about the firm's business, financial statements, biographies of officers and directors, detailed information about their compensation, any litigation that is taking place, a list of material properties, and any other material information. Next, listed firms have to provide annual financial reports. In addition, half-yearly or quarterly financial reports may be required. The purpose of financial reporting is to ensure comparable, transparent, and reliable information about firms. Finally, shareholders have to disclose acquisitions (and disposals) of shareholdings beyond the 5 per cent threshold. In that way, firms can identify their major shareholders.

The conduct-of-business rules for markets are laid down in a raft of EU Directives. MiFID contains inter alia rules on transparency of trading. It covers trading from regulated markets (i.e. stock exchanges) to multi-trading facilities (MTFs), i.e. systems that bring together multiple parties (e.g. retail investors or other investment firms) that are interested in buying and selling financial instruments and enable them to do so. This has increased competition among exchanges, MTFs, and investment firms, giving them a single passport to operate throughout the EU on the basis of authorisation in their home Member State. MiFID also facilitates in-house matching. Under certain conditions regarding pre-trade transparency and best execution, banks and investment firms are allowed to 'match' trades of customers internally. As already indicated, as of January 2017, MiFID II and MiFIR will apply. The new framework introduces a market structure which closes loopholes and ensures that trading, wherever appropriate, takes place on regulated platforms. It introduces rules on high-frequency trading, improves the transparency and oversight of financial markets – including derivatives markets – and addresses the issue of excessive price volatility in commodity derivatives markets. It will also improve conditions for competition in the trading and clearing of financial instruments.

The Market Abuse Directive (2003/6/EC) harmonises the rules for insider trading and for market abuse. It requires closer cooperation and a higher degree of exchange of information between national authorities, thus ensuring the same framework for enforcement throughout the EU and reducing potential inconsistencies, confusion, and loopholes. Moreover, as of July 2016, the Market Abuse Regulation (596/2014/EU) will apply. The new rules on market abuse update and strengthen the existing framework to ensure market integrity and investor protection and will replace the existing Market Abuse Directive (2003/6/EC). This regulation aims at ensuring that the EU regulatory framework keeps pace with market developments, such as the growth of new trading platforms, over the counter trading, and new technology such as high-frequency trading, strengthens the fight against market abuse across commodity and related derivative markets, explicitly bans the manipulation of benchmarks (such as LIBOR), and reinforces the investigative and administrative sanctioning powers of regulators.

The Prospectus Directive (2010/73/EC) requires that prospectuses provide investors with clear and comprehensive information. This directive makes it easier and cheaper for companies to raise capital throughout the EU on the basis of a single prospectus approved by a regulatory authority ('home supervisor') in one Member State.

Finally, the Transparency Directive (2004/109/EC) requires that all securities issuers must provide annual financial reports within four months of the start of the financial year. As for the contents of the financial reports, the EU has adopted the International Accounting Standards (IAS) – now referred to as International Financial Reporting Standards (IFRS) – through IAS Regulation (1606/2002/EC). The IAS provides a single set of comparable global accounting standards issued by the International Accounting Standards Board (IASB).

12.4 Supervisory structures

The organisational structure of financial supervision is in the process of change in most EU Member States. All countries used to have a sectoral model of financial supervision with separate supervisors for banking, insurance, and securities reflecting the traditional dividing lines between financial sectors. Furthermore, financial products are converging. Banking as well as life-insurance products, for example, serve the market for long-term savings. Because of the blurring of the dividing lines between financial sectors, cross-sector models of supervision have emerged. There are two main cross-sector models of supervision: a functional (or 'twin peaks') model and an integrated model.

In the *functional model*, there are separate supervisors for each of the supervisory objectives: prudential supervision and conduct of business. Referring to these two objectives, the functional model is also known as the 'twin peaks' model (Taylor, 1995). In some countries, especially in the euro area where central banks have transferred their responsibility for monetary policy to the ECB, the central bank is responsible for prudential supervision. In other countries, a separate agency is responsible for prudential supervision.

In the *integrated model*, there is a single supervisor for banking, insurance, and securities combined (or, put differently, one supervisor for prudential supervision and conduct of business combined). There are two modes of the integrated model. Denmark and Sweden have adopted a fully integrated model without central bank involvement in financial supervision. In Germany and Austria, the central bank still has a role in banking supervision. The functional model combines the objectives of macroprudential supervision and microprudential supervision, leaving conduct-of-business supervision as a separate

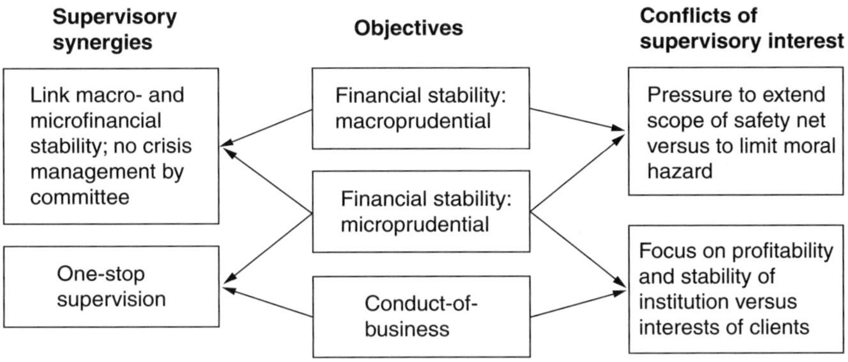

Figure 12.5 Supervisory synergies and conflicts
Source: Kremers *et al.* (2003)

function. The integrated model combines the objectives of prudential supervision and conduct-of-business supervision, leaving macroprudential supervision (financial stability) as a separate function that is usually performed by the central bank.

Kremers *et al.* (2003) have developed a framework to analyse the trade-offs by listing the synergies and conflicts of supervisory interests of both models. Figure 12.5 summarises these potential synergies and conflicts. The first synergy in the left panel of Figure 12.5 results from combining macroprudential supervision and microprudential supervision of financial institutions. The synergy between stability issues on a micro level (at the level of the financial institution) and a macro level (economy-wide) refers to the possibility to act decisively and swiftly in the event of a crisis situation. Crisis management usually requires key decisions to be taken within hours rather than days. Combining both micro- and macroprudential supervision within a single institution ensures that relevant information is available at short notice and that a speedy decision to act can be taken if necessary.[5]

The second synergy in Figure 12.5 is 'one-stop supervision', i.e. the synergy between prudential supervision and conduct of business. This relates to the fact that it confronts all types of financial institutions with one supervisor only for prudential and conduct-of-business supervision. Furthermore, synergies in the execution of supervision are exploited by combining different supervisory activities within one institution.

The first potential conflict of interest between macroprudential supervision and microprudential supervision relates to the possibility of lender-of-last-resort operations (LoLR) by the central bank. How to balance the pressure to extend the benefits of LoLR operations (avoiding systemic risk, like a financial panic or bank runs) to all financial institutions against its costs (moral hazard)? The answer adopted by many central banks is to limit the possibility of LoLR operations to banks, which are subject to systemic risk (see Chapter 10). Then LoLR operations are not available to insurance companies. However, when financial groups integrate, it may become more difficult to separate the banking part of financial institutions that justify the possibility of LoLR operations.

The second potential conflict of interest between prudential supervision and conduct-of-business supervision relates to the different nature of their objectives. The prudential supervisor will be interested in the soundness of financial institutions including profitability, while the conduct-of-business supervisor will focus on the interests of clients. Mixing up both responsibilities of financial stability and conduct of business could lead to incentives for the supervisor to give prevalence to one objective over the other. By separating the supervisory functions, the conduct-of-business supervisor is ideally situated to supervise possible conflicts of interest between a financial institution and its clients, since it will focus only on the interests of the clients. Furthermore, the stability objective is consistent with preserving public confidence and may require discretion and confidentiality, which could be counter-productive to the transparency objective.

12.5 Financial supervision in Europe

A key element in the design of the institutional framework for financial supervision is the appropriate level of (de)centralisation. Until recently, national supervisory agencies in the EU Member States were in charge of the supervision of all financial institutions. With the start of the Banking Union this has changed for banks in the euro area. Supervision of other financial institutions (insurance companies, pension funds, and banks located in countries outside the euro area) is still primarily the responsibility of national supervisors. However, at the EU level several supervisory authorities have been created.

Drawbacks of national supervision

National supervision, within an integrated financial system, has several drawbacks. Even though regulation concerning financial supervision has increasingly become European, various technical rules are still determined at Member State level, and there are considerable variations between Member States. Even where rules are harmonised, application can be inconsistent. This fragmented supervision undermines the Single Market, imposes extra costs for financial institutions, and increases the likelihood of failure of financial institutions with potentially additional costs for taxpayers.

Schüler and Heinemann (2005) have calculated the cost of fragmentation of financial supervision in the EU-15. Their results indicate increasing economies of scale in supervision. Comparing a structure with 15 national supervisors with a cost-efficient European supervisory framework, they predict cost savings of some 15 per cent.

Another drawback of national supervision is the potential for conflicts of interest among national supervisors. While large cross-border financial institutions increasingly operate on an integrated basis, with key decisions taken at headquarters, supervisors are examining the national parts of these institutions. The home supervisor as consolidated supervisor is coordinating the national supervisory efforts to minimise the potential for regulatory and supervisory arbitrage. The national supervisors also perform joint risk assessments of the large cross-border financial institutions, resulting in a joint supervision plan. But there are no legally binding mechanisms to deal with potential conflicts of national interest.

An example of a potential conflict is the distribution of capital (or liquidity) in a financial services group. The host supervisor may request full capitalisation of the host subsidiary, while the home supervisor may request to maintain capital at the group level and to keep the capitalisation of subsidiaries at the minimum level. Supervisors may also have diverging views on how to remedy shortcomings of a financial institution. Supervisors can easily settle on a joint action when they agree. But when there are (lasting) differences, the various supervisors all have the legal power to take enforcement action under their national mandate and this may result in sub-optimal outcomes.

These coordination problems pose the question of whether supervision should be done at the national level or the European level. The basic argument in favour of moving to a European structure is that it might be difficult to achieve simultaneously an integrated and a stable financial system, while preserving national supervision and crisis management with only decentralised efforts at harmonisation (Thygesen, 2003). This is an application of the classical trilemma in monetary policy in which policy makers are confronted with three desirable, yet contradictory, objectives: fixed exchange rates, capital mobility, and independent monetary policy. Only two out of

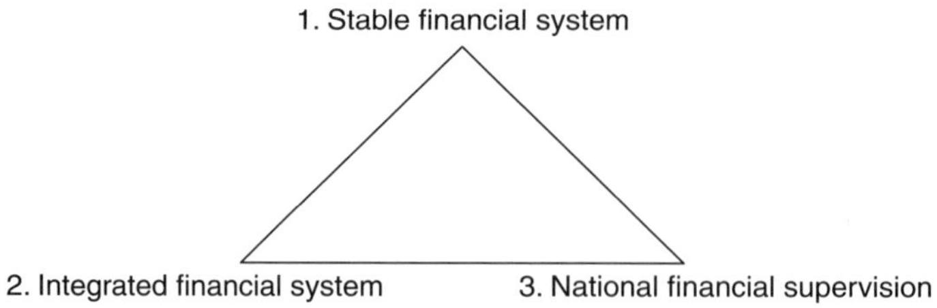

Figure 12.6 The financial trilemma
Source: Schoenmaker (2013)

the three objectives are mutually consistent, leaving policy makers with the decision about which one they wish to give up: the 'trilemma'. A similar trilemma occurs in financial supervision (Schoenmaker, 2013). Figure 12.6 illustrates the three incompatible objectives of the financial trilemma: (1) a stable financial system; (2) an integrated financial system; and (3) independent national financial policies (see Chapter 13 for more details and a full treatment of the financial trilemma model).

An argument against moving to a European solution for financial supervision and resolution at the present time could be that the degree of financial integration does not yet justify such a move. However, as shown in previous chapters, many financial markets (in particular wholesale markets) are almost fully integrated. The infrastructures to support financial markets are also integrating, albeit at a slower pace. There is also evidence for increasing cross-border penetration of banks and insurers. Emerging pan-European financial institutions give rise to cross-border externalities arising from the (potential) failure of these institutions. The increasing presence of financial institutions from other EU countries undermines the capacity of host authorities to manage effectively the stability of their financial system.

European Supervisory Authorities

In October 2008 the European Commission mandated a High Level Group chaired by former managing director of the IMF, Jacques de Larosière, to give advice on the future of European financial regulation and supervision. The Group presented its final report on 25 February 2009 and their recommendation provided the basis for the new European financial supervisory framework.

The de Larosière Report (2009) concluded that the supervisory framework needed to be strengthened to reduce the risk and severity of future financial crises. The de Larosière Group recommends creating a European System of Financial Supervisors, comprising three European Supervisory Authorities (ESAs): one for the banking sector (European Banking Authority, EBA), one for the securities sector (European Securities and Markets Authority, ESMA), and one for the insurance and occupational pensions sector (European Insurance and Occupational Pensions Authority, EIOPA). The de Larosière Group also recommended establishing a European Systemic Risk Board (see Chapter 13), monitoring and assessing potential threats to financial stability that arise from macroeconomic developments and from developments within the financial system as a whole.

The underlying rationale for setting up the ESAs was to ensure closer cooperation and exchange of information among national supervisors, facilitate the adoption of EU resolutions to cross-border problems, and advance the coherent interpretation and application of rules. By preparing uniform standards and ensuring supervisory convergence and coordination, the ESAs should shape the further development of a single rule book applicable to all 28 EU Member States and thus contribute to the Single Market. The ESAs started their operations in January 2011.

The powers assigned to the ESAs include the following:

- developing draft technical standards as well as guidance and recommendations;
- resolving cases of disagreement between national supervisors, where legislation requires them to cooperate or to agree;
- contributing to ensuring consistent application of technical rules of EU law, including through peer reviews;
- a coordination and enforcement role in emergency situations.

Figure 12.7 illustrates the three ESAs: EBA based in London, EIOPA in Frankfurt, and ESMA in Paris. It also reflects that the ESAs work closely with the national supervisory authorities. As such, this network combines national supervision with coordination at the European level to foster harmonised rules as well as coherent supervisory practices and enforcement. Through the Joint Committee, the three ESAs cooperate and ensure consistency in their practices.

In addition to indirect supervisory powers, ESMA also exercises direct supervisory powers over financial players with a pan-European profile, currently Credit Rating Agencies and Trade Repositories (see Chapter 8). This direct supervisory role may be expanded towards other pan-European players, such as central counterparties and cross-border stock markets (e.g. Euronext and OMX, see Chapter 5).

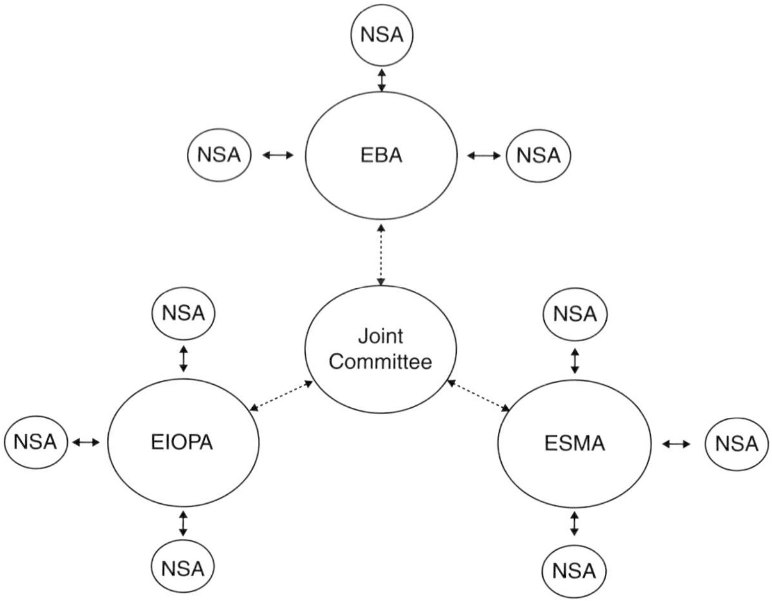

Figure 12.7 The European Supervisory Authorities work closely with the National Supervisory Authorities (NSAs)

Banking Union: the Single Supervisory Mechanism (SSM)

As described in Chapter 3, euro-area leaders decided in June 2012 to establish a Banking Union, which is generally understood to consist of the following four interrelated building blocks:

- a Single Rulebook, consisting of a set of harmonised legislative texts that all financial institutions in the EU must comply with. These legislative texts range from capital requirements to rules for the recovery and resolution of banks;
- a Single Supervisory Mechanism (SSM), which places the ECB as the central microprudential supervisor of banks in the euro area and in those non-euro Member States that choose to join the Banking Union;
- a Single Resolution Mechanism (SRM), which applies to all banks covered by the SSM. Its purpose is to ensure an orderly resolution of failing banks with minimal or no costs for the taxpayer; it will be discussed in Chapter 13;
- a financing regime for exceptional situations, including a Single Resolution Fund (SRF), ESM direct recapitalisation, and, at least, an alignment of deposit guarantee schemes (DGS).

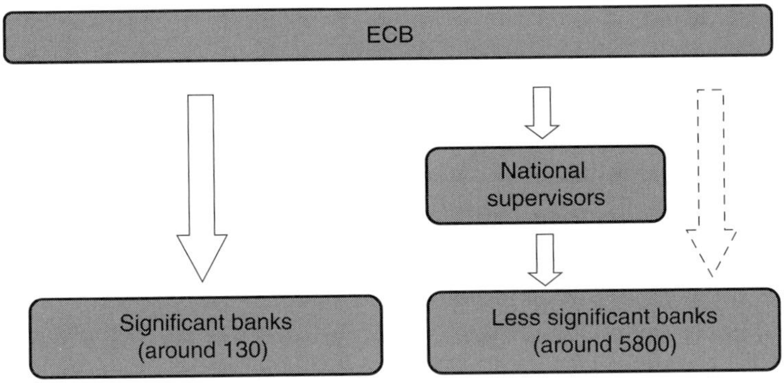

Figure 12.8 The Single Supervisory Mechanism (SSM)

Since November 2014, the ECB directly supervises so-called significant banking groups, while in principle national supervisors will continue to monitor the remaining banks (see Figure 12.8). The main task of the ECB and the national supervisors, working closely together within an integrated system, is to ensure that the single rulebook is applied consistently and coherently and, where necessary, ensure timely corrective action when a bank is in breach of, or about to breach, regulatory requirements. As such, the ECB is responsible for ensuring the safety and soundness of the European banking system, thereby contributing to financial integration and stability in Europe.

Under the new system of supervision, the ECB directly supervises around 130 significant banking groups, representing almost 85 per cent of total banking assets in the euro area. The significance of these banking groups is based on: (i) the total value of their assets, (ii) the importance for the economy of the country in which they are located or the EU as a whole, (iii) the scale of their cross-border activities, and (iv) whether they have requested or received public financial assistance from the European Stability Mechanism (ESM) or the European Financial Stability Facility (EFSF). Moreover, in each participating country, at least the three most significant banks are subject to direct supervision by the ECB, irrespective of their absolute size. The ECB indirectly supervises less significant banks in the participating countries, which number approximately 5,800 in the euro area. This entails that these banks continue to be directly supervised by the national supervisory authorities. However, the ECB can decide at any time to take over the direct supervision of any one of these banks.

The ECB has the power, among other things, to grant or withdraw the authorisation of all banks under the SSM, assess acquisition and disposal of holdings in banks, and ensure compliance with all prudential requirements laid down in EU banking rules. While the ECB directly supervises significant banks, national supervisory authorities are still involved in the day-to-day supervision. Given their experience in supervision and their local proximity to the banks, the national supervisory authorities assist the ECB in performing its supervisory tasks as well as in enforcement procedures. The so-called *Joint Supervisory Teams* (JSTs) are one of the main forms of cooperation between the ECB and national supervisory authorities. For each significant bank, a team is formed of staff members of the national supervisory authorities involved in supervising that bank and staff members of the ECB. The team is coordinated by the ECB. These teams are responsible for the day-to-day supervision of significant banks and carry out on-site inspections. The main tasks of the JSTs are to perform the risk analysis of the supervised entity or group and to propose the supervisory programme and the appropriate supervisory actions.

Setting-up the SSM required changes to the ECB's organisational structure to ensure a separation between monetary policy and supervisory tasks. The governance of the SSM is based on a *Supervisory Board*, acting under the overall responsibility of the ECB's Governing Council. This Supervisory Board consists of: (i) a Chair, appointed for a non-renewable term of five years; (ii) a Vice-Chair, chosen from among the members of the ECB's Executive Board, (iii) three ECB representatives, and (iv) one representative of each participating Member State. The main responsibilities of the Supervisory Board are the planning and execution of the ECB's supervisory tasks and proposing draft supervisory decisions for adoption by the Governing Council. Decision-making within the SSM is based on a procedure known as 'non-objection', which means that if the Governing Council does not object to the draft decision prepared by the Supervisory Board within a defined period of time, the decision is deemed adopted.

Prior to assuming the responsibility for supervision under the SSM, the ECB carried out a *Comprehensive Assessment*, consisting of: (i) an asset quality review (AQR), to enhance the transparency of bank exposures by reviewing the quality of banks' assets, including the adequacy of asset and collateral valuation and related provisions, and (ii) a stress test performed in close cooperation with the European Banking Authority (EBA), which examined the resilience of banks' balance sheets to stress scenarios (see Box 12.4).

Box 12.4 The Comprehensive Assessment

The Comprehensive Assessment aims to scour banks' books for hidden problems, test their ability to withstand crises, and force weak banks to either raise more capital or close. The ECB hopes that the assessment will clear up lingering doubts about the health of banks in the euro area, so that banks can raise funds more easily and increase lending. Lack of credit, especially in troubled countries like Greece and Italy, has been a severe impediment to growth in the euro area.

In the first phase of the assessment, the Asset Quality Review (AQR), teams of examiners pored over the books of the 130 most important banks in the euro area, covering approximately 82 per cent of total bank assets. The aim of the review was to uncover hidden problems, such as bad loans that banks had not disclosed. The AQR conducted by the ECB and national competent authorities (NCAs) examined whether assets were properly valued on banks' balance sheets as of 31 December 2013. It made banks comparable across national borders by applying common definitions for previously diverging concepts and a uniform methodology when assessing balance sheets. More than 6,000 experts across the Single Supervisory Mechanism examined more than 800 individual portfolios in detail, among other things thoroughly analysing the quality of the credits of 119,000 debtors of banks.

In the second phase of the assessment, the banks were subjected to stress tests intended to measure banks' ability to withstand a crisis, such as a severe recession or turmoil in global financial markets. The stress test used both a baseline and an adverse scenario for testing banks' resilience to stress. In the baseline scenario, the EU economy develops in line with the European Commission's economic projections up to 2016; in the adverse scenario, macroeconomic developments clearly deteriorate. The stress test was performed by the participating banks, the ECB, and NCAs in cooperation with the European Banking Authority (EBA). The EBA also designed the stress test methodology, while the adverse scenario was developed by the European Systemic Risk Board (ESRB) in cooperation with the NCAs, the EBA, and the ECB. Banks were required to maintain a minimum CET1 ratio of 8 per cent under the baseline scenario (as for the AQR) and a minimum CET1 ratio of 5.5 per cent under the adverse scenario. Previous stress tests in the euro area failed to restore confidence because some banks that passed them later collapsed. For instance, Dexia required a taxpayer-financed bailout in 2011 only months after passing a stress test administered by the EBA.

Box 12.4 (cont.)

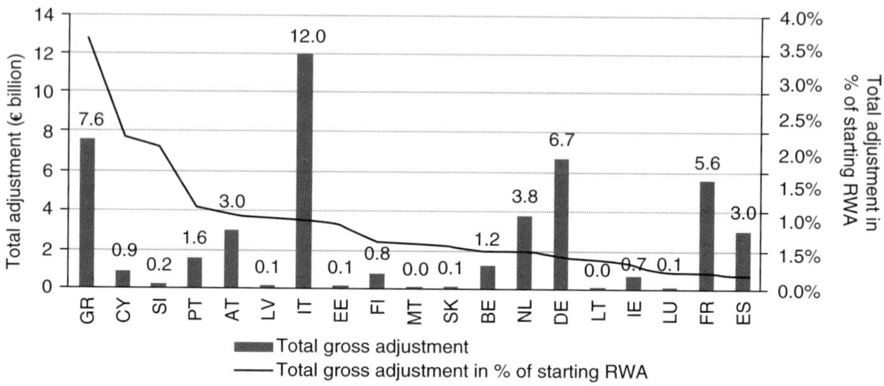

Figure 12.9 Gross AQR adjustment by country
Source: ECB

The outcomes of the assessment were published by the ECB on October 26, 2014. The AQR showed that as of end-2013 the carrying values – or book values – of banks' assets need to be adjusted by €48 billion, which will be reflected in the banks' accounts or prudential requirements (see Figure 12.9). Furthermore, using a standard definition for non-performing exposures (any obligations that are 90 days overdue, or that are impaired or in default), the review found that banks' non-performing exposures increased by €136 billion to a total of €879 billion.

The assessment found a capital shortfall of €25 billion at 25 (mainly small and medium-sized) banks (see Figure 12.10). Twelve of the 25 banks have already covered their capital shortfall by increasing their capital by €15 billion in 2014. The comprehensive assessment also showed that a severe scenario would deplete the banks' top-quality, loss-absorbing Common Equity Tier 1 (CET1) capital by about €263 billion. This would result in the banks' median CET1 ratio decreasing by 4 percentage points from 12.4 to 8.3 per cent.

Capital shortfalls should be covered within six months for those identified in the AQR or the baseline stress test scenario, and within nine months for those identified in the adverse stress test scenario. Shortfalls revealed by the AQR and the baseline stress test scenario may only be covered by Common Equity Tier 1 (CET1) capital instruments. The use of Additional Tier 1 (AT1) capital instruments to cover shortfalls arising from the adverse stress test scenario is limited, depending on the trigger point of conversion or write-down.

Box 12.4 (cont.)

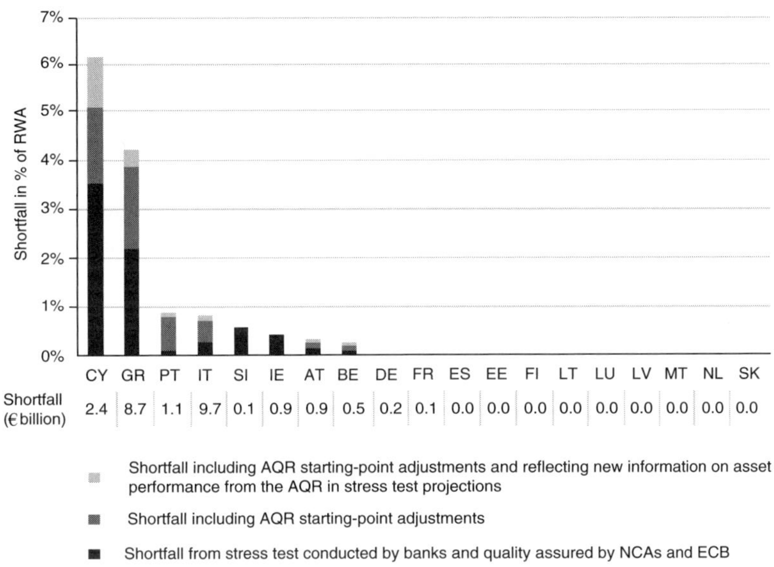

Figure 12.10 Capital shortfall by country
Source: ECB

Challenges for financial supervision

With the start of the Banking Union, financial supervision in the euro area has been changed very rapidly. This section discusses several challenges that financial supervisors face.[6]

EU versus euro area

In the SSM there is, of course, the issue of participation of EU Member States outside the euro area. This tension was, to a certain extent, resolved by giving the authorities of non-euro-area Member States the option to participate in the SSM. By giving non-euro-area Member States full membership and voting rights in the Supervisory Board – the body responsible for the preparation of decisions on supervisory matters – they are placed on an equal footing with euro-area Member States. The role of the ECB Governing Council in the SSM is reduced to the possibility of accepting or rejecting the decisions of the Supervisory Board. Still, non-euro-area Member States are of course not involved in the ECB Governing Council decisions.

Another issue in this context relates to the distribution of responsibilities between the ECB and EU28 institutions, such as the European Banking Authority (EBA) and the European Systemic Risk Board. For instance, as both the EBA and the ECB are developing supervisory manuals, overlaps and/or conflicts between the two sets of supervisory rules may occur. How these possible tensions play out in the future and what consequences they have remains to be seen, but they are evidently of crucial importance for the future of financial supervision.

Transparency and accountability

The global financial crisis has raised questions concerning the accountability of financial supervisors. It became clear that information regarding the supervisory activities and the impact of these activities was inadequate to assess the degree to which supervisors were fulfilling their mandate adequately. Calls were made to give the public and the legislative and executive branches of government more insight as to whether supervisors were performing the right tasks and whether they were performing their tasks well.

Transparency refers to an environment in which the objectives of policy; its legal, institutional, and economic framework; policy decisions and their rationale; data and information related to policies; and the terms of agencies' accountability are provided to the public in a comprehensible, accessible, and timely manner (IMF, 2000). Transparency is thus a crucial component for ensuring accountability. Although other arrangements concerning accountability naturally exist, information concerning the conduct of supervisors is essential for the assessment of their performance. As for the SSM, the channels for accountability include: (i) hearings and exchanges of views with the Chair of the Supervisory Board in the European Parliament and in the Eurogroup, in the presence of representatives from participating Member States whose currency is not the euro, (ii) answers to (written) questions from Members of the European Parliament (MEPs) and EU Council members addressed to the Supervisory Board Chair, and (iii) the submission of an annual report on its work to the European Parliament, the EU Council, and the Eurogroup.

Various arguments can be put forward as to why transparency of banking supervisors may be beneficial (Liedorp *et al.* 2013). First, transparency may enhance the legitimacy of the supervisor. As a supervisory authority is an independent organisation in which unelected officials take important decisions, ensuring legitimacy is vital. Especially in times of financial turmoil, the legitimacy of the authorities responsible for banking supervision is crucial. Transparency may thus also safeguard an adequate degree of independence for the supervisor. By making actions and decisions transparent, chances for undue interference based on an inaccurate perception of the supervisor's conduct are reduced. Second, transparency may increase the predictability of the supervisor, which, in turn, may stimulate banks to adhere to existing regulation.

However, there are also important arguments in favour of secrecy about banking supervision. First, the revelation of information about a financial institution does not function as a neutral mirror of the firm's financial position, but may in fact trigger events that influence that position. This is the 'reflexive nature' of financial markets, meaning that market participants' perspectives on financial markets may in fact drive financial market activity. For instance, exposing liquidity problems at particular firms may freeze the inter-bank market or trigger bank runs, in effect worsening the firms' liquidity problems. A good example is the money market turmoil starting in the summer of 2007. Second, financial supervisors face more restrictions in being transparent than monetary policy makers. For instance, due to legal restrictions, many supervisors cannot reveal much information on individual financial institutions. However, there seems to be room for improvement, as supervisory transparency in the United States is greater than in the EU (Gandrud and Hallerberg, 2014).

Expectations and demands of supervision

Supervisors have to strike a balance between different demands of multiple actors. In fulfilling their mandate, they have to pay attention to expectations of the legislative and executive branch, the supervised institutions, depositors, and the 'general public'. These demands may shift over time and may be conflicting. The legislative branch of government may, for example, expect the supervisor to guarantee firms' compliance with existing policy in order to prevent incidents from happening, but may also expect the supervisor not to put too big of an administrative burden on financial firms. The executive branch may focus on the efficiency of supervision, paying attention to the possibilities of achieving maximum results with a minimum of costs. The supervised firms expect the supervisor to put trust in their compliance with rules and norms and therefore not be too intrusive, while at the same time expecting the supervisor to guarantee compliance with rules and norms of other financial firms. Depositors expect the supervisor to guarantee that their money is safe, thus in effect expecting the supervisor to prevent bankruptcies at all times. Finally, the general public expect the supervisor to be able to guarantee financial stability and prevent financial turmoil from occurring.

Based on a survey in the Netherlands, Van der Cruijsen *et al.* (2013) show that 63 per cent of the respondents (totally) agreed with the view that supervisors have to ensure that banks never go bankrupt. A problem with this expectation is first that given the dynamic nature of financial markets, preventing financial failure at all times is impossible. In fact, it could be highly counterproductive if the supervisor would make 'preventing defaults at all times' a core part of its supervisory strategy, as it would introduce moral hazard problems, both at the level of firms and financial services customers.

Van der Cruijsen *et al.* (2013) also report that a majority of the respondents think that supervisors should inform the public when a bank has problems. However, such a message could undermine confidence in the financial institution or even the financial system. The supervisor will therefore be cautious in communicating problems at financial firms, as this could prove to be counterproductive. Hence, also on this front the supervisor will fail to fully live up to public expectations.

These findings suggest that supervisory authorities should more actively communicate the limits of supervision to the larger public. The timing of this is always difficult. Risks may build up in the financial sector when the economy is on the rise, (over)confidence is gaining the upper hand, and attention for risk mitigation is subdued in favour of potential lucrative opportunities. In such circumstances, the public is less receptive to supervisory warnings, especially when these come with new restrictive powers for the supervisor.

Regulatory capture

The financial crisis of 2008/2009 demonstrated several shortcomings in existing financial sector regulation and supervision. However, some observers go further, blaming financial regulators and supervisors – the 'Guardians of Finance' – for the financial crisis of 2008/2009. For instance, Barth *et al.* (2012, p. 5) argue that 'the Guardians of Finance adopted policies that induced financiers to take excessive risk . . . and the Guardians too often chose not to reform their destabilizing policies, even though they had the power and time to do so'.

One of the reasons put forward why the 'Guardians of Finance' allegedly failed is *regulatory capture*. Nobel laureate Stigler (1971) argued in a seminal article that all regulatory and supervisory agencies tend to respond to the wishes of the best-organised interest groups, in particular the industry they regulate and supervise. When public officials favour the regulated industry's interest over the public interest these officials are 'captured' by the industry and this is referred to as regulatory capture. Captured regulators and supervisors will thus be lenient towards the sector they are supposed to independently regulate and monitor. Regulators may, for instance, pursue strategies to minimise industry costs rather than strike an appropriate balance between those costs and overall public benefits, while supervisors may apply rules inconsistently and exempt individual firms from regulatory requirements. Indeed, there is evidence that in the run-up to the financial crisis lobbying by the financial sector had an impact on financial sector regulation. For instance, there is evidence that Basle II has been influenced by the financial sector lobby so that it became much weaker than its predecessor (Claessens *et al.*, 2008).

Capture may not only occur through special interests directly influencing officials, but also through a more subtle internalisation of the objectives, interests, and values of the financial sector. Indeed, Barth *et al.* (2012, p. 38) point out that 'even well-intentioned, incorruptible officials might be subject to the same human psychological factors that induce referees and umpires in sport to conform to the interests of the home crowd'.

12.6 Conclusions

This chapter has identified three market failures in financial services that justify government intervention. First, consumers may be less informed than financial institutions. Financial supervision (both microprudential supervision and conduct-of-business supervision) addresses this problem of asymmetric information. Second, the malfunctioning of a part of the financial system may have an adverse impact on the financial system as a whole. Macroprudential supervision aims to foster financial stability and to contain the effects of systemic failure. Third, certain players in the market may exert undue market power. Competition policy seeks to protect consumers against exploitation of market power.

Microprudential supervision aims to protect consumers by ensuring the safety and soundness of financial institutions. As financial institutions are becoming more complex, supervisors are moving away from direct control to methods that provide incentives to financial institutions to behave prudently. The Basel capital adequacy framework allows banks to use their internal models to manage the risks and to assess the minimum capital required as a buffer against these risks. Conduct-of-business supervision focuses on how financial institutions deal with their customers. Information provisions ensure that consumers get the right information about financial products. In addition, there are guidelines for objective and high-quality advice to protect the interests of customers. Conduct-of-business rules also promote fair and orderly markets.

The organisational structure of supervision is changing across the EU. Countries are increasingly moving from the traditional sectoral structure (with separate banking, insurance, and securities supervisors) to a functional model (with a prudential and a conduct-of-business supervisor) or an integrated model (with only one supervisor). The functional and integrated models can better cope with market developments, such as the development of complex financial products and the emergence of financial conglomerates.

Finally, the European financial landscape is integrating. In response, financial supervision in the EU has undergone a major reform. The establishment of the ESAs was merely the overture to truly EU-based supervision. Now, with the Banking Union in place, the ECB is responsible for day-to-day supervision of around 130 significant banks, representing almost 85 per cent of total banking assets in the euro area. The ECB will indirectly supervise less significant banks in the participating countries, which number approximately 5,800 in the euro area. However, the ECB can decide at any time to take over the direct supervision of any one of these banks.

Notes

1. The €5 billion loss at Société Générale in 2007 due to the alleged fraud of a rogue trader is an exceptional example of the failure of internal controls in a bank.
2. While prudential supervision aims to minimise the risk of failure, it cannot eliminate the risk of a failing bank in a market economy.
3. Directive 2013/36/EU and Regulation (EU) No 575/2013.
4. The integrity and competence of financial institutions is not listed here as a specific conduct-of-business element. Fit and proper rules are general requirements that are

applied in both prudential and conduct-of-business regulation. Section 12.2 explains these rules.
5. The Northern Rock crisis in 2007 indicates that crisis management by two institutions may not be very effective. According to Buiter (2007), the coordination between the Bank of England and the FSA has been wanting.
6. This section draws heavily on Cavelaars *et al.* (2013).

Suggested Reading

Admati, A. and M. Hellwig (2013), *The Bankers' New Clothes – What's Wrong with Banking and What to Do about It*, Princeton University Press, Princeton and Oxford.

Goodhart, C. A. E., P. Hartmann, D. T. Llewellyn, L. Rojas-Suarez, and S. Weisbrod (1998), *Financial Regulation: Why, How and Where Now?*, Routledge, London.

Haldane, A. and V. Madouros (2012). 'The Dog and the Frisbee', *Paper presented at the Federal Reserve Bank of Kansas City's 36th economic policy symposium 'The Changing Policy Landscape'*, Jackson Hole, Wyoming.

References

Admati, A. and M. Hellwig (2013), *The Bankers' New Clothes – What's Wrong with Banking and What to Do about It*, Princeton University Press, Princeton and Oxford.

Bank for International Settlements (1997), *Core Principles for Effective Banking Supervision*, BIS, Basel.

(2006), *Core Principles for Effective Banking Supervision*, BIS, Basel.

Bank of England (2014), *The Financial Policy Committee's Review of the Leverage Ratio*, Bank of England, London.

Barth, J. R., G. Caprio, and R. Levine (2012), *Guardians of Finance.* Making Regulators Work for Us, MIT Press, Cambridge, MA.

Benston, G. J. and G. G. Kaufman (1996), The Appropriate Role of Bank Regulation, *The Economic Journal*, **106**, 688–697.

Besley, T. (2007), The New Political Economy, *The Economic Journal*, **117**, 570–587.

Buiter, W. (2007), Lessons from the 2007 Financial Crisis, CEPR Discussion Paper 6596.

Cavelaars, P., J. de Haan, P. Hilbers, and B. Stellinga (2013), Challenges for Financial Sector Supervision, *DNB Occasional Studies* **6**, DNB, Amsterdam.

Claessens, S., G. Underhill, and X. Zhang (2008), The Political Economy of Global Financial Governance: The Cost of Basle II for Poor Countries, *The World Economy*, **31**(3), 313–344.

de Larosière, J. (2009), Report of the High-level Group on Financial Supervision in the EU, European Commission, Brussels. Available at: http://ec.europa.eu/internal_market/finances/docs/de_larosiere_report_En.pdf (accessed 13 February 2012).

Dermine, J. (2006), European Banking Integration: Don't Put the Cart before the Horse, *Financial Markets, Institutions & Instruments*, **15**(2), 57–106.

Dowd, K. (1996), The Case for Financial Laissez-Faire, *The Economic Journal*, 106, 679–687.

European Commission (2007), *Green Paper on Retail Financial Services in the Single Market*, EC, Brussels.

(2013), *Capital Requirements – CRD IV/CRR – Frequently Asked Questions*, EC, Brussels.

(2014a), *Banking Union, Restoring Financial Stability in the Eurozone*, EC, Brussels.

(2014b), *Economic Review of the Financial Regulation Agenda*, EC, Brussels.

ESFRC (2005), *Reforming Banking Supervision in Europe*, Statement No. 23, Frankfurt am Main.

Gandrud, C. and M. Hallerberg (2014), Supervisory Transparency in the European Banking Union, *Bruegel Policy Contribution 2014/1*, Bruegel, Brussels.

Goodhart, C. A. E., P. Hartmann, D. T. Llewellyn, L. Rojas-Suarez, and S. Weisbrod (1998), *Financial Regulation: Why, How and Where Now?*, Routledge, London.

Haldane, A. and V. Madouros (2012), 'The Dog and the Frisbee', *Paper presented at the Federal Reserve Bank of Kansas City's 36th economic policy symposium 'The Changing Policy Landscape'*, Jackson Hole, Wyoming.

International Monetary Fund (2000), *Supporting Document to the Code of Good Practices on Transparency in Monetary and Financial Policies*, Washington, IMF.

Kremers, J. J. M., D. Schoenmaker, and P. J. Wierts (2003), Cross-Sector Supervision: Which Model?, in: R. Herring and R. Litan (eds.), *Brookings-Wharton Papers on Financial Services: 2003*, Brookings Institution, Washington DC, 225–243.

Lastra, R. M. (2006), *Legal Foundations of International Monetary Stability*, Oxford University Press.

Le Lesé, A. and S. Avramova (2012), Revisiting Risk-Weighted Assets – Why Do RWAs Differ Across Countries and What Can Be Done About It?, IMF Working Paper 12/90, IMF, Washington, DC.

Liedorp, F., R. H. Mosch, C. A. B. van der Cruijsen, and J. de Haan (2013), Transparency of Banking Supervisors, *IMF Economic Review*, **61**(2), 310–335.

Llewellyn, D. (1999), The Economic Rationale for Financial Regulation, *FSA Occasional Paper 1*, Financial Services Authority, London.

Merton, R. C. (1995), Financial Innovation and the Management and Regulation of Financial Institutions, *Journal of Banking and Finance*, **19**, 461–481.

Mishkin, F. S. (2000), Prudential Supervision: Why is It Important and What are the Issues?, NBER Working Paper 7926.

Nieto, M. J. and L. D. Wall (2007), Preconditions for a Successful Implementation of Supervisors' Prompt Corrective Action: Is There a Case for a Banking Standard in the EU?, Banco de España Working Paper 0702.

Pagliari, S., (ed.) (2012), *Making Good Financial Regulation: Towards a Policy Response to Regulatory Capture*, Grosvenor House Publishing, London.

Quintyn, M. and M. W. Taylor (2003), Regulatory and Supervisory Independence and Financial Stability, *CESifo Economics Studies*, **49**(2), 259–294.

Schoenmaker, D. (2013), *Governance of International Banking: The Financial Trilemma*, Oxford University Press, New York.

Schüler, M. and F. Heinemann (2005), The Costs of Supervisory Fragmentation in Europe, ZEW Discussion Paper 05–01.

Stigler, G. (1971), The Theory of Economic Regulation, *Bell Journal of Economics*, **2**, 3–21.

Taylor, M. (1995), *Twin Peaks: A Regulatory Structure for the New Century*, Centre for the Study of Financial Innovation, London.

Thygesen, N. (2003), Comments on the Political Economy of Financial Harmonisation in Europe, in: J. J. M. Kremers, D. Schoenmaker, and P. J. Wierts (eds.), *Financial Supervision in Europe*, Edward Elgar, Cheltenham, 142–150.

Van der Cruijsen, C. A. B., D. Jansen, J. de Haan, and R. H. J. Mosch (2013), Knowledge and Opinions about Banking Supervision: Evidence from a Survey of Dutch Households, *Journal of Financial Stability*, **9**, 219–229.

CHAPTER

13

Financial Stability

OVERVIEW

Against the backdrop of the 2007–2009 financial crisis, this chapter discusses the growing importance of macroprudential supervision, which focuses on the stability of the financial system as a whole and therefore on the monitoring and assessment of so-called systemic risk.

The chapter sets out the key features of the conceptual framework for macroprudential supervision. The framework starts with identifying the risk dimensions, also known as pillars. The first pillar (time-series dimension) examines financial imbalances, for which a cyclical approach is appropriate. The second pillar (cross-sectional dimension) looks at externalities, for which a structural approach is appropriate. The failure of a large financial institution, for example, poses an externality to the financial system. Another externality is the interconnectedness of financial intermediaries.

The next stage is to design macroprudential instruments or tools to achieve the intermediate targets. On the cyclical side, countercyclical capital buffers and real estate related instruments are applied to achieve the intermediate targets of containing credit growth and house price rises. On the structural side, capital surcharges and resolution plans are applied to achieve the intermediate target of stable global systemically important financial institutions. This chapter also discusses the emerging institutional architecture for macroprudential supervision in the EU and the US.

Finally, this chapter touches upon the issue of crisis management and resolution, discussing the main reactive instruments that can be considered in crisis situations. The new Banking Union crisis management framework is analysed in detail. An important element is transferring responsibility for resolution from the national level to the Single Resolution Board at the European level, mirroring the Supervisory Board of the ECB discussed in Chapter 12.

LEARNING OBJECTIVES

After you have studied this chapter, you should be able to:

- explain the concept of macroprudential supervision and the difference between micro- and macroprudential supervision
- explain the concept of systemic risk and describe what makes financial systems prone to this risk
- understand the two pillars of macroprudential supervision
- describe the key instruments used by macroprudential authorities to prevent the build-up of systemic risk
- describe the principal features of the crisis management and resolution tools, including bail-in
- explain why improvised cooperation leads to an insufficient level of recapitalisation in the case of a cross-border failure and why this calls for a Banking Union approach.

13.1 Financial stability and macroprudential supervision

Macro- vs. microprudential supervision

Although microprudential and macroprudential supervision are closely related, the financial crisis of 2007–2009 highlighted the important distinction between both concepts (see Hanson *et al.*, 2011).

Microprudential supervision has traditionally been the key focus of supervisory authorities. The intermediate objective of microprudential supervision is to supervise and limit the distress of individual financial institutions, with the ultimate objective of protecting the customers of the institution in question. The fact that the financial system as a whole may be exposed to common risks is not (fully) taken into account. However, by preventing the failure of individual financial institutions, microprudential supervision aims to mitigate or prevent the risk of contagion and the subsequent negative externalities related to a possible fall in the confidence in the stability of the financial system.

Macroprudential supervision focuses on the soundness of the financial system as a whole. The intermediate objective of macroprudential supervision is to limit financial system-wide distress, with the ultimate objective of protecting the overall economy from significant losses in real output (see

Table 13.1 Macroprudential versus microprudential supervision

	Macroprudential	Microprudential
Intermediate objective	Limit financial system-wide distress	Limit distress of individual institutions
Ultimate objective	Avoid output (GDP) costs	Consumer (investor/depositor) protection
Correlations and common exposures across institutions	Important	Irrelevant
Characterisation of risk	Seen as dependent on collective behaviour ('endogenous')	Seen as independent of individual agents' behaviour ('exogenous')
Calibration of prudential controls	In terms of system-wide risks; top-down	In terms of risks of individual institutions; bottom-up

Source: Borio (2003)

Table 13.1). While risks to the financial system can in theory arise from the failure of one financial institution, the much more important systemic risk arises from a common exposure of many financial institutions to the same risk factors.

Macroprudential analysis must therefore pay particular attention to common or correlated shocks as well as to shocks that may trigger contagious knock-on effects. Moreover, macroprudential supervision should take account of the interactions between financial institutions and their environment (i.e. other institutions, financial markets, infrastructure and the real economy) as well as the dynamics with which imbalances may build up over time.

As such, the macroprudential perspective assumes that the risk of a shock is (partly) generated and amplified within the system (i.e. the risk is *endogenous*), while the microprudential approach focuses on institutions' vulnerability to threats emanating from their environment (i.e. the risk is *exogenous*).

Moreover, in order to avoid financial system-wide distress, the macro-perspective takes a top-down approach to calibrating prudential controls by identifying risks in the system as a whole, calculating the contribution of each financial entity and then applying the relevant macroprudential tools. By contrast, the microprudential approach is bottom-up, setting the prudential controls in relation to the risk of each individual financial entity.

Systemic risk

Macroprudential analysis and supervision focuses on the monitoring and assessment of so-called systemic risk within the financial system. The term *systemic risk* refers to the risk that an event will trigger a loss of economic value or confidence in a substantial part of the financial system that is serious enough to have significant adverse effects on the real economy.

In the absence of systemic risk, the financial system is stable, i.e. the financial system is in a condition in which it is capable of withstanding shocks and the unravelling of imbalances, thereby mitigating the likelihood of disruptions in the financial intermediation process which are severe enough to significantly impair the allocation of savings to profitable investment opportunities (ECB, 2007).

There are two key features of systemic risk: a structural and cyclical feature. First, as set out in Chapter 1, the financial system is composed of: (1) intermediaries, (2) financial markets, and (3) financial infrastructures. Intermediaries are connected with each other through direct transactions; through similar investment; and financing decisions with third parties. Financial markets, in turn, are connected with each other through the trading activities of financial intermediaries. From a structural perspective, systemic risk relates to the risk that these interconnections and similarities render emerging financial instability widespread in the system (ECB, 2009). Second, the complex network of financial connections is extended through the savings and financing needs of all economic actors. By reallocating savings from individuals and sectors with a surplus of funds to individuals and sectors in need of funds, the financial system plays a key role in the economy. From a cyclical perspective, systemic risk relates to the risk that financial imbalances – in the form of credit and liquidity cycles – can build up in a boom period leading to bubbles, which, when they burst, may translate into adverse effects on growth and welfare in the economy at large.

There are a number of additional features of financial systems that make them particularly prone to these forms of systemic risk (ECB, 2009):

(1) The possible negative externalities from risk taking by financial intermediaries. These arise when a financial institution does not take into account that if it takes more risk, and is thereby more prone to failure, it is more likely to impose costs on society. These costs may not only arise because of the failure of an individual institution, but in particular because of possible spill-over effects to other institutions and markets.

(2) Transactions in financial markets are subject to asymmetric information in which one party often does not know all that it needs to know about the other to make correct decisions (Mishkin, 1992). This may create problems in the financial sector in two ways:
   (i) Before the transaction enters into force there is the risk that potential borrowers who are most likely to produce undesirable (adverse) outcomes are selected (*adverse selection*), and
   (ii) After the transaction is entered into force, the borrower may have incentives to invest in projects with high risk in which the borrower does well if the project succeeds, but the lender bears most of the loss if the project fails (*moral hazard*).

(3) The financial system is characterised by powerful feedback and amplification mechanisms, which may reinforce shocks within the system. For example, illiquid assets, maturity mismatches between assets and liabilities and leverage amplify the force with which problems of one financial institution are pushed through the complex network of exposures. Moreover, sizeable amounts of debt relative to capital and short-term funding may have dramatic effects in stress situations.

13.2 Macroprudential policy

Conceptual framework of macroprudential supervision

While fostering financial stability is the ultimate objective, intermediate objectives or targets need to be specified to make macroprudential policy operational. The macroprudential policy strategy relates intermediate objectives to indicators and instruments (see Figure 13.1). The European Systemic Risk Board (ESRB; see section 13.5) has identified four intermediate objectives, which aim at mitigating systemic risks to financial stability that follow from:

- **Excessive credit growth and leverage.** Excessive credit growth has been identified as a key driver of asset price bubbles and subsequent financial crises, with leverage acting as an amplifying channel.
- **Excessive maturity mismatch and market illiquidity.** Reliance on short-term and unstable funding may lead to fire sales, market illiquidity, and contagion when the financial cycle turns.
- **Direct and indirect exposure concentrations.** Exposure concentrations make a financial system (or part of it) vulnerable to common shocks, either

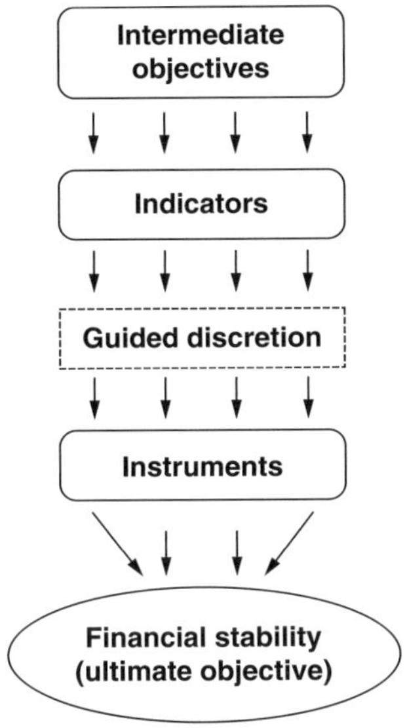

Figure 13.1 Macroprudential policy strategy
Source: ESRB (2014)

directly through balance sheet exposures or indirectly through asset fire sales and contagion.

- **Misaligned incentives and moral hazard.** This includes risks associated with systemically important financial institutions and the role of implicit government guarantees (ESRB, 2014).

Macroprudential monitoring and analysis aims at reviewing potential threats to the stability of the financial system, stemming from the real economy, financial institutions, financial markets or financial infrastructures. This should enable the relevant authorities to gain better insight into the development of imbalances, such as asset price bubbles or vulnerabilities stemming from financial innovation, as well as the degree to which the financial system itself is capable of absorbing such risks.

The monitoring and analysis should in particular focus on (Borio, 2010):

- how aggregate risk evolves over time, i.e. the *time dimension*, and
- how risk is distributed in the financial system at a given point in time, i.e. the *cross-sectional dimension.*

The key issue in the time dimension is how system-wide risk can be amplified by interactions within the financial system as well as between the financial system and the real economy. This is what the cyclical dimension of systemic risk is all about. In good times, agents tend to underestimate risk and, subsequently, overinvest. This overinvestment is fuelled by credit. The credit cycle is in its upward swing. In bad times, the reverse happens: agents become more risk averse and reluctant to invest. In the extreme, this may accumulate in a credit crunch, where banks are withholding credit for new investment. The first two intermediate objectives of macroprudential supervision as identified above fall within the cyclical dimension.

The key issue in the cross-sectional dimension is how to deal with the structural features of systemic risk, i.e. the common exposures across financial institutions. These arise either because institutions are directly exposed to the same or similar asset classes or because of indirect exposures associated with linkages among them (e.g. counterparty relationships). Common exposures are critical because they explain why institutions can fail together. The latter two intermediate objectives of macroprudential supervision as identified above are within the structural domain.

The monitoring process should pay specific attention to any sources of non-diversifiable/systematic risk in the financial system. Hence the importance of common exposures across institutions and of possible symptoms of generalised overextension in balance sheets during economic expansions and macro risks.

The subsequent assessment of risks consists of two stages. First, the potential risks are being ranked in order to see in which areas action is most needed. Second, the identified risks are being linked to possible mitigating policy instruments, which then have to be used. These actions may vary from one situation to the other, depending on the relevant risk.

Finally, evaluation is of importance to ensure that the mitigating action is actually followed up and, if necessary, adjusted.

Cyclical versus structural policies

The role of cyclical macroprudential policy is in mitigating the build-up of financial imbalances at an early stage. *Herding behaviour*, i.e. the tendency for individuals to mimic the actions of a larger group, can lead to financial imbalances at the macro level. An example is the dotcom bubble in the late 1990s when investors were frantically investing huge amounts of money into internet-related companies, even though most of these dotcoms at the time were not making high profits. Another example is the housing price bubble in the United States and some European countries that was a central element in the 2008/2009 financial crisis. How to avert the build-up of this kind of imbalances?

Financial markets are forward looking. As with monetary policy, the key to credibility of macroprudential policies will be in influencing expectations. Once market participants know that policy makers will step in to stabilise financial imbalances when they are building up, these imbalances may not build up in the first place. A further analogy with monetary policy is that effects of macroprudential policy will be uncertain and difficult to measure. Experience over time will help in the clarification of objectives and operating paradigms, as it has in the case of monetary policy (BIS, 2010).

Structural policies are of an entirely different nature. They change the institutions of the economy, through discrete policy reforms, and ultimately aim to improve its long-term growth potential. Examples include changes in the structure of financial institutions (see the discussion on the separation of retail banking from investment banking), static surcharges for systemically important financial institutions (SIFIs), and the deposit-guarantee system. Under this heading, one may also include reforms to the financial infrastructure, such as central counterparty (CCP) clearing and real-time gross settlement (RTGS) as explained in Chapter 7.

Structural policies are more suitable for addressing the cross-section dimension of systemic risk that originates from externalities in the financial system. Spill-over effects can arise from interconnections within the financial system. Insofar as the spill-over effects are not internalised by financial institutions, they are called externalities. The underlying interconnections can be direct or indirect. Prime examples of direct interconnections are interbank exposures through the wholesale payment system or interbank market (see Chapter 5) and, more broadly, counterparty exposures between financial institutions. An example of an indirect interconnection is common exposures. If financial institutions invest in the same asset, such as housing or the oil industry, they will be simultaneously hit by a housing or oil price shock. Even if all individual institutions diversify their portfolios, common exposures may result if they behave in a similar fashion.

Figure 13.2 illustrates the two risk dimensions, or pillars, of the macroprudential framework (Schoenmaker and Wierts, 2011; Galati and Moessner, 2014). The first pillar (i.e. the time-series dimension) is financial imbalances, for which a cyclical approach is appropriate. The second pillar (i.e. the cross-sectional dimension) is externalities, for which a structural approach is appropriate. The cyclical and structural pillars are not fully independent of each other. When the two-pillar strategy is applied, authorities must therefore do a cross-check when analysing financial stability developments. Shin (2010) shows, for example, that excessive asset growth and greater reliance

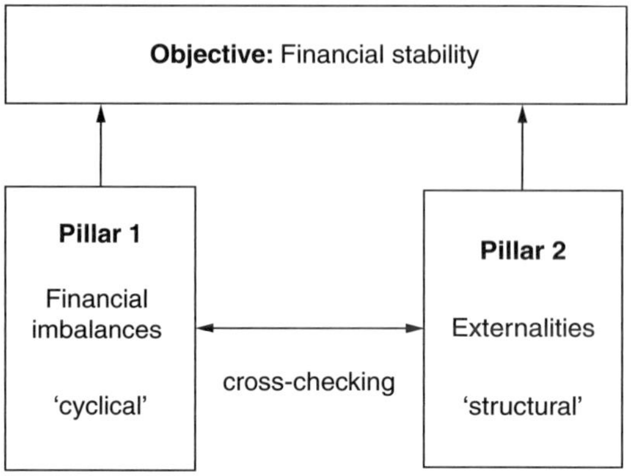

Figure 13.2 Two-pillar strategy for macroprudential policy
Source: Schoenmaker and Wierts (2011)

on non-core liabilities (wholesale funding) are closely related to interconnections between banks. In a boom when credit is growing rapidly, the growth of bank balance sheets outstrips available core funding (retail deposits), and asset growth is mirrored in the greater cross-exposure across banks (wholesale deposits).

13.3 Macroprudential indicators

Indicators

Central banks regularly come up with risk assessments, such as those reported in their financial stability reports, to identify the sources of systemic risks and their transmission channels. These assessments are typically based on a broad range of information and analytical methods, including macroprudential stress tests. Selecting a targeted set of key indicators that capture the identified sources of systemic risks helps monitoring and assessing the build-up of these risks (ESRB, 2014).

An assessment of risks often starts by analysing the financial cycle. Borio (2014) shows that the financial cycle is best described in terms of credit and house prices; it tends to have a lower frequency than the traditional business cycle, and its peaks are closely associated with financial crises (see Chapter 2). Information about the stage and direction of the financial cycle is crucial for assessing vulnerabilities in real time. Mian and Sufi (2014) advise to pay extra attention to household credit, within the broader

Panel A: Cyclical pillar

Intermediate target	Excessive credit growth and leverage		Excessive maturity mismatch and market illiquidity
Indicators	Credit-to-GDP gap	Housing credit, housing prices	Structural funding ratio, short-term liquidity stress indicators

Panel B: Structural pillar

Intermediate target	Exposure concentration	Misaligned incentives
Indicators	Indicators for large exposures, interconnectedness, price contagion	Size, complexity, substitutability and interconnectedness of SIFIs

Figure 13.3 Mapping intermediate objectives and indicators
Source: Adapted from ESRB (2014)

category of private credit. Household credit is mainly used for mortgages. With fluctuating house prices and fixed mortgages, consumption can be volatile. In times of rising house prices – often fuelled by the availability of cheap credit – consumers may spend the over-value of their house. By contrast, in times of declining house prices, consumers are holding back spending, in particular when the value of the house becomes lower than the mortgage (also called negative equity). If many homeowners have negative equity, mortgage banks can be faced with increasing non-performing loans. Notably if homeowners have to sell their property once they lose their job or due to changes in their private life (a divorce, for instance), they may not be able to pay back their loan.

Figure 13.3 summarises indicators for each intermediate objective. Panel A shows the indicators under the cyclical pillar. Credit-to-GDP, housing credit, and housing prices are key indicators of excessive credit growth and leverage. In an empirical test using 38 indicators, Alessi and Detken (2014) find that bank credit-to-GDP, household credit to GDP, and house price growth rank high in identifying excess credit growth. The structural funding ratio (see Chapter 12) and short-term liquidity indicators are important for maturity mismatches and illiquidity.

Panel B shows indicators under the structural pillar. The indicators of exposure concentration are only indicative; more testing needs to be done to find the appropriate indicators for large exposures, interconnectedness, and price contagion (ESRB, 2014). By contrast, much work has been done on systemically important financial institutions (see below).

Systemically important financial institutions

To compute the effect of potential threats to the system as a whole, macro-prudential authorities also need to have a good understanding of what developments in the abovementioned indicators mean for the position of so-called *systemically important financial institutions* (SIFIs). These are financial institutions, whose disorderly failure, because of their size, complexity, and systemic interconnectedness, may cause significant disruption to the wider financial system and economic activity.

Because of this, these institutions are often considered '*too-big-to-fail*' (TBTF). Failure of a large bank is supposedly more feared by supervisors than failure of a small bank, since the former is more likely to result in macroeconomic externalities. For a long time, TBTF banks have received a de facto government guarantee, which leads to a moral hazard problem. As banks know they will be rescued, they have an incentive to take more risks. Such a government guarantee also reduces market discipline by decreasing investors' incentives to monitor and price the risk taking of TBTF banks. As a result, TBTF banks have been able to borrow at costs that do not adequately reflect the risks inherent to their operations (see Strahan (2013) for a review of the TBTF literature).

SIFIs vary in their structures and activities, and hence in the nature and degree of the risks they pose to the international financial system. For example, the collapse of Lehman Brothers, which at the time was not considered to be 'systemic' or TBTF by US policy makers, demonstrated that the disorderly failure of a global financial firm may have strong spill-overs across markets and affects financial stability and national economies around the world.

The assessment methodology for SIFIs comprises five broad categories:

(1) *Cross-border activity*: captures the global footprint of a financial institution. It measures the importance of a financial institution outside its home jurisdiction and is an indicator of the international impact of its distress or failure.

(2) *Size:* looks at the amount of services provided by a financial institution and can be measured by its assets or equity, in absolute terms or as a proportion of GDP. Size may serve as a first indicator of systemic relevance, although institutional size by itself is not sufficient to determine whether an institution is systemically relevant. For example, a large firm may not pose a systemic problem if it is not interconnected or if substitutes are available for its products. Therefore, interactions among the factors also are important in identifying systemically relevant institutions.

(3) *Interconnectedness*: looks at the possibility of financial distress in one institution or market spreading to others through provision of funds and services, funding, confidence factors or exposures through common risk factors.
(4) *Substitutability*: looks at the extent to which other institutions or parts of the financial system can provide the same services if one or more institutions were to fail. A lack of substitutability could pose a systemic threat if the services provided by the failed institution or institutions are of critical importance to the functioning of other institutions or the financial system (e.g. payment and settlement systems).
(5) *Complexity*: looks at the group structures and business models of financial institutions, as the complexity and integrated nature of many financial institutions makes it very difficult not only to manage and supervise SIFIs but also for orderly resolution in the event of their failure.

Stress testing

An important tool to enhance the authorities' understanding of possible vulnerabilities within individual institutions as well as the overall system is to execute a so-called stress test. In stress tests the implications for individual banks' financial positions under several macroeconomic scenarios are examined, taking the banks' exposures and business models into account. The results of such a test show the sensitivity of the portfolio to one or more shocks. Stress tests can be useful because historical data often does not provide sufficient information about the behaviour of markets under extreme events (Hilbers and Jones, 2004).

System-wide stress tests measure the sensitivity of a group of institutions or even an entire financial system to common shocks. The objective is to identify common vulnerabilities across institutions that could undermine the overall stability of a financial system. Compared to stress test for individual banks, the focus is more macroeconomic in nature, because authorities are often interested in understanding how major changes in the economic environment may affect the financial system as a whole.

These system-wide tests can complement stress tests conducted by individual institutions, while also acting as a cross-check for other types of analysis. Stress tests can also be preceded by an asset quality review (AQR), to enhance the transparency of bank exposures by reviewing the quality of banks' assets, including the adequacy of asset and collateral valuation and related provisions.

Table 13.2 Instruments under the cyclical pillar

Intermediate target	Excessive credit growth and leverage			Excessive maturity mismatch and market illiquidity	
Key instruments	Counter cyclical capital buffer	Capital instruments: – leverage ratio – by sector (real estate, intra-financial)	LTV/LTI caps	Stable funding restrictions	Liquidity charges

Source: ESRB (2014)

13.4 Macroprudential instruments

The financial crisis of 2007–2009 revealed a need for macroprudential instruments or tools to mitigate the build-up of systemic risk in the financial system. The entry into force of new EU prudential rules (the CCR/CRD IV package, see Chapter 12) on 1 January 2014 provides the macroprudential authorities in the EU with a new set of instruments to address systemic risk. Within the Banking Union, macroprudential policy remains a responsibility of the national designated authority, with the ECB having the possibility to impose higher (i.e. more restrictive) requirements.

Cyclical pillar

Table 13.2 specifies the instruments under the cyclical pillar. It contains time-varying instruments for effectively stabilising financial imbalances that cause risks to financial stability. The cyclical pillar of financial imbalances is divided into intermediate targets for credit and liquidity (or maturity mismatch) cycles. If asset growth is debt financed (i.e. credit), declining asset values will trigger default when the value of the asset drops below the level of debt. This first default may trigger further defaults. By contrast, if assets are equity financed, falling asset prices may be absorbed by the investors without necessarily triggering a default (e.g. the dotcom bubble of 2000).

Some instruments, such as the *countercyclical capital buffer* and the *leverage ratio*, are system-wide, while others, such as *sector risk weights*, are sector-specific (ESRB, 2014). Some instruments aim to constrain financial institutions (e.g. capital instruments), while others directly affect borrowers

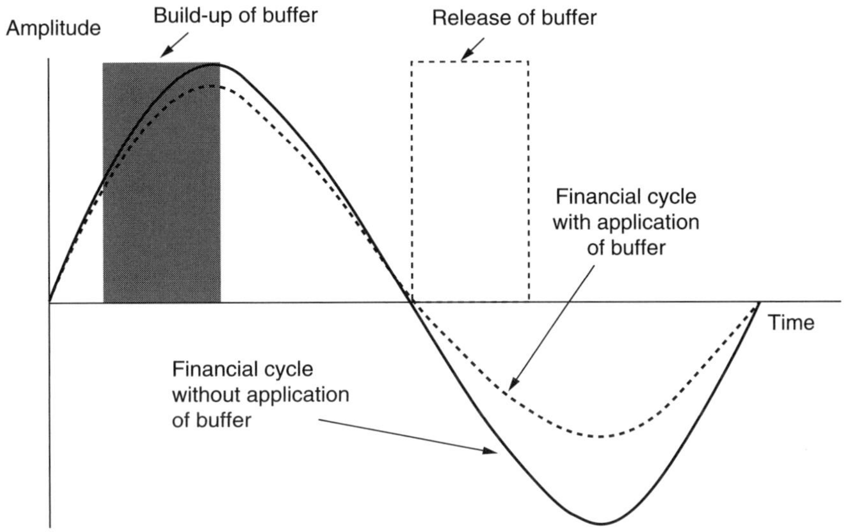

Figure 13.4 Stylised transmission of buffers over the financial cycle
Source: ESRB (2014)

(e.g. *caps on loan-to-value* and *loan-to-income*). Box 13.1 discusses country experiences with these instruments.

The macroprudential instruments under the cyclical pillar can dampen both the upswing and the downswing of the financial cycle (see Figure 13.4). It is important that the countercyclical buffers are increased timely to slow credit growth in the upswing phase. But it is equally important to release buffers in the downswing. This requires a macro approach, as more micro-focused supervisors tend to tighten capital requirements when times get worse.

The CCR/CRD IV package provides for the use of:

- the *countercyclical capital buffer*, to counteract the effects of the economic cycle on banks' lending activity (see Chapter 12);
- the macroprudential use of Pillar II, i.e. the ability to impose additional requirements on a specific bank following the supervisory review process or on a group of banks with a similar risk profile;
- *national flexibility measures*, allowing national authorities to impose stricter prudential requirements in order to address systemic risk. When making use of this flexibility, Member States need to notify and justify a more stringent measure to the Commission, EBA, and ESRB;
- *real estate-related instruments*, e.g. Member States retain the possibility to set higher risk weights for real estate lending, thereby being able to address real estate bubbles;

- two new *liquidity buffers*, i.e. a Liquidity Coverage Requirement (LCR) and a Net Stable Funding Requirement (NSFR) (see Chapter 12);
- a *leverage ratio*, as a backstop mechanism to limit the growth of the total balance sheet as compared to available own funds.

Other instruments which are under national legislation, and may not be a responsibility of the designated authority, include:

- the *loan-to-value (LTV) ratio*, which limits the extension of mortgage credit beyond a particular fraction of the value of housing collateral, and so restricts losses in the event of a default;
- the *loan-to-income (LTI)* ratio, which limits the extension of mortgage credit beyond a multiple of borrowers' annual income, thereby lowering the probability of default.

A common approach to implementing LTV and LTI restrictions is via an outright cap, prohibiting financial institutions from extending mortgage credit beyond the cap. In such a way these restrictions can help mitigate the risk that credit-fuelled bubbles in the housing market arise. Calibrating and adjusting LTV or LTI restrictions requires national authorities to ensure an appropriate trade-off between financial stability benefits, economic activity, and societal preferences for home ownership (BoE, 2011). An alternative approach would be to require banks to fund high-LTV or high-LTI mortgages through higher amounts of capital, i.e. via higher-risk weights.

Structural pillar

Table 13.3 specifies the macroprudential instruments under the structural pillar. It contains instruments for effectively addressing risks to financial stability due to externalities within the financial system, i.e. within financial institutions, market transactions, and financial infrastructures.

Table 13.3 Instruments under the structural pillar

Intermediate target	Exposure concentration	Misaligned incentives	
Key instruments	Large exposures restrictions (by counterparty, sector, geographic)	SIFI capital surcharges	Systemic risk buffer

Source: ESRB (2014)

Box 13.1 Recent experience with macroprudential measures

While the CCR/CRD IV package introduced EU-wide macroprudential measures in 2014, the use of macroprudential instruments is not new. In the period from the Second World War until the financial deregulation of the 1980s, many countries closely regulated credit markets using instruments which resemble the macroprudential policy tools discussed today. From the 1990s onwards, macroprudential policy measures have been most actively used in emerging markets, particularly in Asia in the aftermath of the Asian financial crisis. Lim *et al.* (2014) find that some of the most common macroprudential measures were effective in a cross-section of 46 countries between 2000 and 2010. More specifically, tightened LTV (loan-to-value) and LTI (loan-to-income) ratios, reserve requirements, dynamic provisioning, and ceilings on credit growth (also in foreign currency) all seem to reduce the pro-cyclicality of credit growth. The Hong Kong Monetary Authority (2011) finds that adjustments to LTV caps have been effective in reducing systemic risk that stems from boom and bust cycles in the property market. However, recent evidence suggests that caps on LTV ratios are more effective in dampening household leverage than mitigating credit growth or property price growth.

The reserve requirement (or cash reserve ratio) is a central bank regulation, employed by many central banks, which sets the minimum fraction of customer deposits. It requires that each commercial bank must hold balances at the central bank as reserves (rather than lend out), and can thus limit credit growth. Dynamic provisioning, also called forward looking loss provisioning, is the adjustment of banks provisions for defaults on loans for the effects of the economic cycle, so that provisions will be increased during booms, to allow for the possibility of a downturn, and provisions will be lower during a recession, as there is less room for worsening.

A number of European countries have also implemented macroprudential policies to mitigate risks related to foreign currency lending (especially prevalent in the Central and Eastern European countries). More recently, a number of countries have adopted measures to increase financial system resilience and mitigate the further build-up of risks related to housing markets and household indebtedness in a low interest rate environment (ECB, 2014).

Table 13.4 provides an overview of macroprudential tools targeting housing market imbalances. The table shows that in the Central and Eastern European countries the adjustment of reserve requirements has been the most common macroprudential measure adopted to curb both excessive credit expansion and foreign currency lending. Banks are then required to keep more liquidity in reserve and use less for lending, which should have a dampening effect on credit growth. However, within the euro area, with a single, centralised monetary policy, reserve requirements cannot be used as a tool to target excessive credit growth in individual countries.

Box 13.1 (cont.)

Table 13.4 Implementation of macroprudential policies targeting housing market imbalances

	Counter-cyclical capital buffer	Risk weights measures	Provisioning measures	Reserve requirements	LTV ratio	LTI ratio
Belgium		X				
Bulgaria		X	X	X		
Croatia	X		X	X		
Denmark					X	
Estonia		X		X		
Greece						
Hungary				X	X	
Ireland		X				
Latvia				X	X	
Lithuania				X	X	
Netherlands					X	X
Norway	X	X			X	
Poland				X	X	
Romania			X	X	X	
Slovakia				X	X	
Slovenia				X		
Spain		X	X			
Sweden		X			X	
Switzerland	X	X				

Source: ECB (2014)

With regard to measures aimed at addressing housing market imbalances, a cap on LTV ratios appears to be the most common solution. A LTV cap increases the borrower's equity stake in the property, which creates incentives to service the loan and lowers the bank's losses in the event of borrower default (so-called 'loss given default'). Both of these effects improve the resilience of the financial system and can potentially also lower mortgage credit growth. A related, but less frequently used, measure is a cap on the LTI ratio, which limits the size of the debt (or the cost of servicing the debt) relative to the borrower's income. Adjustments to (mortgage) risk weights and bank provisioning rules have also been introduced in a number of countries (ECB, 2014).

Stricter large exposure requirements (as well as sectoral capital requirements for intra-financial exposures) can be used to address interconnectedness and contagion (ESRB, 2014). These restrictions are microprudential measures that can be further tightened for a macroprudential purpose. They can be applied via Pillar II on a sector basis to reduce banks' exposure to a particular sector or asset class. They may target both direct exposures and excessive (indirect) interconnectedness among financial institutions, thereby reducing contagion risk.

The second instrument is a *capital surcharge for SIFIs*. Because of their size, complexity, and systemic interconnectedness, the failure of such institutions would imply large risks to financial stability. The FSB (2010) recommends that SIFIs should have higher loss-absorbing capacity than the minimum levels agreed in Basel III. The FSB takes the lead on the designation of a financial institution as a SIFI and the height of the surcharge. Chapters 10 and 11 report the list of global systemically important banks (G-SIBs) and global systemically important insurers (G-SIIs) in 2013. These lists are annually updated. So far, only capital surcharges for G-SIBs have been determined, which range from 1 to 2.5 per cent (see Table 10.7).

Another structural instrument for SIFIs to reduce the moral hazard of TBTF are the newly developed resolution plans (Avgouleas *et al.*, 2013). The overall objective of resolution plans is to provide authorities with a strategy for resolving a failing bank, with the aim of: (i) ensuring the continuation or orderly wind-down of a bank's critical economic activities, (ii) minimising the disruption of financial stability, (iii) containing moral hazard, and (iv) limiting the risk of exposing tax payers to losses. It must be possible for a bank to be resolved in a way that ensures that shareholders and unsecured creditors bear comparable losses to the kind they would suffer in the event of a normal insolvency, rather than benefiting from a public bailout as a consequence of the immediate need of preserving financial stability or the continuation of essential services (see also section 13.5).

Capital surcharges for systemically important institutions should reflect the potential losses to society of systemic risk from large and interconnected institutions (ESRB, 2014). The FSB's SIFI framework only applies to global financial institutions. National authorities can designate domestic financial institutions as domestic SIFIs. If needed, national authorities may use the *systemic risk buffer* in response to structural vulnerabilities, including the level of private debt or the size of the banking sector. This is an optional buffer on all or a subset of institutional (see Box 12.3)

13.5 Macroprudential architecture

One of the key lessons from the 2007–2009 financial crisis was that the supervisory arrangements had placed too much emphasis on the supervision of individual firms, and too little on the macroprudential side. In order to strengthen the supervisory arrangements on both sides of the Atlantic, the EU and US authorities established new bodies responsible for macroprudential supervision, i.e. the European Systemic Risk Board (ESRB) in the EU and the Financial Stability Oversight Council (FSOC) in the US. Moreover, at the global level G20 leaders decided to establish the Financial Stability Board (FSB).

European Systemic Risk Board (ESRB)

The ESRB is responsible for the macroprudential oversight of the EU's financial system, defined as contributing to the prevention or mitigation of systemic risks that arise from developments within the financial system and taking into account macroeconomic developments, so as to avoid periods of widespread financial distress.

The ESRB comprises a General Board as its decision-making body, a Steering Committee which sets the agenda and prepares the decisions, a Secretariat, as well as an Advisory Technical Committee and an Advisory Scientific Committee (ASC). While all relevant stakeholders are represented within the ESRB, a prominent role has been granted to central banks, i.e. the majority of the voting members of the General Board are central banks, the Chair is the ECB President, and the ECB also provides the Secretariat as well as analytical, statistical, administrative and logistical support to the ESRB.

The ESRB tasks include: (1) the collection and analysis of all information relevant for macroprudential oversight; (2) the identification and prioritisation of systemic risks; (3) the issuance of warnings where such risks are deemed to be significant; (4) the issuance of recommendations for remedial action; (5) the monitoring of the follow-up to warnings and recommendations; (6) cooperation with the European Supervisory Authorities (ESAs), including the development of indicators of systemic risk and the conduct of stress-testing exercises; (7) the issuance of confidential warnings on emergency situations addressed to the European Council; and (8) coordination with the IMF and the FSB, as well as other macroprudential bodies. Although ESRB recommendations are not binding, the parties addressed are obliged to respond under the principle of 'comply or explain'. In other words, they must follow the recommendation, or explain why they are not doing so.

Developments in EU Member States

The Capital Requirements Regulation (CRR) and Directive (CRDIV) introduce new macroprudential tools and require Member States to set up a 'designated authority' for macroprudential supervision. While all Member States have designated a national authority to conduct macroprudential policy, not all made the same choice. The ASC of the ESRB distils four main institutional models for the allocation of the formal powers for macroprudential supervision:

1. the ministry of finance (or economics);
2. the central bank;
3. the financial authority;
4. an ad hoc committee.

Table 13.5 shows that the central bank has most often been designated as the responsible authority. While several European central banks combine monetary policy and supervisory tasks, they typically have separate departments for financial stability (macroprudential) and financial supervision (microprudential). In these cases, there is an organisational separation between the macro- and microprudential tasks. In some countries, the stand-alone financial authority has been designated for macroprudential policy, while in others the responsibility for macroprudential instruments is shared between different authorities.

There is only one case (Denmark) where the Ministry is directly in charge. It should be noted that the Danish Financial Supervisory Authority is also an agency of the Ministry of Business and Growth in Denmark.

Table 13.5 Institutional models for macroprudential authorities (in numbers and %)

Agency	Ministry of finance	Central bank	Financial authority	Committee
Euro area	0 (0%)	13 (68%)	5 (26%)	1 (5%)
Non-euro area	1 (9%)	7 (64%)	2 (18%)	1 (9%)
Total	1 (3%)	20 (67%)	7 (23%)	2 (7%)

Note: The table covers the 28 EU Member States and the Banking Union
Source: ASC (2014)

The SSM makes the ECB an additional player for the countries that participate in the Banking Union. While the national designated authorities have the power to apply the macroprudential tools, the ECB has the power to set tighter requirements than national authorities. The ECB has established a Financial Stability Committee to advise the Supervisory Board and the Governing Council on the appropriate macroprudential stance.

Finally, in a few cases, a committee has been designated as the responsible authority. In these cases, the committee has direct responsibility for the application of macroprudential instruments. The Minister of Finance or the Central Bank Governor typically chairs these committees. Moreover, in several cases Financial Stability Committees have been established to foster adequate coordination and align the actions of the various agencies. The remit of these committees is to identify risks to financial stability and make recommendations with respect to these risks. These recommendations can for example be directed towards one or more relevant national authorities, which can subsequently act by making use of the statutory instruments at their disposal.

Financial Stability Oversight Council (FSOC)

As established under the Dodd–Frank Act, the Financial Stability Oversight Council (FSOC) in the US should provide comprehensive monitoring to ensure the stability of the nation's financial system. The Council is charged with identifying threats to the financial stability of the United States; promoting market discipline; and responding to emerging risks to the stability of the United States financial system. It is chaired by the Secretary of the Treasury and its members comprise representatives from the Federal Reserve, the federal financial regulators, as well as state regulators (the latter being non-voting members).

The tasks of the FSOC may be summarised as comprising three sets of powers (Enria and Teixeira, 2011):

(1) Coordination powers: the FSOC has the duty to support coordination and information sharing among its members;

(2) Advisory powers: the FSOC may issue recommendations for regulatory policy. In particular, it may recommend new or stricter standards for interconnected institutions including non-banks, as well as financial products and markets posing a threat to financial stability. The FSOC may also issue recommendations to the US Congress to close regulatory gaps;

(3) Systemic powers: the FSOC has the possibility to require consolidated supervision of non-bank financial institutions and to designate specific financial market infrastructures (e.g. payment, clearing and settlement) as systemic, so as to make them subject to regulatory oversight. Finally, the FSOC also plays a role in the possible breaking up of institutions that pose a 'grave threat' to financial stability.

The ESRB and the FSOC have a number of broad similarities. They both have analytical functions regarding the monitoring of the emergence of systemic risks and in this context the ability to share and collect information on the financial system. However, the main difference between the two is the ability to intervene directly in the financial system. The ESRB does not have such powers, while the FSOC can bring institutions and market infrastructures within the scope of regulatory oversight and determine whether the Federal Reserve can act in the context of its important new power to break up financial institutions.

Financial Stability Board (FSB)

The FSB has been established by G20 leaders at their summit of April 2009 to coordinate the work of national financial authorities and international standard-setting bodies and to develop and promote the implementation of effective regulatory, supervisory, and other financial sector policies. It gathers national authorities responsible for financial stability in significant international financial centres, international financial institutions, sector-specific international groupings of regulators and supervisors, and committees of central bank experts.

The FSB was established as the successor to the Financial Stability Forum (FSF), with a broadened mandate to promote financial stability. Among other things, the FSB is working on strengthening the oversight and regulation of shadow banking as well as ensuring that global systemically important institutions have sufficient loss-absorbing capacity when they fail. This 'total loss-absorbing capacity' (TLAC) is vital to ensure that systemically important banks can be resolved with a minimum or no use of public funds.

13.6 Crisis management and resolution

The financial crisis of 2007–2009 forced Member States to grant public support to banks at an unprecedented scale. According to IMF estimates, crisis-related losses incurred by European banks between 2007 and 2010 are close to €1 trillion or 8 per cent of the EU GDP. Moreover, between October 2008 and December 2012, the Commission approved close to €600 billion or 4.6 per cent of EU 2012 GDP in state aid measures in the form of recapitalisation and asset relief measures (EC, 2014).

While clearly necessary at that time to prevent widespread disruption, the financial crisis highlighted that public authorities lacked effective instruments to intervene at an early stage. Moreover, in those cases where a bank would fail, new instruments were needed to rescue a bank's critical functions, with minimum or no recourse to tax-payers money.

The Bank Recovery and Resolution Directive (BRRD; 2014/59/EU) contains the new crisis management framework for banks in Europe. It provides authorities with more comprehensive and effective arrangements to deal with failing banks at the national level, as well as cooperation arrangements to tackle cross-border banking failures. Key elements of the BRRD are (EC, 2014):

- *Preparation and prevention*: banks and resolution authorities are required to draw up recovery and resolution plans on how to deal with situations that may lead to financial stress or the failure of a bank. If authorities identify obstacles to resolvability during the course of this planning process, they can require a bank to take appropriate measures, including changes to corporate and legal structures, to ensure that it can be resolved with the available tools in a way that does not threaten financial stability and involve costs to taxpayers.
- *Early intervention*: supervisory authorities are granted new powers enabling them to intervene if a bank faces financial distress (e.g. when a bank is in breach of, or is about to breach, regulatory capital requirements), but before the problems become critical and its financial situation deteriorates beyond repair. These powers include the ability to dismiss the management and appoint a temporary administrator, as well as convening a meeting of shareholders to adopt urgent reforms and requiring the bank to draw up a plan for the restructuring of debt with its creditors.
- *Resolution:* this occurs at the point when the relevant authorities determine that a bank is failing or likely to fail, that there is no other private-sector intervention that can restore the institution back to viability within a short time frame, and that normal insolvency proceedings would lead to financial instability. Resolution means the restructuring of a bank by a resolution authority, through the use of resolution tools, to ensure the continuity of its critical functions and restoration of the viability of all or part of that institution, while the remaining parts are put into normal insolvency proceedings. The objective of resolution is to minimise the extent to

which the cost of a bank failure is borne by taxpayers. The resolution tools at the disposal of the resolution authority include the power to sell or merge the business with another bank, to set up a temporary bridge bank to operate critical functions, to separate good assets from bad ones, and to convert to shares or write down the debt of failing banks (*bail-in*). These instruments are discussed in more detail below.

- *Resolution fund:* Member States are required to establish an ex ante funded resolution fund. Contributions are raised from banks in proportion to their liabilities and risk profile, so as to reach a target funding level of at least 1 per cent of covered deposits. The fund should primarily be used for these resolution costs that cannot be funded via bail-in, e.g. the financing of a bridge bank. However, the BRRD agreement provides that after these stakeholders have borne sufficient losses (i.e. 8 per cent of the liabilities of the bank under resolution) through write-down or conversion, in exceptional circumstances the resolution financing arrangement may bear the remaining losses, but only up to 5 per cent of the bank's liabilities.
- *Cooperation and coordination:* the BRRD also provides a framework to improve cooperation between national authorities. When a cross-border banking group would fail, this framework should enable national authorities to coordinate their resolution measures and come to the most effective outcome for the group as a whole. Cross-border resolution may indeed give rise to coordination failure, as countries focus only on the externalities within their own country. Box 13.2 explains the financial trilemma model, which makes it possible to compare the efficiency of the different resolution mechanisms.

Resolution tools

The first tool that can be used in case of the failure of a bank is to effect a private-sector acquisition, whereby parts of the bank can be sold to one or more purchasers without the consent of the shareholders. In these cases, the resolution authority can act as honest broker, especially given the time constraints under which most problems have to be solved and the potential information asymmetries that exist.

If a private-sector solution is not immediately at hand, the resolution authority can transfer parts of the bank to a temporary structure (such as a 'bridge bank') to preserve essential banking functions or facilitate continuous access to deposits.

Box 13.2 The financial trilemma*

Schoenmaker (2013) develops the financial trilemma, which states that (1) a stable financial system, (2) international banking, and (3) national financial policies for supervision and resolution are incompatible. Any two of the three objectives can be combined but not all three; one has to give. The financial stability implication of international banking is that national financial policies are no longer adequate. Effective international cooperation for banking supervision and resolution is needed. In Europe, the Banking Union provides the necessary cooperation for banking policies.

The financial trilemma model formalises the systemic effects of bank failure. The policy instrument in this model is a contribution of funds t by the authorities (ministry of finance and/or central bank) to recapitalise a failing bank. The model considers the ex post decision whether to recapitalise or to liquidate a bank in financial distress. The choice to continue or to close the bank is a variable x with values in the space $\{0,1\}$, whereby $x^* = 1$ indicates recapitalisation and $x^* = 0$ closure.

Next, B denotes the social benefits of a recapitalisation and C the costs of continuing the bank activity. Among other things, the social benefits of a recapitalisation may include those derived from maintaining financial stability and avoiding contagion. A minor, idiosyncratic bank failure (for example, Barings) would pose no systemic problem.

Single-country setting

A social planner recapitalises a failing bank only when the total social benefits of an intervention are larger than the net costs: $B > C$. This is the efficient resolution line in Figure 13.5. Private-sector solutions are preferable in case of banking problems to reduce moral hazard. Only when the private sector cannot deal effectively with an emerging banking crisis do the authorities need to decide on the appropriate action.

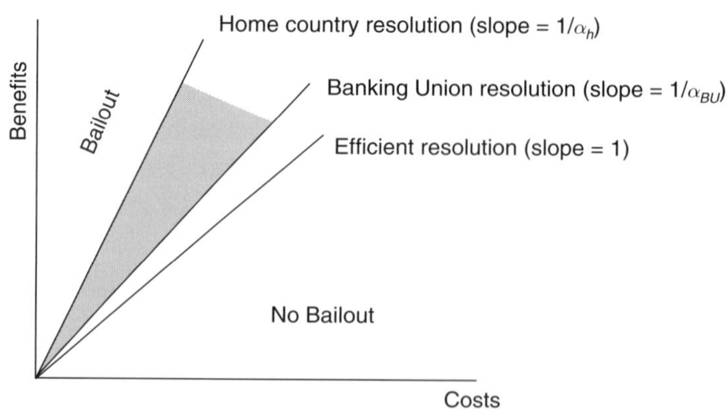

Figure 13.5 Equilibrium outcomes for different resolution mechanisms
Source: Schoenmaker (2013)

Box 13.2 (cont.)

Multicountry setting

In a multicountry setting, the social benefits can be decomposed into the benefits in the home country with fraction α_h of benefits, in the other European countries with fraction α_e, and in the countries in the rest of the world with fraction α_w. These fractions sum up to 1. A cross-border bank is only recapitalised if a sufficient contribution from the different countries can be collected on a voluntary basis. This is an interpretation of improvised cooperation, as in Freixas (2003). The different countries meet to find out how much they are ready to contribute to the recapitalisation, denoted by t. If the total amount they are willing to contribute is larger than the costs, the bank is recapitalised.

The optimal decision for each independent country j is to maximize:

$$x^* \cdot (a_j \cdot B - t_j) \tag{13.1}$$

so that

$$x^* = \begin{cases} 1 \text{ if } \sum_j t_j - C \geq 0 \\ 0 \text{ if } \sum_j t_j - C < 0 \end{cases} \tag{13.2}$$

The only choice variable for country j in this game is the size of its contribution t_j. Equation 13.1 shows that country j can maximise its benefits minus its contribution, by minimising its contribution. If every country only makes a minimal contribution to the recapitalisation, it is difficult to raise sufficient funds to meet the costs (Equation 13.2). This game, in which every country announces its contribution, has a multiplicity of equilibria. In particular, the closure $t_j = 0$, $x^* = 0$ is an equilibrium provided that for no country j

$$a_j \cdot B - C > 0 \tag{13.3}$$

Equation 13.3 indicates that no individual country is ready to finance the recapitalisation by itself, as the benefits for each country are smaller than the overall costs. In that case, every country reduces its contribution basically to zero. The closure equilibrium can occur (even if recapitalisation is efficient $B > C$) because part of the externalities fall outside the home country. This is shown in Figure 13.5 as the home country resolution line.

Solutions

Schoenmaker (2013) models two solutions to this coordination problem. The first is a supranational mandate for financial stability. The decision is taken by a supranational

Box 13.2 (cont.)

body, which can charge the participating countries applying some general criteria to share the burden. The optimal decision for the European supranational body is to maximise:

$$x^* \cdot \left((a_h + a_e) \cdot B - C \right) \tag{13.4}$$

so that

$$x^* = \begin{cases} 1 \text{ if } (a_h + a_e) \cdot B - C \geq 0 \\ 0 \text{ if } (a_h + a_e) \cdot B - C < 0 \end{cases} \tag{13.5}$$

The European body improves on the improvised coordination, as all European externalities ($\alpha_h + \alpha_e$) are incorporated in the recapitalisation decision (see the Banking Union resolution line in Figure 13.5). Chapter 10 quantifies these externalities for the biggest European banks: $\alpha_h = 0.53$ in Table 10.2 and $\alpha_{BU} = 0.73$ in Table 10.6 (note that BU refers to the home country and the rest of the BU). In efficiency terms, the Banking Union leads to an efficiency improvement of 58 per cent compared to the home rule, as the home rule is at a distance of 0.89 (=1–1/0.53) from the efficient benchmark of 1 and the supranational setting is at 0.37 (=1–1/0.73) from 1. Note that 58 per cent = (0.89 – 0.37)/0.89.

A second solution to the coordination failure is to create binding rules among European countries. Goodhart and Schoenmaker (2009) explore ex ante mechanisms for burden sharing.

Another option is to separate assets between a 'good' and 'bad' bank through a partial transfer of assets and liabilities. As a result, the bank in distress is split in a 'good' bank that retains the performing assets, and a 'bad' bank that receives the remaining assets (also labelled *toxic assets*) that are subsequently restructured or liquidated. Bank creditors can either be left with the 'bad' bank and undergo losses as part of the liquidation or be transferred to the 'good' bank, which may entail that their claims are reduced or converted into equity.

The latter process, which is not only applied in situations in which a failed bank is split into a 'good' and a 'bad' bank, is generally referred to as bail-in. The main aim of this instrument is to stabilise a failing bank in order for it to continue its critical functions, with minimal or no use of public funds. Bail-in enables authorities to recapitalise a failing bank through the write-down of liabilities and/or their conversion to equity, so that the bank can continue as a going concern. To ensure that institutions always have sufficient loss-absorbing capacity, the BRRD provides for resolution authorities to set *minimum requirements for own funds and eligible requirements* (MREL) for each institution, based on its size, risk, and business model. It is foreseen that in 2016 the European Commission will introduce harmonised rules with respect to the MREL.

The resolution authority will first write down all shareholders and then follow a pre-determined order in bailing in other liabilities. It potentially applies to all liabilities that are not backed by assets or collateral. However, bail-in will not apply to deposits protected by a deposit guarantee scheme, short-term inter-bank lending, or claims of clearing houses and payment and settlement systems (that have a remaining maturity of seven days), client assets, or liabilities such as salaries, pensions, or taxes. In exceptional circumstances, authorities can choose to exclude other liabilities on a case-by-case basis, if strictly necessary to ensure the continuity of critical services or to prevent widespread and disruptive contagion to other parts of the financial system, or if they cannot be bailed in within a reasonable time.

The write-down will follow the ordinary allocation of losses and ranking in insolvency (see Figure 13.6). Equity has to absorb losses in full before any debt claim is subject to write-down. After shares and other similar instruments, it will first, if necessary, impose losses evenly on holders of subordinated debt and then evenly on senior debt-holders.

Deposits from SMEs and natural persons, including in excess of €100,000, will be preferred over senior creditors. The Deposit Guarantee Scheme (DGS, see below) will in turn rank above these. In extreme situations, the DGS may have to make a cash contribution in the amount by which covered deposits would have been written down had they not been exempted from the bail-in tool.

It should be noted that, in order to protect the interest of creditors, the BRRD includes the principle that no creditor should be worse off under resolution than it would have been had the bank been wound up under normal insolvency proceedings. This principle entitles creditors to compensation if it is determined that the amount they end up recovering is less than what would have been the case of the bank had simply been placed into insolvency (for example, because the resolution authority decides to exclude certain liabilities from bail-in).

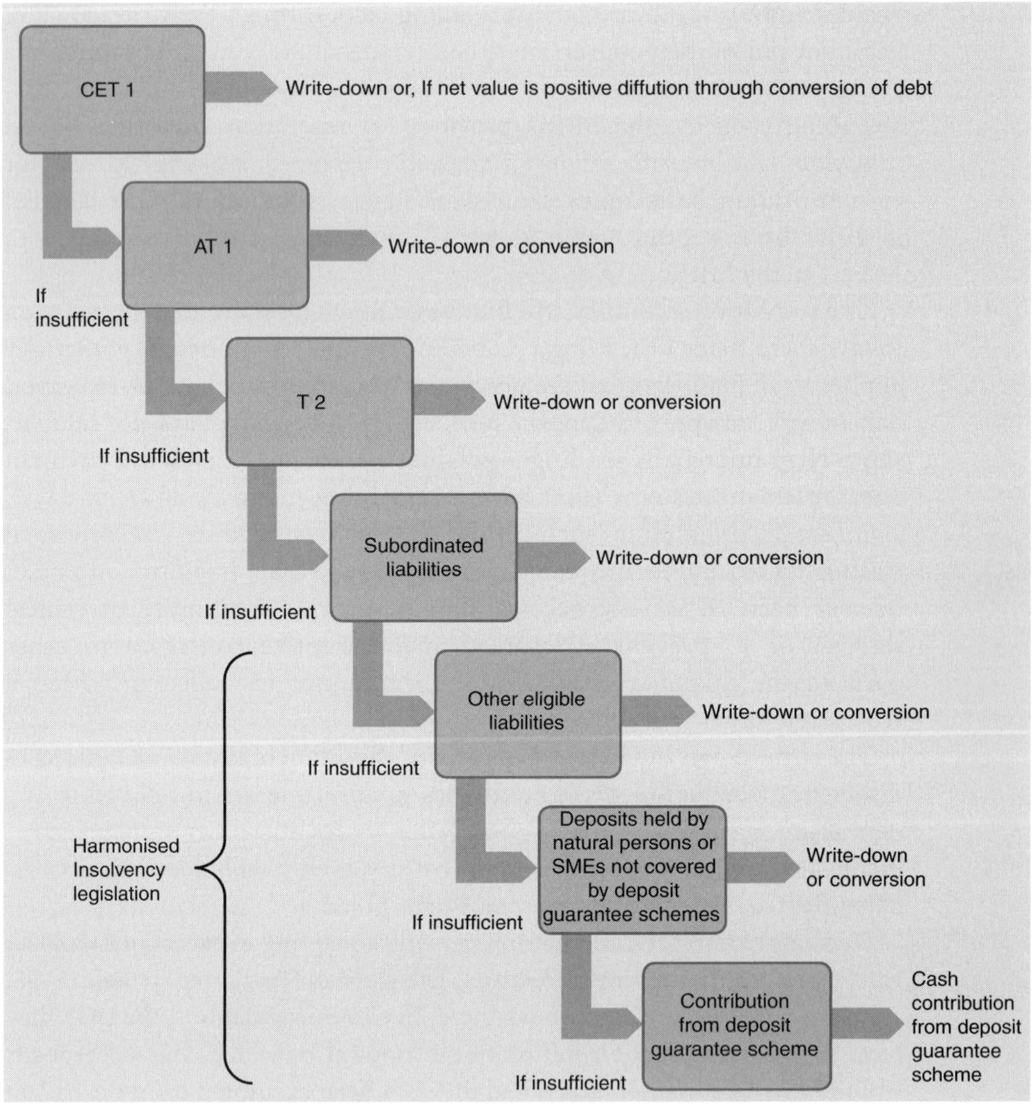

Figure 13.6 Hierarchy of claims in the bail-in procedure
Source: Bundesbank (2014)

Goodhart and Avgouleas (2014) provide a critical evaluation of the bail-in process. They argue that bail-in regimes may fail to fully eradicate the need for an injection of public funds if there is a threat of systemic collapse, because a number of banks have simultaneously entered into difficulties, or in the event of the failure of a large complex cross-border bank.

Other relevant instruments

Emergency Liquidity Assistance

Banks can receive central bank credit not only through monetary policy operations, but exceptionally also through Emergency Liquidity Assistance (ELA) provided by a central bank. Within the euro area, ELA means the provision by a NCB of central bank money and/or any other assistance that may lead to an increase in central bank money to a solvent bank or banking group that is facing temporary liquidity problems, without such operation being part of the single monetary policy. Responsibility for the provision of ELA lies with the national central bank(s) concerned. However, the Governing Council of the ECB may restrict ELA operations if it considers that these operations interfere with the objectives and tasks of the Eurosystem.

Deposit Guarantee Schemes

Deposit Guarantee Schemes (DGS) reimburse a limited amount of deposits to depositors whose bank has failed. The DGS Directive (2014/49/EU) ensures that deposits are covered up to €100.000. Moreover, it stipulates that banks will have to pay in to the schemes on a regular basis (ex ante), and not only after a bank failure (ex post). Target level of each DGS is a minimum of 0.8 per cent of the covered deposits in a Member State, to be reached within 10 years. The directive also aims to gradually reduce repayment deadlines from 20 working days to 7 working days. A pan-EU DGS is currently not under discussion.

Banking Union: the Single Resolution Mechanism (SRM)

The Single Resolution Mechanism (SRM) is the second pillar of the Banking Union and introduces centralised decision-making and a centralised resolution fund, rather than the decentralised approach based on the BRRD. The SRM Regulation (EU/806/2014) applies to all banks established in the Member States participating in the Banking Union.

The SRM will be fully operational as of 1 January 2016, with its main institutional components being the Single Resolution Board (SRB) and a Single Resolution Fund (SRF), to which all banks in the Banking Union contribute. The SRB has the status of an EU agency and has its seat in Brussels. Figure 13.7 provides an overview of the overall structure of the SRM.

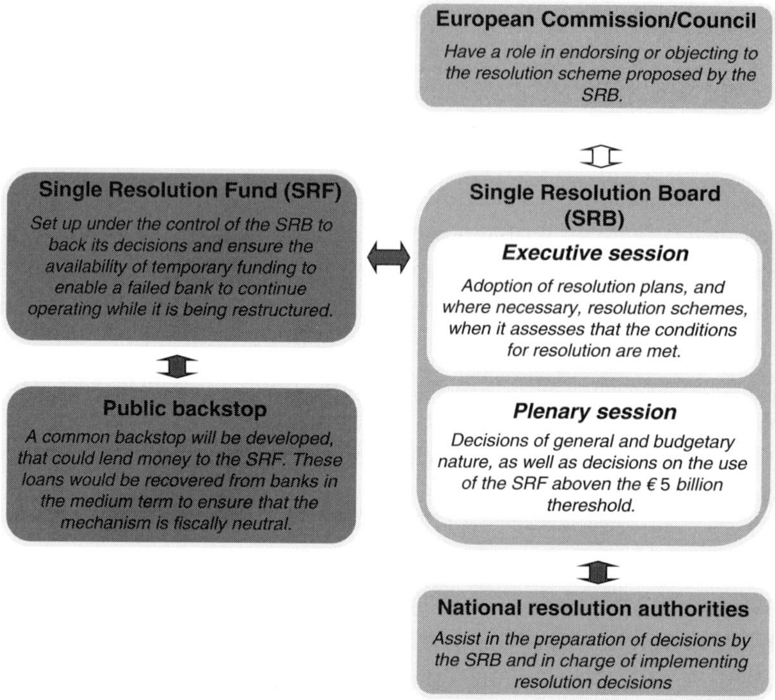

Figure 13.7 Overall structure of the Single Resolution Mechanism

In line with the SSM, the SRB is directly responsible for the resolution planning and resolution of banks directly supervised by the ECB, as well as cross-border groups. The national resolution authorities remain responsible for all other banks, with the exception of those situations in which a resolution scheme foresees the use of the SRF. In such a case, the SRB becomes the relevant resolution authority, regardless of the size of the institution.

The SRB will operate in two sessions:

- In its executive session, the SRB takes the key preparatory and operational decisions for resolving individual banks, including use of the SRF, and the decisions addressed to national authorities, as they are responsible for implementing the decisions of the SRB. In its executive session, the SRB consists of the Chairman of the SRB, the Vice Chair, four permanent members, and the relevant national authorities in the countries where the troubled bank is established. The representatives from the ECB and the European Commission will participate in the process as permanent observers.
- In its plenary session, the SRB takes all decisions of general and budgetary nature. Moreover, the plenary session is involved in individual resolution

cases, if a contribution of the SRF is required above a €5 billion threshold. The plenary session consists of all of the above representatives, except for the fact that in this session all national resolution authorities participating in the Banking Union are represented.

The SRF consists of contributions from all banks established in the Member States participating in the Banking Union. The idea of such a fund is not to replace private investors in absorbing losses and in providing new capital to a bank, but to give temporary financial support through guarantees or loans to ensure the viability of the critical functions of a bank while it is being restructured.

The SRF has a target level of €55 billion, to be reached within 8 years, and can borrow from the market or from third parties if decided by the SRB. During the transitional phase, the SRF is composed of national compartments, which are gradually mutualised. During these years, bridge financing can be made available by individual Member States and lending between national compartment is possible. The Eurogroup and Ecofin ministers adopted a declaration stating that a common backstop will be developed, thereby facilitating borrowings by the SRF. It should be noted that these loans are to be recovered from banks in the medium term so that tax payers' money is not involved.

So how would this structure operate in practice? Upon notification from the ECB that a bank is failing or likely to fail, the SRB first determines whether the conditions for resolution are met. The three relevant conditions in this respect are: (i) that a bank is indeed failing or likely to fail, (ii) that there are no alternative private solutions, and (iii) that a resolution action is necessary in the public interest. Once these have been confirmed, the SRB will adopt a resolution scheme, including relevant resolution tools and any possible use of the Single Resolution Fund.

Given the fact that the SRB is an EU agency, the Commission and, to a lesser extent, the Council have a role in endorsing or objecting to the resolution scheme proposed by the SRB. Where one of them objects to it, the Board would have to amend the resolution scheme. The overall decision-making process may not last any longer than 32 hours, so as to ensure that a bank can be resolved over the weekend.

National resolution authorities assist the SRB in preparing its actions and they are in charge of implementing the resolution decisions in line with national company and insolvency law. Member States are thus integrated into the overall structure with respect to the preparatory and implementation stages related to banks in their jurisdiction. The implementation of resolution decisions is closely monitored by the SRB and the latter can directly address executive orders to troubled banks if national authorities do not comply with one or more aspects of the resolution decision.

13.7 Conclusions

The 2007–2009 financial crisis highlights the crucial importance of effective crisis management tools as well as macroprudential supervision, focusing on the soundness of the financial system as a whole.

As a rule, macroprudential supervision focuses on risks that may trigger a loss of economic value or confidence in a substantial part of the financial system that is serious enough to have significant adverse effects on the real economy. This requires the monitoring and analysis of the way in which: (1) risk is distributed in the financial system at a given point in time, i.e. the cross-sectional dimension, and (2) aggregate risk evolves over time, i.e. the time dimension.

Several indicators are being used for financial stability analysis, with key variables being credit growth or the credit-to-GDP ratio, the ratio of banks' non-performing loans to total loans and changes in property or asset prices.

Particular attention is being paid to monitoring possible risks within systemically important financial institutions (SIFIs), whose disorderly failure, because of their size, complexity and systemic interconnectedness, may cause significant disruption to the wider financial system and economic activity. Stress tests can be an important tool in this process, measuring the sensitivity of a group of institutions or even an entire financial system to common shocks.

Various efforts have been launched at the national and regional level to strengthen macroprudential arrangements, often by establishing new bodies responsible for macroprudential supervision, e.g. the European Systemic Risk Board (ESRB) in the EU, and the Financial Stability Oversight Council (FSOC) in the US.

In Europe, the Banking Recovery and Resolution Directive (BRRD) provides resolution authorities with common powers and instruments to resolve a failing bank in an orderly manner, while preserving critical bank operations with minimal or no use of tax payers' money. In this respect, the bail-in tool enables resolution authorities to write down or convert into equity the claims of shareholders and creditors of banks that are failing or likely to fail. Next to these resolution tools, the BRRD also provides resolution authorities with preparatory and preventative as well as early intervention instruments.

The Single Resolution Mechanism (SRM) is the second pillar of the Banking Union, alongside the Single Supervisory Mechanism (SSM). This ensures that both supervision and resolution are exercised at the same level within the Banking Union. The SRM consists of a Single Resolution Board (SRB), with broad powers in case of bank resolution, and a Single Resolution Fund (SRF), ensuring the availability of temporary funding to support the restructuring of a failing bank.

Suggested Reading

Borio, C. (2010), Implementing a Macroprudential Framework: Blending Boldness and Realism, Bank for International Settlements, Basel.

European Systemic Risk Board (2014), *Flagship Report on Macro-prudential Policy in the Banking Sector*, ESRB, Frankfurt am Main.

Galati, G. and R. Moessner (2014), What Do We Know about the Effects of Macroprudential Policy?, De Nederlandsche Bank Working Paper 440.

Hanson, S. G., A. K. Kashyap, and J. C. Stein (2011), A Macroprudential Approach to Financial Regulation, *Journal of Economic Perspectives*, **25**(1), 3–28.

Schoenmaker, D. and P. Wierts (2011), Macroprudential Policy: The Need for a Coherent Policy Framework, Duisenberg School of Finance Policy Paper 13.

References

Advisory Scientific Committee (2014), Allocating Macro-Prudential Powers, *ASC Report 5*, ESRB, Frankfurt am Main.

Alessi, L. and C. Detken (2014), Identifying Excessive Credit Growth and Leverage, ECB Working Paper 1723.

Avgouleas, E., C. Goodhart, and D. Schoenmaker (2013), Bank Resolution Plans as a catalyst for global financial reform, *Journal of Financial Stability*, **9**, 210–218.

Bank for International Settlements (2005), *Central Bank Oversight of Payment and Settlement Systems, Committee on Payment and Settlement Systems*, BIS, Basel.

(2010), *Macroprudential Instruments and Frameworks: A Stocktaking of Issues and Experiences*, CGFS Papers 38, BIS, Basel.

Bank of England (2011), Instruments of Macroprudential Policy, *A Discussion Paper*, Bank of England, London.

Borio, C. (2003), Towards a Macroprudential Framework for Financial Supervision and Regulation?, *CESifo Economic Studies*, **49**(2), 181–216.

(2010), *Implementing a Macroprudential Framework: Blending Boldness and Realism*, Bank for International Settlements, Basel.

(2014), The Financial Cycle and Macroeconomics: What Have We Learnt?, *Journal of Banking and Finance*, **45**, 182–198.

Bundesbank (2014), Europe's New Recovery and Resolution Regime for Credit Institutions, Monthly Report, June 2014.

Čihák, M. and E. Nier (2009), The Need for Special Resolution Regimes for Financial Institutions – The Case of the European Union, IMF Working Paper 09/200.

Crowe, C., G. Dell'Ariccia, D. Igan, and P. Rabanal (2011), How to Deal with Real Estate Booms: Lessons from Country Experiences, IMF Working Paper 11/91.

de Larosière, J. (2009), Report of the High-level Group on Financial Supervision in the EU, European Commission, Brussels. Available at: http://ec.europa.eu/internal_market/finances/docs/de_larosiere_report_En.pdf (accessed 13 February 2012).

Enria, E. and P. G. Teixeira (2011), *A New Institutional Framework for Financial Regulation and Supervision*, University of Milan.

European Central Bank (2007), Progress Towards a Framework for Financial Stability Assessment, speech by José-Manuel González-Páramo, Member of the Executive Board of the ECB, OECD World Forum on 'Statistics, Knowledge and Policy', Istanbul, 28 June.

(2009), Text of the Clare Distinguished Lecture in Economics and Public Policy by Mr Jean-Claude Trichet, President of the European Central Bank, organised by Clare College, University of Cambridge.

(2014), Recent Experience of European Countries with Macro-Prudential Policy, Special Feature in *Financial Stability Review* May 2014, ECB, Frankfurt am Main.

European Commission (2009), *An EU Framework for Cross-Border Crisis Management in the Banking Sector*, EC, Brussels.

(2014), *EU Bank Recovery and Resolution Directive (BRRD): Frequently Asked Questions, MEMO/14/297*, EC, Brussels.

European Systemic Risk Board (2014), *Flagship Report on Macro-prudential Policy in the Banking Sector*, ESRB, Frankfurt am Main.

Financial Stability Board (2010), *Reducing the Moral Hazard Posed by Systemically Important Financial Institutions*, FSB, Basel.

Freixas, X. (2003), Crisis Management in Europe, in: J. J. M. Kremers, D. Schoenmaker, and P. Wierts (eds.), *Financial Supervision in Europe*, Edward Elgar, Cheltenham, 102–119.

Frydl, E. and M. Quintyn (2000), The Benefits and Costs of Intervening in Banking Crises, IMF Working Paper 00/147.

Galati, G. and R. Moessner (2014), What Do We Know about the Effects of Macroprudential Policy?, De Nederlandsche Bank Working Paper 440.

Goodhart, C. A. E. (2005), How Far Can a Central Bank Act as a Lender of Last Resort Independently of Treasury (Ministry of Finance) Support?, paper presented at the Norges Bank conference on Banking Crisis Resolution – Theory and Policy, 16–17 June, Oslo.

Goodhart, C. A. E. and E. Avgouleas (2014), *A Critical Evaluation of Bail-Ins as Bank Recapitalisation Mechanisms*, CEPR Discussion Paper 10065.

Goodhart, C. A. E. and D. Schoenmaker (2009), Fiscal Burden Sharing in Cross-Border Banking Crises, *International Journal of Central Banking*, **5**(1), 141–165.

Hanson, S., A. Kashyap, and J. Stein (2011), A Macroprudential Approach to Financial Regulation, *Journal of Economic Perspectives*, **25**(1), 3–28.

Hilbers, P. and M. Jones (2004), *Stress Testing Financial Systems*, International Monetary Fund, Washington DC.

Hong Kong Monetary Authority (2011), Loan-to-Value Ratio as a Macroprudential Tool – Hong Kong SAR's Experience and Cross-country Evidence, BIS Research Papers 57.

International Monetary Fund (2011), *Macroprudential Policy: An Organizing Framework*, Background Paper, IMF, Washington DC.

Lim, C., F. Columba, A. Costa, P. Kongsamut, A. Otani, M. Saiyid, T. Wezel, and X. Wu (2014), Macroprudential Policy: What Instruments and How to Use Them? Lessons from Country Experiences, IMF Working Paper 11/238.

MacDonald, R. (1996), *Deposit Insurance*, Centre for Central Bank Studies, Bank of England, London.

Mian, A. and A. Sufi (2014), *House of Debt: How They (and You) Caused the Great Recession, and How We Can Prevent It From Happening Again*, Chicago University Press, Chicago.

Minsky, H. (1982), *Can 'It' Happen Again? Essays on Instability and Finance*, M.E. Sharpe Inc., Armonk (NY).

Mishkin, F. S. (1992), Anatomy of a Financial Crisis, NBER Working Paper 3934.

Organisation for Economic Co-operation and Development (2002), Experiences with the Resolution of Weak Financial Institutions in the OECD Area, OECD, *Financial Market Trends*, **82**.

Schoenmaker, D. (2013), *Governance of International Banking: The Financial Trilemma*, Oxford University Press, New York.

Schoenmaker, D. and P. Wierts (2011), Macroprudential Policy: The Need for a Coherent Policy Framework, Duisenberg School of Finance Policy Paper 13.

Shin, H. (2010), *Macroprudential Policies Beyond Basel III, Policy Mimeo*, Princeton University.

Strahan, P. (2013), Too Big To Fail: Causes, Consequences, and Policy Responses, *Annual Review of Financial Economics*, **5**, 43–61.

Turner, A. (2009), *The Turner Review – A Regulatory Response to the Global Banking Crisis*, Financial Services Authority, London.

CHAPTER

14

European Competition Policy

OVERVIEW

This chapter provides a concise overview of European competition policy, with a focus on financial services. The chapter first defines competition and describes the objectives of EU competition policy, i.e. the maintenance of competitive markets in the EU, as well as the single-market objective. The ultimate goal of competition is to offer consumers greater choice of products and services at lower prices (i.e. to enhance consumer welfare).

The second part of the chapter analyses the economic rationale for competition policy by examining the difference between a perfectly competitive market and a monopoly. In a competitive market, prices are 'competed' down and goods or services are produced in the least costly way. Firms are price takers. In a monopoly, there is a single seller in the market who can exert undue market power. The monopolist thus has significant power over the price and is a price setter.

The third part of the chapter elaborates on the four tools of EU competition policy, i.e. the elimination of agreements that restrict competition and abuse of a dominant position, the control of mergers and acquisitions, the liberalisation of monopolistic sectors, and control of state aid. The application of the state aid rules in the 2007–2009 financial crisis is reviewed.

The fourth part of the chapter discusses a framework for investigating abuse of dominance. One of the elements of this framework is the so-called 'Small, but Significant Non-transitory Increase in Prices' (SSNIP) methodology, which is used to define the smallest market in which a hypothetical monopolist would be able to impose a small but significant non-transitory price increase (the relevant market). The relevant market for various financial services is discussed.

The final part of the chapter provides a brief description of the dual legislative and enforcement system for competition policy in the EU.

LEARNING OBJECTIVES

After you have studied this chapter, you should be able to:

- describe competition and competition policy
- explain the economic arguments for having competition policy
- reproduce the different tools of EU competition policy and explain how these relate to financial markets
- describe the process of assessing a dominant position
- understand the institutional structure of competition policy in the EU.

14.1 What is competition policy?

Competition can be defined as a market situation in which firms or sellers independently strive for the patronage of buyers in order to achieve a particular business objective, e.g. profits, sales, and/or market share (OECD, 1993). Competition forces firms:

- to become (more) efficient;
- to offer greater choice of products and services; and
- to offer these products and services at lower prices.

Ultimately, competition gives rise to increased consumer welfare and allocative efficiency (the latter will be discussed in more detail in section 14.3). Moreover, the level of competition is an important aspect of financial-sector development and, in turn, economic growth (Claessens and Laeven, 2005).

Generally, *competition policy* aims to ensure that competition in the marketplace is not restricted in a way that is detrimental to society (Motta, 2004). In practice, authorities establish a set of rules and policies aimed at safeguarding competition, as a means of enhancing economic welfare and ensuring efficient allocation of resources. However, the aim of competition policy should not be to eliminate market power, as the prospect of enjoying market power is an important driver for innovation and efficiency. Still, as will be discussed in section 14.4, firms are prohibited from abusing market power.

Competition policy is one of the pillars of the EU's internal market policy. By combating distortions of competition between firms, competition policy creates the preconditions for the proper market functioning with the aim to enhance overall consumer welfare. Moreover, safeguarding competition in the EU is an important instrument to promote further market integration, e.g. by taking away barriers for entry or exit, and the application of non-discrimination principles for new entrants. The objective of EU competition policy is therefore twofold (European Commission, 2000). The first objective of competition policy is the maintenance of competitive markets. Competition policy serves as an instrument to encourage industrial efficiency, the optimal allocation of resources, technical progress, and the flexibility to adjust to a changing environment. In order for the Union to be competitive on worldwide markets, it needs a competitive home market. Thus, the Union's competition policy has always taken a very strong line against price-fixing, market-sharing cartels, abuses of dominant positions, and anticompetitive mergers. It has also prohibited unjustified state-granted monopoly rights and state aid measures which do not ensure the long-term viability of firms, but distort competition by keeping them artificially in business. The second is the single-market objective. An internal market is an essential condition for the development of an efficient and competitive industry. The European Commission has used its competition policy as an active tool to prevent this (i.e. the erection of barriers to trade), prohibiting, and fining heavily the parties to two main types of agreement: distribution and licensing agreements that prevent parallel trade between Member States, and agreements between competitors to keep out of one another's 'territories'. The provisions of the Treaty on the Functioning of the European Union (TFEU) specifically require EU policy makers to 'act in accordance with the principle of an open market economy with free competition, favouring an efficient allocation of resources'. Roeller and Stehmann (2006) argue that with the progress made towards realisation of the internal market, the relative importance of the market integration goal has declined. As a result, policy statements increasingly focus on efficiency, consumer welfare, and competitiveness. Nevertheless, competition policy may be an effective instrument to strengthen integration in certain segments of the financial market.

At the EU level, competition law is enforced by the European Commission (more specifically, the Directorate General for Competition), while at the national level the national competition authorities are responsible. Section 14.5 will discuss the organisation of EU competition policy in more detail.

14.2 The economic rationale for competition policy

According to Motta (2004), the basis of competition policy is the idea that monopolies are 'bad'. Although this might sound somewhat simplistic, examining the difference between perfect competition and a monopoly (i.e. the two extremes in a marketplace) is useful to explain the economic rationale for competition policy.

A *monopoly* can be defined as a situation where: (1) there is a single seller in the market, (2) there are no (close) substitute products or services, and (3) there are barriers to entry for potential sellers. As a result of these characteristics, a monopolist has significant power over the price, i.e. he or she is a *price setter* rather than a price taker. The ability of a monopolist to raise and maintain a price above the level that would prevail under (perfect) competition is referred to as *market* or *monopoly power*. Generally, the exercise of market power leads to reduced output and loss of economic welfare. However, monopolies do not necessarily have to be a bad thing. A good example is a *natural monopoly* where a single firm can produce at lower costs than a situation in which there are two or more firms. According to the OECD (1993), natural monopolies are characterised by steeply declining long-run average and marginal-cost curves such that there is room for only one firm to fully exploit available economies of scale and supply the market.

Figure 14.1 shows the welfare effects of market power, by comparing the total surplus at the monopoly price with that at the perfect competitive (marginal-cost) price.[1] Under perfect competition, the price of the goods or services produced equals marginal cost (P_c = MC) and the goods or

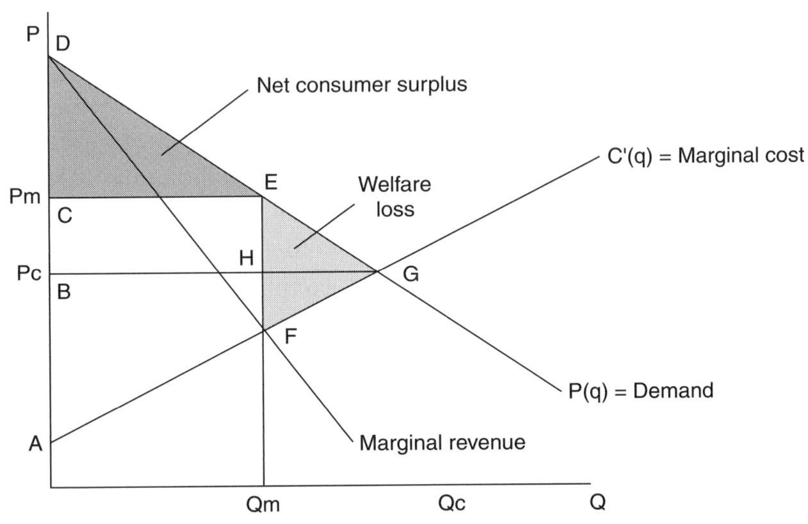

Figure 14.1 Welfare loss from monopoly
Source: Tirole (1988)

services will be produced in the least costly way. At the opposite, the monopolist sets output at the level where marginal cost equals marginal revenue (MC = MR) in order to maximise its profits. Tirole (1988) shows that the total surplus is equal to the sum of the consumer surplus and the producer surplus (or profit), or to the difference between total consumer utility and production costs. In Figure 14.1 this surplus is represented by the area DGAD under marginal-cost pricing and by the area DEFAD under monopoly pricing. The difference between the total surplus under monopoly and the surplus under marginal-cost pricing is the *welfare* or *deadweight loss* (given by triangle EFG in Figure 14.1). This welfare loss represents the overall opportunity costs to society arising from monopoly pricing. In addition, part of the consumer surplus under perfect competition, BCEH, is transferred to the monopolist in the form of excess profits.

So what does this entail in practice for competition policy? Figure 14.1 shows that having one firm (or very few firms) serving the market generally leads to a welfare loss for society. Competition policy should, however, not try to maximise the number of firms that operate in a market, because firms will then not be able to optimise the scale or magnitude of their output, which results in an average cost per unit of output that is higher than would be the case in a more concentrated market. Motta (2004) stresses that:

(1) competition policy is not concerned with maximising the number of firms; and
(2) competition policy is concerned with defending market competition in order to increase welfare, not defending competitors.

Should competition authorities then strive for perfect competition? Since the notion of perfect competition can in practice be highly restrictive in terms of policy making (OECD, 1993), the goal of competition policy should be a more realistic target such as *workable competition*, i.e. trying to create the preconditions for the proper operation of markets and ensure that firms do not abuse a dominant position. Although there is no generally accepted definition of workable competition, all authorities involved in competition policy seem to make use of some version of this concept. According to the OECD (1993), workable competition is a notion which arises from the observation that since perfect competition does not exist, theories based on it do not provide reliable guides for competition policy. Criteria for judging whether competition was workable are wide ranging, e.g. the number of firms should be at least as large as economies of scale permit, promotional expenses should not be excessive, and advertising should be informative.

For competition authorities it is important to have insight into the market power of firms and the level of competition in a specific market. There are various ways to quantify the level of market power. A well-known indicator is the *Lerner Index* (LI), which measures the degree to which a firm is able to price its products above marginal costs. The Lerner Index is a more accurate measure of market power than concentration measures (such as the Herfindahl Index and the CR5 ratio). Nevertheless, it poses some challenges. For instance, if the LI is relatively high it may still be hard to judge whether this indicates market power or superior efficiency. Moreover, in practice the LI is hard to calculate, as information on marginal costs is often not readily available. The LI is given by the following formula:

$$LI = (Price - Marginal\,Cost)\,/\,Price = 1\,/\,\varepsilon \tag{14.1}$$

where ε is the price elasticity of demand [$\varepsilon = -(\Delta Q/\Delta P)(P/Q)$]. The key determinant of market power is the elasticity of demand. The greater ε is, the greater will be the reduction in quantity demanded when the price rises. This entails that the higher the elasticity of demand, the lower the market power of the respective firm. In the case of perfect competition, P = MC and the LI equals zero. The higher the value of the LI, the greater is the firm's market power.

A method to assess competition in a market is the H-statistic of Panzar and Rosse (1987). This test statistic examines the relationship between a change in a firm's input prices and the revenues earned. The basic idea behind this indicator is that firms employ different pricing strategies in response to changes in input costs depending on the market structure in which they operate (see Table 10.4 for the H-statistic in banking).

Even in the absence of a monopoly, dominant positions might arise (Motta, 2004). The latter can, for example, be due to *sunk costs,* i.e. costs which, once incurred, cannot be (easily) recovered. Sunk costs lead to barriers to entry as well as to exit, as the existence of these costs increases an incumbent's commitment to the market and may signal a willingness to respond aggressively to entry (OECD, 1993). In this respect, offering financial services via the Internet or via intermediaries has the potential to improve contestability of markets by lowering sunk costs and barriers.

In other cases a dominant position may arise as a result of *lock-in effects* or *switching costs*. These are costs that customers face when changing from one supplier to the other. The higher these costs, the more difficult it

Box 14.1 Competition in banking

Analysing competition in the banking sector is quite complex (OECD, 2009). On the one hand, the general argument in favour of competition in terms of cost minimisation and allocative efficiency applies to the banking industry. On the other hand, as in numerous other markets, the standard competitive paradigm may not work fully because of features like asymmetric information in corporate relationships, switching costs, and networks in retail banking. In retail banking, switching costs for customers are very important, and reputation and branch networks may act as entry barriers. In corporate banking, established lending relationships and asymmetric information give financial institutions some market power vis-à-vis both firms and investors.

For a long time competition policy was actually applied very cautiously in the banking sector. It was seen as a special sector, where business was heavily influenced by the monetary and regulatory policies of Member State authorities rather than by market forces.

An important, and partly unresolved, question concerns the link between competition and stability. Until the 1980s, the prevailing view was that competition worsens stability. In particular, intense competition was perceived to favour excessive risk taking thus leading to a higher risk of individual bank failure, and regulation was believed to help mitigate this perverse link. Recently, the view on the potential trade-off between competition and stability has become more balanced. However, the results of empirical studies linking competition and stability are still ambiguous. Structural and non-structural measures of competition are found to be both positively and negatively associated with financial stability, depending on the country and the sample analysed and the measure of financial stability used (OECD, 2011). So while competition may not be responsible for fragility, it should take account of the specifics of banking, and not only in crises.

As will be discussed in the next section, the role of competition policy in crisis situations is to keep the markets open, check the distortions introduced by possible rescue packages, weed out inefficient institutions, and remove artificial barriers to entry. In the banking sector particular attention should be devoted to fostering entry in a post-crisis scenario. Vives (2011) argues that all of this calls for close cooperation between supervisory and competition authorities.

becomes to switch. The existence of switching costs can give substantial market power to existing suppliers. For example, the absence of account number portability increases switching cost of customers who would like to change banks. As a result, switching costs in retail banking are relatively high (see Box 14.1 for more information on competition in banking).

Finally, dominant positions can be a result of *network effects*. As shown in Chapter 7, the addition of a new participant to a network increases its value for all participants. This means that the value of the services and products offered to the participants depends on the number of other participants purchasing the same services and products. The existence of network externalities can lead to lock-in effects and make it hard for potential competitors to successfully enter the market.

According to Motta (2004), competition policy is also needed because firms may resort to actions that increase their profits but harm society. One example of such behaviour is *collusion*, which refers to any formal or informal agreements to raise or fix prices or to reduce output in order to increase profits. When explicitly formalised, these agreements are referred to as *cartels*. Firms may also display *predatory behaviour*, which refers to the situation in which one firm drives out its competitors by setting very low prices (sometimes even below costs). As soon as the predatory firm has driven out its competitors and has discouraged new entry into the market, it can raise prices and earn higher profits. Other types of *exclusionary behaviour* include investing in extra capacity, foreclosing access of rivals to crucial inputs, tying and bundling, and price discrimination. *Tying* refers to the practice of making the purchase of product A conditional on the purchase of product B. *Bundling* refers to the practice of selling two or more products or services in a package. *Price discrimination* occurs when customers in different segments are charged different prices for the same good or service, for reasons unrelated to costs (OECD, 1993). However, this type of exclusionary behaviour is effective only if customers cannot profitably resell the goods or services to other customers. Finally, as will be discussed in the next section, mergers and acquisitions may also reduce competition.

14.3 Pillars of EU competition policy

The objective of EU competition policy was first set out in the Treaty of Rome (1957), where it was indicated that one of the activities of the Community includes establishing 'a system ensuring that competition in the internal market is not distorted'. In general, EU competition policy has the following objectives:

- the elimination of agreements which restrict competition and of abuses of a dominant position (*antitrust*);

- the control of mergers and acquisitions between firms;
- the liberalisation of monopolistic economic sectors; and
- the control of state aid.

Antitrust

The two main pillars of EU competition law are Articles 101 and 102 TFEU. Article 101 prohibits agreements and concerted practices with an anticompetitive object or effect on the market, while Article 102 prohibits abuse of a dominant position.

The Treaty on the Functioning of the EU (TFEU) prohibits 'all agreements between undertakings, decisions by associations of undertakings and concerted practices which may affect trade between Member States and which have as their object or effect the prevention, restriction or distortion of competition within the common market'. Actions prohibited under Article 101 can take the form of:

- direct or indirect fixing of purchase or selling prices or any other trading conditions;
- limiting or controlling production, markets, technical development, or investment;
- sharing markets or sources of supply;
- applying dissimilar conditions to equivalent transactions with other trading parties, thereby placing them at a competitive disadvantage; or
- making the conclusion of contracts subject to acceptance by the other parties of supplementary obligations which, by their nature or according to commercial usage, have no connection with the subject of such contracts.

Box 14.2 provides two decisions in the domain of Article 101. The first example is the decision of the European Commission to prohibit MasterCard's multilateral interchange fees[2] (see Chapter 7 for a discussion on interchange fees). The second example is related to the price measures by the Groupement des Cartes Bancaires in France that – according to the Commission – hindered the issuing of cards at competitive rates.

Article 101 applies to horizontal as well as vertical agreements. *Horizontal agreements* are made between competitors in the same product market, while *vertical agreements* are made between firms operating at different stages of a certain production or distribution chain. However, exceptions can be made for those agreements that improve the production or distribution of goods or that promote technical or economic progress. Moreover,

Box 14.2 Article 101 cases: MasterCard and the Groupement des Cartes Bancaires

MasterCard's intra-EEA multilateral interchange fees

Chapter 7 indicated that the use of interchange fees is the subject of several regulatory and antitrust investigations. In December 2007, the European Commission published its findings on the multilateral interchange fees (MIFs) for cross-border payment card transactions with MasterCard and Maestro branded debit and consumer credit cards in the European Economic Area. The Commission concluded that MasterCard violated EC Treaty rules on restrictive business practices, as its MIF inflated the cost of card acceptance by retailers without leading to proven efficiencies. It was, however, stressed that MIFs are not illegal as such. According to the Commission, a MIF in an open-payment card scheme such as MasterCard's is compatible with EU competition rules only if it contributes to technical and economic progress and benefits consumers. In 2008 the European Commission also opened formal antitrust proceedings against Visa in order to establish whether its MIF constituted infringements of Article 81 (now Article 101 TFEU).

Price measures by the Groupement des Cartes Bancaires

In 2007 the Commission decided that the Groupement des Cartes Bancaires (France) had infringed the EC Treaty rules prohibiting practices which restrict competition. The Groupement had adopted price measures that hinder the issuing of cards in France at competitive rates by certain member banks, thereby keeping the price of payment cards artificially high to the benefit of the major French banks. According to the Commission, consumers were the victims of this illegal practice, depriving them of cheaper cards and a more diversified product offering. The decision ordered the Groupement to annul the measures concerned with immediate effect and to avoid taking any measures with a similar purpose or effect in the future.

Source: European Commission (2007a, 2007b)

such agreements should benefit consumers and should not unnecessarily eliminate competition.

Article 102 prohibits abuse of a dominant position. This article states that '[A]ny abuse by one or more undertakings of a dominant position within the common market or in a substantial part of it shall be prohibited as incompatible with the common market in so far as it may affect trade between Member States.' A firm is in a dominant position if it has the ability to:

- set prices above the competitive level;
- sell products of an inferior quality; or
- reduce its rate of innovation below the level that would exist in a competitive market (European Communities, 2003).

However, it is not illegal under EU competition law to hold a dominant position, since this can be obtained by legitimate means of competition. Still, competition rules forbid companies to abuse their dominant position. The next section will discuss a framework for investigating abuse of dominance. A well-known example of an Article 102 case was the decision of the European Commission that Microsoft had abused its dominant market position by leveraging its near monopoly in the market for PC operating systems onto the markets for work-group-server operating systems and for media players (European Commission, 2007c). Microsoft was fined €497 million for infringing the EC Treaty rules on abuse of a dominant market position. Because of non-compliance with certain requirements set out by the European Commission, the fine was subsequently raised to €899 million in 2008.

Examining mergers

The second element of the EU's competition policy is the examination of mergers, in order to assess whether they may lead to less competition. Merger control regulation has existed since 1989. The EC Merger Regulation[3] adopted in 2004 sets out rules for mergers and acquisitions of companies, which could have the possibility to restrict competition. In this respect, Article 2(3) of the Regulation states that: '[A] concentration which would significantly impede effective competition, in the common market or in a substantial part of it, in particular as a result of the creation or strengthening of a dominant position, shall be declared incompatible with the common market.' *Dominance* has been defined by the European Court of Justice (ECJ) as 'a position of economic strength enjoyed by an undertaking which enables it to prevent effective competition being maintained on the relevant market by affording it the power to behave to an appreciable extent independently of its competitors, customers and ultimately of its customers'.[4] However, the new EC Merger Regulation prohibits every merger which significantly impedes effective competition, i.e. the ban is not confined to 'dominant firms'. It therefore takes account of the argument that even in the absence of a dominant position a merger may also have serious anti-competitive effects.

As for the enforcement of merger rules, general principles have been established to ensure an efficient division of work. Mergers with a Union dimension are investigated by the European Commission. The main requirement for a merger having a Union dimension is that the combined aggregate worldwide turnover of the merging companies is over €5 billion and that the aggregate Union-wide turnover of each of at least two of the undertakings concerned is more than €250 million.

A merger may also have a Union dimension if the following turnover criteria are met: the combined aggregate worldwide turnover of all undertakings is more than €2.5 billion, and the aggregate Union-wide turnover of each of at least two of the undertakings concerned is more than €100 million, and in each of at least three Member States the combined aggregate turnover of all the undertakings concerned is more than €100 million, and in each of at least three of these Member States the aggregate turnover of each of at least two of the undertakings concerned is more than €25 million. A merger of such a dimension can subsequently be assessed in a single procedure by the European Commission (one-stop-shop principle), instead of different assessments by the Member States involved.

But if each of the undertakings involved achieves more than two-thirds of its Union-wide turnover within one and the same Member State, the merger is in principle examined by the competition authority of that country (as it is supposed to be better placed to examine the potential effects). Both merger-regulation thresholds are summarised in Tables 14.1 and 14.2. Below these thresholds, the national competition authorities in the EU Member States may review the merger. However, the European Commission can also examine mergers, which are referred to it by the national competition authorities or the undertakings involved. In the latter case, agreement of all relevant national competition authorities is needed.

Table 14.1 Union dimension – threshold I

Undertaking	A	B	A + B
Worldwide turnover			> € 5 billion
Union turnover (UT)	> €250 million not 2/3 of UT in one and the same Member State	> €250 million not 2/3 of UT in one and the same Member State	

Table 14.2 Union dimension – threshold II

Undertaking	A	B	A + B
Worldwide turnover			> € 2.5 billion
Union turnover (UT)	> €100 million not 2/3 of UT in one and the same Member State	> €100 million not 2/3 of UT in one and the same Member State	
Turnover Member State 1	> € 25 million	> € 25 million	> €100 million
Turnover Member State 2	> € 25 million	> €25 million	> €100 million
Turnover Member State 3	> € 25 million	> €25 million	> €100 million

Apart from competitive reasons, potential mergers and acquisitions between financial institutions may also be blocked for prudential reasons. The '*prudential carve-out*' allows supervisory authorities to block proposed mergers and acquisitions if the 'sound and prudent management' of the targeted firm(s) could be put at risk. Initially, the margins of this requirement were defined rather broadly and on several occasions the carve-out was used in a protectionist manner. After the takeover battle for the Italian bank Antonveneta in 2005, in which then-governor of the Italian Central Bank Antonio Fazio tried to block the purchase of Antonveneta by ABN AMRO, the Council and the European Parliament endorsed a proposal in 2007 to tighten the procedures that supervisory authorities have to follow when assessing proposed mergers and acquisitions. Directive 2007/44/EC, sometimes referred to as the Qualifying Holdings Directive, comprises a list of criteria on the basis of which prudential supervisory authorities should assess the acquiring company, e.g. reputation of the proposed acquirer, reputation and experience of the management, financial soundness, compliance with EU Directives, and risks related to money laundering and terrorism financing. Moreover, the assessment period is reduced from three months to 30 days.

Liberalisation of monopolistic economic sectors and state aid

Governments can also introduce restrictions on competition by granting national businesses exclusive rights to provide certain goods or services, or by providing public aid to businesses.

Based on Article 106 TFEU, the European Commission is responsible for monitoring public undertakings and undertakings to which Member States grant special or exclusive rights (thereby establishing monopolistic sectors). The European Commission also has the power to address government actions which may distort competition in the internal market. Under this heading, the European Commission plays a pivotal role in opening up markets such as transport, energy, postal services, and telecommunications to competition.

Firms receiving support from their government are likely to obtain an unfair advantage over their competitors. State aid is therefore forbidden by the Treaty, unless it is justified by reasons of general economic development. The rules concerning state aid have been laid down in Articles 107, 108, 109 TFEU. The objective of state aid control is to ensure that government interventions do not distort competition and trade inside the EU. It strives to find the right balance between on the one hand the advantage for the aid recipient and the achievement of a policy objective (e.g. economic development, job creation, financial stability) and on the other the competitive distortion created in the market (i.e. the disadvantage for the competitors). In this respect, state aid is defined as an advantage in any form whatsoever conferred on a selective basis to undertakings by national public authorities. Therefore, subsidies granted to individuals or general measures open to all enterprises are not covered by TFEU and do not constitute state aid. In order to ensure that these rules are respected and exemptions are applied equally across the EU, the European Commission is in charge of monitoring state aid.

During the financial crisis and the euro crisis, Member States took several measures to support the European financial sector. Some of these measures were directed towards individual institutions (capital injections, asset solutions; see Figure 14.2), while others were general (guarantee schemes, liquidity operations; see Figure 14.3). They reduced the default risks among financial institutions and thus helped to safeguard financial stability. However, the interventions had distortionary effects, because the rapid unfolding of the crisis and market failures complicated the proper design of support policies.

Since the beginning of the 2007–2009 financial crisis, the European Commission has provided detailed guidance on the criteria for the compatibility of temporary crisis-related support measures with Article 107 TFEU. Through the application of state aid rules, the Commission tried to ensure that distortions of competition within the internal market were limited to a minimum despite the important amounts of state aid and that beneficiary banks were restructured when necessary.

Aid instrument	Used	
	In € billion	As a % of 2012 GDP
Recapitalisation measures	413.2	3.20%
Asset relief measures	178.7	1.39%
Total	591.9	4.6%

Figure 14.2 Total recapitalisation and asset relief measures, 2008–2012
Source: European Commission

Aid instrument	Peak outstanding amount (2009)		2012 outstanding amount	
	In € billion	As a % of 2012 GDP	In € billion	As a % of 2012 GDP
Guarantees	835.8	7.10%	492.3	3.82%
Other liquidity measures	70.1	0.59%	42.2	0.33%
Total	906.0	7.7%	534.5	4.1%

Figure 14.3 Total outstanding guarantees and other liquidity measures, 2008–2012
Source: European Commission

Between 1 October 2008 and 1 October 2013 the Commission took more than 400 decisions authorising state aid measures to the financial sector. In the period 2008–2012, overall capital support amounted to €591.9 billion or 4.6 per cent of EU 2012 GDP (see Figure 14.2).

The guarantees and other form of liquidity supports reached its peak in 2009 with an outstanding amount of €906 billion (7.7 per cent of EU 2012 GDP). As is shown in Figure 14.3, the outstanding amount has dropped to €534.5 billion in 2012 (4.1 per cent of EU 2012 GDP).

Prominent state aid decisions include the approval by the Commission of the plan submitted by the Irish authorities to jointly wind down Anglo Irish Bank and the Irish Nationwide Building Society over a period of ten years. Another example is the German Landesbank WestLB, where it was decided that the bank should be split up, and the remaining assets and liabilities transferred to a bad bank in order to be wound down. As such, WestLB would no longer perform banking activities and only continue to provide asset management services. Moreover, a small part of the activities of WestLB was taken over by Landesbank Hessen-Thüringen. Moreover, banks which relied heavily on state aid can be allowed to stay on the market where parts of their activities have a realistic prospect to return to viability, provided that they considerably reduce their size and substantially change their business model to focus only on the viable activities (European Commission, 2012). This approach is well illustrated by the approval of the restructuring of the German Bank Hypo Real Estate, as this bank will shrink to 15 per cent of its pre-crisis balance sheet and phase out a number of business activities.

Table 14.3 lists large banks (assets of more than €250 million in 2007) that received state aid. During the crisis, 14 large banks received state aid. In three cases, two ailing banks were merged as part of the restructuring deal. This was the case for Lloyds Bank (taking over HBOS), Commerzbank (taking over Dresdner), and Banque Populaire Caisse d'Epargne (renamed to Groupe BPCE). As part of the approval of state aid, the European Commission forced banks to downsize. With the exception of Groupe BPCE, the banks with state aid have downsized significantly. The overall downsizing is 18 per cent (decline measured from 2007 to 2011). The EU banking system grew over this period with 9 per cent, so that the growth difference between the sector as whole and the banks listed in Table 14.3 is a staggering 27 per cent.

Restructuring during the financial crisis followed three main principles: (1) the return to long-term viability without state aid, based on a sound restructuring plan; (2) burden sharing between the bank/its stakeholders and the state; and (3) limitation of competition distortions, usually through structural (divestitures) and behavioural measures (acquisition bans or limitations on aggressive commercial behaviour). In anticipation of the implementation of the Bank Recovery and Resolution Directive (BRRD) and the start of the Single Resolution Mechanism (SRM), the European Commission adapted its temporary state aid rules for banks in 2013. The main changes were aimed at improving the restructuring process and the level playing field between banks. As a result of these changes, banks are required to work out a sound plan for their restructuring or orderly winding down before they can receive any recapitalisations or asset protection measures. Moreover, in case of capital shortfalls, bank owners and junior creditors will be required to contribute as a first resort, before banks can ask for public support.

Table 14.3 Large banks with state aid

Banking groups	Assets of separate banks in 2007 in € billion	Total assets in 2007 in € billion	Total assets in 2011 in € billion	Difference 2007–2011 in per cent
1. Royal Bank of Scotland (UK)		2,587	1,801	–30%
2. Lloyds Banking Group (UK)		1,389	1,160	–16%
2a. Lloyds Group (UK)	481			
2b. HBOS (UK)	908			
3. Commerzbank (Germany)		1,116	662	–41%
3a. Commerzbank (Germany)	616			
3b. Dresdner Bank (Germany)	500			
4. ING Bank (Netherlands)		994	961	–3%
5. Fortis (Belgium)		767	Split up	
6. Groupe BPCE (France)		707	1,138	+61%
6a. Caisse d'Epargne (France)	434			
6b. Banques Populaires (France)	273			
7. Dexia Bank (Belgium)		605	413	–32%
8. Landesbank Baden-Würt (Germany)		443	373	–16%
9. Bayerische Landesbank (Germany)		416	319	–23%
10. KBC Group (Belgium)		356	285	–20%
11. WestDeutsche Landesbank (Germany)		287	168	–41%
Aggregate difference state aid banks		8,900	7,280	–18%
Aggregate difference EU banking system		41,062	44,818	+9%

Note: Banks with stated aid are selected on the basis of size: assets over €250 million in 2007. In some cases, two banks were merged as part of the restructuring. Assets of the separate banks are reported in the first column. One bank (Fortis) was split up and ceased to exist. Another bank (WestDeutsche Landesbank) was dissolved in Summer 2012.
Source: Schoenmaker (2013).

Van den End *et al.* (2009) argue that setting conditions for support cannot always prevent that the level playing field between supported and non-supported institutions is affected and that undesirable shifts in capital flows occur. To reduce such negative side effects of support, it is important that the support policies are market compatible, unambiguous and timely withdrawn through an appropriate exit strategy.

14.4 Assessment of dominant positions

Under Article 102 TFEU and the EC Merger Regulation, competition authorities need to examine abuse of dominance. This section discusses how competition authorities may examine (potential) abuse of dominant positions, using a framework suggested by the UK Office of Fair Trading (OFT, 2001). This approach consists of three steps (see Figure 14.4):

1. Assess whether there is a plausible market definition under which the firm under investigation has a high market share.
2. If there is a plausible market in which the firm might be dominant, conduct a full analysis of the economic effects of the practice under investigation.
3. If competition is likely to have been significantly damaged or if there is a prospect of such damage, issue a decision that describes and demonstrates the adverse economic effects of the business practice. Alternatively, if the conduct is not harmful, issue a decision giving the reasons why the business practice under investigation does not constitute an abuse of a dominant position.

The three steps will be discussed in more detail. Although Figure 14.4 depicts an ex-post investigation of possible abuse of dominance, similar investigations can be done ex ante in case of a proposed merger or acquisition.

Step 1: Identify the relevant market

The main purpose of market definition is to identify in a systematic way the competitive constraints that the firms involved face. A market is defined in both its product and geographical dimension (European Commission, 1997). The relevant *product market* is said to 'comprise all those products and/or services which are regarded as interchangeable or substitutable by the consumer, by reason of the products' characteristics, their prices and their intended use'. Moreover, the relevant *geographical market* 'comprises the area in which the undertakings concerned are involved in the supply and demand of products or services, in which the conditions of competition are sufficiently homogeneous and which can be distinguished from neighbouring areas because the conditions of competition are appreciably different in those areas'.

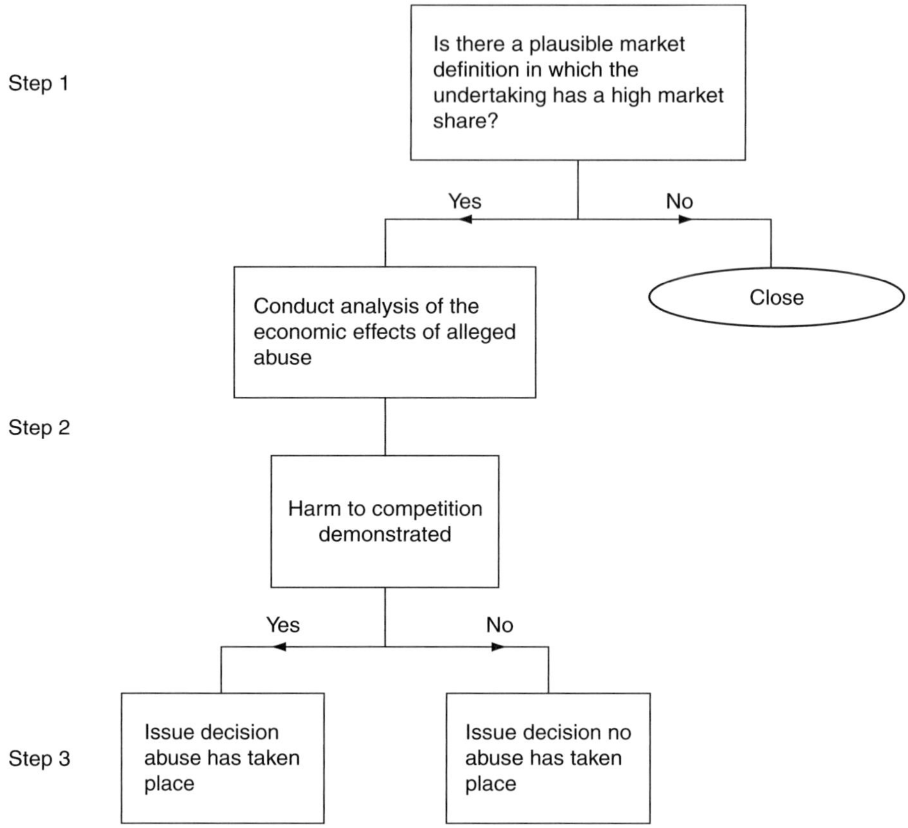

Figure 14.4 Flowchart for undertaking abuse-of-dominance investigations
Source: Office of Fair Trading (2001)

A very common methodology to define the relevant geographical market is the *Small, but Significant Non-transitory Increase in Prices* methodology (European Commission, 2004). The SSNIP methodology is used to examine whether some goods produced within a specific area constitute their own relevant geographical market. The first step is to assume that the respective goods or services are produced by a hypothetical monopolist. Subsequently, the question is asked whether it is likely that this monopolist can earn a profit by increasing prices by 5–10 per cent (i.e. small but significant) for a period of not less than 12 months (i.e. non-transitory).

If the answer is yes, then the candidate goods form their own relevant geographic market. If the answer is no, because consumers substitute away from the candidate markets as they are able to purchase the same good in neighbouring regions or because producers from other regions enter the market, then the relevant geographical market is larger than the goods for the candidate market. The thought experiment is subsequently repeated with a larger geographical area and continued until the answer to the question posed is affirmative. At that stage, the relevant geographical market is composed of all areas included in the last experiment. When it is difficult to assess whether goods which meet the same needs of the consumer belong to the same market or not, price tests (looking at price co-movements) can be used to evaluate the extent of the relevant candidate market.

Whether or not a price increase is profitable depends on the sales volume that is lost following the price increase, i.e. the extent to which a consumer can substitute away from the candidate market (see Box 14.3 which explains the algebra of the SSNIP methodology). The quantity of lost sales depends on the following two aspects:

- the availability of substitute products (i.e. *demand-side substitutes*); and
- the ability of other firms to supply these products (i.e. *supply-side substitutes*).

Once the relevant market has been defined, market shares and concentration indices have to be calculated. There are no thresholds for defining dominance set by law, but the ECJ has argued that dominance can be presumed in the absence of evidence to the contrary if a firm has a market share persistently above 50 per cent. However, a firm with lower market shares may also be dominant, particularly if it faces competitors that are much smaller. The OFT (2001) stresses that despite having a high market share, a firm may not be dominant if one or more of the following conditions hold:

- there are very low barriers to entry into the relevant market and the threat of potential entry is sufficient to discipline firms with high market shares;
- the nature of competition within the market is such that very intense competition exists even where there are very few players; and
- the nature of the buyers in a market and the volumes that they purchase are such that they can exert significant countervailing power against a firm with a high market share.

Also, a high concentration ratio does not necessarily point towards a lack of competition. Claessens and Laeven (2004) estimate competitiveness indicators for banks in a large cross-section of countries and find no evidence that banking-system concentration is negatively associated with competitiveness. In fact, they find some evidence that more concentrated banking systems are more competitive. The latter may be the result of fierce competition in the preceding period, as a result of which the overall banking system has become relatively efficient. Claessens and Laeven (2004) conclude that a contestable

Box 14.3 Algebra of the SSNIP methodology*

Profits (π) beforehand (denoted with subscript 0) are equal to revenue (price (P) times quantity (Q)) minus total costs (average costs (C) times Q):

$$\pi_0 = (P_0 - C_0)Q_0 \tag{14.2}$$

A change in the price ($\Delta P = P_1 - P_0$) leads to a change in quantity demanded ($\Delta Q = Q_1 - Q_0$) and may also lead to a change in the average costs of production ($\Delta C = C_1 - C_0$).

This gives a new level of profits:

$$\pi_1 = (P_1 - C_1)Q_1 \tag{14.3}$$

The change in profit is given by:

$$\begin{aligned} \Delta\pi = \pi_1 - \pi_0 &= (P_1 - C_1)Q_1 - (P_0 - C_0)Q_0 \\ &= \Delta P Q_1 + (P_0 - C_0)\Delta Q - Q_1 \Delta C \end{aligned} \tag{14.4}$$

Note that when $\Delta P > 0$, it is expected that $\Delta Q < 0$. The issue is when $\Delta\pi$ will be less than zero. It is convenient to rewrite (14.4) by dividing through P_0 (note that this does not matter as $\Delta\pi < 0$ if $\Delta\pi/P_0 < 0$), yielding:

$$\frac{\Delta\pi}{P_0} = \frac{\Delta P}{P_0}Q_1 + \frac{P_0 - C_0}{P_0}\Delta Q - \frac{Q_1}{P_0}\Delta C. \tag{14.5}$$

Suppose average costs is constant (i.e. it does not depend on the amount produced) so that $\Delta C = 0$. Then,

$$\frac{\Delta\pi}{P_0} = \frac{\Delta P}{P_0}Q_1 + \frac{P_0 - C_0}{P_0}\Delta Q \tag{14.6}$$

Thus, a price rise will be profitable if:

$$\frac{\Delta P}{P_0}Q_1 > \frac{P_0 - C_0}{P_0} - \Delta Q \tag{14.7}$$

that is, if the increased price charged on the new (lower) quantity is greater than the lost margin on the decrease in quantity. If there are economies of scale, it is also necessary to work out:

$$\frac{Q_1}{P_0}\Delta C. \tag{14.8}$$

If, for example, $\Delta C > 0$ when $\Delta Q < 0$, the increase in price on the new quantity needs to be greater than the lost margin on the decreased quantity plus the higher costs of the new quantity.

Source: Geroski and Griffith (2004)

system may be more important to assure competitiveness than a system with low concentration (see Chapter 10).

Step 2: Abuse of dominance?

Once it is clear that a market can be defined in which the respective firm has a dominant position, the economic effects of (possible) abuse should be examined. Abusive conduct generally falls into one of the following categories (OFT, 2004):

- conduct which exploits customers or suppliers (for example, through excessively high prices); or
- conduct which amounts to exclusionary behaviour, because it removes or weakens competition from existing competitors, or establishes or strengthens entry barriers, thereby removing or weakening potential competition.

In the first case, it may be possible to identify abuse by analysing the profitability of the respective firm. However, profitability figures may be hard to interpret (OFT, 2003). For example, when are profits too high or too low, and what is the relevant time period to consider? And if high profits are found, are they due to market power or to superior efficiency? Profitability figures should therefore be cautiously interpreted and other economic indicators – such as productivity, the advertise-to-sale ratio, prices, and the level of innovation – should also be analysed.

The economic impact of exclusionary behaviour on the market requires a detailed analysis of, among other things, barriers to entry and switching costs. The challenge is to make a distinction between what can be seen as behaviour under normal competition and what can be labelled as abusive practices. In this respect, the OFT (2001) distinguishes between conduct that inflicts harm to competition and conduct that inflicts harm to competitors. Demonstrating harm to competitors is important only when it leads to adverse impacts on consumers. Harm to competitors does not necessarily have an adverse impact on competition. It must therefore be determined whether the conduct represents normal business practice (i.e. lawful competitive behaviour) or abusive behaviour.

Step 3: Issue decision

If no harm to competition can be demonstrated, competition authorities refrain from any intervention. However, if (possible) harm to competition can be proven, competition authorities may impose administrative sanctions, like imposing a fine, prohibiting a proposed merger or acquisition, or requiring additional concessions for the proposed merger or acquisition.

An interesting example of the latter is the proposed merger between the two Swedish banking groups FöreningsSparbanken and SEB in February 2001. The merger of these two banking groups would have created Sweden's leading financial group with market shares in a number of markets in the range of 40–60 per cent. According to the European Commission (2001), the merged entity's large customer base and extensive branch network would have placed it well ahead of its closest competitors in Sweden. In reaction to the preliminary views of the European Commission set out in its Statement of Objections, FöreningsSparbanken and SEB announced in September 2001 that they would withdraw their merger application, claiming that the concessions (e.g. forcing the banks to significantly reduce their market shares) would jeopardise the value of the proposed merger. The European Commission (2001) argued that it should not have been a surprise that it had considered the market as national.

To define the market for banking services to households and SMEs as national is standard practice for antitrust regulators worldwide. In previous cases involving banking mergers the European Commission has raised concerns where market shares were considerably lower (30–35 per cent). Moreover, in 2001 the UK authorities blocked a merger between Lloyds and Abbey National which presented significantly lower combined market shares (27 per cent for household accounts). The subsequent takeover of Abbey National by the Spanish banking group Banco Santander in 2004 did not raise any competition concerns as these banks were (mostly) active in different countries.

Table 14.4 provides some indications on the relevant geographical market for various financial services. The relevant market for retail banking and

Table 14.4 Relevant geographical market for financial services

National	European	Global
Retail banking & insurance		
	Wholesale banking & insurance	
		Re-insurance
	Stock exchanges	
		Investment banking

insurance is national. Retail banking consists of banking services for consumers (e.g. payment services, consumer credit, and mortgages) and SMEs (e.g. payment services and loans). Retail insurance for consumers and SMEs is also very much a local business with significant differences between countries. The relevant rules for retail insurance products, such as their fiscal treatment, the social security framework, and the liability legislation, are national. The relevant market for motor and health insurance is thus clearly national. Markets for wholesale banking and insurance for large firms are European or even global. Corporate customers are looking for tailor-made solutions for their business and are approached by banks and insurers across Europe. There is a shift to global solutions for more specialised services for large firms. Re-insurance, for example, is a global business. A small group of large re-insurance companies from Europe (in particular Germany and Switzerland) and the United States dominate the global market. Investment banking is also a global business. Leading investment banks – located primarily in New York and London – offer underwriting services and advice for mergers and acquisitions. Finally, the relevant geographic market for stock exchanges is shifting. Not too long ago, each country had its own stock exchange where nearly all domestic companies were listed. The market is consolidating at the European level (Euronext, OMX; see Chapter 5).

The borderline between geographical markets may in practice be less distinct than is suggested by Table 14.4, e.g. the relevant geographical market for large firms can also be defined at the national rather than at the European level.

14.5 Institutional structure

The enforcement of EU competition policy remained largely unchanged from 1962, when a highly centralised authorisation system for all restrictive agreements was established (Monti, 2003a). However, since May 2004 the enforcement system has become more decentralised as the national competition authorities and national courts have become (increasingly) involved in the enforcement of Community competition law. Figure 14.5 gives an overview of the dual legislative and enforcement system in the EU.

Before the introduction of the Community competition law in 1958, most Member States did not have a competition policy regime in place. Competition policy has been established at the Community level, and

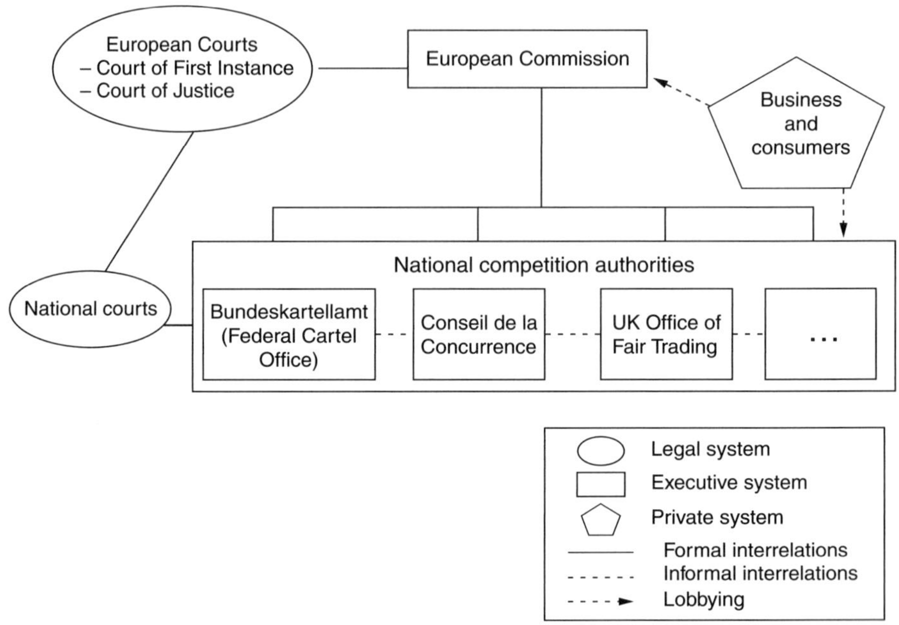

Figure 14.5 Enforcement of EU competition policy
Source: Based on Budzinski and Christiansen (2005)

many Member States created their own legislation and enforcement agencies, while gradually obtaining more enforcement powers originating from EU legislation. The development of competition policy differs from that of financial supervision. The latter was traditionally organised at the national level and has only recently been centralised with the introduction of the Banking Union. Within the current EU competition policy system, EU institutions occupy a central position. The European Commission enjoys the right of initiative in the legislative process, which confers agenda-setting power to it (Schmidt, 2000). Moreover, as shown in section 14.3, the Commission has specific powers in enforcing Community competition law. The application of EU competition law is supervised by the European Court of First Instance (ECFI) and the ECJ. The ECFI is an independent court attached to the ECJ which rules on competition cases in the first instance. Decisions of the ECFI can be appealed to the ECJ.

Effective enforcement of EU antitrust rules requires close cooperation between the EU and national institutions. According to Smits (2005), they have to cooperate in finding evidence for infringements and inform each other about investigations, so as to ensure both an efficient division of work and an effective and consistent application of EU competition rules. For this reason, the European Competition Network (ECN) was established in 2004. Within this network, EU competition authorities work together, exchange information, and allocate cases. Monti (2004) argues that the ECN reflects that in an integrated economy collaborative competition enforcement is more effective than isolated efforts. Given the dual structure of EU enforcement, general principles have been established to ensure an efficient division of work (Monti, 2003b):

- as a rule, competition authorities of the Member States will be well placed to deal with cases that have a major effect on the territory of their Member State;
- where a suspected infringement has its main effects in the territory of two or three Member States, these authorities should consider working together on a case;
- where a suspected infringement has larger geographical scope, the Commission is likely to be best placed to deal with a case.

As for the sanctioning regime, Smits (2005) argues that the absence of a clear regime to impose sanctions for infringements with out-of-state effects is an omission which requires close collaboration among national competition authorities. Another element which needs to be remedied, according to Smits (2005), is the absence of a common leniency platform, as currently individual applicants need to approach as many authorities as the number of markets that may be affected. However, in 2006 the ECN Model Leniency Programme was introduced. Although it does not provide for a one-stop shop, it diminishes discrepancies and allows for summary applications in case of applications in multiple jurisdictions, notably with the European Commission.

The EU's competition policy is different from that in other countries. Box 14.4 illustrates this by comparing competition policies in the US and the EU.

14.6 Conclusions

Competition policy is one of the pillars of the EU's internal market policy and played an important role during the financial crisis of 2007–2009. By combating distortions of competition between firms, competition policy aims to create the preconditions for the proper functioning of markets. Moreover, safeguarding competition is an important instrument to promote further market integration, also within the financial system.

Box 14.4 Antitrust policy in the EU and the US

Ginsburg (2005) argues that Sections 1 and 2 of the US Sherman Act cover largely the same ground as Articles 81 and 82 of the Treaty of Rome (now Articles 101 and 102 TFEU). Moreover, the US Clayton Act is roughly comparable to the EC Merger Regulation. In practice, EU and US competition policy are exhibiting more and more similarities. In this respect, Martin (2005) poses that the EU is moving along the same path trod by US antitrust a quarter of a century ago: from a reliance on maintaining the ability of equally efficient competitors to compete as a way of getting good market performance towards an explicit, case-by-case assessment of the impact of a business practice on market performance, or of a proposed merger/structural change on expected market performance.

Still, there are important differences between antitrust policies in the US and the EU. According to Rosch (2007), one of the main explanations for these differences is that the policies are based on different schools of thought. While US antitrust policies are based on 'Chicago School economics', those of the EU policies are built on 'post-Chicago School economics'. The basic assumption of the first is that markets are by their nature efficient and that a monopolist will never be able to keep out competitors. Chicago School scholars therefore argue that: (1) firms alleged to be engaged in predatory pricing are more likely to be engaged in profit-maximising conduct that is efficiency-enhancing instead of efficiency-impairing, and (2) even if a firm is trying to engage in predatory conduct, the market is likely to adjust. However, according to post-Chicago School scholars, firms do engage in strategic behaviour to undermine (potential) rivals and active antitrust policies are therefore needed. In addition, Rosch (2007) argues that where the Chicago School tends to advocate a hands-off approach, post-Chicago scholars favour a 'light-touch' regulatory approach. In practice, this entails that EU enforcement agencies challenge certain actions of monopolists, while US agencies and courts rarely (successfully) challenge certain exclusionary practices, such as vertical restraints and predatory pricing.

Competition forces firms to become (more) efficient, offer greater choice of products and services, and offer these products and services at lower prices. Ultimately, this gives rise to increased consumer welfare and allocative efficiency. The level of competition is also an important aspect of financial-sector development and, in turn, economic growth. However, firms can benefit from anti-competitive behaviour and may try to scale down competition. The European Commission and the National Competition Authorities therefore aim to:

- eliminate agreements which restrict competition;
- prevent abuse of a dominant position;
- make sure that mergers and acquisitions do not harm competition;

- liberalise monopolistic economic sectors; and
- prevent illegitimate state aid, as witnessed during the 2007–2009 financial crisis.

As for the prevention of abuse of a dominant position, this chapter discusses a framework for abuse of dominance investigations. One of the elements of this framework is the 'Small, but Significant Non-transitory Increase in Prices' (SSNIP) methodology, which is used to define the smallest market in which a hypothetical monopolist would be able to impose a small but significant non-transitory price increase (the so-called relevant market). Finally, the institutional structure of EU competition policy is explained. It is shown that enforcement of EU competition policy has become more decentralised and the dual enforcement system requires close cooperation between the European Commission and the National Competition Authorities.

Notes

1. The OECD (1993) defines perfect competition using four conditions: (1) there is such a large number of sellers and buyers that none can individually affect the market price, (2) there are no barriers to entry and exit, (3) buyers and sellers are perfectly informed about production and consumption decisions, and (4) products are homogenous.
2. The multilateral interchange fee is a fall-back option, which can be used when the issuing and acquiring banks are not able to bilaterally agree on an interchange fee.
3. Council Regulation (EC) No 139/2004 of 20 January 2004 on the control of concentrations between undertakings.
4. Case 27/76 *United Brands Co and United Brands Continental BV v Commission* [1978] 1 CMLR 429.

Suggested Reading

Bikker, J. A. and J. W. B. Bos (2008), *Bank Performance: A Theoretical and Empirical Framework for the Analysis of Profitability, Competition and Efficiency*, Routledge, London.

Motta, M. (2004), *Competition Policy; Theory and Practice*, Cambridge University Press.

Vives, X. (2011), Competition and Stability in Banking, *Oxford Review of Economic Policy*, **27**(3), 479–497.

References

Bikker, J. A. and J. W. B. Bos (2008), *Bank Performance: A Theoretical and Empirical Framework for the Analysis of Profitability, Competition and Efficiency*, Routledge, London.

Budzinski, O. and A. Christiansen (2005), Competence Allocation in EU Competition Policy as an Interest-Driven Process, *Journal of Public Policy*, **25**(3), 313–337.

Claessens, S. and L. Laeven (2004), What Drives Bank Competition? Some International Evidence, *Journal of Money, Credit and Banking*, **36**, 563–583.

(2005), Financial Dependence, Banking Sector Competition, and Economic Growth, *Journal of the European Economic Association*, **3**(1), 179–207.

European Commission (1997), *Commission Notice on the Definition of the Relevant Market for the Purposes of Community Competition Law*, EC, Brussels.

(2000), *XXIX Report on Competition Policy*, EC, Brussels.

(2001), *Commission Takes Note of Merger Withdrawal by Swedish Banks (SEB/FSB)* (press release), EC, Brussels.

(2004), *The Internal Market and the Relevant Geographical Market – The Impact of the Completion of the Single Market Programme on the Definition of the Relevant Geographical Market*, Enterprise Papers No. 15, EC, Brussels.

(2007a), *Antitrust: Commission Prohibits MasterCard's Intra-EEA Multilateral Interchange Fees* (press release), EC, Brussels.

(2007b), *Anti-trust: Groupement des Cartes Bancaires Restricts Competition by Hindering the Issuance of Cards at Competitive Prices* (press release), EC, Brussels.

(2007c), *Antitrust: Commission Welcomes CFI Ruling Upholding Commission's Decision on Microsoft's Abuse of Dominant Market Position* (press release), EC, Brussels.

(2011), *Report on Competition Policy 2010*, EC, Brussels.

(2012), *Report on Competition Policy 2012*, EC, Brussels.

European Communities (2003), *Glossary of Terms used in Competition Related Matters*, EC, Brussels.

Gelauff, G., I. Grilo, and A. Lejour (eds.) (2008), *Subsidiarity and Economic Reform in Europe*, Springer, Berlin.

Geroski, P. and R. Griffith (2004), Identifying Antitrust Markets, in: M. Neumann and J. Weinand (eds.), *International Handbook of Competition*, Edward Elgar, Cheltenham, 290–305.

Ginsburg, D. H. (2005), Comparing Antitrust Enforcement in the United States and Europe, *Journal of Competition Law and Economics*, **1**(3), 427–439.

Martin, S. (2005), US Antitrust and EU Competition Policy: Where Has the Former Been, Where is the Latter Going?, University of Aveiro Working Paper in Economics 27.

Monti, M. (2003a), *The New Shape of European Competition Policy, Speech given at the Inaugural Symposium of the Competition Policy Research Center, How Should Competition Policy Transform Itself?*, Tokyo.

(2003b), *EU Competition Policy after May 2004, Fordham Annual Conference on International Antitrust Law and Policy*, New York.

(2004), Competition Policy in a Global Economy, *International Finance*, **7**(3), 495–504.

Motta, M. (2004), *Competition Policy; Theory and Practice*, Cambridge University Press.

Office of Fair Trading (2001), *The Role of Market Definition in Monopoly and Dominance Inquiries*, OFT, London.

(2003), Assessing Profitability in Competition Policy Analysis, OFT Economic Discussion Paper 6.

(2004), *Abuse of a Dominant Position – Understanding Competition Law*, OFT, London.

Organisation for Economic Co-operation and Development (1993), *Glossary of Industrial Organisation Economics and Competition Law*, OECD, Paris.

(2009), Competition and the Financial Crisis, *Paper prepared for the OECD Competition Committee*, OECD, Paris.

(2011), Bank Competition and Financial Stability, *Report prepared for the G20 workshop 'The New Financial Landscape'*, OECD, Paris.

Panzar, J. and J. Rosse (1987), Testing for 'Monopoly' Equilibrium, *Journal of Industrial Economics*, **35**, 443–456.

Roeller, L.-H. and O. Stehmann (2006), The Year 2005 at DG Competition: The Trend Towards a More Effects-based Approach, *Review of Industrial Organization*, **29**, 281–304.

Rosch, J. T. (2007), I say Monopoly, You say Dominance: The Continuing Divide on the Treatment of Dominant Firms, is it the Economics?, paper presented at the International Bar Association Antitrust Section Conference in Florence. Available at: www.ftc.gov/speeches/rosch/070908isaymonopolyiba.pdf (accessed 13 February 2012).

Schaeck, K. and M. Čihák (2008), How Does Competition Affect Efficiency and Soundness in Banking? New Empirical Evidence, ECB Working Paper 932.

Schmidt, S. K. (2000), Only an Agenda Setter? The European Commission's Power over the Council of Ministers, *European Union Politics*, **1**(1), 37–61.

Schoenmaker, D. (2013), Post-Crisis Reversal in Banking and Insurance Integration: An Empirical Survey, *European Economy – Economic Papers* 496, DG ECFIN, Brussels.

Smits, R. (2005), The European Competition Network: Selected Aspects, *Legal Issues of Economic Integration*, **32**, 175–192.

Tirole, J. (1988), *The Theory of Industrial Organization*, MIT Press, Cambridge (MA).

Van den End, J. W., S. Verkaart, and A. Van Dijkhuizen (2009), Distortionary Effects of Anticrisis Measures and How to Limit Them, *DNB Occasional Studies*, **7**(3).

Vives, X. (2011), Competition and Stability in Banking, *Oxford Review of Economic Policy*, **27**(3), 479–497.

Index